GERMANY'S TRANSIENT PASTS

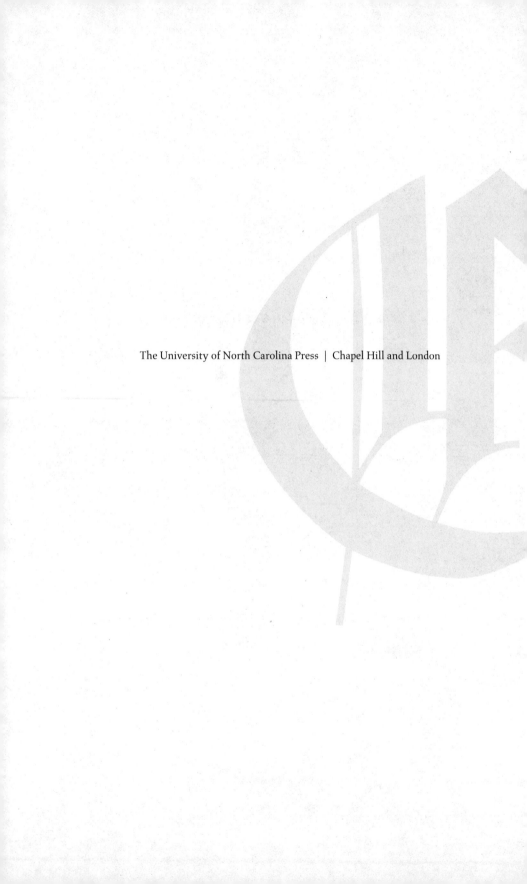

The University of North Carolina Press | Chapel Hill and London

GERMANY'S TRANSIENT PASTS

PRESERVATION AND NATIONAL MEMORY IN THE TWENTIETH CENTURY

RUDY KOSHAR

Designed by April Leidig-Higgins

Set in Aldus by Keystone Typesetting, Inc.

Manufactured in the United States of America

The paper in this book meets the guidelines for permanence and durability
of the Committee on Production Guidelines for Book Longevity of the
Council on Library Resources.

Library of Congress Cataloging-in-Publication Data
Koshar, Rudy. Germany's transient pasts : preservation and national
memory in the twentieth century / by Rudy Koshar.
p. cm. Includes bibliographical references and index.
ISBN 0-8078-2398-8 (cloth: alk. paper)
ISBN 0-8078-4701-1 (pbk. : alk. paper)
1. Germany—Cultural policy. 2. Historic preservation—Germany—History
—20th century. 3. Group identity—Germany—History—20th century.
4. Architecture and state—Germany—History—20th century. I. Title.
DD67.K67 1998   363.6'9'0943—dc21   97-36877 CIP

02 01 00 99 98   5 4 3 2 1

CONTENTS

ILLUSTRATIONS

ILLUSTRATIONS

his is a book about old buildings and memories of national community. Although I did not know it then, the idea for this study began in the 1970s, when I was still researching my doctoral dissertation on Marburg, a small university town in Germany. It was obvious in those years that Marburgers, like their counterparts in similar cities throughout West Germany, were much more concerned about the historical ambience of their community than at any time since the end of World War II. Involved in a research project with a quite different focus, I had little opportunity to pursue this observation then. My interest in how people enhanced the historical qualities of their towns and cities took on more distinct shape only in the early 1980s, when as an assistant professor of history in Los Angeles, I observed what appeared to be a most unlikely movement to preserve historic landmarks, from Craftsman houses to McDonald's hamburger stands, in this, the most unhistorical of U.S. cities. By the middle of the decade I became fascinated with the revival of the concept of *Heimat* in German culture. Inadequately translated as "home" or "homeland" or even "nation," *Heimat* had become the leitmotif of so many cultural practices, encompassing cinema and literature as well as architecture and urban planning, that it was necessary to focus not on the phenomenon in its entirety, but on specific strands. The preservation of historical buildings, a movement with modern roots in the nineteenth century that gained impetus from the recent *Heimat* revival, was a fitting candidate.

I remembered that in the 1970s large parts of the historic core of Marburg had become construction sites as many half-timbered houses and other buildings underwent a costly and time-consuming renovation. I was interested not only in the buildings but in the language and symbols used by preservationists, officials, and members of the wider public who supported or criticized the revival of the city's historic *Oberstadt*. These individuals were as concerned with the integrity and meaning of the *practice* of preservation as they were with the landmarks themselves. They saw an intimate connection between the visual and historical texture of their city's buildings, the process of maintaining and restoring monuments, and the larger issue of what they, as citizens of a local and national community, remembered and represented. The emotional investments Germans made in such practices convinced me this was a worthy subject for research and raised the question of how such efforts had developed in the past. The topic was all the more intriguing in light of the argument, widespread then as well as now, that since 1945 Germans had suppressed a painful history of Nazism, war, genocide, and political division. Did the popular interest in historical buildings grow out of a protest against such suppression? Or was it another example of the German inability to "master" a murderous past? Or was it in some way related to practices and traditions that ultimately had little to do with such issues?

The unexpected unification of Germany thrust historic landmarks, especially those of the former East Germany, onto the political stage. Still, most commentators overlooked the fact that the struggle over monuments had become unusually contentious on both sides of the border almost twenty years previously, and that *this* struggle in turn had even deeper historical roots. All this suggested that a narrative covering the period from roughly the end of the nineteenth century to the 1970s would reveal important changes and continuities in how a single country imagined itself in time. During this period, preservation grew from a movement supported mainly by government and the middle strata into a popular "cult of monuments" endorsed by workers, tourists, and many others. Reunified Germany was thus continuing and elaborating a tradition that had its own peculiar history. I discovered quickly that although information about the technical, touristic, and art-historical aspects of the subject was plentiful, historical scholarship on German preservation as a cultural movement developing over a long period of time was almost completely absent.

The flowering of a new cultural history, in the United States, England, and France particularly, made the subject all the more appealing, especially because this research focused on conflict over symbols, language, and modernity. A growing international scholarship on collective memory provided further impetus, encouraging me to think systematically about how cultural "property" was used to facilitate or hinder a shared sense of the past in the modern world. The *Heimat* revival in Germany was after all about memory, about stimulating a sense of continuity but also about forgetting painful moments in the past. Although this book wears its theory lightly and chooses rather pragmatically between various concepts, it remains indebted to the interdisciplinary discussions that have shaped current studies of culture and memory.

Many institutions and individuals have aided my research and writing along the way. A fellowship from the John Simon Guggenheim Memorial Foundation along with a Faculty Research and Innovation Fund grant from the University of Southern California and a summer fellowship from the German Academic Exchange Service funded the early stages of my research. After my move to the University of Wisconsin, the Institute for Research in the Humanities provided a valuable semester's leave from teaching responsibilities, and summer salary support from the Graduate School as well as a Vilas Associates' Award furthered my studies. In addition, a summer fellowship from the Max-Planck-Institut für Geschichte, Göttingen, capably sponsored by Alf Lüdtke, helped me complete the last stages of the research, and a Jean Monnet Fellowship from the European Forum of the European University Institute in Florence, Italy, allowed me to complete the first full draft of the manuscript. I want to thank Heinz-Gerhard Haupt, Michael Müller, and Stuart Woolf, the codirectors of the European Forum's yearlong program on regions and national identity, for their support and intellectual stimulation, and for giving me the chance to write in a sun-drenched office overlooking an ancient olive orchard in the Tuscan hills. I am also grateful to many colleagues in Europe and the United States for their useful comments and suggestions on various parts of my research. In addition to the individuals already mentioned, they include Hermann Bausinger, Geoff Eley, Steen Bo Frandsen, John Gillis, Martin Jay, Harry Liebersohn, Robert Moeller, Hans Mommsen, Michael Robinson, Adelheid von Saldern, Klaus Tenfelde, Frank Trommler, and Hans-Ulrich Wehler. I also want to thank Lewis Bateman and Ron Maner of the University of North Carolina Press for their continued interest in my research, Vernon Lidtke and Michael Geyer for their useful reading of the manuscript for the press, and Stephanie Wenzel for her judicious copyediting.

Numerous archives and libraries made possible my work. It is impossible to mention by name the individual members of the staffs of the Nordrhein-Westfälisches Hauptstaatsarchiv in Düsseldorf and Kalkum; the Archiv des Landesverbandes Rheinland in Brauweiler; the city archives of Bonn, Cologne, and Düsseldorf; the university libraries of Cologne and Göttingen; the library of the Max-Planck-Institut für Geschichte; the archive of the city conservator's office in Cologne; the European University Institute library; the J. Paul Getty Conservation Institute in Santa Monica, California; the

Library of Congress; and the libraries of the University of California in Los Angeles, the University of Southern California, the Claremont Colleges, and the University of Wisconsin, Madison. In addition, for their assistance in my search for photographic material, I want to thank the Institut für Denkmalpflege of the Niedersächsisches Landesverwaltungsamt, the Oberstadtdirektor of Münster, the Presse- und Informationsamt of Frankfurt am Main, the Presse- und Informationsstelle of the Rheinische Friedrich-Wilhelms-Universität of Bonn, the Universitätsbibliothek Tübingen, the Rheinisches Bildarchiv in Cologne, the Institut für Kunstgeschichte der Universität Wien, the Deutsches Historisches Museum, the Zentralinstitut für Kunstgeschichte in Munich, Art Resource in New York City, and the Bildarchiv Foto Marburg. Thanks also to Klaus Klott for his work in helping me collect this material.

Most of all I am thankful to my family, Judy, Drew, and Annie, whose emotional support and good humor during our travels have always enlightened and enabled my studies. This book is dedicated to them.

GERMANY'S TRANSIENT PASTS

INTRODUCTION

t one corner of the Old Market Square in Cologne stand two attached houses, numbers twenty and twenty-two, that have not only a long history but a history of being preserved.[1] According to research by the city archivist Keussen in 1913, a large house, nicknamed "Pretzel on the Apple Market," stood at this location in the thirteenth century. It was divided between two owners, one the patrician family Vetschulder. Subsequent owners combined and redivided the houses, using them for residential and commercial purposes, until 1580, when the stonemason and later guild representative in the city council Benedict von Schwelm built the attached houses that still stood at the site before World War I. But these houses and others like them were in grave danger in 1913, as unprecedented economic growth in Cologne threatened to destroy old "middle-class" (*bürgerlich*) architecture in order to make space for new commercial firms, and as updated building ordinances made the renovation of ancient structures financially impossible. These developments threatened to eat away at Cologne's medieval *bürgerlich* past. But it was not only social change that aroused fears about the fate of the houses. Over the preceding two decades, mainly for political rather than economic reasons, many Germans had begun literally to revisualize the townscapes of everyday life in the still-young German empire, regarding vernacular structures such as the two houses on the Cologne Old Market Square as "documents of stone" whose reading created an awareness of a long national heritage.

Despite this apparently deep shift in the optic identity of the nation, the houses on the east side of the market square were slated for demolition, a prospect that angered preservationists in various voluntary groups and government agencies. Fortunately, according to *Die Denkmalpflege*, the national journal for historic preservation founded in 1899, Cologne mayor Max Wallraf and city council representative Carl Rehort came up with a plan. Members of the elite Rhenish Association for the Preservation of Historic Sites, Wallraf and Rehort agreed to have the city renovate "Zur Brezel" and "Zum Dorn," as the attached houses had become known, and sell them to the Bakers' Guild, which would use the houses for headquarters and apprentices' lodgings, while the ground floor would be used for a restaurant. The renovation was costly and complicated, including the demolition of the insecure front walls, whose old stones were numbered as they were removed, then replaced in the same relation to one another when the wall was reconstructed.

The history of the houses' preservation does not end there. Alter Markt 20/22 was badly damaged in World War II, when Cologne survived 262 air attacks and more than 90 percent of the old city core was destroyed. Undoing such destruction became a national political cause and a matter of local pride. Correspondence from June 1943 in the Cologne conservator's office indicates that the interior of Zur Brezel was completely gutted by fire and that the city undertook limited preventative measures to see the house through the bombing. But it was clear that Benedict von Schwelm's old house would need more than the kind of protection it received in 1913.

In 1949 the city agreed to pay builder Ludwig Eltz to reconstruct the house. Eltz was enthusiastic about the project because he loved working on old buildings, and having recently resettled in Cologne from Paderborn, he was anxious to start a construction business in the badly destroyed Rhenish city. In 1951 Arnold Nellessen, who had gained the property after an unspecified family conflict over inheritance, applied to the city to use part of it to continue running the restaurant that had been there since before the war. Basing his appeal on a "moral imperative" to carry on the "family tradition," Nellessen said the restaurant would have a menu appropriate to a *"bürgerlich* house." But Nellessen was unable to finance further renovation, and in 1955 yet another individual, Willi Gerbeck, applied to the city to run a small wine cellar in the building. Like Nellessen, Gerbeck emphasized business and moral interests, but his language carried more visible reminders of the Nazi era. He stressed the need to restore historic buildings such as Zur Brezel in order to avoid the "return of asocial conditions" that appeared in this district before urban renewal under Nazism. Intentionally or unintentionally, Gerbeck evoked not the memory of medieval *bürgerlich* Cologne but the "sanitizing" urban projects and concern for national morality of the Nazi era.

The city's involvement in such efforts continued in the next decades, although not without ambivalence. In 1955 the city conservator wrote that

Alter Markt 20/22, Cologne's medieval past as a scrubbed and
painted urban jewel of the 1980s (photo: Judith L. Koshar)

the sums needed simply to maintain the house, provisionally set at 68,000 marks, were much too high considering that renovation of architecturally more valuable buildings such as the city hall had been stalled because of lack of funds. Nonetheless, because the houses gave the east side of the market square an unmistakable "accent"—and had done so for centuries despite their altered form—rebuilding continued, although the conservator insisted that the city as well as the property owner be informed that extensive financial aid for the project was not a precedent for other rebuilding plans. Starting in 1986 Zur Brezel underwent further renovation, and it still stands at its thirteenth-century corner, although it is now a scrubbed and painted architectural jewel peering out at tourists as they amble by on the market square. It is a monument to preservation as much as it is a monument to some publicly resonant version of a perdurable German past.

For every famous or politically notorious landmark in postwar Germany there are dozens of Zur Brezels, just as there are many buildings that were protected at one time but demolished or not reconstructed in a later period. To tell their story would be to include most of the elements I have already mentioned: potential or actual destruction; the layering of historical periods of renovation, rebuilding, and protection; constant and sometimes contentious negotiations between conservators, mayors, property owners, and preservation societies; and the overlay of personal, local, and national visions of collective being. The protection of historic sites such as Zur Brezel opens a world of images and relationships speaking to larger issues about the perceived role of the past in everyday life and definitions of community identity.

Why have Germans regarded buildings such as these worthy not only of financial intervention and state protection but of moralistic commentary on the basis of national identity? What ideas, institutions, and practices made it possible in the first place to regard such buildings as historical? Did the Zur Brezels of Germany symbolize a coherent national past on whose meaning everyone could agree? Or did they connote multiple and transient pasts whose significance was dependent on the context in which they were protected and the uses to which they were put? What has the preservation of such historical buildings revealed about the status and function of history and memory in modernity? These and other questions inform the following study, which considers the history of German historic preservation as a form of national "memory-work" (*Erinnerungsarbeit*) from the late nineteenth century to the mid-1970s.

Historical buildings gained new importance as national symbols as the Cold War ended and seemingly anachronistic national and ethnic identities reappeared with new vigor in post-Communist Europe. Yet beginning already in the late 1960s, a "forceful turn" to the preservation of such objects had occurred in Germany, England, France, Australia, the United States, and several East European countries.[2] Germans were in the forefront of this worldwide movement, and by 1975 West Germans were convinced that one of every twelve buildings in the Federal Republic had historical value. It is unclear if this number increased or decreased after unification, but there can be little doubt that since 1990 Germans have debated the merits of preserving or even reconstructing many objects of historical interest, from industrial artifacts and former concentration camp sites to the Imperial Palace of Berlin and dilapidated urban ensembles in the former German Democratic Republic.

Scholarship has followed this public interest. We now have studies or works in progress on the history of protecting numerous historically valuable sites and artifacts in Germany, most though not all dealing with former concentration camps or other sites associated with Nazism.[3] For Europe as a whole, there is an array of theoretical and historical studies of monuments in the restricted sense of structures built specifically to recall a personality, concept, or event in the past, or what influential Viennese art historian Alois Riegl called "intentional" or "intended" monuments.[4] This literature is a subgroup of a much larger public and academic concern with memory and identity, for Germany and Europe as well as the United States, for material culture as well as other areas.[5]

Recent scholarship on monuments has been rich and highly enlightening, but it has also unintentionally demonstrated that war monuments, busts and statues of famous historical figures, national monuments, and memorial spaces account for only a small part of the built environment's "commemorative capital," its capacity to foster an awareness of the past. A morally necessary phenomenon, the already mentioned focus on the fate of Nazi concentration camp sites in postwar German memory is one of the most visible, perhaps the most visible, example of this restricted vision. Urban planner Kevin Lynch once argued that the built environment consisted of paths, edges, districts, nodes, and landmarks, all of which potentially referred to individual as well as collective memories, "private" as well as "public" images of community.[6] Cultural geography's current interest in social practices in a spatial "context in its fullest sense" is a measure of how broad scholarly treatments of physical environments might be in considering not just the making of memory but any historically specific human action.[7] By focusing primarily on intentional monuments, scholarship has narrowed our view of the variety of spaces in which memory-work is carried out, and the historical study of memory has suffered consequently.[8] In this book I try to broaden the scholarly view of "monuments" to concentrate on structures and sites previously overlooked or incompletely explored in most recent writing on modern German and European memory.

As the foregoing suggests, scholarship on German memory of Nazism has constituted a large part of recent debates on national memory and identity, as evidenced in the many useful studies of the former West Germany's "historians' debate," a harsh public controversy of the 1980s over the memory and historical significance of the Holocaust.[9] But just as the focus on intentional monuments has narrowed our view of the physical contexts in which memory-work has taken place, the emphasis on German memory of Hitler and National Socialism has narrowed the terms of scholarly discussion on the history of collective memory in Germany over the past century. It is morally and intellectually important to ask if Germans have dealt fully with the history of Nazism and the Holocaust. But what of other "vectors" of memory,[10] and what of other historical periods in German memory? How reliable can our insights into the memory of Nazism be if we do not know more about the broader history of public memory of which Nazism is such a crucial part? This study considers one of these important but neglected vectors of German attempts to create a meaningful past.

Conceptually, the cumulative impact of much recent research has been to sharpen scholarly analysis of the differences between memory and history, a subject for which French sociologist Maurice Halbwachs's work in the first half of the century was paradigmatic. Halbwachs argued that collective memory worked when coherent groups kept alive their defining traditions, legends, and myths, but that history took over when the strands of tradition were broken. Historiography thus became a reduced or eviscerated form of orientation to the past, less emotionally resonant than memory and less capable of serving as a point of identity with larger collective goals. Monuments, landscapes, and symbols figured prominently in collective memory formation because in Halbwachs's view they provided a concrete image of perdurability that legitimized group identity over time. Halbwachs also recognized that even when it was most personal and subjective, memory depended on collective processes of conscious recall, narrative, and selection shaped by conversations with others. The adult remembered early childhood, but only after these memories were sharpened and verified by pictures, stories, sights, and sounds accumulated in interaction with friends and family.[11] All memory, individual and collective, was truly group-based *Erinnerungsarbeit*. Halbwachs had laid the conceptual foundations for the study of the social history of memory formation.

Influenced by Halbwachs, French historian Pierre Nora developed the concept of "sites of memory" (*lieux de mémoire*) to understand how and why monuments and other landmarks had become so important in group memory formation in the 1970s and 1980s. He argued that late in the nineteenth century the French Third Republic established a dynamic symbiosis between memory and history. This symbiosis broke down early in the twentieth century, he wrote, as an increasingly "critical" history, or what might be called historical memory, was divorced from the tradition of national memory by the forces of a secularizing society. Cut from its relation to national heritage and oriented toward the study of social process, history became specialized and more sociological while memory became increasingly personal, psychological, and obligatory.[12] Monuments, literature, or even sports events in turn became evocative nodes of crystallized group memories in cultural environments that no longer supported national memory formation of the kind that characterized the nineteenth century. Sites of memory proliferated, frantically and without the nurturing focus that French national identity had given it, because the earlier social and political contexts of memory had dissolved.

From my point of view, Nora's concept of sites of memory encompasses so many objects and images as to make it impossible to use systematically. The concept also bears little relation to how historical actors described various landmarks and traditions. More generally, Nora exaggerates the degree to which both history and memory no longer interacted and contributed to national heritage and tradition in the course of the twentieth century. National identity, the feeling that individuals within a nation constitute an enduring unity, has most often been defined in historical terms, whether those of professional historians or ordinary citizens, although the manner in which the past has been evoked varies from country to country and from time to time. Since at least the 1960s, historical and collective memory have been evoked in ways that stress personal, ethnic, gender, social, and other identities more forcefully, but the nation has not been eviscerated as a leading point of crystallization for collective memory-formation. Nor has the symbiotic relationship between history and memory been weakened, as events in Europe since 1989 have suggested. Rather, the quality of this symbiosis has changed, in part due to the greater role of the electronic media and technological change. This book will provide one detailed empirical example of the way in which a sense of German nationhood has persisted but changed over time through the continued interactions between history, as represented here in officially prescribed and "scientifically" legitimated practices of historic preservation, and national memory, as represented in both the preservationists' and the public's embrace of historical buildings.

The nature of nationhood is an important historical and political issue in the study of collective memory-work. Scholars think of the nation as a constitutive "road" to modernity,[13] a troublesome term for which I offer a definition in Chapter 1. But what role does memory play in the nation and, by extension, in modernity itself? Students of nations and nationalism have criticized an older tradition of scholarship that saw nations as inevitable, virtually organic, and universal entities drawing on relatively fixed traditions based on objective characteristics. They argue instead that nations have been "invented" or "imagined," and that traditions and memories have been manipulated to give nations an entirely fictitious ambience of continuity and stability.[14] Scholars most often see nations as modern occurrences whose claims of being rooted in primordial cultural relations must be seen as the lies they are. In this regard, older arguments of "false consciousness," or of a mis-relation between significance and action, continue to influence scholarship. Anthony Smith has occupied a middle ground between the older scholarship and the new, emphasizing the deep historical and ethnic roots of national myths and traditions, but conceding the necessity of extensive collective effort in the modern period to mobilize such traditions in the process of identity construction.[15] In this view the nation is "constructed," but behind its artifice lie reservoirs of memories, objects, and images whose use and evocation potentially unleash an array of commonly held emotions that are more than the reflex of current action. Nations may be imagined, but nationalist speech makers, preservers of historic sites, and composers of national anthems do not have unlimited scope to invent and manipulate cultural images inherited from the past because those images exert an unmistakable pull on the present. The nature of that pull remains a matter of concrete historical research.

I find that Smith's approach provides necessary balance in a field that—perhaps due in part to a cumulative misreading of the notion of invented traditions—has moved too far in the direction of a "constructivist" argument. At the same time, the relational and contingent features of any form of identity construction must not be overlooked, for the resonance of any inherited myth, narrative, or tradition is finally dependent on the effectiveness of its repeated performance. The "discursivity" of the nation is not in doubt in this approach, in my opinion, but the actual scope of social engineering, the degree to which ideologues and state agencies can get populations to imagine or invent the nation, is delimited by historical factors. I demonstrate in the following pages that although preservationists often cooperated in the wholesale transformation and even destruction of historical buildings, they also insisted on a role for history and historical accuracy, and they were thus among the key groups to delimit—if at times only potentially—the space in which construction of national identity and memory took place. Fully involved in national memory-work, preservationists nonetheless claimed to be stewards of a material culture whose forms could not simply be manipulated ad infinitum. I argue that there was something to that claim. I also demonstrate that the process of imagining the nation is itself not quite as abstract as Anderson and others insist, since it takes place in historically and spatially specific spaces (often the local community or neighborhood), evolves with the rhythm of specific social relations (defined in class, gender, ethnic, and other identities), and is instantiated in specific objects such as historical buildings and monuments. If a constructivist argument, or at least the "hard" version of such an argument, emphasizes abstraction and imagination, my approach stresses the density and substantiality of national memory-work.

Because the nation has been an enormously successful, if violent and dangerous, path to modernity, scholars have quite usefully stressed that national memory-work has had both retrospective and anticipatory qualities. Memory serves not only to legitimize the nation historically but to give it a purchase on the future, to ground the nation in a historical narrative whose ending is even more ineffable than the beginning. More specifically, popular attachments to the memory and traditions of the nation have often been associated with "a specific belief in responsibility toward succeeding generations," as Max Weber wrote with characteristic acuity.[16] This belief applies to the preservation of political prestige as much as it does to the preservation of national landmarks. Just as individual identity is considered to be the result of negotiation between past experience, present self-awareness, and anticipation of future action, national identity is seen as a product of contest and negotiation involving the alignment of past, present, and future in some meaningful relationship. The writing of a history book, the preserving of an old building, or the making of a film with a historical theme all project the past into the future, all carry on the ill-defined sense of responsibility to successors, and all in fact rob the past of its specificity and capture it for future action. I note these future-oriented and "modernist" qualities of the past throughout this study.

The balance of the growing literature on national identity and memory is mixed. Much remains to be done to explicate whether or how national continuity has been defined, how and why the building of meaningful continuities has taken place in specific areas of cultural politics and in specific historical contexts, and how memories have been used to promote or delegitimize national and social identities. More specifically, much remains to be done to demonstrate the varied *uses* of national memory, its appropriations by elites as well as ordinary people, and its function in shaping the emotional life of all members of the national community.[17]

Cultural theory and cultural history provide a valuable point of departure for addressing such issues.[18] Much recent cultural history has moved away from seeing culture as a whole system, as Clifford Geertz does, stressing instead the idea of differential appropriations of "cultural goods," as in Pierre Bourdieu's work.[19] With reference to my subject, such post-Geertzian research presupposes that national memory and its artifacts may have very different meanings for different groups. Memory and tradition therefore represent not just sources of power for elites but also a potential source of noncompliance or even resistance for the powerless. National symbols, which are based on "any object, act, event, quality, or relation which serves as a vehicle for a conception" or meaning of the nation, may have a multiplicity of interpretations. The uses of national memory and symbols need to be considered both strategically and tactically, "from above" and "from below."[20] Elites must not be seen as homogeneous or without serious internal disagreements, just as workers, peasants, the lower middle classes, minorities, and women must not be regarded as coherent or stable voices of resistance or noncompliance. Differences within elite circles are of particular interest in this study, which focuses on preservationists as members of the German educated middle classes whose rhetoric and practice differed in important ways from those of other state and social elites. In considering such gradations of appropriation, moreover, memory and identity must be seen not as residual elements of power relations but as processes that both mirror and produce those relations in all their complexity and indeterminacy. This intrication of culture and power, indeed the notion of cultural politics as such, has been a particularly useful theme in the still-undefined but rich field of interdisciplinary cultural studies research.[21]

I consider national memory as a type of collective and public memory, which consists of "narrative-practical modes of discourse"[22] whose goal is to facilitate shared identities by situating collectivities (nations, states, regions, cities, classes, genders, business corporations, religious institutions, or voluntary associations) in meaningful historical sequences. Since historical sequences include the notion of past, present, and future, public memory looks forward as it directs its gaze backward in time. Public memory in the modern Euro-American world is neither exclusively spontaneous nor fully constructed from above, neither exclusively the product of primordial cultural relations nor of artifice manufactured by the guardians of an official memory. Its appearance must be explained, not assumed, but its appearance is hardly created out of nothing, just as its appearance can be exploited in unpredictable ways by individuals and groups in society. It structures and is structured by a process of conflict and negotiation involving people, objects, and images: the state, regions, cities, the history profession, monuments, flags, kitsch, museums, television and film, commemorative festivals, political parties, and numerous social groups—all working in a complex series of practices whose outcome is dependent on both the weight of experience and the contingencies of power relations.

I argue that conflicts over the public memory of the nation—and therefore over the role of memory in modernity—have produced not the national continuity of ideologues' fantasies but a malleable yet consistent discourse about continuity. In other words, proponents of national identity have developed changing ways of talking and acting that employ a coded language, delimit a field of knowledge, and order and define objects and people within it.[23] Although they were constrained by discourse, historical individuals were not passive "language-effects" but, rather, active users and modifiers of a language beyond which they moved at key moments of change and tension.[24] In preservation we are dealing with a discourse whose field of knowledge was (and remains) architectural history and whose favored objects were historic buildings notionally signifying a coherent national heritage. I argue that this heritage was compelling to its producers and recipients even when the daily practice of preservation revealed the nation's shaky material and ideal grounds. The Zur Brezels of the world existed for the proponents of heritage, and such sites could be made to resonate as symbols of an enduring common past despite their unhinged moorings and uncertain futures. The active formation of these transient pasts, narratives whose conflictual making and unmaking redefined and anchored national continuity throughout the century, is the focus of this book.

Old buildings have mattered in national memory-work. My study deals with the language and actions of state agencies, voluntary associations, and individuals that protected historic buildings and mobilized public support for architectural heritage of the kind that captured the imagination of admirers of Zur Brezel. In this regard, my book is about one significant corporate participant in the process of formation of transient national pasts.

Recently several scholars have pointed out the importance of heritage preservation to Anglo-American political culture. Additionally, M. Christine Boyer has published an impressive and imaginative study of historic preservation's place in the changing urban and historical imagery of the Western world. But her book offers very little information about the everyday practices of preservation, and its fundamental concern is a critique of postmodern urban planning of the 1980s and 1990s, from which it reads the history of urban and architectural images back in time.[25] As in the United States and England, architectural preservation in Germany (referred to most often as *Denkmalpflege*, or *Denkmalschutz*) dealt directly with a very small part of the built environment, but its impact in all these societies was much wider because theoretically it touched on all aspects of the optic identity of towns, regions, and the nation. Moreover, it could claim to be more important to public memory than other cultural activities were because it dealt with large, expensive, and functional artifacts.

There is a large literature on historic preservation in Germany, much of it dealing with techniques and policies or, in a more popular vein, with the touristic attractions of historic sites. More analytical literature on the subject has dealt with specific issues in architectural history, urban policy, local history, or state administration rather than with problems of cultural history, collective identity, and memory.[26] Among the most informative scholarly works dealing with the history of German preservation are von Beyme's and Diefendorf's studies, which do not focus specifically on preservation but treat it in the context of the rebuilding of German cities after World War II. Michael Siegel has usefully considered the protection of monuments as public policy, but he does little to elucidate the daily machinery of preservation or the contingent nature of definitions of the past and of monuments. Godehard Hoffmann's research on "Rhenish Romanesque" style is massively detailed, but it focuses only on the restoration of churches in the Rhineland before World War I. The many publications of the German National Committee for Historic Preservation have been informative but also disparate in terms of their subject matter and conceptual address. Important works by Brix, Durth and Gutschow, and Beseler and Gutschow have considerably broadened our understanding of the subject, but they still operate from inside the practice of preservation, as they should, since Beseler, Durth, and Gutschow in particular are among the leading voices of cultural protection in contemporary Germany. Winfried Speitkamp's very informative research considers preservation organizations and state agencies in a wider context of modern German state policy. A significant advantage of Speitkamp's work is that it offers a more differentiated picture of preservationists' attitudes toward modernity, rejecting an earlier scholarship that put preservation squarely on the side of reactionary antimodernists and cultural pessimists. But Speitkamp's research necessarily concentrates more on an administrative-bureaucratic history than on the role preservationists played in national memory-work, it intentionally leaves out information on historical buildings per se, and it covers only the period from 1871 to 1933.

On balance these useful works have still done too little to give us a more synthetic view of historic preservation in relation to other forms of cultural politics over the greater part of the twentieth century. They have not considered the protection of monuments in the broadest sense in its relation to changing definitions of the nation or (with the partial exception of Speit-kamp) in its fuller orientation to modernity. No scholarly study of German preservation has explored the appropriation and cultural uses of historic buildings by their users, the tourists, workers, postcard collectors, and many others who viewed, visited, and worked in historic buildings. No study has focused explicitly on the differing gradations of appropriation of historic buildings by preservationists themselves. Above all, scholarship has done little to consider preservation as a discourse that did not simply protect monuments but that revisualized and imparted meaning to objects and space, creating monuments in an attempt to have Germans see historical buildings for their national significance. Treating monuments more often as data rather than as texts, this scholarship has focused too little on the key words, images, and institutions that have made it possible to talk about and define historical buildings in the first place. I intend to discuss the historical building as both empirical evidence and discursive resource, exploring how the two dimensions have interacted over time.

My aim is not to write an institutional history, although there is much about institutions in the following pages. Nor do I plan to make systematic statements about art-historical significance and artistic styles. Preservation research is full of such commentary, and I do not try to duplicate or expand on this rich body of literature on the architectural history and formal charac-teristics of monuments and sites. Instead my approach probes certain "ico-nological" moments of historic places, to use the term of the great art historian Erwin Panofsky, because it looks for underlying attitudes toward the past and the nation in preservationists' attempts to create and make meaning of monuments.[27] I craft a narrative showing how preservation worked in German public memory and collective identity for much of the twentieth century. My modus operandi must therefore be one of relatively broadly focused group portraits rather than of exquisitely detailed individual studies. I discuss the period from the 1890s, when historic preservation became part of a middle-class "cult of monuments," to 1975, when European Cultural Heritage Year signaled that preservation had become a popular movement whose institutions and rhetoric looked very much like those of contemporary unified Germany. The last chapter and the conclusion of my book thus open a window on the present, and to have continued my narrative beyond 1975 would have necessitated a very different, perhaps less historical and more publicly engaged book. In any event, this chronology represents a departure from most writing on twentieth-century German politics and culture, since despite numerous exceptions, scholarship remains fixated on the tried-and-true chronological markers of German political history: 1914, 1918, 1933, 1945, 1949, and now 1989. The point, of course, is not to ignore these important dates or deny their relevance—this study uses them to give structure to a number of chapters—but to consider how the distinctive chronology of one important form of cultural politics intersected with them and either relativized or reinforced their significance. My study demonstrates that the history of historic preservation in Germany over this period is best described as a continuity of interstitial changes broken only by a substantial quantitative and qualitative shift in the late 1960s to mid-1970s.

I discuss the institutional bases and public discourse of conservators, art historians, architects, urban planners, and cultural officials. These groups may have differed in outlook and aims, but they shared an identity as preservationists and thus became objects of my study, when through words and actions they contributed to the restoration, maintenance, or even reconstruction of architectural monuments. In keeping with this logic, I distinguish preservationists from those interested in maintaining natural sites or landscapes in the broader sense of the term, whose work was related to but never synonymous with that of preservation as I define it. I want to know how the practice of architectural preservation emerged in specific political and disciplinary contexts and how preservationists shaped and were shaped by prevailing discourses of national identity. I consider the intentions of these groups as well as the reception of their activity and national-political views by workers, farmers, tourists, urban property and business owners, journalists, and politicians. Did the memory-work of these groups coincide with or challenge the memory-work of preservationists in government agencies and allied voluntary groups? Because preservation was and still is largely a product of the cultural politics of federal states and provinces in Germany, I draw rather more on material from one crucial region, the (formerly Prussian) Rhineland, an area unusually rich in monuments, active in preservation, and full of national significance. Only Bavaria, steeped in a long tradition of cultural-political exceptionalism, is comparable to the Rhineland in the number and quality of its historical buildings. In addition to the Rhenish focus, I include information from other parts of Germany, the former East Germany, Europe, and North America.

My definition of historic buildings is derived from the German concept of the *Denkmal*, which is wider than the Anglo-American term "monument." I focus in particular on the architectural monument, or *Baudenkmal*, which in German usage may include ruins, churches, notable public buildings, urban residential and commercial buildings, vernacular structures such as peasant houses and workers' settlements, and industrial buildings such as windmills and (more recently) factories. The term has even been extended to entire urban fabrics, as when Germans speak of the "city-monument" (*Stadtdenkmal*). Throughout the study I focus not on some a priori concept of the architectural monument but on changes in the way Germans have used the term and included or excluded various objects or sites. At some moments, in part in response to public pressure, many disparate subjects such as historical street names and war monuments have been grist for the preservationist mill, and I have considered such topics when necessary. Even then my treatment of historical buildings must remain highly selective.

The definition of "preservation" remains a matter of dispute, but when I use the term I refer to a spectrum of interventions in the physical integrity of movable or immovable objects considered to have historical value. Such interventions may range from the maintenance of historic sites without any substantial modifications of the object, which is arguably the most commonly held sense of the term, to conservation and consolidation, step-by-step reconstitution, adaptive use of old buildings to new social requirements, full reconstruction of a vanished building, or replication of an extant artifact.[28] This definition mirrors the broadening of preservation in the Euro-American world over the past century. This is a significant development, needful of explanation, in my narrative of transient pasts. It is common to distinguish preservation from conservation, the former referring to the "museumification" or isolation of sites, the latter to integration of those sites into modern uses. I employ "preservation" as a working term that encompasses conservation and other interventions because by the late nineteenth century it had already taken on conservationist perspectives, in theory if not always in practice. It thus made sense to retain the (in the United States) more common usage but also stress its changing nature.

Broad strata of the population are oddly indifferent or blind towards the most valuable kinds

of study aids of historical research, towards the documents of stone that have come down to us,

the architectural monuments and everything that goes with them. . . . And nevertheless, slowly it

has dawned on people that short-sighted actions must be stopped, that for monuments there is

also validity to Bismarck's golden words that it is of greatest harm to a nation when it allows the

living consciousness of its connection to its heritage and history to fade.

—Otto Sarrazin and Oskar Hoßfeld, 1899

ONE | DOCUMENTS OF STONE

 istoric preservation became a significant public activity in Germany between the 1890s and the outbreak of World War I. The protection of historical buildings had many precedents, but in these years it became more organized and potentially more popular. Once the concern of Romantic intellectuals and a handful of state officials, historic preservation was now transformed into a vector of modern cultural politics whose main official representatives helped to shape a national optics, a way of seeing the nation in the physical environment. In achieving this position, official preservation had to distinguish its methodologies, institutions, and political relationships from those of earlier forms of preservation without cutting its ties to the past. Preservationists had to define a sense of nationhood at a time when the still-young Second Empire itself explored new ways of creating emotional attachments to the national state. And they had to create a place for themselves in a society in which a once relatively coherent *Bürgertum*, or middle stratum, had given way to a multiplicity of cultural consumers whose understandings of historic buildings did not always match those of official preservation. In the late empire, protecting documents of stone—tangible links to an enduring past increasingly defined

in national terms—thus required new institutions, new patterns of national memory-work, and new forms of public engagement. These institutions, patterns, and forms would survive for much of the twentieth century despite the violent discontinuities of German political history.

Toward a National Optics

"Modernity" signifies the historical epoch in which, for an increasing majority of inhabitants in Europe and then other parts of the globe, an asymmetry between "hope" and "memory," or between the "horizon of expectation" and the "space of experience," becomes the fundamental condition of societal relationships.[1] Experience is "present past, whose events have been incorporated and can be remembered," whereas expectation is "the future made present" that "directs itself to the not-yet." Before modernity, hope and memory worked in a rough balance. But after the seventeenth century, and then more forcefully after the French Revolution, industrialization, and the rise of territorial nation-states, hope disengaged from memory. Anticipation of the future worked without deferring primarily to the authority of remembrance. "Progress" came to signify this twin movement of an optimistic opening toward a future relatively unbounded by experiential factors and a simultaneous weakening and potential evisceration of the past.

As progress created and anticipated new societal resources outside experiential boundaries, the past became an object of continual reflection and "the institution of memory . . . became a critical preoccupation of the effort to think through the present." Nineteenth-century thinkers increasingly defined the age through "a disciplined obsession with the past" marked by the feeling that "recollection . . . ceased to integrate with consciousness."[2] Individuals turned to the past to scrutinize it for its otherness, to revise it in response to the constant shock of the new, and to study it "scientifically." "Critical" and "genetical" narratives heightened a sense that history worked to distance humankind from the space of experience that held progress in check. Critics of progress used the past's otherness to ridicule the present, to insist that embattled tradition persisted, and to create visions of a future world in which memory once again resonated.[3] But even such criticism called attention to the dominance progress had over the past, just as it called attention to the thoroughly modern character of the now enduring obsession to dispose of, evoke, and arrange the past.

Nations and national states were not merely products of this modern condition but constitutive elements of it. Progress, economic growth, and technology not only widened the gap between hope and memory but also were defined in national terms, just as the desire for tradition and memory would lead observers to seek national examples and origins for contemporary successes and failures. Under such conditions, and sometimes with considerable delay and doubt on the part of state authorities, national memory became a potential resource in the state's attempt to create a cultural authority that rivaled and then replaced that of the church and the monarchy. Based on notions of the state as guarantor of Christian values, and of state-run education teaching the rudiments of national history and civic loyalty, modern "cultural politics" stemmed from and shaped the national state's drive for emotional legitimacy.[4]

The disarticulation of hope from memory and the simultaneous institution of memory as a cultural-political strategy assumed a specific shape in Germany. Although reactions to the French Revolution and industrialization transformed German society in the nineteenth century, it was national unification in 1871 that represented the greatest departure from experience for Germans. The cultural nation's authority, which had depended on a multicentered vision of German politics, was diminished (though certainly not extinguished) in favor of a unitary nation-state. The new state was neither wholly a descendent of the First Empire of the medieval age (which had existed in severely weakened form until 1806) nor wholly consistent with the wishes of the German national movement, led mainly by the *Bürgertum*. Reich elites would try to close this gap between past and present by stretching "the short, tight, skin of the nation" over their still-inchoate creation.[5] This entailed the reshaping of German memory to account for the rise of the new empire, a project that historians such as Heinrich von Treitschke took up with considerable public effect. It should be noted that Germany found national unity less historically unprecedented than Italy, which lacked the institutional fundaments for nationhood that German speakers had in the Holy Roman Empire, the German Federation, and the Customs Union. In England, France, Italy, Japan, and the United States, moreover, there was "a roughly comparable phase of obsession with national memory and its underlying myths" from 1870 to 1914.[6] German national unity represented a significant historical departure, and the resultant embrace of national memory was intense and contentious. Yet neither the departure nor the embrace were unique to German culture.

The proponents of a vigorous national memory faced not only the political challenge of creating the empire but also immense social change, as Germany was transformed into a global industrial leader. The resultant social tensions changed the party politics of the Prusso-German Reich into a complex game of maneuvers, uneasily managed by Chancellor Otto von Bismarck until 1890 but then increasingly bungled by successors who were much less adept at exploiting class, confessional, regional, and party divisions. Responding to these tensions, various groups labored to establish more emotional and popular attachments to the German nation than existed in the two decades after 1871. From above, Wilhelm II, who came to power in 1888 and valued national symbolism more than Bismarck did, endorsed the idea of the "culture state" (*Kulturstaat*), which Treitschke and others used to construct an interventionist cultural model for the Second Empire. Under Wilhelm II, the empire founded research institutes and schools abroad in an effort to demonstrate German superiority and enhance the loyalties of Germans outside the nation. At home the Reich, the federal states, and communities built art academies, museums, monuments, and archaeological institutes, which not only served functional purposes but also worked as symbols of national accomplishments in the historical and human sciences. More systematically than before, they also protected historic buildings, of which Wilhelm II was particularly fond.[7]

Still, the Reich was inconsistent in its direction of cultural policy due to the Kaiser's unbounded incompetence, corrosive social divisions, and above all the constitutional structure of the Prusso-German state, which left cultural politics in the hands of the federal states, provinces, and cities. For the elites of such "subnational" entities, local loyalties could enhance, modify, or weaken emotional attachments to the nation, depending on specific historical circumstances. Too, the late Empire saw a general mobilization of public life, making more kinds of memory possible but also allowing alternative readings of the German past based on class, region, confession, gender, and the "ethnicity" of Jews, Poles, Danes, Alsatians, and French within the Reich. Given this complexity, it was impossible for the Kaiserreich to emulate the more centralized French Third Republic, which at the turn of the century adopted eighteenth-century rococo as the style most representative of the national patrimony in architectural restorations, museums, and luxury crafts. No such coherent strategy was possible in the more complex cultural-political landscape of the Kaiserreich, although at the end of the century Wilhelm II expended much energy promoting neo-Romanesque as the national style in new architecture and historic restorations.[8] Nonetheless, a German optic identity did develop.

If the military and the aristocracy quite rightly took credit for the martial victories that created the new German state, the *Bürgertum* had played a key role in the making of a culturally identified German nation and in national memory-work. Since at least the eighteenth century, a humanistic respect for the cultural achievements of the past defined a large part of the classically trained or university-educated *Bürgertum*, who called themselves "the cultured," or *Gebildeten*. Respect for the past was combined with a liberal belief in the possibility of unending material advance through which hope led memory into a utopia of economic and moral well-being. In the late Empire the role of the *Bürgertum* in national memory-work was affected by its changing social makeup. Unlike the Italian *borghese*, whose "humanistic" social structure and political strength persisted well into the twentieth century, the German *Bürgertum* was being transformed by a rapidly changing industrial society creating new patterns of wealth, status, and education. Moreover, liberal political parties, the champions of the *Bürgertum*'s cultural and economic interests, were challenged in the political sphere by the rise of Social Democracy, political Catholicism, and populist anti-Semitism. Despite such changes, the tradition of defining power in cultural terms remained relevant for many parts of the middle strata, and thus different groups within the Protestant *Bürgertum* searched—without a unified strategy—for extraparliamentary alternatives to their eroded electoral power and splintered social makeup.

Nationalist festivals, associations, and monuments suggested one route to extraparliamentary power. But there were also more specifically cultural alternatives, such as historic preservation, protection of historic homelands (*Heimatschutz*), nature conservation, "life reform," industrial design, and cultural entrepreneur Ferdinand Avenarius's Dürerbund, a group whose "ethical idealism" was to be used to uncover an essential and popular Germanness based on culture and history. Influenced in part by Nietzsche's impact, the cultural criticism of writer Julius Langbehn and philologist Paul de Lagarde gave voice to such activities. Much of cultural criticism was based on the distinction between culture (*Kultur*) and civilization (*Zivilisation*), the former referring to values and techniques associated with classical training, profundity, tact, and authenticity, and the latter with practical learning, rationality, and mass culture. Conservative cultural critics identified capitalism, democracy, socialism, and often Jewishness with civilization, and they contrasted the urbanized present with a presumably more organic rural past whose qualities could be symbolized in everything from medieval castles to peasant costumes. Although they did much to increase the late imperial *Bürgertum*'s preoccupation with memory, critics such as Lagarde by no means got the *Bürgertum* to view contemporary society in unabashedly pessimistic terms.[9]

If both cultural pessimism and a continued liberal belief in unending progress shaped the *Bürgertum*'s views, then so too did what may be called a conservative hopefulness. Christopher Lasch has argued that optimism characterizes the "modern conception of progress," which is based on "the promise of steady improvement with no foreseeable ending at all."[10] The analogue to Reinhart Koselleck's concept of hope, optimism may be contrasted with hopefulness, which Lasch sees as stemming from prophetic views of history in Judeo-Christian beliefs, and which modern notions of progress have misused to argue for the possibility of secular utopia. Hopefulness "rests on confidence not so much in the future as in the past," argues Lasch. This confidence derives "from early memories—no doubt distorted, overlaid with later memories, and thus not wholly reliable as a guide to any factual reconstruction of past events—in which the experience of order and contentment was so intense that subsequent disillusionments cannot dislodge it." Such memories do not guarantee stability in the present or future; indeed, they accept that tragedies will occur. Nonetheless, the "experience of order and contentment" derives from a tradition of confidence in which some form of limited justice, some manner of partial resolution, will be possible, though it is not the resolution of secular utopia, unlimited growth, or the premodern organicism of cultural pessimism. This metapolitical or prepolitical point of view could be found in Germany in the thinking of individuals at numerous points on the political spectrum, from left liberals such as theologian-politician Friedrich Naumann or sociologist Ernst Troeltsch to the more conservative devotees of *Heimatschutz*. Uncertainly adjudicating between Koselleck's poles of hope and memory, a *bürgerlich* hopefulness worked throughout German preservationist discourse for much of the twentieth century.

The cultural practices of the *Bürgertum* were not merely compensations for the lack of political power or for the damages of modernity. Rather, such practices imparted meaning to a collective effort embedded in a tradition that was much more than an "invention." The goal was to shape a national memory that would have wide emotional resonance for a polity seeking orientation to the past and future in a time of significant change. But just as the state was unable to settle on a unified national style in architecture, *bürgerlich* social groups were unable to unite around a single cultural-political program of memory-work. Many would have agreed with Reich chancellor Bethmann Hollweg, who wrote historian Karl Lamprecht in 1913 that "we are not sufficiently secure in or aware of our culture, our inner being, and our national ideals."[11] Yet in one sense even this point needs to be qualified by noting again that all these initiatives, whether from conservative or from more progressive groups, sought inspiration from a revived sense of the national past. Constructing a broad campaign to modernize craft and industrial design in the late empire, the Deutscher Werkbund aspired "to restore the lost moral and aesthetic unity of German culture" as much as pessimistic or nostalgic groups did.[12] The advocates of a more emotionally compelling national memory-work marched in the same army, if they did not always fall into drill formation; theirs was a unity of sentiment and purpose if not of form, content, and method.

The formation of a national optics, a multifaceted way of seeing the historical nation in the physical environment, highlighted this emergent unity of sentiment. Having precedents in the Renaissance's desire for images, the late nineteenth century saw the emergence of a culture more saturated than before with visual stimuli. Urban communications and transportation networks created a need to "read" more public symbols, commercial markets created compact advertising messages designed for visual seduction rather than contemplation, and the realistic images of photography and film created new possibilities for visual memory.[13] Most important for our purposes was the national state's need to create objectified symbols of national identity that offered a point of contact and easily recognized visual referent for many disparate groups. The myth of a national community originating in the mists of time increasingly depended on the saturation of local communities with visual markers of the nation's perdurability. Emperor Napoleon I had anticipated the new age decades before by saying, "You must first of all speak to the eyes."[14]

In Germany the Kaiser and the Reich, the provinces, the cities, voluntary groups, and many individuals were involved in an often contentious effort to speak to the eyes of the new nation's citizens. Of all the artifacts produced by the emergent national optics of the late Empire, the most unusual were gargantuan national monuments that began to dot the German landscape in the last decades of the nineteenth century.[15] These included monuments to Arminius the Cheruscan (the *Hermannsdenkmal*) in the Teutoburg forest (1875); the Niederwald monument above the Rhine, which commemorated unification (1877–83); the centenary monument for the Battle of Nations in Leipzig, which was inaugurated in 1913 and considered by some the most illustrious example of that "fine barbarism" that served as a model for nationalist enthusiasm in the last years of the empire; and numerous statues of Wilhelm I, who for many symbolized official German nationalism. The era also saw the building of the grandiose avenue of heroic sculpture, the Siegesallee in Berlin, finished in 1901 and dedicated to the Hohenzollern princes, as well as the neo-Renaissance Reichstag building (1884–94), which served as an intentional national monument even if, strictly speaking, it belonged to the world of architecture. By 1906 Germans had erected more than 300 Bismarck monuments in a cult of commemoration for the Iron Chancellor.

Germany was not the only country to have many national monuments, but their sheer number and size (the Leipzig monument was ninety-one meters high) suggests a more substantial collective need for such objects. Their iconography indicated that nationalist myth and monumentality had become dominant motifs. Completed in 1896, the Kyffhäuser monument's massive base and statuary drew on popular folk myth of medieval emperor Friedrich Barbarossa, whose long subterranean slumber awaiting the renewal of German glory was ended with Wilhelm I's unification of Germany. This is one of many examples of the way medieval imagery continued to link postunification Germany with its preunification traditions. The *Hermannsdenkmal* commemorated the victory of Germanic chieftain Arminius over Roman occupiers in the first century A.D. Its sword was directed not against Rome but France, whose many enduring conflicts with Germany were thereby transformed into a product of a hereditary and deep-seated ethnic animosity rather than concrete historical circumstances. Replete with classical allegories and military figures, heavy neobaroque and neoromantic Wilhelm I monuments transformed the Prussian monarch into a figure beyond history, as did Bismarck monuments, which often achieved a similar effect through more modernist abstract motifs.

Often built atop mountains or in forest clearings, the national monuments had less effect on German visual identity than did urban fabrics as a whole, a second element of the national optics of the era. In the 1890s, ideas about the proper appearance of cities were undergoing a significant shift, thanks to Viennese town planner Camillo Sitte. Before Sitte, planners and architects followed the theories of Georges-Eugène Haussmann, the Alsatian civil servant who reshaped Paris at Napoleon III's behest. In Haussmann's work monumental buildings were isolated not only to provide "light and air," goals that became synonymous with twentieth-century functionalist planning, but also to refer the observer to history. The isolation of the historic building paralleled the optical characteristics of the single monument, whose placement disconnected it from social interactions. This approach entailed "disencumbering" buildings (in German, *Freilegung*, literally "laying free") from their surroundings, which meant that the preservation of historic buildings was very selective. Reinforcing the tendency to emphasize the monument isolated from its milieu, German architect Hermann Maertens's influential spatial aesthetics assumed the perspective of the single individual's static gaze at a building, which was comparable to how the educated middle class contemplated a painting in nineteenth-century art museums.[16] The result was that planning destroyed the milieu of monuments, often consisting of ensembles of "lesser" buildings that later generations would see as historically valuable.

Sitte attacked this spatial optics, although he shared Maertens's and Haussmann's belief in town planning as a tool for educating the masses and making aesthetic matters an autonomous part of planning discourse at a time when public hygiene and transportation needs dominated practice. Sitte was concerned with the aesthetic character of medieval, Renaissance, and baroque city squares. "In the cold traffic-swept modern city of the slide rule and the slum," wrote Carl Schorske of Sitte, "the picturesque, psychologically comforting square can reawaken memories of the vanquished burgher past." Sitte thought this "spatially dramatized memory" could inspire future generations to reawaken community in a rational society.[17] Instead of the universal, static observer contemplating a masterpiece, Sitte's ideal urban viewer took account of individuality, context, and the changing relationship between urban environments and their dwellers. This led him to attack disencumbering. His views became daily coinage for planners, officials, and preservationists in Germany, France, and Belgium at the turn of the century. But this was a temporary victory; proponents of light and air would still dominate urbanist thinking until well into the twentieth century, only to be challenged by a revival of Sittian perspectives, often wearing the conceptual clothing of postmodern theory, in the 1960s.[18]

Sitte also opened the way for more subjective and post-historicist views of the past, because he allowed planners to experiment with historical styles without being wedded to the historically "true" models that constrained Haussmann.[19] Sitte's approach could add to the resources of a national optics because it logically led to a multiplication of buildings that should or could be preserved—or to a multiplication of new monuments, squares, and historical buildings—as part of the historic fabric of a city. History could be more ubiquitous, and individuals could see themselves more readily in urban squares and monuments designed to strengthen national memory. Whereas Haussmann's view stressed monumental history, therefore, Sitte's was potentially more antiquarian. Nietzsche argued that the monumental species of history wanted inspiration across the millennia; the antiquarian, piety for the everyday. The monumental wanted movement toward greatness; the antiquarian, contentment and repose. These goals made antiquarians direct their gaze not only at the mountaintops of human achievement, the stuff of monumental history, but at the everyday foothills, where one found "the trivial, circumscribed, decaying and obsolete." For "the preserving and revering soul of the antiquarian man," wrote Nietzsche, "the history of his city becomes for him the history of himself; he reads its walls, its towered gate, its rules and regulations, its holidays, like an illuminated diary of his youth and in all this he finds again himself."[20] The antiquarian species of memory, as represented in Sitte's urbanistic views, brought the enduring and tangible past within the reach of Everyman.

During the second half of the nineteenth century, German architecture, a third important component of the emergent national optics, developed along the same eclectic and historicist lines that English and U.S. "Victorian" architecture did. Like Haussmann's disencumbering restorations, this architecture reflected a desire to capture pure historical styles that referred people to the values and inspirations of a specific moment in the past. Around the turn of the century, architects Alfred Messel, Peter Behrens, and Paul Bonatz fought for simpler, cleaner architectural forms and new orientations to the cultural heritage. Although their ideas were neither homogeneous nor uniformly successful, they shared an antipathy to historicism without abandoning historical references and without ignoring the persistence of historical tradition. "Using the vocabularies of the older styles, chiefly Gothic and baroque, in new, more orderly, and more vigorous combinations," writes Barbara Miller Lane, "the progressive architects gradually derived from them a set of forms which were at once novel in appearance and visually related to the past."[21] "Abstraction from historicism" took varied forms, including Messel's Wertheim department store in Berlin in 1904, Behrens's Mannesmann Works building in Düsseldorf in 1912, and Paul Schultze-Naumburg's residential designs.

Before World War I there were more radical proponents of the cleaner, simpler style, to be sure; among them were individuals that became leaders of "new building" (*Neues Bauen*) after the war, such as Walter Gropius and Bruno Taut. But generally before the war there was cooperation between the more mainstream proponents of abstracted historicism and the more innovative personalities, a cooperation based partly on the Werkbund. "The architects within the Werkbund thought of themselves as working together to improve the nation's industrial culture," Lane writes, "and this outweighed their differences."[22] These architects had a more relaxed sense of obligation to the omnipresent historical models of the past than their nineteenth-century predecessors had. "Reject the past, but do not sever its bonds to the present" was their motto. They thereby endorsed hope fully but maintained a place for memory in the form of a highly personal obligation to the picturesque, as Sitte had used the term. At the same time, they stressed modern social needs and were thus part of the differentiated early turn to modernist functionalism.[23]

The drive to protect valued local cultures and landscapes, or *Heimatschutz*, intersected with all of these developments, but it also marked its own territory. The roots of *Heimatschutz* can be traced in part to Romanticism's emphasis on the impact physical environments had on identity, to which the first folklorist, Wilhelm Heinrich Riehl, added an important supplement. For Riehl the nation was a total entity defined by four Ss: tribe (*Stamm*), language (*Sprache*), custom (*Sitte*), and settlement (*Siedlung*). Riehl's interest in the last of these gave his work a special relevance for the admirers of historic buildings. A proponent of the traditional peasantry as a backbone of German identity, he thought preindustrial physical settings (including forests and fields) were not only beautiful but functionally superior to industrial ones. His "conservative criticism of modernity" was unpalatable to the national-liberal professors who dominated the German university, while his interest in folklore put him at odds with the then dominant scholars of political history. Nonetheless, *Heimatschutz* spokesmen referred to Riehl as a spiritual father. Riehl himself served as Bavarian conservator of monuments late in the nineteenth century, and one of his Munich university students, Georg Hager, went on to serve in the same position in 1907 while also becoming a noted art historian and leading *Heimatschutz* spokesman.[24]

The *Heimatschutz* movement got started in 1903 when Berlin music professor Ernst Rudorff published a call to unite Germany's cultural, historical, preservationist, and nature conservation groups in the Deutscher Bund Heimatschutz.[25] Founded in Dresden in March 1904 and chaired until 1914 by Paul Schultze-Naumburg, the group had the support of famous economists Carl Johannes Fuchs and Werner Sombart, Hamburg museum director Alfred Lichtwark, geographer Friedrich Ratzel, painter Hans Thoma, Dürerbund chair Ferdinand Avenarius, architect Theodor Fischer, and many others. Like preservation societies, with which its organizations were allied or sometimes identical, it acknowledged the German state's accomplishments in cultural politics but said there was still room for voluntary initiative. Preservation of historic sites was only one of its goals. Influenced by John Ruskin's and William Morris's aesthetic-social critique of English capitalism as well as by the French "Société pour la protection des paysages de France," it was also interested in promoting traditional building forms, conserving natural sites, collecting folk art, and promoting new land use patterns. Given this list, the movement's reputation for dreamy utopianism, often derived from concentrating narrowly on Rudorff's vivid prose or focusing one-sidedly on *Heimat* art and novels, is unwarranted. *Heimatschutz* had practical goals based on the idea that aesthetically pleasing landscapes were socially meaningful. It had small, visible organizations that attracted a professional and civil service constituency that before World War I may have amounted to more than 30,000 dues-paying members.[26]

Heimatschutz had sweeping aspirations: "Let us create a Bund of like-minded people throughout Germany whose goal is to maintain an undamaged and untainted German race [*Volkstum*]," the group's founding statement read, "and to protect from further misfortune what is inseparable from that mission: the German homeland with its monuments and its poetry of nature." Imbued with this spirit, *Heimatschutz* publications sought maximum publicity, and in 1907 the organization's newsletter announced that in Germany 300 newspaper articles monthly dealt with some aspect of *Heimatschutz*. The movement gave voice to a growing concern about the visual integrity of German cities, roadsides, and countrysides. Its emphasis on the "look" of Germany shared much with the socially liberal Werkbund's concern over German design culture. Its stress on the total environment made it compatible with planners' and preservationists' focus on ensembles rather than isolated landmarks. Because the purview of *Heimatschutz* was broader than that of any of the activities discussed so far, its goal of being a point of intersection for all groups involved in creating a national optics was theoretically well founded, if practically unrealized. Still, it managed to consolidate the resources of preservation and environmentalist groups more successfully than did its British counterparts, who were stuck in an unwieldy web of overlapping associations. Because it stressed new uses of cultural and natural resources rather than strict separation of valued areas from social change, it was compatible with efforts to find innovative ways of relating to German history without forsaking the advantages of industrial society.[27]

Beyond this, the movement's goal of creating an undamaged and untainted German race, promulgated energetically by Schultze-Naumburg, had serious implications. It contained a mythic element, a call for a return to origins, as all of the areas surveyed so far did. But here myth entered the world of racial politics, which took on more organized shape in the late Kaiserreich. Conserving the visual integrity of the nation intersected broadly with attempts to conserve racial characteristics and to give politics a "biologistic" basis. Yet the racial message came through unevenly. *Heimatschutz* conservationism had an impact wherever the *Bürgertum* envisioned Germany in the total physical environment; racialism was neither necessary nor inevitable when supporting such goals. The movement's influence among the educated classes was much wider than membership numbers suggest, and it had support from conservative figures in provincial regimes as well as social liberals, Garden City activists, and other bourgeois reformists.[28] The diversity of such groups and interests worked against the brutal uniformities of a racist worldview. What is more, the practical goals of the movement could overshadow the tendency toward ideology and a racialization of national memory.

Whereas the builders of national monuments, town planners, architects, and *Heimatschutz* supporters often spoke to different interests and audiences, they shared a fundamental desire to create new orientations to the German past and new emotional bonds between members of the nation. They shared a desire to step out of the nineteenth century without jettisoning its most important accomplishments and institutions. They believed in hope, but they felt that modernity's ceaseless evisceration of the past could be counterbalanced. They believed in the possibilities of the future and in the healthy and life-enhancing limits of the past. They shared a belief that creating a vibrant optic identity for the nation was central to attaining national political goals. Historic preservation shaped and was shaped by these practices.

Preservation and National Life

Building on traditions of cultural politics in the territorial states, German intellectuals and state officials of the first half of the nineteenth century had already turned their attention to historic preservation. Among the leading influences were Goethe, who departed from tradition in 1773 by writing that an entire building could unintentionally become a "monument," and the Prussian Law Code of 1794, which systematized the legal structure of the monarchy and gave the state the right to protect historically important buildings without setting up a legal apparatus to do so. More than these influences, the aftermath of the French Revolution stimulated public interest in monuments, as, following Thomas Nipperdey, "the consciousness of revolutionary breaks and losses[,] ... the demand for history and continuity, and thus the feeling for 'monuments' of the past, gained ground, especially after 1815." The famous architect and Prussian building official Karl Friedrich Schinkel gave voice to such feelings when he wrote that a nation without historic buildings was "strangely naked and bare, like a new colony in a previously uninhabited land." Concentrating more on Prussian than national identity, Schinkel argued that each district of the monarchy should appoint an expert for preservation much like the provincial conservators Prussia would later have, and he trained Ferdinand von Quast, a young architecture student who became Prussia's first conservator of monuments in 1843.[29]

Among the key postrevolution projects in monument preservation was Prussia's restoration from 1817 to 1830 of the deteriorated Marienburg fortress, the main building of the Deutscher Orden, knightly colonizers of the East, until 1457. Slated for demolition, the historic ruin was the object of a public campaign for preservation, to which the Prussian state acceded. Social pressure in 1827 also motivated Prussia to protect the castle ruin Drachenfels in the Siebengebirge, which was threatened by destructive stone quarrying. Working to enhance its prestige in the newly acquired Catholic Rhineland, the mainly Protestant Prussian state also renewed efforts in 1823 to complete the Cologne cathedral, finishing the project only in 1880 with many private donations and much public sympathy. Bavaria's commitment to historic preservation was even greater than Prussia's, due to the personal interests of Ludwig I, the monarchy's desire to integrate new territories, and a need to provide a Catholic counterweight to Prussian cultural politics.[30] Although both Prussia and Bavaria stressed their national mission, their officials finally placed more emphasis on monarchical and provincial loyalty than on German heritage. Nonetheless, in both states, monument preservation contributed to a sense of the enduring resonance of the past in the present.

Prussia and Bavaria remained leaders in historic preservation, but Baden, Hessen-Darmstadt, Oldenburg, Lübeck, and Bremen also passed noteworthy legislation during the nineteenth century, using cultural politics to legitimate themselves to their populations and against their more powerful neighbors. Such efforts were comparatively limited, as all the German states lagged behind the French in appointing conservators and inventorying monuments. Money was in short supply, and most of the major preservation projects relied on donations and lotteries. Expertise was lacking, as most preservation relied on voluntary labor, and liberal notions of property hindered state efforts to protect historic buildings. In 1871 only Prussia, Bavaria, Baden, and Württemberg among the federal states had central agencies for monument preservation. After Prussia formed an all-volunteer Central Commission for the Research and Maintenance of Monuments in 1853 to assist the state conservator, its forty-two members met exactly two times before it was dissolved in 1891. Officials had a narrow view of historic architecture, concentrating mainly on a few key monuments in government hands, and attempts to expand legal protection to privately held monuments encountered resistance from legislators and property owners.[31]

The journal *Monument Preservation* (*Die Denkmalpflege*, or *DP*) was published for the first time in 1899. Its appearance was symptomatic of developments in the previous two or three decades and constitutive of major changes still to come.[32] Published by the Prussian Ministry of Public Works and inspired by the idea of *Kulturstaat* activism, the *DP* was the first periodical to respond specifically to public interest in historic preservation. One of the first editors was Oskar Hoßfeld, an architect, university lecturer, and Prussian building official who later played a role in drafting legislation affecting historical buildings and forming the *Heimatschutz* movement. Hoßfeld and his coeditor wrote in the journal's first number that despite the importance of the "historical sciences" for all nations, many Germans were "indifferent or blind . . . towards the documents of stone that have come down to us, the architectural monuments and everything that goes with them." So serious was the indifference, the editors averred, that it created doubts about the "cultural achievement that our age so readily claims for itself." Traffic planning and public health policy, disencumbering and destructive restorations, and selfishness and an unthinking desire for the new promoted such indifference. But matters were improving, as both state initiatives and public awareness were growing. People had begun to heed the "golden words of Bismarck," according to the editors, that it was "of greatest harm to a nation when it allows the living consciousness of its connection to its heritage and history to fade." They were convinced that a fundamental reason for preservation's new influence was to be found not only in functional responses to destruction but in a new sense of the nation. Previous generations of preservationists were also motivated by national aims, but they derived their identity from an "undefined Romantic sensibility" rather than the "firm ground of a strong national consciousness" that had evolved in the present.

This shift in sensibility was registered more substantively in "The Protection and Preservation of Monuments in the Nineteenth Century," an address given at the university in Strasbourg by art historian Georg Dehio on 27 January 1905.[33] Born in the Baltic in 1850 and trained by historians Leopold von Ranke and Heinrich von Sybel, Dehio taught art history in Königsberg, Strasbourg (from 1892 to 1918), and Tübingen. He was best known as the compiler of a five-volume survey of German monuments funded by the royal government and completed in 1912, which was widely used as a guide to German historic buildings by preservationists and tourists alike. Having assembled the Gideon's Bible of German monuments, Dehio became a visible public symbol for the preservationist cause, and by the time of his death in 1932 he was recognized as someone who had written for specialists as well as the cultured classes as a whole.[34] Celebrating the birthday of Kaiser Wilhelm II at the university of this Alsatian city on Germany's western frontier, Dehio's speech was delivered before an audience consisting of the monarch himself, faculty, and students. It was the first such academic presentation to deal exclusively with the subject, indicating monument preservation's new status.

Dehio's speech outlined the state of the discipline, beginning with praise for Wilhelm II's support for preservation, but then assuming a critical tone unusual for such celebratory addresses. Monuments were being destroyed at an alarming rate because the modern age was shaped by the French Revolution's "fanaticism of reason," which obliterated historic places "on principle, to the honor of the Enlightenment and the promotion of the living." "The stream of modern economic life" furthered destruction, treating monuments as obstacles and gulping "them down one piece after another from day to day." Even more threatening was the tendency to disencumber monuments and restore them to a presumed historical purity. This had been the dominant practice of preservation for most of the nineteenth century but had been under steady attack since at least the 1880s. "Restora-

Georg Dehio: "What a bounty of historical life still radiates from eight centuries of the past mirrored in the [Strasbourg] cathedral." (photo: *Die schöne Heimat* [1916], 38)

tion" was the "illegitimate child" of historicism whose practitioners, the "doctors of monuments," were "more dangerous than the sickness itself." This moved Dehio to say that the first "commandment" of preservation was "conserve, do not restore." This commandment was best symbolized in the 800-year-old Strasbourg cathedral, whose "bounty of historical life" was well reflected in its many historical accretions, which contrasted starkly with the "cold, archaeological abstraction" that the stylistically "purer" Cologne cathedral had become through its restoration and "completion."[35] To allow national architectural symbols to endure in all their authenticity, conservation, not restoration, was the preferred practice, in Dehio's eyes.

Dehio stressed that preservation was motivated above all by a political goal. "We conserve a monument," he said, "not because we consider it beautiful, but because it is a piece of our national life. To protect monuments is not to pursue pleasure, but to practice piety. Aesthetic and even art-historical judgments change, but here an unchanging criterion is found."[36] Dehio thereby attacked the restorationists, who favored historic buildings not for their historical evolution per se but for the aesthetic qualities of particular architectural styles in the past. He also made an implicit attack on Alois Riegl's idea that not national-historical significance but the "age

Georg Dehio: "We conserve a monument not because we consider it beautiful, but because it is a piece of our national life." (photo: Universitätsbibliothek Tübingen)

value," or *Alterswert*, of buildings caught the imagination of people. Influenced by an emergent tradition of Viennese preservation that questioned absolute standards of beauty, Riegl argued that historical additions on monuments were documents of the "artistic intention" of past ages. These additions were increasingly valued by the public because of the simple fact that they were old and they reflected a building's passage through time. Historical or artistical importance as well as national consequence were secondary considerations. Opposed to any form of restoration, Riegl favored a radical conservation policy by which buildings were maintained but eventually allowed to deteriorate and amortize their full age value "naturally." Although he supported this critique of restoration and by no means discounted other motivations for preservation, Dehio thought Riegl had replaced national memory with hedonistic contemplation of decay for pleasure-seeking individuals uninterested in collective visions of the past.[37]

Cultural-national identity thus reigned over all other reasons for saving old buildings, becoming the one truth that persisted while other interests resonated within and around it. For Dehio, preservation meant proactive pursuit of national goals. He used the more assertive term "protection" of monuments (*Denkmalschutz*) rather than "care" or "maintenance" (*Denkmalpflege*) to describe this project. Although the roots of preservation lay in a conservative impulse to guard against revolutionary historicide, it also required official action to restrict liberal property rights. "I know of no other name for [preservation]," stated Dehio, "than socialism." Leading preservationists such as Dresden art historian Cornelius Gurlitt had also stressed a proactive drive to enhance "social well-being," although for Gurlitt protecting old buildings was a "conservative practice" devoted to "spreading beauty over the entire country with a liberal hand." Dehio was not in any case the only member of the German *Bürgertum* to argue for a conservative-national notion of socialism.[38]

Although Dehio had drawn a stark picture of threats to German historical property, his emphasis on national life and socialism struck a hopeful tone. Noting preservation's reliance on municipalities, schools, and the press, he asserted that "in every stratum . . . the feeling should spread that a *Volk* that has many old monuments is a grand *Volk*." This "recognition of the right of the dead for the good of the living" would be ensured with public action, which would also address preservation methodologies. Educated about the evils of restoration, Germans would rediscover a "clear and uniform architectural and artistic conviction." From that moment, Dehio predicted, "the tributary that had erroneously branched off from the stream of creative art and threatened our old monuments under the name restoration, will return to its natural channel."[39] Dehio thus viewed the relationship of past and present in Enlightenment terms, regarding history as the raw material for a cautionary tale that would lead to a more progressive age of "socialism" oriented to national goals, enlightened public activity, and conservation rather than restoration. The history of preservation thus reproduced the wider societal tendency to place hope above memory even when memory was to be saved from oblivion. Still, by making national memory-work the primary motivation of preservation, Dehio voiced a belief that the past would nurture and sustain future actions. In expressing this belief, he not only synthesized for his listeners the brief history of modern German historic preservation up to that point but also laid out an agenda of hopefulness for the future.

Micropolitics

What institutional relations characterized preservation at the time of Dehio's address? Although *Denkmalpflege* had "developed into its own professional branch," according to a popular lexicon in 1906, the process was still incomplete. Legislation had no systematic method for protection of historic places, and "concerning the basic principles of preservation," the lexicon read, "opinions are still divided." Significantly and accurately, the entry did not portray preservation as a product of specifically German concerns but rather as one manifestation of a modern and international movement including Greece, France, Austria, and other countries.[40]

Among the still-debated "basic principles" to which the lexicon referred was official preservation's definition of the historical building. Conservators and officials were interested above all in what may be called public symbols, objects such as monumental buildings, formal gardens, and historic urban squares that inspire observers and draw them into a larger community. Public symbols may be contrasted with "fields of care," ensembles of objects and spaces such as old urban quarters or "lesser" historical places that are entrenched in daily life. Fields of care are more "antiquarian" than public symbols because they inspire affection for valued social interactions and the memories to which they give rise rather than reverence or awe.[41] Heuristic categories rather than social realities, public symbols and fields of care, like the monumental and antiquarian species of history to which they could be related, would overlap in preservationist practice and public opinions. But like Haussmann's monumental buildings—and despite the influence of Sittian contextualism—an architectural monument was in this period still regarded primarily as an isolated public symbol with definitive artistic or historical value.

Public policy replicated this view. Inventories of historic buildings suggested greater awareness of monuments, but they often did more to narrow perceptions of the past than widen them. The inventories reflected official memory's sense of historical architecture because they were cooperative efforts undertaken by conservators and local *Bürger*, such as a pastor and three local nobles in Geldern in 1891, and they were often subsidized with government grants. The 1894 inventory for Düsseldorf city and county concentrated on the Middle Ages; avoided almost all architecture built after the early nineteenth century, which meant almost all neoclassicist buildings; and was only 172 pages long. By contrast, the interwar inventories of Cologne and Münster would have almost 600 pages each for "profane" monuments alone. Quasi-state organizations such as the Rhenish Association for the Preservation of Historic Sites (Rheinischer Verein für Denkmalpflege und Heimatschutz, or RVDH) adopted an increasingly catholic view of monuments, but before World War I most of the group's subsidies for preservation went to historic churches, of which there was an abundant number in the Rhineland.[42] In Prussia inventories and the Rhenish group relied heavily on the support of the provincial assemblies (*Provinzialverbände*), which were answerable to the provincial parliaments (*Landtage*). In this period the parliaments were regulated by a three-class voting system giving disproportionate power to manufacturers, nobles, and high-level civil servants from the National Liberal and conservative parties. Official preservation thus answered to the fiscal authority of elites whose view of the cultural heritage was marked by a "longing for beauty" based on a narrow canon of monuments.[43]

Nonetheless, the emphasis on a more visually resonant sense of national life and the general public awareness of monuments worked to expand definitions of the historical building. Heinrich Lezius, the author of a 1908 book on preservation law, argued that "also objects without any art-historical value and which merely refer to historical events belong among those things important to historic preservation." In Saxony preservationists had begun to protect "technical monuments" such as old foundries, windmills, and waterwheels, while in Lüneburg the Old Crane, used for loading and unloading ships since the fourteenth century, became a favored historical object.[44]

As the perception of monuments changed, so too did preservation law. In part due to its federalist heritage, Germany had no national preservation legislation of the kind France or Greece had, although such legislation was debated from the Kaiserreich to the Federal Republic. Still, German preservationists were not without legal power, being able to draw on building ordinances and police regulations. The first decade of the twentieth century was crucial because many laws were passed that defined legal protection for historic buildings for decades to come.

Two landmarks were the Hessian law of 1902 and the Prussian law of 1907, which set the parameters for other legislative acts in Saxony, Baden, Württemberg, Oldenburg, and Bavaria. Studied not only in Germany but throughout Europe, the Hessian law was a good example of how smaller German states used cultural politics to compete with their more powerful cousins.[45] A response to public pressure since the 1880s, the Hessian law provided for the drawing up of a list of protected monuments, like the French *classement*, by a council of monuments with representatives from the churches, history societies, and owners of historic properties. It stated that private or corporate owners of monuments could be fined or even imprisoned for altering a listed site without state permission, although there was no apparatus for compelling owners to enter this arrangement save that of the little-used threat of expropriation. Unlisted monuments were subject to compulsory purchase, and the "milieu" (*Umgebung*) of monuments could also be protected. Coming on the heels of 1902 legislation controlling "disfigurement" (*Verunstaltung*) of "outstanding scenic areas," the 1907 Prussian law also potentially protected the milieu of a monument and provided for compulsory purchases, although it did not create a *classement*. Unlike the Hessian law, which put landmarks under direct legal protection, Prussian legislation was based on traditions of aesthetic policing derived from the Prussian Law Code. Its most significant feature was that it empowered local communities to pass preservation ordinances. It also stimulated debates about the meaning of disfigurement, a fuzzy term seemingly applicable to any change in the physical environment with which one disagreed.[46] No one questioned the darker meaning of the term, which, like contemporary and later forms of racism, relied on imagery of the "degeneration" (*Entartung*) of a previously organic coherence marred by modern commerce and industry.

Preservation followed the tripartite organization of German cultural politics in which the provincial (in Prussia) or state cultural ministry was the highest authority for the protection of historic sites, the administrative districts (*Bezirke*) the next highest, and counties and independently administered cities the lowest. Conservators were strategically nested in this structure of authority, being responsible to the state or provincial cultural ministries but dealing extensively with lower officials. Bavaria appointed a general inspector of monuments in 1835, but his authority was limited, compared with that of the first Prussian conservator of monuments, appointed eight years later. Baden appointed a conservator in 1853; Württemberg, in 1858. In the Hamburg city-state, officials such as museum director Justus Brinckmann, responsible for the first authoritative inventories of monuments in the area, did the work of conservators without being offi-

Paul Clemen, first conservator of monuments in the Prussian Rhine province, 1893, and a leading innovator in German preservation until his death in 1947 (photo: Archiv der Rheinischen Friedrich-Wilhelms-Universität Bonn)

DOCUMENTS OF STONE

cially recognized. In Prussia after 1891 provincial conservators were elected by preservation commissions (with representatives of provincial government, voluntary associations, and churches) and approved by the cultural ministry. Before World War I Prussia had a single state conservator and fourteen provincial conservators. Whether the conservator had substantial autonomy, as in the Prussian Rhineland, or was de facto head of a commission for monuments, as in Saxony, he was to embody the qualities of a good civil servant, which with reference to Reinhold Persius, Prussian state conservator from 1886 to 1901, meant "a feeling of obligation to do one's duty, conscientiousness, and joy in work coupled with moderation and consistency of thinking."[47]

What did conservators do? The Prussian Rhine province, consisting of the administrative districts of Bonn, Cologne, and Düsseldorf, serves as an example.[48] Benefiting from the decentralization of provincial government in Prussia in 1875, the Rhine Province had its first conservator in 1893, Paul Clemen, who represented both the Prussian conservator of monuments in Berlin and Rhenish self-government, which now devoted much attention to setting up museums and protecting monuments.[49] The first substantial job for the conservator was to inventory Rhenish monuments, a project that produced thirty-one volumes by 1924. The act of naming, a key part of preservation practice because it defined a field of inquiry, was thus at the heart of the conservator's mission. The provincial conservator worked with a very small staff and oversaw a limited group of sites. Elected by the provincial commission, he (only males acted as conservators in the Second Empire) also cooperated with voluntary groups that subsidized and supported preservation projects. He was asked to educate the public as well, which meant giving lectures, publishing newsletters, keeping a small library, and visiting numerous historic sites, activities that gave him an almost ethnographic perspective on local culture. Although conservators constituted a small group of officials, their influence widened considerably through such public contacts.

Appointed at age twenty-seven, Clemen was perhaps the most important conservator in German history.[50] Responsible for over one-quarter of all historic buildings in the Prussian monarchy, he had more monuments from the medieval period under his supervision than any conservator in Europe. Besides serving as the Rhenish conservator from 1893 to 1911, he was the founder of Bonn university's art history institute, organizer of the German art conservation (*Kunstschutz*) program during World War I, and chair of the annual preservation congress, the Tag für Denkmalpflege, from 1923 to 1932. His book *German Art and Historic Preservation: A Confession*, published in 1933 but including essays and addresses from the preceding two decades, was a central text of German preservation in the first half of the century, containing detailed discussions of preservation goals as well as a rudimentary semiotics of monuments. An exchange professor at Harvard in 1907, Clemen admired and wrote expertly on French medieval architecture and read John Ruskin, H. G. Wells, Oscar Wilde, and Le Corbusier. He would help to reestablish official preservation in the Rhineland after World War II until his death in 1947. Unusual because of his multifaceted activity over such a long period of time, Clemen nonetheless fit the mold of the conservator as both specialist and cultural generalist, a pattern Ferdinand von Quast, first Prussian conservator from 1843 to 1876, initiated. At the same time Clemen symbolized and furthered a trend toward the professionalization of the conservator's office.

Of the many institutions and voluntary associations that specialized in the advocacy of Germany's architectural heritage, the most important on the national scene before 1914 was the Tag für Denkmalpflege, an annual conference growing out of the Association of German History and Antiquities Societies. Begun in 1900, the conference created an open public forum for debate, and thus it reflected the key controversies of historic preservation in a less diluted form than the more technical *DP* did. Newspapers gave substantial coverage to the conferences, whose proceedings were published in book form, often with tasteful *Jugendstil* motifs. A diverse assemblage of individuals attended the conference, which included professional discussions, tours, social events, and lectures on the history of the city in which the event was held. At the 1901 conference in Freiburg, there were ninety official participants; twenty-seven were federal and municipal officials, and twenty-three were university professors. The others were university students, architects, conservators, directors of archives and museums, artists and writers, and members of the free professions.[51] Gaining adherents from throughout Germany as well as Austria and Switzerland, the Tag grew substantially in the years before World War I, and the last prewar conference in 1913 had 700 people in attendance.

Mostly all the official participants at the conferences were men, although women, many of whom were spouses of the attendees, went to lectures by noted architects or conservators as part of the evening social programs. Males predominated in provincial preservation societies, too, even when the less professionalized nature of these groups led to a broader social and gender mix.[52] So-called beautification societies (*Verschönerungsvereine*) such as the large Pfälzerwald Verein actively recruited women but did not elect them to positions of authority. In the national *Heimatschutz* movement only about 5 percent of the membership consisted of women; in the elite RVDH, less than 4 percent. Exclusion of women from the ranks of architectural preservationists was not just a German proclivity but was typical of the movement in the United States as well. But in the United States, women had been in the forefront of preservation either earlier in the nineteenth century, as the Mount Vernon Ladies' Association led a campaign to preserve George Washington's home, or more sporadically at the turn of the century, as when the Daughters of the Republic of Texas preserved the Alamo. Whether they were increasingly marginalized as in the United States or excluded from the beginning as in Germany, women failed to take a leading role in preservation because of the defeat of amateurism and the victory of a professionalizing, male-dominated discipline of architecture.

One of the key preservation associations in Germany was the already mentioned RVDH, founded in 1906 in the historic Gürzenich assembly hall in Cologne.[53] An "allied" association of the Bund Heimatschutz rather than a provincial branch, the RVDH was unique within the *Heimatschutz* movement because it focused primarily on saving historic buildings. It was firmly embedded in Rhenish power relations due to its importance to the Prussian state's attempt to assert cultural and political authority over a Catholic majority and a restive working class. As the group's 1906 program read, the association wanted to assist the state in preserving the "lovely charm" of the Rhineland against the "inartistic and coarse features" of society, putting special emphasis on the less well known monuments of Rhenish towns that had "meaning for the history of the community and its inhabitants." With fewer than 2,000 members, the RVDH was small, but its elite stance and close contact with state authority gave it influence far beyond its size. The board of directors included a retired district president, two judges, a Cologne banker, and two university professors, one of whom was Clemen. Honorary members included all major figures from provincial self-government as well as the Catholic archbishop of Cologne. A list of eighty-two signatories had leading notables from government, education, the aristocracy, and business, while among forty-eight large donors to the group, thirty-one were commercial councilors (*Kommerzienräte*), bankers, or manufacturers. The Kaiser added to the ambience of power by sending the association a note of congratulations on its creation. All this gave the RVDH that "snob appeal" enjoyed by similarly well-heeled preservation groups not only in Germany—the Association for the Preservation of German Castles, founded in 1899 and led by Bodo Ebhardt, castle restorer and close associate of Wilhelm II, is a good example—but also in France, England, and the United States.[54]

The RVDH prefigured a firmer national coalition between *Heimatschutz* and official preservation. Five years after the founding of the association, the

One of Cologne's most famous monuments, the fifteenth-century Gürzenich
assembly hall, site of the 1906 founding of the elite preservation society RVDH
(photo: *Große Bürgerbauten deutscher Vergangenheit* [1916], 91)

Salzburg preservation congress initiated biannual joint meetings of the two movements, whose differences reflected why each participant was interested in what the other had to offer. *Heimatschutz's* more expansive view of cultural politics meant it also had an indistinct view of historic buildings as such, and it was significant that Schultze-Naumburg never published a systematic statement on the methods of architectural preservation. *Heimatschutz* often engaged in quiet negotiation over preservation laws and building ordinances, but it also had a strident and attention-getting tone in public debates stemming from its more heated nationalism and relative independence from official circles. It was common for *Heimatschutz* publications to attack the "wretchedness" of those who violated the group's aesthetic standards and to ridicule opponents' arguments.[55] Contemplative and scholarly by comparison, preservationists working in state, provincial, or municipal agencies nonetheless gave *Heimatschutz* specialized information and a more direct line of influence to official cultural politics. In return, preservationists derived a broader public forum for their agenda by exploiting *Heimatschutz's* wide activities and assertive image. Still, one must not overdo the contrast. *Heimatschutz's* evolution into a popular mass movement combating historicide was more potential than real in this period, and architectural preservation was already rethinking its social role before *Heimatschutz* became its ally, as noted in 1908 by Schultze-Naumburg, who wrote that "with its own growth historic preservation [*Denkmalpflege*] had greatly expanded its program."[56]

Preservationists widened their concept of the historical building, passed more assertive legislation, gave conservators substantial influence, and created an infrastructure for significant public action. Such efforts impressed Edinburgh art historian G. Baldwin Brown, who in 1905 argued that Germany was about to become the European leader in maintaining national architectural heritage, and who wrote that German preservationists successfully implemented their public aims because they were not "extremists" or amateurs but "practical men who are familiar with the exigencies of modern life." Yet obstacles remained. State fiscal support for historic preservation was hard to come by, and the annual preservation congress had to campaign extensively to get an annual grant of 100,000 marks from Prussia. One sympathetic parliamentary deputy, Graf von Hutten-Czapski, observed that "no state with any monuments to speak of gives nearly so little for historic preservation as we do." "Rich France spends three million francs annually," said the deputy, "poor Italy a million lire, and here one thinks of 100,000 marks as being too much. Millions in national heritage are being lost by saving a few thousand marks each year." Debates over preservation legislation in state parliaments were rancorous, as in Württemberg, where representatives championed the "personal freedom of the individual property owner" against preservationists. Cities empowered to pass ordinances protecting historic buildings as a result of the Prussian law made uneven use of their right; in the Prussian Rhine province 150 towns had passed preservation ordinances by 1911, whereas just 38 had done so in Schleswig-Holstein by 1922. Even in the Rhineland the provincial conservator and the RVDH negotiated strenuously with cities, threatening to withhold subsidies for preservation projects if magistrates failed to pass ordinances.[57]

Scrutiny, License, and Control

Promoting national life through preservation of documents of stone entailed not only the building of a public infrastructure but also identifying the nation and its history. But to what nation would preservationists refer in the light of the uncertainties that hampered the new empire and the emergent quality of their own discourse? Discussing England in this period, Philip Dodd wrote that "a great deal of the power of the dominant version of Englishness . . . lay in its ability to represent both itself to others and those others to themselves." This "representation worked by a process of inclusion, exclusion and transformation," he stated, a dynamic of "scrutiny, license and control" by which groups tried to define the historical and cultural meaning of the nation.[58] The ability of preservationists to represent the nation to themselves and their audiences also rested significantly on their own narratives of scrutiny, license, and control.

Scrutinizing society for its "nationness" in the context of the late empire meant a selective appropriation of modernity. If the nation was a vector of modernity, then the level and quality of nationhood itself reflected the ability of Germans to establish a dynamic and creative relationship to the tendencies of a modern society. For preservationists, railway building and architectural modernism were two contemporary developments that significantly affected the optic identity of the nation. Although preservationists attacked materialism and unlimited urban growth, they also accepted that new modes of transportation and communication such as railways were quite literally roads to modern nationality. Unlike English cultural critic John Ruskin, who decried "the iron veins that traverse the frame of [the] country," many preservationists were aware that railways could be used to rediscover the past's surviving traces in the present. In a piece titled "Ramblings through Old Towns," a *DP* writer praised the "magic" of the "modern express train" that enabled him to traverse the nation and arrive in Würzburg for the beginning of a journey through historic Franconian and Swabian communities. "Yesterday at work on the lazy northern Nogat," he marveled, "today on the rushing Main where one sees the townscape encircled by rich vineyards and hilltops!"[59] The railway knit the nation together, creating social relations through which Germans would experience themselves sharing a rediscovered past beyond town, region, and countryside. The creation and spread of something new, the railroad, allowed something quite old, the nation, to extend its influence.

Like the railroad, architectural modernism was a threat as well as an opportunity. Leading preservationists and *Heimatschutz* representatives selectively adopted architectural modernism in an attempt to exploit its advantages and control its disruptive tendencies. All additions to historic architecture "had to eventually subordinate themselves to the artistic totality of the historical ensemble," maintained Paul Clemen, but at the same time historicism's "hypertrophy" of the past, its overwrought need to ape historical styles, had to come to an end. This critique of historicism led Clemen to support the prewar architectural modernism of Messel, Behrens, Bonatz, and the young Schultze-Naumburg. Following Clemen's balanced embrace of the new architecture, the RVDH gave a positive reception to industrial buildings in the modernist vein for German General Electric, the Krupp firm, and other corporations. Cornelius Gurlitt was another leading proponent of modernist architecture in historic preservation. An art historian and professor in Dresden whose academic writings filled ninety-seven volumes from the 1870s to the 1930s, Gurlitt was an outspoken critic of restoration. Like French preservationists who were inspired by Art Nouveau, he advocated *Jugendstil* modifications on historical architecture because they fit the irregular lines of ancient buildings. He criticized the Paris of Haussmann and the Vienna of the Ringstraße, but he still advocated modernist planning as long as it combined beauty and utility. Although his cultural influences included Langbehn, he also read Ibsen, and he was noted for the tolerance with which he studied new artistic styles. His pre–World War I writing revealed the varieties of architectural modernism before it became one-sidedly associated with interwar expressions of that phenomenon.[60]

Preservation as such was seen as an aspect of modernism whereby all advanced "cultural nations" gained new awareness of their architectural heritage, as the editors of *DP* pointed out in their introductory volume. This position brought German preservationists into an international sphere of inquiry through which they gained an often critical perspective on their own society's ability to promote national memory. When preservationists studied international legislation, landmarks, and literature, they did so in part to highlight deficits in their own country. When a *DP* writer attacked the disencumbering of a Lausanne cathedral, he did so in terms that did less to criticize Switzerland than to cast light on domestic debates over resto-

"A citadel of Germanness in the East in the Middle Ages," the Marienburg before completion
of its second major restoration of the nineteenth century, begun in 1882
(photo: *Die schöne Heimat* [1916], 129)

ration practice. A Bonn professor's praise of Bologna's "love of *Heimat*," reflected in its careful restoration of buildings threatened by economic development, had a similarly domestic function for German cities in the throes of expansion.[61] Against such international standards, German modernism, as reflected in historic preservation, was seen by its protagonists as unfulfilled or only partial.

Simultaneously, criticism of how non-German societies handled national symbols strengthened a sense of German superiority over other nations, as when the history of the Marienburg's reconstruction highlighted German disdain for Polish culture. The Marienburg's first modern restoration from 1817 to 1830 stimulated Prussian patriotism, but the second phase of rebuilding after 1882 linked it more closely with German public culture and Wilhelm II himself, who visited the fortress fifty times, lived in it for short periods, and attended historical costume balls there. "This castle was a citadel of Germanness in the East in the Middle Ages," said the Marienburg *Landrat* and delegate to the Prussian parliament Döhring in 1886. "Its restoration and maintenance will in the future also strengthen Germanness . . . against any assault from other nationalities." *DP* did not go as far in using nationalist rhetoric, but it still endorsed the fortress as a national monument, noting that the Marienburg had been restored to the form it had "in

DOCUMENTS OF STONE

the time of the last heroic defense against Polish domination in 1457," and pointing out that its preservation had overcome "centuries-long neglect and devastation" at the hands of a notionally deficient and decidedly unmodern Polish cultural administration.[62]

Preservationist scrutiny extended "upward" toward other nations but also "downward" toward German regions and cities. With variation in time and scope, a cultural renaissance of the region or locale took place in the late nineteenth and early twentieth centuries in Germany, the United States, Italy, and France. In Germany the territorial states and Prussian provinces were more often administrative and political entities rather than culturally identified areas. But there was nonetheless a revived sense that the nation was based on a hierarchy of numerous and enduring historical regions and cities. A multicentered vision of Germany thus reappeared not as a reaction to the modern German state but as a fundament of a new and more intense emotional bond to the nation. Preservation groups contributed to this development, as when the RVDH stated that "because of the abundance and importance of its artistic and historic monuments, the Prussian Rhineland undoubtedly takes the premier place among all German lands." Perdurability gave the Rhineland a unique legitimacy, for it contained monuments "from the period of Roman culture up to the nineteenth century," and thus its landscape was a virtual "historical map of world history." In addition, the Rhineland's "almost American" tempo of economic development and its strategic placement between France and the rest of Germany gave the region an added significance.[63]

Protecting landmarks within this hierarchy of places translated local diversities from the past into national similarities in the present, as in the case of Lübeck, the site of the annual preservation conference in 1908.[64] The *DP* noted Lübeck's historical peculiarity as a Hansa city and stated that the town's unique qualities could be seen in its buildings, which many observers would regard as "strange, at first." Marine air and other climatic conditions resulted in an architecture that did not appear in "simple or modest forms," at least externally, but that, on closer examination, had a deep "inwardness." The Marienkirche, begun in the twelfth century, was of particular interest; it was the first north German brick structure to be erected according to the French model of Gothic cathedrals. The interior of the church showed that "also here an art of the highest expression was in evidence." Inwardness and high artistic achievement meant that Lübeck could legitimately be considered as "the most German" of cities, a unique and ancient pearl apprehended through a local narrative that somehow embodied a general Germanness.

When developed in relation to a city or a region in this way, the discourse of Germanness had a "colonialist" quality. Western colonization of non-

"The most German" of cities, according to *Die Denkmalpflege*, Lübeck had a city hall consisting of several parts (the oldest, *left*) built between 1230 and 1572 and restored from 1872 to 1891. (photo: *Große Bürgerbauten deutscher Vergangenheit* [1916], 101)

Western lands has been based on a construction of Orientalism, a representation that makes the Other different and mysterious in terms of the colonizer's own discourse. In preservationist discourse a "colonial" vision evoked fascination with the "secret of times of earlier ages" revealed by a walk through historic Koblenz or the "unique spell" ancient Trier cast over the cultured observer who knew where to look. In such usages town and region were populated by "phantasmagoria of other times" whose existence was rediscovered in an act of colonialist memory-work.[65] Apprehending historic places in German towns and regions became as exotic as conquering far-off lands in Africa or the Far East. The nation's ability to apprehend such exotic places close to home was no less a measure of modernity than was colonialist conquest abroad.

This archaeological moment was enhanced when it was associated with personal memories and religious sensibility. Childhood and youth, like the artifacts of ancient worlds, were seen as times that are mysterious, distant, and only partially recoverable to the adult world. Preservationists argued that national identity could be enhanced by protecting historic landmarks that aroused feelings of "love and attachment to the places where one grew up, to the things and the environment [that made] the earliest impressions

DOCUMENTS OF STONE

in the eye of the growing child." Religious metaphors buttressed the region's strangeness also. Notions of piety for the past, already grounded in Romantic thought, were well known in the wider culture, as they were in the United States, where officials and tourists regarded historic sites as sacred places of religious and natural mystery. Some German preservationists compared the architectural monuments of a particular region with those of Christianity's holy sites: Mt. Sinai, Golgotha, or the Sea of Nazareth.[66] The origins of a national religion were to be uncovered in numerous local sites of historical significance just as the Christian religion's origins could be located topographically in the archaeology of the Holy Land. Mystery and self-discovery interacted in such preservationist explorations of historic places.

German *Bürger* were the colonialists and archaeologists in these discursive negotiations, and it was *bürgerlich* identity that worked most insistently in historic preservation. Medieval castles and churches were among the most cherished objects of the preservationist pantheon. These were the remains of a religious, dynastic-territorial, and aristocratic past in a society undergoing secularization and commercialization. It would be mistaken to see *bürgerlich* attraction to such artifacts as an example of the feudalization of the German middle classes, who according to a long tradition of historiography wanted to ape the aristocracy or merge with it.[67] Bourgeoisification (*Verbürgerlichung*) is a somewhat more useful concept when it is applied to groups such as the RVDH or the Association for the Preservation of German Castles, which bought, restored, and used medieval buildings for entirely new purposes. But even this concept captures only part of the story. When preservationists protected medieval churches, for instance, they were maintaining artifacts whose history was intimately connected with the development of the German *Bürgertum* itself. Medieval townscapes were dominated by church steeples, symbols not only of the priestly estate but of the power of town administrations that financed such projects either wholly or in part. The turn-of-the-century *Bürgertum* was different from the artisan-*Bürger* that created such structures, but the argument of historical lineage was also much more than imitation of aristocratic ways.

Like many European and American intellectuals who voiced nostalgia for a rural past, German preservationists valued the presumed coherence of the countryside. But national memory in the preservationist key also had a strong urban valence in Germany, as it did in England, where Ruskin and Morris set up the preindustrial city as a model for the future, and in Italy, where restorations of preindustrial cities took place in the attempt to construct Italian nationhood.[68] German preservationists now began to protect more urban commercial and residential structures, medieval urban fortifications, and industrial artifacts. The RVDH's urban program concentrated in

Dresden, Germany's popular "Florence on the Elbe," and one of many referents
of German urban romanticism (photo: *Die schöne Heimat* [1916], 101)

part on "fortifications of small cities on the Rhine and in its hinterland,"
while *DP* published articles or whole editions on big cities such as Nuremberg, Berlin, Aachen, Cologne, Dresden, Düsseldorf, Erfurt, and Danzig.
The urban focus was often used by preservationists to praise historically
conscious city administrations, business leaders, and architects who advanced the cause of monument protection. In such instances the practice
of preservation itself—its sponsors, theoreticians, and audiences—took center stage, diminishing the buildings themselves to symbols of *bürgerlich*
cultural-political influence over the making of the nation.

German urbanism had the same mythic functions for preservationists as
ruralism had for others. The previously mentioned article on Nuremberg
began with the words, "Among the few cities of Germany that have preserved their unique character of old until the present, Nuremberg must
always be counted among them." Praising the use of "blue stone," similar to
Belgian granite, in Aachen architecture, city building inspector Eduard Adenaw noted that this material "had developed closely with Aachen buildings
for centuries." Beyond their undisputed art-historical accuracy, such comments also associated historic townscapes with ancient origins, giving them
an aura that transcended the everyday destructiveness of a society built on

hope more than memory. In this tradition ancient urban ensembles objectified a collectivity whose origins were to be found in a past beyond history.[69]

Like the political parties and nationalist associations of the *Bürgertum*,
preservation groups wanted to garner public support. "Right now nothing is
more popular among the educated classes," wrote Friedrich Naumann in
1902, "than the demand that the entire *Volk* should be initiated into the
secrets of seeing life from artistic perspectives." Preservation was one such
artistic perspective, and many preservationists fully endorsed popular education, departing from the more authoritarian visions of a minimally educated populace blindly following its leaders held by cultural pessimists such
as Paul de Lagarde. Paul Clemen was not alone in believing that by promoting the memory of historical vernacular architecture in the Rhineland,
modern-day artisans and workers could be taught to build according to the
presumably higher standards of these traditional models.[70]

Yet even for preservationists, popular education was to occur under conditions that revealed the educators' deep distrust of "uncultured" strata.
In parliamentary debates advocates of more stringent preservation laws
stressed "how little taste the great mass has," as a member of the Prussian
upper house put it. Rural people received especially heavy criticism because
of their alleged impiety toward the past, a paradoxical situation given the
assumption of many *Heimatschutz* devotees that country people had a sense
of tradition that urbanites lacked. "The rural dweller has no idea at first
about what historic preservation wants," wrote *DP* editor Hoßfeld. Rural
church congregations were some of the most impious because they often
preferred new churches to historic ones. "I will not say that in all the indus-
trially developed areas the old churches should be maintained," said an
observer of the Jülich region in the Rhineland, "but in many cases one could
have been satisfied with a good expansion [of the existing church]." City
dwellers did not escape criticism either. Like the larger cities of previous
decades, many smaller towns began to tear down their medieval walls at the
turn of the century to make way for traffic, a development that caused much
exasperation among preservation officials. "Every preservationist knows
what wars we fight with the municipalities," said one official at the 1901
Freiburg conference, "to maintain these landmarks of old military values,
these traces of the memory of urban autonomy, these elements of picturesque beauty."[71] Rural and urban dwellers alike failed the test of cultural
taste as determined by the emerging national optics of the late Empire. They
would have to learn the evocations associated with Germanness and assume
their assigned subordinate position within its discourse. They would have to
learn to love the past in the way all moderns did.

Cutting across the social discourse of historic preservation were unintended narratives of gender. The nation-state's highly modern preoccupation with long memories could be seen as a cultural-political parallel to male bourgeois autobiographical conventions through which the masculine subject is situated in time as the offspring and perpetuator of a distinct family line. From this perspective the preservation of national landmarks was analogous to the male heir's stewardship over the family name and estate. From a quite different perspective comes the idea that the crypt and apse of medieval churches carried imagery of the womb-cavern shared by ancient forms of sacred architecture throughout the world. This imagery symbolized a feminine principle in architecture shaped by ideas of independence, equality, peacefulness, nurturance, fertility, birth, death, and transformation. This Jungian interpretation leads to the argument that preservationists overlooked or repressed this principle when they failed to point out historic architecture's ancient feminine imagery.[72]

But one can find a more concrete way to analyze the gender aspects of preservation.[73] Those preservation officials who cheered city administrations for passing preservation statutes, repainting the deteriorated facades of historic houses, and retaining the historic morphology of towns at the same time overlooked living conditions in old city centers. The boosterism of city officials notwithstanding, these conditions worsened as city-building created elegant shopping ensembles alongside deteriorating residential areas in and around the old urban cores. Faulty plumbing, inadequate heating, and a lack of ventilation and light all contributed to slum conditions whose main victims were women, children, and the elderly, whose lives revolved more around the physical space of the home than male workers' did. These conditions were most often described as "picturesque" (*malerisch*), a term that has been culturally coded as male in Western societies since its inception. "The picturesque retained the assumptions of gender given to it by its founders," writes James Buzard, "who imagined a male art of seeing that could correct and complete what a feminized landscape held forth." The landscape was coded female because it was beautiful, natural, capable of arousing great emotion, but also incomplete, chaotic, and in need of an organizing principle provided by the male observer. In the case of scenic old towns, the feminized landscape consisted of half-timber houses, narrow streets, and busy market squares—all completed through a combination of preservation and blindness to the social reality in and around them.

A correlate of the emphasis on picturesque settings was a metaphorical language that interwove the themes of masculinity, public life, and national interest as binary opposites to femininity, private life, and the home. One evocative example comes from a 1907 article on the historic half-timbered

Rhenish half-timbered architecture worked as a symbol of the family and local nation. This house from the seventeenth century stood on the market square of the small town Bacharach. (photo: *Große Bürgerbauten deutscher Vergangenheit* [1916], 4)

house (*Fachwerkhaus*) in the Rhine and Mosel regions, which contrasted "international competition, where it is necessary to marshal all one's powers and struggle ruthlessly" with "a place for the heart, a place no longer only left to itself with an indulgent smile but respected with the pride one would have for one's home." This "place" was the realm of "historic preservation [and] defense of *Heimat*." "What are these," wrote the author, "but pious searching and loving care for old family heirlooms from the olden days of one's ancestors."[74] This statement reflected the ideology of separate spheres, which depicted the "national" nation in terms of war and international competition and the subordinate "local" nation in terms of the warmth of the family. If the former was identified with the male, vigorous and equipped for ruthless battle in public life, the latter was identified with the sphere of reproduction and the woman, who was seen as a nurturing and civilizing force caring for family heirlooms that fostered private identity in a male-centered world.

To the extent that most preservationists still favored protection of grand public symbols over vernacular architecture, they reinforced this division of masculine and feminine, the public and the private, in daily practice. Men cared for women by ensuring that there would be public spaces where notionally feminine characteristics of emotion, sensitivity, and maternal love were represented. It is difficult to miss such motifs in rhetoric that praised the organic qualities and sleepy anachronisms of old cities still not completely touched by industrialization. These, according to one advocate of heritage protection, were "bewitched princesses—one should not wake them." In the words of another preservationist, the historic city manifested the "loved, venerable maternal countenance."[75] Nonetheless, males were conducting the feminine work of nurturing monuments likened to family heirlooms of the nation, and thus preservationists not only adopted a position of masculine superiority in relation to women but one of inferiority in relation to the other males who did the more masculine work of war and public life.

It is hoped that the preceding has demonstrated that preservationist representations of the nation emerged from the still inchoate cultural-political aims of the Kaiserreich. Yet preservationists also often envisioned a nation *potentially* different from that proclaimed by the Kaiser or by other elites, and they disagreed among themselves as well, as demonstrated in debates over historical restorations. The dominant technique of preservation throughout the nineteenth century, restoration stripped monuments of their historical accretions, returning them to what was seen as their authentic historical style, which for many Europeans meant Gothic for most of the century, but increasingly could include Renaissance, Romanesque, and other styles as well. Advocates of conservation, including Dehio, Clemen, Gurlitt, and many others who gained increasing ascendancy as the century waned, were as interested in historical authenticity as the restorationists were, and they used the same positivist methods of research. They were not flatly opposed to restoring old buildings—Clemen thought Ruskin's description of restoration as a "lie from beginning to end" too dogmatic[76]—but they favored selectively preserving sites and ruins to reflect the workings of history.

Of the many debates over such issues that shaped this period, the controversy over the restoration of the Alsatian castle Hohkönigsburg was one of the most revealing because it engaged the Kaiser and his allies, professional preservationists, and the public.[77] A badly deteriorated ruin given to Wilhelm II in 1899 by the city of Schlettstadt in Alsace, the Hohkönigsburg became the object of one of the costliest historical restorations in the Empire, requiring 2.3 million marks before it was completed in 1908. The Kaiser devoted much of his personal attention to the restoration of Romanesque churches in the Rhineland his first decade on the throne, but by the turn of the century he became more interested in historical castles. The Hohkönigsburg was of particular interest to Wilhelm II because it was seen as a kind of Western counterpart to the Marienburg, a potentially useful resource for Germanizing the Alsatian frontier, and an effective symbol of the monarchical presence in a site with a long history of dynastic authority. A plaque in the restored castle read, "Here, where Hohenstaufen and Habsburger ruled, walls and towers are once again vigorously resurrected by a third royal line, the Hohenzollerns." No one mentioned that the castle had been destroyed once in the fifteenth century because its occupant had become an unbearable robber knight who terrorized the surrounding lands. Although the peripatetic monarch wanted to use the structure as a temporary residence during his travels, the castle would be restored as a museum (also like the Marienburg), which local officials hoped would be a boon to the area's tourism.

The project was controversial from the beginning. The man responsible for the restoration was Bodo Ebhardt, architect, restorer, and close associate of the Kaiser, who did not have reliable architectural diagrams for the project until a drawing of the castle before its complete destruction in 1633 was found by accident in 1907, just a year before work was finished. Tearing away the weeds and trees that had enveloped the ruin, Ebhardt reconstructed the upper stories and roof of the structure on the basis of still-extant parts and undertook a total reproduction of the watchtower, destroyed in 1557. Although the 1907 drawing demonstrated that Ebhardt had made a relatively accurate reconstruction, his work was roundly attacked. One critic, the author of a book on the Kaiser, focused on the watchtower,

The restored south side of the Alsatian fortress Hohkönigsburg. "Here, where Hohenstaufen and Habsburger ruled, walls and towers are once again vigorously resurrected by a third royal line, the Hohenzollerns." (photo: Bildarchiv Foto Marburg/Art Resource, New York)

writing that "millions were sacrificed to this dream. The old ambience has disappeared, the new building does not conjure it into being again." The *Frankfurter Zeitung* regarded the Hohkönigsburg as an unusually serious case of a "restoration vandalism" that had been spreading over Germany for decades. Parliamentary representatives balked at the cost of the project, which was to be covered by Reich, Alsatian, and royal funds.

In 1899 *DP* criticized the overly "modernized" Wartburg, the restored Thuringian castle where Luther had fled his enemies, and published an article endorsing criticisms of the "theater Gothic" that characterized the first stage of the Marienburg's restoration. It was thus unsurprising to find that Hohkönigsburg was also criticized in this quarter. When Ebhardt discussed his plans in an unofficial evening lecture at the preservation congress of 1900 in Dresden, he aroused considerable debate, and Clemen stated that "all representatives of German historic preservation are agreed that actual restoration work must be suppressed." At the 1901 Freiburg congress, participants voiced their resentment about how Prussian state secretary Robert von Puttkamer, answering the many critics of the restoration, had implied publicly that the previous year's congress was in favor of Hohkönigsburg. They pushed through a resolution stating that the congress wished to take no position at all on the restoration, an abstention based less on divided opinion than on the fear that preservationist institutions would be manipulated by politicians seeking support for questionable architectural projects. Dehio summed up the deliberations adequately by noting that Hohkönigsburg had many opponents among preservationists.

Opposition notwithstanding, seven years later Hohkönigsburg opened with a great celebration in which the Kaiser, seated under the historical copy of a sixteenth-century military tent, reviewed a festive costume parade that represented the most famous personalities from the castle's history. A "speaking history book" reminded the royal audience that in Friedrich Barbarossa's time Germans were the "master race [*Herrenvolk*] of the world." The Kaiser himself rose to address the audience. "Like the Marienburg in the East," the Hohkönigsburg would be "a symbol of German culture and power into the distant future." It would "serve the many thousands who, in a reverent look back to the past, would for their own enjoyment and edification make the pilgrimage to this site of the Kaiser's power."

It was fitting that Wilhelm II should have had the last word, for despite the heat Hohkönigsburg had generated, the fire from which the debates originated masked a greater unanimity on the nation's past and future than appearances suggested. Restoration and conservation were outgrowths of historicism, which by itself could be associated with a variety of ideological positions, from socialism to monarchism. Supporters of either approach

Viennese art historian Alois Riegl, who, in response to the advocates of restoration, wrote in 1903 that "the pure and redeeming impact of natural decay must not be arbitrarily disturbed by new additions" to monuments (photo: Institut für Kunstgeschichte der Universität Wien)

stressed that the substance of the building, the *Bausubstanz*, was subject to many destructive tendencies in the modern age. The cultural capital that nurtured national memory was in a state of constant decline. This sense of threat was often expressed in medical metaphors, as when engineering professor Landsberg wrote in 1910 of the "sickness" of historic buildings. The medical language of preservation intersected broadly with the notion of the nation as a remembering, living entity in possession of its own cultural symbols. If the property, the *Bausubstanz*, can age and pass away, then so too can the nation that derives its identity from remembering and consuming this cultural heritage. The sickness of aging buildings refers to the sickness, real and potential, of the nation, which if it is not aged and forgetful now, will be so in the course of time. It is likely that the public-health inflection of preservation gained impetus from the end-of-century trend toward biologized politics.

The historical school of restorationists treated national artifacts' illnesses by insisting on pure reconstructions in which the old could be not just preserved but given back its youth and perpetuated beyond its normal life expectancy. Ebhardt represented this view, although it could be argued he was far more cautious in such matters than other restorers had been. Conservationists placed little faith in the possibility of making past ages come alive again in new or rebuilt stone. They wanted to keep the patient alive as long as possible not through radical surgery but through preventive medicine that allowed for natural aging. Their approach held out the possibility that, just as Riegl would contemplate the end of the monument through natural decay, the nation would *potentially* contemplate and accept its own historical contingency, if not its certain decline. In practice, like the restorationists, they stepped back from considering this disturbing possibility, and even when they opposed some restorations, they accepted or remained silent about others, suggesting that they, too, wanted to project the nation backward and forward into the mists of time. At the end of the methodological debate, then, their scrutiny, license, and control led them to embrace the same ideal of mythic national longevity that the Kaiser proclaimed, somewhat too inelegantly, from the restored walls and towers of the Hohkönigsburg.

Multiplication and Appropriation

The Hohkönigsburg debate and other previous examples have alluded to public attitudes toward preservation held by individuals who, without engaging directly in the practice of protecting historic places, either participated in preservation groups or expressed more general interest in historic buildings through a multiplicity of activities. Just as preservationists disagreed among themselves and with their political allies, the preservationist public often used and interpreted historical buildings in ways that did not coincide exactly with official views. From what points in the culture did this preservationist public emerge, and what were its distinctive views?

Newspapers were an important source of information for those concerned with preservation activities. They reported extensively on historical buildings, often focusing more on techniques of classification or restoration than on the finished project or its national-historical significance.[78] This more "scientistic" approach to monuments embedded the historic place in a memory of technological achievement that may or may not have had a specific national valence. As such it was part of a larger cultural phenomenon whereby an industrial age considered technical processes themselves to be of equal or even greater concern than their outcome. Nipperdey derived such fascination with technical matters from a European "vulgar-progressivism" that shaped the history of technology, planning, and urban policy.[79] Even when a cultural activity such as preservation was seen as an antidote to the denationalizing effects of industrialization or urbanization, its critique was expressed in the idiom shaped by these effects. This relationship could be seen in professional preservationist discourse as well, and thus no significant distance existed between official preservation and its audiences on this score.

Such technical interests notwithstanding, lay opinion most often concentrated on the general "feel" of historic places, evoking emotions aroused by looking at local cityscapes, as in Eduard Broil's 1913 *Kölnisches Tageblatt* article on Cologne, in which the author praised the city's "steeples and turrets, which tower toward the heavens from the numerous churches and chapels." Quoting an ancient Roman adage, Broil wrote, "If you have not seen Cologne, you have not seen Germany."[80] This approach was also characteristic of Euro-American touristic appropriations of historical buildings, which stressed ambience rather than a documented historical significance. This way of seeing was widespread at the end of the nineteenth century even among individuals who were cogent critics of the political and cultural life of the Kaiserreich. Left-liberal politician and reformer Friedrich Naumann, a cofounder of the Werkbund and advocate of authenticity in German design culture, was one such highly visible critic.[81] Naumann could accept some heavily restored historic places with as little ambivalence as the most popular tour guides or picture books did. Writing in 1908 about Rothenburg ob der Tauber, the much restored and famous Franconian town dating back to the twelfth century, Naumann admitted that here "the Middle Ages stand before us in a rather polished and purified form" and that it was "questionable . . . as to how much of brave little Rothenburg belongs to

"If you have not seen Cologne, you have not seen Germany." The cityscape at night.
(photo: *Die schöne Heimat* [1916], 16)

medieval times." Still, the city stimulated an emotional response shaped by a love of medievalism and a conflation of naturalistic and historic imagery. "We stand here at the wall, as there in the distance the magnificent golden sun sets," he wrote. "Here we saw the full moon over the blue crenelated battlements of the old Imperial City, the same sun under which apples ripened during the Middle Ages and the same moon that filled these crenels with silver light in the days of Barbarossa."[82]

Naumann's language was touristic because it focused uncritically on the foreground characteristics of historic places. This way of seeing historic buildings was facilitated by the spread of the tourist industry, now more attractive and available to members of the middle *Bürgertum* in particular. Tourism's rather indistinct appreciation of particular buildings was well represented in tour guides. When the 1906 Baedeker described Cologne, for example, it referred to the cathedral as the "greatest work of Gothic architecture," quoted Georg Forster's naturalistic metaphor from 1790 that the interior of the structure was "like the trees of a primeval forest reaching for the sky and split into a crown of boughs above," and dutifully recorded the size of the enormous structure.[83] Yet it also stressed the significance of trade, steamboats, suburban development, and the new harbor of the Rhenish city, and it described the historic district around the cathedral as "somewhat cramped and gloomy." In such instances the evocation of an important national symbol and its milieu relativized the importance of national lon-

Although he thought the Middle Ages were present in a "rather polished and purified form" in the famous Bavarian town Rothenburg ob der Tauber, Friedrich Naumann still praised the city for its natural beauty and mythic ambience. (photo: *Die schöne Heimat* [1916], 60)

gevity, a value preservationists emphasized. Nowhere did the Baedeker mention that many preservationists considered the cathedral too ugly and contrived to be regarded as "the" national symbol of Germany and the "greatest work of Gothic architecture."

This was an industrialized or "panoramic" mode of perception, to use Dolf Sternberger's term, a way of seeing "the discrete indiscriminately" that paralleled the perspective one had from the window of a train.[84] It is worthwhile to ponder the considerable national-political effect of this optics. The Cologne cathedral was as much the symbol of the failure of German national identity "from above" in the nineteenth century as it was a symbol of success, but this fact was not mentioned in tour guides. At the turn of the century the Marienburg fortress was being championed by German intellectuals and politicians as both a "bulwark of Germanness in the East" in the past and a tool for neonationalist aggression in the "Eastern marches" in the future. But the official guide to the fortress used a more reserved language, emphasizing the cultural-historical features of the burg instead of its nationalist significance. Visitors to the popular celebration of the Hambach Festival in June 1914 at the Hambach castle received little in the way of historical education, and unsurprisingly the organizers of the festival distanced themselves from the aims of the original radical-liberal Hambach participants, 30,000 of whom had come to the site for the first time in 1832 to swear their commitment to German national unity.[85] Touristic appropriations filtered out such direct political references, allowing the nation to become a depoliticized panorama that was seen as indiscriminately as the buildings themselves.

Even if the specific political resonance of a historic site was avoided or suppressed, tourism had a positive political potential. Dean MacCannell has argued that tourism is "a way of attempting to overcome the discontinuity of modernity, of incorporating its fragments into unified experience."[86] For European tourists in the heyday of the nation-state, those traveling within their own borders may have found national identity to be one of the vehicles through which this unified experience could be created. Tourism may have done much to increase the potentiality that pictures of the nation—captured in part in historical castles, market squares, and grand cathedrals—would have a specific and direct referent in experience, a way of building solidarity in an increasingly fragmented society. This solidarity functioned as myth, a way of seeing and remembering without reference to the messy historical contingencies that created the historic sites in question. But this hardly reduced the reality of what was seen or experienced. It remains an open issue whether Germany, as a new and dynamic nation experiencing the most profound tensions of modernity, relied more on tourism than did other European countries to give its inhabitants a direct and mythic sense of the nation. Whether or not it did, "national orientations"[87] in tourism depended more on the active appropriation of historic places by individuals who labored to see Germany than on a passive acceptance of the arguments of preservation officials.

Tourism was still largely a matter of upper- and middle-class audiences and therefore very much a function of the distribution of economic and cultural resources. It thus offers one of the most important examples of how affirmative responses to old buildings produced results that could be at variance with the national goals of most preservationists. Among the key words of preservationist discourse as reflected in its publications and conferences were taste, balance, and modesty (*Schlichtheit*). Preservationists shared these values with other cultural reformers, such as the members of the Werkbund and the *Heimatschutz* movement. But a big part of the touristic consumption of historic places increasingly took its cue from the monumentalism and spectacle of public culture under Wilhelm II, himself an avid tourist of historic sites and the nation's "first consumer." Wilhelmine cultural excess turned tourism into a form of conspicuous consumption. The Kaiser's favorite preservation projects were lavish restorations of castles and fortresses such as the Marienburg or Alsatian Hohkönigsburg, projects that the annual preservation conference and other groups either debated heavily or voiced their doubts about by remaining icily silent. Industrial groups and the educated middle classes were among the main financial backers of preservation, and they were increasingly prone to "luxury" or to regarding "culture" (*Bildung*) as property. The desire for cultural lavishness turned Germany's topography of historical buildings into a vast department store of consumer items, the products of which ranged from real monuments to representations of those monuments, like the expensive leatherbound book *Die Wartburg*, a cultural history of the famous historic fortress in Thuringia that was almost three decades in preparation and published in 1906 in German and English in a limited edition of several hundred copies.[88]

Consumers of such items had a "social power over time,"[89] based on income and education, that enabled them to enjoy and know historical places in ways that the new consumers of memory and culture, the lower middle classes, rural communities, and even some workers, could not. The entry of these new consumers in the leisure and memory markets was in fact one of the factors that made conspicuous consumption a rational form of social differentiation for groups that wanted to keep the new, inferior consumers at arm's length. Preservation was dependent on the increasingly luxury-oriented *Gebildeten*, a dependence some preservationists would question seriously only after World War I. This dependence created social fissures between preservationists and less well-to-do groups. What was thus seen as a patriotic act of nurturing historic places by *Gebildeten* could be seen by others as a symbol of social inequity, and thus of national disunity.

As noted earlier, tourism also entailed the increased circulation and consumption of images of historic sites, which was part of a general increase in the number and quality of images available to the general public. Photography played an important and specific role in this process with reference to historic buildings. Because railways had done much to blunt the sensuous qualities of travel, photography's apparent renewal of detail made it a useful medium for recapturing a sense of immediacy. This aura of truthfulness thus potentially gave photographs of historic buildings a legitimacy they could not have in a written text or drawing. Publications such as the famous *Blaue Bücher* illustrated book series, which originated in the pre–World War I period and featured many high-quality black-and-white photographs of historic and natural sites, needed almost no text to convey this sense of inescapable reality.[90]

Postcards had a related but different function. The European postcard industry took off in the second half of the nineteenth century, and Germany was the leading producer and consumer of such images. Preservation groups

Commerce, technology, and the past in postcard imagery of Halberstadt, a city in the Harz
(photo: Gynz-Rekowski and Schulze, *Harzansichten*, 11)

adapted quickly to the new commercial art, as the elite RVDH and other associations put together commemorative collections of historic places for paying members.[91] For others, postcards made specific buildings concrete and real for the sender as well as the recipient. They were often purchased at the site itself, and therefore created a closer association between the purchaser and the building than publications such as the *Blaue Bücher* or *DP* did. They often had a social ambience, including scenes of daily life in historic town centers. Postcards from the Harz region from the turn of the century included the scenes of forests, castles, and serene roofscapes (*Dachlandschaften*) we would expect to find in such idealizing productions. Yet one could also buy animated pictures of the busy Breiteweg in the historical center of Halberstadt, pulsing with commercial activity, or of the same town's Holzmarkt, with its *Rathaus*, a scene punctuated by electricity and tram lines across the horizon and an airplane flying overhead. Such scenes placed historic buildings not in some dreamy, preindustrial past or in tasteful settings appropriate to *bürgerlich* culture, but in the hustle of modern commercial life.[92]

Because such scenes were designed less to demonstrate the historical character of specific landmarks than to give the sender or receiver of the card an authentic feel of what it was like to be at the site, they connoted a more tactile sense of place than more academic representations could, a more accessible avenue to the national community of feeling being built. These differences notwithstanding, postcards added to the popularity of historical images and contributed to that general public interest preservationists hoped would redound to the advantage of their cultural-political vision. Moreover, because postcards increasingly offered the chance to send messages, individuals could personalize their involvement in the national (and international) circulation of historical images in ways they could not by paging through the *Blaue Bücher*. Yet personalization presupposed that the national historic site being pictured was a medium rather than a goal, a photographic mechanism whereby personal contacts were upheld rather than the specific point of departure for such contacts. Appropriated in this way, historic buildings always became antiquarian fields of care before they became monumental public symbols.

Personalization and commercialization also occurred in the assembling of collectors' picture cards (*Sammelbilder*).[93] In the 1890s the consumption of such cards rose dramatically as they were included in packages of cocoa, chocolate, and meat extracts, and as manufactured albums in which card series could be completed were promoted. Initially a juvenile hobby, card collecting eventually became attractive to adults, though before 1914 mainly to those of the better-off *Bürgertum* who could afford such relatively expensive products. As cigarette and margarine producers began including the cards after 1918, collecting became widespread among workers and peasants. By 1900 the Stollwerck firm sold 100,000 albums yearly, its domestic sales of chocolate and cocoa more than doubled, and the number of cards distributed reached 50 million yearly. Although *Sammelbilder* featured a great variety of images, natural and historic sites were common subjects, and insofar that they became increasingly accessible, they democratized and commercialized historical imagery by being associated with relatively inexpensive goods. But they also furthered the tendency toward spectacle and elaborate visual stimulation that one could find in Wilhelmine culture's weakness for luxury.

Photographs, postcards, and collectors' cards worked in the same way that the stamp album, the "do-it-yourself museum" of the nineteenth-century, had.[94] They promoted individual activities of classification and ordering of representations that had national-historical significance. If they produced a sense of national pride, they did so on the basis of active and "democratic" appropriation rather than passive acceptance of the national meaning given to historic places by the authorities.

In a now classic formulation of the effect of such maximization on perception, Walter Benjamin argued that a proliferation of images robbed natural, artistic, and historic sites of their "aura," their quality of being uniquely placed in space and time.[95] Many of the processes already discussed multiplied the number of representations of sites in quantities unknown in earlier historic periods. If he regretted the "de-auratization" of images, Benjamin nonetheless was willing to concede the progressive and even revolutionary effects of new forms of representation, particularly in cinema. Preservationists were either less enthusiastic about them (as in the case of the effects of tourism) or unwilling to concede they were important to consider at all (as with *Sammelbilder*). On the other hand, they embraced photography, which as we have seen was regarded as a technique that restored the detail and foreground imagery of preindustrial ways of seeing.[96]

Historical societies and other groups that studied provincial or local history also multiplied images of historic buildings. Such associations had been in the forefront of historic preservation earlier in the nineteenth century, but their direct influence over preservation policy waned as states and specialized voluntary groups gained dominance in this area. Still, local societies continued to have a strong interest in historical buildings. Research was one of their most popular activities, as exemplified in the work of the Association for the Study of Lübeck History and Antiquities, which in 1895 carried out a survey of remaining Old Saxon peasant houses in the region that gained a lively public response. In Frankfurt am Main in 1897 a new Society for Research on Jewish Monuments organized similar activities in an effort to create a topography of Jewish cultural history. Museum exhibits were popular, and groups such as the Old Cologne Association could report that its 1909 display of historical miscellany, paintings, and photographs of local buildings attracted 1,500 people in a single day. Many museum collections were put together by well-informed amateurs who were involved in a growing commerce of historic objects that was a local and petit bourgeois version of the international art trade. Many historical societies had less interest in preserving historic landmarks than in possessing and displaying reproductions of them. Their sense of the past was more proprietary than that of officials involved directly in preservation. Although provincial and municipal conservators often had close contact with the large museums, they had little to do with the small ones, and they openly lamented the fact that local collections developed with little official oversight.[97]

Local collections were criticized for what was seen as a disorganized eclecticism and superficiality that fragmented the public image of the past.[98] Such criticism was based on an anxiety that hundreds of local collectors and museums were situating themselves in historical time according to principles that were questionable to those who tried to dominate German memory. Leading preservationists insisted that the path to more complete protection of historic buildings and artifacts went through a widened perception of those buildings; monuments made sense not as isolated museum pieces but as parts of a larger historical and social ensemble. The work of the local collectors and history societies may have done more to further this change in perception than preservationists admitted even when it did not deal directly with historic buildings. Local collections aroused passionate interest in history and tried to present artifacts in the context of the local and regional past. In doing so, such institutions played a big role in the positive reception and consumption of historic buildings even if it was a role many officials were unwilling to concede them. Above all, they were important vectors of translation between local, regional, and national memories.

I have stressed tensions arising from mainly affirmative responses to and uses of historic sites. What of more ambivalent or critical appropriations? City governments, churches, and industrialists were among the main supporters of the national heritage, but these groups also put up much resistance to the preservation cause. A key source of conflict between city magistrates and official preservation was the protection of medieval fortifications. Urged on by propertied interests, city assemblies wanted to do away with all or part of city walls, but by the last third of the century plans for demolition of medieval fortifications encountered opposition from a strengthened preservation movement. Nuremberg and Cologne were among the major cities in which bitter debates took place, but by the end of the century smaller communities experiencing growth also saw disputes over city walls. The outcome of such local battles was mixed. Nuremberg kept almost all of its medieval walls intact, while Cologne reached a compromise in which just three disencumbered gates and a sample of the wall would be all that remained.[99]

Churches quite rightly saw themselves as stewards of some of Germany's most magnificent historic places, but they were interested above all in the use of those places for liturgical and social purposes, replacing old altars or dispensing with valuable artifacts with little consideration for their historical significance. In the Prussian Rhine province and Lower Saxony, church officials in need of larger spaces for growing congregations made modifications on historic churches without getting necessary permits or without waiting for the permits to be issued. In the opposite direction, consolidation of parishes and congregations in depopulated rural areas led to the abandonment of country churches, and in the half-century up to 1911, twenty-eight of the sixty existing medieval churches in the Rhenish county of Düren were torn down in a pattern of destruction preservationists claimed was typical. More than a matter of neglect, the churches' differences with preservation extended to the legislative sphere. Catholic church officials in particular feared state encroachments on their corporate power, and they were among the strongest opponents of efforts to strengthen the legal regulation of historic places in Prussia, Baden, and Bavaria.[100]

Conflicts over historic churches often drew ordinary congregants into the fray, reflecting opposed meanings of historic buildings. In 1908 an otherwise minor local conflict over the Petri church in Kulmbach aroused controversy in the national preservation press when a local schoolteacher named Spitzenpfeil forcefully opposed plans to top off the church's bell tower with a steeple it had lacked since the fifteenth century.[101] According to officials, not only would the steeple give the church a long-needed aesthetic harmony, it would improve a structure whose historical value was minimal due to destructive nineteenth-century restorations. Spitzenpfeil railed against what he saw as an assault on a "symbol of the Protestant spirit." Obviously, said Spitzenpfeil, the church fathers of past centuries had wanted no part of that "flight from the world" symbolized by steeples reaching toward the sky, and those who advocated "completing" the church did violence to this memory. The director of the German National Museum in Nuremberg, Gustav von Bezold, saw the schoolteacher's defense as an example of an uninformed and overzealous public interest in preserving old buildings simply because they were old, unintentionally highlighting Riegl's idea that "age value" above all regulated popular appropriations of historical buildings. Spitzenpfeil's reading of the symbolism of church towers may have been wrong, but von Bezold's attack indicated that in some cases specialists in the field were willing to manipulate the past far more than ordinary people were. Indeed, the attack revealed that for von Bezold it was not a matter of history at all, but one of aesthetic harmony, whereas for the embattled local schoolteacher, a field of care, defined by locally experienced community identity and Protestant memory, was at stake.

As for the relationship between history and the economy, preservationists could either benefit from or be disadvantaged by economic growth, depending on the regional context. In the Rhineland, economic development threatened many historic buildings but also produced the capital that was needed for donations to preservation associations. In relatively undeveloped northern Hesse, historic places were less threatened, but there was also less money available to maintain them. Preservation would not have had a substantial public voice without the financial resources provided by the bourgeoisie and the aristocracy, but it was these same groups, especially those wealthy bourgeois who built historicist villas on urban peripheries, who wanted to have building ordinances relaxed so that they would have the freedom to add "old German" half-timbering, antique columns, and medieval turrets to their impressive homes. Industrialist Alfred Krupp's massive Villa Hügel in Essen was one of the most outrageous examples. In part, their demand for freer architectural forms revealed a *bürgerlich*-liberal memory whereby the national community grew organically by harmonizing many diverse interests.[102] But this view potentially and practically contradicted the aims of preservationists who by the last prewar decade opposed such historicist imitations on the grounds they created an inauthentic relationship with the German past and an inappropriate environment for the realization of preservationist goals.

More direct opposition to preservation came from many different points on the economic spectrum. The League of Industrialists (Bund der Industriellen) and the Central Association of German Industrialists (Zentralverband deutscher Industriellen), major industrial groups in Germany's burgeoning global political economy, as well as several chambers of commerce, staunchly opposed vigorous preservation legislation or sought significant exclusions from it. The league also organized agencies that directly opposed *Heimatschutz* efforts to limit advertising near historic and natural sites. Urban property developers actively defended their right to destroy historic places. As city-building went forward in the late Empire, historical urban architecture either deteriorated step-by-step as speculators awaited good opportunities to sell their buildings to developers, or facades were painted and restored, often in historical styles that simultaneously increased the rents of longtime inhabitants or made the buildings more attractive to prospective buyers. In many instances buildings were simply torn down in a "massive wave of demolitions" of the kind that shaped the Cologne city center in the two decades before World War I.[103]

Resistance of city governments to preservation ordinances gained impetus in part from the resistance of local property owners.[104] In Trier the local press and the House and Property Owners' Association argued against the proposed passage of a local ordinance on preservation, claiming it would mean "difficult material hardships for Trier citizens." "They investigate and survey, make sketches, photograph, and make models," a local critic said of Trier preservationists, "and then they say the house must be maintained, it has historical value." The fear in many such cases was not only of material hardship but of loss of local authority to experts or cultured outsiders, which could mean conservators, preservation association officials, and the supporters of *Heimatschutz*. "The townscape is supposed to be protected," said a schoolteacher opposed to preservationist efforts to get Jena to pass a local bylaw against defacement of historic buildings. "Now Jena has little to do with Berlin; here we have a townscape that consists mainly of shabby buildings. It would be better to see to it that the buildings were improved." For the schoolteacher, historic preservation was an assault on local indepen-

A center of preservation activity, the historical city Trier also saw much opposition to the protectors of monuments. (photo: *Große Bürgerbauten deutscher Vergangenheit* [1916], 8)

dence, a misunderstanding of local social and economic needs, and an attempt to belittle the community. To save Jena's "picturesque" old districts as national landmarks was not only to overlook the local community's memory of social and economic inferiority; it was also to put obstacles in the way of overcoming it.

I have left German workers until the end of the chapter because, as in many other areas of cultural policy, they were largely excluded from debates over historic preservation and *Heimatschutz*. This did not mean they were not targets of cultural-national politics. Nationalist groups tried to mobilize their loyalties through festivals and monuments, city and state governments linked local or dynastic tradition with nationalist causes through popular pageants, and preservationists announced they wanted to educate the popular classes and arouse their allegiances. The effects of such efforts are difficult to gauge, but we know that consciousness of class division was not as all-pervasive among workers as Social Democratic leaders claimed, and workers both within and outside the socialist movement felt a sense of positive identity with the nation. For their part, workers participated in a form of symbolic preservation, exemplified when they occupied the historic central square or marketplace of a city in Social Democratic demonstrations, or in efforts to recontextualize German history by engaging it for a socialist future.[105] But symbolic preservation was hardly the main aim of socialist politics, nor was a socialist cultural politics as such a central goal of the trade union and party leadership.

Direct commentary on or criticism of monument preservation within working-class culture was rare. Socialists remarked on differences between workers' and preservationists' attitudes toward picturesque old urban districts, but they had a rather marginal interest in urban renewal at this time, due in part to prewar Social Democracy's sporadic interest in communal politics. Active protection of the national architectural heritage was a matter for states and the *Gebildeten*, and workers were in any case more concerned about the rigors of everyday life. When commentary on historic places did occur, however, it reflected both local resistance to and acceptance of *bürgerlich* appropriations of historic places. Just before the centennial of the Leipzig Battle of the Nations in the Napoleonic wars, the Social Democratic newspaper *Rheinische Zeitung* printed a sweeping attack on the historical memory of the *Bürgertum*, which was to celebrate the anniversary in a lavish ceremony in the Cologne cathedral. "In the very same cathedral a solemn holy service of mourning was held in 1848 for the victims of the Berlin barricade fighting," the article read. The local *Bürgertum*, Catholic and Protestant alike, had lost sight of the radical history of liberalism, in the eyes of the commentator, who argued that such "national days of commemoration" showed how the *Bürgertum*'s political ideals "today lay broken before the overflowing strong-box." It was not uncommon to see socialist or radical commentators criticize the *Bürgertum* for its nationalist festivals, just as it was not uncommon for Marxist cultural critics such as Franz Mehring to deride the *Bürgertum* for giving up its earlier role as cultural leader of the nation to pursue material well-being.[106] In the case of the Cologne cathedral, a national shrine played a direct role in symbolizing what the observer saw as the *Bürgertum*'s sacrifice of its liberal ideals to the conspicuous misuse of a historic landmark. Here was a clear instance of the way in which the conspicuous consumption of the past divided rather than united the nation.

But the nation remained, as an alternative rather than an accomplished fact. The linking of the memory of 1848, Berlin, and Cologne established the national parameters of the critique and accepted the cathedral as a referent of national memory. But the accusation of willful misuse occurred with reference to a landmark that was as much about Cologne and the Rhineland as about Germany. Just as preservationists and their audiences mixed different memories without separating them, worker critics unintentionally also spoke on many different planes of identity.

Commitment of official preservation to the exemplary consumption of historic buildings as products of the historical evolution of national life faced a spectrum of public responses, from open (and at times problematic) enthusiasm to indifference or even open critique. Such responses did not preclude the growth of official preservation as an important part of the emergent national optics, nor did it preclude the unstable but marked development of a more emotionally resonant national memory. But the vision of a nationally shared past—which was really an unplanned national memory created by negotiation—was dependent above all on appropriations over which organized cultural policy had incomplete control. National memory appeared not as a coherent, single orientation to the national past and future but as a multiplicity of orientations, a multiplicity of possible nations, linked to social, institutional, and local interests. The popularity of historic places depended as much on their varied social uses as on the anxious policies of conservators, cultural officials, and association leaders in the preservation movement. The dispersion of the nation defined the strength of an official national memory—and its substantial limits. Insistent that their practices had wide public appeal, preservationists would grapple, often unsuccessfully, with this productive tension for decades to come.

> Like Laudomia, every city has at its side another city whose inhabitants are called by the same names: it is the Laudomia of the dead, the cemetery. But Laudomia's special faculty is that of being not only double, but triple; it comprehends, in short, a third Laudomia, the city of the unborn.
>
> —Italo Calvino, *Invisible Cities*

TWO | CITY OF THE UNBORN

orld War I seemed to point neither to the past nor to the future but only to itself, the "front experience," and to the immense, unexampled killing that propelled it. This effect created a sense of time's standing still, a feeling of suspension that compelled pacifist Ernst Barlach to commemorate the war dead in floating figures of mourning such as the one he crafted during the Weimar Republic for Güstrow.[1] The war was thus profoundly threatening to the idea of historical continuity, national or otherwise. On the other hand, there was a sense not of discontinuity but of return, as wartime symbolism drew on historical imagery in the "fortress truce" (*Burgfrieden*), the memory of the Wars of Liberation, and the rediscovery of the distinctive "Germanness" of historic south German baroque and rococo churches. Thomas Mann exhorted Germany to think of itself as Frederick the Great. The present suggested a unique historical experience, therefore, but memory called on the distant past, as Germans of 1914, living in their own embattled Laudomia, acted out the drama of medieval battles or the campaigns of 1813 in an attempt to preserve themselves and their unborn for that third Laudomia, the one of the national future whose model would not be an enervated Wilhelmine

culture but, rather, the front experience. The resort to mythical "first things" in moments of national crisis was not new in Europe. But the urgency with which it took place was, and the inconclusiveness that resulted from so much blood and energy shocked many Germans into realizing how far away they were from having anything resembling a widely shared national memory that offered a point of orientation in the modern world. This realization could not fail to affect the representatives of official preservation policy and their audiences.

Rules and Transgressions

Georges Bataille was a scholar, essayist, early surrealist, and pornographer. The point of departure of his work on modern culture was that social order rested on an ambiguous relationship in which transgressions typically reinforced the interdictions they were designed to upset.[2] The interdiction on killing one's neighbor was violated in war, but one violated it in order to reaffirm the interdiction, just as one reaffirmed the interdiction to have the opportunity to violate it. More than before, German national identity in World War I was based on such violations. This gave it a character much different from the one it had in the Kaiserreich. German national tradition (any national tradition) was certainly not without a history of military killing, and the empire had come into being as a result of three wars. Yet national identity in the politics and daily life of the Kaiserreich rested more on the potential for killing than the actual act, and it allowed for a limited degree of contestation between different collective actors and different versions of identity. War changed this, and hence the militaristic tradition of Prusso-German national identity returned to occupy a central place in the political culture. The *Burgfrieden* was the proper metaphor for the nation in war because it suggested military vigilance; it promised to give Germany a national solidarity the prewar period had been unable to produce (the Kaiser proclaimed that political parties ceased to exist and only "German brothers" remained); and it connoted a deep continuity with a medieval past.

Yet this was a new war, based on new weapons and technologies, supported by new forms of state organization, propelled by new social constituencies within the military, and energized by new forms of popular appeal. The unprecedented nature of the battle was reflected in the fact that soon after the war euphoria dissipated, a major debate among German publicists took place over the meaning of "Germany" and the "German Fatherland." The question "What is German?" was on every articulate citizen's mind. In part because of this confusion the conflagration was also seen as a cultural war, or what Germans referred to as a *Gesinnungskrieg*. Despite the importance of organizing military production, securing access to raw materials, and gaining new territory, many German state officials and intellectuals thought of the war in terms of a global battle between civilization and *Kultur*, capitalism and German socialism, sinners and saved—however those oppositions would be defined. At home, meanwhile, this etched-in cultural contrast inspired artists and writers to hope for a transformation of an ill-defined German culture, indeed a resonant definition of Germany as such, that built on reform efforts begun before the summer of 1914. They hoped for socially relevant art that forsook the influence of what were seen as French styles, such as Impressionism. They hoped that the *Volk*, and not artists bent on innovation for innovation's sake, would determine the cultural tenor of the nation.[3] Such efforts bespoke a deep insecurity on the part of the main protagonists of the cultural war, the *Bildungsbürgertum*, whose painters, graphic artists, and Protestant pastors hoped to see a war-driven apocalypse in German culture leading to a decisive increase in their power.[4] "Thou shalt not kill"—a key premise for a nation defined in Christian terms—was violated in the hope of reasserting the diminished power of those who lived by this commandment.

The cultural war exposed monuments and other cultural treasures to new dangers. Before the modern era, looting or destroying historic buildings was a privilege of the victorious soldiers. After the Napoleonic wars, international law, based in part on ideas of the social contract, recognized that war was conducted by states and their military forces rather than by societies as such.[5] Along with humanistic conceptions of a shared, international cultural heritage, this led statesmen to condemn plundering another nation's art and architecture. These ideas found international legal expression in the unratified Brussels declaration of 1874 and the Hague Convention of 1907. Allowing for the demilitarization of areas rich in cultural monuments and works of art, the 1907 convention assumed one could distinguish between military and civilian zones, and it allowed military authorities to attack schools, churches, hospitals, or monuments if those buildings were used for military purposes. This happened in 1914 when the Germans determined that the Reims cathedral was being used as a military observation post. Historic buildings were to be marked with appropriate symbols to signal their protected status to attackers. This potentially added to the rich if frightening symbolic landscapes of modern warfare. "Pageantry is scarcely the word to use," said J. B. Jackson of the everyday military symbolism he saw in World War II, "but it comes to mind when I recall the display of signs and notices that covered almost every lamp post and tree in the military landscape."[6] The comment applies to World War I as well.

These measures were never implemented. As prophylactic devices such symbols were irrelevant anyway in the context of a radically democratic war in which everyone had the chance to be killed, soldier as well as civilian, and any building could be destroyed, the bunker as well as the cathedral. The length and mechanized nature of fighting as well as the use of airplanes in the last stages of the war exposed human beings and the built environment to unexampled threats. Based on the idea of frightfulness, German war policy heightened destruction of cultural treasures in France and Belgium, where, for example, the Germans razed Louvain and its library, founded in 1426 and containing 280,000 volumes and collections of valuable incunabula and medieval manuscripts. This was only one of the most sensational cases, and hundreds of less internationally known monuments were destroyed in the East and West by both sides. Excepting the war zone of west Flanders, over 20,000 buildings were destroyed in Belgium, where planners had no previous experience to help them confront the immense tasks of reconstruction. There was war damage in thirteen departments in France, a modest figure by the standards of World War II, when more than sixty departments had damage, but a novel and disturbing development in the context of the Great War. In heavy fighting in East Prussia, the only region where the war was fought on German soil, more than 30,000 buildings were lost, among them historically important examples of peasant and bourgeois architecture, estate homes, and twenty-two important churches.[7] States, cities, and other authorities debated how to reconstruct the built and natural environments in all these areas. The gravity of destruction was well known to German military and civil authorities from the opening weeks of the war as they undertook incomplete efforts to protect art treasures and monuments in the occupied territories.

Military and economic policies designed to marshal resources within the warring states contributed to the destruction of artifacts. All the belligerents needed metal reserves as never before, for example, and although Germany had sufficient supplies of iron, it produced only a little more than 5 percent of the copper the enemy did. Calling for self-sacrifice to overcome metal shortages, Wilhelm II promised to melt down some of his own monuments in a gesture that may have brought a secret sigh of relief from those who hated the gargantuan monumentality of Wilhelmine public culture. The first agency to deal systematically with such shortages in Germany was formed in May 1915 in the Prussian Ministry of War. It requisitioned metal objects such as kitchen utensils and church bells, and when its work was completed, 19 million households and more than 40,000 churches and religious institutions were affected. Almost all tin and copper objects that were of any interest to historic preservation were seized, and it was estimated that by January 1918 half of all church bells in Germany had been committed to "higher service for the Fatherland," as pointed out by Prussian cultural official Friedrich Trendelenburg.[8]

Artifacts and War Machines

How did German preservationists respond to the war's novel patterns of destruction? From 1914 to 1918 there was much business as usual among preservationists, as reflected in the pages of *DP*, which continued to publish articles on international developments in historic preservation, yearly reports of preservation activity in the German states, and profiles of key preservation officials of the past and present. Preservation practice also continued as before. In Frankfurt am Main the outbreak of the war caused the city magistrate to discontinue funding for several new projects, but ongoing work on local monuments continued. In 1916 county officials in Hadersleben in Schleswig continued prewar plans to create an open-air museum of peasant architecture, partly to provide additional employment during the war. For some preservationists even the new practical problems created by the war represented no deep methodological break with the past. Lawyer and preservation activist Friedrich Wilhelm Bredt thought that "the war did not bring anything completely unfamiliar [and] that in and of themselves . . . rebuilding of the destroyed areas and the commemoration of the war dead represented no technically new tasks."[9]

If there was nothing technically new about the tasks of preservation in World War I, the war clearly did have an effect on its micropolitical capital. War prevented German preservationists from having more than one major national conference, held in the Bavarian city Augsburg in 1917 and attended by more than 300 people. Only three of the twelve sessions were devoted chiefly to problems of wartime preservation, but these were among the key presentations, including Clemen's address, "Historic Preservation and Heimatschutz in the Western and Eastern Theaters of War," and a panel titled "Historic Preservation and the Seizure of Metal Objects and Artifacts for Military Uses."[10] A sense of discontinuity was everywhere. Referring to the last wartime congress in Dresden in 1913, chair Adolf Oechelhaeuser opened the Augsburg event by saying "probably not one of us had a sense of what violent events, what difficult tests, would confront us before we would be able to come together again."[11]

The impact of war on local organizations was equally obvious. At first the war dampened sociability, an important aspect of that conspicuous consumption on which elite preservation societies relied. Noting "the difficult times," the RVDH decided not to hold a big ceremony celebrating its tenth anniversary in 1916.[12] But the organization was dedicated to the patriotic cause, and like its counterparts in Bavaria and Saxony, it published war-related issues, or *Kriegshefte*, the first of which was a collection of essays titled "War and Art." The organization also extended its activities to Alsace and Lorraine, where no *Heimatschutz* group existed before the war.[13] Such action was fueled by the conviction that the war gave preservation and cultural stewardship a new significance. In its first issue of 1915 the *Mitteilungen des Rheinischen Vereins für Denkmalpflege und Heimatschutz* wrote, "Wartime brings our mission new tasks. If the preservation of individual historical monuments or other purely local efforts seem momentarily less urgent, then for historic preservation the broader demands of our time open up a future that is that much greater."[14]

New opportunities could be seen in a number of key areas. Allied with academics such as historian Friedrich Meinecke and many other public figures, preservationists took a leading role in answering international criticism of Germany's destruction of French and Belgian monuments in the battlefield. This criticism began in the opening weeks of the war and reached truly massive proportions in France, England, and later the United States. Of the German bombing of the Reims cathedral in September 1914, Henry James said it was "the most hideous crime ever perpetrated against the mind of man." French public figures attacked *les Allemands destructeurs* for their acts of violence against Reims, Arras, Senlis, Louvain, Soissons, and other communities, signing a protest that included the names of Maurice Barrès, Georges Clemenceau, Claude Debussy, Anatole France, Andrè Gide, Matisse, and Auguste Rodin. In the last months of the war, in the French publication *Matin* senator Lucien Cornet warned that for every act of German destruction there would be French retribution; Germans would answer for Douai with Freiburg, for St. Quentin with Cologne, and for Lille with Frankfurt.[15]

Preservationists responded to international criticism swiftly. Soon after the German attack on the Reims cathedral, the Academia di san Luca and the Associazione artistica internazionale in Rome criticized the German army and appealed to Germany and the other warring powers to "uphold the principles of humanity in the conduct of the war."[16] This drew a strong rejoinder in December in *DP* from Felix Wolff, former imperial conservator in Alsace-Lorraine, who repeated the German army's argument that the cathedral was being used to direct French bombardment against German infantry. "There can be no question of an apology," wrote Wolff. "What do the signatories [of the appeal] really expect from a war that costs hundreds of thousands of lives, that destroys thousands of human habitats?" The German army would have done the same as the French to defend its position, argued Wolff. In a war in which the Christian principles "love your neighbor" and "thou shalt not kill" no longer apply, "there historic preservation must also abdicate." It was a matter of "sorrow and indignation" for the Germans that academics and artists of other nations would believe that the German *Volk* would plan "an intentional and wanton destruction of artistic and historical values." Because of "its love and respect," for monuments, wrote Wolff, Germany would win the cultural war even if the military contest was still in doubt.

Preservationists also gained influence in direct cultural service for the government war effort.[17] In September 1914 at the urging of general director of Prussian museums Wilhelm von Bode, the Prussian Culture Ministry set in motion efforts to catalog and protect movable art objects threatened by the fighting in Belgium and France. Otto von Falke, director of the Museum of Applied Arts in Berlin, was put in charge of this project. German officials worked directly with Belgian authorities from the Commission Royale des Monuments et des Sites in such efforts. Historic places also received attention, although they proved to be much more difficult to protect. In October 1914 the Prussian Culture Ministry appointed Paul Clemen to be in charge of monument preservation in occupied Belgium, a post that was extended to France in the next month, to the eastern front later in the year, and in January 1917 to all areas occupied by the German military. As a Reich commissar, Clemen's task was threefold: to report what had been destroyed, to oversee and record what efforts at preservation and maintenance were planned and undertaken, and to alert military commanders to the needs for cultural preservation. Approximately twenty-five German specialists and their support staffs worked at the front and in other parts of military zones on such projects.

Clemen also played a central role in a meeting of seventy German, Austrian, Hungarian, and Swiss art historians, military officers, and legal experts in August 1915 in Brussels, where further international protection for cultural monuments in wartime, including the setting up of an international commission to protect monuments in war, was discussed.[18] German organizers had hoped that representatives from entente countries would also participate, but this proved impossible. The conference had little impact in its time, but its deliberations continued to have an effect on preservation thinking in later decades. The short-term outcome of the conference suggested not only that the intransigence of the warring states made cultural protection impossible but that the nature of total war had outrun all legal codifications for protection. More broadly, the conference evoked Bataille's notions once again, as it was Germany, the chief transgressor, that appealed to the international community for more ambitious rules governing wartime cultural protection.

Monuments at war: a 1917 aerial photograph of the damaged Reims cathedral (*above*),
attacked by German artillery, and a 1918 photograph (*opposite*) of French efforts to reinforce
the cathedral's historic statuary (photos: Clemen, *Kunstschutz im Kriege*, 1:56–57)

CATHÉDRALE DE REIMS

Statues décorant le porche Nord de la façade. — État avant la guerre.

Cliché des Monuments historiques.

CATHÉDRALE DE REIMS

Les mêmes, le 30 décembre 1914, après l'incendie causé par les obus allemands.

Cliché Capitan.

The German destroyers: French propaganda illustrates the condition of statues on the north facade of the Reims cathedral before (*top*) and after attack by German artillery. (photo: *Les Allemands destructeurs*, 15)

Such service brought preservationists into conflict with government authorities and with each other. Due in part to patriotic loyalty, preservationist dissatisfaction with wartime destruction was expressed in rather indirect or ambivalent terms. It could be expressed in what von Falke referred to in 1919 as Clemen's official charge to make "repeated and forceful admonition" to military authorities to be vigilant about cultural preservation.[19] Von Falke's emphasis on repetition and force suggested the great obstacles wartime preservation faced in carrying out its duties. It could also be expressed in only slightly veiled public comments such as the one made by Clemen in 1917. "Who among us responsible for looking after the interests of preservation in the war," said Clemen, "has not repeatedly been forced to look on with bleeding hearts and bound hands as the care of historic buildings has been left to heavy artillery, both of the enemy and of our own?"[20] The reconstruction of damaged cities and towns also generated internal debates, as preservationists disagreed about the mode of restoration of Belgian monuments and whether restored East Prussian buildings should have stepped gables and oriels.[21]

Open tensions between government and preservationists also surfaced in the requisitioning of bells.[22] In this case the memory of the Wars of Liberation played a powerful role, although it had a paradoxical effect. Speaking at the Augsburg congress, Prussian cultural official Trendelenburg said that "the willingness to sacrifice compares to the liberation of one hundred years ago," referring to the many bells, pots, pans, and other domestic utensils the German people gave up for military use. Nonetheless, preservationists were worried about requisitioning, particularly as it affected private individuals and communities. What effect would the seizure of inherited copper utensils and other heirlooms have on the popular sense of *Heimat*? asked preservation officials from Schleswig-Holstein, Westphalia, and the Rhineland. And what about church congregations that gave up valuable metal artifacts, including historical bells? By summer 1915 preservationists had raised many objections, and by autumn the Prussian Ministry of Culture had alerted the Ministry of War about their concerns. By early 1917 the state had charged preservationists with the task of classifying bells according to their historic and artistic value, an immense task of inventorying that resulted in many historic objects being saved.

Debates over war cemeteries and monuments also engaged historic preservation because individual graves at the front or at home as well as public monuments were subject to many of the same criteria for individual design, siting, and relationship to the surrounding environment that historic buildings were. Organized by the Reich War Ministry but subject to much public discussion and confusion of administrative responsibilities, the commemoration of the war dead underwent a decisive change in Germany in World War I. Whereas throughout the nineteenth century soldiers were buried in either individual or collective graves at the front without necessarily being identified, only in World War I did individual graves including both the body and the name of the dead become standard practice for all fallen soldiers, although in some cases officers still got preferential treatment by being separated from the others or being buried on higher ground than regular soldiers. World War I accelerated and codified the soldier's right to be remembered in the same way that civilians were, namely as individuals whose grave markers were meant to refer to a particular life and a unique, irreducible life narrative. Here memory could be deeply individual, as the past became an unfathomable web of individual life stories extinguished at the moment of sacrifice. It is possible that American practice in the Civil War provided the model for Europe and Germany on this score, but this was unacknowledged in Germany during World War I.[23]

Historic preservation tried to control such commemorative art by influencing decisions about where to place memorials and plaques and how to design them. Most conservators and preservation associations supported efforts to reform the way Germany remembered the war dead, disavowing allegorical monuments of the past in favor of "cleaner" styles based on classical, "Germanic," and Christian symbolism. This attempt was based above all on a negative image of war monuments built after the Austro-Prussian and Franco-Prussian wars.[24] Criticism of these overblown, historicist, and allegorical monuments was a counterpart to the larger disparaging evaluation of nineteenth-century architecture and the supposedly chaotic orientation toward the past for which it stood. To ensure that the past would not be repeated, official preservation formulated a strategy on several fronts. There was the Rhenish Advisory Board for the Commemoration of War Dead, which sent circulars to county officials and mayors advising them on such matters. It also sponsored a competition among Rhenish architects, which brought a much greater response than expected, to promote better designs for monuments. The national *Heimatschutz* association set up a similar advisory body. Friedrich Wilhelm Bredt advocated the adaptive reuse of empty churches and castle ruins for such commemorative purposes, the former being appropriate because of their associations with eternity and their usually central location; the latter, because of their association in the popular mind with heroism and bravery. *Heimatschutz* official Werner Lindner, who had made the issue of war commemoration a personal crusade, advocated the use of already existing historic fountains as war monuments. Fountains had been a popular setting for monuments because they associated commemoration with a symbol of new or renewed life.

Lindner also wanted to put commemorative plaques in churches, schools, workplaces, offices, and fraternity houses so that memory of the war could be more properly integrated in daily life.[25]

Toward Laudomania?

A large part of preservationist discourse agreed with nationalist and state propaganda that situated the German nation in a new relation to past and future and reevaluated German history in the light of the war. But this project consisted of narratives and metaphorical usages with different emphases and meanings. For some preservationists the war taught the simple historical lesson that the German nation endured through struggle against all hostile forces. In February 1917 Friedrich Carl Heimann, city conservator and vice-chair of the Central Cathedral Building Society of Cologne, gave a speech before that club on the occasion of its seventy-fifth anniversary.[26] The organization was patronized by many noteworthy Cologne citizens, including Cardinal Antonius Fischer, who was honorary chair, Mayor Max Wallraf, and numerous well-known businessmen and bankers. Noting that the club motto was "Harmony and Perseverance," Heimann asserted that it was precisely these traits that were needed now. "As long as there has been a German history, when has there been a more important and difficult problem to solve than in our day, when Germany is called to struggle and surrounded by its enemies?" The motto of an organization seeking completion of a national symbol in the nineteenth century became the motto of new warrior "knights and tribes," who ensured that the homeland would remain a "mighty fortress" on the way to peace. Since at least 1915 this same sense of "holding out" had become an important motif of war commemoration also, as the inscriptions for fallen soldiers' graves emphasized perseverance and survival of national values as such rather than heroic victory for a definitive national goal.[27]

In the eyes of some preservationists, holding out meant that old monuments took on a new meaning. For Bodo Ebhardt, the experience of war demanded that Germans view castle ruins in a particular and, above all, aggressive way. Not romantic contemplation but Teutonic ferocity was the appropriate response to the sight of broken-down German castles. Ebhardt said ruins on the Rhine banks "teach us what our fate would be if the hordes of our enemy descended upon us again. . . . Think of the picturesque image of the Heidelberg castle ruins . . . and let it, along with the silenced and deserted towns and castles of the Pfalz[,] . . . be a call to hatred, revenge, and to battle to the bitter end."[28] In this approach the sense of achievement grounded in a monumental view of the past also carried with it a deep fear of the consequences of not aggressively fighting one's enemies. Significantly, despite Ebhardt's ties with the Kaiser, his preference for war monuments combined classical and Germanic motifs that linked 1914 with imagery of ancient Rome rather than with the memory of Prussian struggles against the French in 1813.[29]

Ebhardt was already known for his nationalist rhetoric before the war, and thus his aggressive reevaluation of German castles was not entirely unprecedented. But often the recontextualization of monuments by preservationists occurred more subtly and in more unexpected contexts. Such was the case at the 1917 preservation conference in Bavarian ministerial official Eduard von Reuter's narrative of the adaptive reuse of a Munich landmark.[30] Introduced as an example that had truly national significance for all Germans concerned with the direction of historic preservation, von Reuter's tale dealt with the thirteenth-century Augustine Church, or Augustinerkirche, which as part of a complex of buildings including a cloister and other structures in the northwest part of the Munich *Altstadt*, was owned by the Bavarian state since secularization in 1803. Used for various official purposes since that year, the buildings were vacated in 1897, and when a new police administration building was approved for the cloister's site in the first decade of the twentieth century, the question of whether to tear down the older structures or preserve and adapt them to new uses became urgent.

Von Reuter noted that officials, architects, preservationists, newspapers, and business groups all had opinions about the Augustinerkirche and the milieu it anchored. In view of the complex's proximity to the city's central business district, some local officials argued that the land should be crisscrossed by new streets and given "to the speculation of private builders with the goal of achieving the maximum possible financial profits for the state." Such plans seemed to be reinforced by prevailing art-historical judgments, represented by individuals such as Munich art professor Franz von Reber, who argued that the exterior of the Augustinerkirche was "extremely prosaic" and of little value as an architectural landmark because it had been thoroughly renovated in Renaissance style under the elector Maximilian's direction in 1620. Efforts to find a more direct historical value also failed, as earlier in the century researchers in the church's subterranean levels had turned up many human skeletons but no remains of famous personalities from the past. The press gave voice to "public frustration" and "the indignant voice of the people," clamoring to have the buildings demolished and citing the public cost of a complex that seemed to have no contemporary value. Among the defenders of the buildings were many of Munich's artists and the architect Gabriel von Seidl, member of a newly appointed Bavarian commission for monuments in state possession, who maintained that the church and cloister gained their importance from being part of a larger historical ensemble that included the fifteenth-century Frauenkirche, whose twin towers gave the Munich *Altstadt* a distinct accent, and the sixteenth-century St. Michael's Church, one of the outstanding Renaissance churches of Europe north of the Alps and an enduring symbol of the Counterreformation.

The issue might have turned into a major controversy; but goodwill prevailed, and in 1914 well-known Munich architect Theodor Fischer, enjoying the support of the Bavarian conservator, completed the restoration and adaptive reuse of the Augustinerkirche, which the Bavarian Interior Ministry had decided to preserve and integrate into the surrounding official and commercial activity. Fischer restored the building in a way that struck a compromise between the representatives of "material" and "ideal" interests, but more significantly for von Reuter, one of his by no means radical modifications to the site became the focus of Germany's anticipated victory in the war. The interior of the Augustinerkirche was divided into street-level shops, upper-floor offices, a concert and assembly hall, and even a gymnastics hall for a local club, leading von Reuter to say triumphantly that "the goal of finding practical uses for the entire interior down to the last cubic meter was achieved." Historical frescoes that could not be saved were photographed by the Bavarian conservator and then destroyed to make way for the interior's new uses. One side of the exterior gained more rounded arches to accommodate shop windows, but in general there was minimal change on the outside of the building. One of the most significant modifications was a terrace and stone balustrade above street level that Fischer constructed on the south side of the building to accent the difference between the lower and upper floors and create a vibrant public space related to the commercial district below. It was this terrace that represented the architect's uncanny anticipation of things to come for von Reuter.

"Is it not as if he had looked into the future when he thought of this plan?" said the Bavarian official of the architect. "Hopefully the day is not too far away when the terrace will be occupied by a festive mass of people, who with jubilation, flowers, and waving handkerchiefs, will greet the heroes returning to the *Heimat* and the work of peace after years of fighting . . . and unheard of victories and events." Fischer's impressive but otherwise ordinary labor of adaptive reuse was now reevaluated as a prophetic act for the edification of the Augsburg conferees. The outcome of a prewar dynamic of conflict, deliberation, and compromise was transformed into an architectural representation of the German Laudomania. The ordinary workings of Bavarian cultural politics were turned into an anticipatory drama whose conclusion would be the extraordinary victories of the German army. But of course the drama had a very different outcome, and the jubilant victory celebration on the terrace of the renovated Augustine church would never take place.

Later, all but the outer walls of the church were destroyed in World War II, adding yet another indignity to von Reuter's prophetic narrative. After being secured in 1948, it was finally restored—as the site of the German Hunting Museum—in the 1960s by architect Erwin Schleich (whom we will meet in another context later in the book).

Preservationists' rethinking of German history could assume an even more proactive and programmatic character, and when it did, it resulted in a call for the Germanization of the past. Language itself was winnowed so that its national essence could be adapted more effectively to the political cause, for example. Already before the war, Germany had seen various groups try to strip the German language of what were considered foreign accretions in much the same way that restorationists stripped baroque additions to Gothic cathedrals. This effort gained new influence in the war, and preservationists rallied to the cause. In 1916 the *Mitteilungen des Rheinischen Vereins für Denkmalpflege und Heimatschutz* printed an article by architect Borggreve of Düsseldorf, who likened the foreign words of architectural discourse to the "dry, fallen leaves" of late autumn.[31] Borggreve praised former *DP* editor Otto Sarrazin as one of the most effective combatants in this battle, noting that he published two books on language in the architectural profession and building trades, areas where foreign words were particularly plentiful and where Germanization was necessary. In six detailed pages Borggreve suggested German alternatives to foreign architectural terms, including the replacement of *Salon* with *Saal* or *Empfangssaal*, *Boudoir* with *Zimmer der Frau*, and *Entree* with *Eingang*. The list included German equivalents for foreign words for types of buildings (residences, hotels, restaurants, scientific clinics, and theaters), building parts, building materials, and architectural plans. Borggreve himself was struck by the " '*embarras de richesse*' " that one confronted when considering terms for the interior and layout of a building. Making such replacements meant "going back to the pure sources that Nature had implanted in the spiritual life of each nation." Insisting on this return to the source was of course compatible with the larger notions of an essential Germanness. Focusing on language itself took the activity of purification to the very fundament of daily life, something deeper and ultimately more powerful than economic interest or politics, indeed something that made it possible to articulate meaning in the first place.

In border regions such as Alsace-Lorraine, Germanization had a particular urgency, and here one writer in *DP* undertook detailed historical studies not only to demonstrate the Germanness of half-timbered houses in this region but to discount analyses that saw significant Norman-French influence on Germanic architecture. Plans to commemorate the centennial of Prussia's absorption of the Rhineland in 1815 altered as the event became a symbol of *German* national pride rather than of Prussian-Rhenish cooperation, a transformation the RVDH promoted.[32] But even less politically fraught regions and architectural styles were open to an active and intentional process whereby they were made to seem more German. Bavarian state conservator Georg Hager called for a reevaluation of south German baroque and rococo churches, which "mirrored the German soul just as well as the Gothic churches." For Hager, who spoke at the Augsburg conference, Gothic architecture meant a separation from nature, while rococo and baroque were in harmony with it. Cornelius Gurlitt agreed with Hager, saying that the best counterargument to the French claim that German culture never produced anything original could be found in baroque landmarks such as the Würzburg castle, "a work of architecture that no nation of the world had imitated."[33] Glorifying south German baroque put Gurlitt and others at odds with expert opinion on war monuments, where the general trend moved against baroque influences.

The reevaluation of the national past among preservationists extended to the use of new metaphors and figures of speech to give meaning to the war experience. At the 1917 Augsburg conference, Clemen expressed the new situation in terms of metaphors of the built environment in which soldiers and officers suddenly became architects of a new Germany, founders rather than stewards, creators rather than destroyers. "And the men who are out there holding the iron front," Clemen asked the conferees, "are they not at the same time the most daring master builders, who are constructing the house of the new Germany, and the military commanders the new teachers—historians, mathematicians, philosophers—and artists?"[34] Here acts of destruction by German soldiers were reevaluated as efforts to build the house of the new Germany. Preservationists had used healing metaphors before the war, but now were explicitly linked to wartime action. Adolf Oechelhaeuser, also using the Augsburg event as his forum, stated that in the midst of "the most terrible of all wars," the German people had not lost the ability to fulfill its "great cultural tasks," which included aiding Belgian reconstruction. "As victors," said Oechelhaeuser, "[we] know not only how to wound but also how to try to heal."[35] Later in the conference another participant compared the preservationist to a *Wundarzt*, an older term for "surgeon" that also brought together the conservationist metaphor with the imagery of a bleeding, war-related wound.[36] Germany's soldier-architects knew how to inflict pain, pierce the flesh of the enemy, and draw blood. But after this necessary viciousness, it knew how to bring the injured enemy back to health, a wiser though defeated—and perhaps sublimely deformed— opponent. We wounded the enemy, said Oechelhaeuser, in order to heal him; we heal him in order to wound him. Following Bataille's notion of cultural order and interdiction, the enemy's historic places had to be destroyed in order to be preserved, just as they would be preserved in order to be destroyed again. The intimacy of destruction and conservation, love of the past and a desire to wipe it out completely, came to the surface in such metaphorical language in a way that was impossible in peacetime.

The use of language to Germanize the past and create new metaphorical relationships between preservation practice and war depended on a set of oppositions between Germany and its Other, as a typical feature of nationalist discourse took on historically specific characteristics in the Great War. The metaphors of soldier-architects and battlefront physicians suggested that widely accepted contrasts between the cultured and the uncultured continued to work despite the apparent irrelevance of social differences in the *Burgfrieden*. Preservationists and other members of the educated classes participated willingly in state efforts to gain popular support for the war effort, thereby reinforcing their self-image as elite cultural brokers. But the role of the cultured extended to the battlefield as well, particularly in the argument of the civilizing mission of the German army. Clemen's 1915 report in Brussels on battlefield preservation distinguished between "brave troops" and "officers who loved and understood art" who managed "to snatch many art objects from ruin."[37] The cultured/uncultured pairing was thus reinforced in the heat of battlefield action, with relation not only to the enemy but also to domestic soldiers. Regular troops were admirably brave, but it was the officers, often advised by Clemen himself, who genuinely loved and understood the art they saved.

Cultured Germans did not just protect monuments but also furthered the indispensable scientific work of classifying and inventorying. German preservation research in Poland and Lithuania produced valuable inventories of monuments, several books, and a number of exhibits. The Generalgouvernement in Warsaw commissioned research on historic buildings in Polish towns, a project that resulted in a handbook for Polish monuments that Clemen hoped would be as important as the guide to Egyptian monuments produced by Napoleon's expeditions a century before. He also noted that the collections of photographs and sketches of monuments on the Western front would take their place as more valuable and lasting documentary sources after the war than more plentiful but ephemeral works about war experiences.[38] Here science assumed its rightful place of superiority over the merely popular memoir literature that began to appear.

The cultured/uncultured opposition would also work in the remembrance of the war dead. Preservationist criticism of past war monuments had an egalitarian aspect because it was linked to the desire to make monuments more accessible to the public and avoid a formulaic allegorical language whose meaning required a deeper knowledge of myth and history than most ordinary Germans could muster.[39] "What can a simple peasant lad do with complicated allegories, especially when they are taken from the ancient world?" asked Lindner. The new monuments should try to tap the "soul of the *Volk*" with a "secret power" that would inspire "patriotic feelings and the spirit of German heroism." In keeping with *Heimatschutz* perspectives, Lindner advocated artisanally produced monuments with simple themes that appealed to the ordinary craft worker or peasant.[40] But the rhetoric of good taste reasserted the claim of the cultured class to superiority by giving it the task of shaping popular expressions of grief. And usually such expressions were found wanting. When the parents of a fallen soldier donated a bell to their church with their son's last words—"Fret not for me, dear Mama"—Robert Hiecke told the Augsburg preservation congress these "horrible lines" represented a marked "fall" from the sublime beauty of commemorative inscriptions from earlier centuries. Rhenish preservationist Bredt, author of a history of cemetery art, showed more sensitivity, saying he avoided juxtaposing good and bad examples of gravestones and monuments in his book because it could easily insult the families of the dead.[41]

When transferred to the international stage, the opposition between the cultured and uncultured became a new and more chauvinistic opposition between Germany and its enemies. Dehio's 1905 references to the French "fanaticism of reason" now returned as a weapon in identifying who the real perpetrators of "art vandalism" were, as the French were reminded of their seventeenth-century army's looting of historic places and the French Revolution's "suicidal frenzy of destruction" of the country's "most venerable historical monuments."[42] Clemen displayed special hate for the Russians, whose barbarism would in his view be justification enough for extending German hegemony in the East.[43] They had left behind a "brittle crust of filth" in Vilna, the Bonn scholar wrote, and they showed a complete lack of understanding for the historical treasures of the East. Russians had ripped out all the historic bells of Riga, just as they had in Vilna, not bothering to categorize them according to quality, as the Germans had done so laboriously at home, said Clemen. They had hauled away monuments such as the Herder busts and the gigantic equestrian statue of Peter the Great, commemorated in 1910 as a symbol of Riga's 200th year of unity with Russia. In what Clemen called a symbolic act, the equestrian statue had sunk with the ship that carried it into Riga bay. The Russians destroyed over 30,000 buildings in more than 20 cities, almost 600 villages, and 300 estates in East Prussia. This was done without military justification and without resistance from the population, said Clemen, a fact that made German annihilation of Belgian architecture seem "not so great."

A belief in cultural superiority emerged also from preservationists' direct interactions with enemy populations. Belgian reconstruction planning was subject to much conflict between architects, city administrations, preservationists, and the government in exile.[44] As reflected in commentary at the Augsburg convention, German officials were astounded by "the passive resistance of the people"; their "bad habits in architecture and daily life"; the "unbelievably deficient understanding, even among the better-off social strata, of hygienic needs in housing and town planning"; and the lack of historic preservation, for which there was "hardly a trace" of sensitivity among the "broad masses." Cornelius Gurlitt suggested that a few German cities have "stewardship" over Belgian cities, as in East Prussia, so that the reconstruction of those communities would take place in line with Germany's "sounder artistic principles."[45] Germany would try to teach Belgium how to preserve its historic buildings, said preservationist Rehorst, and how to construct quality architecture, partly by giving Belgian architects tours of German cities.[46]

As before the war, most preservationists avoided openly racist remarks, although they were not unwilling to allow their public forums to be used for extreme chauvinism. At the Augsburg conference, Bavarian state minister Eugen von Knilling, making one of many responses to enemy criticism of the German army's destructiveness, complained that Germany had to put up with "daily insults" from "Russian illiterates, Parisian Apaches, African fetish worshipers, and the remaining human scum one finds in the enemy camp" who accused Germany of barbarism. But Germany would persevere in its cultural mission, having "too much natural reverence for the cultural treasures of foreign lands to forget that they must respect and protect the common property of the entire educated world so long as the bitter necessity of war allows it."[47] There was hearty applause for this language, according to the published protocol of the meeting.

Preservationists' enthusiastic response to von Knilling's reference to "the common property of the entire educated world" reminds us that in their haste to answer international criticisms, German preservationists wanted to emphasize not only their (superior) Germanness but their loyalty to an Occidental community. In such instances nationalistic thinking became the inferior Other to a more international outlook. In an imaginary dialogue, published in a 1914 art journal, between a German officer and his prisoner of war, a French officer, the German officer, a lawyer, revealed a detailed knowledge not only of French but of English and Dutch architecture and art. In contrast the Frenchman, also a lawyer, had never seen an Impressionist painting and knew little of German museums' enthusiastic reception of French modernism. The German pointedly concluded that the French were "still only Frenchmen," while the Germans were Europeans whose love of culture would be exemplary for coming generations. German adherence to European memory thus gave the nation a special purchase on hope. "You live in the past," said the German, "we in the future."[48] The RVDH gestured in a similar direction when the editors of one of its wartime publications wrote they wanted to respond to nationalistic French criticism "without constantly ringing the national bell," and despite the chauvinism of the Augsburg conference, speakers there repeatedly stressed they wanted to *avoid* the nationalism of their wartime opponents and make purely objective assessments of what had been destroyed and what could be protected.[49]

Gender identities again shaped preservationist discourse in the war. Debates over war commemoration revealed preservationists' desires for "masculine" and "truly German" monuments characterized by "modesty and simplicity" of design, especially on the battlefield.[50] But the masculine principle dominated war remembrance on the home front as well. When historic buildings such as churches were transformed as sites of memory for the war dead, as happened in a number of cities, those that specifically remembered women's plight during the war were few. One could mention the exceptions that proved the rule, such as the Maximilianskirche in Munich, devoted to the "holy courage of sacrifice of hundreds of thousands of mothers and wives, who heroically sacrificed all their maternal and conjugal happiness on the altar of the fatherland."[51] But women played a particularly significant role in remembering the fallen as they discussed their losses with pastors and priests, decorated gravestones and monuments with flowers or pictures, lit candles in church chapels, and openly cried during church services commemorating the dead. Germany's historic places were suddenly transformed into fields of care as they became sites of an unprecedented outpouring of female emotion. Preservationists participated fully in excluding such expressions of grief from their imagery of the nation, concentrating instead on masculine sacrifices for the fatherland.

I have stressed how preservationists participated in the strengthening of national consciousness in a variety of ways. But the picture would be incomplete without noting preservationists' strong sense of self-consciousness about both German national identity and their own contribution to cultural renewal. Preservationists referred again and again to the French charge of

Attacks on the aggressors' memory: vandal-damaged German war monuments in France (*above and opposite*) during World War II (photos: Clemen, *Kunstschutz im Kriege*, 1:71, 73)

CITY OF THE UNBORN

barbarism, denying it and using it ironically, but also often revealing that it struck a sensitive nerve about national characteristics. One German respondent to the charge analyzed the historical roots of the term, concluding that Romance cultures had always regarded Germanic cultures as barbaric by definition.[52] Discussing the problem of metal siding for rural and small-town buildings in the Bergisches *Land* of the Rhineland, an issue of concern for preservationists who wanted new buildings to adapt to historic surroundings, architect Hermann Pflaume decried the increasingly common practice of covering half-timbering with zinc or sheet-iron, asking, "Are we then really the barbarians that foreign opinion would like to make us out to be?"[53] This may have been a self-serving attempt to use the barbarism argument against one's domestic enemies. Yet its use in this context reveals that for the Rhenish architect it had a substantial rhetorical bite in a subject that was literally and figuratively miles from the war.

Self-consciousness was perhaps most pronounced on the subject of German soldiers' graves and cemeteries on foreign soil. In 1916 army captain Wilhelm Rolfs claimed that French people were impressed by the cleanliness, uniformity, and natural beauty of German war cemeteries.[54] Clemen was less sanguine. There would be many German war cemeteries throughout Europe after hostilities, he said in 1917. "In later years they will only be tolerated by a hostile population that will be all too ready to cast a critical eye on these artistic productions." Thus their design and siting were of utmost importance. "The estimation of a nation, as for an individual, depends on how it views itself in its greatest moment."[55] This statement revealed less concern about properly honoring the dead than about honoring them in a way that would stand up to the criticisms hostile groups would make of German culture.

One cannot avoid the mental image of a German kneeling before the grave of a fallen soldier but also casting a wary eye around to see who was watching. Here memory had its deeply self-interested gaze fixed on the national future. But one needs no skip of the imagination to envision this scene, for Wilhelm II embodied the nervous national identity of the period with reference to war monuments. Intensely involved in the planning of a commemorative site for German, French, and English soldiers in the military cemetery of St. Quentin in 1915, the Kaiser personally selected Greek warriors as statues for the structure, fearing that if they were portrayed as German soldiers in uniform, French officials would have them altered after the war. The use of Christian motifs was similarly self-interested. All nations could appreciate the call to Christian mourning found in German cemeteries and thus be dissuaded from obliterating or altering the commemoration of the war dead. In fact, the self-consciousness of Clemen, William II, and many other German officials was logical. Even before the end of the war, French people vandalized German war cemeteries, and several French journalists argued that sumptuous German cemeteries distorted memory of the battlefield's bloody realities.[56]

In the forefront of wartime propaganda, preservationists nonetheless expressed reservations about the effects of nationalist rhetoric on historic buildings. A prime mover in efforts to get the German army to preserve architectural and movable monuments, Berlin museum director Wilhelm Bode criticized German intellectuals who, mirroring their foreign counterparts, called for compensation for war damage in the form of art treasures or other cultural properties. In October 1915 Darmstadt building official Heinrich Wagner warned that wartime nationalism threatened the identity of historic streets because local officials wanted to rename them in honor of military heroes. "If one wants to commemorate princes and military leaders in street names," wrote Wagner, "one should take the names of newly laid-out streets or name streets after them where there will be no loss of local and provincial history if the old name disappears. Each locale has plenty of such places."[57] Too much nationalism threatened historic places just as decisively as too little did.

Anxiety over such matters was connected ultimately with preservationists' continued fears about the relevance of their activity to the German nation. "The healthy, strong impulse of our time must lead us to the point," wrote Werner Lindner of historic fountains as war monuments, "that new monuments will be involved in as lively a way as possible in the being and force of everyday life [*Alltag*]. Their purpose would be misguided if they were appropriate only to the exalted ambience of the commemorative festival, if every moment they did not call out quiet, powerful, subliminally persistent reminders of unforgettable deeds and events to the individual."[58] Here the tried-and-true opposition between "dead" and "living" monuments worked to help Lindner express a need for war commemoration that had a continued impact on daily life, a *völkisch* resonance. But it is not too much of a distortion to replace "new monuments" with "historic preservation," which for Lindner and others should also have a connection to the being and force of everyday life. Would the war establish this connection once and for all, as the Kaiserreich had not? Was Laudomania's city of the unborn finally realizable as a popular entity?

The Being and Force of Everyday Life

Beyond the cultural politics of state agencies and specialized voluntary groups, the preservationist public was highly agitated for most of the war. "As rarely before, perhaps as never before," stated an RVDH official in December 1914, "the public has been preoccupied with voluminous reports and discussions of historic buildings, their protection, and their destruction."[59] French consumers bought academic condemnations of German destructiveness, just as Germans bought literature defending German policy and accusing the French of being the real destroyers of culture. German book buyers made the RVDH's 1916 book *Cemetery and Monument* the best-selling publication that group ever produced, even though it was very expensive and did not deal directly with the burning subject of soldiers' graves and monuments but, rather, with the general history of German cemetery art. Germans found their newspapers full of nationalistic poetry dealing with monuments, such as Rhenish novelist Rudolf Herzog's "Cathedrals in Enemy Land," published in November 1914 in the *Kölnische Zeitung*, which combined reverence for the cathedral of Antwerp with a celebration of the black-white-red flag flying over it. The postcard industry literally added fuel to the fire, though not entirely honestly. One Geneva company produced a falsified postcard of the Reims cathedral with entirely fictional flames and an equally fictional hole caused by a German bomb blast.[60]

One consequence of such public enthusiasm was the emergence of a radical nationalism that was more organized than anything seen until then among the audiences who supported preservation and its related activities. An example may be found in the Reich Federation for Heimat Art

(Reichsbund für Heimatkunst), founded in May 1918 and supported by art-ists, writers, and leading members of the professional classes.[61] A cultural-political parallel to the radical nationalist Fatherland Party (Vaterlands-partei), the Reich Federation was far more radical in its language and goals than historic preservation or *Heimatschutz*, although it was embedded in the same cultural-political milieu, just as the Fatherland Party radicalized argu-ments and demands found in the bourgeois parties.

The goal was to bring together all *Heimat* associations in a national work-ing group that promoted an "authentic, great art of the homeland, a German *Heimat* culture."[62] Founders argued this was the right moment to decide whether Germany would adhere either to an international "superficial cul-ture" or to a "truly indigenous art." The "German spirit" achieved its "posi-tion of global power" in the Middle Ages, said the Reich Federation, but in the intervening period it was threatened by foreign influences. The war created an opportunity for "rebirth." Hans Much, one of the leading spokes-men of the organization, thought this meant Germany had to "unlearn" more than it had to remember.[63] It had to forget its educational system's one-sided emphasis on "Greek and Roman cultures and their imitation in classicism" in order to see that "the spirit of Germany's greatest cultural period, the Hansa spirit, must again be made to live." Much used the well-known distinction between civilization and *Kultur*, insisting that the "Aryan race"—a term rarely seen in preservationist literature on historic architec-ture at this time—should resist the pull of civilization in great cities such as Berlin, which were nothing more than "cultural archives" where *Kultur* died. Architecture, "the highest expression of general culture," would figure prominently in the group's agenda. If Berlin was the negative pole of Ger-man architectural culture, planner and architect Fritz Schumacher's "monu-mental brick buildings" in Hamburg offered a good example of the positive side. Throughout German cities, "brick Gothic" was the solution to the Berlin-style rental barracks, the "symbols of Mammonism." Throughout the countryside, "ancient Lower German [*plattdeutsch*] brick construction" would lead Germans back to true native art.

Despite the appearance of such groups, softer symbolic uses of historic architecture, more patriotic than radical nationalist, were still more nu-merous and effective in this period, just as they had been before the war. One of the effects of government calls for national solidarity was a con-tinuation of the return to the region or the locale begun in the empire. Often promoted by veterans' associations and other civic groups, the placement of plaques commemorating the war dead in churches, synagogues, town halls, and market squares redirected attention to the losses local parents, wives, siblings, and children now mourned. Local-historical legends and historic architecture appeared as symbolic trappings for campaigns to collect donations for war-related causes, as when Brandenburg province in 1917 issued two series of twenty-four postcards depicting monuments, ancient peasant dwellings, and historic streetscapes to raise money for the war disabled.[64] Wartime *Heimat* literature in towns and cities throughout Germany reminded readers that they should keep up interest in local history and culture while "many sons of the homeland from the North Sea to the Alps, from the Danube to the Baltic, kept a dutiful watch so that fatherland and *Heimat* would be protected against the horrors of war," as a 1917 *Heimat* book dealing with Liebenburg and Wölteringerode near Goslar expressed it. The sacrifice of the sons obligated the producers of *Heimat* literature to offer their work as a "sign" to young people at home to have "understanding" for *Heimat* history and monuments, and as a source of security to older people, whose life experience told them "that the roots of national power were solidly anchored in the soil of the *Heimat*."[65] The discourse of local identity thus served to link the home front and the battlefield, reminding soldiers of their true homes and reminding those who stayed behind of their duties while the soldiers were away. Such evocations were far removed in mood and substance from the apocalyptic images of those who saw the war as a world-historical struggle between two inimical cultures—or two races.

Whether one finds hard or soft appropriations, radical nationalism or more benign patriotism, the war did little to reduce battles over the public uses of historical architecture. Indeed, the new public emphasis on nationalist idealism gave such conflicts a more contentious edge. "The '*Burgfrieden*' should not be an excuse for concealing certain acts of destruction during the war—not by the army—that are undertaken in complete silence," read one art journal commentary on the dismantling of the Main River bridge in Frankfurt. Torn down to make way "for God knows what kind of modern piece of clumsy work," the bridge stood in the way of the city's program to modernize local streets and adapt municipal bridges to increased commercial traffic on the Main River. "We too have our enemies at home," the scathing article stated, "he injures us not with canons and war propaganda but with 'public favors.'"[66] This criticism cut in two directions, as the term *Burgfrieden* in quotes suggested that the wartime call for patriotic unity was a farce even as it ridiculed the municipality in the light of the battlefield's higher morality.

It is fitting that the Main River bridge should have occasioned such rhetoric, for the old structure was more than a local curiosity or an example of the still-incipient genre of technical monuments.[67] Originally built mainly out of wood from nearby royal forests in the thirteenth century, the bridge, with its many rounded and graceful arches spanning the busy river, had become "an historical symbol of the first order." Traversed by warring troops throughout the centuries and used to fire cannon shots to warn local citizens of approaching armies, the bridge had also served as the point from which Frankfurter set off showy displays of fireworks to celebrate royal coronations and other events. Goethe praised the bridge for its "length, solidity, and fine appearance" as he fondly remembered his youthful strolls in the Hessian city, thereby entering the artifact into the German pantheon of architectural landmarks. A key switching point in Frankfurt's centuries-old function as a center to east-west and north-south commercial traffic, the bridge had in the nineteenth century become "a popular symbol of the unity of northern and southern Germany." Nothing could stop the destruction of the bridge, and thus, just as Germans mourned the war dead, the preservationist public could do nothing more than "take leave of this, the real symbol of the city."

The presence of larger numbers of war-injured did not fail to bring historic buildings into the harsh light of public debate as well. One unusual example comes from the controversy over a national architectural museum.[68] In 1917 Professor Hermann Schütte of Hildesheim proposed that disabled construction workers and artisans be put to work building models of historical buildings. Rural craftsmen would make models of peasant houses on a scale of 1:20, while craftsmen from small cities would make models of facades of *Fachwerk* houses on a 1:5 scale. Their handiwork would then be collected as an exhibit in a memorial hall containing the works of war-injured architects, construction workers, and craftsmen from the woodworking and metal industries. Covering the history of German architecture from the fifteenth century to the early nineteenth century, it would commemorate veterans' accomplishments while also calling attention to the continued influence of the historical models. As a whole, the exhibit and the museum would serve as an educational tool for students at technical universities and building trades schools and for schoolchildren on field trips. Ultimately the project could lead to the creation of a new industry that occupied war-injured in the production of models of historical buildings.

Heimatschutz representatives expressed many strong reservations about the project, saying that Schütte had not considered sufficiently its organization and implementation. They worried that a collection of historical models would do little either to preserve a memory of the past or to influence builders to construct good housing in the future. They raised questions about the misuses of the project, warning against plans to allow cities to use the historical models as a tourist attraction, which would bring out "romantic-picturesque" sentiments. They raised doubts about how the models would be selected, about the qualifications of the war-injured who would construct the models, and about overall supervision. Finally, they doubted there were sufficient spatial or financial resources to create the kind of national museum Schütte envisioned. If anything was to come of the project, then these issues would have to be addressed by those with experience in such matters, namely architectural preservationists and their *Heimatschutz* allies. Although there was support for the plan among the Augsburg conferees in 1917, preservationists such as Gurlitt made similarly harsh criticisms, and finally the conference rejected the idea of a national architectural museum, suggesting that a provincial museum would be more practical.[69]

Another area of concern was the fate of historic church bells, which exercised the representatives of official preservation but also stimulated popular anxieties. "Never have people done so much research on bells," said one observer in 1917. "Never had popular fantasy dealt with bells so much." This was the background for heightened disputes between the state and the churches and between churches and official preservation. Church bells were the objects of rich associations in German culture, and the *Bürgertum* in particular had grown up with literary and other images of these artifacts in classical texts such as Goethe's *Faust*, where peeling bells symbolized childhood, doom, or the death of Faust himself. Church congregations were frustrated with government requisitioning not only because they had to give up their bells, but because the government initially did nothing with them, leading church representatives to ask if it was necessary to take the bells down so soon.[70] By the last year of the war they looked for replacements for their departed bells, very often finding them in ones made of cast iron rather than bronze. For most churches, Protestant more than Catholic, the cast iron bells were cheaper and more readily available. This alarmed preservationists, who said that the new bells were more costly than presumed, musically inferior because of their harsh tones, and ethically offensive because they represented cost saving in an area of German life where only deep religious conviction and beauty should matter. According to preservationists the choice was unpatriotic as well because it failed to take account of future military needs for bronze. The conclusion was that church congregations should have patience until they could replace their beloved historical bells with new bronze ones.[71]

Beyond such disagreements, the war stimulated substantive proposals for new uses of historical buildings to evoke a national memory. Although the growing antiwar mobilization helped to build a critical atmosphere in which new ideas prospered, most proposals for truly innovative monuments came from sources other than the left-wing parties. Preservationists had done much to foster the search for alternatives, and we have seen that Werner Lindner advocated using historic fountains as war monuments in 1915, arguing they were just as appropriate as "equestrian statues, trophy groups, and other allegorical representations," precisely the objects favored in Wilhelmine public culture.[72] Somewhat more conventional was the movement to transform historic churches into sites of commemoration honoring the war dead. The first example in this genre was the Maximilianskirche in Munich, but there were also plans for Nuremberg, Frankfurt am Main, and Cologne to use other older or newly built churches for this purpose. Although the Munich church was distinguished by its attention to mothers and widows, plans for other commemorative churches called for more traditional themes. This was shown by former high school teacher Walter Rothes's 1916 pamphlet, which outlined possible future models for an attentive public.[73]

Rothes was convinced that the war called for monumental forms of commemoration. Although Gothic-style churches were appropriate because they were associated with authentic German tradition, Romanesque, baroque, and Renaissance churches were much more useful in Rothes's eyes. Such churches offered more wall space for huge frescoes, the best vehicle for monumental themes, and Romanesque architecture was doubly appropriate because its compact forms gave churches "a fortress-like appearance." Demonstrating the continued pull of mythic ways of seeing, Rothes argued that commemorative churches should have massive wall paintings using biblical and allegorical images. Good angels struggling against bad; Cain and Abel; David and Goliath; Daniel in the lion's den; Albrecht Dürer's scenes of the Apocalypse; King Herod's killing of the innocents; allegorical depictions of German troops dressed not in field gray but in colorful garrison uniforms; U-boats, zeppelins, and massive field artillery—all could be worked into a monumental cycle of paintings. Since the site was a church, nationalist hatred would be rejected. "The very original idea of having portraits of enemy princes, military leaders, and diplomats standing in Hell on Judgment Day would go too far," wrote Rothes. Modernist architecture would not be excluded, because steel and glass construction offered exciting possibilities for creating monumental lighting effects. Not once mentioning veterans' groups or the everyday conditions of the war-injured, Rothes concluded, "One must never forget: something extraordinary, immeasurably grand and sublime, and powerfully influential for future generations should come into being."[74]

Rothes's vision was grandiose, but it was not a striking departure from artistic tastes inherited from the prewar era. By contrast, many Germans joined a movement to find alternative monuments to the fallen and the war-injured, who were not to be merely remembered or honored but fully enveloped in the German future. *Heimatschutz* organizations, the Dürerbund, land reform advocates such as Adolf Damaschke, and several cities (Stuttgart, Düsseldorf, Ulm, and Essen) undertook plans to settle returning veterans on land that could be rented cheaply and built up with low-interest loans and other financial incentives. The land was to be found in rural areas where agriculture and small gardens were possible, which made such plans more economically feasible but also compatible with the antiurban view of the past some *Heimatschützer* had. The Garden City movement also advocated homes for veterans. The first such garden city appeared in Königsberg as part of the rebuilding of East Prussia. Garden City houses were often dispersed, had two or three rooms and a garden, and were patterned on what were thought to be ancient Germanic models.[75]

Few commentators laid out a more fully developed alternative form of commemoration than Hans Kampffmeyer did.[76] A state building inspector from Karlsruhe, Kampffmeyer wanted to gain public and financial backing for an entirely new kind of monument that drew on the above-mentioned influences and captured the "spirit of [the] time," which demanded commemoration of "the great and the good." Commemorative plaques in city halls and churches, and oak trees planted in honor of the war dead were worthy attempts, but they fell short of what was required. Germany certainly did not need another "large-size Niederwald monument" or a mountain transformed into a war monument, which had been seriously suggested. This last-named possibility "would not have been German, but American." The best solution was a peace city—"a great new city that embodies the cultural, social, and economic strivings of the best German men and women as completely as possible."

Kampffmeyer laid out his plan by detailing how he would select the site, raise money, buy the land, attract inhabitants, give the community an economic base, and construct its buildings and infrastructure. He sent his plans to representatives of industry and commerce, architects, painters and writers, educators, social workers, and trade union representatives. In 1918 he published both his plan and the various responses to it in a seventy-eight-page booklet. Many reacted to Kampffmeyer's suggestions by agreeing that Germany had too many "dead monuments of iron and stone." This was the view of Dr. Brüdders, director of the German Insurance Bank in Berlin, but also of Konrad Haenisch, a Social Democratic Prussian *Landtag* representative and later minister of culture in the Weimar Republic, who said that the peace city was "in fact worth much more than all the monuments of iron and stone that we have had to tolerate since 1870." Exasperation to move beyond these stultified forms of commemoration united the respondents as few other issues did.[77]

But some respondents argued that not everything about German monuments was to be rejected, and that in fact it was the quality of Germany's old medieval cities that should inspire Kampffmeyer's project. Architect Paul Schmitthenner, later a vociferous critic of functionalist architecture, stated this quite explicitly. "The old city originated centuries ago," he wrote, "and many generations have worked on it. What therein was formed and what became the expression of *bürgerlich*, commercial, intellectual, and religious life, is clear, simple, [and] uncomplicated." Today, everything had changed. "Architectural tradition and artisanal talent are lacking, the 'personal' steps into the foreground everywhere, even when no personality stands behind it." Peace City might offer a solution, a "way . . . to win back what has been lost, the way to 'the beautiful German city.' "[78] For Schmitthenner, Peace City was a potentially "living" monument that could give Germans an authentic link with the past and an inspiring model of the future.

Bruno Taut, who would distinguish himself in the early Weimar Republic as an extreme representative of new architecture, was as enthusiastic about Germany's "beautiful cities" as Schmitthenner was. Of course, Taut's language was much different. For Schmitthenner, the clarity of historical cities offered cherished values in the revival of the German *Volk*. Taut did not use this term, referring instead to "the great common spirit." But like Schmitthenner, who argued that not commissions and advisory boards but a single genius in a "higher comradeship" with several trusted allies should carry out the project, Taut advised Kampffmeyer that only a powerful individual who avoided "everything smacking of compromises" could realize Peace City. He mentioned that his own about-to-be-published book, *Die Stadtkrone*, shared Kampffmeyer's wish for a "renewal of our urban conception."[79] For architects at opposite ends of the political spectrum, the old city pointed the way to new forms of commemoration implemented by a cultural elite unburdened by past conflicts.

Although they would not have been as visionary as Bruno Taut, preservationists would have shared Kampffmeyer's respondents' longing for new ways of using the past in the future. They shared with them a love for the historical city and a desire to have its clarity speak to a confounded nation. The myth of the authentic historic city could be put into the service of remembering the war. But as this chapter has shown, the desire for a revival of the past, which had begun in the Kaiserreich and continued in the war, took place in a context in which both present and future were mortgaged to the moment. Disagreements arising in the process of public appropriation of monuments demonstrated furthermore that the path forward to the past was obtruded. The new/old city of the unborn remained a chimera.

"Space," "Homeland," "Style"!

To hell with them, odious concepts!

—Bruno Taut

THREE | MODERNIST CRUCIBLE

he Weimar Republic lasted only fourteen years. Its failure stemmed less from a German inability to give democracy a home than from the tensions of a classically modern society buffeted by the historically specific crises of unprecedented world war, sharp political upheaval, and unusual economic hardship. It was a modernist crucible, in the sense of being a severe test, with a German difference. If World War I seemed to have been an unprecedented break with the past, the Weimar Republic offered little chance of redemption. The impact of military defeat was as total as it was sudden. Political revolution in the wake of war drove a wedge between past and present. Though uneven in their impact, inflation and hyperinflation, both ultimately products of the war, created both hardship and the fear of even more unprecedented economic disaster. The Republic was hammered from the moment of its inception by political terrorism from both the extreme right and left. Even the supposedly calm years of the Republic from 1924 to 1929 were marked by a developing agricultural crisis and the evaporation of the electoral support of the liberal middle-class parties. The economic depression starting in 1929 thus destabilized an already unsteady polity. Cultural modernism, having begun in the nineteenth century but gaining a more critical edge in the war, now also burst forth on the Republic to create extraordinary ferment in architecture, painting, cinema, literature, drama, and popular culture. Architect Bruno Taut's attack during the early Republic on the "odious concepts" that continued to shape German architecture and urban design was a fitting battle cry for the most radical proponents of cultural experimentation.

Nonetheless, the Republic was not doomed from the start. Supporters as well as opponents of Weimar were aware that the new entity had provided continuity with the Kaiserreich by preserving German geopolitical integrity. The Weimar Constitution provided stability (or repression, depending on one's point of view) as well as a commitment to the cultural-political autonomy of the provinces, a key factor in maintaining preexisting cultural practices, including historic preservation. The economic growth of the 1920s was impressive, if superficial. It took the economic depression and the resultant state crisis to bring about the collapse of a political structure whose future was bleak but hardly foreordained. Ultranationalism in the form of the Nazi Party (Nationalsozialistische Deutsche Arbeiterpartei, or NSDAP) was both a symptom and, once it gained increasing electoral support after 1930, a cause of the deep political crisis. When Hitler came to power in 1933, he argued that Germans would regain the future by reconnecting the broken cords of national memory. Many preservationists, self-appointed defenders of national tradition, rejoiced when Hitler came to power, but as this chapter shows, they were not so unhappy with the Weimar Republic as to make their support for Nazism a foregone conclusion. Still, they, like so many Germans unsettled by the tensions created by the modernist crucible that was Weimar, had deep doubts about the survivability of the national polity, doubts to which Nazism would eventually respond in dangerously creative ways.

Mixed Blessings

Uncertain about what the relationship between the cultural and political nation would be and shocked by the political violence that accompanied Weimar's beginning, preservationists did not know what attitude to take toward the Republic at first. They bemoaned the fall of the Empire, which for Clemen and many other preservationists had provided political legitimacy for the protection of national heritage. The period from the abdication of the Kaiser to the ratification of the Weimar Constitution in August 1919 was particularly tense. When the constitution was passed, preservationists recognized that the Weimar Republic had moved well beyond the Kaiserreich by articulating the Reich's and the states' formal support for the protection of cultural property. Article 150 of the Weimar Constitution stated that "the monuments of art, history, and nature, and the landscape, enjoy the protection and guardianship of the state."[1]

Impressed by such constitutional guarantees, speakers at the annual conference of preservationists in the Thuringian city of Eisenach in 1920 adopted a relatively positive stance in matters related to the institutional standing of heritage protection in the new system. They cautioned about getting involved in "political discussions . . . that are completely foreign to historic preservation." At the same time legal scholar and Center Party representative Konrad Beyerle, discussing a conference committee's resolution to the Weimar government at the Eisenach event, suggested that the new state might open hitherto unavailable chances for political influence. The new system was not going to be a "formal democracy," said the resolution, but would be based on "cooperative work of all estates" in which "the voice of an independent cultural group free of all political stereotypes" would perhaps have more influence than before over legislation and administration of the cultural heritage.[2]

Rooted in part in a continued allergy to party politics, preservationists hoped that the cultural practices of the *Bürgertum* could be adapted to the new political context, making it easier to carry out the cultural nation's memory-work. The 1920 resolution hoped that the new state would depart from "the unlimited maintenance of the legal power of the property owner" that had placed so many obstacles in the way of heritage protection in the past. Beyerle said he was encouraged that "the emphasis on social thinking in the new legal order has not bypassed the concept of property." He pointed out that preservation's desire for a new social consciousness had nothing to do with communism but, rather, with stewardship over the "precious conservative cultural goods of the German nation" and Naumann's "social ethos." Echoing Dehio's 1905 argument about the "socialist" elements of preservation, Beyerle said that if "mammon's striving for profit" was one outcome of the revolution, then so too was the belief that "private property is not an absolute end in itself."[3]

The constitution gave preservation official sanction, but it also left it in an ambiguous legal state.[4] Article 150 was a programmatic statement that had no substantive impact on preservation legislation in the federal states and cities, save for laws passed in Hamburg and Lippe-Detmold in 1920. For the most part, it served as a moral weapon, as when the 1925 annual preservation conference, protesting new Reich tax legislation that hurt owners of historic property, reminded Berlin authorities that Article 150 provided for consideration of the economic burdens of preserving historic monuments when fiscal laws were drafted.[5] Although Reich ordinances of 1919 and 1920 regulated the sale of German art to foreign buyers and gave added protection to historic places, legislation remained inadequate, leading some preservation groups once again to take up the prewar call for a national preservation law, a *clausula generalis* for the Reich and the states that coordinated preservation regulations and went beyond use of local building and police ordinances. But the general law never materialized, and the federal states drafted new, systematized preservation laws that were never implemented, thanks in part to the opposition of the churches. In the late 1920s the ability of the state to protect historic buildings was weakened by a Reich ruling specifying that declaration of a building as a monument obligated the authorities to compensate the owner for the economic burdens of preservation. Discussions of this ruling indicated that although the theoretical right and obligation of the state to intervene in property for such purposes were more strongly accepted than before, the limits to intervention were still substantial, and the contradictions that could emerge between individuals and public authorities were still considerable.

Most provincial and local authorities exploited the ambiguity of preservation law to operate much as they always had. As before the war, cultural policy was largely (and increasingly) the matter of the provincial governments, but unlike the prewar era, in which Wilhelm II clumsily promoted a nationalist monumentalism, the Weimar state was culturally neutral. The Weimar Republic would encourage culture from the center, and indeed it unsuccessfully attempted to provide a more centralized national-state focus for disparate cultural policies so as to suppress particularist and even secessionist ambitions. Except for a short-lived attempt right after the war to create a specifically republican cultural politics, however, the Reich would not promote a particular *kind* of culture, leaving this to the state bureaucracies, which acted as peripheries to Berlin but as centers to the numerous communities and institutions they governed.[6] The cities did much the same, and some urban communities, such as Hamburg, never a kind place to historic preservation before the war, passed legislation that established a conservator's office and went well beyond previous laws against "disfigurement."[7]

The changed relationship between church and state also affected historic preservation in the Republic. Initially preservationists feared that the reorganization of church-state relations would result in increasing loss of historic property held by churches and increasing state inability to oversee monuments in church hands. But anxieties about "radical socialist programs for separating [church and state]" were quickly allayed. By September 1920 Beyerle could proclaim, "All in all today we can state with satisfaction that the danger to church cultural property—excepting the enormous rise in the number of thefts—is not as great as it appeared to be under the direct pressure of the revolutionary disturbances." Preservationists were also satisfied that a July 1924 law on the administration of Catholic Church possessions gave states the possibility of more direct intervention in the churches' handling of cultural property.[8]

Preservationists also expressed concerns about the future of former princely holdings, especially art treasures and architecture. Noble houses and palaces were valuable not only because they represented Germany's aristocratic heritage but also because they served an important art-historical function. With the revolution an estimated 115 larger palaces and their surrounding buildings fell into the hands of the *Länder* via the Reich government. Sixty-seven dated from the late seventeenth and early eighteenth centuries, constituting the major part of Germany's profane historic architecture from the early modern period.[9] The economic crises of the postwar period made the protection of such artistic treasures difficult for both private owners and public corporations. The already mentioned 1919 decree prohibiting unauthorized sales of German artwork abroad and a September 1920 Reich decree on the dissolution of family entail earned moderate support from preservationists in late 1920, although they also insisted they had not been brought into the decision-making process enough.[10]

If legal developments suggested the chance for protection, there were still many difficulties in deciding what would be done with the palaces. Bodo Ebhardt gave the extreme version of everyone's fears: the castles would fall victim to the "evil and fanatical shortsightedness of political cliques and the fanaticized oppositionist elements of our people."[11] Most preservationists displayed greater calm. Still, although they were willing to adapt to the new times, they continued to believe in strictly demarcated historical styles and time periods, and they insisted that new uses for these architectural traces from the past should fit earlier historical intentions as much as possible. The castles were designed not only for utilitarian purposes but for princely representation as well, and their history imposed limits on contemporary reuse. In taking this position preservationists were still thinking their way into previous historical periods, using memory as a path to the past rather than as a key to the present. Such historicism brought them into conflict with other institutions and groups, which had different needs and interests.

Speakers at the Eisenach conference opposed plans for dividing the castles into small apartments or making homes for the war-injured out of them. Similarly inappropriate was the turning over of castles to local "rabbit breeding clubs" or to "party politics." The Eisenach conferees were cautious but generally positive about using them for administrative and educational purposes. Fifty of the castles in the hands of the states had already been transformed into museums—an arts and crafts museum in Karlsruhe and a museum for the history of territorial princes in Darmstadt—a development which was promising but also filled with technical difficulties. By 1930 the "castle problem" had not been definitely resolved, and ten years of preservation of these structures in the Republic led Rudolf Esterer of Bavaria to the conclusion that many government preservationists had made about every other area of their work: each dispute or doubt had to be considered on a case-by-case basis.[12]

Legislative-political issues, relations between state and church, the castle problem—preservationist policy in all these areas finally came down to a question of material and economic resources. Preservationists replicated the larger national discourse by pointing to Germany's bitter poverty after World War I, but they also conceded that their material situation was mixed rather than uniformly bleak. The material shortages were real enough, especially right after the war, when preservationists looked with horror at the plundering of monuments for wood and the theft of art treasures from historic churches. Associations such as the RVDH were "fully disorganized" as a result of the inflation (but also because of the French occupation of the Rhine and the deportation of key government personnel). More broadly, the Reich and provincial governments made a commitment to historic preservation in a way the Kaiserreich had not, but they did not have the financial resources to put commitment into effect. Inflation and depression hurt both public and private owners of monuments, making everything from costly restoration to basic upkeep prohibitively expensive. By 1930 the great cathedrals of Cologne, Speyer, Xanten, and Mainz were overdue for repairs that had been put off because of economic obstacles. As before, preservationists felt that the groups and state agencies responsible for preserving Germany's monuments were doing only the bare minimum.[13]

Yet they did not lose sight of the country's considerable material advantages. The war had been fought mainly on non-German soil. Only in East Prussia did Germany face some of the same economic problems of reconstruction that confronted France, Belgium, and other countries. The shortage of state funds for protecting historic buildings would have the ironic effect of ensuring that certain damaging modifications would not be financed. Dehio's trope of the preservationist as great destroyer had less resonance in these straitened circumstances.[14] Unemployment caused by a downturn in reconstruction or restoration work could be partially balanced by increased demand for artists, architects, and craftsmen in building war monuments. There was some justification to *Deutsche Kunst und Denkmalpflege* (DKD) contributor Wilhelm Ambros's 1932 claim that despite many material shortages, it was an exaggeration to speak of a "crisis of monument

preservation."[15] The new age had brought mixed blessings rather than un-
alloyed disasters.

Beyond the question of economic and legislative issues, there was a clear
anxiety about preservation's future as a cultural-political institution and
arbiter of German memory. Although the 1930 preservation conference
gained much of its notoriety from its stymied debates over the Cologne
cathedral, it also devoted much attention to the question of how preservation would train the next generation of conservators, architects, artisans,
and administrators.[16] Demographics told the story. Preservation's key leaders, the members of the heroic generations of the Kaiserreich, had either
passed away or were very old. Influential Rhenish preservationist F. W.
Bredt had died in 1917. The head of the annual preservation congress since
1907, Adolf von Oechelhaeuser, died in 1923. Eduard zur Nedden, chair of
the RVDH since its founding in 1906, died in 1924. Stettiner Hugo Lemcke
retired in 1924 at age ninety, having been the sole conservator of the Prussian province of Pomerania since 1894, the year in which Prussia created the
post. Georg Dehio was seventy-five years old in 1926, when the last volume
of his monumental history of German art appeared. The art historian represented preservation's link with its early nineteenth-century origins, for it
was said that as a youth he had seen Rome "still with the eyes of Winckel-
mann, Goethe, or Wilhelm von Humboldt." He died in 1932. Gurlitt was
eighty years old in 1930. Though still very active, Clemen was sixty years
old in 1926.[17] Given the age profile of so many key figures, it is unsurprising
that the twenty-fifth anniversary of groups such as the RVDH in 1931
should have been cause for celebration as well as concern over what the
future held.[18]

The war and Weimar created new problems for preservationists, but the
lines of continuity between the Empire and the Republic cannot be mistaken. One such connection was the persistent tension between the reality
of preservation practice and a wider social vision. Still focused on a narrow range of monuments, the annual preservation conference continued to
sponsor panels on more traditional preservation themes such as the restoration of churches, while *DP* published articles on similar facets of preservation work. Among the ninety-eight most important preservation projects of
the Prussian Rhine province in 1925, fifty were for churches and eighteen
for church-related objects. Only thirty were for profane structures, including mainly city walls and castle ruins. The cost of subsidizing these first two
categories of artifacts accounted for nearly three-quarters of the provincial

budget for monuments. Of 171 grants made for preservation projects by the Reich, state, province, and RVDH in the Rhineland in 1929, 101 were for churches and related artifacts.[19]

Nonetheless, many preservationists continued to insist that monuments should be seen not as isolated museum pieces but in their dynamic interactions with a changing society, and that not just famous landmarks but also lesser monuments and entire historic districts should be grist for the preservationist mill. Not individual monuments, grand or modest, but contexts and relationships were the stuff of preservation for these individuals. A big part of the 1928 preservation congress in Würzburg and Nuremberg was concerned solely with the relationship between "the historical city and the contemporary age," the title for the first plenary session of the conference.[20] Prior to the congress, *DP* featured articles titled "The Nuremberg Old City in a Developing Greater Nuremberg," "A Munich Example of Contemporary Building in the Historic City," "The Historic City and the Contemporary Age" (by modernist architect Ernst May, who also spoke at the 1928 event), and "The Kassel Oberneustadt as an Architectural Monument."[21] The last-named article dealt with a six-block ensemble laid out in the seventeenth century as a Huguenot settlement by Hessian Duke Karl according to plans by influential architect and Huguenot refugee Paul du Ry. The RVDH devoted more attention than before to technical monuments, an interest that also occupied the 1930 annual conference and *Heimatschutz* groups. For the RVDH, too, such concerns were part of a larger social agenda that included attention to the history of previously neglected constituencies, such as the peasants of the picturesque but backward Eifel region. All this corresponded to the tendency to see cultural politics as an aspect of the national state's social responsibility.[22]

Preservationism's wider ambit was in part a response to a broader public thirst for monuments, and in order to respond to this demand, the federal states and provincial agencies took an even greater role in historic preservation than they had in the Empire. Indeed, the fall of the Kaiserreich and the contentious birth of the Republic had made it not only possible but desirable for the states and provinces to resort to regional culture as a source of integration and political legitimacy, all the more so in border areas exposed to interactions with other national communities. Moreover, the greater role of the national government in all areas of social and cultural policy mobilized the federal states, which wanted to protect their cultural autonomy. In 1925 Edmund Renard reported that since the war, "the provincial government has given increasing support to the [RVDH] because it recognizes the association's importance in practical matters of monument preservation."[23] Of nearly 1 million marks spent for historic preservation in 1929 in the

Prussian Rhine province, all but roughly 6,000 came from the central authorities and Prussia, from the provincial administration, and from lotteries organized by Prussia and the province. Perhaps because of this key institutional backup, the RVDH reported substantial membership gains by the early 1930s. But it also warned that its work should remain independent from the province, and its spokesmen, referring to their greater reliance on public authorities, reminded members that the difficult economic situation would result in choices that were sometimes painful to the friends of preservation. Here, too, preservation's socially minded ambitions faced severe fiscal realities. At another level heightened reliance on state authorities was reflected not only in funding decisions but in the appointment of Robert Hiecke, Prussian conservator of monuments, to the chair of the annual preservation conference in 1932, an appointment that led one Cologne journalist to wonder aloud if preservation had finally become completely integrated in the Prussian state's "cultural bureaucracy."[24]

Buoyed by greater ambitions, public support, and dependence on state agencies, preservationists continued to seek partners in related fields. During Weimar, preservation groups established good relations with the burgeoning nature conservation movement and the Catholic Congress for Christian Art (Tagung für christliche Kunst), founded in 1920. But *Heimatschutz* was still the most significant ally and the best vehicle for gaining wider influence. Involved in many areas of German cultural politics, the Bund Heimatschutz business report of 1931 noted that its representatives participated in national debates over architectural design, ran campaigns against the "ruin of landscapes and townscapes," published books and pamphlets on traffic problems and home design, collected material from 10,000 questionnaires dealing with the condition of technical monuments, counseled city officials, and discussed various urban planning projects. This hardly exhausted *Heimatschutz* work, for its local branches, among which one of the most active was the Westphalian Bund, were involved in youth education, radio programs, local museums, collections of folk songs, and contacts with Germans outside Germany.[25]

Despite being identified with nationalistic antimodernism and racism in the Weimar Republic, *Heimatschutz* leaders such as Paul Schultze-Naumburg, one of the most extreme nationalists, in 1931 stressed the importance of "objectivity" (*Sachlichkeit*) in all matters pertaining to new and historic built environments. *Heimatschutz*'s enemies were "indifference and false sentimentality," opponents shared by historic preservationists as well as by many advocates of modernist functionalist architecture. *Heimatschutz* spokesmen and their preservationist allies reminded audiences of these cognate interests as often as possible. When the Society of Friends of German

Heimatschutz was formed in May 1929, its language was moderate, stressing the movement's desire to find "the balance between good tradition and sound progress." The society's honorary members included Reich interior minister and Social Democrat Carl Severing, and the group's signatories and donors included notables from academics, business, and government who were by no means identified exclusively with the nationalist right or with vigorous antimodernism. Among Rhenish preservationists associated with the new association were the ubiquitous Clemen, Rhenish provincial director (*Landeshauptmann*) Johannes Horion, and Düsseldorf judge and RVDH chair Franz Schollen.[26] This mainstreaming of the *Heimatschutz* movement was the source of preservation's positive relationship with it.

Yet the racist elements of *Heimatschutz* discourse were even stronger than before. Schultze-Naumburg and nationally known critic of the Bauhaus Konrad Nonn, later an editor of *DP*, did not shrink from using a language of racial identity that was also appearing with increasing frequency in other fields in Germany in the late 1920s and 1930s. Such individuals often focused on architectural modernism as the Other to sound racial identity. A racialist form of social conservation found support in preservation circles, especially in the ideas of writer Karl Wagenfeld, founder of the Westphalian Heimatbund in 1915. Wagenfeld believed that only the maintenance and development of "tribally [*stammlich*] based landscapes" would prevent Germans from becoming "strangers in the Fatherland."[27] What was most dangerous about such words and the actions associated with them was not extremism per se (although this was serious enough) but the fact that they were accepted, more widely in Weimar than before, among the "best and the brightest" of the population, including leading preservationists. The adoption of such language was due in part to a growing sense of threat to the national community.

The Vulnerable Nation

A new vulnerability characterized national memory from the point of view of both the wider culture and preservation in this period. As a consequence, one of the central attributes of German public memory in this period was a longing for a mythic sense of national history and national totality. In German intellectual life, this desire was widespread, most notably among the proponents of a conservative revolution whose intellectual roots lay in the Kaiserreich but whose thinking was decisively shaped by the war experience. An appropriate literary symbol of this tendency was Oswald Spengler's *Decline of the West*, which defined "decline" as mythic "fulfillment." No less driven by such needs was Nazi Alfred Rosenberg's *Myth of the Twen-*

tieth Century, which appeared in 1930 glorifying Germanic legends and gods and arguing that such stories should provide a model for contemporary Germany.[28] Public practices reflected a broader popular basis for myth. Begun in the Kaiserreich, Reich Founding Day became the site of praise for the achievements of Wilhelm I, Bismarck, the rise of an industrial economy in Germany, and the persistence of an essential Germanness that war and revolution could not obliterate. The Rhineland's thousand-year celebration of 1925 was designed to convince not just Germans but also the international community and especially the French that the German nation had historical roots beyond contemporary political contingencies.[29] Weimar cinema was well known for its grimy social dramas, but it also featured historical dramas based on myth and legend—such as those by the famous film production company UFA, or Universum Film A.G., on Frederick the Great and Ernst Lubitsch's historical pageants—and *Heimat* films that anchored viewers in timeless landscapes of rural fields and *Fachwerk* cities, filmic evocations of a more settled past.[30]

This environment could not fail to affect the perspective of preservationists even when they recognized the stability of historic preservation as an institution. Whether they used the flatter language of the *DP* to refer to the "change of governmental relations" or the more hyperbolic words of Center Party representative Beyerle, who spoke of the immediate postwar period as a "time of upheaval and transformation of all values" in which "art, history, and the appearance of the homeland" were in danger, preservationists stressed the extreme vulnerability of historic sites, and hence of the national past itself, during the violent founding of the Weimar Republic. Of course, the nation had been vulnerable in the Kaiserreich and World War I, but at that time there had been a political leadership (at least until the end of the war). Now the state appeared to be without any direction at all. At the 1920 Eisenach conference Oechelhaeuser set the tone by saying the "ship of state" appeared to be "leaderless and beyond hope."[31]

Again and again the Eisenach conferees proclaimed their anxieties about how far the cultural nation had drifted from its historical moorings. The problem was neither money nor economic hardship per se, but a general moral malaise. The new Prussian conservator of monuments, Robert Hiecke, argued that because of the war, a "crude way of thinking" spread over the nation. This resulted in a complete disregard of heritage, one of those finer things always vulnerable in times of war and political dissonance. For the Berlin official the nation's new immortality was sadly summed up in the ransacking of the historic castle Ludwigstein by a *Wandervögel* group and in the destruction of the ruin of the Cistercian cloister Chorin, a famous thirteenth-century Gothic brick masterpiece, by ruffians. Money for the

The public longing for myth and continuity encompassed not only great urban monuments and political festivals but vernacular architecture as well. These street scenes (*above and opposite*) from the small town Duderstadt in the 1920s appeared in a publication subtitled *Pictures from a Thousand-Year-Old City*. (photos: Jaeger, *Alt-Duderstadt*, 17)

protection of historic buildings was in short supply after the war, said Hiecke, but people were spending more on the movies than on preservation. What did this say about the nation's priorities? Such questions hardly constituted special pleading on the part of preservationists, for the leading cultural politicians of the Weimar Republic, Konrad Haenisch, Social Democratic cultural minister of Prussia, and Carl Heinrich Becker, his undersecretary and later cultural minister, a professor and a supporter of the left-liberal Democratic Party, also insisted that cultural and moral renewal was the key to the survival of the German nation after the war.[32]

Deeply rooted in German political culture, the trope of heightened vulnerability led preservationists to fashion a redeployed story of redemption. If the nation was in danger, it would have to stabilize itself by new efforts of recovery. More than fantasy or invention, this narrative gained symbolic force from specific objects of brick, wood, and stone built by people with whom one could feel a common bond. For the Eisenach conferees, the Wartburg castle, a medieval fortress perched more than 400 meters high on the Wartberg that served as the site of the conference, was such a symbol

because it had risen from the "ashes and rubble" of its prior state of deterioration in the nineteenth century to become "what is for we Germans a cultural treasure of *Land* and nation." The site thus worked to support a prescriptive narrative. The "beginning" of the narrative, as before, was rooted in a combination of myth, German lore, documented history, and images of memory. Oechelhaeuser talked of the Wartburg, whose origins could be traced back in legend to the eleventh century, as "this sacred place . . . consecrated through art and history, through sagas and poetry." The sight of the Wartburg brought about immediate, spontaneous, and naturally "German" memories. "Involuntarily one's thoughts turn back to the times when the German minnesinger came together in noble competition under this roof at the court of the art-minded Thuringian Dukes," said Oechelhaeuser, referring to the legendary medieval musicians who met at the Wartburg.[33] Even if the ship of state was leaderless, the ability to draw on the natural resources of the German soul, to achieve in a way that only monumental history allowed one to achieve, was again present. "German diligence and energy, German intelligence, science, and art have still not been destroyed as driving powers of our *Volk*," Oechelhaeuser reminded the conferees. "The conviction is growing," he said, that "not everything is lost yet if everyone works seriously . . . on the reconstruction of what has been destroyed, on the re-strengthening of German economic life, and on the recuperation of the

The Wartburg, "this sacred place . . . consecrated through art and history," a symbol of German national perdurability in the Weimar Republic (photo: *Deutsche Burgen* [1927], 56)

soul of the German *Volk*."[34] Such imagery suggests that the discourse of rebuilding (*Wiederaufbau*) would not be totally new when it emerged in even more extreme conditions after World War II.

Dehio had said that preservation depended on the nation's interest in its history; great peoples had long memories, and preservation awaited the German people's declaration of its greatness. For many preservationists the nation had become the *Volk* community (*Volksgemeinschaft*), a term fraught with new political and racist connotations. According to Franz Graf Wolff Metternich of Bonn, who was Rhenish conservator of monuments from 1928 to 1950 as well as a Nazi Party member, an artifact could claim to be "a monument . . . if from an educative or aesthetic standpoint it has a meaning for the *Volksgemeinschaft* based in the past but still living in the present." The interest in vernacular architecture, technical artifacts, and other more modest monuments fit into this perspective because it was part of that "totalistic thinking of preservation" that encompassed historic buildings as well as works of art and museum artifacts.[35] The more insistent the *Volksgemeinschaft* became in its demands on citizens' memory, and the more vulnerable it felt itself to be, the more all-encompassing the definition of monuments would become.

If nationalist and racist discourse reverberated more widely among preservationists through such redefinitions of the nation, it also could be limited or recast in a variety of ways. One limit can be found in preservationists' continued loyalty to the idea of service to a European, not just an ethnic and national, heritage. "Despite the many differences in ethnic starting points," wrote respected Michelangelo scholar and former Austrian preservation official Dagobert Frey in 1930, "preservation and *Heimatschutz* present themselves as a specifically European problem: that of the protection and upholding of Occidental culture in the all-encompassing development of humankind."[36] This commitment to humankind in a time of growing nationalist antipathies was significant.

Another limit on more radical nationalist thinking was preservationists' willingness to compromise with the needs of a modern commercial society, which so often represented civilization's inferiority to German *Kultur*. The 1930 preservation congress in Cologne was so willing to accept modern traffic needs that *Oberbürgermeister* and, later, West German chancellor Konrad Adenauer, an active participant in the proceedings, exhorted the conferees not to give in to the idea that the automobile was the "absolute power in the whole city." RVDH official Max Schlenker, also an official of the so-called Langnamverein, an important industrial pressure group, argued for a "rationalization" of preservation based on the realization that "the economy is destiny."[37] Like *Heimatschutz*, historic preservation looked for balance between its vision of national heritage and the forces of economic growth and materialism. But because many *Heimatschutz* spokesmen's stronger commitment to racist-national thought led to antimodern conclusions, preservationists' desire to compromise with modern commercial life was more convincing.

Even more revealing was the preservationist response to architectural modernism, one of the most important areas of cultural experimentation in the Republic and ostensibly one of the greatest threats to historical tradition. In this field the prewar consensus between historicist and progressive architects had broken down. The tradition of abstracted historicism continued, but it had a vital competitor in new building as represented in the work of Walther Gropius, the famous architectural school the Bauhaus, and mass "functionalist" building projects by Ernst May, Bruno Taut, and others.[38] The modernist Weissenhof settlement overlooking Stuttgart was a point of crystallization of conflict between the two traditions.[39] Constructed as an ensemble of single-family houses, apartments, and row houses by the Werkbund in 1927, Weissenhof attracted as many as 20,000 visitors a day when it was open to the public from July to October of that year. Its participants considered Weissenhof to be a window on the future and a symbol of hope not only for Germany but for modern society. Its critics, among whom

Heimatschutz representatives and less experimental architects were some of the loudest, argued that the project—shaped by flat roofs and horizontalism—had little to do either with German architectural tradition and national memory or with climatic conditions of northern European life. The more extreme critics saw Weissenhof as an affront to German racial identity, noting with disdain that an ironic postcard of the settlement featured "camels, lions, and the colorful street life of an Arabian village." Against the experimentation and perceived disorderliness of the Weissenhof, one critic contrasted the "balance and calm" of the nearby Kochenhof settlement of Stuttgart, originally intended in 1933 as the reorganized Werkbund's first exhibit of Nazi architecture.[40]

Many preservationists heartily attacked architectural modernism. Cornelius Gurlitt, by the Weimar era a grand old man of preservation, had been a vigorous prewar advocate of modernist additions to historic buildings, but in 1930 he said he could no longer counsel such additions for restorations on architectural treasures such as the eighteenth-century Zwinger complex in Dresden because the nature of modernism had changed. By this he meant that architectural modernism's commitment to the historical had been cut, a telling though arguable criticism. Echoing the accusations of Nazis that the new architecture was a form of "cultural Bolshevism," Richard Klapheck, a member of the RVDH and of the Rhenish Monuments Council, wrote of the "aping of Soviet ways in Stuttgart" with reference to Weissenhof.[41]

Yet there was much more openness to the new than one might at first think. Klapheck made a point of distinguishing between experimentation with new forms and building materials, which was to be welcomed by preservationists, and unproven claims about the superiority of flat roofs and new building, for which he thought the Stuttgart exhibit stood. In 1930 Gustav Lampmann, editor of *DP*, attacked the *Heimatschutz* movement for its "authoritarian" approach to current debates over architecture and preservation. One had to concede the "strong power of expression of new building" and the "sound, native understanding" it had begun to foster "in broad strata of the *Volk*." To the extent that *Heimatschutz* learned to accept and facilitate this healthy popular outlook, to work as genuine nurturing of *Heimat* based on "functionality and economy" rather than only as defense of *Heimat*, "it steps down from the authoritarian podium from which until now it has believed it could teach the *Volk*, in order to mingle with the *Volk* and promote, with them and from them, that which develops itself actively."[42]

Featuring a panel that included modernist Frankfurt planner Ernst May, who would later build new urban centers in the Soviet Union, and traditionalist Theodor Fischer of Munich, the 1928 preservation conference was very instructive in this context. The debate over new building was vigorous, but it was set up precisely to promote discussion, to let both sides have their say, rather than to create a platform from which architectural modernists could be attacked, as the chair of the conference, Paul Clemen, pointed out. It was the representatives of *Heimatschutz*, such as Tübingen economist Carl Johannes Fuchs, who used the most contentious language at that meeting, portraying the struggle between new building and traditional styles as a struggle between civilization and *Kultur*. In contrast, municipal building official Gerhard Ritter of Leipzig noted that the differences between May and Fischer were not that great and that consequently "the fire department found no reason to intervene." Several of May's critics did not oppose new building as such but, rather, his contention that German urban dwellers had become "nomads" whose mobility required a new architecture for the masses. Their argument was that German cities had in fact not changed as drastically as advocates of new building claimed. Not architectural modernism in general but new building in particular should be rejected because it was a temporary response to a time of hardship and panic that would eventually fade away.[43] It should be noted that this criticism of new building was based on a historical view in which threats to the enduring stability of the historic city were less serious than most observers assumed. It was a call not for feverish action or rigorous struggle but for caution, balance, and an awareness of the limits imposed by historical continuity. Weimar could have used more appeals of this kind, especially on the conservative-nationalist side, where most preservationists stood.

Preservation's less heated response to modernism was expressed in everyday practice as well. Recognition by the leading figures of the Rhenish preservation lobby, including Clemen, Renard, Klapheck, and Busley, that "no representative of the modern tendency" sat on the Rhenish Monuments Council in 1928 suggested an awareness of modernism's potential resonance if not acceptance of its claims. More substantively, in 1930 and 1931, Lübeck citizens debated a plan to allow pacifist artist Ernst Barlach to sculpt sixteen figures for the west front of the Katharinen-Kirche. The municipal council for monuments voted for Barlach's proposals, with two dissenting voices, against the protests of the Bund Heimatschutz, which argued that the "highly modern figures" would destroy the physiognomy of the historical building. The Lübeck senate chose to take the council's advice and go ahead with the project. When the famous Old Castle of Stuttgart burned down in 1931, the *Land* conservator found himself in agreement on restoration plans for the fourteenth-century Renaissance symbol of the city not only with conservative Theodor Fischer of Munich but also with Paul Bonatz, a leading exponent of historicist abstraction and for a short time a member of the Social Democratic Party (SPD). The castle would be restored

Damaged by fire in 1931, the Old Castle of Stuttgart, symbol of the city, was completely restored by 1936. (photo: *Deutsche Burgen* [1927], 10)

by 1936 by traditionalist Paul Schmitthenner.[44] Here and elsewhere preservationists tried to build bridges to cultural modernism even when they endorsed critics' attacks on the flat roof, artistic abstraction, and other expressions of cultural experimentation for which Weimar was known.

Building bridges. This is what *Heimatschutz* and many other cultural-political movements had wanted to do since the Kaiserreich, but now even more so in an age of political mobilization and heightened national vulnerability. One *DP* writer said that preservationists should form a more powerful "association encompassing all German regions" to carry its message of the necessity of national memory to the public.[45] But historic preservation was somewhat like the bourgeois parties of Weimar: full of intentions to be more popular, willing to criticize itself and others about "old school" techniques that looked down disparagingly on the *Volk*, but unable to realize the move to popular action in practice. Like the *Bürgertum* from which they came, preservationist spokesmen were deeply ambivalent about appealing to the masses. Love of nation was still something to be taught from above rather than in cooperation with a wide array of groups from

MODERNIST CRUCIBLE

below; remembering the national past was something that had to be closely monitored and controlled.

Such ambivalence was vividly expressed in the varying positions leading preservationists took on the problem of public action at the 1920 preservation conference. Hiecke continued to emphasize that the *Volk* had to be educated about the need for historic property, a need they were unable to see because of "party fragmentation" and "megalomania." They had to be taught that a historic building was not a luxury but an "inalienable part of one's self" and a "cultural good necessary for life."[46] Jena professor Paul Weber was not very confident about the possibility of this project, stressing the gulf that existed between educated groups and workers. "Manual workers [*Handarbeiter*] are now the dominant power in Germany," he said, "and as long as this great mass is not drawn along for our interest, we will always be meeting only among ourselves." A participant in the Thuringian Adult Education School (*Volkshochschule*) program titled "Wartburg Week" earlier in the year, Weber recalled how he had tried to interest "industrial workers and young female workers" in tales of Luther, the minnesinger, and the dukes of the Wartburg. "This week was thoroughly instructive for me" said Weber. "That which educated people understand under the category Romanticism does not exist for the modern industrial laborer. No bridge leads to the other side. . . . The worker mistrusts all that." Weber's solution was not more education but more love—for one's fellow German and for the nation as a whole. Von Oechelhaeuser, director of the Association for Continuing Education in Karlsruhe, expressed sympathy for Weber's standpoint but argued that it was useless to invite workers to the conference because its "serious, scientific work . . . cannot be done and understood by the layman." As for promoting love of nation and building bridges to popular classes, said Oechelhaeuser in direct contradiction to years of speeches and conferences, this was not the congress's job. Such tasks belonged to "other popular organizations."[47]

The Eisenach conference took place at the beginning of the Republic, when class tensions were exaggerated. But little changed in preservationists' views of their public standing in the course of the next decade, and at the last annual preservation conference held during Weimar, in Cologne from 16 to 19 September 1930,[48] official preservation's ambivalence about popular opinion was still evident. The issue this time was the restoration of the Cologne cathedral, for which public interest ran high since the famous monument had been the centerpiece of the thousand-year anniversary of the Rhineland in 1925 and of celebrations of the departure of French troops from Rhenish cities a year later. The RVDH stimulated further interest in

1927 by publishing a volume of essays titled *The Cologne Cathedral in Danger*.[49] The cathedral continued to function as a national symbol, being praised for its essential Germanness, which in one writer's eyes consisted mainly of its ability to take the French Gothic it copied to a new level of "verticality."[50] It was touted as a national-political weapon that in the past as well as the present functioned as "the sign of a harmonious holding together of all German tribes, the symbol of a united German Empire."[51] Such symbolism had added political significance in view of the Nazi Party's stunning electoral success in Reichstag elections two days before the opening of the 1930 conference, a success that would open more than two years of bitter political conflict and uncertainty.

No one was happy with the condition of the cathedral. Late nineteenth-century disencumbering left the giant structure standing free in the middle of a traffic island in one of the busiest parts of the city. Air pollution, traffic, and a constant stream of tourists damaged the building. Telephone and tram lines crisscrossing the surrounding streets enmeshed the landmark in a gray-black web. Gustav Decker's 1927 painting *Cologne: The View from the Fürstenhof to the Cathedral Square* captured perfectly this melancholic ensemble.[52] Complicated restoration work on the buttresses and the west choir, the original part of the structure, stirred controversy over how weathered and damaged stones were to be replaced.[53] Critics demanded that the authorities outline a new set of principles for carrying out further restorations. The 1930 preservation congress debated such issues, but it was clear from the proceedings that preservationists' expectations were at odds with those of others.

Speakers at the conference openly agreed with those who saw in the cathedral not an art-historical masterpiece but a national symbol and a place of worship. This was hardly a concession, since preservationists had always thought the cathedral was ugly. But instead of outlining general principles on the cathedral and other projects—instead of using it as a "paradigm," as one critic put it—the conference got involved in complicated discussions of chemical treatments of stone, of the merits of certain kinds of interior lighting, and of the style in which individual parts of the church should be restored. Unlike the 1928 conference, the "radical-modern" argument was never heard in Cologne because its proponents were not invited. For many preservationists the cathedral's restoration was *not* a test case for preservation as a whole, and thus the absence of modernists was logical, though politically fraught.

There was little appreciation among the conference participants that 1930 was also the fiftieth anniversary of the completion of the cathedral. In the eyes of Dagobert Frey, overlooking this date represented official preserva-

Gustav Decker's 1927 painting *Cologne: The View from the Fürstenhof to the Cathedral Square* captured the melancholic ensemble of which the cathedral was the centerpiece.
(photo: Museum Ludwig Köln, 221 904)

tion's distance from the popular appropriation of the cathedral as a national symbol. Specialized discussions were legitimate, to be sure, but according to Frey official preservation had missed a chance to advertise its cause and arouse more public interest in its contributions to the nation. "Historic preservation and *Heimatschutz* should not become specialized matters of a small group of professionals," wrote Frey, "they must stay in touch with all the social strata and status groups of the broad public."[54]

Stung by attacks from within and without, conference officials defended their procedures in correspondence with government officials. They criticized the press for its reports on the conference, repeating the already widespread opinion among preservationists that big public meetings such as the Cologne congress were inappropriate for debating such issues. They organized a smaller conference of experts and officials (including Cologne mayor Adenauer and the Catholic hierarchy) in December 1930, which, away from the harsh light of public debate, outlined a set of more general plans for restoration work on the cathedral.[55] But they continued to defend their treatment of the monument, which ultimately depended on the strategy of careful replacement of original parts of the structure with restorations that followed the spirit rather than the exact form of the building. The Cologne cathedral was certainly typical of great historic buildings situated in urban centers, they insisted, but once again it was not a paradigm of German monuments as such. The heralded motto of German preservation, "Conserve, do not restore," stopped at the doors of this monument. As before, said the meeting's participants, historic preservation could not offer any really general principles, but only difficult choices based on case-by-case considerations.

This was not a message that meshed neatly with ebullient demands for a nationalist cultural politics of identity and memory. Yet on a deeper level it was consistent with such demands. The cathedral should not be exposed to dangers inherent in modernist additions to historic architecture or to a conservationist logic, which in its Rieglian mode meant the eventual death of this towering national symbol. Because the cathedral was as pure a symbol of the nation as one could find, rules for its maintenance could be suspended. Like the notionally "special path" of the nation it symbolized, the cathedral enjoyed a *Sonderweg* of cultural protection. Stated in such terms, it is clear that preservationist anxiety over the cathedral was a cognate of anxiety over the nation, now more uniquely vulnerable than ever. It was fitting that this juxtaposition of two sets of anxieties found expression in a cloistered meeting of officials pushed to articulate their principles by public and professional displeasure with the national conference.

Only to Be Sincere

The Cologne debates showed that official preservation's problem was not a lack of popular interest in historic buildings and the past but, rather, too much. In addition, this interest assumed forms that preservationists found politically and culturally threatening. More than in previous eras, public appropriations of historic buildings in the Weimar period had a certain ferocity, whether based on love or hate, that put the subject of national history and symbols at the center of political culture. Some Germans were motivated to revisualize monuments radically in this context, as in Ernst

Ernst Stern's 1919 lithograph of the Brandenburg Gate depicted the monument as if it moved with the rhythm of the political agitation going on around it. (photo: Deutsches Historisches Museum)

Stern's 1919 lithograph of the Brandenburg Gate in which the famous landmark was depicted as if it moved with the rhythm of gunshots and political violence going on around it. Such efforts were part of a ferocious search for sincerity, a need to see through artifice, whether one found it in politics or in historical buildings. For advocates of new building, sincerity was to be gained in an architecture that overcame the "crinoline and wigs" of the nineteenth century, as architect Erich Mendelsohn's poem "Why This Architecture?" put it in 1928. For the advocates of historic buildings, sincerity was no less passionately desired, although it was to be found not through an allegedly ahistorical modernism but through love for the national past. For them as well as for modernists, Mendelsohn's lines, written on the occasion of the opening of the modernist Schocken (today, Horten) Department Store in Nuremberg, rang true:

> Not to be somehow against our Beautiful Fountain or impious to Saint
>   Sebaldus.
> Not to throw a stone in the Nuremberg Museum.
> Only to be sincere.
> You do demand sincerity?
> From your friends, from everyone?

But you want to be tricked by the things around you, by your house,
 your builders?[56]

Cultural modernism's attitude toward historic buildings set the tone for
critical avant-garde intellectuals. For Dadaists of the world war and the
immediate postwar era, the world could no longer be seen in terms of
tradition. Transiency reigned over all people, images, and things. Tristan
Tzara, Romanian poet of the Dada movement in 1918, said Dada was "abolition of memory . . . abolition of history." For George Grosz and the radical
Neue Jugend circle, one had "to be made of rubber," for it would take that
kind of flexibility to live in the modern world. Amid the chaos of modernity,
"a Gothic church might any day be replaced by a department store."[57] But
this was no reason for despair, said Dadaists. It was to be accepted, welcomed, and viewed as the absurdity it surely was.

But even among the radical proponents of change, history was not abandoned. Modernist architect Bruno Taut was an admirer of Germany's historical cities, but his admiration led to critical perspectives on German monuments, as when he supported Kampffmeyer's Peace City in World War I.
Taut had controversial, if short-lived, experience in preservation and was
associated with Cornelius Gurlitt briefly when both men were coeditors of
the journal *The Art of Town Planning Past and Present* (*Stadtbaukunst alter
und neuer Zeit*), although he left it after Gurlitt criticized him for his extreme views. His attitudes toward historic preservation were more complicated than many scholars have thought, just as the scope of his thinking
went beyond architecture to include interior design and furniture.[58] For a
short time in the 1920s city architect in Magdeburg, Taut was in the early
days of the Republic a utopian critic of "tradition," arguing that concepts
such as "space," "homeland," and "style" had to be annihilated. "To hell with
them, odious concepts!" he wrote. "Destroy them, break them up! Nothing
shall remain! Break up your academies, spew out the old fogies, we'll play
catch with their wigs! Blast! Blast!"[59]

Comparable to the revolutionary slogan of the early USSR, "Peace to the
factories, war on the palaces,"[60] this rant was connected on one side with
Taut's utopian visions of crystalline architecture. But there was also an
effort to disassociate historic buildings not only from a vague sense of
tradition but from a specific nationalist discourse that, after World War I,
had revanchist desires for lost German territory in both East and West. In
the January 1920 edition of his periodical *Frühlicht*, he wrote,

Frühlicht considers the old architecture neither in national nor in antinational terms. The image of history is also a product of fantasy, and
indeed it is often a very dangerous one, since it appears in "layers,"

which in and of themselves may be genuine, but whose selection and meaning depend entirely on the immediate standpoint. Before the war one regarded the beauty of cultural sites in the East, Danzig, Posen, Thorn, Breslau, etc., as a product of the tension of racial differences and mixtures, but today one tries to claim those places, as well as Straßburg, Xanten, and elsewhere, exclusively for Germany. The danger of this approach, colored by immediate attitudes, is immense; current political passions can hardly be calmed this way. Starting with apparently harmless cultural considerations, desires for reconquest are aroused, and war after war is the unavoidable outcome. We should now know what war means. And even if the French, the Poles, etc., have railed against us, and continue to do so, that is only a reason for not imitating such stupidities.[61]

Taut's argument undercut nationalist readings of historic architecture, claiming that historic places, whether those of "lost" territories or of more secure areas, were not "national" in the sense of being exclusively the property of one national group. Yet Taut had not abandoned national identity as a foundation of his political language, and his practical solutions to preservation problems reflected his respect for historic places that had national significance. During his tenure in office, Taut championed a modernist restoration of the Magdeburg citadel that retained the baroque articulation of its inner wall but also transformed the important landmark into a "show terrace." Praising medieval towns and rural imagery, he advocated the use of color on historic buildings, saying that the past used lively colors throughout the physical environment. This "retrospective historicism" was not unique to Taut but ran throughout the modern movement.[62] His campaign for more color was controversial, not least because Taut saw an analogy with the political situation of the early Republic. "I find a parallel in the retreat from uniform, deadening gray and the return to exterior color," he wrote in a contentious appeal of 1919 signed by many well-known modernist architects, "and the retreat from the expansionist tendency of the world-encompassing, materialistic power politics of the officer caste and the return to the small-scale perspective of the settled, at-home citizen who lives a healthy life on his plot of land."[63]

Such ideas prompted much criticism in Magdeburg and elsewhere; but the call to color did have a noticeable effect on other groups, and it was an effective means of dealing with older buildings at a time when more ambitious forms of maintenance were out of the question due to material shortages and inflation. Moreover, despite Taut's radicalism, his perspective intersected with a quite conservative view of modern society in which tradi-

Modernist Bruno Taut's use of colorful facades in a historical ensemble
in Magdeburg (photo: Junghanns, *Bruno Taut*, plate 126)

tion, rural imagery, and the local were seen as superior to the expansionist, world-encompassing point of view. Here and in many other places there was considerable agreement—nearly a national consensus—between modernist critics and the defenders of tradition. But in Taut's thinking, the global perspective belonged to the expansionist warrior class, not the "internationalist" planner or the socialist, as it did in conservative discourse. Here a critical use of history, and a symbolization of newly colorful historic buildings, was turned against the military class, which in a conservative reading could be linked to the very provincial values that Taut saw as antipathetic to the German war machine. This way of thinking prefigured critical forms of *Heimat* discourse and preservationism of the 1970s.

The point is even clearer if we consider one of Taut's criticisms of the Magdeburg cityscape, published in *Frühlicht* in the spring of 1923. "How then does the heritage of 'our fathers' look?" he began. "I stood in the tower of the cathedral and saw no organism. The old, the churches, stand like shriveled up flowers in a desolate field of weeds. And where one no longer saw an old street, no organic, fine mass of roofs . . . there was now a sheet of ugly blocks in which one has used a knife to cut absolutely straight streets." The imagery of a desolate field of weeds choking historic buildings was one from which preservationists could have taken heart had it not been wedded to a combination of preservation and futuristic planning that conservators and their government allies found threatening. For later generations of preservationists, however, Taut, like Walter Benjamin, was an important predecessor in the critical uses of monuments.

If Taut's work may be taken as an indicator of how far some German intellectuals had taken the critique of national-historic places without necessarily abandoning the nation as a point of reference, then the evolution of social tourism can be read as a cognate phenomenon in everyday life. Upper-class and middle-class tourism were, of course, well developed in the nineteenth century, and the beginnings of working-class tourism can be found before World War I. Although workers and the lower middle classes would not be part of the mass touristic market until after World War II, the 1920s and early 1930s saw more and more workers as tourists. Tourism may be considered part of the process of "becoming public," whereby people have the opportunity to observe modern social processes, events, and institutions firsthand.[64] To the extent that the processes and objects workers viewed had a distinctively historical character, tourism was one path through which workers gained access to public constructions of memory.

For the workers' movement, the most important touristic organization was the Friends of Nature Tourists' Association (Touristenverein Naturfreunde), originally founded in Vienna in 1895. At one point in the 1920s the German Friends of Nature had more than 100,000 members. This was no insignificant number, but it was small when compared with the mass tourist market or to the number of German workers. Not solely a leisure-time organization, the group's touristic efforts were devoted mainly to getting workers out of the cities and into the countryside, the "college of life," where by 1933 volunteers in the organization had built more than 200 Friends of Nature houses. The Social Democratic Party distrusted the Naturfreunde, as it did many cultural organizations, which in the eyes of party leaders diluted socialist political action. In the last years of the Weimar Republic the SPD also carried out what amounted to a purge against Naturfreunde who supported the Communist Party.[65]

The Naturfreunde contributed to social tourism by seeing natural and historic sites through "class" binoculars. Starting around 1910 with the writings of Gustav Hennig, the concept of social touring became more widespread. Combining elements of the elite grand tour and the journeyman apprentice's wandering, the idea was that the traveler did not just look at beautiful sites but also studied people and social situations to gain critical insights into the fabric of everyday life. This was attractive to writers in the workers' movement, who developed the idea in the 1920s and 1930s in trips in Germany, the USSR, and Africa. "Social touring is the fathoming of the social aspect of the landscape through which one wanders, with all its crises, cares, artistic creations, and technical accomplishments," wrote Georg Schubert in the Hessian Naturfreund magazine in 1932. Theoretically any area could be toured socially, not just places of unusual natural or historical importance. The critical thrust of social touring emerged from its ability to destroy "the impression . . . that history, the economic as well as the political and cultural, consists of a mosaic of the destinies of worldly and religious princes." The goal was to tear down the "smoke-screen of the *bürgerlich* picture of history" and arrive at a class-based perspective.[66]

Despite its critical perspective, social tourism, like Taut's discourse, had points of contact with nationalist ideology. There was a long bourgeois tradition of getting off the beaten track of tourism, a striving for a more authentic and unique experience than that of standard touristic travel.[67] Social tourism shared the bourgeois passion for touring natural and historic sites, although it often selected sites different from those of the middle classes. It said nothing about abandoning a national perspective even when it stressed the international brotherhood of workers and working-class tourists. It agreed with preservationists about the need to see touristic sites in their larger social context. Like social tourists, thoroughly middle-class preservationists were arguing that not the individual monument but the monument in a larger net of social and national relations was the proper perspective. But it parted company on the class issue, although it remains a matter of contention how thoroughly a class perspective dominated the daily workings of social tourism.

Walter Benjamin was a kind of social tourist—albeit an enigmatic and highly demanding one—in his writings on European cities and architecture. They reveal his ability to capture the social reality of historic buildings and street scenes—indeed, the morphology of whole cities. Writing as a Jew and a leftist intellectual, Benjamin was much more willing than preservationists to extract a critical-political meaning from historic architecture. Benjamin wrote briefly but critically of historic German church bells, speaking of "the chimes that on Sundays spread such deep melancholy over our cities."[68] More generally, he read a secret history of barbarism in European monuments, noting that each historic place was built on the backs of countless numbers of laborers. "There is no document of civilization," he wrote, "which is not at the same time a document of barbarism." His attack on historicism and championing of critical memory, articulated most powerfully in 1940 shortly before his death but prefigured in his earlier writing, pierced the heart of preservationist discourse.[69]

Nonetheless, it is interesting to note that Benjamin saw some of the same things in the historic city that preservationists saw. His writing contains many examples of the anthropomorphizing of buildings, and he was fascinated with the "magical" and "auratic" qualities of historic sites. Of several "old-fashioned" buildings in Berlin he wrote, "They have much knowledge of our childhood," an observation similar to that of preservationists when they associated historic places with memory of youth. "Anti-scrape" (or antirestorationist) preservationists would have nodded with understanding had they read the 15 December 1926 entry in his Moscow notebook concerning the famous St. Basil's Cathedral, whose inside, he wrote, "has not only been emptied, but eviscerated like a felled deer, and turned into a 'museum' attraction for mass edification."[70] This reenacted the well-worn preservationist trope of living and dead monuments, although it did so with a chillingly evocative prose for which Benjamin has become widely known.

Critical statements about the preservation of historic places could also be heard within the political classes of the left. Not that leftist politicians were always doubtful about the value of historic buildings. Social Democratic speakers in the Prussian *Landtag* in 1921 argued that the cultural minister should adopt "planned economy" principles to protect endangered historic buildings and to make more conservators' jobs full-time positions. When the issue of the maintenance of the badly deteriorated Goethe House in Frankfurt came up in the *Landtag* in late 1922, a time of increasing economic hardship, Social Democratic politicians explicitly supported the right-wing liberal German People's Party initiatives to get more financial support for the building and its holdings. Nonetheless, the stewards of historic places more often came in for harsh attacks from the left. Social Democratic politicians were unremittingly critical of the "propagandists for tourism and 'historians,'" who advocated protection for historic sites such as the restored Hannover *Altstadt*, whose "brightly colored facades" hid indefensible hygienic conditions.[71]

Such critical assessments of historic places by traditional or organic intellectuals on the left operated at a distance from the everyday workings of preservation. Among the examples discussed in the preceding paragraphs, only Taut was directly involved in preservation, and then only for a short time and with rather obscure results. If we move to critical perspectives from within the groups that had more direct connections to heritage preservation, we get a stronger impression of how bitterly contested such issues had become in the wider public.

I noted that the 1930 preservation conference in Cologne failed in part because the public response to it was so overwhelmingly critical, convincing many that the conference had outlived its function. If we examine this public reaction in more detail, we find layers of even more vociferous public dissatisfaction. An unidentified writer for the newspaper *Düsseldorfer Nachrichten* pointed out that the opening greetings from officials and academics at the conference were so lengthy that one had the impression it was preservationists not monuments that needed "tender handling."[72] This struck at the heart of official preservation's connections to the state and the country's academic elite. The conference opened with praise for recent preservation work on the Cologne Kartäuser Church, a fourteenth-century Gothic jewel with eighteenth-century additions whose baroque features were further emphasized by restoration from 1923 to 1928. For the *Nachrichten* observer, in contrast, the history of this monument was an example of how first the French, then the Prussians, and now the preservationists—practicing "secrets of the preservationist witch's kitchen"—had ruined a "shrine." No wonder they use the term *Denkmalpflege* rather than *Denkmalschutz*, said the writer, for the first term was a euphemism for carrying out any operation on a monument including "falsification." Significantly, when the church was restored after World War II, the baroque fittings and decoration were eliminated.

This bitter attack on restoration—or what many were calling "repair" (*Instandsetzung*)—culminated in an assault on preservation of the Cologne cathedral. The "ineffectual congress" demonstrated that the protectors of the monument were not using "the appropriate medicines of a highly developed science of the pharmacology of buildings materials [*Baustoffpharma-*

zeutik]" to conserve the monument. Instead they were replacing old sections of the cathedral bit by bit, including buttresses from the original medieval part. Applied to the city's historic architecture as a whole, this method would mean that "in about six years—if in the meantime it does not rain fire and brimstone—[Cologne] will possess the biggest collection of sparkling, brand-new antiquities in the entire world." The words are chilling considering that only a little more than a decade after they were written, fire and brimstone fell on not just Cologne but many other German cities. The writer warned that restoration through replacement of sections of the cathedral was not the answer—even when preservationists tried not to copy the medieval portions in all their detail. The only reliable way to save the landmark was through the "untiring art of healing practiced by the doctor." Even when commentators gave the congress credit for having had some "partial successes," the public response remained highly critical, not only because of restoration technique but because of official preservation's distance from its public. "For a long time already historic preservation has no longer been the exclusive property of those who feel called to it," argued one observer. "It is a matter of course of public opinion."[73]

One month after the 1930 congress the debate fired up again, this time on the occasion of the fiftieth anniversary of the great festival of October 1880 that celebrated the completion of the cathedral two months previously. Writer and critic Karl Jatho's 16 October attack in the *Düsseldorfer Nachrichten* repeated some of the criticism already put forward in the previous weeks, but this time in more vituperative and anti-Prussian terms. The anniversary would remind people of "the holy act of that great brotherhood of artists" that built the cathedral. They would symbolically rise from their graves addressing the "present-day Prussian preservationist and cathedral master architects" with the warning, " 'Hands off! You shall not kill our work before its natural death!' " One day later in the *Kölnische Volkszeitung* another article on the anniversary appeared, this time not dealing with restoration of the cathedral but with Catholic memory. The writer remembered that many Catholics, above all the Catholic clergy and politicians, stayed away from the October 1880 celebration because of their bitterness over the treatment of Catholics in Bismarck's *Kulturkampf* of the previous decade.[74] Such commentary revealed how brittle was the layer of national symbolism that enshrouded the weathered exterior of the Cologne cathedral.

The tone of the cathedral debates was unexceptional in a Germany that was being rocked by political contention. In early 1931 Baden architects, artists, and university professors attacked state conservator Fritz Hirsch for his practice of restoring badly deteriorated castles in Bruchsal, Karlsruhe, Rastatt, and Schwetzingen with exterior colors that critics thought were

Die neuen Glocken von St. Jacobi

Gefallenengedächtnisglocke   Kinderglocke   Phot. A. Schmu

Bells and German memory: a 1925 postcard depicts two new church bells for the Gothic Jacobikirche of Göttingen, one dedicated to the memory of the war dead (*left*), the other a "children's bell." (photo: author's collection)

inappropriate. One building was painted red with white window frames. The issue of how to paint historic buildings had been contested since early in the Republic, and preservationists themselves were divided on the problem. But in the early 1930s such public debates became cockfights: "There must be a corpse," wrote one observer sympathetic to the Baden restorations. "It fits so well with today's violent methods of political argument," he continued, "that also here one becomes even intransigent and vehement . . . that one questions totally every thought and intent of the opposition."[75]

Such passionate struggles also occurred over war commemoration. As Germans remembered the almost 2 million soldiers killed in the war, they saturated preexisting buildings with plaques, crosses, and inscriptions on church bells. There were also two great surges of monument-building to commemorate the dead, one in the first five years of the Republic, the other beginning in 1929. In the first, largely Christian themes of mourning dominated, whereas in the second phase more nationalistic themes obtained.[76] As they had been in the war, preservationists were active in national debates over the design, siting, and meaning of such monuments. Cornelius Gurlitt, acting as chair of the Association of German Architects and Art Historians, made key interventions in contentious debates over a failed Reich war memorial, and Robert Hiecke was among the committee members who decided to commission architect Heinrich Tessenow to transform Schinkel's classicist Neue Wache into a war monument. Built in 1817–18 as a military guard station and symbol of Prussian victory over Napoleon, the Neue Wache was later a memorial to Nazi heroes, an East German monument against war and fascism, and then a controversial memorial to all victims of World War II commissioned by the newly unified Federal Republic and dedicated in 1993.[77] The Tessenow project was not only a heavily debated artistic event but a public anomaly. An opening in the roof of the famous Berlin landmark shed dramatic light on a simple block of black Swedish granite decorated with a silver oak wreath. At the foot of the block was a stone carrying the dates of the war. Such simplicity had a negative effect on the public's ability to identify with the monument. "Would popular taste have conceded to stronger accents?" asked one observer, who noted that the monument lacked "the proper emotional supports, the symbols." And people voted, uncertainly, with their feet: "The *Volk* streams in, docilely takes off its hat, but then with a certain embarrassment stands around the block, around which an all too orderly circle of donated wreaths lay."[78]

Aside from criticism and open public debate, Germans continued to use historic buildings in ways that paid little attention to preservationist concerns or interpretations. The main difference between the Weimar Republic and the Empire was not only the scale of use but also the quality, which reflected a more commercialized and mobile society agitated by a contentious party politics and a need to find balance in the sureties of national myth.

There was disturbing evidence that many Germans, among them groups that preservationists thought of as allies or audiences, simply disregarded preservationist thinking on the nation and memory. The Rhenish Monuments Council was alarmed that in the economic crises of the late Republic, churches and museums intentionally avoided legal limitations on the sale of artifacts to foreign buyers.[79] Preservationists used moderate tones in their dealings with the business community, but their tolerance was often unrequited, as breweries, oil companies, cigarette makers, and margarine producers vigorously resisted efforts to control commercial advertising on or near historic architecture. Castles throughout Germany were reused as youth hostels, in which more than 4 million people stayed in 1931; but youth groups did little to support preservation per se, and from the preservationist perspective they treated historic buildings with little respect, wrecking them when things got out of hand but more often simply ignoring elders' counsel of caution.[80] This was not Dehio's idea of piety for the national past and its symbols.

Political groups continued to rely on historic buildings for important symbolic effect, and the historic city of Weimar's associations with democ-

A touch of the Middle Ages: Nuremberg appealed to the Nazi Party because of the city's "old German ambience," reflected here in a view of the central square in the interwar period. (photo: Bildarchiv Foto Marburg/Art Resource, New York)

racy and learning were of considerable significance to the Republic's founding and broader political meaning. But it was the nationalist right that made particularly effective use of historic sites, just as it was the right that dominated nationalist myth during the Republic. Now more than before the war the Marienburg served as a point of condensation for anti-Polish, "frontier" ideology and a symbol of militaristic and nationalist versions of monumental history. Already in World War I Hindenburg had become closely associated with the fortress through Wilhelm II's naming of one of its gates after the war hero. In Weimar this association became stronger as the Reich president's eightieth birthday was celebrated in conjunction with the completed restoration of one of the towers, and Hindenburg was named an honorary citizen of the city of Marienburg. All this took place in spite of the ambivalence of the Marienburg conservator, who, like most other conservators, worried about where to draw the line between taste and pure propaganda.[81]

Nuremberg became even more important as a symbol to the nationalist right in the late Republic. Thanks to good traffic connections and a police chief sympathetic to right-radical politics, the Bavarian city became the site of National Socialist Party rallies in 1927, when the party was still a minor force. Nazi rallies later became known for their use of Albert Speer's grandiose architecture. But Nuremberg was a candidate for such scenes also because its centuries-old history as host to the Imperial Diet of the Holy Roman Empire gave it an important symbolic presence, and because the "touch of the Middle Ages" and "old German ambience" of its historic city center, its ringing bells, narrow streets, and stands of half-timbered houses, appealed to the Nazi Party's "backwards-oriented drive forward." Exploited but also felt deeply by many Nazi leaders, the popular wish for sincerity in all spheres of life gained fitting expression in evocations of Nuremberg's place in the long continuities of German history.[82]

More variably than in the political sphere, historic buildings continued to work as cultural capital for many groups. Weimar commercialism promoted this trend, as reflected in the innovative modernist poster art of the era, which abstracted from the physiognomy of historical cities in appeals to tourists to spend three days in Munich or other cities. But among the best examples of the conspicuous consumption of historic places by the *Bürgertum* is the Association for the Preservation of German Castles. One of the group's most visible activities was the annual castle tour, which included guided visits to castles and fortresses throughout German-speaking Europe, including Austria.[83] The weeklong June 1928 tour had 116 participants, mostly retired military officers, estate owners, members of the free professions, businessmen, and their spouses. Club members paid 200 marks to go on the tour; guests, 50 marks more. The tour announcement stressed the Germanness of the Rhine. "What place draws Germans to it more today than the Rhine?" it read. "There the treasures of old German culture and the walls of castles, rich with memories, are inexhaustible." The group visited the famous thirteenth-century Marksburg in Braubach, the only fully preserved medieval fortress of the Rhineland; the restored thirteenth-century fortress Genovevaburg in Mayen near Koblenz; and Roman artifacts in Trier. Big cities were not slighted, as the itinerary included Düsseldorf, Aachen, and Koblenz.[84]

Most importantly for our purposes, the tour displayed itself for all who were willing to look. City officials met and entertained the tour participants wherever they visited. Banquets, ceremonial greetings, lectures, and a variety of other activities filled the itinerary. Bodo Ebhardt, longtime chair of the club, made a point of stressing that the participants were "well prepared" and always "enthused about the tours"—real connoisseurs of history and of the sites they visited. Newspapers carried accounts of the tour's visits to various cities, and each year's tour was written up in the association newsletter, *Der Burgwart*.[85] One of the highest forms of charity in biblical tradition is anonymous giving. If club members' historical knowledge had been charity, it would have been of a less exalted kind in the Christian hierarchy. Historical knowledge and a taste for tradition were here freely displayed and openly flaunted.

Ebhardt claimed the tour always received strong support from the author-

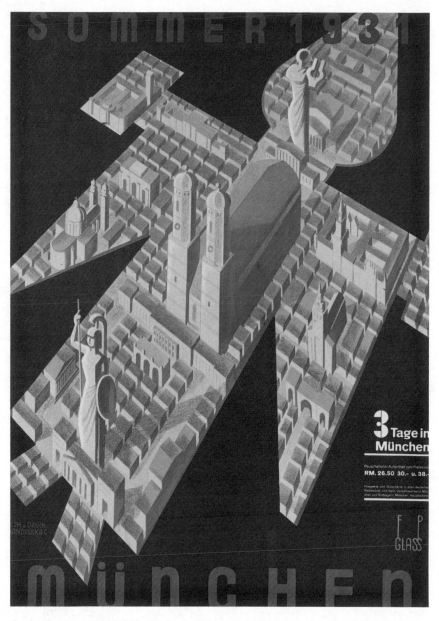

Consuming cityscapes: a 1931 advertisement for three-day tourist packages abstracts, in modernist fashion, from Munich's historic physiognomy. (photo: Deutsches Historisches Museum)

The thirteenth-century Marksburg, near Braubach, the only fully intact medieval fortress in the Rhineland, and a favorite site in the annual tour of the Association for the Preservation of German Castles. (photo: *Deutsche Burgen* [1940], 24)

ities.[86] But the club's relationship with conservators and other members of the preservationist lobby was not always smooth. The tensions had much to do with Ebhardt's aggressive restorations of fortresses and castles, a practice that brought him into constant conflict with antiscrape groups before the war. I cannot say whether such tensions continued to create bad blood between the association and Rhenish preservationists in the Weimar Republic. But bad blood there was. When Ebhardt invited the Prussian Rhine province administration to participate in the 1928 tour, provincial conservator Renard counseled against sending a representative to the tour, referring to unspecified "activities of the association and its leaders that strongly run counter to the interests of historic preservation." One can only wonder if the group's aggressive nationalism and display of its cultural capital also violated the preservationist commandment "Thou shalt not be tactless."

Further down the class structure, collectors' cards continued as a form of plebeian cultural capital. After the production of *Sammelbilder* collapsed in the war and postwar inflation, cigarette and margarine companies provided them in the late 1920s and early 1930s. A "true flood of commercial card series" appeared on the market as Reemtsma, Haus Brinkmann, and other cigarette companies competed for what was becoming a much larger and more plebeian group of consumers. Historic buildings remained a popular theme. German castles were of particular importance at a time when imagery of military security and national myth were widespread. *Sammelbilder* also functioned as substitutes for tourism, especially for the lower middle and working classes. Buyers of a 1931 Stollwerck album were encouraged to collect pictures of Rhineland cathedrals, castles, ruins, and landscapes. By doing so they would supposedly gain the same proprietary sense of the national heritage that tourists acquired when they traveled to various historic sites. "You are a German," read the Stollwerck album, "and the Rhine, that is your river."[87]

Yet it is possible that the cards also diminished the effect of historic buildings on the popular imagination. Historic places were just one of a much vaster assortment of themes including sport, film, theater, women, literature, dance, and nature. Later images of war, the 1936 Olympics, and the Hitler cult would add a new layer of vivid images. As they became increasingly varied and colorful, *Sammelbilder* seemed to point more to anticipation of the future than to the repose of the past. A 1924 album titled "Then and Now: From the Half-Timbered House to the Skyscraper" depicted urban skyscrapers with a zeppelin flying overhead and a modern port in the background. In an insert at bottom right was a half-timbered house in a typical *Altstadt*; the insert on the bottom left had a picture of Liebig's Meat-Extract. The old house was reduced to the background in an image that linked the commercial product with progress and activity in the modern age.[88] Moreover, it portrayed an urban future of "American" skyscrapers, a vision whose relevance to Germany preservationists and urban planners often vehemently denied.[89] Aside from pointing to these shifts in audience and imagery, the issue with collectors' cards for nation-thinking preservationists remained what it had been before the war: they were a highly personal, uncontrollable appropriation of historical imagery thoroughly immersed in commercial life.

Weimar-era tourism presented some of the same problems. Strengthened by the economic recovery and more widespread use of the car in the later 1920s, tourism struggled once the full impact of the depression occurred. But for some areas of Germany, economic crisis meant that tourism became an even more important resource. In 1932 tourism was seen as the answer to the western Rhenish Eifel region's long-term poverty and need for "frontier" security. Plans for industrializing the region had to be postponed in the economic crisis, and one solution was to exploit the area's numerous fortresses, cloisters, and former noble residences to bring in income. The Eifelverein, a *Heimat* organization with more than 14,000 members, supported such plans. The normal activity of the club itself had been a spur to local consumption of historic places for much of the previous decade, and its use of historic places reflected a touristic sensibility that was often foreign to the more austere gaze of the preservationist. When it held its annual meeting in the thirteenth-century town of Mayen in 1928, the association had the local Genovevaburg lit up with floodlights that offered "local inhabitants and visitors enchanting images." Eifelverein officials were advisers in a regional competition promoting improvements in photographs for travel souvenirs. The club reported that the Eifel historic museum had had over 40,000 guests since its opening in 1921. On the last afternoon of the assembly the city had a historical parade with 500 participants in traditional peasant dress. A festival at the castle followed, attended by local people, club members, and tourists. Its goal was the memory of a military victory against the French in 1673.[90] Here memory paraded on a local stage whose organizers offered entertainment, color, and evocations of historical events.

Such local appropriations of historic places present a picture of tremendous variety. A final example comes from the small town of Markt Rohr in Niederbayern, whose 1,276 inhabitants celebrated the 1,000-year history of their community in June and July 1926. Although the Festschrift printed for the festival began with a poem evoking the powers of the past—"Memory strengthens, memory heals, and frees!"—it also noted that there had been disagreement as to whether the town was founded in 858 or 926.[91] The ancientness of the town, whatever its true chronological age, was as always

The thirteenth-century Genovevaburg, source of enchanting images for *Heimat* groups in the Eifel (photo: *Deutsche Burgen*, [1940], 23)

closely linked to its visual appropriation. The opening page of the publication carried a drawing of the silhouette of the townscape and its single dominant church tower, a motif repeated throughout the publication.

Local town leaders made a direct appeal to tourism in organizing their historical program, welcoming guests "from near and far." They also linked the festivities simultaneously to the war and the future, reminding visitors that "this celebration should be dedicated to our fathers and the fallen heroes, to the living and coming generations."[92] What this combination of functions meant in practice, however, was a colorful melange of historical images. The festival opened with a Saturday evening festival accompanied by ringing bells and cannon fire. Sunday morning there was a memorial church service, then official greeting of guests of honor in front of the *Rathaus*. In the afternoon there was a historical parade through the old town. Later in the week there were shooting matches with prize competitions, a play (*The Monk of Rohr*), a memorial church ceremony for the war dead of the town, a motor caravan organized by a local branch of the German Automobile Club, a cattle and pig show with prize competition, a gymnastics competition, daily one-hour tours through the historic Cloister Church, and daily "festivities of all kinds" on the festival grounds.

The historical parade was a particularly rich—some would say chaotic—

layering of images, including nearly 200 participants and eighty horses.[93] The parade featured two mounted heralds; two individuals portraying King Heinrich and Duke Arnulf, both mounted; a local orchestra and other musicians peppered throughout the procession; a person portraying the founder of the local cloister in 1133; a figure representing Bishop Heinrich of Regensburg and the prelate Reimer, donors to the town of its historic thirteenth-century church bell; a float depicting the granting of market rights to the town by Kaiser Ludwig of Bavaria in 1347; a fifteenth-century hunting party; citizens dressed as the eighteenth-century builders and painters of the Cloister Church in its present form; a float depicting the weaving trade in the eighteenth century; the mounted Emperor Napoleon I, who had stayed a single evening in the town in April 1809; marching men portraying the first local civil militia in 1848; the town's first postal wagon from September 1870; marchers representing soldiers of the Franco-Prussian War; marching soldiers from 1914; and the local gymnastics group. There was also a children's parade with 160 participants, all portraying different occupations and social types, including washwomen, smithies, cooks, agricultural laborers, tailors, members of an early nineteenth-century Kaffeeklatsch, gypsies, and peasants in historic costumes. The children's parade concentrated more on social history; the adults', on political events.

The Festschrift also described the history of the town's historical buildings, including its Romanesque parish church. But this was less an art-historical lecture than a narrative of the building as a symbol of the town's victimization and persistence through war, occupation, plague, and economic crises. In the Thirty Years' War "fanatical Swedes" destroyed the twelfth-century church and cloister. Not until 1722 was the structure rebuilt. The massive church tower held the oldest bell in Bavaria. In the nineteenth century, when the cloister was dispossessed, the cemetery on the north side of the parish church lost its lovely stone portal including sculpted figures that evoked the "frailty and transitoriness of human life." The portal and other valuable artifacts were sold for ridiculous prices and used for paving stones or foundations for new buildings. Although the portal now graced another nearby cemetery, other local monuments met humiliating fates. One gravestone of a "pious count who was also a patron of the cloister" was "installed in a tavern—in such a manner that men and animals disgraced it with excrement."[94] The narrative added further information on the local *Rathaus* and the building of a war monument in 1873. But it also reported a major fire in the eighteenth century, the first public telephone service in 1903, and the toll of World War I, which resulted in the "hero's death" of thirty-four local sons.

It is impossible to tell what Germany's leading preservationists would have thought of Rohr's extraordinary ramble through historic sites, costumes, periods, and events in the summer of 1926. Markt Rohr was unexceptional in its treatment of history. This form of commemoration, often built around key local historical sites, could be found not only in community celebrations but in the festivals of churches, voluntary societies, and trade unions. This was the kind of emotional evocation of the past bordering on kitsch many preservationists had in mind when they bemoaned their own distance from the *Volk*. But it was also a textbook example of how the age value of historical landmarks blended with other immediate interests and considerations to create not tact but a more naive rendering of a living past. Too, although Rohr appeared in this narrative as a German town participating in German history, the program evoked everyday life far more than it did national grandeur. The town acted for the glory of Germany, but it was the town itself that survived the events depicted in this narrative of vulnerability and survival. This form of sincerity had an unmistakably local ambience.

Markt Rohr's homespun historical pageantry was hardly as challenging as Bruno Taut's harsh words were to the "odious concepts" that gave meaning to German culture. But its quality and form suggested that the Republic was indeed a modernist crucible in which not only the most radical proponents of the future had their say but also the provincial and local defenders of tradition, however that was defined. Preservationists working in government departments and quasi-state associations tried to balance themselves between these and many other expressions of simultaneous pessimism and longing for a new political, cultural, and moral sincerity. Yet their continued allegiance to the language of nationality, *Volk*, and authenticity—to the idea of *Kultur* as a superior expression of an essential German perdurability—inevitably placed them on the side of those who envisioned a polity stripped of social democratic and liberal ideals. Preservationists' conservative hopefulness put them in the company of those whose hope depended on authoritarian-nationalist and racist renderings of German memory. Yet even in this company, preservationists such as aging art historian Clemen or dedicated cultural bureaucrat Hiecke were uncomfortable. Accepting the argument that Germany's documents of stone gained their moral resonance from a revived and transformed *Volksgemeinschaft*, most defenders of the country's architectural monuments still balked at the idea of appealing broadly to the German people, just as they had before the war. Whether they regarded the German nation from the heights of the weathered, decaying Cologne cathedral and the mystic, legend-enshrouded Wartburg or viewed it from the streets of homely towns like Markt Rohr, the preservationists feared stepping into the cacophony of mass-based cultural politics in the modernist key. Hopefulness was, after all, based on the idea not of utopia but of partial, compromised political resolution gained through hardship and even tragedy. What political and cultural viewpoint could be more fitting for practices and techniques decided by case-by-case investigation of historical places rather than sweeping agendas and breathless manifestos? The preservationist message was hardly designed for those who wanted unblinking sincerity, immediately and without compromise. Preservationists' hesitancy, a cultural-political diffidence, would even move their radical nationalist allies within and outside the Nazi Party to attack them for holding their own versions of odious concepts grounded, above all, in an allegiance to history. But that part of the narrative belongs to the next chapter.

A new generation will transform the monuments of heroes and commemorative groves into sites of pilgrimage for a new religion, where German hearts will be molded again and again according to a new myth. At that moment art will suddenly conquer the world anew.

—Alfred Rosenberg, *Myth of the Twentieth Century*

FOUR | WHERE GERMAN HEARTS ARE MOLDED

lfred Rosenberg concluded the second book of his best-selling tome with the above lines. Although Hitler regarded Rosenberg's thought as quirky philosophizing, the Nazi theorist captured an aspect of the dictatorship directly relevant to this study. Referring to the war monuments and other commemorative landmarks of the regime, Rosenberg thought of such sites of memory as a source literally to reproduce new hearts imbued with love for Germany and a sense of religious-mythic existence.[1] Rosenberg had specific sites in mind, and many Nazi ideologues thought that *Thingstätte*, outdoor forums for plays and concerts designed specifically to promote Germanic myth and racial ideology, were especially appropriate for regime goals. But anything would do. Art, architecture, film, the new autobahns, painting, monuments, historic buildings in the broadest sense—all theoretically contributed to the constant production of such emotional attachments to a political-racial religion. The act of producing new hearts, a cultural revolution of the most radical kind, lay at the core of a discourse of performance, or *Leistung*, which refers to the whole range of practices necessary to creating and representing new Germans. Present since at least the age of stunning economic success after

1870, this discourse gave the 1930s a particular meaning for Germany, one of heated recovery, reconstruction, growth, and militant security. It thus shaped memory also, since it not only drew a line of demarcation between the insecurities of the past and the more hopeful present, but it also provided a cultural imagery that a later period of growth and security, most significantly that of the 1950s, would draw on in unacknowledged but important ways.

Historic buildings, previously painstakingly protected to create an orientation to the past and future, quickly became part of this discourse in ways that will be considered in the following chapter. Before doing so, it is useful to point out an important shift in the political use of historic buildings in this period. Although politicians had tried to use memory to lead Germans back to essentialized tradition, to envelop memory in myth, Nazism's principle of performance radicalized the process. In previous political uses, memory had never been entirely obliterated; it remained embedded somewhere in the interstices of governmental and public appropriations of the past. Aiming to create new hearts at every moment, the regime tried to obliterate memory's always potential noncompliance with contemporary political needs. This violence at the core of Nazism's approach to the past had important implications for the practice of historic preservation.

The Culture of *Leistung*

The dominant aspect of the Third Reich was its devotion to a mythic racial identity based on the constant production of emotional attachments to the regime. In this respect it shared the thirst for myth that all parts of German society had during the war and the Republic. But 1933 signaled a specific discontinuity. Economic growth, improvement of infrastructure, military expansion, population growth, and the breaking down of old social and political loyalties—these were not simply legitimized by myth. Rather, myth redefined them, turning them into resources for the real goal of the regime, the eternal production of new hearts and the performance of rituals of loyalty, including mass slaughter, in support of that production. "Performance" was the concept and reality that achieved this. Performance was needed in economic growth because the country had to be brought back from economic depression. It was needed in military production, because despite Hitler's profession of peaceful intentions, he had chosen war. It was needed in urban planning, because here Hitler wanted to remake the urban fabric of Germany to reflect the grandeur of the race. It was needed in culture, where film, photography, painting, architecture, and sport created idealized representations of (mostly male) German racial identity, ways of thinking and speaking through which Germans represented themselves as superior beings to one another and to inferior Others.

The well-known concept "reactionary modernism" fails to capture the dynamic of Nazi Germany because it leaves in place nineteenth-century dichotomies of progress and reaction, modern and traditional.[2] Nazism aimed to destroy these opposed terms and create new ones that enabled the racial nation to adapt to a world of global economic competition, unremitting technical advance, and continuous cultural revolution. The performance principle, or *Leistungsprinzip*, regulated this approach to past and present. It was neither modern nor reactionary but genuinely beyond these categories or any combination of them. In this sense Nazism's claim to being revolutionary was fair. Moreover, the *Leistungsprinzip* was unremittingly violent. Those members of the *Volk* community who were weak performers, those who were *leistungsschwach*, deserved help and indoctrination. Those who were considered unredeemable or hostile to the production of new German hearts—Slavs, Jews, Communists, Socialists, dissident Christians, homosexuals, and gypsies—were killed.

Performance did not necessarily mean that the forms in which it was represented were entirely new. Consciously and unconsciously, supporters of the Nazi regime drew on preexisting historical models, displaying their reverence for Germanic cultic imagery in the *Thing* movement at one moment or embracing medieval imagery at another. The Nazi regime centralized cultural authority, but it praised provincial self-government and regional loyalties as parts of the Germanic heritage. When Leni Riefenstahl's Stormtroopers (Sturmabteilung, or SA) answered the national call to duty in her regime-financed film *Triumph of the Will*, they announced their presence according to their historical regions. Nor was the use of historical and mythic imagery independent of the many internecine struggles that characterized all spheres of Nazi policy. A fierce opponent of Rosenberg's radical uses of history, Joseph Goebbels insisted that although 1918–33 was to be considered "criminal," it would be against the regime's interests to apply "National Socialist yardsticks to all of German history and its heroes." This meant one could not represent "Goethe as a Freemason and poisoner of Schiller, and Mozart as a victim of poisoning . . . and all of them together as Freemasons."[3]

Generally, *Leistung* in the cultural realm, as defined by Goebbels in a 15 November 1933 speech at the Reich Chamber of Culture in Berlin, was based on the realization that "people" were the "source of strength" of all art and that "the statesman's activist way of thinking must return as the artist's instrumental way of thinking." The cultural realm was therefore to work according to the same principles of action, commitment, and monumental achievement that underlay political conquest. Cultural *Leistung* depended on the abilities of the artist, the genius of artistic talent, and not on "dilettantes" who were committed to the National Socialist cause but who failed to rise above mediocrity. Heroic artistic achievement—cultural performance in a monumental-mythic key—would occur in the Third Reich only according to the highest artistic standards used to judge performance in the past. But it would be based on "fresh blood," young artists who "have nothing in common with the past, which we have left behind us." This artist "must create new forms."[4] Goebbels thus squared the circle, portraying the artist as both artistically liberated and politically obligated.

Considering the effect of film on modern perception, Walter Benjamin used the urban built environment as a metaphor to explain a new relationship between the human eye and mechanical means of representation. "Our taverns and our metropolitan streets, our offices and furnished rooms, our railroad stations and our factories appeared to have us locked up hopelessly," he wrote. "Then came the film and burst this prison-world asunder by the dynamite of the tenth of a second, so that now, in the midst of its far-flung ruins and debris, we calmly and adventurously go traveling."[5] In this passage Benjamin unintentionally revealed an important affinity between the modern, filmic eye and the National Socialist vision of urban space and architecture. The dynamite of the tenth of a second matched the Nazi desire for speed and performance. The metaphorical ruins of the city viewed through the camera's eye matched the notional and real ruins of Nazi urban projects, to say nothing of the ultimate consequences of Nazi warmaking. Yet modernist and Nazi visions were not identical. The Nazis wished to see the urban world "exploded" in the process of creating new buildings that spoke a National Socialist message beyond modernity.

This had enormous implications for the protection of historic buildings, which even before the destruction of World War II were under much more stress in the Nazi dictatorship than they had been in Weimar despite the regime's often-proclaimed commitment to tradition. Theoretically, they were under stress because of new Nazi-inspired planning initiatives, represented in the formation of the Reich Office for Area Planning in 1935 and, later, more radically in the General Plan East, the goal of which was to "Germanize" occupied Eastern territories and liquidate "unwanted" populations.[6] Through such agencies, which in typical Nazi fashion often competed with one another, Germany entered a new stage in its history in which, like other Western countries though with different timing and different political goals, a more radically efficient distribution of goods and services in space became a primary objective. Tied to National Socialist racial-political goals, such planning meant that the monument became one resource among many in a web of planning contexts whose key principles were not those of tact or piety but of performance and accountability in the service of radical national ideas. Even if the regime's ultimate aims of racial war and German hegemony were self-defeating and irrational, its planning strategies depended more than ever on the efficacious mobilization of land, labor, and capital. For many planners and technocrats, greater rationalization and efficiency were even more possible in the East, where in contrast to Western territories the preexisting social and urban forms of "inferior" populations could be destroyed with impunity and new German settlement patterns constructed *di nuovo*. Because the General Plan East was based on the vision of a largely agrarian society, it entailed the theoretical and, as in Warsaw, actual destruction of much urban heritage.

In urban planning Nazism created a racist conglomerate of ideas constructed out of Garden City traditions, conservative-technocratic theorizing of the 1920s, and even the expressionism of radical thinkers such as Bruno Taut. Hitler himself admired Haussmann's remaking of Paris under Napoleon III. By 1936 urbanistic thinking had shifted from a *völkisch*-organic to a more technocratic inflection. Meanwhile, limited urban renewal schemes were undertaken in Frankfurt am Main, Braunschweig, and Kassel, and a monumental rebuilding of key urban ensembles was begun in Berlin, Munich, Nuremberg, and elsewhere. Had Nazi planners been able to carry out their visions, they would have remade German cityscapes with entirely new time referents. Each major city's physiognomy would not be dominated by the traditional structures of church and *Rathaus* but by new "urban summits," or *Stadtkrone*, of Nazi buildings. A city that was also the capital of a Nazi Party district (*Gau*) would have a "*Gau* forum" made up of such structures. Urban planners from varying political positions had used the concept of *Stadtkrone* before Nazism, but now this idea became a centerpiece of urbanistic thinking. Hitler himself bemoaned the lack of such architectural summits in *Mein Kampf*, writing that "our big cities of today possess no monuments dominating the city picture, which might somehow be regarded as the symbols of the whole epoch." Despite Hitler's intense wishes to build new *Stadtkrone*, this project had hardly gotten off the ground by the outbreak of the war.[7]

Nazi-era urban planning revealed a rather conventional and historicist side in such thinking. It was not that Nazism took up the program of the historicist architects who so adamantly attacked new building in the 1920s, for the regime virtually ignored the work of these supporters. Yet the NSDAP did try to situate itself specifically in the flow of German history through various architectural and planning initiatives. Nazism claimed it had achieved a cultural revolution, and its place in history would be marked quite directly by buildings that referred the observer to National Socialist rule. The same assumption was working when Nazi officials opposed renaming historic streets after Hitler. Except for key avenues and squares in some of the major cities, only newly reconstructed or new streets designed by the regime itself should carry the name of the Führer. Even the autobahns, symbols of the regime's productivity, led one Nazi journalist to consider German roads in relation to their Roman, Napoleonic, and nineteenth-century precedents, a perspective that moved the writer to argue that the Third Reich had opened "the greatest epoch of road building in all of history."[8]

But urban planning also moved beyond previous historicist assumptions by creating new cultural-political functions for regime buildings, highways, districts, squares, and, indeed, entire cities. In the Munich Königsplatz, where the Nazi martyrs of the Hitler putsch in 1923 were reburied, urban space was not shaped by nineteenth-century perceptions in which monumental buildings stood more or less isolated from one another, "freed up" to be appreciated singly for their historical and contemporary meaning and oriented to their surroundings precisely as monuments that stood apart from the rest of the urban fabric. Instead, the square as a whole became isolated from its context, refashioned as a monumental ensemble of Nazi party buildings whose relationship to the rest of the city was one of authority and domination rather than interaction, contemplation, and communication. Hitler had the Königsplatz covered with more than 20,000 square meters of granite slabs so that it could be used as a forum for mass meetings. This new sense of the square demeaned the past while also manipulating it through the use of classicist motifs on government buildings, museums, and memorials.[9] At a more comprehensive level, whole urban fabrics were torn from their previous historical associations and transformed into total symbols of a myth-inspired racial community: Munich was the capital of the Nazi movement; Nuremberg, the city of party rallies; Goslar, the center of peasantist "Blood and Soil" ideology; Braunschweig, the mecca of Schutzstaffel (SS) chief Heinrich Himmler's cult of the medieval Welf duke Heinrich the Lion; and Berlin ("Germania"), the capital of Hitler's new racial empire.

Although party officials disliked his socialist tendencies and tried to limit his public appeal, Gottfried Feder was the most influential urban planner in the Third Reich. His ideas also signaled planning's striving for revolutionary new goals. Feder praised past urban forms but also stressed the need for modern cities attuned to the performance principle and radically efficient uses of time and space. His *The New City*, published in 1939, was based on

WHERE GERMAN HEARTS ARE MOLDED

extensive studies of German cities by coworkers and students, who were trying to establish a new "art of city planning" derived directly from the social structure of urban populations. In a time of biologistic thinking, urban social structures inevitably were interpreted according to Nazi principles of race hierarchy and racial performance. For Feder, the "degenerate big city" was the "death of the nation," as one of the section headings of the book proclaimed. The frightful threat of racial degeneration and death was to be met with radically new urban forms enabling the nation not only to revive itself but to dominate others. Echoing the ideas of Garden City theorists and many others, Feder argued the ideal city was much smaller, about 20,000 people, and its historical model was the medieval town, whose organic structure and rhythm were products of a radical orderliness completely foreign to the chaotic "architectural liberalism" started by the French Revolution.[10] The solution to contemporary urban-liberal forms was not a return to the Middle Ages but, rather, protection for what had been handed down from the past in combination with modern technologies for renewing—Feder advocated large-scale urban renewal projects—and expanding contemporary big cities according to organic principles. Stripped of their more explicit links to racial concepts, Feder's ideas were very important in reconstruction planning during and after World War II, having influenced Hamburg planner Konstanty Gutschow and others in the following decades, and they did not differ radically in many respects from those of planners in other Western nations.[11]

One of the most notorious areas of Nazi cultural practice was architecture. Like many previous critics of German architecture and planning, Nazism condemned the historicist eclecticism of the nineteenth century, claiming it represented individualism, race mixing, and capitalist speculation. But Nazi architectural theory was just as eclectic as that which it replaced. Searching for organic forms, it drew on not only the pre-1830 classicist and regionalist traditions of conservative architects but also on modernist models based on prewar innovators such as Peter Behrens.[12] The chaos of influences was masked by the appeal to simplicity, grandeur, and manliness. National attitude replaced substance under cover of an apparently uniform monumentalism. At its root, the goal of monumentalism was to be *völkisch*, which in practice meant that architecture should be built so as to promote maximum popular mobilization in the regime's festivals and meetings.

Architecture was one of the best areas in which the proponents of *Leistung* could find a natural outlet for their aggression. When important party figures supported key architectural projects, a veritable blitzkrieg of destruction and construction took place. When plans for the renewal of the area immediately surrounding the Brandenburger Tor were implemented,

The performance of the Reich's building plans: after Hitler laid the cornerstone for the House for International Tourism in Berlin on 14 June 1938, workers at sixteen separate construction sites in the city commenced their labors while singing the *Deutschlandlied*. (photo: Heiss, *Bei Uns in Deutschland*, 97)

large swaths of residential housing were eliminated. Building sites such as those for the Reich Air Force Ministry in Berlin or the complex for the annual Nazi Party rallies in Nuremberg required immediate removal of what had been standing before and rapid building of the new structure. In the first case, construction teams tore down an entire ensemble of historic buildings on the Wilhelmstraße, including the old Ministry of War; in the second case, there were specific plans to get rid of pine and spruce trees in favor of oak trees, which were better symbols of power and permanence and were in any case favored by proponents of more Germanic influences in architecture. At the building site for the air ministry, three shifts worked around the clock, as workers contributed practically as well as symbolically to the imagery of *Leistung*.[13] In Munich, tenth-of-a-second destruction was extensive. It included the tearing down of classicist palaces and other buildings in and around the Königsplatz and a nearby famous church in the Sonnenstraße as well as less drastic actions like "cleansing" building facades of their floral *Jugendstil* styles.[14]

The Third Reich also created new monuments, many linked to Nazism's

WHERE GERMAN HEARTS ARE MOLDED

fascination with death and heroism in the past.[15] Building on the Weimar-era nationalist cult of Albert Schlageter, a German terrorist executed for sabotage by the French in 1923 in Düsseldorf, the Nazis erected statues, busts, and simple wooden crosses commemorating this German hero. The tenth anniversary of his execution in May 1933 saw especially heated adulation for Schlageter, whose memory was conflated with memory of the war dead. The Nazis sponsored many veterans' monuments that, unlike those of Weimar, glorified war and created images of strong, fighting males as racial politics said they should be rather than as they were. In these structures classical and realistic motifs were common. The myth of the battle of Langemarck in Belgium, where young German soldiers were said to have sung "Deutschland, Deutschland über alles" as they went to the slaughter, was one of the most widely used sources for such narratives. Having taken virtual control of war commemoration, the National Association for Veterans' Graves (Volksbund Deutsche Kriegergräberfürsorge) used the imagery of medieval castles to create *Totenburgen*, collective veterans' monuments set on hilltops and consisting of massive stone architecture. This medievalism also found expression in the Westphalian castle Wewelsburg, which was to be the hub of the SS's neofeudal empire of warrior knights; the transformation of the twelfth-century Braunschweig cathedral St. Blasius into a "national site of pilgrimage" for adherents of the legend of the medieval Welf duke Heinrich the Lion (who had founded the church and was presented in official ideology as a Hitler-like "leader personality" of an earlier age); and the use of the Marienburg to symbolize the return of Polish lands to their rightful owners. Creating a psychotopography of the Nazi city, the regime printed a tourist guide leading people through the various "sites of memory" of the National Socialist "struggle over the Reich capital" Berlin that included the burned-out Reichstag, various pubs where SA men were killed by Communists, and the theater on Nollendorfplatz where the SA disrupted the first showing of the "traitorous Jewish-American" film *All Quiet on the Western Front* in 1930.[16]

The result of such initiatives in planning, architecture, and monument building was a violent "negative preservation,"[17] a *démontage* of large parts of the built environment with various goals in mind. One goal was the eradication of certain elements of history from public memory. This occurred as early as 1932 in Dessau in the state of Anhalt, where the Nazis had just come to power and where they removed a monument to Jewish philosopher Moses Mendelssohn, who had been born there.[18] The regime was especially ruthless in its handling of reminders of the Weimar Republic. The Nazis erased street names commemorating the "November criminals," as one Reich Chancellery decree of April 1933 put it, and replaced them with

DER BRAUN-
SCHWEIGISCHE
STAATSDOM
MIT DER GRUFT
HEINRICHS
DES LÖWEN

EIN VORBILD
GEGENWARTSNAHER
DENKMALSPFLEGE
IM NEUEN DEUTSCHLAND

Nazism recontextualized historic landmarks such as the Braunschweig cathedral, which became
a site of pilgrimage for the cult of Heinrich the Lion, a "leader personality" of an earlier age.
The subtitle of an article in the glossy *Die Kunst im Deutschen Reich* in which this photo
appeared reads, "A model for relevant historic preservation in the new Germany."
(photo: *KDR* 3, Folge 11, Ausg. A [November 1939]: 358)

either names of Nazi Party dignitaries or the original name, if it was deemed
to have historical value. In 1936 in Neutempelhof in Berlin, a Weimar-era
Garden City, they renamed streets after World War I flying aces as part of a
campaign to obliterate the Republic's accomplishments and legitimize future war.[19] In Poland the Germanizing of street names in the Generalgouvernement or, much more violently, the burning of the Warsaw Castle as a
symbol of the Polish nation in 1944 (to say nothing of the destruction of
three-quarters of all buildings and more than nine of every ten historic
landmarks in Warsaw and the killing of 700,000 Warsaw residents), are just
two examples of a brutal negative preservation.[20]

Creating a Nazi psychotopography: this dramatic picture provided the cover to a tour guide, *We Travel through National Socialist Berlin*, in which national landmarks and sites from the history of the Nazi movement were combined to form a new optic identity and collective memory for the city. (photo: Engelbrechten and Volz, *Wir wandern durch das nationalsozialistische Berlin*)

Although negative preservation entailed unprecedented destruction, its goal was also to preserve enough of the old to remind observers of the complete triumph of the new. This was one of the motivations of the infamous art exhibit on "degenerate art," which displayed the works of modernist artists as examples of a decadent artistic culture on which Nazism now closed the door. These paintings were eventually destroyed, auctioned, or lost, but short-term preservation had served its function, particularly when it was put on display. This aspect could also be seen in the Reichstag fire of 1933 and the massive destruction of synagogues in 1938. In the case of the Reichstag fire, unplanned but exploited by the Nazis, the structure was left standing despite some support for its being rebuilt, though without the architectural features that symbolized Germany's previous "internal disorientation," to use the term of one architectural writer.[21] It remained a tourist attraction and a highly symbolic ruin, "dead" but still evocative of the political turbulence of pre-Hitler Germany and thus a reminder of the chaos that always threatened German culture.

In the case of the synagogues, many were burned to the ground in the euphemistically named "Reich Night of Broken Glass," which in Berlin alone resulted in the destruction or damage of forty of the city's fifty Jewish places of worship. But many synagogues were left standing as ruins, as in the case of the massive Oranienburger Straße synagogue, dedicated in 1866 and the most important such Jewish structure in Berlin. Damage to this landmark would have been much greater had a local police officer, more concerned about artistic value than racial politics, not driven away marauding SA men and called the fire department. The synagogue could still be used for Passover in 1939, only to be extensively damaged in a late 1943 bombing. The Levetzowstraße synagogue in Berlin was also only lightly damaged in 1938, used as a deportation center for those being shipped to extermination camps in the East, then severely damaged but still left intact as a ruin in the war. In both instances, World War II finished what the SA had started. However, while they stood as ruins, these burned-out hulks were fitting symbols of the larger racial-political goals of the regime: to exterminate Jewish life in Europe but to preserve enough of Jewish culture to signify Germany's total triumph over the racial threat.[22]

Less well known by historians but perhaps even more important to the everyday life of Germans were the Reich Labor Ministry's urban renewal projects (*Sanierung*). Limited urban renewal schemes were tried in Hamburg after the cholera epidemic of 1892 and in Stuttgart after 1900, and the first comprehensive planning guide to what was then called inner urban ex-

WHERE GERMAN HEARTS ARE MOLDED

pansion appeared in 1921. In Nazi Germany urban renewal occurred mainly from 1933 to 1936, before the regime was fully committed to economic autarky and military expansion, and before it concentrated more fully on grandiose projects to create new cities (The City of the "Strength-through Joy" Car, The City of Hermann Göring Industries) or remake old ones. But urban renewal schemes were also worked out during World War II for cities in the occupied Eastern territories, often with the help of officials who had organized *Sanierung* projects in German towns. Some renewal projects for German towns had been prepared well before 1933 but had not been carried out, partly because of a lack of funds but also because city governments of the Weimar Republic had concentrated on new housing rather than the revival of old districts. Hamburg was the main exception to this rule in the 1920s. Designed in general to adapt preindustrial, urban infrastructures to industrial needs, renewal could include the restoration of old buildings, the creation of parks and other open spaces, the widening of streets, and the destruction of whole ensembles of buildings to reorganize transportation networks. Legislation and plans for renewing the central cores of German cities after 1933 included Berlin, Braunschweig, Breslau, Cologne, Frankfurt am Main, Hamburg, Kassel, and Lübeck.[23]

Urban renewal spoke to many different interests. It satisfied the anti–big city, pro-medieval inclinations of some parts of the intelligentsia, including preservationists, planners, and architects who had opposed Weimar city governments that spent money on new housing developments. These groups romanticized the notionally organic social relations and picturesque cityscapes of historic urban centers. Urban renewal appealed to the economic interests of small retailers and artisans, who saw it as a chance to attract tourists and new investment.[24] It appealed to planners, investors, mayors, and tourists who wanted to unclog traffic in historic city centers and link them to the autobahns. It met the interests of those who stressed the need for better hygienic and social conditions in historic downtowns, where the poor, the elderly, criminals, and prostitutes challenged *bürgerlich* aesthetic and moral preferences. Before the Nazi period, social-hygienic arguments had been used by Social Democratic supporters of urban renewal, and therefore post-1933 renewal projects could be used to appeal to these now-silenced groups as well.[25] Too, it had a military rationale because it decentralized populations vulnerable to aerial bombing.

Finally, it had a specific appeal to some National Socialist leaders, who saw in the old city districts a new living space, or *Lebensraum*. The new space was an inner-city analogue to the vast stretches of *Lebensraum* that would be not only imagined but conquered for healthy "national comrades" in the East. Nazi advocates of urban renewal were motivated by many of the goals already mentioned, but they were especially anxious to demonstrate the regime's decisiveness and performance. It meant a lot to the regime to be able to say that urban renewal had been "aggressively undertaken," as one observer stated for Aachen in 1941.[26] Moreover, in places such as Berlin and Hamburg the Nazis wanted to punish Social Democrats and Communists by "renewing" their neighborhoods, which in effect meant actively displacing inhabitants from working-class quarters that had opposed Nazism and scattering them to the margins of the city. One Nazi Party spokesman said in 1934 that the neighborhoods of Berlin needed to get rid of their "asocial and traitorous elements," while a year later another party leader insisted that "the misery-ridden quarters must disappear completely." Owners of "renewed" properties in Cologne and other cities had to sign a contract stating they would rent apartments only to "morally unobjectionable Aryan *Volk* comrades." In Polish Łódź, brutal wartime urban renewal was carried out even more forcefully against "undesirables," mainly Jews and Poles. Here "Germanization demanded . . . a new order from the ground up, for people as well as things," in the words of the city building director.[27]

Decisiveness, *Leistung,* and political hatred could neither overcome the many contradictions of urban renewal nor consistently define the role of historic buildings in the regime's vision of racially pure cities. Representatives of the heavily antiurban *völkisch*-organic side wanted to remove most historic buildings in city centers, leaving only a few grand public symbols. Others, such as planner Fritz Schumacher, much admired by many preservationists, defined "German cultural property" to include many vernacular structures. Those who thought in military terms wanted to disperse buildings to make them less vulnerable to aerial bombing and poison gas attacks, a perspective that did not agree with National Socialist advocates of clusters of monumental buildings housing the agencies of party and state.[28] Hitler himself was little interested in "ordinary" urban renewal, turning his attention instead to more megalomaniacal schemes. Only a fraction of what was planned was carried out, in part because the regime's interest turned to other projects. Although many supporters of urban renewal saw it as a way of strengthening small business and handicrafts, it appears that small business declined in the renewed districts. World War II added the biggest contradiction, as by 1943 most of what had been renewed in the previous ten years was or would be destroyed or severely damaged.

Berlin is the most notorious example of urban renewal, but it was an exception because its imperial-political goals far outweighed normal objectives of getting better housing and stimulating investment. It was different from either the nineteenth-century renewal of Paris by Haussmann or the renewal of Rome by Mussolini, being far more ambitious because it emanated from a vision of the city not as the capital of an industrial power but as the center of a world racial empire. Unlike Rome, with its classical artifacts and dramatic Via dell'Impero, or Paris, with its considerable stock of medieval architecture, Berlin had little really old architecture to regenerate or destroy and too little really monumental architecture to satisfy Hitler's tastes.[29] For the Führer the plan was to create "a city for the indefinite future that was worthy of a thousand-year-old people with a thousand-year-old historical and cultural heritage." Nazi chief architect Albert Speer worked to realize this vision, although he suppressed his admiration for austere Greek and Prussian classicism to satisfy Hitler's more baroque-influenced interest in classical monumentality.[30] Other cities made references to myth in their discussions of renewal projects also, as when Frankfurt am Main's plans were discussed in the context of that city's impending thousand-year anniversary.[31] Yet no other urban project could boast of such claims on the past and future as those made for Berlin. No other city so decisively associated the transformation of urban physiognomy with an ideology of global racial struggle.

Functional equivalents to these major efforts could be found in the regime's village beautification programs. These enlisted public support to maintain historic peasant architecture, plant trees and shrubs in small towns and hamlets, and clean up farms and workshops so as to make them appealing to the ever more mobile tourists of Hitler's Germany. But Nazi "cleansing" of the built environment did not stop with barns, village streets, and stables. Civilian cemeteries were also to be made more architecturally uniform, simpler in style and design, and above all more appropriate for their roles as "sites for the national cult."[32] Even the dead were to perform service for the regime's architectural and planning goals.

Heritage preservation appeared to find direct support from Nazism. Like Wilhelm II before him, Hitler became the most famous consumer of German culture in general and historic architecture in particular. He made much of his love of monumental buildings, characterizing the Vienna Ringstraße as an "enchantment" and speaking of "the magical spell of the sites of Mecca and Rome," which he had never seen when he wrote about them in *Mein Kampf*.[33] It seemed to matter little that for the Führer personally, most parts of the German townscape were expendable. Except for the grand cathedrals and city halls, wrote Hitler, historic medieval cities consisted mainly of "swarming frame, wooden, and brick buildings, which even today, with the tenements climbing higher and higher beside them, determine the character and picture of these towns."[34] Such disparaging views of vernacular buildings notwithstanding, the overall feeling of the regime seemed to favor everything for which architectural preservation stood.

The Nazi Party addressed preservationists directly, coordinating their organizations, fitting them into the short-lived Reich Association for Heritage and Heimat (Reichsbund Volkstum und Heimat, or RVH) and assuring them of a special role in a "cultural revolution" that demanded "conservation in the grand style." The journal *Architecture*, architectural supplement of *Art in the German Reich*, edited by Albert Speer, ran lavishly illustrated features of historic buildings and praised provincial and municipal conservators. Preservationists benefited from urban renewal programs that seemed to realize lasting demands for a revival of historic city centers, from a 1934 campaign to control advertising in the countryside, from 1936 legislation that created stricter guidelines for new building in historic districts, and from the adaptive reuse of old buildings by party and Hitler Youth groups. These and other measures seemed to legitimize the regime's claim that it had "unchained" communities such as Aachen from decline after "the great purification" of 1933 by saving historic downtowns, promoting local festivals, and creating or maintaining *Heimat* museums—actions that, not incidentally, were placed on the same moral plane as the regime's attacks on "cultural depravation" allegedly caused, in the case of Aachen, by the departed French occupation troops and "their substantial female entourage."[35]

Despite the selective destructiveness of Nazi urban planning, despite Nazi unwillingness to endorse a completely historicist architecture, and despite the rampant consumerism of German public life in the 1930s, both preservationists and the NSDAP could easily think of the dictatorship as a serious proponent of heritage conservation. Reinhard Bentmann argued, "Seldom has historic conservation . . . seen better times than in Germany after 1933."[36] There is something to the argument, if one keeps in mind the contradictions that characterized preservationism's placement in the cultural politics of Nazism.

Performance-Oriented Preservation

On the face of it, the discourse of *Leistung* reshaped the everyday practice of historic preservation. Held as part of a national conference of the RVH, the 1933 Kassel preservation congress had just one theme: "Protection of Monuments and the Homeland in the Rebuilding of the Nation." This was designed to demonstrate the institution's commitment to the national cause and to contrast the Kassel conference with earlier conferences, but especially with the Cologne event of 1930, the potential political thrust of which was dispersed by technical discussions and a proliferation of subthemes. Preservationists found themselves meeting against the (for them) unusual backdrop of mass political ardor, as the RVH festivities opened with torchlight processions by the SA, SS, and Hitler Youth. The aura of performance deeply affected the Kassel conferees, who reported that no previous meeting had ever made such demands on their time and concentration.[37]

Commitment to the new regime found further expression in the coordination of preservation groups in the RVH and in the generally greater visibility of *Heimatschutz* thinking in all areas of historic preservation. Linked to the Strength through Joy organization in the German Labor Front, the RVH was led by former Hitler Youth and Nazi student leader Werner Haverbeck. Its goal was to bring together all groups dealing with *Heimat*-related activities in a central party organization under the sponsorship of Hitler's representative Rudolf Heß. It included offices for *Heimatschutz*, nature conservation, preservation of monuments, folk music and dance, peasant costumes, and artisanal culture. The head of its office for monuments was Prussian conservator Robert Hiecke. But the RVH was dissolved in 1935, as its leaders clashed with Rosenberg's activist group, the Kampfbund für deutsche Kultur, and as officials of the established *Heimat* associations found the Reich organ too worker-oriented and populist. Still, the influence of *Heimatschutz* continued to grow as the Deutscher Bund Heimatschutz, in cooperation with Nazi Party organs, took over the RVH's responsibilities, asserting influence over provincial *Heimat* activity and forging new understandings between it and provincial self-government organs that were badly weakened by Nazi centralization. Meanwhile the RVDH endorsed *Leistung* as the most important signifier of cultural policy, announcing its commitment to "genuine performance" and to having "an echo in the wider landscape" of German public life.[38]

Publications dealing with historic preservation also reflected the new political situation. In 1934 the first number of *Deutsche Kunst und Denkmalpflege* appeared under the direction of Burkhard Meier and Konrad Nonn, both editors of the predecessor journal in the Republic. Though its tone and content reflected its Weimar-era heritage, the journal now featured old German script and a subscription price that was lowered by one-third. Its opening editorial, "Historic Preservation in the Life of the People," pointed to its desire for more popularity, dividing its audience into experts, helpers, and the general public and noting that more than before it wished to mobilize these helpers to bring the preservationist message to "the broad strata of the *Volk*." Publishers of inventories of monuments also tried to make their work more accessible. The long-awaited inventory of the Cologne cathedral, compiled and edited by Paul Clemen in 1937, had many illustrations, a low price, and a commitment to the "widest circulation." The first edition quickly sold out, and in 1938 a new one appeared.[39]

A 1937 lexicon mentioned that historic preservation had seen a substantial "widening of the concept of the monument."[40] This development seemed also to fit Nazi wishes for a greater popular resonance, as historic preservation turned to the saving of vernacular rural and urban architecture more than before. Such activity was prefigured in earlier preservation law and practice, but it was now not only more salient but also more imbued with nationalist overtones. Nuremberg city planners had preserved many vernacular structures in the *Altstadt* since the late nineteenth century, but they did so in Nazi Germany because, as the *DKD* put it, saving these buildings was an issue that touched "every German who loves the great monuments of his national history." Basing its policy on a 1920 preservation ordinance, the city of Hamburg preserved mainly middle-class housing and, in rural areas consolidated with the municipal district after 1937, peasant architecture that reflected the "popular heritage [*völkische Erbe*]." The transformation of an ensemble of farm buildings dating from the early nineteenth century into a "museum village," the first major open-air museum on German soil, in Cloppenburg in Lower Saxony in 1934, derived from a similar impulse, as did unrealized plans originating before World War I but continuing in the 1930s to create the country's first open-air museum of technical monuments. The Baden conservator added fuel to this populist fire by announcing in the late 1930s that the most important goal of his office was to protect "the small and medium cities and rural communities with their monuments, as well as the picture of the village in the entire region."[41]

Developments in other fields supported and strengthened this expansion. The national architects' association, the Deutsche Gesellschaft für Bauwesen, undertook a campaign to catalog and study German peasant architecture, a project begun by its predecessor organization in 1891 but now found deficient in coverage and analysis.[42] There were more than 2,000 *Heimat* museums in Germany in 1936, and it had become common for them to concentrate not only on some of the traditional traces of *Heimat* culture but also on collections of "the artifacts [*Denkmäler*] of the entire work culture of the peasant"[43] or on industrial artifacts. In 1938 the small city of Viersen, a twelfth-century settlement northwest of Düsseldorf, was just starting a local museum depicting the development of the community from a cluster of rural artisans' workshops into an industrial town. The Rhenish town of Rheydt, north of Bonn and able to trace its history to the ninth century, took a similar course with its *Heimat* museum, in which the history of the local textile industry and its buildings and work implements would be on display.[44] To the extent urban renewal affected fields of care and the historic housing stock, it also reinforced more populist definitions of monuments.

If the regime appeared to have established an entirely new context for the practice of heritage protection, some things went along as before. Preservation's legal status in the Nazi period changed almost not at all compared with Weimar, although Prussian and Reich ministries were merged and all preservation activities became centralized under the Reich cultural ministry. A Reich preservation law was once again debated but never passed. In 1936 all ordinances prohibiting the disfigurement of historic districts and scenic environments were brought under a single law, but this did little to change preservation's legal standing or its use of such ordinances. The Nazi regime passed legislation in August 1933 making it possible to restrict the use of private property more than before, but preservationists made little use of the Law for the Expropriation of Property for the General Good, relying instead on the general language of *Volksgemeinschaft* to put pressure on people who owned existing or potential historic landmarks.[45] In such instances, established notions of the national good proved more serviceable to preservationists than did more radical Nazi variations on the theme.

Held jointly with *Heimatschutz* groups, the 1936 preservation conference in Dresden was indicative of the new/old situation. Nazi official and provincial director Heinz Haake opened the congress saying that although the purpose of the event was just as before, preservation was "now more distinctly shaped with a view to the interests of the race and *Heimat*."[46] Lecture topics reflected the new view, encompassing nature and technology in road building, the protection of half-timbered architecture, nature conservation legislation, the maintenance of historical gardens, the protection of peasant architecture, the restoration of historic art objects, urban renewal and historic districts, the provincial museum for folk art in Saxony, and a general overview of historic preservation in Germany. The overview was given by Robert Hiecke, who would be praised in the postwar era for concentrating on the professional goals of the conservator rather than the ideological goals of the regime.[47] Direct ideological references were certainly not absent from Hiecke's address as he praised Hitler and lauded urban renewal in Lübeck, Trier, Leipzig, and Dresden, where "cleansing" urban environments of the "sins of past times" was deemed particularly successful. He congratulated SS chief Himmler for supporting the restoration of the tomb of Heinrich I in the Quedlinburg Cathedral, a "national holy place from the great past . . . of the first German Reich." Yet much of Hiecke's reportage to the 400 participants dealt with the normal workings of the preservationist apparatus. Hiecke was hopeful that the Reich preservation law would soon be implemented (it was not); that the definition of monuments would continue to widen without making historical values "absolute"; that "conserve, do not restore" would remain the motto of preservation even when some restoration would be allowed; and that conservators would adapt monuments to contemporary uses. None of these concerns was either new or particularly indicative of the fraught political situation. Rather, they inspired Hiecke to ask the conferees to "recall one more time the basic philosophy that should dominate the entire practice of preservation. Its foundation is and remains piety for historical values."[48] What did this suggest about preservationists' sense of national identity?

Privileged Marginality

DKD writer H. K. Zimmermann argued in 1938 that his contemporaries no longer thought in terms of "a mechanical and therefore incessant and unlimited 'progress,'" a statement intriguingly similar to postmodernist viewpoints of the 1970s and 1980s. But unlike more radical postmodernists, who would advocate the ironic citation of historical influences, the lesson for Zimmermann was that one could once again "learn from history."[49] Moreover, in contrast to postmodernist suspicion of all totalizing worldviews, for many preservationists Nazi ideology became the key regulator for cultural politics. In this Nazi-inflected mobilization of national memory within hope, there was room for much agreement between the regime and preservation but also for much dissonance, particularly in the dominant metaphors used to describe the nation as a historical entity.

The sense of a break in national history was decisive. For some, an end to the sense of living in a time of transition between periods of organic wholeness, a key trope inherited from the nineteenth century, appeared to be imminent. This was a variant of the idea that destructive, nineteenth-century "progress" had finally come to an end. When preservationists met for their Kassel conference in 1933, Nazi cultural official Apffelstaedt of Düsseldorf told the audience no one had greeted Hitler's rise to power more than the advocates of preservation and *Heimatschutz*. "After much casting about in ideologies that were isolated from the real world and that almost led to the dissolution of the entire national organism, after years of criminal and snobbish degradation of popular practices," said Apffelstaedt, "the concepts *Volk* and *Heimat* once again circulate in the thoughts of the German people."[50] This was a gross distortion of the recent past from the point of view of historic preservation, which found an anxious but relatively stable institutional home in the Weimar Republic. But it was an all too useful genetical narrative whose key function was to distinguish the present stage of national culture from the one just concluded, and to demonstrate that Nazism offered the hope of ending that sense of transitoriness that made contemporary life so culturally toxic. The feeling of having overcome a painful era of transition extended to the use of monuments, as when landmarks such as Frederick the Great's elegant palace and park, Sanssouci, built between 1745 and 1747 by architect Georg Wenzeslaus von Knobelsdorff in Potsdam, regained their prominence as sites of a national religion. "Sanssouci is once again at the center of nationalist festivals," wrote the Berlin National Gallery's Paul Ortwin Rave in 1934. "The past winter's Hitler Youth regiment's consecration of the colors will remain unforgettable. Lit by floodlights, the Sanssouci hill rose in blinding radiance, as if enchanted, out of the evening shadows."[51]

Linked to the sense of overcoming was a new opening to racist language. "Keenly listening for the voice of his own blood," said Apffelstaedt at the Kassel conference, "the German man begins to get a sense of his own great past."[52] The sense of living in historical time that had once been part of a healthy cultural-national identity was now a result of the "voice of the blood"; national culture was replaced by racial stock. Although most preservationists did not go as far as the self-described "political soldier of the Führer" Apffelstaedt in the use of such grotesque language, they were hardly immune to Nazism's political-biological discourse. The Kassel conference also featured an address by famous art historian Wilhelm Pinder, much closer to preservation circles than Apffelstaedt. Pinder saw the historical city as the material outgrowth of the "tribe," or *Stamm*, the "expression of [its] *Volkstum*."[53]

The concepts of "cleansing" or "purification," both captured in the German word "to clean [*reinigen*]," offer even more direct examples. In March 1934 preservationists and *Heimatschützer* participated in a campaign organized by the RVH, Strength through Joy, and the Reich Interior Ministry aimed at ridding the countryside and historic sites of advertising, a longstanding goal of historic preservation, with the slogan "Germans, cleanse the image of your *Heimat*." Critical of the "liberal commercial spirit" that covered natural and historic sites with inappropriate swaths of color and verbiage, the campaign wanted to create a physical environment in which "every right-thinking German can once again feel healthy."[54] This language found direct support in urban renewal programs, whose collective name had a hygienic or biological connotation insofar that renewal could refer to the health of an urban "organism." Hans Vogts, city conservator in Cologne in 1933 and an "unpolitical" man in the eyes of his successors, nonetheless openly called for a *Sanierung* of buildings and a "purification [*Bereinigung*] of the image of the city" in the rather seedy Rhine Quarter (also called the

Martinsviertel) near the Cologne cathedral. This included eliminating un-desirable people and replacing them with "valuable national comrades." Such goals were realized in practice, as two-thirds of all renewed properties changed hands in Cologne, and owners were contractually obligated to the city to rent only to morally fit "Aryan" persons.[55]

Vogts was no National Socialist. His interest in urban renewal stemmed mainly from a genuine concern for the future of the German city and a wish to make preservation deal with more than "the maintenance of a single building." Taking part in urban renewal schemes meant that the protectors of historic places could be intimately involved in the "national economy and social policy." But one did not have to be a Nazi to use racial language, be-cause racial thinking permeated so many areas of society. Moreover, Vogts's distaste for the pickpockets, prostitutes, and swindlers of the Martinsviertel was shared widely by the general populace.[56] The line between "purifica-tion" of buildings and neighborhoods and "ethnic cleansing" is distinct, but it could be crossed when a murderous racial politics became the regulator of projects to renew urban districts.

In this period official inventories of monuments took up the themes of mythical decline and transience, also signifiers of National Socialist ideol-ogy. Prepared before 1933, the inventory for the city of Speyer featured a preface by well-known Bavarian conservator Georg Lill that struck a tone thoroughly in line with National Socialist discourse. Justifying the sheer monumentality of the book's size (815 pages), Lill wrote that the inventory consisted not just of descriptions of present-day Speyer but of monuments destroyed in the city's turbulent history. "Speyer's physiognomy rises up like an image in the mist from the ruins of the past, as with so much of Ger-man history," wrote Lill. "So it is that ethical-national motives are stronger than art-historical and topographical principles in order to create not an inventory of that which exists in the present but an overview of what once was."[57] Lill created a virtual city in this passage, a community like the second city of the dead in Calvino's evocative description of the imaginary Laudo-mania. In one sense such ghoulishness was thoroughly consistent with the larger project of preservation, a cultural practice that in spite of itself re-mained fixated on the dead rather than the living. But regardless of the Bavarian conservator's intention, this was also imagery fitting for a regime that designed buildings to retain their grandeur as ruins. Just ten years later, the once-whole physiognomy of many German cities would indeed arise like an image in the mist of the cruel winters of postwar Germany.

Racialist and mythic discourse supported an expansion of the definition of monuments beyond that which any previous period had seen, a develop-ment to which the sheer length of the Speyer inventory gave unmistakable

Bavarian conservator Georg Lill on the Speyer cathedral, 1934: "At no other such building do the monumental architectural ideas of one of the greatest periods of German history, the era of universal power of the Holy Roman Empire, crystallize so distinctly." (photo: *Deutsche Dome des Mittelalters*, 33)

expression. The expansion of the number of objects under consideration by preservationists also suggested that the image of national community had been extended horizontally and vertically, and here, too, inventories were indicative of the trend. The forty-first volume of the inventory for Westphalia, published in 1935, concentrated on post-1700 "profane" monuments for the city of Münster and included many vernacular buildings. Much of its photography departed from the practice of previous inventories by situating monuments in everyday contexts. We find a little girl standing in front of a sixteenth-century house on the Rothenburg, cars parked in front of a row of eighteenth-century residences on Ägidiistraße, and flowers in front of a 200-year-old house in the Wilmergasse. Although most photos in this and other inventories featured the monuments themselves and were without human figures, there was now enough of a human presence, a social ambience, that reflected a sense of the nation "living" its historic places.[58] That the nation was now interpreted in the biologistic terms of Nazi discourse transformed such ambience into regime propaganda. When the German public called for a wider understanding of monuments in the 1970s, one of the embedded but unacknowledged meanings of this vernacularist tradition was a biologistic sense of national community.

If preservationists' sense of the nation was deeper and wider, national memory was now also an object of greater manipulation. In Cologne from 1933 to 1938 the renewal of the Martinsviertel resulted in much destruction, as sixty-five buildings were torn down and many others substantially modified. Whole houses were moved to different lots. Pieces from the destroyed buildings were used liberally to redecorate new or restored houses, as when a nearly 300-year-old iron wall tie from one house was used on another because it fit well with the new structure's window frames. A beautiful, richly decorated lintel from the eighteenth century found in the cellar of one destroyed house was placed in the entrance of a shop at a nearby site. Planners used uniform street lanterns for the entire quarter and replaced the old blue enamel street signs common throughout the rest of Cologne with chiseled limestone signs of the kind that graced some early nineteenth-century cities.[59]

Contemporary conservators as well as their successors understood that such modifications made the renewed district not only a referent of past ages but principally a monument to preservation of the 1930s. Hans Vogts had reservations about what had been done to public memory at the moment he was involved in the renewal project, saying in 1936 that "naturally it is not to be overlooked or avoided that in their totality these measures do away with much of the district's picturesque charm, its patina of age."[60] Yet this play with the past did little to detract from urban renewal as a project of national memory. Rather, it reinforced a process whereby National Socialism transformed memory through performance and tenth-of-a-second destruction. Above all, from the point of view of its potential popular resonance, it aimed to make history more entertaining, less threatening, and generally "cleaner" than the very "dirty" history Germans had gone through in the previous two decades.

Preservation was not an isolated instance of the expanding leisure industry's impact on historical memory. The increasingly popular *Heimat* museum "had stopped being a site for the idle musing of the eccentric," read a 1936 account. "Everywhere we see the effort to make 'dead' things come alive for the *Volk*."[61] There is no lack of examples of how this effort to make the history of the *Volk* lively also resulted in much manipulation. The *Heimat* museum of the village of Goch, site of an eleventh-century settlement hard on the Dutch border, moved into a historic patrician house in 1938, planning to use its courtyard for the reconstruction of a small *Bürger* residence torn down in another part of the town that would serve as a facsimile of a cigar maker's workshop. The Rhenish city Wesel planned a "museum district" that included not only a newly restored room of the garrison headquarters where Frederick the Great met his father after the prodigal son had run away, but also "a pottery workshop . . . in which every museum visitor has the opportunity to study the making of beautiful and authentic pottery; a completely new kind of museum exhibit."[62] The pottery workshop was an early example of something that has now become an international trend, namely a kind of historicist science fiction in which the attempt is made not just to preserve historic sites but to replicate past lifestyles and techniques. Building in part on the increased public interest in technical monuments of the 1920s, these museums planned exhibits designed to attract not the cultured but a less educated and sophisticated audience. In short, they wanted to appeal not to connoisseurs but to mass consumers of a new social history whose ultimate referent was the *Volk*.

Preservationists and museum officials were not just accommodating public demand. They were also intuiting an important shift in the way Germans had begun to visualize the nation. A 1938 discussion of "the art of lighting effects" and "light-painting" in the Vienna University Church considered not only how to make it easier for congregations to read their hymnals but how artifacts such as historical altars might be presented effectively to the general public. An assistant in the provincial conservator's office of Bonn wrote the district president in Aachen in 1941 advocating modifications in plans for routing the autobahn junction near Aachen. The proposed minor rerouting toward the west would not only save the moated, late medieval fortress Kalhofen, slated for restoration when peace came, but also create an "especially charming" view for the autobahn driver, who would gaze at the Kalhofen garden from his or her window.[63] In these and many other instances a more aestheticized and consumerist display of monuments was being proposed, one that suited a secular transformation of the referents and means whereby Germans imagined themselves as a nation. One could make the same argument about how Nazism used war monuments, or the way Speer aestheticized Nazi Party rallies with his "cathedral of ice" created by upturned floodlights, an interesting parallel to preservationists' use of light to display medieval landmarks. But this more consumerist approach to preservation was ultimately woven more deeply into the way Germans were seeing their environment and each other, indeed in the way they were experiencing the nation.

These shifts in consuming, seeing, and signifying have parallels elsewhere. In the United States, which was decried by many Germans as a "country without history," the 1941 Historic American Buildings Survey included the following subject headings: "barns and sheds, blacksmith shops, canal locks, convents, dairies, dog-run-type buildings, fences, fire stations, furnaces, jails, kilns, observatories, pounds, railroad stations, shot towers, well structures, and windmills." Americans, too, had widened their vision of the role of material culture in national memory, in theory if not

The autobahn as a window on the commercialized history and landscape of the nation. Constructed from 1937 to 1939, this autobahn bridge by celebrated architect Paul Bonatz framed a monument in Limburg an der Lahn. (photo: Friedrich Tamms, "Paul Bonatz," *Die Baukunst*, December 1942, 228)

entirely in practice. Indeed, they were well ahead of the Germans in considering industrial artifacts as objects of historic interest. Their approach to preserving these things had also become more activist, or to put it negatively, more manipulative. In 1926, just as the restoration of Williamsburg was being planned, Henry Ford began to assemble Greenfield Village in Dearborn, Michigan. Interested in a more practical and engaging form of historical memory than that given by schools, Ford reassembled ninety old buildings to represent U.S. development through invention, agriculture, and technology.[64] Like some of the Germans we have discussed, Ford was engaged in the commercial mediation of national memory through historic preservation. Commenting on the Williamsburg project, Viennese professor Hans Tietze wrote in 1936 that "historical-unhistorical" artifacts represented an American sense of authenticity that was foreign to most European societies.[65] That there were significant differences between U.S. and European appropriations of the past cannot be denied. But Tietze failed to point out that Germans had also gone a long way toward manipulating historic buildings and artifacts for a public whose gaze was increasingly shaped by the visual imagery and emotional draw of a commercializing society.

Taking a somewhat longer view, it is a considerable distance from the

German examples to history theme parks and other mass-market phenomena of the 1980s and 1990s. But such phenomena are on the horizon in Hitler's Germany and elsewhere in the Western world in ways they were not just a generation before. One of the great differences, beside those of scale, geography, and social use, was that the Rhine quarters, *Heimat* museums, and artistically illuminated historic cathedrals of the 1930s were inflected by the hypernationalism of the Hitler regime. Still, to the extent that historic preservationists funded, advised, and oversaw many such projects, they were fully engaged in the playful selling of what had become anything but a playful national history. When Nazi Party officials entertained foreign guests in Frankfurt am Main, they invariably treated them to a chicken dinner in one of the many good *Altstadt* restaurants and then strolled through the half-timbered fantasy world of the recently renewed historic center.[66] The juxtaposition of fun and barbarism, kitsch and death, is frightening, but one must see through it to realize that Nazism was not determining but rather following a secular development. Molding new hearts for the regime entailed techniques of public presentation and manipulation of national history shared widely with all societies undergoing the vigorous development of a consumer culture.

Despite their contribution to the regime, most preservationists never tried to articulate their work fully with the cultural policies of Nazism. Their aim was to situate themselves securely in the political culture but also to establish distance from it. Of course this not only could be said for many forms of cultural politics; it also matched Goebbels's view of the relationship between culture and power. The propaganda czar of the Third Reich was convinced that intellectuals needed room to maneuver if the national culture was not to seem unilaterally steered from above. But preservationists wanted even more distance. They strove for what I have called elsewhere (and with a different emphasis) a privileged marginality:[67] privileged because the work of protecting historic buildings was already imbricated with the language of state cultural policy and elite social networks, but marginal because National Socialist hegemony over cultural politics was unquestioned, because historic preservation neither resisted it actively nor regretted serving it during the dictatorship, and because preservationists believed their agenda was different from that of other cultural institutions because of the nature of preservation practice and the objects and images it engaged. Above all, preservationists considered their work marginal because, their adaptation to contemporary developments notwithstanding, they felt that protecting historic buildings put them at odds with a future-oriented, fast-moving society that had abandoned the nineteenth-century idea of linear progress for a racist utopia beyond modernity. Sixty years earlier Nietzsche

A site for strollers and guests of the Nazi regime, the historical fantasy world of the Frankfurt am Main *Altstadt* as it appeared in the 1930s (photo: Bildarchiv Foto Marburg/Art Resource, New York)

disparagingly referred to the "history-hungry" of his age who became "walking encyclopedias" crammed with knowledge of bygone "ages, customs, arts, philosophies[, and] religions."[68] Preservationists wanted history to engage "life," but there was enough of the nineteenth century, enough of the historicist history-hungry in them to make Nietzsche's harsh judgment applicable to the 1930s. Preservationists now turned this approach to the past into a resource, a cultural-political weapon that had important implications for their view of the nation.

Many preservationists insisted that "practical conservation," the application of preservation theory in daily life, remained "an art of the single case and a science of the borderline that barely tolerates any principle that cannot be contradicted or at least found to have exceptions." The cautious, case-by-case nature of preservation was hardly conducive to the desire of Nazi hierarchs for tenth-of-a-second performance. The conservator was a combination of administrator, art historian, architect, and diplomat. He was called to advise religious congregations that wanted to remodel parts of a historic church and to help city mayors adapt historic buildings and ensembles to traffic needs. "In such cases," Breslau professor Dagobert Frey wrote, "the conservator cannot be satisfied with policing functions; rather he must advise, assist, and help others to have some backbone. One could speak of a pastoral preservation."[69]

The pastoral metaphor regulated preservationists' sense of their contribution to national identity. As in all metaphors, certain "entailment relationships" were at work here.[70] If the preservationist was like a pastor, then his audiences, which potentially included the whole German *Volk*, were congregations whose worship was shaped by the formal attributes of a liturgy. The pastor used vestments and artifacts—indeed, the church as a whole—to continue liturgical traditions and engage the loyalties of the audiences. Historic buildings were key artifacts of the national congregation's liturgical practice. Preservationists were the pastors who ensured that such artifacts would not only be available but would be used properly.

Such imaginary relationships suggested that nineteenth-century traditions of spiritualizing national identity were still important even if they found a point of engagement with Nazism's racialization of the nation. The difference between the two paradigms, between spiritualization and racialization, was vividly reflected in the artifacts that best represented them. Although preservationists concentrated more systematically than ever on peasant buildings and urban vernacular ensembles, they had not forsaken their love for the cathedrals of Cologne, Speyer, and other cities. Medieval Christian architecture above all still served as the regulator of preservationists' national vision. Conversely, for Nazism, although medieval townscapes still worked as backdrops to the mobilization of the nation, it was the Nuremberg parade grounds or the Berlin Olympic stadium that most evocatively engaged the imagination of the *Volk*. Between the hushed tones of worshipers and tourists in the Cologne cathedral and the roars of massed crowds of the Berlin stadium there were, of course, important similarities; both emanated from people who were spectators of and participants in national "total works of art." Journalist William Shirer realized this when he likened the atmosphere of a 1934 Nuremberg party rally to the religious fervor of a Christmas service in a great Gothic cathedral.[71] But the differences were more striking than the congruences, and they were not only a matter of style. The churchgoer ideally contemplated his or her place in God's creation in the national church, but the comrade of the racial community shouted mindlessly to demonstrate allegiance to the mass. Within this difference, preservation's pastoral metaphor, the product of a larger set of historical relationships, intentionally set limits to Nazism's racialization of past and present.

Cultural Revolution?

How might one characterize the representation and appropriation of historic buildings by those outside the circle of history-hungry preservationists up to World War II? Did such representations support or hinder the cultural revolution? To address these questions, it must be emphasized that Nazism aimed not only to instrumentalize historical places but also the people who viewed them. At first glance historic places and their users and admirers appeared to have been thoroughly under National Socialist control in party festivals and rallies. Historic buildings were prominent in the festival culture of Nazism because many party functions took place not in new stadiums but in the historic centers of cities and towns. Film and painting often prescribed how these mass spectacles and urban settings were to be imagined. Of all the regime-supported representations of historic buildings in the Third Reich, Riefenstahl's filmic images in *Triumph of the Will* of massed audiences filing through the decorated Nuremberg *Altstadt* during the 1934 party rally were perhaps some of the most interesting artistically. Riefenstahl's work was realistic. The Nazis favored realism because it was ostensibly more understandable to the masses and supposedly more useful in preparing people for future action, as when realistic motifs on war monuments were thought to stimulate support for the war to come.[72] Yet Riefenstahl's marching columns past Nuremberg historic houses presented an ideal of contemporary enthusiasm and national solidarity. Creating new German hearts relied not on pictures of the real per se but on prescriptive, myth-inspired pictures of what the real should be. Historic buildings increased a sense that the ideal had become the real in Riefenstahl's cinema because they could be associated with the tangible and seemingly unmovable reality of the nation itself.

There were, of course, other less representational views of historic architecture associated with Nazi festival culture, such as Paul Herrmann's 1942 painting *The Flag*. This work reduced Munich's well-known historic cityscape to a shadowy mass of geometric shapes and turrets framing the 1923 Beer Hall putschists, with Hitler among them.[73] Like the cult of Schlageter, the Munich putsch was part of the cycle of celebrations and rituals organized by the party. Werner Rittich, coeditor with Speer of *Art in the German Reich*, said of this "historical picture" that "here the representation of the March of November 9 develops into a picture in which celebration and honor, responsibility informed by an awareness of fate, energetic will to life, past and present, action and participation, resonate together to become a unified whole." With its abstraction from the specific outlines of the Munich cityscape, *The Flag* was even more historical-unhistorical than Willamsburg or renewed German urban districts were. Nonetheless, it situated the myth of the Beer Hall Putsch in a wider national narrative because it evoked the well-known physiognomy of one of Germany's most pictured cities.

The drive of Nazi festival culture to instrumentalize monuments as well as masses involved directing the populace to perform its appointed role in spectacles of racial-national solidarity. It is necessary to emphasize how Nazi use and public reception of historic buildings were transformed in the process. Historic buildings had been a backdrop for many different kinds of festivals in the past. But just as Nazi architecture was designed to dominate public spaces, historic buildings, when recontextualized in Nazi collective action, were literally designed to leave participants speechless, to end communication. When the NSDAP celebrated a new Schlageter monument in Düsseldorf in May 1933, the party organ *Volksparole* vividly described the role the city center played in bringing about public adulation: "The dignity of the festival, its size and importance, made its impression on the cityscape. No house without flags, no streets without rows of facades decorated in greenery.... Never before had Düsseldorf, indeed, one could say, never before had a city in Germany seen a richly colorful spectacle such as this. Words no longer suffice, the eyes cannot grasp everything. Incalculable masses of spectators and marching columns in brown, black, gray and blue."[74]

Nazi instrumentalization of historic buildings gained popular support outside the cycle of official festivals and rallies. The widened view of historic places supported by urban renewal projects found additional resonance in popular publications such as primers that portrayed entire cities—Greifs-

Paul Herrmann's *The Flag* reduced Munich's historic cityscape to a mass of geometric shapes. (photo: Zentralinstitut für Kunstgeschichte, Munich)

wald, Regensburg, Berlin, Goslar, Hamburg, Munich—as "sites of memory of [Germany's] heroes and the deeds of its heroes and people." Public interest in monuments of social history corresponded to National Socialist wishes to create more popular attachment to a wide range of historical places. Wesel's previously mentioned historic pottery workshop in a local

An end to communication: the decorated Nuremberg *Altstadt* as background to the spectacle of seemingly endless marching columns of SA men in 1933 (photo: Heiss, *Bei Uns in Deutschland*, 52)

museum received "great applause" from visitors, and the Geldern county museum's exhibits of peasant artifacts gained enthusiastic responses from German as well as Dutch tourists.[75] Popular interest in peasant culture was of course ironic at a moment when many rural youth used groups such as the Hitlerjugend to escape the rigidity of country life, when many rural people grew increasingly disillusioned with the regime's economic and cultural policies, and when during the war urban dwellers fleeing from the bombs created friction with rural hosts when they found the countryside lacking in modern amenities.[76] The construction of a peasant past, both a National Socialist strategy from above and a popular movement from below, passed right by the social reality of German rural life.

Although museum-goers and tourists were interested in urban, technical, or peasant artifacts, Germans did not abandon their love for the more traditional public symbols of national history. Party publications such as the glossy *Art in the German Reich* ran many well-received features on the traditional monuments of German architecture. The most popular touristic outing within the Nazi leisure organization Kraft durch Freude was the one- or two-day trip to a German resort or a city with many famous landmarks. The *Blue Books* and other illustrated publications continued to present romanticized visions of the most famous German landmarks and landscapes stripped of people and conflict, although they often did so with the most up-to-date technical means, as in one of the Langewiesche volumes on aerial views of German cities and the countryside. The Drachenfels, with its famous castle ruins, remained "the most visited mountain in Europe," and its popularity was enhanced by plans for a "modern restaurant and hotel with all amenities that will be accessible to the entire *Volk* and affordable for every pocketbook."[77]

Nazism reduced monuments and their audiences to instruments of a politics of racial performance, but audiences also willingly participated in this process. Local populations took part in decorating market squares and buildings along parade routes, an action made easier by the distribution of free decorative material to private houses, as when people in Tübingen, Rothenburg, and other Swabian towns got greenery to decorate their houses for the First of May celebration in 1933. The Nazified names of the streets used in such processions were also often products of popular action rather than National Socialist direction. Soon after Hitler was appointed chancellor, Germans renamed streets, squares, and public buildings after the Führer. Preservationists worried about this trend when it obliterated historical place names, but so did Nazi leaders, who in a decree of April 1933 asked Germans to "refrain from altering historical markers" and reminded them that "only that which the national revolution has itself built for the future can carry its name and the names of its leading figures." German manufacturers produced mugs, playing cards, and postcards linking Nazism with national monuments such as the Brandenburg Gate, and by May 1933 officials had become so anxious about the flood of "tasteless national symbols" that they began a campaign to elevate public taste. Germans' interest in both vernacu-

„Das ganze Deutschland soll es sein!"

Nazi kitsch included postcards of famous landmarks, as when the Brandenburg Gate and other artifacts were used to symbolize affinities between Hitler and Bismarck. By May 1933 officials had assembled enough questionable items to create a small museum of "tasteless national symbols." (photo: Württembergisches Landesmuseum) lar architecture and grand public symbols was encouraged by the regime, but such love for historical places was also based on established cultural traditions.[78]

No better example of the relationship between prior memory-work and Nazi goals could be given than *Heimat* culture, which remained one of the key areas for popular appropriations of historic architecture. Here Nazism provided the context for activities that existed well before 1933 but lacked the political focus Nazism gave them. There was no shortage of *Heimat* associations in the Third Reich. In 1938 Aachen county (not including the city) had eleven such associations ranging in size from 12 to more than 100 members. The county also had a historical society with 50 members; five branches of the Eifelverein, the largest with 250 members; and an association for the protection of birds, with 80 members.[79] The range of activities was wide and varied. *Heimat* associations supported and advised "family researchers," or *Sippenforscher*, who used archival materials, birth and death notices, and even heirlooms to research family histories. Promoted by Nazi racial policy, which required applicants for state and party offices to submit "ancestor charts" proving Aryan heritage, professional and amateur family researchers built a cottage industry linking the antiquarian and the national, familial, and racial memory. Avid participants of *Heimat* groups, schoolteachers were among the most active collectors of archaeological artifacts for public and educational purposes. Regime campaigns to beautify cities and villages also received much fanfare from *Heimat* associations, as when the *Heimatverein* "Alde Düsseldorfer" exhorted its members to support the local NSDAP's 1941 campaign for the "cleansing and correction of disfigurement" of historic buildings and squares.[80]

After all the regime's efforts to create a cultural revolution, a large part of local cultural activity was still organized by rather unremarkable groups that existed before 1933. Celebrating fifty years of existence in 1938, the Eifelverein is a good case from the Rhineland.[81] Its leaders boasted that it had been unnecessary to "coordinate" the club in 1933 because it had always stood for "*Volk, Heimat*, and the Frontier." Leading members of the NSDAP and state officials belonged to the organization throughout the dictatorship. In the dark days of 1944 its language was completely fascist, expressing love for the "Führer, steely hard in his will and decisiveness to hold out, come what may." Yet right alongside this unambiguous commitment to Nazism, the organization's actual use of historic places had more to do with the past than the present. As it had before 1933, the *Verein* promoted the Eifel as a tourist attraction, a goal that meshed perfectly with Nazi efforts to beautify towns. As before 1933, the club's *Heimat* almanac remained a popular item precisely because its focus was on "the history, culture and economy of *the*

Eifel"—and not on some larger area with which local people had trouble identifying—as one official reminded the NSDAP in 1937.[82] Publication of the association newsletter, support for preservation projects on various monuments, and membership meetings all remained part and parcel of the homely machinery of *Heimat* culture. It is difficult to say how deeply Nazi ideology intervened in the Eifelverein's ongoing use of local history, but it is certain that local use continued in forms on which the regime had little effect. Nazism could be accommodated within the work of this particular association just as it could be sloughed off after 1945. No necessary connection existed between thinking *Heimat* and advocating Nazi goals.

Artistic representations and popular appropriations of historic buildings may have strengthened the National Socialist cultural revolution, but not all Germans were convinced that Nazism obligated them to love such national symbols. The Nazi regime spent far less on public housing policy than the Weimar Republic did, especially after the push to rearm in 1935–36, and its campaigns to beautify cities and towns were based in part on the practical need to get public institutions and private property owners to contribute voluntarily. Here there was an ambiguous record. In Tübingen a local newspaper admitted that village beautification initiatives in the surrounding area "had not exactly aroused distinct enthusiasm in each and every community." In Rothenburg ob der Tauber a special program, Hilfswerk Alt-Rothenburg, had to be organized in 1937 to help the city restore its many historic walls and towers. Part of the plan was to get private property owners voluntarily to do more to keep up "the cultural property entrusted to them" by the nation and contribute more financially to the project. As of 1939 the results were disappointing.[83]

In these and other instances Nazism did little to get the German people to cross the line preservationists had always had difficulty getting them to cross: the line separating a general cultural interest in historic places from a willingness to make large-scale, long-term financial sacrifices to protect them. This was due in part to the fact that the Nazi Party's desire for performance put it on the side of antipreservationist concerns just as often as not, especially when it came to economic issues. Public criticism of the "sheet metal pestilence" that spread sheet metal siding and roofs over historic buildings and scenic areas was met by the regime with halfhearted attempts at regulation, partly because the sheet metal industry had done much to convince Nazi leaders of its economic importance.[84] Ostensibly designed to control advertising in the countryside, Goebbels's Advertising Council of the German Economy actually opened more opportunities for advertisers in 1934, and when Westphalian factory owner and *Heimat* activist Wilhelm Münker pressed the regime and advertisers for stiffer regulations, he was placed in protective custody in late 1940.[85] In these and many other instances, public demand for more protection of historic places was met with policies that reflected the hard economic realities associated with the cultural revolution.

Beyond the larger cultural-political struggles caused by Nazism's activities in its triangular relationship with preservation and the economy, the era was punctuated by the same kinds of small daily struggles between property and history that had occurred in previous decades. A 1936 conflict between Rhenish conservator Wolff Metternich and the *Oberbürgermeister* of Aachen over renovations done to the facade of a historic house on the Aachen market square without the conservator's knowledge could have occurred just as easily in the 1920s or before World War I. In this instance a local apothecary had modified the windows and placed the term *Apotheke* four different times on the facade, which Metternich felt was a violation of the local preservation ordinance. In the same year, owners of an Aachen thermal spring fountain listed as a monument, seeking to avoid the notoriety of being called "The Waters for Acrobats," encountered resistance from Metternich when they asked permission to modify the well to make it easier for their elderly rheumatic customers to negotiate the steps to the healing waters. Their plans were approved only after much modification.[86] These rather pedestrian frictions continued to occupy individuals and organizations whose uses of historic places revolved mainly around economic rather than cultural or historical interests.

The foregoing indicates that public uses of historic buildings revealed broad national support for the Nazi cultural aim of molding new hearts imbued with love for Germany. Like Karl Scheffler, who introduced the popular blue book of aerial views of German cities and the countryside, people wanted to "contribute to the idea of a spiritual and cultural unity—in the diverse forms of the German Fatherland and the diverse stirrings of the individual German."[87] Yet the ways in which unity was pursued ultimately had more to do with past experiences than with the radical opening to the future Nazism entailed. No complete Nazification occurred. Long-standing tensions between the preservationist lobby, its elite as well as popular audiences, and the larger society continued. German hearts were still pulled in often contradictory directions by the societal forces that shaped national memory as it developed in reference to the physical environment of towns and cities.

Sodom and Gomorrah

Respected conservator Dagobert Frey reacted to World War II by noting that the "unprecedented victorious advance of German troops" in Poland was beneficial to cultural policy because it rapidly removed historic places from harm's way. Similarly, according to another expert, in Lorraine the expected destruction of both man-made and natural environments along the Maginot Line was avoided because of the "development of the military campaign, which only in isolated instances brought heavy fighting and the destruction associated with it."[88] Such remarks must be seen in the context of assumptions that regarded wartime cultural policy as a cultural mission linked to a permanent political settlement rather than a mere provisional stewardship over monuments in occupied areas. For Poland this had especially brutal overtones, as Frey announced that the thousand-year cultural mission in Poland had entered a "new decisive phase," that Gothic churches in Poland vividly reflected "the overpowering expression of German settlement and the stream of creative German national power," and that the immediate art-historical goal was to "win back" historically rooted German cultural property in the new territories. What damage had been done to important medieval architecture of Warsaw was a result of the "senseless resistance" of the Poles. To carry out rational preservation and prevent further destruction, German cultural officials would conduct a cultural blitzkrieg in which they would "as quickly as possible take over Polish preservation agencies with their archival holdings, photographs, and plans."[89]

Frey reacted opportunistically to the invasion, seeing it as an opening for his own art-historical research on Silesia and Poland. He is credited with having argued successfully against the dynamiting of the Warsaw Castle in 1939 and 1940, but he never questioned the brutal German occupation of the country. In this he was hardly exceptional. A virtual army of cultural officials saw eastward expansion as a great opportunity to advance research and careers, to say nothing of German influence. Berlin art historian Niels von Holst echoed Frey's opportunism when he outlined plans to reassert German influence in the Baltic, where according to von Holst, Latvians and Estonians had labored to remove traces of German history from churches and public squares, and where during a single year of dictatorship the Soviet Union destroyed many historic buildings. In Reval, Riga, and other Baltic communities preservationists would have much to offer in the Nazi-led "new formation" of Eastern cities.[90]

The German army's program for the protection of monuments and art treasures, or *Kunstschutz*, must be seen in the light of this aggressive historical perspective.[91] It began for occupied territories in May 1940 under the direction of the high command of the army, dealing with movable as well as stationary objects. It existed only where regular military governments were organized, including France, Belgium, Serbia, parts of Greece, and, later, Italy, but excluding Norway, Denmark, Holland, and the brutalized Eastern territories. Based on World War I techniques, *Kunstschutz* authorities wanted to protect cultural property from wartime damage and administer monuments and art objects in a way that would not only prevent them from being moved during the war but also make them available to German museum officials, art historians, and collectors. They had some clear successes, protecting more than 500 castles and their interiors in France and assisting local authorities in the restoration and maintenance of historic sites in many other areas. Propaganda films celebrated such actions, portraying the sensitivity and care German officers and soldiers demonstrated for other cultures.[92] As in World War I, German authorities wanted to prove to the outside world they were not barbarians and that the permanent political hegemony of Germans in Europe would not lead to the destruction of its most cherished cultural property.

Rhenish art historian Wolff Metternich was put in charge of *Kunstschutz* in western Europe, serving in this position until June 1942, when he was first put on extended leave and then fired by Hermann Goering. Arguing that no art objects should be removed from Western territories until after a peace settlement, Metternich represented the more "correct" approach to cultural property shared by certain high-ranking military officials. His well-placed caution earned him his dismissal. He was certainly no match for organizations such as Alfred Rosenberg's Einsatzstab Reichsleiter Rosenberg (ERR), whose founding Hitler had ordered. On 30 June 1940 Hitler circulated a memorandum instructing German forces to identify all cultural objects of German provenance with the ultimate aim of returning them to the fatherland. The ERR's official goal was to "safeguard" this property, but its practical effect was to plunder cultural objects left behind by Jews and others. It competed not only with the military, who resented Hitler's order to give the ERR full assistance, but also with other plunderers, most notably the avaricious Goering and his representatives, who fell over one another collecting valuable paintings, furniture, and other artifacts throughout Europe. It was this rapacious activity, and not the less visible but more responsible *Kunstschutz*, that has marked the historical record of German wartime actions toward the cultural treasures of enemy countries.[93]

If the war encouraged preservationists to see *Kunstschutz* in long-term historical perspectives of German cultural might throughout Europe, it also prompted reflections on the longer evolution of monument preservation itself. When the 100th anniversary of Karl Friedrich Schinkel's death occurred on 9 October 1941, it moved Günther Grundmann, writing in the *DKD*, to point out that Schinkel's efforts to save historical places represented the dawn of modern preservation at a time when, as in the present "eventful and hectic" days, all of Europe held its breath as Napoleon returned from his exile on the island of Elba.[94] The unstated message was that German preservation would again be called on to respond to world-historical events. Accordingly, the *DKD* paid much attention to monuments in occupied areas, the growing destruction of German cities, and the battlefield deaths of its contributors and readers. In a 1944 newspaper article Hans Bahn of the Hamburg Conservator's Office portrayed preservationists as fighters in the "battle over art" and exhorted them to be "more dogged" in their efforts to save the "last portal, the last fragment of a gable in the *Altstadt* alleys."[95] Conservators, churches, and city building authorities stored valuable medieval and Renaissance stained-glass windows endangered by wartime bombing and cooperated with the art history research association Deutscher Verein für Kunstwissenschaft to catalog these artifacts and determine what Germany possessed in this long-neglected genre of historic preservation. This effort enabled Germany to catch up with England and France, for art history scholars in these countries had already produced general overviews on the subject.[96]

More extensive actions to protect domestic historic buildings from war damage were hindered by regime efforts to avoid unnecessary disruptions of public confidence. Not until the bombing of Lübeck in July 1942, the first really destructive raid on a German city, did the Luftwaffe's council on civil air defense hold a general meeting in Berlin that planned the protection of cultural treasures. Even when a more deliberate response was developed, it could not be very discriminating except for the most important monuments, since the goal was to clear the rubble for military purposes. Too, Speer's elite staff for rebuilding damaged cities, organized in 1943, was much less interested in monument protection than in solving urban traffic problems. During the years of worst damage, the work of professional conservators was limited by shortages of human and material resources, and their efforts to cope became the stuff of exemplary postwar narratives. Hanna Adenauer, niece of the future West German chancellor and, later, Cologne city conservator, personally arranged to have trucks and drivers transport medieval altarpieces and statuettes from Cologne churches to storage depots outside the city in 1943 and 1944. Public willingness to protect historic objects and buildings was strictly limited, most obviously because the goal for many Germans, even those who were better-off or strategically situated to make cultural policy, was simple survival. Cologne reconstruction began in 1941 when Konrad Adenauer and a few close associates formed a team of experts, but the level of destruction quickly delayed effective action until after the war.[97]

In World War I, Germans had urged French and Belgian cities to take a functional approach to destruction, integrating the war's effects into routine longer-term urban planning. They now applied the same reasoning to the growing piles of rubble in their own cities. The same Hans Bahn who would exhort fellow conservators to fight bitterly to save the last historical gable in an *Altstadt* alley also calmly considered the advantages of intermittent destruction, arguing in effect that the war could accomplish some of the things preservationists had wanted all along. In Hamburg before June 1943, bombing raids destroyed no monument of real importance, and the cleanup enabled preservationists to make mild restorations of buildings. Conversely, the Anglo-American terror raids of July and August 1943, codenamed Gomorrah, caused extraordinary destruction in the old town center, necessitating "a reorientation of preservationist thinking." This did not change the general principle that wartime destruction should be used to accomplish old goals but, rather, made it more urgent. It was true that the war had ended hopes of having a well-integrated "zone for monuments" (*Denkmalzone*) in the center of Hamburg, but many historic buildings were still standing, and many old facades and building parts could be integrated into new ensembles. Some Hamburgers feared that preservation as previously practiced was no longer possible, said Bahn, but in fact preservation could offer "stimulus and impulse" to a rebuilding that would lead the great city "out of the unculture of the last seventy years."[98] Not just for preservationists but for the majority of planners during and after the war, the famous British motto applied: "a disaster, but an opportunity."[99]

Not all Germans reacted so opportunistically to the loss of cultural artifacts. The war caused unprecedented damage to Germany's stock of historic church bells, as some 90,000 bells were either destroyed by bombing or melted down by a regime thirsty for metal reserves. As in World War I, preservationists undertook an emergency inventory and, thanks to Hiecke's negotiations with state agencies, saved the most valuable bells. But an emotional public reaction drove preservation, as church congregations "became aware of the priceless treasure hidden inside their walls."[100] Clergy and other officials hid bells, "lost" keys to bell towers, wrote anonymous letters criticizing the action, held special church services when the bells were delivered, and insulted government officials requisitioning bells. In a small Bavarian town in 1942, women who had been awarded the German Mothers' Cross of Honor for having four or more children threw their medals at the *Landrat* and building inspector who had come to collect the local church bell. The bell was delivered a few days later only after several leaders of the demonstration were taken into custody. The requisitioning reminded some churchgoers of the dark days of World War I, and at one of the special services commemorating the departure of a church bell in 1940, a Protestant congregant was overheard saying, "It is bad luck to fight a war with bells, they tried

WHERE GERMAN HEARTS ARE MOLDED

that in the last war and lost." Behind these reactions was a general feeling that "one was intruding in things that people consider to be sacred," as one clergyman put it in 1942. So unsuccessful was the 1940 campaign obligating communities to report the monuments and bells they possessed that the decree was renewed in 1942 to ensure a more complete accounting.[101]

Such information opens a window on the pain of those who were not just defending a cherished local monument but experiencing the dangers of air warfare. The era of the bombing raids reduced large parts of the population, most consisting of women, children, and the elderly, to getting the bare essentials of everyday life. "We climb across mountains of ruins, rummage through rubble and broken glass, crawl through unknown cellars, tear out other people's boxes and bags," wrote Berliner Ruth Andreas-Friedrich in her diary as she described efforts to find food and clothing. The "intimate community of air-raid defense" built up in one's neighborhood did not support too much thinking about the destruction of an important medieval cathedral or lavish bourgeois residence from the eighteenth century. On the morning after an air raid one could see young men and women dancing and embracing one another against the backdrop of smoking urban ruins; their lives had been spared even if the surrounding buildings had not. Berlin prostitutes used the many irregular spaces created by the ruins of the Kurfürstendamm to attract their customers.[102] Preservationist concerns about historic buildings could not have been more distant from the existence of those struggling to maintain a life, often with the bitter memory of the death of loved ones and the fear of their own death close at hand.

Nonetheless, people were moved by the "painful losses" of historic buildings that preservationists mentioned in otherwise routine reports on the war. After more than one-tenth of the historic Lübeck *Altstadt* was leveled in the Palm Sunday raid of 28 March 1942 by British bombers, Robert Hiecke's references to "the disgracefully ruined heritage of the old Hansa city" suggested not only anger but a sense of finality and widespread shock that affected all Lübecker who had emotional attachments to the destroyed twelfth-century cathedral, the Marienkirche and Petrikirche, and the *Rathaus*. Police, military, and Nazi Party reports noted that despite the populace's despair over the unprecedented destruction, there was no "sense of panic," and the "behavior of the people in the air raid shelters was exemplary." A Rhenish SA official argued that local people were deeply affected by the destruction of their historic buildings. "In quiet sadness and holy anger," he wrote of the typical Rhinelander in 1942, "he sees many of his cultural treasures sink into dust and ashes." The official insisted that people were filled with hate for the English and that their love of *Heimat* was never stronger. The regime needed to believe the public hated the enemy; the true level of bitterness felt by Germans toward Allied forces because of the loss of cultural heritage must in fact have varied tremendously. But there can be little doubt that people understood the extraordinary cultural devastation taking place around them.[103]

This understanding served as a basis for criticism veiled by a sense of fate whose origins observers were incapable or unwilling to articulate. For art connoisseur Udo von Alvensleben, who had close friends alike among those who resisted the regime and those in the military who supported it, the bombing of Berlin, like the evisceration of the culture of "old Europe," was somehow predictable, though perhaps premature. "The image of this destruction appeared to me already during peacetime," von Alvensleben wrote in his diary at the end of 1943, "but I expected it first well after my death." The characterization of war damage as a fitting punishment from heaven became more frequent as the war went on. One Catholic priest near Koblenz in May 1944 told young parishioners he was surprised that "godless cities" such as Hamburg and Berlin were not already flattened just as Sodom and Gomorrah had been. On 20 July 1944, the day of the failed attempt on Hitler's life, Regensburg police arrested a Carmelite father for sermonizing that the destruction of German cities was a holy punishment that would lead the German people back to their lost faith. He was condemned to death, but the sentence was never carried out.[104]

Church leaders also used their buildings as symbols of a new commitment to Germanness, in a successful attempt to increase church attendance and membership. Paradoxically it was no longer Nazism but the church and its physical presence that aroused memory of a common purpose and culture. One Protestant publication in Dessau argued in 1943 that "the Church is a part of our *Heimat* and a part of our entire life, physically, intellectually, and spiritually understood. . . . Our Houses of God in city and countryside . . . our popular hymns and songs . . . our German history . . . our political and social life . . . our entire national culture . . . all of this is unthinkable without Christianity and the Church."[105] When church leaders found support from preservationists and planners to rebuild Germany's damaged places of worship after the fall of Hitler, they were building on a popular religiosity engendered during the war and emotionally attached to such historic sites. Here as in so many other areas, the postwar period commenced during the Third Reich.

To the extent popular reactions to the loss of buildings such as churches can be assessed, the structures were valued as fields of care as much as they were as public symbols. Here, too, memory connoted pain. In the absence of husbands and clergymen called to the front, women played a bigger role in the everyday life of Protestant as well as Catholic churches, just as they took even greater responsibility for raising children and running households. For women more than for men, the church was a central focus of mourning for loved ones and for decorating chapels and monuments commemorating the war dead.[106] For others, losses in the physical environment had a more mundane but nonetheless important quality. "Alde Düsseldorfer" members who read their association's newsletter in 1942 and 1943 found aggressive appeals to stick together in the face of the "enemy terror attacks from the air." But beyond calls for solidarity, there was simply pain. One newsletter lamented "that our club headquarters 'Im goldenen Kessel' was destroyed in the enemy air attack on the night of 11 September 1942. Paintings, the library, mementos, and our beautiful new club flag were exterminated by the flames."[107]

As for top National Socialist officials, their response to such human concerns was to demand superhuman resistance against Western "terror attacks" and "barbarism." Moreover, they demanded that people forget, as when Goebbels wrote of his happiness that Germany's urban heritage was finally being swept away to make room for National Socialist culture, and when a Nazi official closely involved in cultural matters referred to the ruins of German cities as "the security deposit . . . for a happy future for all Germans in a strong Fatherland." Hitler thought that forgetting would mobilize Germans against the enemy, telling Albert Speer that "the less people have to lose the more fanatically they will fight."[108] In such instances Nazi ideologues created a discourse of reconstruction, which was really the discourse of *Leistung* displaced onto the memory of a postwar future. This reconstruction had an inflection much different from the one that was to come in the 1950s, but it had a similar goal: to mortgage a real confrontation with the causes of this terrible destruction for moving ahead, fighting, and rebuilding.

Not only the regime avoided a full accounting of the causes of this terrible damage to German cities. Non-Nazi groups were also willing to trade memory for a new future, to trade mourning for feverish rebuilding. Hitler told his chief architect that the bombing of German cities would make it possible to reconstruct them "even more beautifully than before." This vision resonated. The *Heimat* club "Alde Düsseldorfer" was painfully aware of how the bombing had wounded its Rhenish home, but club officials turned their attention to the future. "We are losing our cultural property, and much of it is irreplaceable, but love and loyalty to our severely tested *Heimat* city remain," read the November 1942 newsletter. "Indestructible will [our city] be in the future as well, the basis for our part in reconstruction [*Wiederaufbau*], which, so we all hope, will enable our *Heimat* and garden city to arise again in new splendor in happier times of peace."[109]

At a time when the machinery of mass death had already begun to work, this hope for the reconstruction of a new garden city on the Rhine was a projection into the future of the act of forgetting this specific, terrible past still unfolding. It was also obscene. Yet from another perspective it was a fitting commentary on the complexities of memory. The Düsseldorf club's hope for reconstruction was based in part on a memory of recent German history in which Nazi officials, participants in preservationist congresses, Hamburg city planners, and many others regarded the 1930s as a period of successful recovery from the political conflict and economic crises of the Weimar period. Armed with such short-term memory, many Germans projected this past onto a future that had to be better than the toxic present in which they lived. This was hardly only a petit bourgeois conceit. Postwar workers in the Ruhr remembering their wartime experiences would link the 1930s and the recovery of the 1950s as analogous periods of stability and security, "good times" broken by the "bad times" of war and postwar hardship.[110] On this point, Germans from very dissimilar backgrounds found a momentary locus of commonality on which they drew in the bitter years to come.

By way of conclusion, it is worth considering somewhat more the implications of this projection. Economic and "moral" recovery under Nazism was based on a total transformation of the past and future, a transvaluation of modernity itself. To project the immediate past of the 1930s into the near, post-Nazi future was to bracket the revolutionary quality of National Socialist politics and the racial war it engendered. To imagine that the unprecedented loss of historical buildings in the war might be compensated by beautiful garden cities, by a return to previous forms of religiosity, or by heightened allegiance to some publicly resonant version of German tradition was to minimize the actual historical discontinuity represented by the piles of rubble. This emergent tendency was, of course, consistent with the logic of Nazism's approach to the past, which, because of its insistence on performance in all areas of life, was far more destructive toward history than its praise of tradition would lead one to expect. Yet such normalization of the war's vast destruction and killing could also be consistent with the more mundane workings of public memory, always highly selective and now increasingly manipulative as commerce took hold more forcefully than ever of the artifacts of history. The admirers and defenders of historical buildings were less seduced by the projected narrative of recovery, but they, too, acquiesced even if their professional calling and conservative hopefulness led them to insist more decisively than others on the need to remember. Their privileged marginality within Nazi culture, a limited though palpable antidote to forgetting, could thus be carried over into the still-uncertain future that everyone longed for in the wake of the bombing. They contributed to what was in fact an impressive public embrace of the past in the years immediately after the war, as we will see. Nonetheless, before the full violence of Nazism's anticipated cultural revolution could be assessed, indeed before guilt could be fully felt and worked through, memory was articulated with a modernized and emergent imaginary of hope. This newly adjudicated relationship between the future and the past is the subject of the next chapter.

Memory resembled the shape of the brain itself, a succession of roundabouts and
curlicues, crosswalks, all of it curling in on itself, worn down like the ancient paths of the earth.
Some were cul-de-sacs, some great thoroughfares, detours, byways. Some were so tightly wound
they were like bracelets of elephant hair, impossible to pick apart without severing the strands.
Severed, the memory died. The soul withered. Memory was never just one large thing but a
multitude of small things. Memory depended on the small details that were wound in, a glass of
pilsener or an electric light, or hedges bending in the wind.

—Ward Just, *The Translator*

FIVE | COMMEMORATIVE NOISE

ilence" has been the dominant metaphor for historical
accounts of the German memory of Nazism in the imme-
diate postwar years. Referring to worldwide expectations
that Germans would mourn for the victims of the Nazi
regime, Jost Hermand makes the point succinctly. "Most
Germans," he writes, "who themselves went through
much suffering, and who during the postwar period were concerned at first
above all with sheer survival, simply said nothing about these things."[1] But
if silence about Nazism obtained in these years, is this an adequate characterization of German public memory as a whole? Had the Germans "repressed their past" completely, as Mary Fulbrook argues?[2] Had they severed
the strands of memory, allowing the public soul to wither and die? My
evidence suggests that if other areas of public memory are considered, then
commemorative "noise" rather than silence would be a more telling metaphor. Whether they discussed the reconstruction of historic buildings or
celebrated historical anniversaries, Germans demonstrated a substantial
interest in the past, "the multitude of small things"[3] constituting memory,
even as they endured severe physical hardship. Those responsible for protecting historic buildings, material referents of the cul-de-sacs, thorough-

fares, detours, and byways through which memory wove itself, were among the voices producing such commemorative noise.

Günter Grass wrote that in the immediate postwar years "there was no collapse, no absolute beginning, just sluggish and murky transitions."[4] This useful perspective allows one to mediate between historiography's all too starkly drawn interpretative choices between the "restoration" of prewar conditions and the idea of "zero hour," a decisive break with the past. Bonn scholar Hans-Peter Schwarz has argued that western German history up to about 1953 was marked simultaneously by the energies of reconstruction and the persistence of prewar history.[5] After 1953–54 the "welfare society" of the 1980s began to take shape, but before this the situation was relatively open-ended, even when people oriented themselves to the "ideas of the postwar period." "Society still seems chaotic," wrote Schwarz of the late 1940s and early 1950s, "development in the relevant sectors is highly uneven, clear patterns do not yet appear." Adopting Schwarz's chronology to Grass's idea of murky transitions, this chapter begins with a discussion of the relationship between reconstruction and public memory from 1945 to about 1953.

Murky Transitions

Over 50 million soldiers and civilians died in World War II, as Russia lost 20 million people and Poland over 6 million. Eleven million people died in Nazi concentration camps, about 6 million of whom were Jews. Germany did not escape the slaughter it unleashed, losing almost 600,000 people in the bombing of German cities alone and nearly 3 million civilians altogether. Not only had the war left untold death and suffering, it continued to plague Europeans well after the end of the fighting. Seven million foreign workers and Allied prisoners of war were still in Germany in spring 1945, and many German prisoners of war would not see their homes for years to come. Roughly 13 million Germans were homeless, most of those who came from the East in the first half decade after the war being women, children, and the elderly.

The war's human toll was grimly mirrored in the unprecedented physical destruction of European urban centers. Four hundred German bombers had leveled most of Warsaw, and in Belgium more than 2,600 cities and towns experienced war damage. The German air force had destroyed the historic city centers of Amiens, Rouen, and Beauvais in France and Rhenen, Middelburg, Wageningen, and Rotterdam in Holland. Many communities in the Soviet Union, Hungary, Yugoslavia, and Greece lay in ruins. In German cities there were 400 million cubic meters of rubble, and more than one-quarter of the country's nearly 19 million residences were destroyed. Total

The Cologne cityscape and cathedral after the bombings. Scenes such as this compelled some Germans to search desperately for "good, humane feelings and clear, rational thoughts." (photo: Rheinisches Bildarchiv, 178475)

losses were reckoned at 35 billion marks, which equaled the average annual domestic income of the German people for the prewar period. The everyday psychotopography of German cities was dominated by ruins. "I look out my window," wrote exiled actor Wolfgang Langhoff after returning to Düsseldorf, "and from across the street empty spaces and the decrepit facades of burned-out buildings stare back at me: a view that in the first two weeks makes the returnee's heart stop, but to which he soon becomes so accustomed that his eyes pass over it as if everything was in the best of shape. What can one do when destruction becomes normal and wholeness abnormal?" A sign of moral degradation as much as it was an imposing physical problem, the vista of rubble led Communist poet and, later, East German cultural minister Johannes R. Becher to wonder aloud if Germans would ever again have "good, humane feelings and clear, rational thoughts."[6]

Yet if the moral problem remained, physical destruction was not as complete as it looked, and especially after the currency reform of 1948 and the beginning of the Marshall Plan, economic trends in the zones about to become the Federal Republic of Germany (Bundesrepublik Deutschland, or BRD) began moving steadily upward. Matters developed more slowly in the East, which would become the German Democratic Republic (Deutsche Demokratische Republik, or DDR). Here Germans began rebuilding from a lower socioeconomic base, they suffered more than the West from territorial dismemberment, they lost valuable resources from Soviet demands for reparations, they were unable to keep educated citizens from moving to the West, they had no equivalent to Marshall Plan aid, and they had architects who were willing to kowtow to Soviet and German Communist ideas on reconstruction.[7]

As this contrast suggests, the pace and character of recovery were shaped by political factors, as sovereignty over the German nation passed first to the occupying powers and then to two German states, whose leaders maintained a rhetorical commitment to a single German nation but undertook different though related policies of reconstruction. West Germans wanted not only to rebuild housing but to etch in capitalist market relations, a strategy that could easily write off cultural property as a legitimate cost. A relatively hands-off policy toward the market meshed well with federalist traditions, as they were understood differently by German liberals and Allied occupiers, and it satisfied those who wanted to avoid a repeat of Nazi centralization. In matters of education and cultural policy this meant a relative abstinence when it came to state intervention, which in turn also reflected the Federal Republic's ambiguous role of representing only part of the cultural nation. In effect state commitment to cultural leadership was less pronounced in the *Grundgesetz*, the Basic Law of the Federal Republic, than

British troops march past German civilians in the bombed-out Münster *Altstadt*.
(photo: Stadt Münster, Presse- und Informationsamt, St. 4.24.2)

it had been in the Weimar Constitution or Hitler's rhetoric. This stood in contrast to the East German Communist Party, the Sozialistische Einheitspartei Deutschlands, or SED, which had a commitment to—if not a well-thought-out plan for—shaping culture according to regime interests that were often sketched in nationalist hues.[8]

Reconstruction of the built environment began during the war, when German, Belgian, French, and other officials drew up blueprints for rebuilding or renewing urban fabrics.[9] Everywhere the need for housing and transportation imposed practical burdens on the planning process, but war destruction made it possible to realize that part of the planning agenda aimed at curing ills the nineteenth century left behind. "The dispersal of the big city is the most decisive element in its recovery," wrote two planners in 1950. "The concentration of masses of people in the smallest areas is the most dangerous inheritance to come down to us from the last century. . . . Responsible planning's chief goal for the present is to attack this fundamental evil."[10] That fascism and war could be connected in the public mind with memories of nineteenth-century urban ills enhanced the argument. Planning departments thus played a big role not only in spearheading reconstruction but also in promoting flight from the immediate past. But this was no uniform rejection of twelve years of Nazi dictatorship, for German planners drew on technocratic traditions that had coexisted easily with Nazism's monumentalist urban thinking. Postwar German planning drew selectively on the recent past, picking up a line of continuity shared with counterparts in other Western states.

Reconstructors did not fail to see what had been lost, but after utopian ideas about the future of German cities were passed around and dropped—architect Heinrich Tessenow and preservationist Adolf Friedrich Lorenz wanted to leave Rostock's many ruins in place, allowing a garden city to grow over the devastation[11]—the emphasis was on practical measures rather than on painful reflection. Adherents of technically modernized cities thus made great headway in Berlin, Hamburg, Kassel, and Hannover, prefiguring the more substantial functionalist victories of urban planning of later decades, and although East German planners used a language of reconstruction directly opposed to that of the West, they shared with Western modernists a desire to have smaller towns and monumental urban centers.[12] Still, in the early years of reconstruction, rebuilders who wanted modernized cities that also maintained a "historical" ambience achieved equal success, notably in Munich, Münster, Rostock, and Dresden. "Traditionalist" and "modernist" paths were unclearly marked, and reconstructed cities were compromises rather than definitively new or precisely restored entities. In some cases there was impressive consensus. "Traditionalist and modernist architects, planners, and citizens agreed," wrote Diefendorf, "that a major historic monument—which usually meant a religious or government building predating 1830—should be preserved if undamaged and restored if only moderately damaged."[13] Decision making looked to both the future and the past. The currency reform of 1948 in the West brought new investment and the destruction of more prewar architecture, for example, but in the same year in Münster radical plans to move the historic commercial district, the Prinzipalmarkt, were abandoned in order to rebuild on the spot. In the Soviet zone extensive wartime destruction of Dresden, Leipzig, and Chemnitz initially gave rise to ambitious goals for remaking historic city centers; but plans to create a substantially new Dresden were toned down, and sections of the *Altstadt* were rebuilt in approximately historical form.[14]

Planners or architects committed to rebuilding historic architecture concentrated on the most imageable landmarks, and in Western cities such as Cologne this meant rebuilding the churches, which Konrad Adenauer identified as the key goal of reconstruction for that community in 1944. Conservators and architects supported this policy, as did businesses catering to the tourist trade. But the issue went well beyond immediate interests. Christian themes of the sacrifice and redemption of Germans dominated the memory of the war in this period, and the churches were fitting architectural settings for such sentiments, which articulated a general postwar revival of popular religiosity whose origins went back to the last years of the Third Reich. Churches had the support of the occupation authorities in all four zones right after the war, in part because they were seen as relatively uncompromised by Nazism. This was inaccurate, since the churches had implicitly or explicitly supported the regime, especially in the early years, but it is also true that they resisted Nazism or did not comply with it through formation of the Confessing Church and the battle against euthanasia. When Bavarians reconstructed the badly damaged thirteenth-century St. Lorenz Church in Nuremberg, then, it was not insignificant that this had been the site of a mass rally against Nazi efforts to take over the Protestant Church in 1934.[15]

Whether traditionalist or modernist solutions for cities were found, whether rebuilding focused on churches or other major landmarks, reconstruction also meant the outright destruction or damage of historic buildings. This was a continuation of Nazism's faulty preservation policies, its "scorched earth" approach in the last days of World War II, postwar military reuse of historic sites, and the rapid clearing of rubble. Too, occupation authorities had a political interest in doing away with the traces of imperial, Prussian, and Nazi history, as did German officials. Thus Hitler's new Reich Chancellery, built with great cost and grandeur by Speer but not irretrievably damaged in the war, was torn down; Hitler's bunker was intentionally buried and closed; and in Munich on the Königsplatz (after much hesitation) Nazi buildings were dynamited. The East German regime destroyed the eighteenth-century Berlin Castle, home of the Hohenzollerns, which was blown up in 1950 after earlier plans for reconstruction were dropped. In this case the regime's apparent victory over the memory of monarchical authority would seem complete just years later when architects of the modernist Council of State Building on the Marx-Engels-Platz incorporated a portal of the Berlin Castle in the new building, constructed from 1962 to 1964. From that portal, it was said, Karl Liebknecht proclaimed the socialist revolution at midday on 9 November 1918. Liebknecht's proclamation was followed two hours later by Philip Scheidemann's declaration of the Weimar Republic from the window of the Reichstag reading room. The so-called Liebknecht Portal would now be an architectural counterdemonstration to the restoration of the Reichstag in West Berlin from 1957 to 1961. In some instances Soviet authorities were more tolerant of politically fraught monuments than German Communists were, as in the case of the Dresden Opera House, which due to connections to monarchical power and the fact that Hitler attended the opera there, was slated for demolition by the SED even though it had not been irretrievably damaged. Impressed by logical argument and substantial amounts of vodka, Soviet cultural officers were cajoled

Doing away with politically unsavory memories. Munich dynamites the pillars of the "Honor Temples," classicist structures on the Königsplatz commemorating Nazi party martyrs of the Beer Hall Putsch, in 1947. (photo: *HEUTE* 2, no. 29 [1 February 1947]: 5)

by several non-Communist Dresdeners to exert their influence to protect the ruin.[16] Many critics argued that even if buildings avoided destruction, their restoration or the rebuilding of surroundings cut all meaningful connections to the past.

It is easy to forget that Nazism's legacy in the physical environment cannot be measured in terms of destruction alone. Average annual building activity during the twelve years of dictatorship matched that of the nineteenth and twentieth centuries as a whole, with a decided bias for architecture reflecting Nazi power. Even then, there were more churches built per year in the Third Reich than in 1900–1933. Many Nazi-era office buildings, highways, factories, monuments, and stadiums survived or were reconstructed. Many symbols of the regime remain embedded in the fabric of material culture to this day—a militaristic fresco from 1940 in a Hamburg army barracks, numerous Nazi symbols and inscriptions on the graves of the Ohlsdorf cemetery outside Hamburg, a swastika implausibly retained over the entrance to a building in a 1930s rural settlement in southwest Mecklenburg, and an excerpt from a Hitler speech in a stained-glass window in a Saalfeld cloister turned into a museum. Twelve years of dictatorship left an imprint on the built environment that was not only not to be excised but which provided positive models in planning, preservation, and engineering. Although occupation authorities and German governments demolished buildings and ruins that recalled the Nazi era, they also often followed the example of Munich, where authorities restored buildings the Nazis had modified by returning them to the form they had had in the dictatorship.[17]

What did western Germans remember in these years of pell-mell reconstruction? In November 1951, 80 percent of the respondents to a survey said that 1945 to 1948 was the worst period of German history in the century, far outscoring the next group of respondents, who made up 8 percent of the total and selected 1939 to 1945. The aftermath of the war and not the war itself had placed an unprecedented obstacle between Germans and their past. Those who identified with the past said they felt the late Kaiserreich was the best period of the twentieth century, which may have been true for those aged sixty and over in 1945. Younger working-class Germans and others would later identify the prewar years of the Nazi period, the "first economic miracle," as a time when jobs were available and relative material security was again a possibility if not a fact.[18]

Focusing on either the Kaiserreich or the later 1930s, different generations saw reconstruction as a vehicle for the return to normality. The rapidity of postwar rebuilding has often been seen as proof that West Germans were fleeing from their past, avoiding the painful process of openly admitting emotional commitments to Hitler and the idea of the racial community. Throughout German society there was indeed a need for moving forward, forgetting, and compensating the wounds of the past with the anticipated material rewards of the present. In April 1945 de Gaulle told the French, "The time for tears is over. The time of glory has returned." Two years later Adenauer unintentionally gave a German response, substituting stubborn action and the promise of prosperity for glory. "To begin and to work, these are endlessly better than a thousand reflections about what one can do or may do, or what one cannot do or may not do," he said in response to discussions over the rebuilding of the Cologne churches. Unyielding action was the future chancellor's reaction to his own ambivalence about the Germans, who in his eyes hesitated between demoralization and determination.[19] This ambivalence was replicated in the way the statement referred to the past. The call for obstinate, nearly frantic labor recalled Nazism's emphasis on performance, yet because of the almost mindless energy it necessitated, it created a deep rupture with recent events and encouraged a headlong rush into the future.

Yet even then there was no general flight from history, as one can see from continued public interest in historic landmarks and cities that gave Germans a sense of deep continuity. In 1948 Cologne celebrated the 700th anniversary of the laying of the foundation stone of the cathedral. In May 1948 Frankfurt and Germany commemorated the centennial of the Frankfurt national assembly and reconstructed the site of the assembly, the Paulskirche, which many assumed would be the symbol of the new postwar democracy, with its capital not on the Rhine but on the Main River. Financial donations to the Paulskirche project streamed in from all over Germany, including the Soviet zone. In all four occupation zones noted cultural figures, from aged liberal historian Friedrich Meinecke to spokespeople of the left-wing Cultural Association for Democratic Renewal of Germany, later a key East German cultural agency, called for a return to Goethe and the humanistic values he represented. In August 1949 the 200-year celebration of Goethe's birth occurred, for which the controversial rebuilding of the Goethe House in Frankfurt am Main was begun in 1946. Like its Western antagonist, the DDR celebrated the anniversaries of its historic cities, as in the case of the former Hansa town Frankfurt an der Oder, 700 years old in 1953, for which commemorative postage stamps featuring the Marienkirche, the *Altstadt*, and the fourteenth-century *Rathaus* appeared.[20] By distinguishing between national heritage (*Erbe*) broadly conceived and a more activist nurturing of tradition, the DDR would try to use such monumental history to build its version of the first socialist nation on German soil.

These events and commemorations marginalized the recent past by establishing heroic continuities, focusing on German survival in the face of insurmountable odds. They worked hand in hand with a developing memory of German victimization that repressed memory of those murdered in the Nazi camps. I say more in the next chapter about the commemoration of victims of Nazism in the built environment. Here it is enough to point out that in the West right after the war, Christian and largely "unpolitical" themes dominated the still-limited construction of places of memory (*Gedenkstätte*). In the East "antifascist" political themes carried the day after an initial period right after the war in which many spontaneous actions, some organized by former camp inmates, tried to keep memory of the Holocaust alive.[21] In neither case was there a full and open confrontation with Germans' identification with Nazism, the first step in mourning *all* victims of the regime.

The city of Nuremberg's handling of the Reichsparteitagsgelände, the huge complex of buildings and spaces designed for the annual Nazi Party rallies, was symbolic of this reluctance.[22] In December 1946, just weeks after the Nuremberg war crimes trial declared the SS a criminal organization, the Nuremberg city council resolved to use the still-intact former SS barracks at the site as an administrative building or even city hall without once considering the building's symbolism and history. (The owner of the barracks, the U.S. army, refused to give up the structure.) In 1950 the badly bombed city used the incomplete Congress Hall, a monumental assembly hall designed to house Hitler's adoring throngs, to celebrate Nuremberg's 900th anniversary without pointing to the structure's awful past. Until well into the 1970s officials avoided all actions that would link the site with the memory of National Socialism or with the history of the city itself; the Reichsparteitagsgelände covered an area fifteen times the size of Nuremberg's *Altstadt*, but tourists complained that signs directing visitors to the site were virtually absent. This unwillingness to remember stands in stark contrast to the general public interest in the past suggested by the preceding information, and we turn to a specific public vector of this interest to examine the juxtaposition of remembering and forgetting in more detail.

Archipelagoes of Memory

What was historic preservation's position in the immediate postwar years, when historical buildings lay in fragments and planners wanted to rebuild as quickly as possible? How did it reconstruct the history of the nation at a time when not only physical well-being but the existence of a political community as such was in doubt?

Preservationists faced economic, political, legal, and social obstacles in these difficult years. Public demand for housing was strong, hardship widespread, and political uncertainty dominant. Reconstruction planning went on over the heads of the preservationists as well as the general populace. Preservation policy was often undertaken by institutions over which preservationists had uneven control. With international financial backing and much domestic support, the Protestant and Catholic Churches had considerable autonomy, for instance, often drawing up restoration plans and hiring architects without input from preservation officials. In Münster and Nuremberg preservationists had substantial influence in planning debates; in Hannover or West Berlin they did not. Single issues such as whether or not to reconstruct Goethe's birthplace in Frankfurt were resolved by the ebb and flow of public discussion rather than by direct intervention by preservationists, who spoke for only one among many constituencies. The 1950 decision to restore the gigantic seventeenth-century Charlottenburg palace in West Berlin, heavily damaged in air raids of 1943, was made not to please a preservation agenda but to respond to the East German regime, which destroyed the Hohenzollern palace in Berlin in 1950–51. In East Germany in the late 1940s, pro-regime advocates of preservation explicitly put the protection of historic buildings in a position subordinate to the reconstruction goals of German Communists and Soviet zonal leaders. When this included Soviet support for the restoration of internationally known landmarks such as the Unter den Linden ensemble in Berlin comprising the Neue Wache, the university, the state opera, and other buildings, then historic preservation resulted as a function of larger political processes.[23]

Preservationists also faced internal constraints. Conservators' staffs had always been small, and postwar shortages of materials and skilled labor made a bad situation worse. Such limits undoubtedly forced conservators to rethink their public functions, as when Lower Saxon state conservator Oskar Karpa referred to his role as a "defense lawyer for monuments."[24] Called in only when an individual is charged with a crime, unable to prescribe prophylactic treatment, the defense lawyer was more reactive than the "doctor for monuments" that had dominated metaphorical renderings of the conservator in earlier decades. The obstacles to preservation were overcome somewhat by the fact that Allied occupiers had an organization for protecting monuments and works of art, modeled after that of the Germany army, that helped to guard important ruins until clearance or reconstruction could take place, and that organizations such as churches could get international assistance. Moreover, like the planning initiatives in which they played varying roles, preservationists had prepared for reconstruction not after the war but during it. Begun as an informal circle in 1941, the Society for the Friends of Reconstruction of Cologne was picking up a thread of continuity when it was founded as a formal organization in December 1945 and introduced to an enthusiastic public half a year later.[25] But these were small compensations in what appeared to be a much larger disaster.

Most preservationist work in the first three years after the war was provisional, dependent on many contingencies, and oriented toward saving "island-like quarters of renewal around a church, a city hall, a market square, [or] a group of buildings," as Bavarian conservator Georg Lill wrote in 1946. This emphasis on archipelagoes of memory in a sea of ruins recalls the narrower approach to preservation that people such as Bonn art historian Paul Clemen, still alive in the first two years after the war, had fought against since before World War I. Although before the war Clemen had insisted on widening the purview of preservation, in general major monumental buildings constructed before 1830 and especially in the medieval and early modern periods were favored in the Kaiserreich. This view of historic architecture now returned. In northern Germany Hamburg's efforts to create a "tradition island" in the *Altstadt* had influence if not always practical results in Hannover, Lübeck, Braunschweig, and other cities. In a city such as Nuremberg, considered a spectacular example of the successful rebuilding of an entire historic city center, clusters of historic churches, museums, and key state buildings were in fact favored by city and state agencies, while restorers and architects of more numerous vernacular and private buildings had to seek financial help elsewhere. In Frankfurt am Main just four reconstruction projects had significant backing: the Goethe House, the famous St. Paul's Church, the cathedral, and the Römer complex of the town hall. In the Soviet zone the tendency to favor such archipelagoes was even more pronounced, as in the case of the already mentioned Unter den Linden ensemble in Berlin or the nearly completely destroyed eighteenth-century baroque Zwinger complex of galleries, pavilions, and gardens in Dresden.[26]

Nonetheless, it is crucial to remember that destruction appeared to be so total, that some urban planners had blueprints for a radical restructuring of transportation networks that would have deformed historic districts drastically, and that utopian plans, such as one for the rebuilding of Würzburg in a different place, threatened to alter German cityscapes beyond recognition. What real hopes did a maximalist agenda for preservation have when in the oldest parts of a city such as Hannover only 32 of the 1,600 preexisting half-timbered houses remained? Limited preservation of archipelagoes of architectural memory was a difficult and contested position in this context. This argument applies even more to the Eastern zone, where on the whole reconstruction favored historical buildings less than in the West.[27]

The more limited agenda was not always obvious from what many conservators said. One of the only provincial conservators to argue aggressively for more consideration of historic places in postwar planning was Westphalian Wilhelm Rave, who stated in 1947 that "an old urban ground plan should be seen as a cultural-historical monument." He drafted the "Principles of Historic Preservation in the Reconstruction of Old Cities," issued by the Monuments and Museum Council of Northwest Germany, which stated that the conservator was to be consulted on measures for preserving "the urban layout, which is often the only remaining evidence of the history of a place." This perspective theoretically increased the power of the conservator, since focusing on the broader historic morphology of the city rather than on single landmarks meant preservation interests would be considered from the outset of reconstruction. A broader point of view was reflected also in East German preservation's interest in industrial monuments, which resulted in a rather precocious inventory including about 1,000 artifacts for Saxony in 1950.[28] Once they moved away from rhetoric and inventories toward practice, however, conservators did not (and could not) follow the logic of these wider perspectives.

Preservationists were not simply responding to constraints and opportunities. Their emphasis on a limited number of key monuments was also a product of a general approach to culture that characterized postwar Europe. Older notions of culture as "high culture," the strict separation of *Kultur* and civilization, universities and schools as islands of humanistic training in a mechanized world—these traditions were reaffirmed decisively, in part as responses to artistic modernism and commercial culture.[29] Protecting only a few historic sites went hand in hand with this return to an elitist notion of culture based on defending a select range of artifacts from a glorious past. This was fully compatible with a long-term change in preservationist thinking inherited by both East and West, namely the transition from narrower art-historical to broader cultural-historical criteria in conceptualizing monuments.[30] The broadening of the concept of the monument associated with this long-term transition now crystallized more generally around highly visible public symbols rather than fields of care.

Cultural-historical criteria were reflected in the West German preservationist response to one of the most ideological cases of monument destruction in the first postwar decade, the East German demolition of the Berlin palace. Aside from the many reasons for saving the building, the most important issue for Western preservationists was the loss of something representative of a particular style and cultural epoch. "[With the razing of the palace] Occidental culture has lost the last work of one of its greatest architects, Andreas Schlüter," read a statement by West German conservators. Considered to be Schlüter's masterpiece, the royal palace reflected the architect's absorption of not only German but French and Italian influences of the late seventeenth century. Similar assumptions informed preservationist work in the East. The bombing of Dresden had been ghastly not only for its human suffering, one commentator wrote, but because it destroyed "the art city" on the Elbe.[31] Broader than nineteenth-century notions of monuments as markers of the evolution of specific artistic styles, this appropriation of monuments was nonetheless a considerable retreat from those more socially engaged ideas about preservation one found in urban renewal schemes and open-air museums in the Third Reich.

COMMEMORATIVE NOISE

Even if preservation could have had a substantial voice in rebuilding, it could not have spoken in a uniform manner. Some preservationists supported modernization and modernized planning, as they did in Frankfurt am Main or Stuttgart, while others did not. In cases such as the 1947 decision of the Frankfurt magistrate to rebuild the Goethe House, the head of the Frankfurt office of Hessian state conservator Hermann Karl Zimmermann accepted reconstruction, saying the Goethe House was more important for its historical-cultural rather than its artistic value, and that, therefore, preservationist criteria of authenticity did not apply. What is more, said Zimmermann, all parts of the building, including its interior furnishings, which had been stored during the war, could be reused in the new version of the structure. In contrast, although Georg Lill did not oppose reconstruction, he did regret its style, saying that not a historical copy but a "completely new design," with a scale appropriate to the artifacts and memorabilia it would house, was the best solution.[32]

Where there was unanimity, it often did not favor broad historic protection. Conservators who argued for protection of the entire historical morphology could legitimize destruction of many buildings and ensembles as long as the general historic form of the city was evoked. This position agreed completely with that of the more historically sensitive planners and politicians who destroyed more than they saved. Many conservators insisted that the criterion of their response to reconstruction was "proportion," or *Maßstäblichkeit*, whether of a single building or of a district or street pattern, but this was a vague concept that hid many variations of meaning and many approaches to the past—and hence as many ways of forgetting as remembering.[33] Because preservation often meant protection of a facade whose interior was rebuilt according to contemporary standards, the loss of historical substance was actually quite large even when preservationists "won" their battles against builders, planners, and politicians. Reflecting the influence of interwar tendencies toward museum-like historic districts, preservationists in the Hamburg Cremoninsel and in Hannover supported the reconstruction of buildings from one area of the city in another to preserve particular types of historical models.[34]

As before the war, preservation gained part of its legitimacy not from protecting monuments but from bearing witness to what was lost or about to be lost. This was no easy task in postwar Europe. Comprehensive wartime reports on destruction had been impossible. During the two decades after 1945, a full account of what had been lost was complicated by the tempo and nature of rebuilding. It took until 1978 for the DDR to produce a comprehensive overview of wartime losses; until 1988 for the BRD. Before this date the only West German *Land* to produce thorough documentation on war damage was North Rhine-Westphalia, although there were partial inventories of damage for individual cities and regions in the late 1940s.[35] Paradoxically, had such estimates been more widely available earlier, there might have been more justification for doing away with historic architecture, since the reports indicated that initial damage assessments were exaggerated.

From a relatively early stage, preservationists working from more limited perspectives realized that the number of totally destroyed and unreconstructible major monuments was small. Writing in *Die Kunstpflege* in 1946, Hans Wentzel noted that with a few significant exceptions all the historically important medieval and Renaissance stained-glass windows in Germany had been safely stored for protection. The real problem was that many buildings from which the windows had been taken were no longer standing. Although Westphalia had been badly hit, Provincial Conservator Wilhelm Rave noted that Allied bombing destruction was uneven in the region. In the county of Büren near Paderborn, the only historic building to have been lost was the "wonderful Wewelsburg," an essentially seventeenth-century fortress that had been detonated not by Allied but by Waffen-SS explosives, and which in any case would later be rebuilt as a youth center. An Eastern observer noted that although Dresden, Nordhausen, and Magdeburg experienced catastrophic losses, many other cities did not. Halle's *Rathaus* was badly damaged, but in general this community remained "the best maintained big city in Germany." Quedlinburg, Wittenberg, and Schwerin had little really serious damage also.[36]

The Rhineland experienced the worst damage of any area, having lost roughly one-third of its residential housing. But even there the situation for historic architecture was not a total disaster. Rhenish conservator Hartwig Beseler maintained that nearly 23 percent of some 3,201 monuments in the administrative districts of Aachen, Düsseldorf, and Cologne were completely destroyed, while another 62.4 percent (1,997 buildings) were damaged considerably. However, he was quick to point out that none of the area's thirty-nine monuments of "outstanding importance" should be written off. Some thirty years later preservationists estimated that the area of future West Germany lost about one-fifth of all historic monuments. But again, this recent estimate stressed that because of restoration none of these were among the most cherished monuments on German soil, except the Braunschweig palace, a three-story, three-wing marvel of baroque classicism built in the 1830s on the basis of an earlier structure and finally destroyed in 1960.[37]

COMMEMORATIVE NOISE

Such estimates were based in part on the more limited sense of historic sites already discussed. But this way of seeing and remembering also had a more specific function in postwar memory. Just as the commemoration of the 20 July 1944 conspirators against Hitler would reduce the issue of resistance to manageable proportions, adopting a narrow view of what was lost made wartime destruction comprehensible and survivable.[38] But just as reducing resistance to 20 July ignored the issues of complicity and ideologically unsavory forms of resistance, the narrow estimates of loss canceled out the tremendous destruction the war reaped on the physical environment as a result of German aggression. In both cases, a narrow thread of memory foreclosed broader, more disturbing experiences and reduced the impact of irreducible events.

Another factor affecting the assessment of damage was that the immediate postwar years had some advantages for those worried about historic sites and natural environments. The blight of advertising in historic town centers and scenic rural areas slowed in the two years after the war due to shortages of money, material, and electricity, although shop owners in some cities took advantage of the bureaucratic confusion by circumventing building bylaws and putting up more advertising. Only when the economy got going again did advertising pick up substantially, so that by the early 1950s advertising had increased not just in urban commercial districts but in residential areas, resorts, and the countryside. The loss of historic architecture and the general austerity of the postwar years stimulated new organizations or revived old ones dedicated to preserving local history.[39] Archaeologists benefited from the destruction of churches because they could undertake digs that had been technically impossible or prohibited before. Architectural historians in the East benefited from a slower pace of reconstruction because it gave them more time to do their research on important monuments.[40] Preservation could look at the postwar years with the same opportunistic eyes that planning departments had, though for different reasons.

In some cases the reconstruction of monuments created structures that were thought to be superior to their predecessors. "It makes one's heart beat faster," wrote Wilhelm Neuß of the Association for Christian Art for the Cologne-Aachen region, "to know that St. Quirin in Neuß has been completely rebuilt, with an interior perhaps even more powerful in its effect than before." St. Quirin was a richly elaborated thirteenth-century church whose reconstruction began just eight days after a 5 January 1944 bombing raid had damaged its vault, central cupola, and part of the roof of the middle aisle. Speaking of St. Remigius in Viersen, another observer made a similar assessment: "The church is really much more beautiful than before. Whoever goes into the church through the main entrance has a picture of the most beautiful harmony before him." Like St. Quirin, St. Remigius, a late Gothic cathedral from the fifteenth century, was under reconstruction before the war ended.[41] Here the war enabled preservationists to improve on the past, making memory more vivid, evocative, and harmonious. The sheer enormity of destruction could be forgotten in the face of such sanitized history.

Institutional arrangements reflected still more complex relations with the past. Having taken note of Robert Hiecke's efforts before 1945 to gain support for a national preservation law, the Standing Conference on Cultural Ministers asked him to draw up a memorandum outlining his views on the subject after the war. No law came into existence, due largely to the Federal Republic's allergy to centralized cultural-political leadership, a long-standing tradition of regional cultural autonomy, and a more immediate reaction to Nazi centralization. The practical effect was a reversion to the Kaiserreich, when Prussia and the Reich made no specific legislative guarantees about the need for protecting cultural property. At lower levels of government, only Berlin, Hamburg, and Lower Saxony failed to mention the importance of preservation of monuments in their constitutions, but only two Länder, south Baden in 1949 (later absorbed into Baden-Württemberg) and Schleswig-Holstein in 1958, passed legislation on the issue. As might be expected, in practice some states did more than others. Assuming its traditional position in the forefront of the preservation movement, Bavaria took an active role in rebuilding historic architecture and spent more than 30 million marks on eighteen key projects in Munich alone from 1945 to 1950.[42]

In terms of personnel, there was substantial continuity with the Nazi and Weimar periods. To take only a few notable examples of some of the key figures, Günther Grundmann had been provincial conservator of Lower Silesia until 1945. He then became municipal conservator in Hamburg in 1950 and served as chair of the group of government conservators, the Association of Land Conservators of the Federal Republic, until 1960. Georg Lill had been director of the Bavarian State Office for Preservation since 1929 and remained in that office until 1950. Lill and Graf Wolff Metternich of Bonn, who had been an important figure in Rhenish preservation before and during World War II, were president and vice-president, respectively, of the association of western German conservators that served as a caretaker organization until a more permanent association was formed in 1950. Robert Hiecke had been head conservator of monuments in Prussia from 1918, a leading official in the Reich Education Ministry after 1934, and a leader until his death in 1952 in the unsuccessful struggle to have a uniform historic preservation law for the BRD. Even the aging Paul Clemen played a role in the reorganization of preservation in the Rhineland in the first two years after the war.[43]

Continuity in personnel was paralleled by continuity in the organs of preservationist public activity. The journal *Die Kunstpflege* appeared in 1946 as a continuation of the *DKD*; but it was published only once, and in 1952 the *DKD* reappeared to take up its pre–World War II agenda, as explicitly stated by its new editor, Josef Maria Ritz, a leading preservation official in the Weimar Republic and Nazi dictatorship.[44] In 1947 the RVDH was incorporated into the Rheinischer Heimatbund (RHB), designed to steer all *Heimat* activities in the region, but soon the elite Rhenish association returned to its original name and its "original goals of 1906," as one official put it. Although the RVDH remained a part of the Heimatbund, it once again concentrated on historic architecture rather than the dispersed folkloristic and cultural activities of the broader *Heimat* movement.[45] As for the tradition of a national preservation conference, forty-seven senior preservation officials from all over Germany met for the first time in Munich in June 1948, but soon political realities undercut initiatives toward German-German organization.[46] Nonetheless, West German conservators organized a yearly conference for the BRD, although it had neither the public resonance nor the broader programmatic impulse that some prewar conferences had had.

In the Soviet zone and East Germany there was substantial organizational continuity despite national division. The demise of Prussia meant the end of the position of Prussian conservator of monuments, but the *Länder* retained the conservator's office, and overall direction of official preservation was given to the cultural ministry in the Soviet zone. A reorganization and centralization of preservation agencies would follow in 1953. The conservators could rely on new officials, the district conservators, whose jurisdiction corresponded roughly to the areas of old Prussian districts, as well as old officials, voluntary assistants present in some communities since before the war, to further their work. Preservation councils organized around conservators, annual congresses, and restoration workshops added to a structure that functioned much as before. Restoration also relied heavily on pre-1945 personnel, as in the case of Hubert Ermisch, who had restored the Dresden Zwinger from 1924 to 1936 and who was given the even greater challenge of restoring it after the war. The big change was in ideology. In the advisory councils for preservation there would be concerted efforts to ensure that not only representatives of the churches but also "antifascist parties," the Free German Youth, and the influential Cultural Association for Democratic Renewal of Germany would be present. This was part of a broader effort to decouple official historic preservation from its "imperialist" past. The DDR's overall commitment to preservation was expressed officially in the 1952

Decree on Maintaining National Cultural Monuments, the first legal codification of historic preservation on German soil after 1945.[47] Neither ideology nor government decrees canceled out the real element of continuity in historic preservation, namely that after the first years of Soviet *démontage* and East German reconstruction, the slower pace of socioeconomic change and funneling of resources toward new building projects allowed old buildings and districts to escape destruction.

Fragments of a Nation

In the bitterly cold winter of 1946–47 in Cologne the Society for Christian Culture held a lecture series in which the rebuilding of the city's churches was discussed by planners, architects, preservationists, clergymen, academics, and city officials before large audiences huddled in the Auditorium Maximum of the university. More than 200 air attacks had destroyed as much as 90 percent of the old historic core of the city, while the larger urban area had lost about 70 percent of its buildings, in which remains only 40,000 of Cologne's nearly 800,000 prewar inhabitants subsisted in 1945. Though still structurally sound, the Cologne cathedral was damaged by bombs and grenades, and one buttress had an eighty-cubic-meter hole in it. The city's famous and artistically even more important Romanesque churches, originating mainly between 980 and 1247 and including St. Andreas, St. Aposteln, St. Cäcilian, St. Gereon, and Groß St. Martin, had been more heavily damaged. There was no debate as to whether the Rhenish metropolis's many churches should be rebuilt; everyone present assumed they would be. Instead the participants offered responses to those who had either advocated leaving the churches as ruins or demanded rebuilding them as exact copies. The participants' rhetoric revealed much about how they envisioned the German nation as it was now symbolized in a damaged, thin thread of cultural artifacts.

Modernist architect and city planner Rudolf Schwarz began his address with the phrase "as fire consumed the churches of Cologne," giving the event the character of a natural, mythic disaster in a far-off time and place. Another participant, Heinrich Lutzeler, said, "He who sows the seeds of total war should not be surprised when . . . he reaps the storm of total war."[48] The motif of natural disaster displaced the war into the world of events over which human beings had no control. The metaphor of sowing seeds presupposed human agency, although it was clear that the speaker was not placing responsibility for the disaster at the door of the audience, but at the door of those unidentified people who had supported Hitler. More than a purely Christian or conservative rendering of the war, this approach could also be found on the literary Left, where Gruppe 47 writers spoke of World War II in terms of biblical metaphors of the flood.[49]

The effect of the disaster was nearly total, leaving only traces of a bygone world. "The world has fallen into pieces," said Hermann Schnitzler, "we see pieces all around; fragments of a world whose wholeness the young hardly, and the old just barely, remember."[50] Here the war was represented as an unprecedented break with the wholeness of the national past, although it was not a total break because the "fragments" of that past remained behind, allowing the nation "barely" to remember a prewar era. What prewar era was being referred to was not entirely clear. It may have been the prewar Nazi period, which would be remembered in many areas of German society as a moment of relative security. In any case, this metaphorics of fragments—of loss and impoverishment—picked up on an important tradition of prewar discourse. But now the thought lines linking present and past were frayed and almost broken, and vulnerability was heightened. If there was ever a time when Germans stood "terribly naked and exposed, like a new colony in a previously uninhabited land," as Schinkel warned they would if they abandoned history, then it was the immediate postwar period.

Debates over rebuilding artifacts such as the Goethe House demonstrated that some preservationists recognized that the nation and its symbols could not be brought back, at least not in their preferred form, and that national landmarks would have to be mourned for and eventually taken leave of, as if "from a dead person," as the opponents of reconstruction of the nineteenth-century museum Alte Pinakothek in Munich argued.[51] Significantly, both structures were rebuilt, suggesting that a potential for accepting the inevitable decline and transmutation of national identities was missed. But in the case of the Alte Pinakothek, architect Hans Döllgast used many original building parts with their patina, partly because of material shortages but also because of the desire not to hide the destruction.[52] Yet this potentially productive way of "reading" the violent history of the nation in the facade of a historical building was the exception that proved the rule, and as the postwar era developed, many critics would demand that the scars of the war incorporated in Döllgast's reconstruction be removed.

The Cologne discussions offer a good example of how preservationists and their allies not only avoided the possibility of taking leave from national landmarks but explicitly opposed it. Adenauer wanted immediate rebuilding, imploring the Cologne conferees to have "more courage, less pessimism" and rejecting others' demands for leaving the heavily damaged steeple of Groß St. Martin as a "memorial to the wickedness of our time."[53] He found support from preservationists, such as Graf Wolff Metternich, who said it was "an absurdity" to suggest that some of the city's damaged

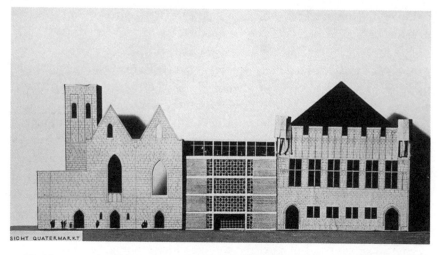

West Germany was reluctant to resituate ruins in the postwar city. An exception was Cologne's heavily damaged seventeenth-century St. Alban's Church, shown here in a model integrating it with the rebuilt Gürzenich assembly hall (*above*) and as a "cultivated ruin" (*opposite*). (photos: Bader, "Zur Denkmalpflege in Nordrheinland," 32; Rheinisches Bildarchiv, Cologne, L 4554/1)

churches should be left as ruins. Ruins were "out of place" in the modern urban fabric, said Metternich, and in any case preservationists did not have to remind Germans of the war. "Without our help," he continued, "we will have enough memorials for generations to come. The churches are places of peace and reconciliation. Everything reminiscent of war and hate should be kept away from them and their surroundings."[54]

This statement contradicted the position taken over the previous decades by many of Metternich's colleagues, who had endorsed memorials and commemorative plaques for the war dead in or near churches after 1918. Of course they had been considering intact churches rather than burned-out hulks, and in any case in 1947 most preservationists sided with Metternich. In Cologne itself ruins such as the seventeenth-century Catholic church St. Alban's, in which sculptor Ewald Mataré's copy of Käthe Kollwitz's moving *Mourning Parents* was placed in 1955 as a monument to World War II, were startling exceptions. Moreover, St. Alban's impact as a permanent "cultivated ruin" was compromised, as it became a set piece in an ensemble including the rebuilding of the Gürzenich assembly hall complex on the busy Quatermarkt.[55] It was not in any case one of the twelve historically important Romanesque churches that, with the towering cathedral, gave the Cologne cityscape its distinctive aura. By rejecting the maintenance of ruins referring directly to the war, preservationists constructed a typical argument for those who chose to forget the recent past, turning those who

wanted a critical memory of war and Nazism into people who wanted to continue the era of "war and hate." The threads of the cultural nation were reknit around themes of Christian harmony and forgiveness, and those who opposed immediate reconciliation were transformed into the (possibly un-Christian and antinational) enemies of the new advocates of peace.

This rhetorical move was also evident in the way preservationists dealt with intra-German relations. Critiques of the East by Western observers contributed to a hardening of attitudes toward the cultural politics of the Soviet zone and the early DDR. Planner and architect Rudolf Schwarz saw himself on "the last line of retreat of the Occident," a "soldier assigned to the last post that can still be defended" from dictatorship in the East.[56] There may have been good reason to see things in this manner, but such attitudes also furthered a dynamic whereby exponents of critical memory, defined as those in both East and West who wanted to remind Germans of past political sins, became the new representatives of war and hate. West German preservationists would gain a more balanced view of the East as time wore on, but in this era they were convinced that East German cultural policy had "little to do with sensitive and intelligent historic preservation," as noted in a 1952 *DKD* article by Berliner Paul Ortwin Rave. All four occupation zones were criticized in this piece, but the East was singled out for reducing preservation issues to purely political considerations, most notably in the destruction of the Berlin palace and the reuse of the baroque Zeughaus, the first building to be erected on Unter den Linden when that byway was being transformed in the eighteenth century from a royal riding path into a monumental street, as the Museum of German History.[57] Critical memory of war and fascism, inspired by Communist ideology and instantiated in the use of many historical buildings, was thus seen as a vehicle for reintroducing the very dynamic of hate it was designed to overcome.

Such criticism notwithstanding, preservationists in the Soviet zone had access to a narrative that potentially confronted the recent past and took leave of a form of national identity that had produced such horror. Historic preservation was to leave behind its "imperialistic" heritage, in the words of Gerhard Strauß, the adviser for preservation to the central German administration in the Soviet zone. It was to overcome its historical deficiency of being a "refuge for large parts of the German intelligentsia, who after the failure of German bourgeois attempts to gain freedom, were satisfied with imagined or bygone worlds." A "transformation of the fundamental standpoint of historic preservation" based on a "new commitment to the truth" and a realization that the ruins of German churches and museums were *not* the "regrettable but accidental manifestations of an otherwise acceptable historical development" was necessary.[58]

But Soviet and East German Communist authorities undercut the potentially positive results of critical memory by placing the war and Nazism in a narrative of monopoly capitalism and imperialism. Moreover, an emphasis on national cultural heritage, developed by the regime as a "class theory of the nation" but appropriated by various groups in different ways, made it impossible to leave behind the basic referents of national-political identity that were at the root of the catastrophe.[59] Even if Communist ideology had openly confronted Germans' emotional attachments to Hitler rather than reducing everything to the ritual of antifascism, the outcome would have been uncertain. The populace gradually became so suspicious of Soviet and regime political goals that open confrontation with the past might have been seen as yet another piece of Soviet Cold War strategy.

The preceding emphasizes what was suppressed in preservationist accounts of the German past. But what were the more affirmative elements in this reconstruction of German memory? We find one answer in a 1948 memorandum of the Rhenish Heimat Association of Aachen in which a monumental narrative of the nation drew on past discursive traditions but also recontextualized them to fit the new situation.[60] An appeal for rebuilding key Aachen monuments such as the severely damaged *Rathaus*, built in the fourteenth century over a part of the eighth-century imperial residence of Charlemagne, the Kaiserpfalz, the document began by stating that "Aachen . . . is an eternally living monument to Charlemagne and his imperial idea . . . for the rebuilding of the Christian Occident after the decline and destruction of the Roman Empire." This move to the plane of European Christianity had been a theme of preservationist discourse before and during the war, when proponents of *Kunstschutz* emphasized their role in saving Occidental culture. It had been a theme of those Germans who had resisted Hitler as well, as former Leipzig mayor Carl Goerdeler and others saw the ruins of Aachen and other German cities as powerful symbols of the bitter challenges facing Western culture as a whole.[61] But now it assumed a more urgent and even progressive valence after twelve years of hypernationalism. One can make a similar statement about regionalism, which reappeared in a more forceful guise. "It is hoped," said the document with reference to reconstruction, "that also in the far-off future there will be an awareness that every city has its own special laws." In this arrangement the nation potentially stood alongside the region, the city, and Europe rather than above them, equal to other emotive appeals to collective feeling rather than predominant.

But just as the Cologne church debates opened the possibility for breaking the nation's hegemony over visions of the past without finally doing so, the Aachen appeal almost reverted to older patterns of national identity. This was evident in terms of language and style rather than explicit political references. Specifically, one finds a continuation of the language of German idealism in the document that parallels other areas of German culture such as literature, and thus suggests how deeply etched the discourse of national identity was in postwar preservationist thought. According to the document, the "Imperial history" was palpable in the present because it was "embodied in livelier and more impressive ways in the Kaiserpfalz . . . than through military reports or laws." This led to a more general statement on the function of the monument, which was seen as an "embodiment of historical memories and holy religious feelings" and the bearer of a "high symbolism and mysterious world of imagination and otherworldly power." These qualities "continue[d] to speak" even when the monument, like the remnants of the Carolingian residence lying deep under the Aachen cityscape, was destroyed or decayed. Even under these conditions, the monument retained the "essence of great national and local memories in the sense of that 'paradise of memory, from which we cannot be driven,'" a quote from the Romantic writer Jean Paul. Fittingly, it was Jean Paul who wrote, "To the French, God has given the land; to the English, the sea; to the Germans only the air."[62] The physical referents of this Edenlike "paradise of memory" consisted not only of whole, damaged, or disappeared monuments and ruins, but also of air, as ineffable as the afterglow of figures on a computer screen. They worked as metahistorical and mythic referents whose world was somehow beyond or above the vicissitudes of past and present.

The persistence of this way of evaluating monuments may suggest that preservationists were restoring discredited nationalist traditions. In fact they were using old words to describe new situations, which meant they were creating new rhetorical constructions. They had not broken with the tradition of the cultural nation, but they had dropped its racist valences; surrounded it with new, more powerful European and regionalist meanings; and retained the cherished language of idealist thought. One must vigorously condemn their repression of the memory of the Nazi dictatorship's victims, but one must also appreciate the effort to reconstruct a national past whose future was by no means assured. This effort was not confined to German conservatives but was embedded in a wider European project. Historian Alan Milward has demonstrated that even the most progressive postwar thinkers advocating new forms of European community reasserted the nation-state as the principal vehicle of political identity. Like the more modest spokesmen of the Aachen *Heimat* group, they were not above using imagery of Europe's imperial past; the visionaries of the European Coal and

Steel Community noted that the new agency included the regions that were formerly part of Charlemagne's Europe.[63]

During the first phase of rebuilding, preservationists continued to rely on the idea that the cultural politics of the nation depended on public support. But how would the cherished bond between preservation and the rest of the nation be reestablished in the new postwar context? One way was to set the record straight on the role preservation played during World War II, just as Clemen had tried to set it straight in response to charges of German barbarism in World War I. Preservationists had "to once and for all inform the public about the heavy responsibilities German historic preservation took on during the war," wrote George Lill in 1946, "in an effort to protect the cultural treasures entrusted to it in the face of disastrous conditions and the often hostile hindrance by culturally ignorant Nazi government agencies."[64] Portraying preservationists as heroic defenders of tradition in the face of Nazi barbarism was at least partly disingenuous, but it reflected how quickly a selective memory of recent events had begun to take hold in the effort to position historic preservation in a more positive light for the German public.

Another path to the nation was to get people to think of culture—even high culture—as a basic necessity of life, just as food ration cards were. When in the late 1940s the mayor of the small Rhenish city Münstereifel defended historic preservation by saying it was not a "hobby of romantic antiquarians and idealists," he was reacting to a widespread criticism inherited from the prewar era but more critically felt in the postwar age of austerity.[65] Responding to the idea that saving historic landmarks was a luxury at a time when many lived in temporary barracks, Bavarian cultural official Christian Wallenreiter put the matter bluntly in an article titled "Residential Building instead of Preservation of Monuments?" He wrote, "Social policy can only be successful if it is shaped by the knowledge that the social question has to do with the totality of existence . . . rather than only with economic matters." This totality of existence was in turn dependent on cultural referents such as monuments, which acted as a spiritual mirror that enabled the "*Volk* to recognize itself."[66]

Both efforts—setting straight the historical record and making an argument for contemporary relevance—were shaped by a persistent element of preservationist discourse, namely, ambivalence about popular participation in the cultural politics of the nation. Speaking before the Association of the Friends of Heimat in Neuß in 1948, Joseph Busley, a North Rhine-Westphalian cultural official, told the audience that although *Heimat* and similar groups contributed to reconstruction, most citizens were called on only for "moral support." "Most of our contemporaries," said Busley, "are not in a position to determine the importance of the restoration of a townscape . . . because of their immediate needs and cares, their deficient education, and their materialistic outlook." Busley argued that Germany found itself in a time "in which large parts of the people rejected every link to the past, in which one has forgotten that an essential part of our culture is comprehended through tradition, in which many people have the opinion that everything must all at once be radically different."[67] In such statements preservationists criticized the vast majority of a nation that would not accept the past preservationists were trying to give them. The cultural politics of notables, still straining to adapt to changed conditions, blamed the victims of historicide for their victimization. In this regard, there was substantial continuity not with the Nazi era but with the late Kaiserreich.

This narrative was deployed in even more critical terms than those Busley used. When Paul Ortwin Rave, who in the Nazi period had praised the nationalist reenchantment of Sanssouci, recounted the first years of reconstruction in Berlin, he began with a sympathetic portrayal of ordinary people who lost their homes, jobs, and loved ones, and whose desperate quest to have a roof over their head could be understood. Yet they were not without blame for the loss of historic landmarks. Making up more than one-third of all workers clearing rubble during the Berlin blockade, the "rubble women," or Trümmerfrauen, in particular acted heroically to clear away the fragments of Berlin architecture. But "where the remains of buildings that may or may not have been ruins still loomed up dangerously, the walls were offhandedly overturned, torn down, exploded, without even asking about the possible age or value of such structures." This criticism cut deeply against the grain of public imagery, as the rubble woman, endlessly photographed for newspapers and women's magazines such as HEUTE and celebrated in Günter Grass's poem "The Great Rubble Woman Speaks," became an icon of the rebuilding process. Still, in Rave's account it was not the women who were ultimately responsible but the building authorities, the Berlin city council, and the Allied authorities.[68]

But criticism of the uncultured was accomplished with a note of considerable self-criticism and retrospection. "The Preservation and Heimatschutz association held many congresses," said Busley in reference to the organization of which he had been a leading member. "[It] raised big sums of money for the maintenance of artistic monuments, but it was not successful in getting a foothold in the Volk."[69] This statement was paired with the usual note of frustration, namely that the efforts of the most important cultural authorities had not been successful "in the protection of entire townscapes as such." But frustration was extended back in time: "The process of systematic destruction of our *bürgerlich* monuments started well before the war. In many cases unfortunately we were satisfied with giving an obituary for a destroyed building." The current state of Germany's bombed cities was thus rooted not in the specific conditions of the war and Hitler's politics but in a longer history of destruction in which preservationists were implicated. As true as this may have been, it replaced recent political horrors with a longer-term narrative of social victimization, explaining Germans' inability to participate fully in national tasks of rebuilding by referring to the economic and urban—but never political—sins of the fathers.

Desire and Doubt

As they had for so long, preservationists wanted wide public support but also doubted the abilities of the German people to make reasonable choices about the fate of national landmarks. This dialectic of desire and doubt was mirrored in public appropriations of historic places. Germans derived no single meaning from their ruined cities and historic sites. As before, many Germans regarded historic buildings with sheer insensitivity. The administrative heartland of the SS state, the Berlin complex of palatial offices, museums, and underground torture chambers known as the "Gestapo terrain," was ransacked for food, clothing, wood, and other materials. Those who took part in the widespread plundering of privately held mansions in the Westphalian countryside obviously shared few of the concerns of either the critics or the supporters of preservation. Many were driven by simple necessity, for there were "briquettes and a crust of bread to scrounge," as novelist Erich Loest wrote. In contrast, U.S. servicemen who stole valuable relics and manuscripts were often motivated only by the lure of profits on the American memory marketplace. GIs who used the ruins as scenic backdrops for photographs of their newly conquered German sweethearts, and German photographers who used piles of rubble for fashion photos in illustrated magazines such as *HEUTE* and *Film und Frau*, needed to say little about their true interests.[70]

But generally—and aside from the fact that saving the traces of Nazi terror left most of them cold—Germans may have been more concerned about the fate of documents of stone in this period than in any other until the 1970s. In the first months after the war postage stamps appeared depicting damaged historic places and calling for donations for repairing and rebuilding. Some used historic buildings to obliterate Nazi imagery, as in the case of a local stamp issued by postal director Hugo Böttcher in Schwarzenberg in Saxony between June and August 1945, which redesigned the ubiquitous "Hitler-head stamps" of the Nazi era by superimposing a silhouette

The ruins carried many different meanings for Germans. In Dresden in 1945 the city became a vast bulletin board as parents and children searched for one another through messages painted on ruined buildings. (photo: Seydewitz, *Zerstörung und Wiederaufbau von Dresden*, unpaginated)

of the famous local castle over the Führer's profile. Government officials attributed the general "lethargy" of many people in badly bombed cities not only to the everyday struggle to get by but to the loss of orientation resulting from the disappearance of historic landmarks. In Cologne there was much public "mourning for what has been lost." Families took outings to the sites of ruins to observe the destruction, in some cases leaving indelible impressions on young people's minds.[71]

Cultural representations reflected and shaped such concerns. Film director Wolfgang Staudte's *The Murderers Are among Us*, released in 1946 as the first of a short-lived genre of "ruin films," used bombed-out Berlin as a backdrop, as did Italian neorealist Roberto Rosselini's 1947 *Germany at Zero Hour*. Cinema was one of the most affordable and popular forms of entertainment in postwar Germany, and the number of film theaters rose from 1,150 to nearly 3,000 in 1948. This medium did much to spread imagery of the country's urban moonscapes, although the impact of Rosselini's film was

Ruins as a souvenir: a U.S. serviceman and his German wife in 1947 at the spot in Munich where they had first met eighteen months previously (photo: *HEUTE* 2, no. 34 [15 April 1947]: 20)

belated, and Staudte used expressionist motifs that reduced the realistic effect of the ruins. Photojournalism was much closer to "the facts" in this regard, although even in this area both German and Allied photographers published highly constructed pictorial images of ruins, horrible scenes of the concentration camps, and photos of U.S. soldiers working to bring a new postwar order to the leveled nation.[72]

Among the critics of historic buildings were public commentators who simplistically equated preservation or reconstruction of historic buildings with a Nazi mentality and modernization with progressive and democratic instincts.[73] As inaccurate as such equations were, they are understandable given the emotions that memories of Nazism aroused. But more sophisticated viewpoints embraced the type of mourning preservationists rigidly rejected without equating a love of history with Nazism. One of the most sensitive critiques of German attachments to national landmarks came amidst one of the least edifying and emotional debates, the controversy over the reconstruction of the Goethe House. Writing in 1947, Walter Dirks, a prominent postwar advocate of socialism on a Christian basis and cofounder of the important journal *Frankfurter Hefte*, argued that any form of rebuilding, whether a restoration or a newly constructed historical copy, would be unacceptable and false because it would obliterate a historical judgment that must not be ignored. Germans should accept this judgment and have the "courage to take leave" of a past in which Goethe was thoroughly impli-

Ruins as a movie set: actress Hildegard Knef (*bottom left*) being filmed in 1947 in the remains of the Munich Regina-Hotel (photo: *HEUTE* 2, no. 38 [15 June 1947]: 16)

cated. "There are connections between the spirit of the Goethe House and the fate of its destruction," wrote Dirks. This Goethean spirit put a premium on classical learning, idealism, and irrealism. More Goethean than Goethe himself, the German people, especially its intellectuals, allowed "the economy and power to run out of control," a situation that had led them down the road to destruction. The German people should now have the courage to acknowledge that "bitter logic" that reduced the Goethe House to ruins and realize that the "verdict of history" was "definitive."[74] Dirks had formulated an appeal to mourn, a call to take leave courageously of a past in which "poets and thinkers" moved all too easily among mass murderers. Rarely was the need to mourn and the concomitant need for democratic reform evoked more explicitly in German public discourse.

Against such arguments, the defenders of tradition mounted their own offensive, most systematically in Frankfurt am Main in the civic group Bund tätiger Altstadtfreunde, which had lost its struggle to have the Paulskirche rebuilt as an exact historical copy instead of with a modernized facade, but would now win the Goethe House controversy. The Bund's supporters argued that saving the *Altstadt* meant saving the "aristocratic core, the vertical structure of the organism of the city of Frankfurt." This was not a call for political reaction, they maintained, but for the realization that modern architectural forms were inappropriate in premodern urban milieus.[75] Georg Hartmann, chair of the foundation responsible for the Goethe House, argued that rebuilding the house was not a lie but an act that evoked a truly great German thinker's contribution to German culture and humanity in general.[76] Everyone understood that the advocates of rebuilding were not arguing that this would be seen as Goethe's real birthplace, he said at the opening of the landmark in 1951. But the house could be and was rebuilt to capture the "old forms and colors" and the original "harmony of scale." This met the preservationist criteria of proportion even though preservationists themselves were ambivalent about the whole scheme. Hartmann's caution notwithstanding, it also claimed an aura of authenticity for the structure that critics said was impossible.

Above all, according to Hartmann, there were "buildings that were more than buildings." The Goethe House needed to be rebuilt because it was a "symbol of the unity of peoples . . . [a] symbol of peace." People throughout the world wanted reconstruction, said Hartmann, who quoted statements from Hermann Hesse, Albert Schweitzer, and Thornton Wilder supporting the new Goethe House. In the context of this transnational interest in the project, the motto of the Goethe House supporters was not "courage to take leave" but "courage to have fidelity" to those humanistic and universalist elements of the German past that had so recently been suppressed. Here the advocates of restoration also supported the spirit if not the letter of preservationist strategy. And they added fuel to the fire of critics such as Dirks and many others, who worried aloud that the restoration of Goethe's house symbolized the restoration of a German national identity that made fundamental democratic reform impossible.

Like the Paulskirche reconstruction and Cologne church debates, the Goethe House controversy engaged the highest levels of German and international public life. The showy ceremony for laying the foundation stone of the rebuilt monument gained international coverage in newsreel features and newspapers, but one commentator writing for the left-wing *Baukunst und Werkform* guessed the perspicacious viewer of the scene might be overcome with the feeling that "in Frankfurt on clear days ghosts made the rounds."[77] There were spirited if not always equivalent battles elsewhere, including the less well documented cities in the Soviet zone before regime orthodoxy settled in, where despite subsequent heroic narratives of rebuilding, much debate arose in city councils and other bodies over what styles reconstruction was to adopt.[78] But there were many other sites of the battle over memory, most of them less internationally famous, in which the defenders of tradition assumed positions that can by no means be reduced to a single common denominator. These sites are in many respects more relevant to the issue of public memory than the Goethe House was because cumulatively they drew in larger audiences and spoke to the general pattern of rebuilding rather than to the reconstruction of a single (albeit nationally and internationally resonant) landmark.

By the late 1940s, for example, defenders of historic buildings began to focus more generally on reconstruction as a negative and destructive process. Almost since the beginning of reconstruction there had been criticism of postwar planning because of corruption, the arrogance of officials, and as in Cologne, the Nazi-era origins of the main reconstruction agency headed by Rudolf Schwarz.[79] But criticism of the loss of historic architecture as such could also be heard as the voices of protest against the razing of damaged historic buildings became more plentiful, more pointed, and more organized. In 1950 the city government of Solingen, near Cologne, decided to destroy the ruin of the historic Goebel House, a palatial two-story building constructed in 1784 as both residence and business address of a tobacco manufacturer that was all but leveled in a bombing raid of November 1944. Local citizens protested vigorously, noting not only that the razing was unjustified because of the condition of the still extant walls of the house, but that city officials' handling of the situation would hardly strengthen the "in any case negligible trust people have for the authorities" because proper permits for the demolition were never gotten. All that remained of the impressive building was the heart-shaped cornerstone, which would be deposited in the city archive. In Düsseldorf by the spring of 1953 a local federation of *Heimat* groups called the Vaterstädtische Arbeitsgemeinschaft had mobilized against what its chair called a "dictatorship of the planners," whose members were guilty of "murder via the drawing board" as they destroyed valuable architecture and cut down mature trees lining important streets and public squares.[80]

Again in contrast to the Goethe House, the issue of what style was best for rebuilt and preserved cities was discussed in real detail only by the more thoughtful critics. When this historicism produced a "clean, balanced architecture of the authentic old city and its modest world of the *Bürger*," as one observer of the Düsseldorf *Altstadt* advocated, conservators could hardly have agreed more.[81] Such *Altstadt* architecture evoked memories of a settled *Bürgertum* still undisturbed by the blandishments and threats of modern commercial societies. For most of the populace, nuanced critiques of architectural style were less useful than a general sense that what looked old was better. This was a popular sense of Riegl's concept of age value transferred into the postwar era. It seemed to make little difference if the old was more or less copied and re-created, as in the case of the Goethe House, which enjoyed substantial popular support despite many intellectuals' criticism of the project. The point was to arouse remembrance per se, rather than to remember something specific, such as the German people's complicity in mass extermination. When the imperative to remember could be combined with direct economic interest, as it was in the case of the Münster retailers' support for the "historicist" reconstruction of the central commercial area, the Prinzipalmarkt, then the chances for reestablishing historic architecture's full age value were even stronger.[82] To the extent defenders of tradition were able to avoid overly schematic or technical discussions of the reconstruction of historic buildings, they were able to speak to such popular desires for a general past mirrored in historic buildings.

Some German cultural officials stated that in the badly bombed cities throughout Germany in 1948 respect for tradition was a rare commodity because "the burden of indescribably difficult conditions of daily existence" made thoughts of "a higher cultural life" impossible.[83] Yet at the level of individual appropriations of historic places, the love of tradition had many uses and many intersections with everyday needs. In the case of Paderborn builder Ludwig Eltz, who in 1949 got a contract from the city of Cologne to rebuild Zur Brezel, two attached half-timbered houses badly damaged in World War II, reconstruction was one part respect for historic architecture and one part economic opportunism for a man trying to start a construction business in the bombed-out Rhenish city.[84] There were many other Ludwig

Age value and a general sense of the past were far more important than historical accuracy in the reconstruction of Münster's Prinzipalmarkt, shown here before World War I (*above*) and as reconstructed after 1945 (*opposite*). (photos: Münster Presse- und Informationsamt)

Eltzes in Germany, where private builders and corporations were often the only ones responsible for rebuilding historic structures outside the select circle of "star" cathedrals and city halls. Politicians, magazines, and newspapers in both East and West celebrated the rubble women's unselfish commitment to clearing up damage to German cities, as they should have, but the need for a food ration card also motivated many individuals whose husbands or fathers were killed or imprisoned and whose children faced hunger. Men cleared rubble as well, often being responsible for breaking off mortar from bricks to be reused in the rebuilding process. Aside from the ration cards that could be gained from such effort, however, young Wolfgang Mischnick, later a prominent Free Democratic Party politician in Bonn, labored as a "stone hitter" on the ruins of the Dresden Hygiene Museum in 1945 so that he could be alongside his father, whose deafness made it impossible to hear warnings for detonations or other demolition work.[85] In such instances the reconstruction and reuse of historic sites depended on the lives, actions, and understandings of an array of people, including not only city officials and the conservator but also the people who lived and worked in the buildings. Here concepts such as "reconstruction" or "memory" were broken down into finer fragments of everyday behavior and

meaning, successive voices, self-interest, familial ties, and constantly transformed appropriations.

For some, and often more pointedly than for most conservators, historic
buildings were to be preserved as inspirations to reconnect with the "better"
part of the German past. This often began with explicitly critical perspectives, particularly in the East, where one critic's account of the "gruesome
destruction of the art city Dresden" typically combined assaults on the
"criminal politics" of Hitler and Anglo-American military forces' "indelible
crime against humanity." In this account Goebbels's happy observation of
March 1945 that one would no longer hear "evening music" in the Zwinger
was put on equal footing with Allied bombing of the defenseless city. But
criticisms of the immediate past appeared in the West as well, often emerging from the direct conflict of local groups over how to remember their
historic artifacts and buildings. A celebration of Mönchen-Gladbach's 600th
anniversary in 1950 drew criticism from one observer, who on hearing the
rhetoric of loyalty to *Heimat* accompanying a display of local historic artifacts, remarked pointedly, "Did not we hear the same thing in Hitler's
time?"[86]

The better Germany could not be envisioned solely by criticizing past
abuses but had an activist and positive side as well. In Berlin there was both
official and popular sentiment for doing away with more than 1,000 street
names referring to Nazi and military figures, and by 1946 local neighbor-

hoods had made so many suggestions to rename streets after resistance heroes or former socialist leaders that the city magistrate stopped accepting proposals.[87] The renaming project foundered in the West, in contrast to the East, where in Berlin and many other cities renamed streets commemorated "personalities from the workers' movement, the antifascist resistance, and socialist reconstruction," as one Dresden guide to historical street names put it. These were the "workers," "heroes of work," rubble women, and "activists of the first hour" who cooperated not only to free Germany from Hitlerism but more specifically to clear away rubble and begin reconstruction. Not all new street names in the East were directly associated with the workers' movement but, rather, struck a more national theme. Less than a week after the creation of the DDR in 1949 the regime renamed one East Berlin street Geschwister-Scholl-Strasse after the brother and sister from Munich who resisted Nazism, were arrested, and were executed in 1943.[88] But what had been popular enthusiasm in the first postwar revulsion against Nazi crimes and an attempt to find all-German symbols of renewal soon became a formulaic state strategy.

There were many examples of public figures who wanted to use German architecture to refer audiences to the positive political tasks of the present. When Cologne celebrated its thousand-year history in 1950, Mayor Ernst Schwering, standing in front of the cathedral before a huge crowd, including dignitaries such as Carlo Schmid, vice-president of the *Bundestag*, told his listeners that the city's historic "sworn brotherhoods uniting artisans and shopkeepers" offered a model of a "free community," a "democracy when democracy still had to be invented." Inspired by this historical spirit, Cologne's reconstruction would work as "a symbol for those forces that could guarantee Germany's reconstruction." Schwering's comment was also a criticism of the present, which could be seen as lacking that true democracy prefigured in Cologne's past. The visual and aural ensemble of the cathedral, the assembled dignitaries, the enthusiastic crowd, and the rhetoric of democracy and reconstruction signaled how thoroughly the cathedral had been recontextualized to serve both positive and critical functions. Just as in preservationist rhetoric, this recontextualization also meant that the developing history of East Germany would be marked as the Other to the West. The same celebration that praised Cologne democracy at the cathedral featured public prayers led by the papal representative pleading that the DDR regime "would not rip down the crosses" from East German churches.[89]

Critical memory could also obviously serve conservative causes. National and provincial representatives of the Deutscher Heimatbund used every opportunity to argue that their message was misused by the Nazi regime. But this effort also had a more distinctly local inflection as supporters of

Heimat groups defended the language of memory, *Heimat*, and rootedness. The mayor of the small town of Mehs who wrote to Rhenish provincial authorities about the reorganization of the RHB in 1948 insisted that pro-Nazis within the organization had done more to hurt the work of historic preservation than anyone else, and that only people who had not joined the NSDAP or who resisted it should be allowed to join the postwar version of the club. The Vreden official who wrote the Rhenish-Westphalian Cultural Ministry in 1949 pointed out that an appreciation of local history and monuments in the county of Ahaus had suffered because of the power of "patriotic history" and "Prussian state thinking"; the postwar period was the time to correct this imbalance.[90] These people assumed critical perspectives on the past, but they did so without giving a full and reflexive account of the roots of National Socialism or Prussianism. Nonetheless, given the discursive tradition in which local *Heimat* groups had been nurtured, it was a considerable cut against the grain, and the potential opening for a larger one.

From such a perspective a conservative Europeanism comparable to that existing among preservationists could also find an appropriate referent in historic buildings for the broader public. Partly under Dutch administration, the county of Rees—like many other counties and cities in these years and like the organizations of expellees[91]—took up "the old tradition" of producing a *Heimat* almanac, replete with pictures of historic buildings on the cover, in 1950. The 1951 almanac included reports and stories advocating "reconciliation and . . . European unity." In 1952 Vreden, also on the Dutch border, planned to celebrate its 700-year anniversary by publishing a comprehensive history of the city, its famous religious foundation, and its monuments, which had been almost completely rebuilt after 40 percent of the historical core had been destroyed by Allied bombing. "With reference to the new European order it is salutary," read the proposal for the history, "to reflect on the damages brought about in particularly affected areas by the age of unnatural and exaggerated national-state splintering of Europe." Significantly, the Vreden proposal attributed popular dissatisfaction with the postwar world not to Nazism or the war but, rather, to the nature of modernity. "It is a danger of modern life," read the proposal, "that historically uprooted and spiritually homeless people are defenselessly exposed to the fashionable trends and slogans of the day." The antidote was to rediscover one's local church, monuments, myth, and tradition to promote not nationalism, as the interwar period had, but the "power of reconciliation and unification of peoples."[92]

The search for "another" Germany mirrored in historic buildings had an even more restorationist inflection than this example for some, although one should be cautious about equating restoration with the absence of change. Let us consider for a moment the situation of elite consumers of historic sites. Very soon after the end of the war the *Kunstfreund,* the connoisseur of fine art, could find much to interest him or her in activities such as the exhibitions of historic stained-glass windows in Stuttgart, Freiburg, and Cologne.[93] Here visitors could view the nation's cultural capital despite or—in the case of glass windows that had been removed to protect them from bomb damage—because of the war in a situation in which the nation as a whole looked poor indeed. At the opposite end of the spectrum of historic sites, in 1951 and 1952 lovers of the *Fachwerkhaus* could go to some sixty exhibits and lectures on that subject held in Kurhessen. Part of the return of "high cultural" sensibilities, such events were also linked to a partial revival of tourism for Americans or better-off Europeans and Germans, who continued to search for that "Romantic Germany" evoked in the 1950 motto of the German Central Administration for Tourism.[94]

The revival of this way of seeing was just one aspect of a larger process whereby representations of historic buildings continued to be surrounded with an aura of tact and good taste, key words of that "affirmative culture" that Herbert Marcuse said sought beauty, truth, and genius in order to stabilize bourgeois rule. In 1952 the Langewiesche publishing house produced another version of its *Die schöne Heimat* picture book.[95] Celebrating the Blue Books series as an "established concept,"[96] the editors stressed that the pictures were designed to appeal not to "reason" but to the "heart," thereby reenacting the old distinction between civilization and culture. Indeed, the pictures were arranged not as an "ordered herbarium" but as a "bouquet of beautiful pictures." The arrangement of photographs was designed to emulate a knowledgeable touristic excursion through Germany, "beginning in the northwest and ending there after having made a giant circle." But this was nothing like a specific itinerary; the point was not "holding to geographical lines"—to do so would have necessitated holding to geopolitical realities—but "a sense of harmony from [viewing] related pictures." It was a touristic experience based on a leisurely organized mix of taste, balance, and harmony. The nineteenth-century *Bildungsbürger,* lover of the cultural nation uncoupled from its political referents, would have found little to disagree with.

Nor would he or she have found the selection or presentation of photos surprising.[97] A cavalcade of black and white cathedrals, half-timbered houses, palaces, and castles passed before the reader's gaze in the 1952 volume; most of the pictures lacked reminders of human use. Strewn through this "bouquet" of public symbols were photographs of modern developments that failed to disturb the harmony of the selection, such as a gently rolling autobahn on the Swabian alp. The caption accompanying the picture of the

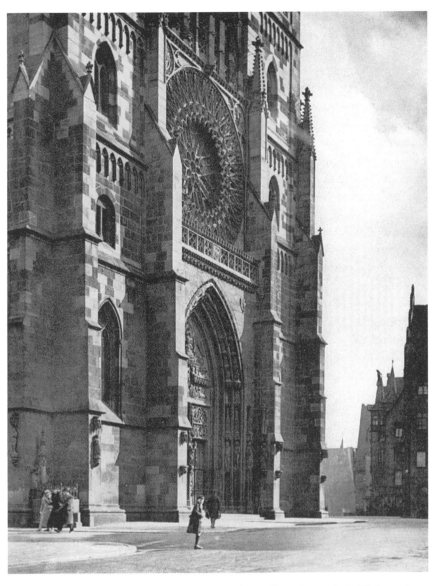

The restoration of established ways of seeing—the famous Nuremberg cathedral St. Lorenz is depicted as it had been before World War II—adapted tradition to the postwar era, creating new forms of West German national identity. (photo: *Die schöne Heimat* [1952], 139)

west facade of the famous St. Lorenz Church in Nuremberg stressed that the church was located in "the second biggest and most industrial city of Bavaria," although there was hardly a view of the truly industrial parts of the city. What is more, the city "had preserved its medieval cityscape until the most recent past." To include this statement without referring to World

War II destruction or the efforts of rebuilding—St. Lorenz itself was heavily damaged, and reconstruction of the massive basilica went on into the 1960s— was to glide over a whole array of painful historical events. The introduction made only vague reference to "destruction during the last war."

The book also retained an older cultural-political perspective. It relied on the classics, in this case the literary authority of early nineteenth-century patriot Ernst Moritz Arndt, to evoke the nation. "Where God's sun first shone," the passage read, "where for you the stars in heaven first gleamed, where lightning first displayed His omnipotence to you and His storm winds first caused holy terror to sweep through your soul, there is your love, there is your fatherland. Where the first human eyes lovingly looked over you in the cradle, where your mother first happily set you on her lap and your father taught you wisdom and Christianity, there is your love, there is your fatherland."[98] Here well-established conventions of linking nature, infancy, mother love, religion, and nation worked in a way that would have been at home before the "last war" had caused its terrible destruction.

Yet the restoration of a tried-and-true way of seeing, talking, and thinking the nation should not hide the fact that *Die schöne Heimat*'s language articulated an important change in public uses of old buildings. Beautiful monuments of centuries past now assumed an updated meaning in the years of postwar reconstruction. As before, the prefigurative element was very strong. It cited its 1915 predecessor on the dustcover, noting that the "task and intention have always been and remain to show *Germany as a unity*."[99] National "unity" referred not just to the tradition of the cultural nation but potentially also to a new political nation that would overcome the transiency of a Germany split by the Cold War and intra-German differences. Moreover, according to the excerpted book review on the back dustcover, the Blue Books stood for "quality, for pride in work and cultural responsibility." It was hoped that such good, *bildungsbürgerliche* qualities would maintain themselves in a "steely diligence" that would help Germans overcome "all economic difficulties"—a viewpoint analogous to the belief in old buildings as economic resources in the Weimar Republic. "Let us vindicate the optimism that is in evidence in the forecast of a purified [*gereinigte*] German future," continued the excerpt, echoing earlier hopes of reconstruction after World War I.

A German "unity," "steely diligence," a "purified future"—the language would have been at home in Nazi Germany. Yet in the new context it reflected a way of seeing that was tied to the developing Cold War, to economic recovery, to democracy as West German elites understood the term, and to an updated conservative modernism that still gained emotional profit from the imagery of premodern and preindustrial culture. The malleability of such traditions rather than their persistence per se is most striking. At the same time, the new use of such imagery acted as only a partial filter of past discursive traditions. The nineteenth century, Weimar, and Nazism were all layered into this appropriation of historic places in a way that few Germans unraveled but which perhaps they sensed.

Significantly, such themes found an echo in more widely accessible appropriations of historic buildings such as *Sammelbilder*. National identity remained a theme of collectors' cards after 1945, although *Blut und Boden* themes from the Nazi era were understandably dropped.[100] There was some idealization of war and the German propensity for military values, but most *Sammelbilder* stressed recovery, the "economic miracle," and German quality work. Historic places remained part of the mix of national symbols. One 1952 card album titled "Beautiful Germany" showed cities and architectural monuments that either had not been destroyed or had been restored. There were no mountains of rubble, and many of the pictures of monuments came not from the early 1950s but from 1932, the year in which the album had first been issued. Just as West German albums stressed idyllic *Heimat* untouched by war, a DDR collector card album from a cigarette manufacturer lauded traditional peasant dress as an antidote to capitalist "fashion." More often, however, DDR albums stressed not historic buildings as national symbols but an egalitarian "German Democratic Republic under Construction," as a 1956 album was titled.

Popular appropriation of historic buildings as national symbols led to critical Europeanist, Marxist, and restorationist-nationalist perspectives, but no point of view could have had wide resonance without the revival of popular antiquarianism. In many instances antiquarianism dealt directly with reconstruction. Motivated by the damage done to its church, city hall, and medieval gable houses, a group of citizens from the lower Rhine city Kalkar, almost half of whose thirteenth-century town center was destroyed, announced the founding of the Association of the Friends of Kalkar in 1947, asking for support from the cultural ministry in its effort to appeal "to the whole world" for help in saving its architectural treasures. But usually the antiquarian impulse had an even wider ambit. In late 1948 Cologne officials could speak of "wildly growing local-cultural activities" crisscrossing the social life of their city, prompting them to think of ways to "steer, order, hold in check, and above all to plan" *Heimat* culture. The thousand-year anniversary of Cologne in 1950 was an especially popular and emotional event as thousands of Kölner assembled in the square in front of the cathedral, which loomed above the piles of rubble surrounding the celebrants.[101] In this context, historic preservation reacted to popular enthusiasms as much as it nurtured and organized them.

This is quite clear for Düsseldorf, where *Heimat* clubs entered territory where more visible and politically fraught groups such as the RVDH still had to tread softly. A small group of members from the Düsseldorfer Jonges had gathered on 8 May 1945, less than a month after the entry of American troops into the city, although they had to await a September British decree allowing assemblies to start *Verein* activity again. Founded in 1932, Jonges met amidst the ruins in its favorite pub "Im Anker," becoming one of the most active and visible local *Heimat* associations in the late 1940s, "like a phoenix from the ashes," as one local history put it in metaphorical language common in this period. In 1947 club president Wilhelm Weidenhaupt, a baker, wrote the provincial cultural ministry, saying the group was ready to broaden its goals after the first difficult postwar years, a strategy cultural authorities had been encouraging since they thought the RVDH was still too vividly remembered as a "definite propaganda instrument of the [Nazi] party." Noting that it wanted to avoid "all misleading phraseology, sentimental (because misunderstood) concepts such as *Heimat* and 'Blood and Soil,' " Düsseldorfer Jonges threw itself into a broad campaign of publication, money collection for German prisoners of war, radio and press activity, involvement in youth groups, and historic preservation. Club membership grew from 600 at the beginning of 1947 to 1,250 in 1951 as youth groups were formed and more than 30 *Tischgemeinschaften*, social circles dating back to 1932, were revived. The club's slide show presentations to the general public dealing with *Altstadt* architecture were particularly well attended.[102]

The majority of Germans were silent about their emotional investments in Nazism and the Holocaust. But they did not turn their back on history. The immediate postwar era was a time of intense political, professional, and public interest in the past, a moment when tremendous efforts were undertaken to reestablish continuities that the war and Nazism seemed to cut definitively. This process was by no means natural or assured. For many Germans at all social levels, both past and future seemed to collapse into a present that was as long as the time until the next rations could be secured. A part of my narrative is therefore a success story describing the extraordinary energies necessary to reconstruct public memories in times of crisis.

Undamaged, restored, or reconstructed historical buildings played a special role in this context, as their size, their association not mainly with specific historic events but with a sense of the past, and their role for national, local, and personal memories provided an objective backdrop to the reconstruction of normality. The question of how historical buildings should refer to the past—a burning issue for intellectuals, planners, and preservationists—was less consequential for the wider public than the question of whether such references should exist at all. Although there were many Germans in government and society who were willing to take leave of damaged or destroyed historical buildings, the majority of people in East and West wanted to preserve, restore, and even reconstruct these material reminders, these places of memory, of a cultural nation. Yet as before the war, there were many cultural nations, many ways of appropriating the national past for contemporary social uses. The measure of success of the idea of the cultural nation was whether it could be adapted and reused in a variety of social contexts.

If the commemorative noise of the period did little to examine critically the roots of the crisis in which Germans found themselves, it underscored and heightened the importance of common national pasts shared by various groups in separate occupation zones as well as in the newly founded states of 1949. The period was restorationist in this sense, but restoration involved change and adaptation, murky transitions rather than simple continuities. Moreover, the continuities were variable, as some groups picked up on unacknowledged traditions from the Nazi period while others, notably many official representatives of preservation, sought connections with pre–World War I Germany. Historical buildings served as malleable referents for these multiple temporalities.

This chapter suggests that the reestablishment of common national pasts was necessary if a more critical engagement with the history of Nazism were to take place. This was as true for advocates of monuments as it was for participants in other areas of cultural politics. Seventy-five years previously Nietzsche had stated that critical history constituted a danger if it was allowed to overpower antiquarian and monumental history. The protectors and reconstructors of historic buildings agreed. The commemorative labors explored in this chapter should therefore be seen as the necessary fundament for a *potentially* critical view of German history in years to come. If this critical potential was unrealized, or if it was not realized in ways that did justice to the victims and their memory, then this was not a product of the unavailability of historical resources or a general public desire to flee the past. In the next chapter we examine the early 1950s to the mid-1960s, an era in which public interest in historic preservation and history in general did indeed decline, and in which the potential for a critical awareness of the historical roots of Nazism seemed even more remote than in the immediate postwar years. In the light of this later evidence, the foregoing is ultimately a narrative of missed opportunities.

O Germany, you're torn asunder

And not just from within!

Abandoned in cold and darkness

The one leaves the other alone.

And you've got such lovely valleys

And plenty of thriving towns;

If only you'd trust yourself now,

Then all would be just fine.

—Bertolt Brecht, 1952

SIX | **SIX | A NORMAL MEMORY** MORY

espite causing massive destruction, World War II also gave many Germans a specific point of reference to the past in the immediate postwar years. The war was a major break, and Germans oriented themselves to prewar times in order to reassert national continuity. Even those who used the war as the opening to a new future looked to a prewar past, as in the case of modernist architects who took inspiration from the interwar architecture of Gropius, May, and Taut. As the reconstruction of German cities moved forward, the direct damages of the war soon assumed a secondary significance, and modern and historical townscapes alike assumed, more or less, their normal silhouettes. Conservators as well as local preservation groups began to fight battles over less famous structures that reconstruction threatened to sweep away. Despite differences in the scope and timing of rebuilding in both West and East, it was no longer possible on either side of the border to focus only on the effects of the war because a subtler war, a battle over the secular process of reproducing German cities, evolved. War damage was mixed with "peace damage," whose effects derived from the "normal" needs of an urban-industrial and Cold War world.

A new and uncertain future—and thus a new and equally uncertain past—intervened between Germans and World War II.

For some the experiences that were most relevant to the new situation were those of the 1930s, when Germans saw a recovery that in context was as unprecedented as the one they were going through in the 1950s. Despite the Nazi regime's insistence on cultural revolution and *Leistung*, recovery's goal had been normality and respite—from World War I, from political chaos, from economic scarcity, and from "racial degeneration." Just as Germans wanted to reestablish what was seen as a prewar normality in the 1930s, West Germans of the 1950s wanted a normal, advanced European industrial nation with the cultural and material security it was thought to entail. Secular destruction caused by economic and urban growth would have to be accepted, at least within certain limits. If a key aspect of critical memory is the desire to create a past in which one would like to originate, then in this era Germans, like their 1930s counterparts, imagined a past in which they played the role not of the shipwrecked Robinson Crusoe but, rather, of the modern consumer.[1] When Bertolt Brecht wrote ironically that "all would be just fine" if only his country of thriving towns and lovely valleys would trust itself, many Germans stripped this passage of its subversiveness, leaving only the sentiment of wanting everything—past, present, and future—to be just fine.[2] From their usual position of cultural off-centeredness, the protectors of historic buildings shared the national thirst for normality.

The New Past

What chronology underlay the evolving past of this era? Ludwig Erhard, the father of the West German Economic Miracle, argued that the postwar era had ended in 1965.[3] Since the founding of the Federal Republic there had been undisturbed Christian Democratic leadership, shaped most successfully by Konrad Adenauer until 1963 and then by Erhard himself until 1966. This was the most sustained period of party-political stability since Bismarck's chancellorship had ended in 1890. The return of economic security and the promise of even greater material prosperity—both within the memory of Germans who lived through National Socialism and the immediate postwar years—were unmistakable. From 1950 to 1961 West German real GNP per capita doubled as industry flourished and the country reasserted its position as a major global trader. An unprecedented housing boom and suburban expansion took place, fluctuating but not slowing substantively until the early 1970s. Traffic-driven cities, tourism, commercialization of leisure time and culture, and the overpowering influence of American tastes in cinema, popular music, and clothing styles all reflected the relative political calm and economic well-being that gave credence to Erhard's chronology.

The DDR was often seen by the West as a counterexample, the Other. But here, too, there was a form of economic miracle based on reconstruction and the stabilization of political life, especially after the building of the Berlin Wall in 1961. Even without the wall, by the late 1950s some East German officials had enough confidence (or lack of realism) to predict their economy would overtake that of the West in the near future. East Germany tried to compensate for its comparative disadvantage with the West by promoting socialist state ownership of property and centralized planning for reconstruction. Such experiments failed abysmally, partly because political considerations constantly overrode sound economic calculation. Nonetheless, one cannot fail to note that in the context of the time, the regime had a right to claim it had provided new hope for people whose memories of the first bitter postwar years were still sharp.[4]

If the postwar world had ended, then a new emotional regime, a new pattern of political-cultural legitimacy, was needed. This placed a premium on symbolism and history. In one respect this was an inheritance from the Nazi era, when everything was permeated with symbolic meaning. Yet the conditions of the period also demanded a new set of symbolic resources. National flags and anthems, stamps and coins, the choice of Bonn and Berlin as capitals, the renaming of streets, and statistical reports of economic growth all had an important symbolic function. Politicians in both East and West also used historic buildings freely in the struggle over symbols. The completed restoration of the "German Kaiserdom," the Speyer Cathedral, in September 1961 gave government and church officials the chance to promote the idea of the German nation's origins in an ancient, "God-fearing, Occidental world" that offered hope for the speedy removal of the "arbitrarily constructed wall of hate" of a "Godless system." Officials on both sides of the wall of hate, constructed only a month before the Speyer ceremony, used historic buildings to make similarly ideological statements.[5]

The struggle over historical symbols also gained urgency from the destructive energies released by economic and social success. In the BRD economic prosperity created a more mobile but also more "alienated" society in which not only critics but also political leaders spoke of a need for a cultural life richer than that offered by liberal consumerist ideology. The German Urban League called for a wider cultural palette in German cities, one of many worthy demands that organization made without having the economic wherewithal to realize it. At the 1956 Christian Democratic Party annual conference in Stuttgart, one delegate painted West German cultural life in provocative terms in comparison with East Germany. "Go over the

The new past appears on the horizon of East German expectations. Under a banner proclaiming, "We are building the new Dresden," Walter Ulbricht speaks at the ceremonial laying of the cornerstone of the city's soon-to-be-reconstructed historic center on 31 May 1953. (photos: Seydewitz, *Zerstörung und Wiederaufbau von Dresden*, unpaginated)

A NORMAL MEMORY

border once and see," he said, "what there is in cultural life, in cultural associations, theater, subventions, and the like. They give out millions, while we make only minimal sums available."[6] This criticism stemmed in part from a traditional *bürgerlich* anxiety that the state was not spending enough to protect *Kultur* from the demons of commercial society. But it also pointed to the specific and uniquely powerful tensions that West Germany's successful normality had brought about, to say nothing of the intimacy with which national images in East and West fed off one another.

The cultural crisis of normality was evident in the transformation of the built environment, where a significant loss of older buildings linking past and present occurred. From 1956 to 1968 the share of all residential buildings in the BRD built before 1918 fell from almost half of the total to less than a third. In the same period the share of residences built after 1948 increased from more than one-quarter of the total to more than one-half. One would expect to see increases in the share new residential housing had in an expanding number of total buildings in this era of rapid reconstruction. Yet reconstruction did not only add new buildings; it also included the tearing down of old ones and their replacement. If West Germans still wanted to see architecture from before the twentieth century—and many still did—the best place to do so in this age of helter-skelter growth was in smaller communities. Cities and towns of less than 100,000 inhabitants contained three-quarters of all residential buildings erected before 1900, accounting for one-fifth of all residential buildings in the BRD in 1968. In East Germany, by contrast, pre-twentieth-century buildings accounted for nearly 43 percent of all residential structures. This was of course not wholly due to regime policy but also to neglect and shortages in the construction industry. In the Federal Republic, villages of less than 2,000 inhabitants had the largest percentage of old buildings; in such communities almost four of every ten residential structures dated from before the turn of the century.[7] Nonetheless, the overall tendency was a continuous reduction in older buildings, and even smaller communities were not left untouched by the destructive *Leistung* of the Economic Miracle.

Proclamations of the end of the postwar era, economic growth, political stability, the need for symbolic and cultural orientation, and destruction of the built environment allowed a new past to intrude between the present and the war. Consciousness of national history and identity was transformed in the process. After reviving the memory of nineteenth-century liberal democracy via its use of political symbols such as the black-red-gold flag, after reasserting the importance of Christian tradition, and after celebrating economic performance as a return to German values, West Germany assumed a hybrid form that made it neither a direct descendant of earlier German history nor something totally new. Just a year before Erhard declared that the postwar period had ended, critic Hans Magnus Enzensberger asked skeptically, "Am I a German?," arguing that for his countrymen, "the extinction of nationality as an objective, socially galvanizing force is comparatively near at hand." Nonetheless, the idea of national identity lived on, shaped in Germany by a combination of pride and self-hate, and no one could predict how the "shadows of former nations" would continue to regulate German and European identities. Enzensberger's solution was a shrug of the shoulders: "I have no wish to quarrel with those who attach more importance to the fact that I am a German than I do. I shall accept this fact whenever possible, and ignore it whenever necessary."[8]

The critic's skeptical acceptance of what he saw as an anachronistic sense of Germanness pinpointed the prosperous nation's uncertain relationship to the past and the future. Growth and dynamism gave a presumably less "national" future a new dominance without cutting away the past entirely. By the end of the period under consideration, many West Germans concluded that the BRD was neither a "transitory stage" on the way to a united Europe nor a short-lived "provisional step" on the way to national reunification.[9] But then what was it? A normal national existence—the ability to say "I am a German" and feel everything was "just fine"—meant that "the future had to be overcome" even if the national past continued to cast a shadow over events.[10]

Analogous developments occurred in the other Germany. After claiming to be a complete break with the past, East Germany began to explore its relationship with German history. This derived from a belief that the German Democratic Republic too had achieved a certain normality as it completed the transition from capitalism to socialism. Focusing on the future, the DDR wanted to stabilize the past so as to portray the "socialist nation" as a natural outcome of German history. This trend toward constructing a "persuasive historical culture" and national myth-building became much stronger in the 1970s under Erich Honecker's regime, but it could be seen in the 1950s as well.[11] Since mid-1952 there had been a stronger emphasis on national tradition in DDR speeches, writings, books, press, radio, and film. Leading members of the regime such as Minister of Education Fritz Lange began publicly to stress the national accomplishments of Prussian official Karl Freiherr vom Stein, Prussian military leader Gerhard von Scharnhorst, and other heroes of the period from 1807 to 1815. In 1953 the regime decided to build the National Research Center and Memorial of Classical German Literature in Weimar, which was dedicated to Marxist research and popularization of German literature from 1750 to 1850. Walter Ulbricht himself called for new, more positive considerations of German history in

1952, saying that "until now German history has been represented so often as the 'German misery.' "[12]

As in the West, the built environment had a role to play. In the wake of the destruction of politically unsavory landmarks, East German architectural writers in 1951 advocated finding a "new national German architecture" whose positive referent was the Soviet Union and whose negative referent was the Bauhaus, which *Neues Deutschland*, using language reminiscent of the National Socialist era, called the "true-blue child of American cosmopolitanism." This view of the past had a triple function. It served to distinguish the evolving "proletarian" architecture of the DDR from the architecture of West Germany. It served to delegitimize East German intellectuals who wanted to adapt the Bauhaus tradition to a socialist future, such as writers Ludwig Renn and Rudolf Leonhardt, or architects Franz Ehrlich and Waldemar Adler, who drew up the first plans for what was to become the major steel-working city Stalinstadt, later Eisenhüttenstadt. And finally, it opened the way to a reevaluation of German historical architecture and monuments in a way that potentially re-created a common ground between the two Germanys. In contrast to the Bauhaus, which had been a source of enormous conflict in the Weimar Republic, Kurt Liebknecht, nephew of Karl Liebknecht and president of the East German Academy of Architecture, offered Schinkel's classicism as the "last progressive architecture" in the German past. By emphasizing classicism, Liebknecht pointed to an epoch whose historical and cultural importance was unquestionable in both East and West. Because preservationists on both sides of the border still identified 1830 as the cutoff point for monuments, they too could agree on Liebknecht's evaluation.[13]

The new architecture would be "understandable to the *Volk* and would be appropriate to its individuality [*Eigenart*] and sense of beauty," as stated in a 1954 handbook. It would depart not only from the "formalism" of the Bauhaus but also from what was seen as the "functionalism" of U.S. architecture. Its ideal was captured in the massive offices, apartment buildings, and monuments lining the Stalinallee (formerly Frankfurter Allee, later the Karl-Marx-Allee) in Berlin, a planned seven-kilometer-long intentional monument to the working-class movement, to be built largely with material from World War II ruins. Of this elaborate streetscape, which was never properly completed, East German poet Johannes R. Becher wrote in 1952,

Name, that everyone knows,
radiating more than ever:
Street—your Monument!
Proud Stalinallee.

Less sanguine observers of such architecture described it as a combination of "speculative baroque" and "barrack classicism" that was related to Berlin planning of the late 1920s and Speer's ideas for remaking the city as the capital of a Nazi world empire. In the early 1950s East German architecture would assume historicist and national forms, while later it adopted more functionalist and notionally socialist characteristics using much-derided methods of prefabricated slab construction (*Plattenbau*). By the early 1960s East German architecture and urban planning followed the path taken not just by other Communist states but also by the West, namely to find more systematic ways to integrate the preexisting urban fabric into plans for the future.[14]

The Central Committee of the SED resolved in 1955 that more needed to be done to research and popularize the vernacular architecture of villages, cities, and counties because "the struggle for the development and victory of a Marxist-Leninist historiography in the German Democratic Republic must also be fought on the terrain of the history of *Heimat*."[15] Cultural monuments, "characteristic documents of the cultural development of a people," as well as technical monuments, whose history reflected the "level of development of the forces of production," were among the most important sources in this turn to local roots. Identity politics was not the only goal of such research, which was also to provide data for town and village planning.[16] As such, an understanding of vernacular urban and architectural forms was to be part of a broader social revolution in which the entire populace was brought into regime-directed cultural activities. This also led to the adaptive reuse of churches as museums and community centers or of the former villas of industrialists, National Socialist chieftains, and big landholders as "Houses of Culture," which numbered about 1,000 in 1958. These were attached to factories or collective farms and had reading rooms, meeting halls, and cinemas.[17]

The future dominated national memory in both Germanys, and thus it is unsurprising to find that both countries had similar approaches to the commemoration of the victims of Nazism in the built environment. On the face of it the two states could not have been more different. In the BRD normalization created an environment in which the commemoration of Jewish and other victims of Nazi extermination had abstract religious motifs, a result of the general valorization of religiosity and "Occidental culture" in the 1950s. These rarely evoked detailed pictures of either perpetrators or victims. Even when a "flood of commemoration" swept over West Germany in later years, it failed to pinpoint German complicity in mass murder or deal effectively with the fate of the victims. Throughout the decades after the war, commemoration resulted from conflicts between Bonn, local citizens' initiatives, political parties, and municipalities. In the East, by contrast, centrally planned monuments such as the Buchenwald concentration camp site, set up as an elaborate *Gedenkstätte* in 1958, or Sachsenhausen, which served as a Nazi concentration camp, an internment camp overseen by the Soviet Union after the war, and an East German memorial center since 1961, were shaped by the prevailing regime ideology of "antifascism." This made victims as well as perpetrators as indistinct as they were in the West.[18]

Revived Institutions

Preservationists shared the wider culture's desire for normality. This was reflected in part in their effort to create narrative closure on the immediate postwar years. Writing in 1952, Hamburg conservator Günther Grundmann looked back at the previous years of reconstruction, noting that "precisely what appeared to be impossible became reality the next day, what was supposed to be absolutely certain shortly became unrealizable." This also applied to preservation, where "much that just a few years before was considered to be restorable was suddenly written off, and much that appeared to be hopelessly lost was more quickly and fundamentally preserved because new points of view and new possibilities suddenly turned up."[19] Grundmann wrote in a particular historical and spatial context: Hamburg possessed little historic architecture, took the modernizing route during reconstruction, and preserved or rebuilt historical buildings in a kind of Hanseatic Disneyland on the Cremoninsel. Yet he touched on a sentiment that many preservationists shared. No previous era presented quite this combination of insecurity and possibility. It was an exciting but unpredictable period that the new era of normality would hopefully bring to an end.

Normalization depended in part on reasserting a prewar optics against a narrower view of monuments that obtained in the immediate postwar years. For most of the preservation lobby, the early nineteenth century remained the unofficial cutoff point for monumental status, and structures erected during the 1920s, to say nothing of National Socialist architecture, enjoyed no legal protection and little disciplinary interest. Preservation laws reinforced this narrowness by categorizing monuments as buildings belonging to an already closed epoch of architectural history.[20]

Yet the expanded views of the prewar age were returning, and the mid-1950s saw increased discussion of the need to protect hitherto neglected artifacts such as peasant architecture, which in the Rhineland resulted in the formation of the area's third open-air museum dealing with rural customs and artifacts in Mechenich-Kommern near Euskirchen. Preservationists also turned their attention to rapidly disappearing historic paving stones in cities such as Hildesheim, Würzburg, and Mölln. Responding to postwar initiatives in industrial archaeology in Great Britain, officials such as Josef Röder, director of the Landesmuseum Koblenz from 1956 to 1975, began systematic protection of "technical cultural monuments." The first comprehensive inventory of extant architecture and artifacts of the industrial revolution in the Federal Republic would not appear until 1975, although provincial inventories, such as that produced by the Landesamt für Denkmalpflege in Schleswig-Holstein in 1969, did include information on technical and maritime monuments, including lighthouses. Meanwhile the Lübeck conservator preserved and studied an early nineteenth-century lighthouse and an eighteenth-century salt warehouse in 1964. In 1961 the association of West German conservators responded favorably to Berlin's renewal and preservation of ensembles of nineteenth-century apartments in the Kreuzberg district, one of the most damaged areas of the city, describing the effort as unusually "worthy of notice." The conservators also pointed out that the Kreuzberg project illustrated a new popular interest in the middle and later nineteenth century, which would increase in unprecedented ways in the next fifteen years. Preservationists debated how far this interest should be accommodated.[21]

In East Germany a shift toward a broader vision of monuments was registered in part in the way regime authorities returned to prewar ideas about the proper disciplinary goals of preservation. As the new system stabilized, it became less interested in eradicating the architectural traces of Nazism and Prussian militarism and more willing to return to a program of protection for "churches, castles, city halls, and *Bürger* residences, that is, the objects of classical historic preservation," as the chief of the Berlin office of preservation in the DDR wrote.[22] This included less emphasis on the restoration of landmarks destroyed by World War II (although many of these had still not been restored) and more on monuments hitherto neglected or underutilized.[23] To carry out its task, official preservation was reorganized in 1953 in the Institut für Denkmalpflege, which integrated provincial agencies into a new hierarchical structure. Distinguishing between the heritage of German history as a whole and those parts of the past that could be integrated into progressive traditions, the regime restored landmarks previously associated with reactionary political history, as in the case of the Brandenburger Tor, which from 1957 to 1959 became a monument of peace stripped of its Prussian symbolism. The shift was also registered in a slippage of temporal borders. If the East German state continued to focus mainly on preindustrial monuments, by the early 1960s it had also begun to consider more recent structures such as the Bauhaus buildings in Dessau. Castigated as a product of American imperialism in the early 1950s, the Bauhaus was rehabilitated in the 1960s and put under legal protection as a historic monument in 1964. Meanwhile, DDR preservationists researched rural and small-town "people's architecture," producing the first comprehensive survey of peasant architecture on East German soil from 1965 to 1968.[24]

Contrasting attitudes toward ruins on either side of the German-German border also reflected the desire for normality. The West allowed few ruins to stand, among them several notable churches: the Kaiser-Wilhlem-Gedächtnis-Kirche and Klosterkirche in Berlin, St. Alban's in Cologne, St. Nikolai's in Hamburg, and the Aegidienkirche in Hannover. Hardly unanimous in their response to such projects, preservationists' attitudes toward the popular Kaiser-Wilhelm-Gedächtnis-Kirche, an 1890s product of Wilhelm II's love of Rhenish Romanesque architecture severely damaged in the war, ranged from "absolute support to clear rejection." As for another famous Berlin ruin, the Reichstag building, they were generally positive about its restoration from 1957 to 1961, although they noted that the heavily simplified exterior of the restored building had an uneven look, since in the early stages of work the architects were unable to get Silesian quarry stone, which architect Paul Wallot had used in the original, and had instead used a combination of old parts and new pieces of Nesselberg sandstone from near Hannover.[25] Overall, conservators were less willing than before to tolerate ruins. "Precisely because of the experience of great destruction in World War II," wrote J. M. Ritz in 1956, "the striving for completeness has grown. The ruin as such no longer has the high status it once had."[26]

The ruin found a more hospitable home in East Germany, where an emphasis on new building marginalized the reconstruction of landmarks. Too, the East German state was not interested in reconstructing churches except when such projects enhanced the regime's political standing or brought in valued foreign currency raised by the Lutheran Church's Special Building Program. But the churches' efforts in this area also had limits, and thus important historical churches in Frankfurt an der Oder, Dresden, Beeskow, Rathenow, Wriezen, and elsewhere remained ruins. Where reconstruction was impossible, churches worked to shore up sagging walls and store salvaged artifacts in anticipation of later restoration. Government conservators discussed "ruins in the city" as a town-planning concept that could be defined and cultivated for later policy initiatives.[27] Ruins were thus integrated into urban fabrics and the planning process although they were not seen in toto as permanent elements. The DDR was planning to have all remaining World War II ruins in the Dresden city center reconstructed by 1990, with the notable exception of the eighteenth-century Frauenkirche, still acknowledged as "one of the most important Protestant church buildings" and the "most important symbol of the Dresden city silhouette." In a city plan-

In 1956 J. M. Ritz wrote, "The ruin as such no longer has the high status it once had."
Whereas this may have been true for West German preservationists, it was not so for the
wider public, who embraced one of preservationists' least favored ruins, the Kaiser
Wilhelm Memorial Church, shown here in two postcards, one before World War II (*left*)
and the other in 1948. (photos: author's collection)

ning document from 1967, authorities earmarked the Frauenkirche ruin for
development as a war memorial. The site eventually received a plaque ex-
horting citizens to join "the struggle against imperialist barbarism, [and] for
peace and happiness of mankind."[28]

Such differences suggested the range of meanings that ruins evoked in
this era. In the West, the rapidly disappearing ruin symbolized the Economic Miracle's ability to cut away most remaining traces of wartime destruction. Normality demanded the end of the ruin as concept and physical
reality. In the East, ruins were more visible and politically instrumental for
the regime's antifascist ideology, but this did not necessarily mean they
signified a greater general interest in keeping alive the memory of German
political folly. For preservationists they may have been embarrassing markers of how insubstantial the preservation cause was in East German cultural
politics; for churches they were vivid reminders of the state's hostility to
religion; and for Western tourists they were yet another example of the
inferiority of Communism. Yet they were also integrated into the everyday

A NORMAL MEMORY

life of the DDR in ways that made them as "natural" as the carefully restored churches and public buildings on the Western side.

As before, preservation's status as an institution depended on relationships with its surrounding penumbra of support groups. This remained true even in the East, where cultural policy was highly centralized. Here government conservators relied on voluntary work, often carried out by members of the Kulturbund der DDR, who assisted in inventorying monuments and had specialized programs on historic preservation and *Heimat* culture. These were the diminished but still relevant East German descendants of the cultured *Bürgertum* that had always supported preservation. They had equivalents in other European socialist states, where volunteers not only cooperated with authorities but sometimes reversed or altered official policies.[29] As for the West, I have noted that the high point of the relationship between historic preservation and *Heimatschutz* occurred in the Weimar Republic and the Nazi regime. There was still sentiment among conservators in the late 1940s and early 1950s to revive the joint congresses of the two groups begun before 1914.[30] But generally preservation distanced itself from *Heimatschutz* at the national level, as *Heimatschutz* disavowed its links with Nazism. Such perspectives on the recent past did not stand in the way of further institutional cooperation between the protectors of old buildings and *Heimat* activists. Nor did it deter the RVDH from being involved in projects with direct relevance for *Heimat* groups, such as a comprehensive program begun in 1960 to catalog Rhenish rural villages.[31]

The Association of West German Conservators formed new contacts with West German restorers' and art historians' professional associations in the 1950s. Mirroring the attitude of West German political culture, the association also stressed the need to bring Germany out of international isolation. In the 1950s it established a close working relationship with UNESCO, and the head of the association, Günther Grundmann, became West Germany's corresponding member with the International Committee of Monuments, Artistic and Historical Sites, and Archaeological Excavations. The association also invited East German conservators to its annual conferences beginning in 1954, although Grundmann was quick to point out that as of 1961 this had not been reciprocated. Still, East German conservators were not isolated in this period, as they worked to establish international contacts with professional preservation agencies in other eastern bloc countries. Selected individuals also took limited advantage of West German conservators' invitations, and some were able to host small groups of West German preservationists in their country, as in 1962 (just one year after Grundmann's complaint) when some thirty employees of conservators' offices in Halle, Dresden, Brandenburg, and Schwerin accompanied Western colleagues on a three-day tour of landmarks in East Germany.[32]

Internally, the new West German association worked on a number of projects, including inventorying, a key aspect of preservationist strategy since the nineteenth century and one of the most important areas in the first ten years of the group's existence. Inventorying had become a contested issue in West Germany. Some argued it was a purely scientific undertaking; others used inventories as necrological substitutes for monuments that were quickly disappearing. Bavarian conservator Heinrich Kreisel warned against both tendencies, noting that inventories were necessary to serve their original purpose as aids to both specialists and the public. Kreisel noted that every week his office received an average of 2 requests to tear down landmarks and another 150 to modify them, and that experts estimated it would take sixty years to research the seventy-five Bavarian counties that had still not been covered. Bavaria was a microcosm of a general German backwardness in this area, as the BRD had nothing to show that was quite as ambitious as the national inventory of French monuments initiated by André Malraux in 1964, which systematically included historic peasant dwellings.[33]

By the early 1960s, conservators' congresses emphasized that the tasks of saving the most famous monuments had more or less been achieved, drawing yet another line under the narrative of the immediate postwar years. It was time to consider more specialized handling of those monuments, such as the matter of the original color of medieval churches, as well as the protection of less publicly visible historic architecture. As widely discussed in this period as inventorying, the question of color and historic landmarks indicated how preservation had opened itself to trends that just thirty years earlier were politically controversial. A radical in his time, Bruno Taut was now praised for his "healthy reaction" to the gray-on-gray treatment of monuments that had prevailed for so long.[34]

A Nation Like Any Other

A discourse of cultural-national normality gave shape and purpose to such institutional arrangements and practices. The opening statement of the revitalized *DKD* stressed that "historic preservation is intimately connected to the spiritual and material life of our *Volk*. Its responsibility is to maintain and preserve the visible signs of those forces without which a nation is incapable of living."[35] Here Germany, a nation that could live without monuments no more successfully than any other, appeared normal, continuous, and thing-like. In contrast to the immediate postwar era, when in fact the German nation was a matter of uncertainty, the nation was now assured some form of existence, albeit one that would be impoverished and vulnerable in the long term without historic landmarks. One could read this subtle shift in emphasis elsewhere, as in the 1952 essay by historian Fritz Rörig published posthumously in the Lübeck historical society journal. Discussing "the city in German history," Rörig noted that "the end of the German city" seemed to have come in World War II. But six years later "the view into the future" was "not without all hope." "If in the future we should manage to live in a morally based, unified entity of the *Volk* and the state," wrote Rörig, "then we can hope for an inner renewal and even new flowering of our cities."[36]

A more elongated view of German national continuity and anticipated future normality was offered in 1952 by Christian Wallenreiter, a Bavarian cultural official, who wrote that through monument preservation, "history, in a concentrated and heightened form, is continuously present, awakening that healthy historical consciousness that does not hamper our development through misuse of the past, but rather through the most natural connection bestows on us its most valuable treasures." "We gaze into this mirror of life," he continued "not because we want to sink into the past, but because we want to guard against sinking into the events of the present, because we want our people to recognize itself."[37] This statement was regulated by a discourse in which the idea of a coherent national memory not only had continued relevance but was projected into a safer future. The preservation of historic buildings was there to help the German people "recognize itself," to see a "most natural connection" between past and present without misusing the past in the way Nazism had. Historic buildings reminded Germans not to remember specific events or injustices but to remember to remember they *were* a people with a commitment to later generations.

To remember specifically would in fact not only have been a departure from a long tradition of memory; it would also have been politically risky. Characterizing Germany as a nation like any other presupposed forgetting the unique and unprecedented events that had taken place just years before. Like any other nation, Germany needed monuments, but how could those monuments possibly recall a past like that of any other nation without forgetting the history that made Germany unlike other nations in Western modernity? By reasserting the structural forgetfulness of historic preservation, Wallenreiter's appeal was able to square the circle created by this dilemma. The normal workings of collective memory, its selectivity and malleability within the limits of specific discursive traditions, could thus be applied to a very unique and destructive history. Monumental and antiquarian modes of memory could be used to suppress the critical mode or that part of the critical mode focused on the war and the victims of Nazism.

Wallenreiter's efforts also pointed to an important shift in the relationship between modes of national memory. If monumental memory had dominated the activities of preservationists in the first postwar years, when the most well-known archipelagoes of memory were reconstructed, then antiquarian memory assumed a stronger if still not dominant role in official preservation in this period. The war's traumatic destruction of historical church bells was widely discussed in this period, for example, and preservationist Ernst Sauermann contributed to the discussion by reminding Germans that Europe as a whole had just gone through a "thirty years' war" stretching from 1914 to 1945, in which bells were among the most important artistic losses. The remaining bells recalled a history of "German industriousness in art" that stretched back to Carolingian times. Walther Zimmerman stressed the pervasiveness of bells in everyday German memory, writing that "especially in the countryside the bells are so intimately tied to the life of the community that they play a big role in the consciousness of each individual. The tone of the bells of one's *Heimat* accompanies each individual's memory, and connects them with the joy and pain of human life."[38]

Historic bells thus reminded Germans of etched-in historical identities based on what were seen as ancient traditions of performance and productivity. They alerted Germans to the hardships they shared with other Europeans, even if these hardships were the direct result of a murderous regime many Germans had enthusiastically supported. They served as points of reference for *individuals* whose aural memories were shaped by the sound of church bells since childhood, reinforcing the close relationship between West German identity and religion in the process. Above all, the discussion of bells as historical artifacts shifted national memory back to a course it had set out on before the war. No longer unilaterally imposed from above, collective memory was now to emerge more spontaneously from evolving social relations and the dynamic of daily experiences. Wallenreiter's mirror of life now reflected a wider range of people remembering a wider array of artifacts and experiences. Antiquarian ways of remembering were supposed to bring national artifacts closer to that life Nietzsche insisted was the basis of historical knowledge.

Many church congregations did not restore or preserve bells but replaced them with exact historical copies. We have noted that after World War II, in the West a general allergy to ruins made full-scale restoration and historical copying a common if not always uniformly accepted practice in architecture, urban planning, and historic preservation itself. To the extent this practice was rhetorically linked with the idea of an increasingly popular national memory, it suggested that the national past could not only be sustained (through conservation or restoration of intact artifacts) in the present but actually reproduced and reinvented from ruins. But historical copying suggested a deep crisis of the ability to remember. The resort to replication and copying revealed that even more drastic interventions were required in order to secure a place for the historical. The Third Reich had manipulated the past through urban renewal schemes, Nazi ritual, and the general culture, but now new forms of manipulation occurred to create a more democratic and latitudinal national community. This postwar nation could be created only on the basis of even more radical negotiations with the past.

Bavaria is a good place to look for such sweeping and systematic interventions to preserve historic sites. Bavaria manipulated the historical traces of a normal nation by reusing and reconstructing Nazi buildings, which in a more political view of history would have symbolized forces that had made national normality inconceivable. In Munich during the National Socialist dictatorship architects tore down four splendid Florentine-style buildings from the nineteenth century on the Ludwigstraße and replaced them with more "monumental" structures. These buildings were severely damaged in the war, but they—and not the Florentine palaces they replaced—were carefully reconstructed after 1945. In 1937 one of Leo von Klenze's beautiful palaces built for the cousin of Ludwig I was torn down and replaced by a building designated to be the new Reichsbank. Completed as the Landeszentralbank only after World War II, its first story appeared in a form that was more or less in the style 1930s planners had envisioned. The landmarks register's official description of the bank stated innocently it was a "neoclassical monumental building adapted to the image of the street."[39] There were comparable examples in Munich and elsewhere, as in Cologne, where more than fifty office buildings were built during the Third Reich. Although Cologne architects tore down many nineteenth-century buildings after the war, they reconstructed the 1930s edifices in the austere neoclassical style the buildings had under Nazism. Insurance companies were especially drawn to the style because they thought it projected security and longevity.[40] But even when Nazi buildings were favored, they stood without reference to their specific political meaning. In either case—the destruction or reconstruction of architecture of the National Socialist era—the effect was to normalize the urban fabric, depoliticize historical buildings, and blunt critical memory.

Not only traces of the Nazi period were being manipulated or eradicated from memory. Shaped by a strong sense of local and provincial identity, Munich Reconstruction Style was lauded by critics, who praised its combining of new historicist architecture with modernization while retaining the basic historical morphology of the city, and its rebuilding of many churches and famous public edifices, such as the Alte Pinakothek, restored from 1953 to 1957. Preservationists' qualms about the rebuilding of Ludwig I's Victory Arch and the elaborate Residenz, whose earliest parts dated from the sixteenth century, were not enough to dampen the generally positive public reaction to Munich's rebuilding.[41] The last major landmark to be reconstructed was the Munich National Theater, built by Karl von Fischer, Max Joseph I's architect, in the early nineteenth century. The *DKD* praised the reconstruction, which lasted from 1958 to 1963, running an article by the main architect, Karl Fischer, and introducing the piece by saying it dealt with "an event as important as it was decisive for German historical preservation" because it was a case in which reconstruction met unusually wide public approval. Fischer himself argued that the decision to reproduce the original building was based in part on the fact that "the National Theater was one of the very few early classical opera houses, a *Bürger* theater of the kind that was possible only after the French Revolution."[42] Art-historical criteria were important in this justification, as the building was representative of a particular architectural style and genre. More broadly, the statement reproduced the link between a city, the genius architect, the nation, and the *Bürgertum*. There had been a broad campaign in the press, radio, and *Landtag* to restore the building, reasserting the link at the level of collective action.

That the link could be made with so little nuance, so little attention to the complexities it masked, is perhaps as surprising as its having been made at all in this period of rapid change in which the age to which the writer referred had been all but buried in World War II. But Fischer was convinced the reconstruction was a success. What is more, he had decided to gear the reconstruction not to the most recent form of the building, but to its original shape before 1823, after which the famous architect Leo von Klenze had made a "reluctant restoration" in the aftermath of a fire. Here again, public action had played a role, as the Friends of the National Theater, a group responsible for much of the campaign to rebuild the structure, had argued strongly for the pre-1823 solution. Not merely the war could be overcome, but the entire period from the early 1820s to the late 1950s. "Through its terrible impact history has created the opportunity," wrote Fischer, "to allow Karl von Fischer's marvelous original concept to appear again."[43] Even though Fischer conceded much to modern needs in the interior of the building and moved the auditorium fourteen meters in order to make room for corridors and cloakrooms, the outside was lovingly restored, masking its artificial character for everyone except perhaps the architectural connoisseur.[44] This was normal national memory with a strong Bavarian inflection.

East German architects reconstructed many landmarks in much the same fashion.[45] The famous German State Opera House, or Deutsche Staatsoper, a major classicist accomplishment of Frederick the Great's architect von Knobelsdorff, was reconstructed as part of East Berlin's most famous historical ensemble on Unter den Linden in the early 1950s and opened to the public with much fanfare in 1955. Like Fischer several years later, the architect in charge of the project, Richard Paulick, one of the leading planners of the monumental core of the developing East German capital, made a fairly arbitrary decision about the historical form the interior of the great building was to have. Arguing that his goal was "the maintenance of the national heritage," Paulick chose not to reconstruct parts of the interior in the rococo style the building had before its destruction. Instead, because Paulick maintained that von Knobelsdorff's interior reflected superficial court tastes and later inferior renovations, he chose to give it a starker, classicist form (with updated technical features) that mirrored the exterior, thus making a speculative leap about the original architect's intention and a deeply critical assessment about the building's history. The reinterpretation of the building extended to the motto over the entrance, which instead of reading, "Fridericus Rex Apolloni et Musis," as it had originally, now disingenuously read, "German State Opera." East German cultural minister Johannes R. Becher said in 1955 that Paulick's creation was an example of a "living reconstruction, that teaches us what it means to renew the old in contemporary form." Today expert opinion sees the building for what it is, namely, an act of historicist speculation.

Preservationists' approval of such schemes at the time they were carried out was often a concession to public taste. One can make this statement with some confidence for the West but also for the East, where in the earlier 1950s at least the defenders of historical architecture argued that popular opinion favored classicist over modernist styles. Popular pressure to reconstruct buildings often supported historicist forms that preservationists had criticized throughout the first half of the century, arguing that reconstruction was too antiquarian, too closed to the new. The public's attraction to such styles was broad and undiscriminating, extending well beyond the theme of postwar reconstruction, as evidenced in the touristic successes of the three ornate historicist nineteenth-century castles—Lindenhof, Herrenchiemsee, and Neuschwanstein—of insane Bavarian King Ludwig II, which attracted more than 1 million visitors annually in the 1950s. This alarmed one prominent museum director so greatly he suggested to the chief conservator of Bavaria that the castles should be made off-limits to tourists and closed by the state in order to protect public taste from further contamination.[46] But the weight of events could no longer be resisted. Tourists wanted to see history, whether in the form of nineteenth-century fantasies or rebuilt urban structures that copied or speculatively reinterpreted earlier styles. "Conserve, do not restore," still the motto of conservators and their allies, had now come to include practices—and a range of disastrous historic events—that could be imagined only as nightmares or apocalyptic visions when the slogan was first used at the end of the nineteenth century. Preservation policy thus evolved reluctantly out of the complex workings of social approval, state policy, and a professional discourse altered to react to and shape impulses from throughout state and society.

The attempt to have a normal memory attuned to public taste even extended to those architectural sites that could potentially call attention to the most abnormal events of recent German history. German synagogues that had survived the Nazi pogrom of 1938 and the war as ruins—the Jewish houses of worship on Fasanenstraße, Levetzowstraße, and Oranienburger Straße in Berlin were some of the most important—were largely ignored after 1945 and then wholly or partly demolished in the 1950s. The *DKD* paid scant attention to these sites, but when it did, the journal blunted—intentionally or unintentionally—the potential effect. Worms was the site of Germany's only medieval synagogue, a structure whose origins dated back to the eleventh century, as well as Europe's oldest Jewish cemetery. The Nazis burned the synagogue down in 1938 and exploded its ruins in 1942. Almost 65 percent destroyed in bombing raids of March and April 1945, Worms managed to rebuild all of its most famous medieval and baroque landmarks, although much of its residential stock from the medieval period was lost. When from 1959 to 1961 the city reconstructed the synagogue with only the foundation, a portal, and the underground baths remaining as original parts, West German conservators accepted the copy without discussion at their 1963 annual meeting. They approved reconstruction not because of the horrific nature of Nazi crimes but because of the unique art-historical value of the original structure, the centrality of Worms Jewry to German Jewish culture, and the fact that most synagogues had been destroyed in the Third Reich.[47]

The point is not that these were not good reasons but, rather, that the conservators missed the opportunity publicly to discuss the larger meaning and effects on German material culture of Nazism's racial war. These were normal reasons for accepting the complete reconstruction of a building whose leveling was anything but the result of a normal event and whose return to historical form effaced the disaster that so irretrievably broke the bond between past and future. Preservationists most often bracketed political narratives out of their work, and consequently the positive nonresponse to the Worms reconstruction was also a continuation of a particular discipline's selectivity toward the past. It might be added that on purely technical grounds the Worms case was very problematic because there were no other early medieval synagogues available for comparison.

The manipulation of historic sites rested on a deep ambiguity about the viability of national memory. Whence came the threat to the nation's ability to remember itself? The effects of World War II were rapidly being effaced in the West, and despite many misgivings and criticisms preservationists went along with the process. As significant parts of the reconstruction became history, society focused less on war than on secular trends. Responding to and shaping this process, preservationists recontextualized a narrative of modernity's threat to monuments, the historical city, and national memory. They focused on the destructive energies of peace instead of war.

The return to this normalizing critique of modern society may be seen in part in the many critical narratives of reconstruction that emerged in this era. For planners, politicians, businesspeople, and many ordinary citizens, reconstruction was a story of heroism. For preservationists it was a more mixed affair, as in the case of heavily damaged Frankfurt am Main, which was modernized and Americanized more intensively than other reconstructed cities. By 1956 most of the rubble from the war had been cleared away, except near the historically evocative Römerberg complex and the cathedral, and the Goethe House and Paulskirche had been rebuilt. Enough change had taken place throughout the rest of the city to enable preservationists to assess what ten years of reconstruction had done. To his satisfaction, H. K. Zimmermann noted that the planned "dispersal" of the city, its transformation into a metropolis of large blocks with parallel skyscrapers, had not been as drastic as originally feared.[48] City planners had taken into account preservationist concerns about the use of pitched slate roofs and avoided tall buildings around the Römerberg. In view of such developments, preservationists were happy to work within the existing discourse of modernism, as they had been since the end of the nineteenth century. A continuous German past could still be remembered from the morphology and scale of the city if not from the content of its individual buildings.

Nonetheless, the disadvantages of Frankfurt's rebuilding outweighed the advantages in Zimmermann's estimation. A growing number of skyscrapers had already begun to dot the cityscape. Building lots were too huge, giving the impression that what was being built for residential purposes were not houses but, rather, groups of houses whose character and siting reminded one of the Weimar-era working-class project. "From the point of view of preservation," wrote Zimmermann, "one would have preferred that even in the architectural forms of our time the fundamental *bürgerlichen* character of the urban space would have persisted, which [here] means a sensitively ordered collection of related but still individually designed 'houses.'" Instead, a deeply problematic "mixture of individualistic and collective tendencies" emerged. Though financed mainly by "collective means," reconstruction never took the next logical step of being directed "from a single agency" that planned centrally and built new buildings "in the same spirit, if also not in the same individual forms, like the residence cities of the baroque era."[49]

Thus the contemporary reconstruction of Frankfurt was held up to the critical mirror of baroque planning, and the contemporary period was found wanting not necessarily because of specific stylistic reasons, but because it lacked the courage to be uniform in its application: "The courage to work toward such a consequence [of greater coherence] appears to be about as unrealizable as the courage to work toward the opposite pole of purely individualized construction."[50] This indecision was clearly expressed in new buildings whose cornices were of uniform height due to building ordinances even when the buildings were very different and even when their facades were animated through more or less arbitrary decorations such as alternating color schemes, stone or glass mosaic, and unusually shaped railings and fences.

All this represented an "inner conflict in the overall scheme."[51] In combination with the argument that the era lacked courage to follow through on a uniform design in the manner of the baroque residence-city, the notion of inner conflict inflated the critique in a way that gave it a more inclusive character. On one level it could be seen as a criticism of West German cultural politics, which allowed individual *Länder*, city planners, and ultimately capitalist market relations to determine the form and pace of rebuilding. Cemented in the first postwar years and in the founding of the BRD, the nation-state's cultural-political abstinence was now bearing its problematic fruit. On another level, it was certainly not the only critique of such planning either for Frankfurt or for West Germany as a whole. Nor was it a critique that focused only on the major cities. Rebuilding in Rhenish small cities such as Xanten, heavily and unnecessarily damaged in the war, was also criticized by the RVDH because reconstruction there quite simply could not produce "architecture."[52]

The criticism also depended on a much older preservationist trope. Clemen, Dehio, and others all had castigated the nineteenth century for its cafeteria-style approach to history, which made it possible for architects, municipalities, kings, and homeowners to choose from any number of historical styles. The problem of the nineteenth century, as Clemen had pointed

A NORMAL MEMORY

out, was that it had no style but only styles, an irresolution incompatible with preservationist visions of the past, when architects and workmen alike presumably knew how to build in the shadow of authoritative but benevolent tradition. Historic preservation had tried to work toward an alternative based both on coherent tradition and an innovative artistic spirit, which many in the Kaiserreich recognized in the first manifestations of progressive or abstracted historicism. Now, in Frankfurt am Main and many other communities, irresolution was again criticized, though not specifically as a result of the proliferation of styles. Instead the problem was that the culture of reconstruction moved between collective and individual perspectives, central planning and individual anarchy, uniformity based on legal means and arbitrary differentiation. Out of the discontinuity of planning in Frankfurt a modern, negative tradition of irresolution emerged, tied to functionalist planning rather than nineteenth-century historicism and restorationism.

This perspective allowed preservationists to reenact their critique not of modernization as such but of the tensions produced within modernization. It represented not an antimodern tirade against the present but a conservative hopefulness whose roots once again take us back to the Kaiserreich. The usefulness of this critique became clear when notions of the future's threat to historic buildings became stronger in the 1950s and early 1960s, stimulating an image of a past beyond modernity's contemporary crises.

A good example comes from preservationists' concerns about rural modernization. This is a subject easily forgotten in scholarship that has naturally focused on urban reconstruction. If one surveyed what remained of "peasant-house [Bauernhaus]" architecture in the West German countryside, wrote Torsten Gebhard, one could see the effect of both neglect and modernization. Farmers, craftsmen, and other owners of rural houses had in some cases neglected any form of substantive upkeep, turning their neighborhoods into "true slums." Here the past had become tawdry and anything but the picturesque rural culture portrayed in evocations of peasant life earlier in the twentieth century. At the same time, some owners of historic rural architecture had developed modern expectations that hardly fit the Bauernhaus: "It is not only that running cold and warm water, electric lighting, toilets and central heating are supposed to be installed in the Bauernhaus, it is also that people say the rooms are too low, too narrow, too dark."[53] A consumerist vision threatened to destroy what was left of Germany's limited and often dilapidated stock of peasant houses, which stemmed mostly from no earlier than the beginning of the nineteenth century.

Even if such buildings escaped neglect or insensitive modernization, they were vulnerable to the dangers of a rapidly changing milieu. This was a period of enormous economic modernization in the German countryside. What happens when a *Bauernhaus* stays the same and everything around it changes? "Does the public then see it only as a curiosity or photo opportunity, in the middle of . . . a fully electrified village, twenty-meter high silos, tractor garages, and all the other technical equipment of the present?" asked Gebhard. All this symbolized "that crisis-ridden relationship contemporary man has to the past." This crisis affected both urban and rural people, but in rural architecture there was still limited hope. When one sees "a village border still free of falsification" or "an undisturbed old village lane," it is not a "romantic feeling that inspires us but rather surprise at the power of that which has grown organically," wrote Gebhard.[54]

Gebhard felt the need to distinguish his reaction to an "organic" historical milieu from that of nineteenth-century Romantics, who had also stressed the shock effect of the past. But this past was in danger of being overwhelmed because its referent was reduced to a single artifact, a photo motif or curiosity for tourists. The specific crisis of the period from this perspective was that preservation and, by extension, the nation could preserve organically developed traces of a German past only in the form of consumer goods no different from the consumer goods that surrounded them. Riegl's age value had been decisively overcome by exchange value. In making this critique Gebhard placed the 1950s in a longer narrative of the destructiveness of economic modernization.

This critical use of history gave rise to a more limited appeal for preservation than one would have heard in earlier eras. The scope of modernization in the countryside was now greater than at any time in the past. In Baden-Württemberg from 1960 to 1970 some 70,000 "peasant enterprises" were lost.[55] The expectations of the preservationist were reduced accordingly. In the 1930s there were incomplete plans for a kind of *classement* of peasant houses, which reflected a desire for systematic preservation. In the 1950s no such solution was called for. Instead, for Gebhard the maintenance of the peasant house would "always be a matter of luck." All that could be done was to turn rural ensembles into parts of *Heimat* museums or open-air museums, save the shells of modernized peasant houses, or carefully record and measure such houses before they were destroyed. To save the *Bauernhaus* in toto would be to save "the peasant order," which was an impossibility. Reaffirming preservationists' obligation "to serve life," Gebhard argued that the goal should be to see that rural culture—"the spirit of order, of proportion, of quality of work and humanity"—continued to inform the modern age.[56]

In this view the national past existed not as an antithesis to the present but as a limited yet integral part of it. The threads linking past and present were almost completely shredded; but they were still there, and their saving suggested that somewhere on the other side of the modern, in the postmodern perhaps, memory and history still had a limited place. But if this was a vision of postmodernity, then it was hardly new in the 1960s. Rather, it had been working in preservationists' conservative hopefulness, which projected potential and imperfect harmony into the future based on a limited realization of past promises.

The presence of another Germany, indeed of another Europe, played a decisive role in the making of normal memory also. West German criticisms of the East German regime's preservation policies could be seen as a continuation of a long-standing critique of Communism's "historicidal" tendencies. This tradition had gained legitimacy from Paul Clemen's interwar evocations of the Soviet Union's science-fiction-like destruction of history.[57] But there was more to it than this. West German preservationists had a strong interest in the East, following developments there with regularity. In 1961 the association of *Land* conservators planned to take a guided tour of preservation sites in the "Eastern zone," but this had to be called off at the last moment in the wake of the building of the Berlin Wall. The following year they were able to tour Quedlinburg, the Harz mountain town famous for its half-timbered houses, *Rathaus*, and remaining medieval fortifications, and several other East German cities, and they were quick to praise the efforts of their Eastern colleagues, whose work was distinguished from the regime's actions. "[East German conservators] care for their monuments conscientiously, rationally, and with great sacrifice," wrote Bavarian Heinrich Kreisel, "they are not the ones who tear down monuments." This allowed Westerners to feel a commonality with their Eastern colleagues beyond contemporary politics, as it was a chance to discuss "concerns of German historic preservation and aesthetics that are near to everyone's heart."[58]

Well before this the short East German past had begun to acquire not only negative but also positive characteristics in Western eyes. West German preservationists stressed that the DDR was built on two layers of ruin, one caused by Hitler, the other by Stalin. They followed the general tone of the political culture of the 1950s by noting the brutality and arbitrariness of Russian troops in the war and the radical destructiveness of the Soviet occupying force. Writing in the *DKD* in 1954, art historian Niels von Holst, who not incidentally was a key figure in Nazi plundering of the Baltic states in the war, argued that in the "central German Soviet zone" a "dynamic-anarchistic" process of revolutionary liquidation of the past was still under way in some areas. This process was much like that of the early days of the

French and Bolshevik Revolutions. Yet von Holst argued this would give way to a more sensitive handling of the architectural heritage, which had already occurred in some cases, as in Dresden, where in the eyes of another West German colleague, reconstruction had by 1955 slowly reached "a gratifyingly high level."[59]

Significantly, for von Holst Soviet officials had made several choices about preserving landmarks against which both West and East German developments looked questionable. Von Holst wondered aloud why the Soviets quite rightly rejected modern traffic arteries in the historic centers of Riga and Reval while West Germany built "obtrusive skyscrapers" next to historic buildings. He noted that in Riga a castle in which many Russian czars had stayed was preserved while the Hohenzollern palace in East Berlin had been torn down. Yet Saxony and Thuringia had recently shown more sensitivity to the artifacts of aristocratic and bourgeois Germany, observed von Holst.[60] By 1989 the historical record would show that alongside the DDR's many successes in historic preservation there was an array of disasters: the deterioration of historic town centers, the massive yet shoddily constructed and barrackslike modernist building complexes, and the ruins of places such as the Frauenkirche in Dresden. Nonetheless, at the time von Holst was writing, there were enough signs that despite East Germany's threatening challenge to German tradition, West Germany's own ability to nurture a national memory was paradoxically called into question by the practices of Communist states.

As the foregoing suggests, even questionable East German preservation policies could be used to highlight problematic West German policies. Preservationists and architects protested vigorously against official decisions to destroy the ruins of the Potsdam and Braunschweig baroque castles in the late 1950s. Responding to an attack on German cultural "barbarism" in the *Neue Zürcher Zeitung*, Günther Grundmann painted both regimes with a broad brush. "We stand as barbarians," he wrote, "indeed as barbarians over here as well as over there, for whom nothing that the past has left us is sacred when it comes to enforcing our political convictions, whether according to the rules of authoritarian or democratic principles." Noting that in Braunschweig a Social Democratic majority in the city council got the decision to demolish the castle passed by just one vote, Grundmann argued that the "cultural context" not only of this decision but of East German policy on Potsdam was linked to the "calumnies of German Nazi historical writing." In this view both West and East suffered from twelves years of Nazism's violent misuses of German memory. And both regimes acted demagogically when they claimed such preservation projects represented undue financial burdens on the people, although they were willing to burden those same populations with the cost of bombers, rockets, and highways.[61]

The door to cultural-national memory remained opened for preservationists, but some of its essential hinges—region, social hierarchy, and gender—were less easily operative without considerable discursive reworking. This was the price of normality. The 1950s saw a revival of *Heimat* values in preservation circles. Proclaiming "*Heimat* lives" in 1956, the RVDH argued that a return to values of local memory was a healthy reaction to Nazism's dictatorial desire to conduct *Heimat* policy "at an official level [*vom grünen Tisch*]."[62] But the region's importance could also be seen elsewhere, as in preservationist responses to reconstruction. In the opinion of one preservationist writing in 1959, Xanten "reconstruction style" was in its earlier stages "good and simple," having achieved a "contemporary relationship with the austere brick buildings of the Middle Ages and the Lower Rhineland" and an "architectural precision comparable to that of the Gothic." This good start was botched later, as Xanten rebuilding fell victim to some of the same problems other cities experienced. Thus even when preservationists criticized rebuilding, as they did in Cologne, whose reconstruction style was otherwise glowingly praised by the *Kölnische Rundschau* in 1955 for its grounding in "architectonic logic and modern planning," their criticism reinforced the idea that local memory had a place in the national scene.[63] Even bad reconstruction styles were bad according to their specific local valences.

Local memory also legitimated a democratic present based on a European community and individual rights—values perfectly integrated in the official rhetoric of BRD political culture. The small town, defined in 1959 by RVDH literature as a community of between 2,000 and 12,000, was seen not as the center of the German soul but as a "fertile soil for a universal human functioning."[64] Linking *Heimat* with universal concerns was hardly unprecedented. The racially inspired *Heimat* of the Nazi era was also based on the notionally universal legitimacy of German superiority. But in the age of the Economic Miracle the link served to highlight democracy, participation, and a sense of individual responsibility. The small-town *Heimat*, now seen as an achieved "school of democracy,"[65] had become the seedbed of the potentially Europeanized, prosperous, historically conscious West German who looked back on his past as a long, bloody, but finally successful quest for the life he was now experiencing. The fit between this vision of the citizen and the liberal-democratic culture of the Federal Republic was difficult. The rooted, responsible, and restorative democrat of *Heimat* was worlds away from the socially mobile businessmen, politicians, and planners who managed the prosperous new Germany from their urban offices. Asserting *Heimat* as a home of settled democratic spirit therefore had a critical potential even when fundamental criticism appeared all but impossible in the age of Adenauer, Erhard, and the Cold War.

Nonetheless, the region's democratic valences allowed an important transformation in the sense of the nation. Through public spaces such as cities and regions, members of the *Volk* community became *Bürger*, the inheritors of notionally objective cultural values and the proponents of civic rights and political duties. For preservationists this term had a specific meaning. Hamburg citizens had a right to preserve historic buildings not because they were "philistines," as was implied by criticism of Hamburg preservation efforts in the modernist architecture magazine *Baukunst und Werkform*, but because they were *Bürger* who had the right to have "a last visible connection to the traces of their history."[66] Being a *Bürger* connoted rights, maturity, and appreciation of the way the past informed the present. This preservationist theme of the need for public participation, linked to notions of an integrated national community in the past, now took on more proactive, civic, and individualist inflections.

Three aspects of this civic memory need to be mentioned briefly. First, the reelaboration of the idea of popular involvement in building pasts came at a time when those pasts seemed more threatened than ever. "The people," in the more civic rather than cultural sense of the term, had arrived only to find that their history had been all but swept away by the Economic Miracle. Still rather unevenly felt in this period, consciousness of this destruction would be a significant spur to civic action in the next decades. Second, a civic sense of public history by no means excluded traditions of social hierarchy based on the uneven distribution of cultural capital. As their key audiences continued to do, preservationists still thought of society in terms of a deep divide between cultured lovers of tradition and uninformed outsiders whose rootlessness was exaggerated by the materialism of the contemporary age. By adhering to values of "the individual" against "the mass,"[67] the new citizen of the BRD, rooted in historically sensitive small and medium-sized cities, became the representative of a new hierarchy. Third, national memory based on civic participation depended on a reelaboration of the gendered imagery of *Heimat*. The dominant culture of the Federal Republic in the 1950s was based in large past on the reaffirmation of conservative notions of gender, bourgeois sexuality, and the family.[68] These values found full expression in preservationist discourse, especially when the rootedness of the local community and nuclear family were praised in typical fashion as the antidote to urban youth problems, alcoholism, and divorce.

The New Past and the Old

A newspaper commentator in Gießen in 1952 divided that Hessian city's long history into two eras, one covering the 800 years preceding the bombing raid of December 1944, the other covering the subsequent 8 years of reconstruction. This viewpoint had a wider public resonance, as many Germans were convinced that the aftermath of the war had created a deep divide in German historical continuity.[69] A glorification of the more distant past was one response. In October 1951 a plurality of respondents (45 percent) said that the Kaiserreich was the best period of German history, although 40 percent mentioned 1933 to 1938. Reinforcing the positive evaluation of the Kaiserreich, more than one-third of survey respondents in January 1950 and August 1952 said that of all "great Germans" Bismarck had done the most for Germany. (Hitler received 10 and 9 percent of the votes, respectively). By 1959, however, only 28 percent of the respondents chose the Kaiserreich and only 18 percent the Nazi period, while 42 percent chose the present. In 1963 the numbers were 16, 10, and 62 percent, meaning that nearly two-thirds of the respondents favored the present over past periods, with the greatest enthusiasm from people between the ages of 16 and 29, while 42 percent of the respondents 60 years of age and older still chose the Kaiserreich. This was combined with a diminishing "national feeling." The percentage of young male respondents who said that they would sacrifice their lives for "Germany, my *Volk*, my *Heimat*, my Fatherland" declined from 1952 to 1956 from 25 to 13 percent. As early as September 1949, 52 percent of the respondents in the American zone, West Berlin, and Bremen said nationalism had no meaning at all for them. The surveys suggested that key words such as "history" and "nation" had a declining resonance in this period.

Popular attitudes toward historic architecture were ambivalent. In October 1956, when survey respondents were asked whether they would favor the reconstruction in its original historical form of a 400-year-old urban *Rathaus* destroyed in the war or its replacement with a modern building, 45 percent said they preferred the historicist reconstruction; but 37 percent said they wanted the modern building, and 18 percent were undecided. Along gender lines, slightly fewer men favored reconstruction compared to the modern solution (42 and 43 percent), whereas 48 percent of the female respondents favored reconstruction compared to 33 percent for the modern

Although West Germans were ambivalent about the past, there was still significant support for historic places, and cities such as Rothenburg ob der Tauber, shown here in the 1950s, remained popular tourist attractions. (photo: Bildarchiv Foto Marburg/Art Resource, New York)

building. Generally, the percentage of respondents favoring the historical reconstruction increased with age, level of education, and social status.[70]

Taken as a whole, the survey data suggested that people were increasingly satisfied with present conditions, that they were more skeptical than before of the power of national history and tradition to give meaning to their lives, but that they were by no means willing to abandon historical orientations. The preservation lobby was among the groups fighting to keep such historical orientations alive. But their work was made more difficult by the notable successes of reconstruction, which encouraged presentist viewpoints and acceptance of what German cities and towns had become in the rush to normality.

As the decade wore on, it was typical to find commentators friendly to business and commercial interests stressing that disagreements over whether cities should have been built in traditional or modern styles were ultimately "meaningless" when seen against the "practical *Leistung* of reconstruction" in places such as Frankfurt am Main. In the opinion of a *Frankfurter Neue Presse* writer, "the Frankfurt Wonder" and "Frankfurt Tempo" reduced specialists' debates to irrelevance. But even when the exchange of critical and affirmative views was taken more seriously, it had a

A NORMAL MEMORY

similar effect insofar that it created distance between Germans and the twelve years of Nazi rule. A 1958 newspaper account of Dortmund's rebuilding showed how critical and affirmative perspectives blended to create this new relationship with the recent past. "There are cities in which reconstruction took place in such a fashion that people already regret their decisions," the article read. By contrast, "the second Dortmund" had made responsible decisions, and its reconstruction had put it on the "road to the future," thanks to "untold efforts and the unerring optimism of its *Bürger* spirit." Such efforts resulted in the creation of a " 'city of work and a city of workers' " that had a "social face and its own cultural vision."[71]

Even when more "historical" cities emerged from reconstruction, the past was relativized when placed against a successful present and future. In 1956 painter Oskar Kokoschka received a commission from the Federal Association of German Industry to paint a picture for the reopening of the Wallraf-Richartz-Museum in Cologne.[72] The product was an almost impressionistic portrait that portrayed historical Cologne's cathedral, the *Altstadt*, and many other old buildings in vibrant colors. But by taking the massive modern tower on the fairgrounds as its point of view, it also made the Rhine River the central focus, a shift in perspective from earlier artistic representations. This enabled Kokoschka to include ships steaming down the Rhine River, a train crossing the Hohenzollern Bridge, and the factories and exhibition grounds of the right bank of the Rhine. Cologne was no longer only historical Cologne but a combination of a "genuine old city" and a "busy metropolis." Pride in the new German city spoke just as clearly in this representation as it did in the newspaper rhetoric on the "second" Dortmund. Kokoschka's representation reenacted the pre–World War I touristic view of Cologne as reflected in the 1906 Baedeker guide, which reduced the cathedral to one of many modern accomplishments of the bigger, better metropolis.[73]

Such triumphalism gave artistic expression to a broad popular recognition of Cologne's ability to chip away at the "Adolf Hitler Mountain," local citizens' derisory nickname for the gigantic pile of rubble dwindling but still standing on the centrally located Neumarkt in 1955.[74] That some urban residents actually began to bemoan the passing of the images and relationships associated with the rubble was further proof that the new dominated the old. In 1954 one could read a bittersweet account of how rebuilding in Frankfurt am Main destroyed more than 150 varieties of colorful European and exotic wildflowers and other vegetation that had grown in the ruins. "Their existence must remain an episode," wrote a *Frankfurter Rundschau* commentator, of the many examples of "rubble flora." "They fulfilled their purpose of covering the destruction with a compassionate cloak whose traces are now gradually disappearing."[75] In previous years the public psycho-

Rubble flora, such as coltsfoot on the Frankfurt Römerberg, were the objects of nostalgia as they gave way to reconstructed buildings. (photo: *HEUTE* 2, no. 35 [1 May 1947]: 11)

A NORMAL MEMORY

topography of German cities had accepted the abnormal as normal, but now the sweeping away of rubble required cultural adjustment.

Rebuilt or developing older cities entered a new phase in which the tensions of the modern were no longer as contested as they had been before the war. Criticism of modern developments was still there, to be sure, but—just as in the case of preservationists' attitudes toward peasant architecture—the modern age seemed to have reduced the space of legitimacy for critique. When a retired railway worker responded to a survey question about the transformation of the university town Göttingen into a modern city, he said, "Change takes place at the expense of the romantic, but—it has to be."[76] This fatalistic modernism put public defenders of historic buildings on the defensive. It was not only in Düsseldorf that *Heimatvereine* interested in saving historic architecture in 1955 were met with a "disparaging smile" because of what was said to be their "exaggerated conservative sentiment."[77] The conservator could be seen as an obstacle when he toed what was perceived to be a purist line in conflicts over cultural protection. In 1960 in Kempen such criticism took a particularly vicious turn when one journalist referred to a "stab in the back" by the *Land* conservator, who had slowed the transformation of the local Franciscan cloister into an administrative building by quibbling over the size of the windows "as if the historical worth of the building depended on [such matters]."[78]

If such popular attitudes reflected impatience with historic buildings and the people who acted as their stewards, public attachments to such structures and what they signified could still be found. The beginnings of a radical social critique of reconstructed German cities were evident in this period, as reflected in well-known writer Alexander Mitscherlich's 1965 polemic against urban life in the BRD. Mitscherlich's discourse on the "unlivability" of German cities attacked the social and psychological ills of contemporary communities deformed by the interests of the state, the economy, and planning. Referring to the city as an "expression of groups and of the history of their rise and fall," Mitscherlich argued that traffic-swept, capitalist German cities did little to offer that psychological settledness that made communities humane.[79] He offered both an explicit and an implicit defense of the sense of community that achieved historic environments symbolized for many Germans. Mitscherlich acted more as a harbinger of later political energy than as a key opinion maker of this period. His longtime identification with the non-Communist Left isolated him from the array of preservation groups and *Heimat* societies that shared his despair over urban ills but not his political agenda. Moreover, his vision of community rested on social-psychological rather than national-cultural criteria despite his references to a "senselessly divided Berlin" that symbolized the

Critics such as Alexander Mitscherlich wrote that planning and growth robbed many postwar West German cities of that psychological settledness that towns of the past had. Two images of the Hildesheim market square in 1900 (*above*) and 1962 (*opposite*) contrast the warmth of an achieved historic town with the gray certainties of the rebuilt city. (photos: Institut für Denkmalpflege, Niedersächsisches Landesverwaltungsamt, Nr. Repro K91-193 and 4258)

larger unlivability of the German nation.[80] Most public support for historical buildings thus still rested on a more conservative basis in this period, and it would only be in the later 1960s and early 1970s that a more direct social-critical voice could be heard among the defenders of historic places.

Such conservative support could be seen in a variety of activities. One was public memory of the destruction German cities experienced as a result of World War II, which gained prominence in the tenth, fifteenth, and twentieth anniversaries of the bombing. Bonn was one of the least damaged cities, but a newspaper account dealing with the fifteenth anniversary of the 18 October 1944 bombing there typified the sense of loss and fortunate survival of monuments most such anniversaries evoked. The account quoted a newspaper piece on the day of the bombing. "Many cultural buildings that in Bonn and beyond have become a concept for the cultural life of the city, such as the Beethoven Hall and City Theater, sank into rubble and ashes.

A NORMAL MEMORY

Even the Bonngasse's Beethoven House, venerated throughout the civilized world as the birthplace of the greatest genius of our city, could be saved from the threatening flames only in the last moment."[81] The article did not comment on the obvious indictment of the "uncivilized" forces that had unleashed their vengeance on the Rhenish town. Nonetheless, the article showed that the sense of identification with these structures was still strong enough that fifteen-year-old words still captured the experience.

The Bonn recollection of World War II was a rather mild expression of a phenomenon that assumed harsher ideological tones elsewhere in the public culture. For those who looked back longingly at the East Elbian estates as the signifiers of "art and tradition," the war in general, and the attack on Hitler's life in particular in 1944, was "the beginning of the end" of a tragic development that transformed the noble mansions and country homes of the Prussian aristocracy into "public buildings, school centers, party locals, and com-

In the 1950s the DDR promoted public memory of the victims of Dresden—grimly shown here in a photograph of piles of corpses after the February 1945 Allied raid—in its ideological struggle against "imperialist warmongers" in the West. (photo: Seydewitz, *Zerstörung und Wiederaufbau von Dresden*, unpaginated)

munity centers of all kinds." Like "naughty children," wrote Bogislav von Archenholz, author of a nostalgic evocation of the "abandoned palaces" of the East, DDR officials destroyed or broke up the libraries, transported the historic furniture, and modified the buildings of the East Elbian landholders. "The wounds scarred over," argued von Archenholz, but "that which is irreplaceable never returns."[82] Significantly, the mirror image of this conservative use of historic buildings could be found in the DDR's propagandistic exploitation of the memory of the war in places such as Dresden. Published first in 1955 and then reissued under a new title in 1982, *Destruction and Reconstruction of Dresden,* by Dresden writer and curator Max Seydewitz, linked the city's horrific bombing in February 1945 with the postwar struggle against "the atomic war being prepared by imperialist warmongers."[83] Replete with gruesome photographs of piles of corpses from the Dresden air raids and grim mountains of rubble, the book also celebrated the reconstruc-

A NORMAL MEMORY

tion of the city as an example of the DDR's appreciation of that "art and tradition" von Archenholz claimed was being destroyed in the holocaust of East Elbian estates. In both cases the memory of World War II was the context for harsh ideological appropriations of historic sites.

There was popular opposition to the destruction of monuments, much of it thoroughly situated in the mainstream of the new political culture of the BRD. Usually such opposition dealt with buildings with mainly local significance. In 1955 in Düsseldorf local *Heimat* and historical societies protested the razing of historic buildings in the expansion of the Justice Ministry Building, but they could not prevent such destruction, prompting a local newspaper editorial to ask, "Where's the democracy there?" This question signaled exasperation with the authorities, to be sure, but it also suggested an indeterminate mix of support for and skepticism about democratic ideals.[84] Public opposition to the restoration of historic buildings could have a similarly critical though ambiguous tone, often in terms that official preservation would have found appropriate. In 1957 the Düsseldorf City Building Office planned to rebuild the 400-year-old *Rathaus*, the so-called Tußmann-bau, named after Duisburg builder Heinrich Tußmann, who may have been the architect of the building in the 1570s. Writing in the *Düsseldorfer Nachrichten*, an unidentified local critic attacked these plans in what amounted to a traditional language of cultural protection. City officials' plans to restore the building inside and outside so as to create more "pomp" and "rooms for representation" for the mayor and city director were simply inappropriate to the "modesty" of a sixteenth-century *Rathaus* built when Düsseldorf had just 3,000 inhabitants. Overlooking this original historical quality of the building constituted a "lack of piety" against which local citizens "should protest strongly." If the city wanted to show "reverence" for the building, it would use it for offices that required less ostentatious displays of municipal power.[85] Here all the well-known facets of preservationist language—tact, piety, reverence, balance, modesty, and adaptation to local circumstances—found expression in a public critique of city hall, both as a place of history and as an institution.

The plans to remodel the *Rathaus* aroused passionate criticism from groups that were not always friends of cultural protection—representatives of local retailers, home and property owners, and local hotel and restaurant owners. Noting that the reconstruction of Düsseldorf had left more historical facades than historical buildings, an accurate assessment, a critic argued that the city's plan was a "sin against the spirit of historic preservation." It took little time to see that the sin was less a distortion of history than a violation of the bottom line. Had the board of directors of a "private corporation" planned to rebuild its offices according to the same ratio of personnel to space, they would have been "fired without notice." The city was building a new administrative building outside the *Altstadt*. Why could the mayor and city director not work there, even if they were separated from other administrative personnel in the old *Rathaus*, just as in "private industry a board of directors would work without being in direct contact with its staff"? In any case, the city's taxpayers, its political parties, and many others had already opposed this plan to have the mayor housed in "a late Gothic facade with baroque trimmings."[86] Here the argument of *Leistung*, so damaging to historic buildings in the Nazi and postwar periods, now allied with the preservation cause.

Whatever the motivation for arguing against the city's plans, the contention was situated firmly on the side of authenticity. In fact, of course, the Tußmannbau was already a heavily remodeled building, a product of the contemporary age rather than of the sixteenth century. Just a month before the Düsseldorf papers debated the *Rathaus*, a local commentator had praised the decision to restore the seventeenth-century Neanderkirche, a "gem of the *Altstadt*" on the Bolkerstraße. "All the ugly modifications and remodelings [of the past] will disappear," said the commentator, who noted that there was much public support for restoration of the church in the style of a traditional "preacher church" of the period from 1683 to 1687 and for its "freeing up." Here the opposite tack, restore rather than conserve, was taken, though with much the same motivation of historical authenticity.[87] No contradiction was pointed out between public responses to the two projects, but then none had to be. The public understanding was extremely malleable, especially since war and reconstruction had created an environment in which the most contradictory manipulations of historic buildings seemed to point in the direction of a valued past whose links with the present were indistinct at best.

Such conflicts could be just as easily turned against conservators and their staffs as against the planners, builders, architects, and officials. When the historic Mevissen-Koch house of Dülken was torn down as part of that city's reconstruction efforts, the incident led one observer to reflect on more than this specific structure. The loss of this monument reminded one of the "failures of historic preservation in Dülken during the last fifty years," a history of failure the writer explicated by recounting four examples since 1906 in which conservators were unable to save historic buildings slated for destruction. The result was spiritual and material poverty, which led to anxious commentary on the uneven distribution of cultural capital in the BRD. "Today we in Dülken lack almost completely the historic buildings from old times which other cities have in such rich abundance," concluded the piece. "It remains a fact that those cities and villages that make an especially good impression on outsiders are the ones that can show them many old buildings."[88]

Outsiders were indeed interested in German cities that had many old buildings. Just as they had participated in debates over the Goethe House in Frankfurt and the Hohenzollern palace in Berlin years before, international observers continued to monitor German policies on monument protection. The city of Potsdam's 1958 decision to tear down its damaged baroque palace, built in the eighteenth century by von Knobelsdorff, elicited protests not only from West Germans but from Richard H. Howland, president of the National Trust for Historic Preservation in the United States, whose telegram to DDR officials argued that the "loss of building would be irreparable disaster." In the same period Swiss commentators added their voice to protests against the destruction of the world famous baroque palace in Braunschweig in 1960.[89] In some cases international pressure saved landmarks from being demolished or inalterably changed. Lübeck's famous twelfth-century cathedral had been badly damaged in the 1942 bombing raid, and in the late 1950s doubts arose as to whether its thirteenth-century Gothic choir could be maintained. A Swiss scholar published an appeal in the *Frankfurter Allgemeine* in 1959 arguing that the cathedral's "linking of Romanesque and Gothic styles, of German and French," made it a far too important symbol to be allowed to fall into ruin. Whether Lübecker were moved by the appeal to Franco-German cultural affinity remained unclear, but they responded to the call, amassing a war chest of 1.5 million marks for restoration of the choir.[90]

International as well as domestic outsiders' interest in historic places was fueled in part by increased travel, as for the first time in European history a mass tourist industry took shape. Touristic travel fed popular antiquarianism in this period in a number of ways. Commercial enterprises used the imagery of historical buildings to make their products more appealing to visitors, who bought beer, wine, cigarettes, silverware, dishes, playing cards, and many other products bearing the image of a local cathedral, city hall, or ruin. In at least one case such commercial activity was credited with keeping up memory of historic places that were still under reconstruction from war damage. A *Die Welt* writer argued in 1961 that Lübeck marzipan firms did much to keep alive memory of how the former Hansa city had looked before World War II by carrying pictures of its seven steeples on their packages. In effect the commercialization of the city's historical skyline provided a bridge between the prewar era and the early 1960s, when the seven steeples were fully reconstructed and the city's normal image returned.[91]

A less openly commercial form of selling historic architecture and artifacts occurred in *Heimat* museums. They remained popular in the BRD, constituting an important source of income derived from the display of historic buildings and artifacts. This applied to the DDR as well, though here ideological arguments were more important than economic ones. In 1965 nearly 80 percent of all museums and 46 percent of all museum visitors were in this category in East Germany. Both percentages would decline in the next decade, but in 1975 there were still 344 *Heimat* museums, 56 percent of all museums, with about one-fifth of all museum visitors in East Germany.[92]

Encouraged by official preservation but also motivated by local impulses, *Heimat* activities remained an important cottage industry in these years. *Heimat* groups continued many of their traditional pursuits, such as co-operation with county administrations in the production and distribution of *Heimat* almanacs, of which there were seventeen with a circulation of 90,000 in the northern Rhine counties alone in 1964. These publications included short pieces on local history, photographs, statistics, nature studies, prose and poetry in local dialects, and articles on the protection of monuments. Their continued popularity was the subject of a Westdeutscher Rundfunk broadcast in March 1964.[93]

The almanacs reflected a deep popular appetite for historical orientation that was sated by the publication of many books on local history and culture. As befit its origins in an antiquarian discourse, this literature was affirmative rather than critical. Yet the critical vein could not be ignored. Walter Gerteis's two-volume *The Unknown Frankfurt* earned scholarly and popular recognition when it appeared in the early 1960s.[94] It combined sketches of local personalities, anecdotes and sayings in the "real Frankfurter" dialect, illustrations and photographs, and entertaining narratives of key historic events from the beginning of Frankfurt to its last days as a "free city" before Prussian takeover in 1866. Historic buildings moved to the center stage, often as symbols of Germany's notionally special political discontinuities, as in the case of the Paulskirche, "this plain building erected for entirely different purposes" from those it would have in 1848, when "overnight it became one of the most famous buildings in Germany."[95]

But more often for Gerteis historic places nurtured a nervous cultural continuity. The last chapter of the book contains a 1909 photograph in which a zeppelin flies over the historic St. Leonhard Church, a thirteenth-century building that incorporated architectural pieces from its Romanesque predecessor. The zeppelin symbolized Frankfurt's industrial progressiveness, a key theme of Gerteis's popular history. But the St. Leonhard Church put such scientific advances in a particular historical context signaled by the title of the chapter. Gerteis's caption read, "Centuries separate the St. Leonhard Church and the zeppelin. But both recall the old Frankfurt generosity. Well-

A 1909 photograph of a zeppelin over the Leonhard church evokes memory of *bürgerlich* patronage for both innovation and tradition in Walter Gerteis's popular local history of Frankfurt, published in 1961. (photo: Gerteis, *Das unbekannte Frankfurt*, unpaginated)

to-do families donated to and founded the church, and the first ever air show of all time, the ILA 1909, was possible only through the guarantee of a million marks from Frankfurt *Bürger*."[96] This tradition continued in the postwar age, when the Goethe House, local churches and hospitals, the opera house, and the university all benefited from local citizens' donations. But was all this definitive evidence for continuity? "We would like to think it is," said Gerteis, who concluded the book with the following: "Possibly when new wealth is being amassed it takes longer for the realization to set in that wealth is an obligation, and that its holders are quite rightly judged by the works they leave behind."[97] Here the unsteady persistence of a specific Frankfurt tradition highlighted the larger national issue of the controversial relationship between wealth and social responsibility, the sticking point of the social market economy mirrored in the simple juxtaposition of a zeppelin and a historic cathedral.

This muted but recognizable potential for critical history in early 1960s narratives about historic places is even more clearly exemplified in a series of articles published in late 1964 and early 1965 in the daily newspaper *Bonner Rundschau* titled "Old Bonn Streets Recall Their Experiences." This series explored the history of Bonn streets, some of which were quite unremarkable and without substantial ensembles of historic architecture. The stories were colorful, humorous, and often filled with interesting vignettes about historical personalities and events in the Rhenish city's long history. They concentrated on a distant and popular history: the origin of the name "Bonngasse" in Roman and possibly pre-Roman history, the destruction and rebuilding of the Rheingasse after the flood of 1784, the development of the butcher trade and other crafts in the Wenzelgasse, and the medieval practice whereby every *Bürger* in the city had the right to brew his own beer in one of the municipal breweries without having "to bow to the taste of other brewery bosses."[98]

The articles' approach to recent history was obtuse at best. The only reference to the destruction of the Rheingasse in October 1944 in a World War II bombing raid came in a short caption to a photograph showing one of the street's half-timbered houses.[99] Even more spectacularly, the article on the Gudenaugasse, which up to 1856 had been the "Jewish alley," did not mention the Holocaust once.[100] This street was one of those avenues that "played no particular role in the present and had no especially noteworthy buildings in the past." But the street had "a not unimportant and characteristic position" in the history of the Rhenish city, which unfolded between the lines of the narrative.

The article explained that Bonn had a Jewish community as early as 1180. Its inhabitants were invaluable to the economic life of the town because they alone were not bound by the church's restrictions on interest and had money available for lending. Non-Jewish residents relied on Jewish moneylenders and often found themselves heavily indebted to them. This resulted in one particularly gruesome incident in 1349, the "battle against the Jews," in which, after Jews were blamed for the plague that had broken out in Bonn and the region, "many" were murdered and the rest driven out. It took thirty years before Jews returned to Bonn, where they built a synagogue and again established a thriving community that nonetheless found itself confined to a ghetto for the first time in 1715. One of the gates to the ghetto led to a street that had "one of the most beautiful" street names in early modern Bonn, the Alley of the Lilies, which had been ironically named because of the foul smell its cesspool gave off. Such irony was common for the time, and citizens in other cities gave such streets similarly appealing names, like Rose Alley or Lavender Lane.

It was a brutally harmless story evoked by a single street in the rather unlikely capital of the Federal Republic of Germany. Yet compared with the other stories in this series, it was the only one to attempt to relate a narrative of the social and cultural identity of a people whose persecution and well-being were closely involved with the history of the German people. That the story could do so little with the contemporary history of mass murder of Jews, and that it handled the distant history of Bonn Jewry so clumsily, should not hide the fact that the structure and content of the story seemed to be trying for something more serious—a critical narrative rather than a string of cute incidents, a tale of destruction featuring German perpetrators rather than one of unproblematic persistence. Here at least was the sign of a potentially critical perspective in the guise of a popular antiquarianism situated in the mainstream of a normal German memory that recalled so much history but yet so little.

This city which cannot be expunged from the mind is like an armature, a honeycomb in whose

cells each of us can place the things he wants to remember: names of famous men, virtues,

numbers, vegetable and mineral classifications, dates of battles, constellations, parts of speech.

—Italo Calvino

SEVEN | THE NEW CULT OF MONUMENTS

rom the late 1960s to the middle of the 1970s, West Germany experienced the beginnings of what Hessian conservator Reinhard Bentmann called a new cult of monuments. "The midlife crisis of a society that is no longer all that young . . . crystallizes in retrospective dreaming," wrote Bentmann in 1975, "in a regression into the lap of history and into the warm stone and wooden heart of old cities." Bentmann criticized the adherents of the new "wave of nostalgia," arguing they were retreating into the past in order to "escape the responsibility of being 'grown-up.'"[1] Despite the harshness of this judgment, the conservator did not condemn the public longing for monuments, saying instead that it needed to be understood, and that official preservation had to work out its own criteria for addressing popular attitudes. Bentmann was undoubtedly too close to events to see that the new cult of monuments was similar to the one Alois Riegl had observed much earlier in the century. Like the pre–World War I reaction to the economic destructiveness of Germany's drive to become a major industrial power, the more recent public desire for historic sites was motivated primarily by a growing critical memory of deep social change in work structures, leisure activities, and the built environment. For

those who focused on historic buildings, there was a growing consciousness that as the Federal Republic prospered, an unprecedented wave of historicide had taken place, a "second destruction" (according to Erwin Schleich) of monuments that went well beyond World War II demolition. The second destruction appeared to create even greater discontinuity with a shared German past than the first one had. Yet this broad realization of continuing historicide was also different from the earlier desire for monuments because it occurred in the wake of a profound destabilization of West German politics, a questioning of the fundamental bases of the BRD's identity. The late Kaiserreich had seen much uncertainty about political identity, to be sure, but the public contestation in the period starting in the late 1960s was broader and deeper. The sometimes violent political mobilization of the period opened an unusually large public space in which many different kinds of commemorative activity, many vectors of memory, could be expressed. Historic preservation's response and contribution to this activity is the subject of this chapter, which covers developments up to 1975, when official preservation's long-standing desire for broad public resonance culminated in European Cultural Heritage Year, an international event designed to raise public consciousness of the significance of historical places, and which simultaneously opened a new, uncertain epoch in the cultural protection of the nation's artifacts.

The New Society

After almost two decades of "crystallization and consolidation," the two Germanys in the mid-1960s entered a period of intense internal transformation.[2] The possibility of national reunification was remote, even if it was a formal goal of the Basic Law, and even if, as novelist Günter Grass said with characteristic candor in 1967, "sleazy politicians" still fostered nationalist hubris.[3] Sleazy politicians openly beating the nationalist drum were in a minority in this period in the West, however, or they were identified with relatively marginal groups such as the German refugees' organizations. This did not mean a sense of national identity had simply given way to other regional or international identities or even to Grass's concept of a new confederation of the two Germanys in something both less and more than the nation-state. Instead, the divergence of the two states was accompanied by efforts to delineate parallel but not entirely incompatible collective identities in which the national past remained an important if (especially in the West) rather understated element of official political discourse. The nineteenth-century German nation now spoke sotto voce in efforts to build a new industrial society on either side of the German-German border.

In the West more than a decade of Christian Democratic (CDU) dominance gave way in 1966 to a "grand coalition" between the CDU, the Free Democrats, and the Social Democrats, then in 1969 to a coalition government between the Social Democrats and the Free Democrats that would last until 1982. This era saw a new emphasis on economic planning and growth, new levels of consumption, educational reform, and an expansion of social welfare. *Leistung* assumed a "Europeanist," interventionist, and democratic face open to the outside world and willing to present itself as a model not of racial superiority but of efficiency and Western values. An equivalent to Kennedy and Johnson's Great Society, the consumption-oriented, democratic nation of the Federal Republic had "movement is everything" as its motto.[4] But the economic and political successes of the grand coalition and Social Democratic governments were gained only with considerable internal political tension. The rise of "extraparliamentary opposition" to the grand coalition, the evolution of student protest against the Vietnam war, the growth of a counterculture directed against a materialist society, and in the mid-1960s the growth of neo-Nazi groups created a feeling of unrest unprecedented in the history of the Bonn Republic. More fundamentally, a growing awareness of the limits of economic growth and rising environmentalist consciousness raised suspicions that the new society was deeply flawed. Political reaction to the violence of the late 1960s and especially to a wave of terrorism that began in earnest in 1974 added to the sense that a "change in tendency," or *Tendenzwende*, was carrying West Germany away from the reformist activism of the new society. Conservatives spoke of an "ungovernable" society that had wanted too much too fast, while Social Democrats and liberals warned of an impending political backlash and doubted the viability of ambitious reforms.

After stabilizing itself by building the Berlin Wall, East Germany entered a period of consolidation and growth as well. Based on political repression punctuated by fragile expressions of dissent, the DDR developed a socialist version of *Leistung* under Walter Ulbricht until 1971 and under Erich Honecker thereafter. The early 1960s saw the development of a New Economic System based on scientific state planning and industrial growth. No longer a primitive peasants' and workers' state overcoming the depredations of war and scarcity, the new system was to be an "achievement-oriented career society"[5] promising material satisfaction, technological advance, and a new form of socialist identity. Built in the late 1960s, the East Berlin television tower, a grotesque needle reaching for the sky without any relation to the surrounding historical landscape, well symbolized the regime's developing technocratic impulse. The leadership's paranoia about political upheaval in Czechoslovakia in 1968 and Poland in 1970 led to quiet dismantling of the

New Economic System as a recentralized, less experiment-minded approach took hold. Yet political repression was less overt than before, and although the economy chugged along more like a cheap Trabant than a sleek Western BMW, relative material prosperity, social stability, and (in the East European context) international leadership gave East German society a precarious legitimacy.

The West gained a new international stature due to its impressive economic and political accomplishments, but it also had the "middle class blues," to use one of left-wing writer Hans Magnus Enzensberger's evocative terms for the sense of dissatisfaction material pleasure brought with it. "We eat the grass / we eat the social product," wrote Enzensberger of the satisfied West German Bürger in 1966, "we eat the fingernails / we eat the past."[6] If this past could be seen in historic buildings, then the West had indeed eaten much of it in the rush to create a new society. During the thirty years after the end of the war the percentage of the building stock dating from before 1840 fell from 27 to 15. In 1968 in villages of less than 2,000 inhabitants four of every ten residential buildings dated from before 1900. But in cities with more than 100,000 this ratio dropped to less than two of ten.[7]

It was easy to see how this had happened. By the early 1970s, West Germans had gone through two phases of postwar rebuilding, each with implications for historic structures.[8] In the first phase, from the end of the war until roughly the mid-1950s, restorative and traditional tendencies had much support in architecture and planning, though not without considerable ambivalence, and many badly destroyed German cities reappeared in a form that gave them something of their pre–World War II character. In the second phase, from the mid-1950s until the early 1970s, extravagant plans for economic growth and the building of new housing, a modified modernist architecture, and traffic-oriented urban planning destroyed broad swaths of historic places. In about 1973 a third phase ensued due to economic recession, the energy crisis, growing dissatisfaction with the modernist rebuilding of the previous decades, and a downturn in the building industry. The effect was to redirect attention to historic buildings and town centers as symbols of bygone ages or as new fields of investment. Urban planning seemed to have made a full turn as the Federal government's 1975 report on urban construction noted that "thinking about conservation" had made unprecedented inroads.[9] A blurring of previous positions was one result, as the progressive and growth-oriented architects and planners of the 1950s and early 1960s became outspoken advocates for conservation of resources.

All three major political parties belatedly tried to capitalize on and shape the middle-class blues. Just as it had taken until the 1960s for the parties to focus systematically on cultural politics and educational reform, and then only because of popular pressure, it took until the late 1960s and early 1970s before the parties began to notice the effects of historicide in the built environment.[10] *Sanierung* became an important response to urban problems in this political context, as municipal politicians undertook a broad campaign to renew their historic centers. The German Urban League adopted the slogan "Save Our Cities Now!" for its 1972 convention. This was a significant reminder of the new social relevance of historic buildings—or more broadly of culture as a social resource—by an institution that historically championed the social needs of workers and consumers. Urban communities devoted financial resources to more "quality of life" issues, and from 1963 to 1975 cities' spending on cultural matters increased more than threefold, a jump much higher than that registered by the federal states. The musical, theatrical, cinematic, and other programs funded by such increases often took place in community "communication centers," which were most often new buildings erected after 1960 but which during the years from 1972 to 1977 could also be restored historic buildings.[11]

Historic urban districts were marred by traffic problems, deteriorated residential and commercial architecture, the departure of younger and middle-aged higher-income groups for rural or suburban areas, and a consequent loss of business and tax revenues. These developments had begun to affect smaller and medium-sized cities in particular, which despite the trend toward big cities still accounted for two-thirds of the West German population in 1974, and whose historic centers differed from those of major cities because they still combined residential and commercial functions. These cities also had more than three-quarters of all pre-1900 residential buildings in West Germany.[12]

The remaking of urban areas gained legal codification in the Urban Renewal Act of 1971, designed to regulate *Sanierung* projects and take "cultural requirements,"[13] including the collective need for historic buildings, into account in all planning. Federal and *Land* governments provided three-quarters of the funding for urban renewal and gave the cities much flexibility in carrying out the nearly 600 projects that had been completed or were under way by 1978.[14] The vast majority of projects dealt not with the most run-down neighborhoods but with those that promised long-term commercial investment and profitable residential property. This gentrification of neighborhoods often displaced the elderly or lower-income groups whose dwellings had been "renewed" and made increasingly attractive to middle-class professionals looking for stylish historic neighborhoods. In Duisburg-Neumühl 14,000 inhabitants had to leave their homes; in Munich's inner city, 73,000; in Bonn, almost 13,000. A "trend toward neatness"—or what Hessian conservator Gottfried Kiesow criticized as the "search for perfection

The programmed and projected look of the postmodern city was enhanced by artificial lighting techniques for monuments such as the fourteenth-century Frankfurt am Main cathedral, shown here in 1965. (photo: Frankfurt am Main Presse- und Informationsamt, Archiv Nr. 1.33.-5)

THE NEW CULT OF MONUMENTS

and renewal"—ensued, in part because corporate franchises, taking over more stores and restaurants in historic centers, wanted pleasant surroundings for their clientele. The result was that some of the most depressed urban areas—deteriorated neighborhoods between commercial centers and suburban peripheries in big cities, for example—were left to their own devices while other more desirable sections received both funding and facelifts in a further advance of the process of staging history already noted for urban renewal schemes of the 1930s.[15]

An increased concern with the appearance of history was reinforced by postmodern architecture, which valued playful (and often superficial) historical citation and the adaptation of new building to surrounding contexts. To the extent they stressed historicist and regional designs as well as meaning and vibrance rather than stripped-down functionalism in the built environment, many postmodern ideas were strikingly similar to those espoused by *Heimatschutz* and preservationist spokespeople since the late nineteenth century. The results of this cross-fertilization were not always satisfying to preservationists or the general public in Germany, however, especially when postmodernism's aesthetic clashed with local needs that architects found prosaic and unoriginal. For many postmodernists the city had become a spectacle, "culling a programmed and projected look" borrowed from cinematic and televisual imagery even more transient than Benjamin's tenth-of-a-second perspective from decades before. The fit between postmodernism and the new interest in restored historic districts was by no means exact, but the convergence between some postmodernist architects and some preservationists was strong enough to signal important shared concerns in Germany and other countries.[16]

Underlying such developments in West Germany was the maturation of a generation that equated the second phase of rebuilding with the insensitive forgetfulness of their parents, whose wish to be prosperous and forget the horrors of Nazism found abundant symbolic expression in the modernist high-rises or department stores that punctured many historic city districts. Embittered by the failure of many political reforms, the new generation sought values of authenticity and the real outside the realm of parliamentary politics—in private life but also in a new identity politics based on neighborhood and region. This resort to a new cultural evaluation of *Heimat* had parallels with the earlier tendency of the *Bildungsbürgertum* to look to natural and cultural environments as spheres of influence that could be dominated when the political sphere offered no such outlets. This connection was denied by the generation of the later 1960s, who self-consciously opposed the sins of their parents and grandparents in a form that nonetheless bore the traces of earlier responses to political conflict. When this opposition took the increasingly frequent form of occupying and restoring *Gründerzeit* residential buildings from the 1870s, it had come full circle.

Nonetheless, one cannot underestimate the bitterness of a postwar generation that saw only their parents' inability to come to terms (if that was possible emotionally) with recent history. This feeling contributed to a broader public reevaluation of German history and a more profound and critical interest in the rise of Nazism and the Holocaust. There had been much public discussion of the Holocaust starting in the first half of the 1960s, when SS bureaucrat Adolf Eichmann's trial in Israel in 1961 and the trial of Auschwitz guards in Frankfurt am Main in 1964 gained media attention, but now interest picked up even more. In 1965 Dachau opened a more realistic and critical exhibit at the site of its former concentration camp, emphasizing how "the murderous system" of mass killing developed.[17] In 1966 Lower Saxony built a museum and documentation center at the former site of the Bergen-Belsen concentration camp, and in 1968 the city of Berlin set up a small memorial and documentation center dedicated to the history of the German resistance. The elaborate and successful exhibit "Questions for German History" opened in the reconstructed Reichstag building in West Berlin in 1971, and in 1974 the Cologne city archive organized an exhibit on resistance and persecution during the Nazi dictatorship. This activity was sporadic when compared with the proliferation of such projects in the 1980s, but one can see the wider scope of the later period prefigured in the earlier one.

If these years saw a more open public discussion of the place of Nazism in German history, important barriers to memory-work still had not been overcome. The public interest in the past was sparked partially by fascination with the 1930s, expressed in literature, film, and popular culture that rode a "Hitler wave," and valorized intellectually by a neoconservative evaluation of Nazism's role in German history shaped by, among others, Hitler biographer Joachim Fest and avant-garde filmmaker Hans-Jürgen Syberberg. But barriers to memory also came from within the intellectual-cultural structures of those who were most critical about the German past. The protesters of the "generation of 1968" had underlined the structural continuities between the Federal Republic and the Nazi period, a historical perspective their parents had been unwilling or unable to see.[18] This had profound consequences throughout the historical profession, where a new social structural history tracing the strands linking Nazism with earlier periods of German history emerged to become a major element in West German academic writing. It had even more widespread effects in society, where the candid appraisal of the past contributed to a kind of compensatory activism of the present, an attempt to make up for the political action that notionally could have stopped the rise of fascism. Yet the new generation stopped short of making a more searching exploration of their parents' and grandparents' participation in mass murder.

This evasion occurred in a number of ways: substituting memory of Kristallnacht for the memory of the Holocaust as a whole; concentrating on the history of German Jews only to the point of their deportation, the point at which for all practical purposes they disappeared from German history; and failing to devote thorough attention to the process of extermination itself in the death camps. What had begun as a full-scale assault on the inability of the older generation to remember its past ended in a "new bond between the generations,"[19] a consensus to avoid the disturbing memory of Germans as perpetrators in favor of the memory of victims, who were powerless to shape memory. The observation of this taboo formed one of the emotional bases for a common West German identity in the 1970s.

In East Germany a period of fairly spontaneous confrontation with the memory of the Holocaust right after the war gave way to an official "antifascist" liturgy of remembrance that saw Nazi extermination policy as a function of monopoly capitalism. Preserved concentration camps in Buchenwald, Ravensbrück, and Sachsenhausen presented visitors with the official line. By the 1970s, antifascist remembrance was transformed more fully into SED propaganda. As in the West, DDR memory of Nazism developed largely without specific reference to the actual historical experiences of the victims. But antifascist ideology was even less likely to focus realistically on perpetrators and victims than West German Holocaust remembrance was. Not only an ideological instrument to shape public images of the past, East German antifascism was "an existentially compulsory historical-philosophical premise [of] state doctrine."[20]

Critical memory-work relating either to the Nazi period in particular or to political history in general operated at some distance from official preservation practices, as I have emphasized throughout the book. Only in a small minority of cases did government conservators and their staffs work on projects with direct relevance to the history of Nazism, as in some of the history workshops discussed below, which were in any case only beginning in the second half of the 1970s. Nonetheless, the critical tone and activity of these years, the wish to understand and illuminate a part of the German past that many considered to have been hidden from public memory, did add an element of urgency to preservation activity. As for the broader context of memory as it related to historic buildings, the general course of modernization and its direct effects on people's daily lives stimulated action more than Holocaust remembrance did. The disruptive effects of social change drove a wedge between an already vaguely remembered past and the present, making the desire for memory more urgent than at any time in the postwar period. In the West this desire was also associated with a new politics of memory in which the nation, as an integral political frame uniting and superseding diverse memories, was replaced by a new and more multi-faceted national construct that served as a cognate of the mobile consumers' society. Where did historic preservation fit in this development?

Demand for Totality?

As in the two decades before World War I, this era saw a flurry of legislative activity as by 1980 all West German federal states had new legislation regulating the protection of historic places. None of the new laws challenged the inviolability of private property, although each followed the Basic Law by stressing the social responsibilities of ownership. Each specified that, as the Baden-Württemberg law read, "public interest" based on "scientific, artistic, and *Heimat*-historical" motivations defined what a monument was.[21] There was similarly significant legislation in the East, where a 1975 law provided for the drawing up of lists of protected buildings at the district and county level in addition to that of the state, which had already issued a roster of "monuments of particular national significance and international artistic value" in 1962.[22]

In contrast to the DDR, where preservation remained highly centralized in spite of some devolution of authority, the *Länder*, private owners, and cities and towns were the major official supporters of preservation in the BRD. A small Federal fund for the protection of "architectural monuments with particular national and cultural significance" did exist, but it covered only isolated historic churches and government buildings. As might be expected in a decentralized system, the amount of money available for preservation in the federal states and towns varied greatly. Bavaria was once again far ahead, giving almost four marks per capita in subventions for the maintenance of nonstate historic sites in 1975, with Baden-Württemberg next at one mark per capita, North Rhine-Westphalia in third place with just less than one mark, and Bremen at the bottom with eighteen pfennigs. There were also regional variations in the types of monuments protected. The Rhineland became a leader in the still-sporadic practice of preserving industrial monuments, as Günther Borchers, appointed *Land* conservator for North Rhine-Westphalia in 1970 and trained in archaeology and architecture, devoted much attention to such artifacts, and as special consultants on the preservation of industrial landmarks were appointed in Münster and Bonn in 1973 and 1974, respectively.[23]

The traditional preservation societies underwent significant change.

Looking for "a different term for *Heimatschutz*," the RVDH joined the Rheinischer Heimatbund to form the Rhenish Association for the Preservation of Monuments and Natural Sites (Rheinischer Verein für Denkmalpflege und Landschaftsschutz, or RVDL).[24] The name change allowed the group to retain its traditional emphasis on historic buildings while also satisfying *Heimatschutz*'s interest in natural landscapes and blurring the distinction between nature conservation and monument protection, as Gothic cathedrals and half-timbered houses were seen (misleadingly, because they are not renewable) as scarce resources similar to rivers and forests. Finally, the new name symbolically freed the group from the long history of nationalist and racist connotations of *Heimatschutz*. That this historical penumbra still caused anxieties can be seen from an unusually defensive statement in 1970 in which the RVDH pointed out that it did not deal with the "interests, wishes, dream images, and whims of a few eccentric, reactionary or dried up antiquarians, but [with] the legitimate wishes and expectations of representatives of conscientious *Bürger*." This defense was not entirely unjustified, since the group had a broader occupational and gender mix than it had had earlier in the century, and it was deeply interested in contemporary issues such as the effects of nuclear reactors and autobahns on historic buildings and natural environments.[25]

The role of the government conservator had by this period become a matter of widespread discussion in both the profession and the public. More than a matter of the conservator's training and professional status (both still ambiguous), the debate touched broader issues of the definition of monuments and the conservator's social role. "The idea of the conservative conservator, the 'gilder of the nation' who shuns the present and sees his task even today as consisting only in the museal protection of a few art-historically preferred monuments, is passé," wrote *Die Zeit* architecture expert Manfred Sack in 1975. "In his place belongs the conservator who enjoys reality, who conceptualizes and practices historic preservation in its connection with the politics of urban development." He may have had in mind someone like Borchers, who as a conservator with special enthusiasm for industrial monuments was using a rapidly produced series of cheap booklets, the Arbeitshefte des Landeskonservators Rheinland, rather than standard bound volumes to publicize preservation issues and arouse public consciousness. Writing in a somewhat more restrained fashion in an important collection of essays on historic spaces in West German life, Erika Haindl argued that popular demands on the conservator were to be welcomed, and that conservators were to be given more interdisciplinary training in social science methodologies and more help in working with citizens' initiatives.[26]

Kiel state conservator Hartwig Beseler took a different approach, arguing that the public was asking too much of the conservator. The conservator's role should be limited, insisted Beseler, and the tendency to inflate the definition of the monument should be resisted. "A downright vehement departure from the single object (which is what the term monument [Denkmal] actually refers to)," wrote Beseler, "has led people to believe in the healing power of vague general concepts like 'ensemble' or the monstrous 'city-monument' [Stadtdenkmal]." The Kiel preservationist noted that in 1970 official estimates put the number of monuments at around 200,000 for the BRD, but five years later this number had grown to 800,000 or even 1 million. Small in comparison with the countries richest in monuments, such as Italy, where a population 13 percent smaller than that of the BRD had an estimated 4.5 million architectural landmarks, this number nonetheless represented a four- or fivefold increase in just a half-decade.[27] Part of this extraordinary inflation could be explained by the growing interest in architecture of the late Second Empire, including monuments of industrial history. If the estimate of 800,000 was accurate, then one of twelve buildings in the BRD was a historic site, one in ten if the higher estimate was accepted, and one in five if only pre–World War II structures were considered. Beseler cautioned that such perspectives would make planning and growth virtually impossible and inflate the conservator's role beyond all practical boundaries. Nonetheless, the idea of the conservator as a cultural generalist, a person of broad learning and sensitivity to contemporary social trends in the tradition of Quast, Clemen, and Hiecke, still appealed to Beseler.

Beseler was criticizing what Christian Democratic mayor of Stuttgart Manfred Rommel, by no means an enemy of preservation policy, called a dangerous public "demand for totality" in preserving the past.[28] Like the neoconservative critics of democracy and welfare-state social policy, some representatives of official preservation worried aloud that public memory had become ungovernable. One could see this anxiety in the way Rhineland-Pfalz conservator Werner Bornheim gen. Schilling dealt with the issue of private property as it was debated with reference to preservation legislation and the right of expropriation in 1973. Bornheim referred to the "curious preference of our time to go around undermining things, including the concept of property. We must protect ourselves," he said, "from becoming stirrup holders for tendencies that completely negate the idea of property!"[29] In this view, contemporary tendencies threatened rather than helped professional preservationists. There was too much memory rather than too little. Government agencies were not to be stirrup holders for radical and uncompromising forms of preservation but, rather, managers of their constituencies' always limited and controllable collective past.

At the turn of the century the conservator emphasized not only administrative and professional tasks but also a moral-educative function that was tied to the *Bürgertum*'s positive evaluation of history. The crisis of historicism and slow dissolution of the *Bürgertum* left this moral-educative element weakened but still intact from the 1930s to the early 1950s. Thereafter, however, specialization, which had always been an element of the conservator's role but never a dominant one, increased. Two decades later, in response to a tremendous upsurge of public enthusiasm for historic preservation, the conservator as cultural generalist was once again a popular trope of public discourse, this time in the form of the politically aware, socially conscious, and professionally interdisciplinary citizen-official. Yet many critics charged that the reemergence of the cultural generalist, when tied to notions of "ensemble" and "city-monument," overwhelmed the appropriate channels of official cultural politics, creating "nonsense" and even a "reactionary" politics that gave the state "an unsuitable influence even down to the smallest detail."[30] It was a situation fraught with contradiction.

If there had been a canon of historic sites up to this period, it disappeared in the popular cult of monuments. Some observers considered this a function of a natural trend whereby each age, armed with more historical knowledge than the last, would consider more structures to be monument-worthy, or *denkmalfähig*. This argument bothered art historian Willibald Sauerländer, a featured speaker at the 1975 *Land* conservators' annual conference in Goslar, who suggested that current interest in historic architecture was the result of a deeper qualitative shift rather than commemorative arithmetic.[31] Behind this inflationary spiral was a reaction to the social changes of a postwar world in which "grayness" took over the cities and "planned wastelands" the countryside, where historical monuments were swallowed up in "a monster landscape of skyscrapers."[32] The rapidity and scope of these changes constituted the fundamental difference between the 1970s and the late Kaiserreich, when an expanded sense of the monument was still connected to the increase of historical knowledge.

The altered context required dramatic changes in the way preservationists conceptualized the monument, in Sauerländer's view. Just as the late nineteenth century replaced earlier aesthetic-patriotic definitions with a scientific-historical explanation, the late twentieth century should find its own interpretation. In doing so, it would have to go beyond Cultural Heritage Year's motto, "A Future for Our Past," which for Sauerländer still smacked of the old historicism. New definitions should reverse the terms of the argument, expressing the idea "only through a preserved past to an urban future." Dehio's "historical existence as such" would have to be replaced by a "socially mediated" focus through which distinctions between great star monuments and vernacular architecture would be less consequential, and through which a "pluralism of concepts" would produce a variety of historic ensembles. These ensembles would be integrated into the everyday life of modern urban dwellers, whose relationship to past and future would be based less on didactic, scientific, and historical approaches to monuments than on a sense of multiple pasts interacting in social and commercial exchanges. Sauerländer argued this approach would protect preservationists from the criticism that concepts such as the "city-monument" would turn the entire urban fabric into a lifeless museum. A social view of the monument would mean not only multiplicity but willingness to accept change, even the "sacrifice of the old, where for clear urbanistic reasons this is unavoidable."[33] Arguing that conservators would have to accept the destruction of monuments was hardly new, but Sauerländer was correct to argue that popular enthusiasm for historic places demanded a well-thought-out response from governments and cultural officials.

If socially mediated preservation meant that government conservators would have to understand the daily interests of their urban and rural constituencies, then this also meant that commercial forces would have a role to play. Although historic places had served as major elements in the new consumers' cityscapes of the twentieth century since well before the 1970s, this development reached a new level as the popular cult of monuments took hold. The staging of history via old city centers was not only supported but actively promoted by some conservators and their allies, who called for the "attractivization" of monuments and historic districts.[34] Yet this trend was by no means unanimously accepted. In the eyes of one critic, aestheticization turned the monument into a "curiosity" rather than an "antiquity," as it had been under the historicist gaze of nineteenth-century viewers. The consumer-friendly "milieu island," increasingly an outcome of urban renewal projects, was only one aspect of this transformation of historic ensembles into what one preservationist called "Disneylands," which became a catchword for almost any programmed (new or rebuilt) historicity.[35] Using a similar language, Die Zeit's Manfred Sack criticized Frankfurt mayor Rudi Arndt's plans to fill in part of the historic Römer complex with modern constructions aping medieval half-timbered houses, calling the project "Rudi Arndt's Disneyland" and the "Mickey Mouse Middle Ages." This view was shared by many conservators.[36] Despite such opposition, conservators and municipal officials, responding to public demand for more socially resonant policies, were among the forerunners in the trend toward commercialization and aestheticization of historic places.

The DDR would have to wait until the 1980s to get such "Disneylands," as the reconstruction of the Nikolaikirche and its milieu at a site associated with the thirteenth-century origins of Berlin demonstrated.[37] In the mean-

Frankfurt's reconstructed Römerberg (June 1979), or what *Die Zeit* critic Manfred Sack called the "Mickey Mouse Middle Ages." Skyscrapers in the background reflect the unprecedented growth of the postwar city. (photo: Frankfurt am Main Presse- und Informationsamt, Archiv Nr. 1.1.-4)

time there was growing doubt about how the regime had handled some monuments in the immediate postwar years, and even within the SED after Ulbricht some officials were willing to criticize the demolition of the Berlin Palace as an act of cultural vandalism. In contrast to the West, regime policy was based less on consumerist fantasy than on the "aesthetic resonance" of a monument and its "role as a carrier of historical information."[38]

In practice this approach tended to limit rather than increase the number of monuments, as with the example of *Jubiläums-Denkmalpflege*, or jubilee-preservation. Beginning in 1967 with the commemoration of Martin Luther

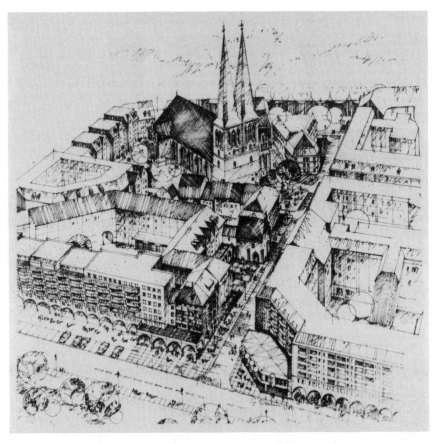

Reconstruction projects such as the Nikolaikirche ensemble, shown here in a 1982
sketch, reflected a belated trend toward historicist "Disneylands" in the DDR.
(photo: Stahn, *Das Nikolaiviertel am Marx-Engels-Forum*, 72)

as a hero of the "early bourgeois revolution," this form of preservation
represented the cultural nation through historic sites chosen for their association with monumental figures of the German past. Birthplaces or other
buildings connected to the lives not just of Luther (Wittenberg and Eis-
leben) but to sixteenth-century Peasants' War leader Thomas Müntzer and
composers Heinrich Schütz (Weißenfels), Händel (Halle), and Bach figured
prominently in such efforts. The reopening of the Bauhaus in 1976 and the
return of the statue of Frederick the Great to its traditional spot on Unter
den Linden in 1980 continued the trend. For some preservationists such
policies skewed the protection of cultural heritage for questionable state
interests. For others there was an indirect benefit, since some preservation,
even when oriented to monumental and national needs, was better than

none, and jubilee-preservation could be exploited to create regime and public support for other projects closer to the preservationist agenda, as when
the Halle office of the East German Institut für Denkmalpflege used the
450-year commemoration of the Lutheran Reformation to gain support for
restoring key historic places.[39] The outcome of such efforts was that whereas
the DDR could demonstrate to the world its devotion to cultural heritage in
a number of highly visible sites, the larger part of its architectural heritage,
such as its many half-timbered cities, deteriorated due to neglect and long-
term planning that condemned it to destruction once new urban building
projects were started. Although jubilee-preservation was based on restoring
or protecting a very limited array of sites, moreover, it demonstrated the
same tendency toward aestheticization shown in Western preservation. Ju-
bilees and the monuments that represented them were, after all, tourist
attractions as well as results of political acts.

Despite state policy, the number of East German monuments did increase,
reaching about 50,000 in the early 1980s and including many vernacular
and industrial structures. This was not an insubstantial number, but it was
small by the standards of a country such as Czechoslovakia, which claimed
to have seven times more protected monuments. From 1950 to 1970 the
DDR spent 16 billion East German marks on the "maintenance and modernization" of old residential housing, but in the first five years of the 1970s the
sum for such purposes had already reached 10 billion. Aside from their
functional role in urban planning, such old residential neighborhoods also
had "cultural and historical values" because they were "traditional sites of
the struggle of the working class." The East German Kulturbund issued a
reader on technical monuments in 1973, which unintentionally revealed
that until this time the peasants' and workers' state had been as haphazard
as the West in saving such artifacts. Still, an inventory of about a thousand
technical monuments existed for Saxony since 1950, the DDR Constitution
explicitly called for protection of landmarks of economic history, and many
lay historians of factories were involved in the protection of industrial artifacts. Efforts to create a Marxist Dehio handbook of monuments that
prioritized workers' housing and peasant architecture ahead of the grand
monuments of the past failed, but the effort legitimated those who sought to
expand the purview of East German preservation.[40]

By contrast to the real and potential expansion of East German heritage, the central list of protected monuments of DDR history, which carried
only the most important East German landmarks of national and international stature from the postwar era, was small indeed. In 1979 it had only
twelve monuments, including the three former concentration camp sites of
Buchenwald, Sachsenhausen, and Ravensbrück; the East Berlin television

tower; a Soviet-inspired peasant settlement begun in Thuringia in 1946; a 1950s dam near Halle; the East Berlin Council of State Building with its "Liebknecht Portal"; and two historical ensembles reconstructed after 1945 on the Alte Markt of Magdeburg and the Thälmann-Platz (returned to its earlier name, Neumarkt, in 1990) in Rostock. Preservation agencies were reluctant to focus on such monuments partly because so many older historical buildings required more urgent attention, and partly because of aesthetic and political distaste for the architectural products and historic sites of the socialist regime.[41]

A Transformed Nation

As the foregoing suggests, DDR regime officials were less self-conscious than their Western counterparts about tying preservation to narratives of the nation or about using educative-patriotic themes. Here the protection of monuments was closely integrated into a socialist cultural politics that wanted "to assimilate the cultural heritage of the German *Volk*, the revolutionary workers' movement, and the humanistic and progressive cultural products of other nations of the world, and to bring about consistently a living connection to everything that is great, forward-looking, and revolutionary." Memory of an international revolutionary tradition was to be linked to historic preservation's "social task," which was "to integrate that which we have inherited into socialist life, to promote knowledge of historical relationships, and thereby to deepen the *Volk*'s understanding of its national traits and its national feeling."[42] Official preservationists were ambivalent about such uses, but they also exploited them when necessary.

At first glance West German preservationists' attitudes toward the nation were diametrically opposed to those in the East. Just as West German politicians emphasized Europeanist themes, official preservation swore allegiance to European rather than to national culture. "Whoever has attentively studied documents associated with the founding of the Rhenish association in 1906," said RVDL chair Hermann Heusch in response to European Cultural Heritage Year in 1975, "certainly knows that precisely this turn toward European history and tradition was and remains an essential element of the association's tasks."[43] True as far as it went, this statement nonetheless rewrote the organization's history in a rather questionable way. Heusch would have been on firmer ground had he noted that although national identity had once been foremost in RVDH thinking, both European and regional moments relativized the national from time to time. Moreover, nation-thinking persisted in preservationist discourse, especially for members of the older generation such as Franz Graf Wolff Metternich. Metternich was the offspring of a Rhenish family with a tradition of public service and sympathy for Prussian interests. He died in 1978, having worked as conservator of the Rhine province from 1928 to 1951, as head of the German army's *Kunstschutz* program in the West, and as an active proponent of preservation in government agencies and organizations.[44] Writing in 1970, he criticized the materialism of the age for undervaluing "the documents of our European culture" and stressed the international context of the "Rhenish people's" existence. Yet when German preservation had to make choices about such perennial issues as the historic milieu of the Cologne cathedral, it did so because this monument was a "visiting card of the German *Volk*."[45]

Metternich's younger colleagues noted an absence of discussion of national identity among West German preservationists. According to Bonn preservationist Georg Mörsch, in European circles this discursive void made the BRD "a distinct outsider when it came to the role played by architectural heritage in the creation of national identity." Yet it was precisely this ostensible lack of "nationness" in preservationist discussions that one had to regard with caution, not because the conservator was to be a nationalist but because national identity remained as a legitimate motivation for cultural politics. "Historic preservation must also be aware of different idealistic or ideological thought systems," argued Mörsch, "in which the need for visible history can be expressed and which are not misguided simply because we do not discuss them at the moment." This perspective meant that professional preservationists had to risk unpopularity by reminding individuals that artifacts such as Bauhaus buildings and architecture from the National Socialist era should also be protected even if there was presently no demand for such things.[46] But it also implied that nationalist motivations for protecting certain monuments were not to be overlooked even when public interest was not strongly shaped by such sentiments. The conservator should think nationally, said Mörsch, even when officials or the people did not.

The complexities of national identity in the BRD are most interesting in an area of public discourse that until the late 1960s had shown relatively little interest in the preservation of historic buildings, namely the Marxist Left. West German Marxist thinkers were influenced in this period by the example of the Bolognese Communist Party, whose slogan was "Preservation Is Revolution." They praised DDR monument protection, arguing that it taught that not individuals but "the society" was the true owner of historic landmarks. They discussed Russian Communist theories of monuments in connection with debates over the possibility of a "proletarian public sphere."[47] But most often they were busy reworking the German Marxist heritage of Theodore Adorno, Max Horkheimer, Ernst Bloch, and Walter Benjamin, who was of particular interest to those neo-Marxists who

Roland Günter: "It is a scandal that in a democracy the majority of the population has to a great extent been kept from the right to have its own history." Two views (*above and opposite*) of the Eisenheim settlement. (photos: Bildarchiv Foto Marburg/Art Resource, New York)

thought systematically about historic buildings. Writing in the spring of 1940, just months before his death, Benjamin made the famous remark that all "cultural treasures . . . owe their existence not only to the efforts of the great minds and talents who have created them, but also to the anonymous toil of their contemporaries. There is no document of civilization which is not at the same time a document of barbarism. And just as such a document is not free of barbarism, barbarism taints also the manner in which it was transmitted from one owner to another. A historical materialist therefore dissociates himself from it as far as possible. He regards it as his task to brush history against the grain."[48]

In this view historic places were part of that same superstructure that clouded social conflicts in ideological pronouncements. The great monuments were also monuments to the resourcefulness of the worker. Abandoned factories or old windmills were not only ruins and scenic traces of a romanticized past, not just "technical monuments," but signs of the inevitable decline of past modes of production. National genius was not only the expression of an irreducible identity but also part of a global history of violent and destructive class conflict, rising and falling productive forces, and changing social relations. Fields of care were not unhistorical even if

THE NEW CULT OF MONUMENTS

they lacked important historic architecture; on the contrary, they were permeated with the history of particular struggles, workers, and neighborhoods. All this could be an important counterweight to cultural nationalism's idealization of historic places even when it retained a sense of national continuity.

A good example of how this critical perspective reworked a sense of national identity was the Eisenheim project, led by the author of the inventory of historic places for Oberhausen, art historian Roland Günter. A member of the left wing of the Social Democratic Party, Günter played a key role organizing a workers' initiative protecting the workers' colony Eisenheim in Oberhausen in the Ruhr. Consisting of nearly fifty buildings at the turn of the century, this settlement had been built in 1844 by the Krupp firm as the first nonstate working-class housing settlement in Germany. It included two-story brick duplexes and other types of structures that were relatively roomy even by contemporary standards—a function of the competitive market for labor in the nineteenth-century Ruhr—and that ranged in quality from "good" (about half of the buildings) to "average" or "poor." The main drawback was a lack of indoor showers and toilets in about half the structures, a condition that local residents and outside supporters insisted could be changed with a modest investment. Darkened by the effects of over a century of air pollution, all the buildings in the settlement had been heavily modified over the years, as workers, pensioners, and housewives left "traces" in garden plots, kitchens, work sheds, and decorations. This form of appropriation (*Aneignung*) represented a true popular usage of a historic field of care that was actually much more than a "living museum," as the otherwise perspicacious conservator Günther Borchers mistakenly called it. Among the 488 persons in 159 households living in Eisenheim was an unspecified number of "guest worker" families, a very high proportion of SPD voters (up to 90 percent), and a substantial group (more than one-quarter) of households living below the poverty line.[49]

What happened in the 1970s in Eisenheim had implications for many similar mining settlements (*Zechensiedlungen*), which numbered as many as 3,000 and included as many as 1 million inhabitants. Many of these historic ensembles were in danger of demolition due to urban renewal and the plans of mine owners, who no longer gained profits from them. In the Krupp settlement of Altenhof, mine owners bulldozed pensioners' houses soon after they died, intimidating the remaining, usually aged inhabitants who did not want to move. One Krupp executive said in 1968, "We have to throw off our ballast of tradition." The Eisenheim initiative began as a research project by university students, Günter, and another *Dozent*, Jörg Boström, to show how capitalism destroyed such settlements, becoming a protest group only in 1972 when owner August Thyssen Hütte AG's plans to demolish the site and build skyscrapers on it appeared ready for implementation.[50]

Günter drew directly on Benjamin when he defended workers' protests, saying that to live in a place was to "leave traces" of one's existence that could be excavated like "a deposit, a stratum" of the earth. "He who seeks to approach his own buried past," wrote Benjamin, "must conduct himself like a man digging." Workers digging for their own past did so in defense of their community, whose relationship to the outside world was like that of a colony to imperialist and capitalist exploiters in Günter's eyes. "Benjamin distinguished between visual and tactile uses of architecture," wrote Günter, and Eisenheim was a pure example of the way in which "touch" rather than "sight"—the preserve of the nineteenth-century lover of historic places—dominated workers' sensibilities.[51] Evident in many modifications to building exteriors, kitchens, and gardens that Eisenheim inhabitants had made over the years, historic traces had different meanings for the workers, housewives, pensioners, and children who made up the bulk of Eisenheim residents than for factory owners. For Günter, this difference demonstrated the absence of "absolute historicity." "The nobility, church, and upper *Bürgertum* have made use of their right to history for a long time," he wrote, "it is a scandal that in a democracy the majority of the population has to a great extent been kept from the right to have its own history, that is from the right for preservation of its historic sites."

Sincerity and naivete mixed with elitism characterized this perspective.

Günter and Boström were convinced that workers' initiatives would work more efficiently than citizens' initiatives because, unlike the latter, workers did not have to elect representatives. "The members of a workers' initiative can be certain that their 'delegate' will represent the general interest of the initiative without being elected."[52] This organicism was coupled with a view of workers as nonadults. Eisenheim's garden houses and small workshops possessed a "cultural value" that would have been denied such structures just twenty years previously. These modest "monuments" evoked Benjamin's comment on children's play: "Children build a world of objects for themselves, a small one within the larger one." Workers' "tinkering [basteln]" became a symbol of the settlement dwellers' childlike simplicity in the face of mine owners' and state officials' selfishness. Still, Günter and his colleagues had identified a deeply personal and tactile form of collective memory that was different from that represented over so many decades of official efforts. "For me a monument is a memento," one retired mineworker told Günter. "When I go walking with my little grandson, then I want to show him the conveyor tower where I and my father worked."[53] Uttered with reference to a workplace, this statement nonetheless also could apply to one of the Eisenheim houses, whose significance was more personal and even physical, more a product of a curatorial approach to the armature of memory, than that of the gentrifiers and commercializers of the age.

The mobilization against demolition generated considerable national visibility as president of the BRD Gustav Heinemann threw in his support for the Eisenheimer. Significantly, the local SPD, the majority party, supported this initiative only hesitantly when it came to providing more than rhetoric, and the trade unions had little interest in a conflict that did not affect workplace politics. By contrast, when the Christian Democrats said anything at all about Eisenheim, they were positive, in part because they had no electoral or financial investment in the matter. In general the regional and national press and television gave the Eisenheimer their most consistent support. *Land* conservator Günther Borchers, Roland Günter's longtime colleague and a strong advocate for preservation of technical artifacts and workers' settlements, also gave full support to the Eisenheim project, in contrast to most other *Land* authorities.[54]

The Eisenheim project suggested that social preservation, the maintenance and renewal of not just the physical environment but also the social networks within and around it, was just as important to some West Germans as historic preservation in the more traditional sense of the term.[55] It also suggested that new forms of national identity were working even when these forms were rather muted. From one side the nation was defined in negative terms. If workers were to preserve their past, said two of Günter's collaborators, then this would take political action. But this was hardly easy, they said, because in Germany there was a "historical aversion to the political and above all to political practice."[56] Thus defenders of Eisenheim would have to educate both themselves and others in a long learning process, overcoming that lack of political sensibility that many thinkers on both the Left and the Right had decried as a specifically German shortcoming for more than a century. In a more positive vein, it was largely a German radical tradition that Günter drew on—mainly Benjamin and Bruno Taut, whom Günter cited as a "socialist architectural theorist" who had once praised Eisenheim as a good example of "sound living conditions."[57] Moreover, when Günter castigated the "scandal" of a democracy whose population did not enjoy a right to its history, it was the problem of a specifically German democracy that led him to this criticism.

There was no advocacy of a new national identity here, to be sure. But the shadow of "Germanness" remained—albeit in a critical, socially responsible, and truly democratic guise—even when other issues were present. Indeed, part of the quality of this Germanness was its intentional avoidance of the issue of national belonging altogether. An attempt to avoid the identity that could not be avoided, identification with the nation thus continued to work at a considerable distance. Enzensberger's resigned shrug to the question "Am I a German?" was paradigmatic in this context.

One finds a comparable perspective in a more scholarly treatment of the traditional objects of historical preservation in a collection of essays, *Lübeck, the Old City as a Monument*, which originated as part of the fourteenth annual German Art History conference in 1974.[58] Introduced and edited by art historian Michael Brix, the essays dealt with the problem of how to specify the concept of the "city-monument." They were aimed at a particular tradition in the history of perceiving and protecting historical townscapes. Lübeck was not just one of the most fascinating examples of historical urban architecture, as most preservationists had agreed for more than a century; it was also a "provocation" whose monuments could not be used to legitimate a "dreamy flight into the past." "A distinctly rational will to order formed the urban morphology," wrote Brix. "Power struggles between the citizenry and clerics motivated rival architectural projects in religious buildings. Even the strongly fluctuating upper stratum of shopowners was not excepted from the struggle for existence, to say nothing of the misery of the underprivileged, who were affected by land speculation and housing shortages. Lübeck demonstrates most strongly that urban architecture should not be conceptualized one-sidedly as a medium of beauty but also an expression of class and interest conflicts and suffering."[59]

Preservationist literature had never been without an appreciation of the relationship between historic buildings and power struggles. But Brix's evo-cation of the medieval city put the emphasis on struggle from below and class interest from above, the part of the equation that had always been subsumed in earlier accounts. Here a Benjaminian emphasis on the barba-rism underlying culture took the specific form of seeing historic preserva-tion in terms of the history of class struggle. In the DDR this perspective was raised to official state policy as not only intellectual discourse but tour-ist literature stressed underlying social struggles in representations of his-toric buildings. In this perspective the "brilliance" of the lower German brick Gothic architecture of a city such as Stralsund, which had become a showcase of DDR preservation due to the well-maintained medieval and early modern buildings of the *Altstadt,* could not hide the "struggle of the lower strata of people against the few families who controlled the city coun-cil" that ran "like a red thread" through local history.[60]

In neither case—and most obviously in the DDR—was there a disavowal of German nationhood. Rather, critical memory was deployed to right a long imbalance in the way Germans regarded places widely considered to be of national and historical concern. For East German tourists the brilliance of historic places was to be integrated in a longer narrative of class struggle that appreciated both the cultural accomplishments and profound social costs of capitalist exploitation. For Brix, "fascination," which in this connection meant a deep and ultimately inexplicable emotional attachment to national architectural treasures in a city such as Lübeck, was not to be done away with but was to be "connected with provocation." Nor would there be a one-sided condemnation of earlier defenders of tradition in preservation and architec-ture. As one of the essays on turn-of-the-century Lübeck showed, the cul-tural program underlying *Heimatschutz* architecture "had been equated in an all too undifferentiated way with the political-reactionary trends of the beginning of this century."[61] We have already seen that East German cul-tural officials were willing to find new approaches to the long tradition of *Heimat* thinking as well.

Such perspectives on political identity transformed the nation into a set of social relationships based on a multitude of often violently opposed interests and orientations to the past rather than a homogeneous entity integrated from above by reference to a single, hegemonic continuity. But this was neither a denationalization of collective memory nor a replacement of na-tional by social history. A nation remained, but its sense of inherited com-munity was now seen as the product of a series of repressed or vaguely felt pasts whose relationship with national memory in the older sense of the term was based less on lines of authority than on a reciprocity of historically shaped but immediately lived experiences.

If preservationists and their allies were transforming the German sense of the nation from the supply side, then the demand side reflected this trend even more dramatically. In a front page editorial in January 1975 the *Frankfurter Allgemeine Zeitung* called the new interest in "the historical" a genuine "people's movement," noting that those who called such memory-work reactionary often forgot that nostalgia was a product of "left-wing discoveries from the time of wildest protest."[62] Opinion surveys showed that West Germans thought historic preservation was an important public activity for which the state had done too little in the past. In 1980 a survey of voting age West Germans revealed that 88 percent of all respondents wanted some form of protection for historic buildings.[63] Among those who favored preservation "women, south Germans, environmentalists, members of the Free Democratic Party, the better-paid, managers and leading civil servants, and younger people" were overrepresented, while the underrepresented included "farmers, middle-income groups, semiskilled or unskilled workers, pensioners, and residents of medium- and small-sized cities." In both the CDU and the SPD it was not the mainstream members but those on the margins who were overrepresented among the advocates of monument protection.[64]

This interest fueled the extraordinary increase in the number of monuments already discussed. "Since every text, grand or humble, is seen to be equally representative of its proper milieu," wrote historian Hayden White of an analogous development in intellectual history, "the very notion of a text that might serve as an especially privileged interpretative model is set aside."[65] More than ever, many different historical buildings became "equally representative" of their milieus in 1970s West Germany. Just as the idea of culture was democratized, the idea of the monument was broadened and made more accessible to many different groups. Breadth and accessibility of meaning also meant that popular antiquarianism assumed a more decentralized and personalized character. Italo Calvino has given us one of the most evocative literary statements of such antiquarianism in his account of Zora. One of Calvino's invisible cities, this community was distinguished by the fact that everything in it was a referent of memory, recalling mnemonic uses of spatial arrangements in the Middle Ages:

> The man who knows by heart how Zora is made, if he is unable to sleep at night, can imagine he is walking along the streets and he remembers the order by which the copper clock follows the barber's striped awning, then the fountain with the nine jets, the astronomer's glass tower, the

melon vendor's kiosk, the statue of the hermit and the lion, the Turkish bath, the café at the corner, the alley that leads to the harbor. This city which cannot be expunged from the mind is like an armature, a honeycomb in whose cells each of us can place the things he wants to remember: names of famous men, virtues, numbers, vegetable and mineral classifications, dates of battles, constellations, parts of speech.[66]

The world's most learned men were those who had memorized Zora, but the city also languished and, paradoxically, was forgotten because it was forced to "remain motionless and always the same, in order to be more easily remembered."[67] Although Calvino's Zora was important to personal memory, it was also a significant referent of collective memory, for its byways and buildings became objects of a decentralized but nonetheless social process of memory formation.

Like Calvino's Zora, the West German built environment became a field of increasingly individualized memory-work with a larger collective meaning. The trend toward more individualized preservation was partly a result of the perceived general inadequacy of institutional support for monuments, partly a sign of the relative lessening of organizations' hold on leisure-time activities. In heavily bombed and modernized Hamburg, antique dealer Eduard Brinkama gained national attention by organizing a campaign to restore classicist buildings in the Pöseldorf area. In the same city, businessman Alfred Toepfer started a foundation that successfully restored baroque half-timbered houses along the Peterstraße, where "slum conditions" had appeared in recent years.[68] Such antiquarian entrepreneurialism spanned the generations, as the Federal President's Scholastic Competition on German History, a successful campaign to create interest in the German past among schoolchildren, was begun in 1974 by *Bundespräsident* Gustav Heinemann and Hamburg businessman Kurt A. Körber. Both wanted to promote a popular interest in history that moved beyond the dry, abstract narratives of professional historians.[69] Sometimes in groups, sometimes singly, schoolchildren embarked on historical projects, sifting through archival material, doing oral history, and exploring historic buildings as highly personal documents of stone. The prize competitions were socialization exercises for young people, who learned to consume the past by "doing" history in organized competitions that prepared them for life in the memory-saturated society.[70] In this regard at least, they shared a lot with their *bürgerlich* ancestors, who instead of going out with microphones and shovels, explored the world with Baedeker or Dehio under their arms. The *Bundespräsident*'s competition created identities that had less to do with a sense of long-term historical continuity than with a horizontal affirmation of social and civic relationships. Nonetheless, as with so many other aspects of the reception of history and monuments in this period, the school competition created resources for a critical engagement with the national past even if, or because, the national was being redefined in the process of "searching for traces."

Another important aspect of the new cult of monuments was tourism, which reached new highs in Europe and West Germany. One observer argued in 1970 that preservation had been transformed from a cultural politics of the state, the universities, and the art academy into a cultural politics of tourism.[71] In Germany the number of overnight stays grew by 60 percent from 1964 to 1975. Heidelberg had more than 360,000 visitors in the 1969 tourist season; Cologne, more than 785,000 visitors; and Goslar, almost 180,000. Non-German tourists made up from 51 percent of the total in Heidelberg to 41 percent in Goslar. But tourism was not confined only to the major historic cities. Tourists patronized the new open-air museum for Rhenish peasant houses in Kommern as well as the Rhenish town of Zons, which sold itself as a historical monument in toto and reported more than 300,000 guests annually. In the Hunsrück region, made famous in the 1980s by the film *Heimat*, tourists flocked to local castle ruins, small historic churches, and peasant houses, a pilgrimage that worried preservationists but delighted mayors, shopkeepers, and travel agents. The DDR also began to see an increase in tourism in the 1970s, reporting that the state tourist office organized over 4 million vacations within the country and over 1 million from East Germany to other socialist states. The office was eager to promote "tradition-rich, carefully preserved historical cities such as Görlitz, Quedlinburg, and Stralsund" for domestic touristic consumption.[72]

The United States was, of course, the largest non-European participant in Western European tourism, sending more than 6 million tourists to the Old World in 1968 and making up about 12 percent of all arrivals and overnight stays in Germany in 1975, second only to the Dutch.[73] Although good dining was a central goal, according to a 1969 Gallup poll, U.S. tourists were also among the most avid visitors to historic places, listing old cities, museums, cathedrals, castles, and medieval fortresses as the most sought-after attractions.[74] Such well-fed tourism—to which Europeans were by no means immune—was oriented more to sightseeing than to traditional *Bildung*. This trend highlighted one of the demand factors that encouraged preservation to stress the visual elements of historic buildings more than before. Tourists wanted to see sites but not necessarily to know their history as comprehensively as the nineteenth-century *Bürger* did. It also suggested that touristic memory-work had a particularly important international component in this era, as many U.S. citizens constructed Europe as their historic origin, viewing the historic sites that symbolized the land of their ancestors. Many younger Americans, reacting to what they saw as the superficial rootlessness of modern commercial society, sought historic sites that created a sense of continuity and heritage, something more real than shopping malls and television. A highly personal search for roots in the honeycomb of memory generated an unprecedented degree of transatlantic traffic.

Gentrification was a related phenomenon because it too was international in scope but also a product of the professional middle class's desire to find new spatial referents in its search for history and identity. The need for an educated workforce in the growing tertiary sector of German cities had put a premium not on income as such but on quality of life issues, as I have noted. This in turn created a strong impetus for humanizing the urban world, which meant in part the restoration and maintenance of historic places that evoked the sense of community of earlier ages. A new urban, professional middle class was creating its own fields of care behind the heavily restored and prettified facades of historic buildings, creating a "bourgeois playground" as part of a broader urban restructuring process.[75] Conservators swallowed hard when they saw how the new urban middle class "preserved" buildings, but they also realized that it was "only this *bürgerlich* stratum that is in the situation to maintain these old houses," as Cologne conservator Hiltrud Kier said of the large nineteenth-century residential buildings in the increasingly popular Cologne Neustadt.[76]

Gentrification could occur in areas such as Neustadt, which was relatively undamaged in World War II and therefore had legitimate historical as well as economic worth for the city, or in cities such as Bonn, where there had been little war damage and where generally less aggressive economic development had left large parts of the urban morphology more or less intact for a long time. The Bonn Südstadt, where one could find streets of three-story residential dwellings mixing classical, Renaissance, and *Jugendstil* motifs built from 1870 to 1910, was an especially desirable area for such investment and a good example of the new interest in once-hated *Gründerzeit* architecture. This neighborhood seemed to recapture an era—which, depending on whom one asked, lasted into the 1950s—when "the street was part of the normal living space, the accepted, safe play area for children. The mother watched the children from the home." In such a historical view, gentrification was tied to a widely felt but personalized need for the notionally simpler values of the protective bourgeois family whose threatened future in the alienated modern city was counteracted by the symbol of "grandfather's house and its decorated facade."[77] There were limits to this movement, and urbanists noted that internationally as well as in West Germany the number of individuals who went "back to the city" was smaller than assumed.[78] But the tendency was strong enough to generate hope and memory across a range of groups and communities.

Gentrification could be seen as part of a long tradition whereby educated members of the middle classes conspicuously consumed old buildings to create social distinctions. This period differed from earlier ones, however, because consumption was so explicitly promoted. Whereas the *Bürgertum* legitimated earlier forms of conspicuous consumption with appeals to *Kultur* instead of civilization, ideal as opposed to material interests, the gentrifiers welcomed commercialization even as they nostalgically looked back to what were thought to be simpler, less commercial times. The mass media furthered this paradoxical process, as pictures of historic places appeared on beer bottles, in advertisements for insurance companies, in television travelogues, and on calendars and book covers. Historical buildings were useful vectors for commercial use because they were familiar, durable, and trusted symbols whose qualities advertisers hoped the consumer would associate with their products. In the 1970s there was "hardly a daily newspaper or an illustrated magazine that did not report regularly on the restoration of picturesque buildings."[79] Here representations of consumption doubled for the actual consumption of historic places that readers wished for or had already accomplished. But this was not only a mass-media phenomenon. A savings and loan bank in the small town of Nümbrecht in the Rhenish Oberberg area made use of the popularity of historic places by sending a multipage Christmas card to its customers that from year to year included pictures of historic rural architecture and customs.[80] From mass-market media to small-town banks, historic places were the glamorous stars of a commercialized public culture.

Recalling his earliest childhood memories of Berlin, Walter Benjamin wrote that he first got to know the city as a "theater of purchases" in which "it first became apparent how my father's money could cut a path for us between the shop counters and assistants and mirrors, and the appraising eyes of our mother, whose muff lay on the counter."[81] Benjamin's theater of purchases was a metaphor depicting one sensitive child's first encounters with the confusing spatial complexity of a world outside the home. Gentrification and commercialization turned the metaphor into reality, transforming entire urban districts and their historic houses into stage sets for new wealth.

The traditional institutions of popular history and preservation continued to grow in these years, as from 1963 to 1968 the membership of history and *Heimat* societies increased by 20 percent, and from 1968 to 1973 by 12 percent. But the appearance of new associations dealing with preservation was one of the most significant aspects of heightened public interest. One of the most long-winded examples was the Study Group for Urban History, Urban Sociology, and Monument Preservation, founded in 1973 by representatives from more than thirty cities in Baden-Württemberg, Bavaria, and Rheinland-Pfalz. It published a periodical, *The Journal for Urban History, Urban Sociology, and Monument Preservation*, whose title was later mercifully changed to *The Old City*. Most new groups were less academically oriented, having more practical and short-term aims, and among these the citizens' initiatives, a key development in the political culture of the former West Germany, were most numerous. Estimates vary, but the number of initiatives in the 1970s probably approached 50,000 and included some 2 million individuals. Encompassing an unusually wide array of interests, those initiatives dealing with architecture and the urban fabric usually focused on single issues rather than all-encompassing schemes—the saving of a particular monument or street, or the effects of new highway construction in a single urban neighborhood. Tactical rather than strategic, the initiatives depended more on small groups of activists than on stable memberships and rigid organizations.[82]

Surveying the local situation, the Bonn *General Anzeiger* noted in April 1980 that citizens' initiatives had grown like "mushrooms" in the capital city in the preceding years. Of those groups concerned with architectural conservation, one of the oldest was a coalition formed in 1969 with the single goal of forcing the city to reroute a planned freeway through the city center. It had 350 members but was essentially the one-man operation of a retired engineer. Another group consisted of "professors, architects, lawyers, historians, and geographers" who worked to uphold the "original character" of Bonn and who collected 4,500 signatures in a petition drive to save an old café. In North Rhine-Westphalia there was much popular interest in technical monuments, and in Bendorf-Sayn in Kreis Mayen-Koblenz individuals from "all levels of education, all parties, and especially from youth" gathered in an Arbeitsgemeinschaft Sayner Hütte. The plan was to restore the Sayner foundry, built in 1769 and then modified many times by various owners, including Alfred Krupp. The restored complex would be used as a cultural center and museum for the history of industrial technology. Until 1972, citizens' initiatives and other similar associations had about 4 percent working-class membership. From 1973 to 1975, thirty-one workers' initiatives appeared in the Ruhr, and more would follow. The Eisenheim project was a pioneer in such developments.[83]

Crossing the borders between citizens' initiatives, working groups to save industrial artifacts, and workers' initiatives fighting for their own versions of historic neighborhoods were alternative cultural centers whose activity often involved the protection of historic buildings. For these groups, loosely united by the slogan "Burn the Opera Houses!," a definition of historic buildings very different from that for official preservation was at work. Seeking creativity and alternatives both to elite culture and to the politicized cultural critique of the student movement, such cultural expression envisioned relations that were untouched by the competitiveness of industrial society.[84] A phenomenon of not only older urban districts but also of run-down suburban fringes, these centers were often organized by architects, academics, artists, social workers, and teachers who wanted to create a space where youth could interact freely without the surveillance of parents, educators, church officials, and the police. Using the street as a symbol of communication and "education for a critical consciousness," the organizers of such centers insisted that youth should be taught they were more than "electoral cattle" for the parliamentary machinery of the BRD. Loosely organized and often distrusted by the authorities, the centers might occupy a former fish auction hall built in 1893 but slated for demolition, as they did in the Volkshaus Fischmarkt initiative in Hamburg St. Pauli, or they might adapt abandoned small shops, as was suggested by the city cultural director of Nuremberg. Although leaders of such initiatives wanted young people from all social classes to take part, up to the mid-1970s they had attracted mainly middle-class youth.

An even more radical form of alternative preservation appeared in the squatters' movements, which continue today in all industrial countries. These movements used the tactic of illegal occupation of buildings against speculative urban land strategies that resulted in the intentional deterioration of many salvageable buildings and districts. As Castells remarked, these tactics represented a radical break between urban dwellers and the state and a direct assault on the principle of private property, the line over which official preservation would not step.[85] The first occupation of a house by squatters in Germany occurred in the Frankfurt am Main Westend in the fall of 1970.[86] This area of Frankfurt had seen much speculation by property owners, who often allowed their buildings to remain vacant and deteriorate while they awaited higher prices from corporations looking for lots on which to build high-rise complexes. The Westend thus not only had a severe housing shortage; it also became the site of many new skyscrapers that gave the Frankfurt cityscape an entirely new—and to many Germans—thoroughly disturbing quality. Led by Til Schulz and three others who had formed a *Wohngemeinschaft*, a kind of urban commune, this action occurred after Schulz was denied an extension of a one-year lease and thwarted in an effort to build a residential center for alternative political practice in "a typical old Westend building with a beautiful *Jugendstil* facade and big, high rooms, most of which had become rather run down."[87]

Schulz noted that the building owner was Jewish, "like many other Frankfurt speculators," and the "more or less open anti-Semitism" of the neighborhood lower middle class created "unwished-for sympathies" for the squatters.[88] Juvenile bravado also characterized the alternative scene, as squatters tested themselves by finding out not only who knew how to do carpentry or electrical wiring but also "who had the courage to stick their hands in a toilet blocked with shit." The protest at Eppsteinerstraße 47 against the landlord's refusal encompassed students, members of a film collective, social workers, hippies, individuals from the antiauthoritarian movement, "Adorno students in search of 'correct' praxis," anarchists, and Turkish and Italian families—about thirty-five people in all.[89] When the protesters barricaded themselves in the five-story building, they announced their plans with placards in several different languages: "The apartments belong to those who live in them! Don't let yourself be driven out of your homes! Organize collective resistance! Drive out the speculators!" It was hoped this would not be an isolated action but, rather, the springboard for a more sustained political drive. The occupation became a media sensation as the participants in the "house collective" renovated and maintained the structure in an atmosphere of "tension and euphoria." Part of the tension came from the threat of retaliation by the owner and the police, who in fact did intervene violently when further house occupations occurred in Frankfurt the next year. But tension also occurred due to internal conflicts between the militant German occupiers and the non-German families and families with many children. Til Schulz finally conceded that the idea of a collective had failed, but he was unwilling to abandon the tactic of occupation, as were many other militants in Amsterdam, Hamburg, Berlin, and other cities in the 1970s and 1980s.

History workshops (*Geschichtswerkstätten*) were (and are) a kind of citizens' initiative involved, among other things, in historic preservation projects. Based on models drawn mainly from Britain and Scandinavia, the history workshop movement belongs more to the 1980s and 1990s, when it flourished and gained academic expression with the support of the practitioners of *Alltagsgeschichte*, or the history of everyday life, such as Ulrich Herbert, Alf Lüdtke, Hans Medick, Detlev Peukert, Lutz Niethammer, and Annemarie Tröger.[90] But one can see the roots of the later period in the 1970s. Beginning with the work of the Project Group on Regional Social History at the University of Konstanz under the directorship of history professor Gert Zang in the second half of the 1970s, the evolution of history workshops gained momentum in 1979 when the Ottensen archive of Hamburg bought an old nail factory as a center for cultural and historical exhibits and research. In 1980 the Berlin History Workshop formed, and in 1983 a national grouping of history workshops with its own journal was set up in Bochum. In 1979 there were similar developments in East Germany, where the Society for Heimat History was formed within the Kulturbund der DDR.[91] These were among the first participants in a "new history movement," a term applying mainly to the West, which included academics but also lay historians who reconstructed repressed or unpublicized histories of workers, women, the elderly, and youth in cooperative projects that invited public participation. The built environment figured prominently in the efforts of such "barefoot historians." Many local history projects got off the ground by defending an abandoned factory, a trade union clubhouse, a nineteenth-century working-class settlement, or a residential street from urban renewal or destruction.

A loosely organized array of groups and interests, the new history movement advocated active historic preservation, or *aktive Denkmalspflege*, that defended traces of a forgotten or repressed past in the built and natural environments.[92] Because they used these material referents to celebrate histories of groups and individuals that were dominated or defeated, they come close to Walter Benjamin's idea of historical materialism in which history is written not "the way it really was" but as it might have been.[93] Constructing the "as it might have been" facilitated grieving, not only for lost buildings and the social relationships they symbolize, but also for lost opportunities of solidarity and identification with history's (and, to the considerable degree such projects dealt with National Socialism, the Holocaust's) victims. These populist preservationists constructed potential sites of mourning, giving Germans a chance to work through, collectively and individually, the traumas of a post-Holocaust world. We have noted above that such attempts were often transformed into ritualistic displays of guilt that suppressed the memory of the victims and German complicity in mass murder. But just as these groups theoretically focused on the "as it might have been," it is important to recognize the potential with which they moved into the byways of collective memory to construct new orientations on Germany's transient pasts.

Formally and substantively, the existence of such groups was a threat to the established preservation societies, which were unprepared to respond to contemporary issues with the same urgency and energy that the initiatives showed. Because the initiatives often did not require the longer-term investment of time and energy that regular association membership demanded, they could draw on relatively short-lived action more readily. In some cases, as in more left-wing history workshops, there was direct ideological and political conflict with the established history or *Heimat* associations. Discussing the attitude of some of the workshops toward the locale, one observer noted that the workshops thought of *Heimat* "as life possibility—not as proof of lineage."[94] Such differences could erupt into nationally visible controversies, as when the more politically engaged members of the movement challenged West German government efforts to create a national history museum in the 1980s.[95]

A Future for the Past

In 1975 Europeans observed Cultural Heritage Year, which was organized by the seventeen member-states of the Council of Europe and seen as a continuation of the council's Nature Conservation Year held five years earlier. The 1970 event illustrated that "environmental politics encompasses all areas of life," including "the preservation and renewal of our historical cities and regions." Based on this connection between natural and cultural resources, Cultural Heritage Year was designed to "heighten Europeans' interest in their common architectural heritage." The motto of the campaign was "A Future for Our Past," which summed up a triple goal: the protection of "historically or artistically important buildings and whole complexes of buildings" that would have "a living function in modern society"; the protection and renewal of the "character" of old cities and villages; and the promotion of preservationist consciousness at the international, national, regional, and local levels. Many different activities would be used to encourage high-quality architecture harmonious with historical surroundings, to clean up inappropriate advertising in historic areas, to promote pedestrian zones in historic city centers, and to promote the beautification of landscape around monuments and historic ensembles.[96]

It was significant that Cultural Heritage Year officially endorsed an approach to preservation for which so many Europeans had fought since the nineteenth century. The point was not to preserve single, great monuments, although these would not be ignored, but to think in terms of ensembles and milieus that would find a place in modern cities and regions. By officially endorsing this approach, Cultural Heritage Year also illuminated how cultural memory had changed. Until well into the postwar period, most European preservationists regarded the period up to about the middle of the nineteenth century as the cutoff point for the preservation of architecture. In the ten years preceding 1975, however, this horizon had slipped, and now, according to a German proponent of Cultural Heritage Year, 1930 was "the present-day limit."[97] The past had moved closer to the present.

The event was planned by a large international committee made up of key representatives of major cultural agencies, including UNESCO and ICOMOS, and chaired by Lord Duncan Sandys, son-in-law of Winston Churchill and head of Europa Nostra, an international association of non-state preservation and environmentalist groups. It featured a well-orchestrated media campaign including television and radio, printed brochures and other literature for distribution to schools and universities, special commemorative postal stamps, and traveling photo exhibitions. It chose forty-five European model cities for special programs that would demonstrate what had already been done and what remained to be done in integrating historical architectural ensembles into modern society. The culminating event was a major international congress in Amsterdam in October.

In Germany Cultural Heritage Year symbolized a major turning point in postwar history, indeed an end to the postwar phase of German rebuilding and a valorization of the new popularity the preservation of monuments had in German life. Writing in *Aus Politik und Zeitgeschichte*, Curt Christoph von Pfuel, a member of the West German Committee for European Cultural Heritage Year, stated that "the reconstruction of German cities after the Second World War is . . . more or less completed." Reconstruction had meant an emphasis on solving the housing shortage and providing for the material needs of the population, but in the meantime Germans had become aware of how much had been lost. Whereas at the end of the war 27 percent of all buildings in Germany had originated in the period before 1840, in 1970 only 15 percent did, a figure that shocked West Germans and convinced the writer "it was high time to bring about a radical change in this area." This realization had already borne fruit. Historic preservation had gained many new supporters before Cultural Heritage Year, and since the late 1960s at least there had been a "reversal in the general attitude toward past and future" in which the value of history in the present was ever more widely recognized.[98]

Germany had five model cities for Cultural Heritage Year, Berlin, Trier, Rothenburg ob der Tauber, Alsfeld, and Xanten. These were selected to give a fair geographical distribution but also to represent a different aspect and set of problems for preservation, including social issues such as the relationship between urban renewal and equitable housing arrangements for moderate- and low-income groups. In addition, Bamberg, Lübeck, and Regensburg conducted parallel programs that offered additional data for contemporary urban problem solving. Hans Meier, Bavarian minister of culture, headed a national committee with thirty-three members drawn from *Bundestag* and *Land* parliament representatives, officials of the West German *Land* conservators' association, churches, youth groups, trade unions, business concerns, the mass media, and the Deutscher Heimatbund. President of the BRD Walter Scheel acted as official patron of the program.

The event was accompanied by many different programs at the national, regional, and local levels, including prize competitions for schoolchildren's proposals for preservation, competitions for various professional preservation and architectural projects, traveling exhibitions, organized debates over impending preservation legislation, numerous publications, commemorative stamps from the *Bundespost*, commemorative coins from the federal treasury, and commemorative medallions in silver and gold depicting each of the model cities from the national committee. DDR officials did not recognize the event or participate in any of its international programs. Nonetheless, even there it had an impact, exerting pressure on the passage of the landmark 1975 preservation law.[99]

The same sense of culmination and new beginning that was apparent at the national level was felt at the regional level. There were plenty of activities, and the Deutscher Heimatbund issued a special publication laying out the year's events among the BRD's many organizations. The RVDL's Bonn chapter took part in the official opening ceremonies of the event in the capital on 21 January, sponsoring excursions to technical monuments in Duisburg and other preservation projects in the model city Xanten on the same day. Its Koblenz chapter used the event to publicize its efforts to protect two historic houses threatened by demolition. The RVDL as a whole celebrated Cultural Heritage Year with a big annual congress in Aachen including participants from Belgium, France, Luxemburg, and the Netherlands. In its annual meeting in June, the Rhenish association's president Hermann Heusch called Heritage Year a "crowning event" in a long history of protecting "Occidental tradition and history." The event also signaled the end of a postwar tradition of historicide. "Thank goodness we have overcome a lack of attention to history," said Heusch. "We are very happy that above all our young people have, perhaps instinctively, understood these signs of the times."[100] After decades of preservationists' lamenting youth's lack of concern for history and monuments, it was a significant statement, whether or not it accurately reflected contemporary cultural activity.

Of course, there were critical voices, and among conservators it was not just Hartwig Beseler who was skeptical. Beseler noted in his report on Schleswig-Holstein's 1975 program that there were no "titanic activities" in his province during the year because preservation officials felt that regional exhibits of historic architecture or other similar events were not worth the time and effort. In spring 1976 at the annual meeting of *Land* conservators, Beseler and others registered a similar skepticism with reference to the plan to have the German National Committee for European Cultural Heritage Year become the German National Committee for Historic Preservation, a step that was eventually taken. Hamburg conservator Manfred Fischer feared this would lead to a "collateral government" for preservation. This response was based primarily on institutional-political grounds, but Beseler quite correctly thought opposition to the year ran deeper. Referring to those who thought 1975 had reduced the opponents of historic preservation to "a silent minority," he asked, "or is it not in fact the majority?" He was referring in part to those many property owners who saw "cultural landscape [*Kulturlandschaft*]" and "city-monument" as notions whose implementation could strangle growth. Beseler, Willibald Sauerländer, and others thought the year's events highlighted public and official disorientation about what in fact a monument was. From another angle, this period also saw a series of ironic commentaries on Cultural Heritage Year's motto, one of the more politically engaged being a 1975 volume coedited by Roland Günter titled *No Future for Our Past?* In this volume Günter argued compellingly that Cultural Heritage Year would not have occurred in some German cities were it not for the agitation of citizens' initiatives, which, he pointed out, nonetheless found no official representation on the national committee.[101]

Criticisms of Cultural Heritage Year also opened a space for significant memory-work that began to explore the deeper impact of Nazism on German society, as exemplified in the work of *Die Zeit* writer Günther Kühne, who raised unpleasant memories about Berlin, one of the model cities.[102] Noting that Cultural Heritage Year saw more applications for permits to tear down old buildings in Berlin than in any previous year, Kühne called attention to the fact that Erich Mendelsohn's famous modernist Universum movie theater on the Lehniner Platz, built in 1926–28, was situated on a plot of land that had recently come up for sale. The site sold for 5 million marks, and the advertisement for the real estate mentioned that the land featured "an old building ready for demolition." "So this is what such urban-architectural qualities represent for some circles," wrote the unbelieving Kühne. Mendelsohn was Jewish, noted the writer, who reminded readers of the Nazis' "rabid policies toward his best buildings." His Columbushaus on the Potsdamer Platz, badly damaged but still usable after the war, was ripped down by East German authorities after the June 1953 uprising. (He might have mentioned that soon after the war another of Mendelsohn's masterpieces, the Schocken Kaufhaus in Stuttgart, was demolished.) There were some attempts under way to save the Universum, including several projects for adaptive reuse, a debate over the architect's buildings led by the SPD in the Berlin senate, and a protest by the Bauhaus archive. But Berlin would remain "a city without memory" if the owners of these properties

THE NEW CULT OF MONUMENTS

were allowed to buy and sell sites as they pleased and if the city lacked effective preservation legislation. The case of the Universum movie house highlighted not only the shortcoming of the current celebration of preservation but also the awful histories contained in the "stones of Berlin." In the case of Mendelsohn's work, in any event, the story had a happy ending, as the building was saved and restored from 1976 to 1981.[103]

In preparation for a decade and inspired by public action surrounding European Cultural Heritage Year, Erwin Schleich's 1978 book on the second destruction of Munich was even more explicit in pinpointing Nazism's dire continuity in the built environment. Part picture book and architectural history and part polemic, Schleich's study showed how postwar historicide had taken its cue not only from the "march of the technocrats" but from Nazi destructiveness, which was the "prelude" to post-1945 planning and rebuilding. Although postwar planners shared the destructive urge of Nazism, moreover, they often tried to kick over the traces of this connection. In the case of the Wittelsbacher Palace, which as the Red Palace had been Gestapo headquarters, they bulldozed this reminder of Nazism away even when it was reparable, as if "they could deny that the Gestapo and concentration camps existed." They also often restored historic buildings that the Nazis had modified back to their National Socialist rather than their pre-Nazi form. In such instances the "classicist-dictatorial" face of Nazi urban planning had been transmogrified into the "stylish modern" face of contemporary planning.[104]

Considering the influence of Cultural Heritage Year, Gottfried Kiesow wrote that "the consciousness for one's own history as an indispensable part of the nation was, after its misuse in the Third Reich, understandably lost and transformed into an absolute lack of history."[105] Kiesow's statement of an absolute lack of history after the war was exaggerated, but it is nonetheless significant that he wrote in the past tense. Moreover, the rebound of historic preservation, valorized and stimulated even more by Cultural Heritage Year, raised the question of whether national identity was on the rebound as well. Preceding information in this chapter suggests that one must answer in the affirmative, and that indeed public support for Cultural Heritage Year was as much a result of a new, albeit transformed, national feeling as it was a stimulus. Indeed, because German national identity now took on more Europeanist overtones, whether it was expressed in respect for "Occidental" culture or support for NATO, it found Cultural Heritage Year a fitting context in which to develop. That Schleich and others brought many Germans face to face with the dark chapters of their past in the middle of an international celebration of European heritage only demonstrated that the experience of Nazism would still have to be confronted—as a deep structure of a specific national memory. The event thus opened a window on the German future, just as national memory-work in the past always had. But this future belongs to the period through which we are living, and its outlines thus remain as inchoate as the past from which it still derives much of its energy and force.

n June and July 1995 the artists Christo and Jeanne-Claude wrapped the Reichstag building. Shrouded in more than sixty tons of a shimmering, silvery fabric secured with ten miles of blue rope, *Wrapped Reichstag* became a major media event similar to earlier projects by the concept artists.[1] Yet there was a difference. Many German political figures, including Chancellor Helmut Kohl, expressed reservations about Christo's idea, saying it would damage the dignity and gravity of a national landmark at a time when the new and still-uncertain German nation profoundly needed such sites. Others lauded the attempt, arguing that wrapping the Reichstag offered humor in a place still haunted by disturbing political memories. Stressing process rather than only the result, Christo said the wrapped Reichstag symbolized the making of a "lighter" national identity, a horizon of expectation in which Germans could laugh at themselves and emerge triumphant from the burdens of their awful history.

Was this the late twentieth-century political equivalent of light beer and low-calorie foods? Or was it a particularly resonant example of an ancient opposition between the heaviness and lightness of identity, an opposition that was the basis of Milan Kundera's influential 1984 novel? Using Nietzsche's perplexing idea of eternal return, Kundera asked his readers to consider how they would feel if the French Revolution occurred not just once but over and over again, allowing Robespierre to chop off heads repeatedly. Such bizarre historical events would take on a new and horrifying perspective because they would lose the "mitigating circumstances of their transitory nature." The terrible weight of the past was bearable precisely because it had happened but once. But Kundera also wrote that transiency has its own costs, its own burdens. To happen only once is not to have happened at all; to live a life without burdens is to dissolve into the nothingness of unlimited freedom, amnesia, and the lightness of air. For Kundera, the only certainty was that "the lightness/weight opposition is the most mysterious, most ambiguous of all."[2]

Inspired in part by the stunning economic payoffs of *Wrapped Reichstag*, which stirred enormous touristic interest, German politicians and other doubters eventually came around to Christo's point of view. The project was a profound success, fun as well as profitable. But they were unwilling to admit, just as Christo was unwilling to see for fear that the originality of his work would be questioned, a basic fact. Transiency, provisionality, and light-ness—words used to describe the visual effects of the shimmering wrapped monument—had been part of German national identity for a long time, even at those moments when it seemed heaviest and most concerned about establishing a centuries-long lineage, a state of eternal return. This has been the argument of my narrative.

I have argued that the preservation of historic landmarks, from grandiose public buildings to modest peasant and working-class houses, has uninten-tionally revealed the indeterminacy, the quality of not leading to a definitive end or result, of German national identity. This has also meant that the national past from which the community supposedly would get its sense of orientation for the future was equally devoid of fixed meaning. The preser-vation of buildings, constantly corroded by the ravages of social change, war, love, and neglect, has symbolized a sense of the nation, constantly destabi-lized by forces beyond its control and therefore promoted again and again, in countless recastings and re-creations, as the key to collective being, the center of gravity of political weight. Like the politicians who insisted that *Wrapped Reichstag* assaulted the dignity of a great landmark, German offi-cials have denied the stubborn transiency of the nation they claimed to represent. But like contemporary politicians, various motivations—money, fame, ideology, and fear of popular denial—have made those officials willing to promote the very forces that transformed the national past, present, and future into shifting strata of contention and uncertainty.

This book has emphasized historic preservation's complex relationship to the changing, unstable optic identity of the nation. Germans have saved historic buildings as landmarks that symbolize a shared national history and by extension a shared national future. This symbolism has operated as part of and in response to an increasingly visual culture of the twentieth century. The look of landmarks, streets, and squares has become the look of the nation, expressed in grand Gothic cathedrals, impressive public buildings, or modest working-class settlements from the nineteenth century. Historic buildings and townscapes have been mirrors in which Germans have seen themselves as products of a common and enduring past, recognized their notionally unique characteristics, and signaled their perceived difference from other national groups. Historic buildings have been used to symbolize other identities, of course. Regional, municipal, masculine, and *bürgerlich* identities have found expression in the discourse of preservation, as we have seen. Yet for most of the period covered here, nation-thinking was said to subsume and regulate these other ways of imagining community. When it went underground, as it were, it did not go away. As both dominant and interstice, national identity has worked in, around, and through the discourse of preservation.

Modernity is the experience of growing asymmetry between dominant hope and marginalized but still resonant memory. In part to provide balance without subverting hope's hegemony, the nation has defined this asymmetry, seeking to control its more radical and unsettling effects and striving to make it explicable to subject populations through both force and aura. I thus agree with Liah Greenfield's recent assertion that nationalism and national ideas are not functions of modernity but constitutive elements of it.[3] Modernity's awful lightness, promoted by its unending production of societal resources outside experiential boundaries, has been countered, evoked, explained, and even facilitated by the nation's unbearable and enduring weight. The future has been a national future; the past, a national past. Although hope has progressively disengaged itself from that space of experience in which the past seemed to orient present action, official national thinking appeared to reintroduce such orientation by providing new legitimacy to memory. Hope's hegemony has not gone unchallenged, just as memory's marginality has never been a foregone conclusion. As a concept hegemony depends on the idea of a moving equilibrium in which contending forces negotiate and struggle with one another over resources whose final distribution is never guaranteed even if one or several participants in the power struggle gain disproportionate influence. To the considerable degree the modern nation is dependent on achieved structures of economic growth, market predictability, and bureaucratic perdurability, hope retained its enormous advantages even though it necessarily relied on and channeled memory for emotional ballast.

All countries experiencing those economic, social, political, and cultural tensions associated with modern history have seen this growing asymmetrical relationship between hope and memory. Yet for reasons that are well documented in the secondary literature, there are some factors that suggest that the relationship between hope and memory has been particularly fraught with tension in Germany. More than in England or the United

States, the countries with which Germany has been justifiably compared since the nineteenth century, nation-thinking in Germany has been contentious, ambiguous in its political colorations, multivalent, and volatile in its capacities to mobilize populations. The cultural politics of nationhood, a variable strategy organized to initiate and maintain emotional attachments to the nation, has thus been a deeply controversial subject throughout the modern period. In turn the link between attempts to foment German national identity and attempts to preserve national landmarks, one recurrent practice in the complex cultural politics of the German nation, was and remains very strong. Nurtured by Romanticism's stress on the physical environment's importance in forming identity, reinterpreted by political figures attempting to rouse national allegiances, and buffeted by the immense destructive power of socioeconomic change and war, historic places have assumed an importance they do not have elsewhere. This is not meant to be another argument about Germany's unique path through history. One could also point to the Poles' or the Czechs' interest in their national landmarks, though for different reasons. It refers, rather, to the real and peculiar historical forces that have made a wrapped Reichstag somehow mean more in context than a wrapped Congress or wrapped Houses of Parliament. This point was reaffirmed a month before *Wrapped Reichstag* was completed, when German cultural officials, preservationists, and historians debated the fate of the former East Germany's monuments in a conference of the German National Committee for Historic Preservation in Berlin, where panelists in a roundtable discussion agreed that many Germans had a particularly sensitive relationship to their monuments and history.[4]

In making this point it is important to stress that visions of the nation as reflected in its historic sites did not persist unaltered. Hobsbawm is quite correct in writing that "national identification and what it is believed to imply, can change and shift in time, even in the course of quite short periods." He goes on to state "this is the area of national studies in which thinking and research are most urgently needed today."[5] Official national memory came to depend more on latitudinal rather than longitudinal lines of authority, that is, on the legitimacy established by everyday social interaction rather than state *dirigisme*. For the period after World War II, this statement obviously applies more to West Germany than to the East. There was a constant ordering and reordering of this vision, just as there was a constant restoration, modification, and destruction of historic places. I have therefore placed emphasis on the fluid construction of national identity in the same way Christo insisted that the process of wrapping the Reichstag was ultimately more important than the end result.

But alteration and process do not preclude persistence. The unwrapped

Reichstag would reemerge to symbolize some of the same heavy traits Helmut Kohl, no lightweight himself, alluded to when he first expressed anxiety about Christo's project. In the literature on national identity, constructivist arguments have overlooked strands of "structuring" continuity, the ways in which process cohabited with and was limited by persistent themes, rhetorics, and symbols. Recurring themes—cultured Germans as pious stewards and interpreters of cultural property, national *Kultur* as a distinctive protectant against materialistic civilization's contaminations, the region's national connotations, hopefulness as a conservative appropriation of the idea of national perdurability leading to partial epiphany, the transiency of party-political regimes and ideologies in relation to some notionally deeper organicist or even racist impulse, specific national myths and legends, and most obviously certain key landmarks and sites—shaped official rhetoric of political community throughout moments of political discontinuity.

Responding negatively to the question of whether one can speak of single national political cultures, Mary Fulbrook quite reasonably argues "there are too many subcultural variations with different bases."[6] Nonetheless, it is the persistence and combination of these variations—many voices speaking the same lines over and over again—that explain in part how the idea of a single, unified national political culture has been so resonant not just in Germany but in the modern world. The experience of a chain of ephemeralities, like so many beads on a rosary, resulted in a living tradition comprising the stories the nation tells itself. In the preceding pages, we have seen that the institutional continuities of preservation made possible the voicing of recurring national themes and narratives. Conservators held to a motto of "Conserve, do not restore," even when they did not follow this method. They continued to nurture a sense of marginality and betweenness in relation to other disciplines and the political process generally, replicating other disciplines' sense of difference. For much of the period covered here preservationists adhered to a cultural nationalism based on *bürgerlich* and masculinist images of *Heimat*. Reinforced by a practice focused on objects that had in fact lasted over great stretches of time, they believed the nation was a recurring, anthropomorphic entity uneasily lodged between a more coherent and meaningful past and a soon-to-be-accomplished resolution of conflict in the future. Yet they also consistently if unintentionally drew attention to those aspects of their practice that belied the fixity of national existence, as when debates over restoration and conservation opened a small window on a future in which the national body's objectified cultural property corroded with time. Future studies of national and other identities will have to consider a more complex dialectic of construction and persistence, lightness and weight, than they have so far. Hobsbawm's notion of the "invention of tradition" was meant to apply to a specific range of social phenomena that became widespread in the last three decades of the nineteenth century. But it has mistakenly come to stand for almost all public representations of national memory and history. Similarly, postmodernism's useful stress on ephemerality has also overshadowed those structures, institutions, and ideas that do not change or, rather, that change more slowly than might normally be assumed. In the Introduction I suggested that Anthony Smith's research on the ethnic origins of nations was a useful corrective to some of the literature on this subject because it focused attention on long-term continuities even if the notion of ethnicity itself was fraught with methodological and political problems.

The complex interaction of persistence and change is clear when one considers what types of objects preservationists cherished. On one hand, this book has traced a narrative of cultural protection in which modest fields of care have come to outweigh grand public symbols in importance. Roland Günter's Eisenheim settlement appears to have displaced Georg Dehio's Strasbourg cathedral. Regenerated urban neighborhoods have come to have more historical significance for some than medieval city halls. Art-historical, cultural-historical, and social criteria for monuments have interacted over almost a century to produce the change, as have transformations in patterns of urban destruction, political conflict, and social interest. In addition, a general expansion of the historical, associated above all with the rapidity of socioeconomic and technological change, has foreshortened the present and bloated the past, constantly corroding the line separating the two, bringing the former ever closer to the latter, multiplying beyond all expectations the number of history-worthy sites and objects. In simple quantitative terms, the triumph of vernacular objects has seemed assured.

Popular access to transportation, tourism, literature, and other media have resulted in changing forms of appropriation of historic places based on quantity and use, literally consuming objects in ways that demand the production of ever more objects. Alarmed by such unprecedented forms of manipulation, preservationists of the past two decades have come to study the management of "attrition on historic artifacts" as a central problem in its own right,[7] although I have offered evidence demonstrating that this concern was already prominent before World War I. Such consumption has in turn also led to greater *bürgerlich* and professional emphasis on conspicuous consumption, partly as response to popular access, partly as a function of the workings of an increasingly commercialized society regulated by the demands of economic performance. From the point of view of preservation, one could speak of rapidly changing desires for the past, which determine what is deemed a historic building or site and what is not without regard to the long existence of particular artifacts. Paul Clemen saw this as a nightmare when, shrinking from the excesses of the Bolshevik Revolution, he asked his readers to imagine a terrible new age when, virtually overnight, all the great landmarks would lose their status as cultural treasures.[8] This book has shown that this changing vision of what is historical can be either a nightmare or a sudden, wonderful dream mediated by the workings of the market in memories.

Yet the great public symbols did not disappear, and the problem of attrition has affected them as much as it has fields of care. The transition from Strasbourg to Eisenheim was by no means a one-way street. Immediately after World War II, the cherished landmarks of the national canon were, if anything, more highly valued than they had been in the preceding five decades or than they would be in the following ones. The DDR restored and maintained many star monuments as well, even as it insisted that vernacular architecture needed more attention in a peasants' and workers' state. As the *Wrapped Reichstag* suggests, the public symbols of the nation have assumed a new importance in German political culture after unification, and plans to rebuild (or, more accurately, re-create) structures such as the demolished Hohenzollern palace and Dresden's Frauenkirche have rightly raised criticisms of the West's architectural revanchism against the East. Postmodern planning's tendency to reduce the city to a chain of polished historical vignettes—not unlike the archipelagoes of memory described in Chapter 5—have reinforced the focus on such grandiose symbols. The vaunted canon of German preservation—cathedrals, castles, and city halls— has after all retained its influence and continues to reap profits for both business and government agencies.

But why were these buildings historical and others not? The history of the buildings themselves or of their occupants had much to do with it. Memory and history constantly modify the past, but the associations between, for example, Goethe's residence and the larger meaning of the great poet in German culture remain as the (not quite) irreducible raw material of such constructions. Too, the great public symbols were large, often centrally located, and expensive artifacts with a tradition of being protected. The construction and maintenance of the Cologne cathedral or the restoration of Marienburg were monuments of cultural politics as much as the buildings themselves were monuments of the national community. But the exigencies of political struggle also played a role. As the nation's sense of how it looked changed, the canon of sites changed with it. As the nation became less the product of states, monarchs, and elites and more the outcome of relations between contending social groups, real or imagined, the sites of memory changed to accommodate the new social dynamic. This meant including new sites of memory, but also devising new ways of looking at old ones. The great cathedrals became not only instances of genius but products of that same *Volk* that produced industrial artifacts, peasant houses, and medieval streetscapes. In East Germany, constant references to the difference between "tradition" and "heritage" regulated this process. The scope of historic places also changed, as not just single objects but whole ensembles were included. As latitudinal forms of authority regulated popular views of the nation, sites of community identity expanded horizontally to encompass more buildings and byways, a more elaborate honeycomb in which personal experience could become articulated with collective sentiment. Although the city-monument became the nightmare of some professional conservators only in the 1970s, it was foreshadowed in theory before World War I and in practice in urban renewal projects under Nazism.

As certain objects have retained their resonance and other new ones gained unprecedented influence, what in fact was remembered over time? Historic preservation is a practice oriented not mainly toward the memory of single events or personalities but toward a general sense of the past, a feeling that something should be remembered although it may not be clear what that is. Lynch wrote of "evidence of time" embodied in physical environments.[9] He was discussing not only monuments or historical time but time significations throughout the everyday urban fabric. Nonetheless, the statement applies to our evidence as well. Landmarks had various meanings for preservation's sense of historical time: the past was threatened, it accelerated, it was expanding, it represented hope for the future, it was to be overcome, it should be repressed, it should be revived. We have focused on how a sense of the nation's enduring past, present, and future regulated inquiry into the evidence of time in the built world.

Critical memory has been present in such perspectives, as when preservationists attacked the effects of social change on notionally organic communities. These narratives held up the industrial present to the yardstick of medieval and early modern history, marking out a less fragmented past in which contemporaries could imagine their origins. For much of the period covered here, such memory evolved under mainly conservative auspices through which the future offered hope rather than optimism, partial release from contemporary problems rather than secular utopia. But more often than not, narratives glorifying the *Volk*'s accomplishments and articulating relations between self and *Volk* dominated. That Germans have felt the need to use landmarks as referents of such mythic narratives suggests, from one perspective, that the problem of German history in the past century has not been silence about the past but noise, not forgetfulness but too much memory. Had the overwhelming noise created by antiquarian and monumental narratives of the past not been so intense, perhaps critical narratives of events such as the Holocaust might have been able to break through more easily and with greater impact. Scholarship requires a great deal more information on the antinomies of this "other" German public memory, the one that did not repress the past but dredged it up insistently in so many variations, before it can understand more fully German cultural history.

Yet even if such narratives of national pride and duration had not been so ubiquitous, the memory of single events would still not have been very salient for those who preserved historic buildings. The public memory of single events has, of course, had a long history, as the deeds of kings and princes were replaced by monuments recalling the heroism, tragedy, and longevity of the *Volk* or, in its East German variation, the working class. Monumental and antiquarian narratives gave substance to this transformation as well. In Germany such populist memory only recently began to include critical narratives of the *Volk*'s direst deeds, including avant-garde critiques of war after 1918 and public condemnation of Nazi mass murder after World War II. Yet we have seen that the Holocaust remained an undigested and problematic aspect of national memory even if, especially during the years from the end of this study to the present, it became a fundamental regulative of all expressions of German collective identity. Historic preservation has been wedded to general and often mythic notions of national accomplishment, and critical memory of single events, especially those in which the national self is not merely challenged but called into question most directly, have never been able to break through into the light of national self-criticism. Such self-criticism would demand the kind of lightness and mournful leave-taking from the nation that most Germans, to say nothing of most moderns, have been unable to bear because of the constitutive nature of the nation in contemporary life. How, after critically sifting through its past, can one take leave of the nation and its history of violence without removing this fundament of modern political community?

I agree with Christine Boyer that "historical phenomena portrayed as 'heritage' are cultural treasures of art carried by the authorities in every triumphal march, and these treasures reek of omissions and suppressions."[10] But one can shift the perspective on this statement to emphasize that acts of omission and suppression also suggest opportunities and individual acts of appropriation. In the *New York Times* article cited above, the subtitle read, "The wrapped Reichstag was whatever symbol one wanted to make of it. And making nothing at all of it was an honorable option." A comment on the indeterminacy of postmodern art, this statement also reminds one of the various uses to which the idea of the nation has been put in the last two centuries. It is doubtful that the much-discussed question of whether certain countries are more nationalistic than others can be addressed with much certainty. But as I have tried to show in the preceding pages, even at moments when nationalistic opinion seems to have run high, Germans' use of historic sites involved an array of meanings over which the national idea could hardly claim complete dominance. And even when nationalism was expressed, this involved the active seizing of the term through both rhetoric and action rather than passive acceptance of nationalist thought as it was handed down by elites and the state. This book has only scratched the surface of such multiple and active appropriations, the tactics of the less powerful and powerless, suggesting their variety if not their full scope and texture.

Such evidence reminds us that all forms of intentional memory have extreme limits, whether they are glorifications of national deeds or condemnations of national crimes. The emotional resonance of memory is defined in part by the degree to which events do not register in consciousness, as Benjamin noted, but that flare up unexpectedly, like Proust's involuntary memory, to give an event or a place a new and startling meaning in relation to both past and present.[11] Official national memory's adoration of certain key landmarks thus always developed slightly out of step with popular appropriations of them. Various groups may have loved, hated, or ignored historic places, but they loved, hated, or ignored them in their own ways, which may or may not have been compatible with official wishes. Similarly, the commemoration of key events or personalities in intentional monuments or in historic buildings broadly defined may actually have substituted for the intense emotional experience of asking how and why history occurred in the way it did and what responsibility the group or individual had in history's outcome. Recent scholarship has demonstrated how Holocaust commemoration has deferred such critical memory, as I have noted. At one level, this kind of substitution or deflection of memory through history can be researched only through finely grained oral testimony of the kind Luisa Passerini has produced.[12] Yet I think the preceding pages have included enough information to suggest that the lack of synchronization between official and popular memory is broad, complex, and worthy of additional detailed study even without the resort to oral history. At the very least, a cultural history of public memory must include the study not only of the production of ideas and symbols, but of their distribution in society and their acceptance, active appropriation, or rejection by others.

Yet the picture of a lack of synchronization must also be qualified. There is much evidence to suggest that official memory's use of monumental and antiquarian narratives found much public support. Germans did see national landmarks as important referents of their own collective existence, their participation in a perdurable community of sentiment bounded by national symbols, traits, legends, and experiences. Even when material interest, loyalty to an association, or leisure-time pursuits got in the way, national allegiances continued to operate in public uses of historic places, just as they did for conservators and their many allies. The weight of national existence could not be denied, even when in the 1960s people such as Enzensberger responded to it with a shrug rather than an outstretched arm, and even when some preservationists identified with the nation in negative rather than positive terms. This study has not condemned such public identification with the nation because, as Kundera's novel reminds us, lightness is as fraught with danger as weight, pure transience as horrific as eternal return. It may be true that political economy, transportation, the electronic media, and computers have rendered national boundaries obsolete. But at least in the emotional lives of moderns and even postmoderns, it is untrue that the nation "is no longer a major vector of historical development," as Hobsbawm has argued.[13]

If Hobsbawm were correct, then how does one account for the flap over *Wrapped Reichstag*? Christo's project suggests that the questions for Germany after unification remain much the same as they have for the past century despite the emergence of so many transient pasts in that period. If *Wrapped Reichstag* is a particularly evocative example of a playful and postmodern form of preservation, then how does it connect to German history? Protecting historic sites has been seen as an important factor in constructing a sense of a common past. But the question of *which* common past—that of a normal nationhood? of a rediscovery of liberal civic heritage? of an unprecedented war of racist extermination? of a shamefully failed Communist dictatorship?—has not been and probably will not be answered soon, by Christo or others. Those arguing for myth, grandeur, and national weight seem to have the upper hand at this writing, just as they have over the past century. Will the preservation of historic sites continue to offer them raw material for this version of the past? Or will open realization of the transiency of all historical perspectives and all efforts at preservation once again corrode this particular frame of identity, leaving a new, chastened, perhaps less violence-prone but still resonant nation in its wake? Noted philosopher Jürgen Habermas has arguably offered the most compelling response to these questions, which define German identity at the millennium. Habermas has argued repeatedly that Germans must disengage politics from culture. They should adopt a "constitutional patriotism" that eschews nationalist politics in favor of liberality, tolerance, and parliamentary authority while also retaining a sense of their cultural identity. In this view, historic places would serve simultaneously as affirmative markers of an enduring cultural tradition and critical reminders that nationalist politics must be rejected in favor of European and democratic perspectives. Habermas's proposal will be debated for years to come. In the meantime, Germany's monuments, from the *Wrapped Reichstag* to the medieval Zur Brezel of Cologne, will continue to resonate as malleable symbols of a nation's volatile making and unmaking.

NOTES

Abbreviations Used in the Notes

ALVR   Archiv des Landschaftsverbandes Rheinland, Brauweiler
APKNS   Institut für Zeitgeschichte. *Akten der Parteikanzlei der NSDAP.* Munich:
          K. G. Saur, 1984. Microfiche.
APuZ   *Aus Politik und Zeitgeschichte*
BAK   Bundesarchiv Koblenz
DAS   *Die Alte Stadt*
DKD   *Deutsche Kunst und Denkmalpflege*
DP   *Die Denkmalpflege*
DPHS   *Denkmalpflege und Heimatschutz*
HASK   Historisches Archiv der Stadt Köln
KDR   *Die Kunst im Deutschen Reich*
MBH   *Mitteilungen des Bundes Heimatschutz*
MRVDH   *Mitteilungen des Rheinischen Vereins für Denkmalpflege und Heimat-
          schutz*
NWHSADü   Nordrhein-Westfälisches Hauptstaatsarchiv Düsseldorf
RHP   *Rheinische Heimatpflege*
RP   Regierungspräsident
RVDH   Rheinischer Verein für Denkmalpflege und Heimatschutz
RVDL   Rheinischer Verein für Denkmalpflege und Landschaftsschutz
SADü   Stadtarchiv Düsseldorf
SKK   Stadt Köln, Konservator
ZRVDH   *Zeitschrift des Rheinischen Vereins für Denkmalpflege und Heimatschutz*
ZVLGA   *Zeitschrift des Vereins für Lübeckische Geschichte und Altertumskunde*

Introduction

1. For the pre–World War I material, see F. Bolte, "Erhaltung alter Bürgerhäuser am
Alten Markt in Köln," *DP* 15, no. 2 (5 February 1913): 13–14. For the post-1945 situation

of the houses, see Ludwig Eltz to Oberstadtdirektor, Köln, 13 March 1949; Arnold Nellessen to Stadtausschuß, Köln, 5 May 1951; and Willi Gerbeck to Oberstadtdirektor, Köln, 23 May 1955, all in SKK, Bez. 1, Bd. 1, Altermarkt 20/22.

2. Relph, *Modern Urban Landscape*, 221.

3. The press is, of course, one of the richest sources for following such debates for the contemporary period. For examples of more historical and analytical treatments, see Behrens-Cobet and Reichling, " 'Bilder erhalten, die den Schlaf stören' "; Berliner Geschichtswerkstatt, *Sackgassen*; Koonz, "Between Memory and Oblivion"; Koshar, "Building Pasts"; Maier, *Unmasterable Past*, esp. chap. 5, which deals with debates over German history museums; Marcuse, "Die museale Darstellung des Holocaust"; Puvogel, *Gedenkstätten für die Opfer des Nationalsozialismus*; Reichel, *Politik mit der Erinnerung*; Till, "Place and the Politics of Memory"; and Young, *Texture of Memory*.

4. See Riegl, "Der moderne Denkmalkultus," 144. The literature is voluminous and still growing. For examples, see Hardtwig, *Geschichtskultur und Wissenschaft*, esp. chaps. 8 and 10; Koselleck and Jeismann, *Der politische Totenkult*; Laqueur, "Memory and Naming in the Great War"; Mosse, *Fallen Soldiers*, esp. chaps. 3, 5, 6, 7, and 10; Mosse, *Nationalization of the Masses*, esp. chap. 3; Nipperdey, "Nationalidee und Nationaldenkmal"; Sherman, "Art, Commerce, and the Production of Memory in France after World War I"; Tacke, *Denkmal im sozialen Raum*; Tobia, *Una patria per gli italiani*; and Young, *Texture of Memory*.

5. Certainly the most internationally visible project in this genre is Nora, *Le lieux de mémoire*, which considers "sites of memory" encompassing monuments, literature, historical buildings, government documents, and other objects. But see Englund's critique of Nora's nostalgia for French grandeur in "Ghost of Nation Past." For an argument that mistakenly sees the current interest in memory as primarily a phenomenon of post–Cold War Europe, see Judt, "Past Is Another Country." For a comprehensive study of national memory in the United States, see Kammen, *Mystic Chords of Memory*; for the recent Anglo-American world, see Lowenthal, *Past Is a Foreign Country*.

6. For an illustrative example of the many references to the past contained in built environments, see Lynch, *What Time Is This Place?*; for the definition of the built environment, see Lynch, *Image of the City*, esp. chap. 3.

7. Peter Jackson, *Maps of Meaning*, 23.

8. For a recent exception to this trend, see Ladd, *Ghosts of Berlin*, which analyzes the layers of German history as reflected in Berlin's built environment.

9. Besides some of the works cited above, see Baldwin, *Reworking the Past*; Diner, *Ist der Nationalsozialismus Geschichte?*; Domansky, "Die gespaltene Erinnerung"; Domansky, " 'Kristallnacht,' the Holocaust, and German Unity"; Eley, "Nazism, Politics, and the Image of the Past"; Evans, *In Hitler's Shadow*; Friedländer, *Reflections of Nazism*; Friedländer, *Probing the Limits of Representation*; Kaes, *From Hitler to Heimat*; Lüdtke, " 'Coming to Terms with the Past' "; and Moeller, "War Stories."

10. For the useful notion of vectors or "carriers" of memory, see Rousso, *Vichy Syndrome*, esp. chap. 6. Rousso defines carriers of memory as "any source that proposes a deliberate reconstruction of an event for a social purpose" (219).

11. Halbwachs, *Collective Memory*. It is more accurate to speak not of memory but of "memory-experiences." The former can include behavior such as learning a skill or acquiring a habit (something both animals and human beings can accomplish), but the latter involve consciously reflecting on past experience and recognizing that "memory is

being experienced." This conscious activity is unique to human beings. See Warnock, *Memory*, 9.

12. See, for example, Carr, *Time, Narrative, and History*, 163–77; Nora, "Between Memory and History."

13. Greenfield, *Nationalism*.

14. See, above all, Anderson, *Imagined Communities*; Hobsbawm and Ranger, *Invention of Tradition*.

15. See Anthony Smith, *Ethnic Origins of Nations*, and Smith's critique of Anderson and Hobsbawm in "The Nation." Schama's *Landscape and Memory*, 15, also stresses the endurance of national myth in landscape traditions, although he fails to consider Smith's work.

16. Weber, "The Nation," 172.

17. On the study of the emotional resonance of nationhood, see most recently, Confino, *Nation as a Local Metaphor*, which supplements Anderson's concept of "imagined communities" with an analysis of collective memory.

18. Chartier, "Texts, Printings, Readings," esp. 171–75; Hebdige, *Hiding in the Light*, esp. 80–85.

19. Bourdieu, *Distinction*.

20. On symbols, see Geertz, *Interpretation of Cultures*, 91; on military metaphors in the study of culture, see Certeau, *Practice of Everyday Life*.

21. Fiske, *Reading the Popular* and *Understanding Popular Culture*; Nelson, Treichler, and Grossberg, "Cultural Studies." On the relevance of cultural studies to scholarship on national identity, see Eley and Suny, "Introduction," esp. 19–32.

22. Carr, *Time, Narrative, and History*, 168.

23. For this definition of discourse, see Foucault, *Order of Things*, 158.

24. I take note of Jerrold Siegel's criticisms of recent studies that reduce subjectivity to a mere outcome of all-encompassing linguistic systems in "Human Subject as a Language-Effect."

25. Dellheim, *Face of the Past*; Hewison, *Heritage Industry*; Kammen, *Mystic Chords of Memory*, 621–28; Lowenthal, *Past Is a Foreign Country*, esp. chap. 7; Wright, *On Living in an Old Country*; Boyer, *City of Collective Memory*.

26. Beseler and Gutschow, *Kriegsschicksale Deutscher Architektur*; Beyme, *Der Wiederaufbau*, esp. chap. 9; Boockmann, "Marienburg"; Brix, *Lübeck*; Diefendorf, *In the Wake of War*; Dölling, *Conservation of Historical Monuments*; Durth and Gutschow, *Architektur und Städtebau der Fünfziger Jahre*; Durth and Gutschow, *Architektur und Städtebau der Fünfziger Jahre: Ergebnisse der Fachtagung in Hannover*; Durth and Gutschow, *Träume in Trümmern*; Durth and Nerdinger, *Architektur und Städtebau der 30/40er Jahre*; Findeisen, *Geschichte der Denkmalpflege Sachsen-Anhalt*; Hoffmann, *Rheinische Romanik*; Huse, *Denkmalpflege*; Institut für Denkmalpflege, Arbeitsstelle Dresden, *Denkmale in Sachsen*; Koshar, "Against the 'Frightful Leveler'"; Koshar, "Altar, Stage, and City"; Koshar, "Building Pasts"; Magirius, *Geschichte der Denkmalpflege Sachsen*; Mai and Waetzoldt, *Kunstverwaltung, Bau- und Denkmal-Politik im Kaiserreich*; Meckseper and Siebenmorgen, *Die Alte Stadt*; Mittig and Plagemann, *Denkmäler im 19. Jahrhundert*; Paschke, *Die Idee des Stadtdenkmals*; Rheinischer Verein für Denkmalpflege und Landschaftsschutz, *Erhalten und gestalten*; Scharf, *Kleine Kunstgeschichte des deutschen Denkmals*; Michael Siegel, *Denkmalpflege als öffentliche Aufgabe*; Speitkamp, "'Ein dauerndes und ehrenvolles Denkmal'"; Speitkamp, "Denkmalpflege und Heimatschutz"; Speitkamp,

"Das Erbe der Monarchie"; Speitkamp, "Die Hohkönigsburg"; Speitkamp, "Kulturpolitik unter dem Einfluß der Französischen Revolution"; Speitkamp, *Verwaltung der Geschichte*.

27. On Panofsky, see Daniels and Cosgrove, "Introduction," 2–3.

28. See Fitch, *Historic Preservation*, 44–47.

Chapter 1

1. See Koselleck, " 'Space of Experience' and 'Horizon of Expectation,' " esp. 271, 272, from which the following quotes are taken.

2. Terdiman, "Deconstructing Memory," 14–15.

3. For the following, see Rüsen, *Lebendige Geschichte*, 39–56. Critical narratives delegitimize other forms of historical argumentation in an attempt to create a discursive space for alternative models. In this case a good example of critical narratives comes from the Enlightenment, which denigrated tradition's hold on humanity. Genetical narratives describe an arc in which an individual or collectivity develops from alien to present forms of life. The Enlightenment's story of humankind's improvement is an example.

4. On the origins of cultural politics, see Abelein, *Die Kulturpolitik*, 193–218.

5. Anderson, *Imagined Communities*, 86.

6. Kammen, *Mystic Chords of Memory*, 284–90, here 284.

7. Abelein, *Die Kulturpolitik*, 106–7.

8. Silverman, *Art Nouveau in Fin-de-Siècle France*, 142–58; Hoffmann, *Rheinische Romanik*, 65–82.

9. Stern, *Politics of Cultural Despair*; Mosse, *Crisis of German Ideology*, esp. pts. 1 and 2. On the uneven effect of cultural pessimism in academics and the wider public, see, for example, Iggers, *German Conception of History*, 128, 240, and Nipperdey, *Deutsche Geschichte, 1866–1918*, 1:591–92, 821.

10. For the following, see Lasch, *True and Only Heaven*, 47, 81.

11. The 1913 letter was reprinted in the *Vossische Zeitung*, 12 December 1915, as quoted in Abelein, *Die Kulturpolitik*, 107.

12. Campbell, *German Werkbund*, 11.

13. On the visual elements of memory, see Terdiman, "Deconstructing Memory," 22.

14. See Virilio, *Vision Machine*, 41.

15. For the following, see Nipperdey, "Nationalidee und Nationaldenkmal," esp. 153–70; Mosse, *Fallen Soldiers*, 48; Hobsbawm, "Mass-Producing Traditions," 274–76; Hutter, *"Die feinste Barbarei"*; Lurz, *Kriegerdenkmäler*, 2:69–76, 436; Schama, *Landscape and Memory*, 109–12; and Tacke, *Denkmal im sozialen Raum*, which is particularly convincing on the *Hermannsdenkmal*.

16. Ladd, *Urban Planning and Civic Order*, chap. 4; Pinckney, *Napoleon III and the Rebuilding of Paris*, esp. chaps. 4, 9; Holston, *Modernist City*, 47–49; Ziolkowski, *German Romanticism and Its Institutions*, 314–17.

17. Schorske, *Fin-de-Siècle Vienna*, 72, 65.

18. Olsen, *City as a Work of Art*, 309; Sutcliffe, *Autumn of Central Paris*, 191.

19. Muthesius, *Das englische Vorbild*, 170.

20. Nietzsche, "On the Uses and Disadvantages of History for Life," 73.

21. Lane, *Architecture and Politics*, 13.

22. Ibid., 27.

23. See Haiko, "Architecture of the Twentieth Century," 9–12.

24. Andreas, "Wilhelm Heinrich von Riehl," 129–30; Nipperdey, *Deutsche Geschichte, 1866–1918,* 1:640; Schama, *Landscape and Memory,* 113–16; Zuhorn, "50 Jahre Deutscher Heimatschutz," 18–19; Hager, "Georg Hager," 489–90.

25. For the following, see Zuhorn, "50 Jahre Deutscher Heimatschutz," 21–24, 28–29. For background, see Bergmann, *Agrarromantik und Großstadtfeindschaft,* but more recently, see Applegate, *Nation of Provincials,* esp. chap. 3, and Rollins, "Aesthetic Environmentalism," which against Bergmann and many others stresses, perhaps too strongly, the socially liberal qualities of *Heimatschutz.* See also Jefferies, "Back to the Future?," and Confino, *Nation as a Local Metaphor,* chaps. 5–7.

26. Rollins, "Aesthetic Environmentalism," 2, 157–58.

27. Aufruf zur Gründung eines Bundes Heimatschutz, as reprinted in Deutscher Heimatbund, *Fünfzig Jahre Deutscher Heimatbund,* 62; "Der Name Heimatschutz," *MBH* 3 (1907): 77; Rollins, "Aesthetic Environmentalism," 106–14.

28. Rollins, "Aesthetic Environmentalism," 166–70.

29. Dölling, "Protection and Conservation of Historical Monuments," 9–10, 12; Muthesius, "Origins of the German Conservation Movement," 37–48; Huse, *Denkmalpflege,* 21; Brix and Steinhauser, "Geschichte im Dienste der Baukunst," 238; Michael Siegel, *Denkmalpflege als öffentliche Aufgabe,* 24; Steinert, "Aspekte der Denkmalpflege in Nordrhein-Westfalen," 7; Epstein, *Genesis of German Conservatism,* 341–52, 372–87; Nipperdey, *Deutsche Geschichte, 1800–1866,* 554; Erich Blunck, "Schinkel und die Denkmalpflege," *DP* 18, no. 4 (15 March 1916): 25–27; Julius Kohte, "Ferdinand v. Quast: Zu seinem hundertsten Geburtstage," *DP* 9, no. 8 (19 June 1907): 57; Speitkamp, "Kulturpolitik unter dem Einfluß der Französischen Revolution," 131–41.

30. Boockmann, "Marienburg," 99–100; Rollins, "Aesthetic Environmentalism," 86–87; Michael Siegel, *Denkmalpflege als öffentliche Aufgabe,* 29–30.

31. Michael Siegel, *Denkmalpflege als öffentliche Aufgabe,* 29–30, 32, 35–40, 39–47; Speitkamp, " 'Ein dauerndes und ehrenvolles Denkmal,' " 176–77; Speitkamp, "Kulturpolitik unter dem Einfluß der Französischen Revolution," 142, 146–53; Brown, *Care of Ancient Monuments,* 57–61, 74–75.

32. For the following, see Speitkamp, " 'Ein dauerndes und ehrenvolles Denkmal,' " 186; Reuther, "Oskar Hoßfeld," 652–53; and Otto Sarrazin and Oskar Hoßfeld, "Zur Einführung," *DP* 1, no. 1 (4 January 1899): 1–2, from which the quotes derive. The *DP* changed its name and emphasis several times. In 1923 it took the name *Denkmalpflege und Heimatschutz.* Later it became *Die Denkmalpflege: Zeitschrift für Denkmalpflege und Heimatschutz* before assuming the title it has today, *Deutsche Kunst und Denkmalpflege,* in 1934, when its format was changed in order to attract a wider readership. The *DKD* has since 1952 been published by the Association of *Land* Conservators, the official body of former West German state conservators.

33. The text of the speech is reprinted as "Denkmalschutz und Denkmalpflege im neunzehnten Jahrhundert," in Wohlleben, *Konservieren nicht restaurieren.*

34. Paul Clemen, "Zum Gedächtnis an Georg Dehio," *DP* 34, no. 1–2 (1932): 76–79; Gall, "Georg Dehio"; Goetz, "Georg Dehio," 1–2.

35. Dehio, "Denkmalschutz und Denkmalpflege im neunzehnten Jahrhundert," 90, 93, 99, 101.

36. Ibid., 92.

37. On Riegl, besides his "Der moderne Denkmalkultus," see Forster, "Monument/Memory and the Mortality of Architecture," and Zerner, "Alois Riegl." On the differences between Dehio and Riegl, see Wohlleben, "Vorwort," 11–14.

38. Dehio, "Denkmalschutz und Denkmalpflege im neunzehnten Jahrhundert," 92; Gurlitt is quoted by Magirius, *Geschichte der Denkmalpflege Sachsen*, 149. Conservative thinkers took up "socialist" orientations more forcefully in World War I, but they were building on prewar precedents, as noted in Klemperer, *Germany's New Conservatism*, 57–58.

39. Dehio, "Denkmalschutz und Denkmalpflege im neunzehnten Jahrhundert," 92, 102–3.

40. "Denkmalpflege," *Meyers Großes Konversations-Lexicon*, 641.

41. I extrapolate here from Tuan, "Space and Place."

42. Clemen, *Die Kunstdenkmäler des Kreises Geldern*; Clemen, *Kunstdenkmäler der Stadt und des Kreises Düsseldorf*; Geisberg, *Die Stadt Münster*; Vogts, *Die Kunstdenkmäler der Stadt Köln*; Hilger, "Paul Clemen und die Denkmäler-Inventarisation in den Rheinlanden," 390–91; Edmund Nedden, "Geschäftsbericht," *MRVDH* 10, no. 3 (1916): 293–98.

43. Lademacher, "Die nördlichen Rheinlande," 680–81; Naumann, *Werke*, 6:78.

44. Heinrich Lezius, *Das Recht der Denkmalpflege in Preußen: Begriff, Geschichte und Organisation der Denkmalpflege* (Berlin, 1908), 2, as cited in Mainzer, "Denkmalpflege im Rheinland Heute," 191; Magirius, *Geschichte der Denkmalpflege Sachsen*, 152; F. Havemann, "Der alte Kran in Lüneburg," *DP* 7, no. 5 (14 April 1905): 35–36.

45. For the following, see Brown, *Care of Ancient Monuments*, 9–10, 44–46, 103–13; Preußisches Herrenhaus, *Stenographische Berichte*, IV. Sitzung, 31 March 1903, 38, 40; "Der neue Gesetzentwurf zum Denkmalschutz im Großherzogtum Hessen," *DP* 3, no. 5 (17 April 1901): 36–39; Tag für Denkmalpflege, *Zweiter Tag für Denkmalpflege*, 22–33; Speitkamp, " 'Ein dauerndes und ehrenvolles Denkmal,' " 188; H. Wagner, "Freiherr von Biegeleben 80 Jahre," *DKD* 41 (1939): 59.

46. See, for example, Preußisches Herrenhaus, *Stenographische Berichte*, XVII. Sitzung, 28 May 1906, 355–61.

47. Speitkamp, "Kulturpolitik unter dem Einfluß der Französischen Revolution," 158; Walter H. Dammann, "Justus Brinckmann und die Denkmalpflege in Hamburg," *DP* 17, no. 5 (14 April 1915): 33–35; "Reinhold Persius," *DP* 3, no. 5 (17 April 1901): 33–34.

48. For the following, see Renard, "Die Denkmalpflege in der Rheinprovinz," 447–48.

49. Unique to Prussia, the twelve *Provinzialverbände* were administrative-political entities situated between the Prussian state on one side and the towns and cities on the other. For background and literature, see Ditt, *Raum und Volkstum*, 15. For the origins and cultural tasks of the Rhenish *Provinzialverband*, see Lademacher, "Die nördlichen Rheinlande," esp. 676–77, 679.

50. For the following, see Hilger, "Paul Clemen und die Denkmäler-Inventarisation in den Rheinlanden," 383–98; Horion, "Paul Clemen und die Rheinlande," 11–16; Lützeler, "Paul Clemen," 281; Landschaftsverband Rheinland, *"Der Rhein ist mein Schicksal geworden"*; Graf Wolff Metternich, "Paul Clemen zu Seinem 70. Geburtstag," *DKD* 38 (1936): 278–80; Verbeek, "Paul Clemen"; Brown, *Care of Ancient Monuments*, 54–55; and Julius Kohte, "Ferdinand v. Quast: Zu seinem hundertsten Geburtstage," *DP* 9, no. 8 (19 June 1907): 57–60.

51. For an announcement of the second congress, see "Generalversammlung des Gesamtvereins der deutschen Geschichts- und Altertumsvereine in Freiburg, 23.–26. Sept. 1901," in HASK, Kulturangelegenheiten 47–52, Nr. 142. Figures are based on "Liste der Teilnehmer," in Tag für Denkmalpflege, *Zweiter Tag für Denkmalpflege*, 3–5.

52. For the following, see Applegate, *Nation of Provincials*, 67; Rollins, "Aesthetic

Environmentalism," 171–72, n. 109; "Verzeichnis der Mitglieder," *MRVDH* 10, no. 3 (1916): 387–427; Dubrow, "Restoring a Female Presence," esp. 159–63; Flores, "Private Visions, Public Culture"; Hosmer, "Broadening View of the Historical Preservation Movement," 122; and Kammen, *Mystic Chords of Memory*, 260.

53. For the following, see "Überblick über die Organisation des Heimatschutzes," *Heimatschutz* 5, no. 1 (1909): 31; Lademacher, "Die nördlichen Rheinlande," 590–633; Rollins, "Aesthetic Environmentalism," 177–78, 240–47; "Rheinischer Verein für Denkmalpflege und Heimatschutz," announcement of founding, 1906, NWHSADü, RP Düsseldorf, 534; Clemen, "Eduard zur Nedden," *ZRVDH* 17, no. 2/3 (February 1925): 105.

54. On snob appeal, see Kammen, *Mystic Chords of Memory*, 261. Ebhardt's association, which still exists today, attracted leading figures from business, the military, the aristocracy, the government, and the professions. See "Vereinigung zur Erhaltung deutscher Burgen, Einladung zur Teilnahme an der Festversammlung deutscher Burgenfreunde," Marksburg bei Braubach a. Rhein, 10. Juni 1906, in NWHSADü (Kalkum), RP Aachen, 980.

55. Borrmann, *Schultze-Naumburg*, 63. For two examples of *Heimatschutz* stridency, see Richard Nordhausen, "Die Nutzbarmacher," *Mitteilungen des Bundes Heimatschutz* 3, no. 5/6 (May/June 1907): 63, which decries the "wretchedness" of Brandenburg provincial officials' plans to make more urban forest lands available for public recreation, and "Verschiedenes," *Heimatschutz-Chronik* (1917): 8, in which an anonymous writer sharply attacks a Hamburg engineer for suggesting some historic and natural sites could tolerate more "disfigurement" than others.

56. Schultze-Naumburg is quoted in Borrmann, *Schultze-Naumburg*, 63. Borrmann uses the quote to stress the impact of *Heimatschutz* on architectural preservation, but in fact it also refers to preservation's independent growth and maturation.

57. Brown, *Care of Ancient Monuments*, 27; Preußisches Herrenhaus, *Stenographische Berichte*, IV. Sitzung, 31 March 1903, 41, and XVII. Sitzung, 28 May 1906, 355–61; "Denkmalpflege und Heimatschutz in Württemberg," *DP* 7, no. 9 (12 July 1905): 75; Scheck, " 'Im Winkel des großen Vaterlandes,' " 259; "Vereinsnachrichten," *MRVDH* 2, no. 3 (1908): 125; *Dürener Zeitung*, 4 December 1911.

58. Dodd, "Englishness and the National Culture," 2.

59. Ruskin, *Seven Lamps of Architecture*, 198; C. Steinbrecht, "Streifereien durch alte Städte," *DP* 1, no. 1 (4 January 1899): 7.

60. Clemen, "Entwicklung und Ziele," 62; Jefferies, *Politics and Culture in Wilhelmine Germany*, esp. chap. 2; "Neuzeitliche Industriebauten," *MRVDH* 4, no. 1 (1910): 26–56; Sutcliffe, *Autumn of Central Paris*, 193; Otto Schubert, "Cornelius Gurlitt"; Gurlitt, "Die Dorfkirche"; Lurz, *Kriegerdenkmäler*, 2:437; Gurlitt, "Der deutsche Städtebau."

61. Otto Sarrazin and Oskar Hoßfeld, "Zur Einführung," *DP* 1, no. 1 (4 January 1899): 1; "Freilegung der Kathedrale in Lausanne," *DP* 7, no. 9 (12 July 1905): 72–73; Walter Bombe, "Denkmalpflege in Bologna," *DP* 16, no. 15 (2 December 1914): 113–16, and *DP* 16, no. 16 (23 December 1914): 121–24.

62. Boockmann, "Marienburg," 112–47, where the author also points out that Polish maintenance of the Marienburg actually made subsequent restorations possible; Otto Piper, "Was zur Wiederherstellung und zur Erhaltung unserer Burgenreste geschehen ist (Schluß)," *DP* 1, no. 11 (30 August 1899): 90.

63. On the renaissance of regions, see Applegate, *Nation of Provincials*, 13–16; Confino, "Nation as a Local Metaphor"; Kammen, *Mystic Chords of Memory*, 181–84; Porciani, "Il medioevo nella costruzione dell'Italia unita," esp. 166–67; and Thiesse, "La

petite patrie enclose dans la grande," esp. 5–9. For the RVDH statement, see flyer "Rheinischer Verein für Denkmalpflege und Heimatschutz," NWHSADü, RP Düsseldorf, 534; on the Rhineland as an international region, see A. von Behr, "Denkmalpflege und Heimatschutz," RVDH brochure to Rhenish elementary school teachers, December 1908, 1, NWHSADü, RP Aachen, 980; on the Rhineland's "almost American" development, see "Vereinsnachrichten," *MRVDH* 1, no. 2 (1907): 36.

64. For the following, see "Zum neunten Tage für Denkmalpflege in Lübeck," *DP* 10, no. 12 (16 September 1908): 89–90.

65. Said, *Orientalism*; E. Müller, "Rundgang durch Alt-Coblenz," *MRVDH* 2, no. 2 (1908): 58; Eduard zur Nedden, "Ein 'Trierer Heft,'" *MRVDH* 3, no. 2 (1909): 67; Gusevich, "Purity and Transgression," 101.

66. On youth and historic places as religious sites, see A. von Behr, "Denkmalpflege und Heimatschutz," RVDH brochure to Rhenish elementary school teachers, December 1908, 1, NWHSADü, RP Aachen, 980; on the United States, see Sears, *Sacred Places*.

67. Kocka, "Bürgertum und bürgerliche Gesellschaft im 19. Jahrhundert."

68. For the following, see Choay, *Modern City*, 102–3; Porciani, "Il medioevo nella costruzione dell'Italia unita," 167–73; "Rheinischer Verein für Denkmalpflege und Heimatschutz," NWHSADü, RP Düsseldorf, 534; "Alt-Nürnberg in Gefahr!," *DP* 1, no. 1 (4 January 1899): 6–7.

69. "Alt-Nürnberg in Gefahr!," *DP* 1, no. 1 (4 January 1899): 6; Eduard Adenaw, "Aachener Bauweise," *MRVDH* 7, no. 3 (1913): 191; Tuan, *Space and Place*, 126.

70. Naumann, *Werke*, 6:78; Paul Clemen, "Die überlieferte heimische Bauweise und ihr Wert für die heutige Architektur," *MRVDH* 3, no. 1 (1909): 26–29.

71. Preußisches Herrenhaus, *Stenographische Berichte*, XVII. Sitzung, 28 May 1906, 357–58; Hoßfeld, "Denkmalpflege auf dem Lande," *MRVDH* 1, no. 1 (1907): 26; Renard is quoted in "Der Rheinische Verein für Denkmalpflege und Heimatschutz," *Dürener Zeitung*, 4 December 1911; Edmund Renard, "Mittelalterliche Stadtbefestigungen und Landesburgen am Niederrhein," *MRVDH* 2, no. 3 (1908): 135; Tag für Denkmalpflege, *Zweiter Tag für Denkmalpflege*, 16.

72. Bernold, "Anfänge"; Lobell, "Buried Treasure," 141, 143.

73. For the following, see Saldern, "Bauen, nichts als Bauen," 8–9; Buzard, *Beaten Track*, 16. One of the best descriptions of urban slum conditions is Evans, *Death in Hamburg*, which also discusses the renewal of urban districts. Hamburg was one of the only German cities to undertake thorough urban renewal in this period.

74. A. von Behr, "Das Fachwerkhaus am Rhein und an der Mosel," *MRVDH* 1, no. 3 (1907): 69–87, here 69–70.

75. The first phrase comes from Albert Erich Brinckmann, art historian and city planner, as quoted by Hartmann, "Städtebau um 1900," 93; the second is from the Bremen Verein "Lüder von Bentheim," as cited in Hartung, *Konservative Zivilisationskritik*, 200–201.

76. Jokilehto, "History of Architectural Conservation," vol. 2, pt. 2, 382.

77. For the following, see F. W. Bredt, "Die vaterländische Bedeutung der Burgen," *MRVDH* 9, no. 1 (1915): 45–58, here 54; Gollwitzer, "Zum Fragenkreis Architekturhistorismus"; Hoffmann, *Rheinische Romanik*, 57–60; Th. Landsberg, "Aufgaben des Ingenieurs bei der Erhaltung der Baudenkmäler," *DP* 12, no. 5 (20 April 1910): 35; Otto Piper, "Was zur Wiederherstellung und zur Erhaltung unserer Burgenreste geschehen ist," *DP* 1, no. 10 (30 August 1899): 79–82, and 1, no. 11 (30 August 1899): 88–91; Speitkamp,

"Die Hohkönigsburg"; Weindling, *Health, Race, and German Politics*, 36–59; Tag für Denkmalpflege, *Zweiter Tag für Denkmalpflege*, 103–18.

78. See, for example, *Kölnische Zeitung*, 30 June 1894; "Vermischtes," *DP* 1, no. 2 (25 January 1899): 19.

79. Horne, *Great Museum*, 17; Nipperdey, *Deutsche Geschichte, 1866–1918*, 1:821.

80. Eduard Broil, "Köln, die Stadt der Türme," *Kölnisches Tageblatt*, 4 October 1913.

81. Domansky, "Der Deutsche Werkbund," 270–71.

82. Naumann, *Werke*, 6:64, 67.

83. See Baedeker, *Deutschland im einem Bande*, 283.

84. Sternberger, *Panorama of the Nineteenth Century*; Schivelbusch, *Railway Travel*, 61.

85. Nipperdey, "Der Kölner Dom als Nationaldenkmal," 169; Boockmann, "Marienburg," 143, 145–46; Applegate, *Nation of Provincials*, 90; Mosse, *Nationalization of the Masses*, 83–84.

86. MacCannell, *The Tourist*, 13.

87. Bausinger, "National Orientations in Tourism."

88. Breckmann, "Disciplining Consumption"; Vierhaus, "Bildung," 547–48; Krauß, *Wiederherstellung der Wartburg*, 58.

89. Bourdieu, *Distinction*, 71–72.

90. I rely here on John Berger, *About Looking*, 49, which is in turn a reading of Susan Sontag's ideas on photography. For an example of the *Blaue Bücher*, see *Große Bürgerbauten deutscher Vergangenheit*.

91. Schor, "*Cartes Postales*"; "Vereinsnachrichten," *MRVDH* 1, no. 3 (1907): 65; "Vereinsmitteilungen," *MRVDH* 2, no. 2 (1908): 46.

92. Examples are in Gynz-Rekowski and Schulze, *Harzansichten*, 8–11, 80–81. Confino stresses only the "coziness" of *Heimat* postcard iconography in "Nation as a Local Metaphor," 66.

93. For the following, see Weyers and Köck, *Die Eroberung der Welt*, 8–26. Thanks to Alf Lüdtke for informing me of this source.

94. Horne, *Great Museum*, 15.

95. Benjamin, "Work of Art in the Age of Mechanical Reproduction"; see also Koshar, "Against the 'Frightful Leveler,' " 13–14.

96. See Schivelbusch, *Railway Travel*, 63.

97. Lenz, "Die altsächsischen Bauernhäuser"; Speitkamp, *Verwaltung der Geschichte*, 93; "Der Verein Alt-Köln," *Localanzeiger*, 24 October 1909; Paul Weber, "Persönliche Denkmalpflege," *DP* 1, no. 6 (3 May 1899): 50; Applegate, *Nation of Provincials*, 47–48; Scheck, " 'Im Winkel des großen Vaterlandes,' " 294; Jacobus Reimers, "Die Museen und die Denkmalpflege in der Provinz Hannover," *DP* 1, no. 1 (4 January 1899): 9–10; Hartung, *Konservative Zivilisationskritik*, 199–200. On the broader development of local history museums, see Roth, *Heimatmuseum*, and Confino, *Nation as a Local Metaphor*, esp. 134–53.

98. See, for example, Lehner, "Das Bonner Provinzialmuseum."

99. Ladd, *Urban Planning and Civic Order*, 126–29.

100. "Vermischtes," *DP* 1, no. 1 (4 January 1899): 12; "Kirchliche Baudenkmäler," *Kölnische Zeitung*, 18 August 1896; Hartung, *Konservative Zivilisationskritik*, 198; *Kölnische Zeitung*, 5 December 1911; Preußisches Herrenhaus, *Stenographische Berichte*, IV. Sitzung, 31 March 1903, 41; more generally, see Speitkamp, *Verwaltung der Geschichte*, 339–64.

101. For the following, see G. v. Bezold, "Übereifer in der Denkmalpflege," *DP* 11, no. 2 (3 February 1909): 10–12.

102. Reulecke, *Geschichte der Urbanisierung*, 103.

103. Rollins, "Aesthetic Environmentalism," 151, 180, 203–5; Speitkamp, *Verwaltung der Geschichte*, 371–72; Nörthen, "Innerlich unsolide, im Äußeren gemein," 54; Kier, "Glanz und Elend," 242.

104. For the following, see Zenz, *Die Stadt Trier im 20. Jahrhundert*, 67; "Denkmalpflege: Pflege der heimischen Bauweise," *MBH* 3 (1907): 82–87, here 82–83.

105. Evidence for working-class membership in the *Heimatschutz* movement is scant, for example, but Rollins, "Aesthetic Environmentalism," 174–75, speculates that the large share (27.6 percent) of unidentified occupations in the Verein für Heimatkunde und Heimatschutz of the industrial and mining region Siegerland meant that workers may have enrolled in the organization. For the rest, see Blessing, "Cult of the Monarchy"; Mosse, *Nationalization of the Masses*, 161–82; Lidtke, *Alternative Culture*, 45; Reulecke, *Geschichte der Urbanisierung*, 96–97.

106. Wünderich, "Von der bürgerlichen zur proletarischen Kommunalpolitik"; "Kölner Jahrhundertfeier," *Rheinische Zeitung*, 15 October 1913.

Chapter 2

1. Lurz, *Kriegerdenkmäler*, 4:356.

2. Bataille, *L'erotisme*; see also Clifford, *Predicament of Culture*, 125–26.

3. Jeismann, *Vaterland der Feinde*, 318; Eksteins, *Rites of Spring*, 79–80, 116–19; Lurz, *Kriegerdenkmäler*, 3:160–62.

4. Vondung, "Deutsche Apokalypse, 1914."

5. Günther-Hornig, *Kunstschutz in den von Deutschland besetzten Gebieten*, 1–7.

6. J. B. Jackson, *Necessity for Ruins*, 13.

7. Tag für Denkmalpflege, *Dreizehnter Tag für Denkmalpflege*, 54; Uyttenhove, "Continuities in Belgian Wartime Reconstruction Planning," 48–51; Baudoui, "Between Regionalism and Functionalism," 35; "Vermischtes," *DP* 17, no. 16 (22 December 1915): 127.

8. Tag für Denkmalpflege, *Dreizehnter Tag für Denkmalpflege*, 152–53; on the 1918 count, see Dethlefsen, "Unsere neuen Glocken," *DP* 20, no. 2 (13 February 1918): 9.

9. Schaumann, "Die Denkmalpflege der Stadt Frankfurt a.M. im Jahre 1914," *DP* 17, no. 13 (20 October 1915): 100–102; "Das Freiluftmuseum in Hadersleben," *DP* 18, no. 3 (1 March 1916): 17–19; F. W. Bredt, "Werden und Wollen des Heimatschutzes," *MRVDH* 11, no. 1 (1917): 17–20, here 19.

10. For the invitation to Clemen's address, see RVDH, "Einladung zur Hauptversammlung [des Tages für Denkmalpflege] am 8. Dez. 1916," NWHSADü (Kalkum), RP Aachen, 980.

11. Tag für Denkmalpflege, *Dreizehnter Tag für Denkmalpflege*, 19.

12. "Vereinsnachrichten," *MRVDH* 11, no. 1 (1917): 3.

13. Ibid., 6; G. Wolfram, "Nationalitätsgrenze und Bauart in Lothringen," *MRVDH* 9, no. 3 (1915): 159–64.

14. "Vorwort," *MRVDH* 9, no. 1 (1915): 5. Speitkamp, *Verwaltung der Geschichte*, 137–42, also stresses the war's impact on preservation and *Heimatschutz*.

15. Henry James to Edith Wharton, 21 September 1914, in *The Letters of Henry James*, 2 vols., ed. Percy Lubbock (London, 1920), 2:420–21, as cited in Eksteins, *Rites of Spring*, 158; *Les Allemands destructeurs*, 1–3; Clemen, "Der Krieg und die Kunstdenkmäler," 7.

16. For the following, see F. Wolff, "Denkmalpflege und Krieg," *DP* 16, no. 15 (2 December 1914): 116–17.

17. For the following, see Falke, "Die Einrichtung des Kunstschutzes," 12–13.

18. See *Stenographischer Bericht der Kriegstagung für Denkmalpflege Brüssel, 1915*.

19. Falke, "Die Einrichtung des Kunstschutzes," 13.

20. Tag für Denkmalpflege, *Dreizehnter Tag für Denkmalpflege*, 47.

21. Ibid., 44–45.

22. For the following, see ibid., 151–57.

23. Lurz, *Kriegerdenkmäler*, 3:5–6.

24. Ibid., 9, 17.

25. F. W. Bredt, "Geschichtliche Bauten und Kriegerehrung," *DP* 19, no. 2 (7 February 1917): 14–15; Lurz, *Kriegerdenkmäler*, 3:126.

26. For the following, see *Kölner Tageblatt*, 15 February 1917, from which this quote was taken; "Vermischtes," *DP* 19, no. 2 (7 February 1917): 15. The membership list is contained in HASK, Kulturangelegenheiten, 47–52, no. 105.

27. Lurz, *Kriegerdenkmäler*, 3:140.

28. Bodo Ebhardt, "Deutsche Burgen als Vorbilder," in *Das eiserne Buch: Die führenden Männer und Frauen zum Weltkrieg 1914/15*, ed. Georg Gellert (Hamburg, 1915), 204, as cited in Applegate, *Nation of Provincials*, 117.

29. Lurz, *Kriegerdenkmäler*, 3:82–83.

30. For the following, see von Reuter's address, "Der Umbau der Augustinerkirche in München," in Tag für Denkmalpflege, *Dreizehnter Tag für Denkmalpflege*, 137–51; for brief historical background on the church, see Beseler and Gutschow, *Kriegsschicksale Deutscher Architektur*, 2:1378; Schleich, *Die zweite Zerstörung Münchens*, 75.

31. Ad. Borggreve, "Über das Fremdwort im Bauwesen," *MRVDH* 10, no. 2 (1916): 264–69, esp. 268, 269.

32. G. Wolfram, "Nationalitätsgrenze und Bauart in Lothringen," *MRVDH* 9, no. 3 (1915): 159–64; Bär, "Zur hundertjährigen Zugehörigkeit der Rheinlande zu Preußen," *MRVDH* 9, no. 1 (1915): 7–10.

33. Tag für Denkmalpflege, *Dreizehnter Tag für Denkmalpflege*, 87, 88, 89, 112, 113.

34. Ibid., 47.

35. Ibid., 46. The congress chair returned to the metaphor in ibid., 82–83.

36. Ibid., 114.

37. Ibid. 39.

38. Ibid., 51, 61.

39. Werner Lindner, "Der Brunnen als Kriegsdenkmal," *MRVDH* 9, no. 2 (1915): 127–36.

40. Werner Lindner, "Denkmäler für unsere Krieger," *Flugschrift des Dürerbundes* 139 (1916): 7–8, as quoted in Lurz, *Kriegerdenkmäler*, 3:17–18.

41. Robert Hiecke made his remarks as a cospeaker for the general theme "Die Beschlagnahme der Metallgegenstände für Kriegszwecke und die Denkmalpflege," in Tag für Denkmalpflege, *Dreizehnter Tag für Denkmalpflege*, 163–64; Bredt, *Friedhof und Grabmal*, 4.

42. Grautoff, "Die Denkmalpflege im Urteil des Auslandes"; J. Knauth, "Die Verheerungen der französischen Revolution am Straßburger Münster," 223–29, here 223, and E. Renard, "Die Zerstörung der Kirchen St. Maximin u. St. Paulin bei Trier durch die Franzosen im Jahre 1674," 230–40, both in the thematic volume "Von Krieg und Kunst," *MRVDH* 8, no. 3 (1914).

43. Tag für Denkmalpflege, *Dreizehnter Tag für Denkmalpflege,* 50, 52, 54.

44. Uyttenhove, "Continuities in Belgian Wartime Reconstruction Planning," 48–51.

45. Tag für Denkmalpflege, *Dreizehnter Tag für Denkmalpflege,* 43–44, 45.

46. Ibid., 80.

47. Ibid., 21.

48. Karl Scheffler, "Kunstgespräche im Kriege," *Kunst und Künstler* 13 (1914–15): 147–48.

49. F. W. Bredt, foreword to "Von Krieg und Kunst," *MRVDH* 8, no. 3 (1914): 183; Tag für Denkmalpflege, *Dreizehnter Tag für Denkmalpflege,* 21.

50. J. Krüger, "Soldatengräber an der Westfront," *MRVDH* 9, no. 2 (1915): 67–79.

51. Rothes, *Kriegs-Gedächtniskirchen,* 3.

52. Wilhelm Waetzoldt, "Der Begriff des 'Barbarischen,'" *Kunst und Künstler* 13 (1914–15): 437–41.

53. Hermann Pflaume, "Die Gefahr der Metallbekleidungen," *MRVDH* 9, no. 3 (1915): 184.

54. Wilhelm Rolfs, *Soldatengräber und Einheitskreuz* (Munich, 1916), 14, as cited in Lurz, *Kriegerdenkmäler,* 3:57.

55. Tag für Denkmalpflege, *Dreizehnter Tag für Denkmalpflege,* 53.

56. Lurz, *Kriegerdenkmäler,* 3:91, 92, 159–60.

57. Published in the Berlin *Lokal-Anzeiger,* Bode's view was excerpted in "Chronik," *Kunst und Künstler* 13 (1914–15): 94; Heinrich Wagner, "Alte Straßen- und Ortsnamen," *DP* 17, no. 13 (20 October 1915): 102–5, here 102.

58. Werner Lindner, "Der Brunnen als Kriegsdenkmal," *MRVDH* 9, no. 2 (1915): 127–36, here 128.

59. F. W. Bredt, foreword to "Von Krieg und Kunst," *MRVDH* 8, no. 3 (1914): 183.

60. Ibid., 184; Rudolf Herzog's "Dome in Feindesland" is reprinted in "Von Krieg und Kunst," 208. The sales of *Friedhof und Grabmal* are discussed by Bredt in "Die 'Mitteilungen' und übrigen Veröffentlichungen des Rheinischen Vereins für Denkmalpflege und Heimatschutz, 1907–1916," *MRVDH* 10, no. 3 (1916): 327.

61. Auschuß zur Gründung des Reichsbundes für Heimatkunst, Bad Homburg vor der Höhe, May 1918, NWHSADü, RP Aachen, 16644. Among the candidates for the central committee were 9 artists and writers, 6 professors, 5 high-level officials, 3 businessmen, 2 teachers, 2 clergymen, and a woman with unspecified occupation.

62. Rundschreiben des Reichsbundes für Heimatkunst, May 1918, NWHSADü, RP Aachen, 16644.

63. Hans Much, "Heimatkultur," address at the founding meeting of the Reichsbund für Heimatkunst, 31 May 1918, NWHSADü, RP Aachen, 16644.

64. Lurz, *Kriegerdenkmäler,* 3:162–63; the Brandenburg series of postcards were discussed in *Heimatschutz-Chronik* 2 (1917): 7–8.

65. Witt, *Engere Heimat,* unpaginated. Originally published in 1883–84, the edition from which these quotes were taken was completed in October 1916 and published in 1917.

66. K. Sch., "Frankfurt A.M.," *Kunst und Künstler* 13 (1914–15): 479.

67. For the following, see B. Müller, "Die alte Mainbrücke in Frankfurt a.M.," *DP* 16, no. 10 (29 July 1914): 75. The author was a professor and museum director.

68. For the following, see *Heimatkunst und Denkmalpflege, gefördert vom Deutschen Hilfsbund für kriegsbeschädigte Bauhandwerker. Eine Ergänzung zur Kriegsbeschädigtenfürsorge im Baugewerbe auf dem Lande und in kleineren und mittleren Städten. Ein Vor-*

schlag von Prof. Herm. Schütte in Hildesheim (Geestemünde: Weserdruckerei, n.d.), as cited in "Ein deutsches Baumodellmuseum und die Anfertigung der Modelle durch kriegsbeschädigte Bauhandwerker," *Heimatschutz-Chronik* 2 (1917): 1–5. See also Lurz, *Kriegerdenkmäler,* 3:187.

69. "Ein deutsches Baumodellmuseum und die Anfertigung der Modelle durch kriegsbeschädigte Bauhandwerker," *Heimatschutz-Chronik* 2 (1917); Tag für Denkmalpflege, *Dreizehnter Tag für Denkmalpflege,* 216–30.

70. Tag für Denkmalpflege, *Dreizehnter Tag für Denkmalpflege,* 155, 191; on bells in *Faust,* see Berman, *All That Is Solid Melts into Air,* 44, 56, 69.

71. Dethlefsen, "Unsere neuen Glocken," *DP* 20, no. 2 (13 February 1918): 9–11. The author credited the Catholic Church with a finer sensibility for the ethical values rooted in appearances and ritual and thus more likely to understand the significance of choosing bronze bells.

72. Werner Lindner, "Der Brunnen als Kriegsdenkmal," *MRVDH* 9, no. 2 (1915): 128.

73. Rothes, *Kriegs-Gedächtniskirchen.*

74. Ibid., 13, 22, 29.

75. Lurz, *Kriegerdenkmäler,* 3:184–86.

76. Kampffmeyer, *Friedenstadt.* See also Lurz, *Kriegerdenkmäler,* 3:186–87.

77. Kampffmeyer, *Friedenstadt,* 43, 53.

78. Ibid., 63.

79. Ibid., 58–59.

Chapter 3

1. Tag für Denkmalpflege, *Dritte Gemeinsame Tagung für Denkmalpflege und Heimatschutz,* 100.

2. Ibid., 19, 21.

3. Ibid., 31–34. See also Speitkamp, "Das Erbe der Monarchie," 17.

4. For the following, see Michael Siegel, *Denkmalpflege als öffentliche Aufgabe,* 51–55.

5. "Der 25. Tag für Denkmalpflege und Heimatschutz zu Freiburg im Breisgau (20. bis 25. September 1925)," *DPHS* 10–12 (1925): 180–82, here 180–81.

6. Michael Siegel, *Denkmalpflege als öffentliche Aufgabe,* 49; Speitkamp, "Das Erbe der Monarchie," 17–18.

7. Grundmann, "Denkmale," 226; Michael Siegel, *Denkmalpflege als öffentliche Aufgabe,* 40.

8. Tag für Denkmalpflege, *Dritte Gemeinsame Tagung für Denkmalpflege und Heimatschutz,* 29, 31; Renard, "Die Denkmalpflege in der Rheinprovinz," 466.

9. Tag für Denkmalpflege, *Dritte Gemeinsame Tagung für Denkmalpflege und Heimatschutz,* 144–45.

10. Ibid., 107, 155–56.

11. Ibid., 168–69.

12. Ibid., 147–156; Rudolf Esterer, "Denkmalpflege an Bayerischen Residenzen und Schlössern nach der Zeit der Monarchie," *DP* 32, no. 3 (1930): 97–103; Speitkamp, "Das Erbe der Monarchie," 16–17.

13. Tag für Denkmalpflege, *Dritte Gemeinsame Tagung für Denkmalpflege und Heimatschutz,* 31; Franz Schollen, "Geleitwort," 1, and Joseph Busley, "Fünfundzwanzig Jahre Rheinischer Verein für Denkmalpflege und Heimatschutz," 68, both in *ZRVDH* 24, no. 2 (1931).

14. Michael Siegel, *Denkmalpflege als öffentliche Aufgabe*, 50.

15. Wilhelm Ambros, "Denkmalpflege in Krisenzeiten," *DP* 34, no. 1–2 (1932): 3–9, here 3.

16. Tag für Denkmalpflege, *Tag für Denkmalpflege und Heimatschutz, Köln*, esp. 171–83.

17. Paul Clemen, "Adolf von Oechelhaeuser," *DPHS* 1–3 (1923): 95–100; Clemen, "Eduard zur Nedden," *ZRVDH* 17, no. 2/3 (February 1925): 105–8; on Lemcke, see "Vermischtes," *DPHS* 1–3 (1925): 31–34; Gustav von Bezold, "Georg Dehio: Eine Würdigung seines Schaffens gelegentlich des Abschlusses seiner 'Geschichte der Deutschen Kunst,'" *DPHS* 1–3 (1926): 28–31, here 28.

18. See, for example, Joseph Busley, "Fünfundzwanzig Jahre Rheinischer Verein für Denkmalpflege und Heimatschutz," *ZRVDH* 24, no. 2 (1931): 39–76.

19. Renard, "Die Denkmalpflege in der Rheinprovinz," 468–70; "Verwaltungsbericht des Provinzialkonservators," *ZRVDH* 24, no. 3 [*Jahrbuch der Rheinischen Denkmalpflege* 7] (1931): 5–16, here 8–15.

20. Tag für Denkmalpflege, *Tag für Denkmalpflege und Heimatschutz, Würzburg und Nürnberg, 1928*, esp. 71–117.

21. O. E. Schweizer, "Die Nürnberger Altstadt im entstehenden Groß-Nürnberg," 57–60; Fritz Beblo, "Ein Münchener Beispiel neuzeitlicher Bauweise in der Altstadt," 60–62; Ernst May, "Altstadt und Neuzeit," 63; and Gessner, "Die Oberneustadt in Kassel als Baudenkmal," 64–69, all in *DPHS* 30, no. 8/9 (August/September 1928).

22. Joseph Busley, typed protocol of Bund Heimatschutz meeting, 10 April 1931, ALVR, 3787; Linse, "Die Entdeckung der technischen Denkmäler"; Speitkamp, *Verwaltung der Geschichte*, 171–86.

23. Renard, "Die Denkmalpflege in der Rheinprovinz," 466; on the states' cultural policies, see Speitkamp, "Das Erbe der Monarchie," 17–18.

24. "Verwaltungsbericht des Provinzialkonservators," *ZRVDH* 24, no. 3 [*Jahrbuch der Rheinischen Denkmalpflege* 7] (1931): 5–16; Johannes Horion, "Rheinischer Verein für Denkmalpflege und Heimatschutz und die Rheinische Provinzialverwaltung," *ZRVDH* 24, no. 2 (1931): 6; Wernher Witthaus, "Denkmalpflege," *Kölnische Zeitung*, 19 May 1932.

25. Typescript of protocol of Vorstands- und Vertreterversammlung des Deutschen Bundes Heimatschutz, Berlin, 10 April 1931, 2–3, 6, in ALVR, 3787.

26. Vorstands- und Vertreterversammlung des Deutschen Bundes Heimatschutz, Berlin, 10 April 1931, and Aufruf der Gesellschaft der Freunde des deutschen Heimatschutzes, May 1929, both in ALVR, 3787.

27. Zuhorn, "50 Jahre Deutscher Heimatschutz," 41.

28. Klemperer, *Germany's New Conservatism*, 76–91, 174; Lehnert and Megerle, *Politische Identität und nationale Gedenktage*, 57.

29. Lehnert and Megerle, *Politische Identität und nationale Gedenktage*, 143–44.

30. Kracauer, *From Caligari to Hitler*, 47–55, 115–19.

31. "Tagung für Denkmalpflege in Berlin," *DP* 21, no. 9 (23 July 1919): 70; Tag für Denkmalpflege, *Dritte gemeinsame Tagung für Denkmalpflege und Heimatschutz*, 21, 16.

32. Tag für Denkmalpflege, *Dritte gemeinsame Tagung für Denkmalpflege und Heimatschutz*, 63; Speitkamp, *Verwaltung der Geschichte*, 171–72.

33. Tag für Denkmalpflege, *Dritte gemeinsame Tagung für Denkmalpflege und Heimatschutz*, 15–16.

34. Ibid., 16.

35. Franz Graf Wolff Metternich, "Die Pflege der Bau- und Kunstdenkmale," in *Der Deutsche Heimatschutz: Ein Rückblick und Ausblick*, ed. Gesellschaft der Freunde des deutschen Heimatschutzes (Munich: Kastner and Callweg, 1930), 228, as cited in Speitkamp, "Denkmalpflege und Heimatschutz," 164; on "totalistic thinking [*Totalgedanke*]," see Busley's intervention in Sitzung des Denkmalrates, 22 December 1931, 3, in ALVR, 11096.

36. Dagobert Frey, "Zum Geleite," *DP* 32, no. 1–2 (1930): 1–2, here 2.

37. Tag für Denkmalpflege, *Tag für Denkmalpflege und Heimatschutz, Köln*, 154; Max Schlenker, "Wirtschaft, Denkmalpflege und Heimatschutz," *ZRVDH* 24, no. 2 (1931): 19–24, here 24.

38. Lane, *Architecture and Politics*, esp. 11–145.

39. Ibid., 119–23; Pommer and Otto, *Weissenhof 1927*.

40. For background on the critics, see Lane, *Architecture and Politics*, chap. 5; on Kochenhof, see "Die Kochenhofsiedlung in Stuttgart: Bauaustellung deutsches Holz für Hausbau und Wohnung," *Monatshefte für Baukunst und Städtebau* 17 (1933): 481–512, here 481, and Lane, *Architecture and Politics*, 210; for "tact," see Tag für Denkmalpflege, *Tag für Denkmalpflege und Heimatschutz, Würzburg und Nürnberg, 1928*, comments by Ernst May, 79, 84, and by Werner Lindner and Paul Clemen, 263–64.

41. "Zwei Beiträge zur Denkmalpflege," *Düsseldorfer Nachrichten*, 16 September 1930; Klapheck, *Neue Baukunst in den Rheinlanden*, 203.

42. Gustav Lampmann, "Vom Heimatschutz zur Heimatpflege: Eine Stellungnahme der Schriftleitung," *DP* 32, no. 1–2 (1930): 50–53, here 52.

43. Tag für Denkmalpflege, *Tag für Denkmalpflege und Heimatschutz, Würzburg und Nürnberg, 1928*, 99–117.

44. Bericht über eine vertrauliche Vorbesprechung des Ausschusses des Denkmalrates, Bonn, 9 January 1928, as well as Bericht über die Sitzung des Denkmalrates, 3 March 1928, both in ALVR, 11096; Hans Pieper, "Die Barlach-Figuren für die Katharinen-Kirche zu Lübeck," *DP* 33, no. 1 (1931): 84–88; R. W. Schmidt, "Der Brand des alten Schlosses in Stuttgart," *DP* 34, no. 1–2 (1932): 40–45; R. W. Schmidt, "Der Wettbewerb zum Wiederaufbau des alten Schlosses in Stuttgart," *DP* 35, no. 1–2 (1935): 51–57.

45. Wilhelm Ambros, "Denkmalpflege in Krisenzeiten," *DP* 34, no. 1–2 (1932): 5.

46. Tag für Denkmalpflege, *Dritte Gemeinsame Tagung für Denkmalpflege und Heimatschutz*, 63, 64.

47. Ibid., 171, 172.

48. An annual conference was planned for Kassel in 1932 but was postponed until the following year.

49. For the cathedral's symbolic importance to the French departure, see "Mitternachtfeier am Kölner Dom," *Kölnische Zeitung*, 1 February 1926; for the RVDH volume, see "Der Kölner Dom in Gefahr," *ZRVDH* 19, no. 3 (1928).

50. J. Sauer, "Der deutsche Dom am Rhein," *Kölnische Volkszeitung*, 26 September 1930.

51. Franz Schollen, "Der Kölner Dom in Gefahr!," *ZRVDH* 19, no. 3 (1928): v.

52. Borger and Zehnder, *Köln*, 302–3.

53. Karl Jatho, "Unstern über dem Kölner Dom," *Düsseldorfer Nachrichten*, 16 October 1930.

54. Dagobert Frey, "Tag für Denkmalpflege und Heimatschutz, 16.–19. September 1930," *DP* 32, no. 6 (1930): 287–91, here 287, 291.

55. "Ergebnis der Beratung vom 9. Dezember 1930 über die Probleme der Denkmalpflege am Kölner Dom," ALVR 11041; for the printed report of the meeting, see Tag für Denkmalpflege, *Tag für Denkmalpflege und Heimatschutz, Köln,* 239–43.

56. Erich Mendelsohn, "Warum diese Architektur?," *Die literarische Welt* 4, no. 10 (9 March 1928): 1, as reprinted in Kaes, Jay, and Dimendberg, *Weimar Republic Sourcebook,* 451–53, here 452.

57. Tzara is quoted in Lewis, *Politics of Surrealism,* 5; for Grosz, see Tower, *Envisioning America,* 65.

58. Michael Siegel one-sidedly places Taut in the camp that saw preservation as irretrievably reactionary; see *Denkmalpflege als öffentliche Aufgabe,* 49; on Taut and Gurlitt, see Lane, *Architecture and Politics,* 233, n. 19; on Taut's expansive view of modernism's impact on interior design culture, see Zöller-Stock, "Bruno Taut."

59. Taut, "Nieder der Seriosismus!," in *1920–1922, Frühlicht,* 11, as cited in Lane, *Architecture and Politics,* 46.

60. Miljutenko, "Wir dürfen nicht geschichtslos werden," 23.

61. Taut, *1920–1922, Frühlicht,* 23. At this time Taut's *Frühlicht* still appeared as part of *Stadtbaukunst alter und neuer Zeit.*

62. Whyte, *Bruno Taut and the Architecture of Activism,* 31.

63. Taut, *1920–1922, Frühlicht,* 101–2.

64. Keitz, "Anfänge des modernen Massentourismus," 182–89; MacCannell, *The Tourist,* 49–50.

65. Upmann and Rennspieß, "Organisationsgeschichte der deutschen Naturfreundebewegung," 69–71; Spode, " 'Der deutsche Arbeiter reist,' " 285–86.

66. *Hessische Naturfreundezeitschrift* 6 (1932): 40, as cited in Buchsteiner, "Arbeiter und Tourismus," 45; second quote is from *Arbeiter-Wander-Reiseführer* (Berlin: Dietz-Verlag, 1932), 9, as cited in Buchsteiner, "Arbeiter und Tourismus," 46.

67. Buzard, *Beaten Track,* esp. chap. 2.

68. Benjamin, "Moscow," 126.

69. Benjamin, "Theses on the Philosophy of History," 255, 256. The theses were not published until 1950.

70. Benjamin, "Berlin Chronicle," 27; Benjamin, *Moscow Diary,* 25.

71. Preußischer Landtag, 81. Sitzung, 10 December 1921, 5708, and 182. Sitzung, 21 November 1922, 13221–26; *Beilage zum Volkswillen,* 23 February 1930, as cited in Jung and Birkefeld, " 'Großes Aufräumen,' " 62.

72. "J," "Geschehenes und Noch-zu-verhütendes," *Düsseldorfer Nachrichten,* 23 September 1930. On the architectural history of the Kartäuser Church, see Beseler and Gutschow, *Kriegsschicksale Deutscher Architektur,* 1:540.

73. Wernher Witthaus, "Gedanken zum Denkmalpflegetag," *Kölnische Zeitung,* 25 September 1930.

74. Karl Jatho, "Unstern über dem Kölner Dom," *Düsseldorfer Nachrichten,* 16 October 1930; Paul Holtermann, "Das Kölner Dombaufest 1880 und die Katholiken," *Kölnische Volkszeitung,* 17 October 1930.

75. Willy Oeser, "Im Brennspiegel: Der Kampf um die badischen Schlösser," *Kölnische Volkszeitung,* 2 May 1931; for the critics, see "Schutz vor Denkmalschutz!," *Kölnische Zeitung,* 11 February 1931.

76. Behrenbeck, "Heldenkult oder Friedensmahnung?"; Lurz, *Kriegerdenkmäler,* 4:221, 281.

77. Lurz, *Kriegerdenkmäler,* 4:51–52, 93–94. The use of this building as a war monu-

ment aroused controversy in the early 1990s when the Federal Republic, using a 1937 Käthe Kollwitz figure, transformed it into a national monument commemorating all victims of the war. This gesture erased significant differences between the victims and excluded Jews by using Christian motifs of mourning and redemption. See Koselleck, "Allemagne," and Reichel, *Politik mit der Erinnerung*, 231–46.

78. B[urkhard] M[eier], "Die Neue Wache in Berlin," *DP* 33, no. 4 (1931): 157–58, here 158.

79. Bericht der Sitzung des Denkmälerrates, Düsseldorf, 4 January 1932, ALVR 11096.

80. On youth hostels, see the figures cited in Spode, " 'Der deutsche Arbeiter reist,' " 285, n. 17.

81. Boockmann, "Marienburg," 147–53; Dr. Kickton, "Die Marienburg," *DP* 24, no. 4 (3 May 1922): 25–31.

82. Reichel, *Der schöne Schein*, 124–26.

83. Bodo Ebhardt to Landeshauptmann, Düsseldorf, 17 October 1927, ALVR, 11109.

84. See the announcement and itinerary, "Burgenfahrt 1928 an den Niederrhein und durch die Eifel," as well as the list of participants, both in ALVR, 11109.

85. See Bodo Ebhardt to Landeshauptmann, 17 October 1927, as well as the itinerary, both in ALVR, 11109.

86. For the following, see Ebhardt to Landeshauptmann, 17 October 1927, and Renard to Joseph Busley, Landeshaus, Düsseldorf, 22 March 1928, both in ALVR, 11109.

87. Weyers and Köck, *Die Eroberung der Welt*, 13, 109.

88. Ibid., 58.

89. See, for example, Max Berg, "Hochhäuser im Stadtbild," *Wasmuths Monatshefte für Baukunst* 6, no. 4/5 (1922): 101–20.

90. "Die Tätigkeit des Eifelvereins," *Kölnische Zeitung*, 5 June 1928; "Die Hauptversammlung des Eifelvereins in Bitburg," *Kölnische Volkszeitung*, 2 June 1931.

91. *Jahrtausend-Feier Markt Rohr*, 27–33.

92. Ibid., 3.

93. For the following, see ibid., 12–14.

94. Ibid., 53.

Chapter 4

1. Rosenberg, *Der Mythus des 20. Jahrhunderts*, 450.

2. Herf, *Reactionary Modernism*.

3. Ditt, *Raum und Volkstum*, 18; Goebbels is cited by Bracher, *German Dictatorship*, 262.

4. "Das Leistungsprinzip in der Kunst," *Kölnische Zeitung*, 16 November 1933; Goebbels's speech is cited in Lane, *Architecture and Politics*, 176.

5. Benjamin, "Work of Art in the Age of Mechanical Reproduction," 236.

6. Rössler, "Applied Geography and Area Research in Nazi Society"; Rössler and Schleiermacher, "Der 'Generalplan Ost' und die 'Modernität' der Großraumordnung," 7–11.

7. Petsch, *Baukunst und Stadtplanung*, 82, 199; Hitler, *Mein Kampf*, 264; Feder, *Die neue Stadt*, 111.

8. On historicist architects, see Lane, *Architecture and Politics*, 215; on street names, see Burkhard Meier, "Zur Umbenennung historischer Strassennamen"; on the autobahns, see Reufert, "Straßen machen Geschichte," *Westdeutscher Beobachter*, 6 July 1940.

9. Petsch, *Baukunst und Stadtplanung*, 87–89; Lurz, *Kriegerdenkmäler*, 5:139–40; on sense in the urban fabric, see Lynch, *Good City Form*, esp. chap. 8.

10. Feder, *Die neue Stadt*, 10.

11. Dirk Schubert, "Gottfried Feder," 210–11.

12. Bültemann, *Architektur für das Dritte Reich*, 30–45; Lane, *Architecture and Politics*, 147–216; Petsch, *Baukunst und Stadtplanung*, 19–21, 187–92.

13. Petsch, *Baukunst und Stadtplanung*, 96–99.

14. Schleich, *Die zweite Zerstörung Münchens*, 10–17.

15. See Baird, *To Die for Germany*.

16. Lurz, *Kriegerdenkmäler*, 5:126, 136, 306, 308–33; Petropoulos, *Art as Politics*, 213; Werner Flechsig, "Der Braunschweigische Staatsdom mit der Gruft Heinrich des Löwen," *KDR* 3, Folge 11, Ausg. A (November 1939): 358–65; Burleigh, *Germany Turns Eastwards*, 194; Engelbrechten and Volz, *Wir wandern durch das nationalsozialistische Berlin*, 49, 210.

17. For the term "negative Denkmalpflege," see Michael Siegel, *Denkmalpflege als öffentliche Aufgabe*, 56.

18. Grossert, "Nachdenken über meine Stadt," 67.

19. Burkhard Meier, "Zur Umbenennung historischer Strassennamen"; Karwelat, "Neutempelhof," 29–34.

20. Burleigh, *Germany Turns Eastwards*, 195–97; Jankowski, "Warsaw," 77–80.

21. See Joseph Tiedemann, "Das Reichstagsgebäude zu Berlin," *Beilage zum "Baumeister"* 31, no. 6 (June 1933): B77–78.

22. Reichel, *Politik mit der Erinnerung*, 202–6.

23. See Petz, *Stadtsanierung im Dritten Reich*, 97, 123; Durth and Gutschow, *Träume in Trümmern*, 1:237–39. For an example from the occupied territories, see Gutschow, "Stadtplanung im Warthegau."

24. Petz, *Stadtsanierung im Dritten Reich*, 7–14.

25. See, for example, Jung and Birkefeld, " 'Großes Aufräumen,' " 61–62.

26. On the *Altstadt* as *Lebensraum*, see unsigned article "Altstadtgesundung und Altstadterhaltung," *Beilage zum "Baumeister"* 10 (October 1936): 210; Peter Schmidt, "Aachen; eine entfesselte Stadt," *Westdeutsche Beobachter*, 19 May 1941.

27. Petz, *Stadtsanierung im Dritten Reich*, 37, 39, 31; Schlungbaum-Stehr, "Altstadtsanierung und Denkmalpflege in den 30er Jahren," 86. The German building official in Łódź is quoted in Gutschow, "Stadtplanung im Warthegau," 240.

28. Petsch, *Baukunst und Stadtplanung*, 192–95.

29. Petz, *Stadtsanierung im Dritten Reich*, 21, 39–46.

30. From Hitler's speech at the Technische Hochschule Berlin, 1937, as cited in Petsch, *Baukunst und Stadtplanung*, 98. On the difference between Speer and Hitler, see Speer, *Spandauer Tagebücher*, 166–67.

31. Alfons Pacquet, "Die Frankfurter Altstadt—Abbau oder Sicherung?," *Beilage zum "Baumeister"* 10 (October 1936): 205–12, here 205.

32. Dr. Janssen, "Die neue Friedhofsordnung für den Regierungsbezirk Koblenz," *Rheinische Heimatpflege* 6, no. 3/4 (1934): 358.

33. Hitler, *Mein Kampf*, 19; Bültemann, *Architektur für das Dritte Reich*, 36.

34. Hitler, *Mein Kampf*, 265.

35. Ruland, "Kleine Chronik des Rheinischen Vereins," 28–34; Burkhard Meier, "Der Denkmalpflegetag in Kassel," 197; "Denkmalpflege und Denkmalschutz in der Rheinprovinz," *National Zeitung*, 20 June 1937; Alexander Heilmeyer, "Neue Wege der Denk-

malpflege," *Die Kunst im Deutschen Reich* 3, Folge 10, Ausg. A (Oktober 1939): iii–iv; Peter Schmidt, "Aachen; eine entfesselte Stadt," *Westdeutsche Beobachter*, 19 May 1941.

36. Bentmann, "Der Kampf um die Erinnerung," 213.

37. See the unsigned report on the conference to provincial officials, 23 October 1933, ALVR, 11041. See also Burkhard Meier, "Der Denkmalpflegetag in Kassel." On the RVH festival, see Durth and Gutschow, *Träume in Trümmern*, 1:239.

38. For background, see Ditt, *Raum und Volkstum*, 210–15; on the Reichsbund's goals and organization, see *Mitteilungsblatt für den Reichsbund Volkstum und Heimat* 1 (Oktober 1933): esp. 2–4; on conflicts with party organs, see Rosenberg to Heß, 2 October 1934, *APKNS*, pt. 1, vol. 2, frames 12600814–15; for the RVDH, see Hans Kornfeld, "Der Rheinische Verein für Denkmalpflege und Heimatschutz und seine neuen Aufgaben," typescript, February 1937, ALVR, 11145.

39. Karl Einhorn, Burkhard Meier, and Konrad Nonn, "Die Denkmalpflege im Volksleben," *DKD* 36 (1934): 1; Clemen, *Der Dom zu Köln*, vii, ix.

40. "Denkmalpflege," *Meyers Lexicon*, col. 918.

41. Heinrich Höhn, "Umgestaltungen in der Altstadt von Nürnberg," *DKD* 36 (1934): 73–77, here 73; Michael Siegel, *Denkmalpflege als öffentliche Aufgabe*, 57–58; Beseler and Gutschow, *Kriegsschicksale Deutscher Architektur*, 1:231; Föhl, *Bauten der Industrie und Technik*, 34; Karl Wulzinger, "Die Badische Denkmalpflege," *DKD* 41 (1939): 52.

42. See Tag für Denkmalpflege, *Tag für Denkmalpflege und Heimatschutz, Dresden*, 85.

43. "Heimatmuseen," 299.

44. Provinzialverwaltung to Regierungspräsident, Düsseldorf, 10 November 1938, NWHSADü, Regierung Düsseldorf, 56235.

45. Michael Siegel, *Denkmalpflege als öffentliche Aufgabe*, 58–59.

46. Tag für Denkmalpflege, *Tag für Denkmalpflege und Heimatschutz, Dresden*, 1.

47. For the following, see ibid., 125–39.

48. Ibid., 139.

49. H. K. Zimmermann, "Gewinn und Verlust der Neuzeit in einer deutschen Altstadt," *DKD* 40 (1938): 177–201, here 177.

50. For Apffelstaedt's designation as a "political soldier of the Führer," see Burkhard Meier, "Der Denkmalpflegetag in Kassel," 197; the quote is from the typescript of the speech "Volk und Heimat," 10, in ALVR, 11041.

51. Paul Ortwin Rave, "Sanssouci," *DKD*, 36 (1934): 49–57, here 49.

52. Apffelstaedt, "Volk und Heimat," 10, ALVR 11041.

53. Durth and Gutschow, *Träume in Trümmern*, 1:240.

54. Cited in Ditt, *Raum und Volkstum*, 225–26.

55. Kier, "Glanz und Elend," 255, and n. 20, 263, where the author quotes Vogts's 1938 use of the term *"wertvollen Volksgenossen"* without noting that this example illustrates how widespread racial thinking was even among preservationists who wanted nothing to do with politics. On changes in property ownership, see Schlungbaum-Stehr, "Altstadtsanierung und Denkmalpflege in den 30er Jahren," 85–86.

56. Kier, "Glanz und Elend," 250; Hans Vogts, "Gesundungsmassnahmen im Kölner Rheinviertel," *DKD* 38 (1936): 298–303, here 303.

57. Lill, "Vorwort," v.

58. Geisberg, *Die Stadt Münster*.

59. Kier, "Glanz und Elend," 254.

60. Ibid., 254, 255.

61. "Heimatmuseen," 300.

62. Provinzialverwaltung to Regierungspräsident, Düsseldorf, 10 November 1938, NWHSADü, Regierung Düsseldorf, 56235.

63. Hermann Grom-Rottmayer, "Neue Beleuchtungsanlagen in der Wiener Universitätskirche," *DKD* 40 (1938): 210–14; Wildemann, office of Provincial Conservator of Rhineland, to RP Aachen, 16 January 1941, NWHSADü, Regierung Aachen, 16819.

64. See Hosmer, "Broadening View of the Historical Preservation Movement," 127–28, 129, 132.

65. Hans Tietze, "Die Wiederherstellung von Williamsburg, Virg., U.S.A.," *DKD* 38 (1936): 100–104.

66. The anecdote is recounted by Frankfurt architect Theodor Derlam, "Aus dem Leben des letzten Frankfurter Altstadt-Baumeisters," 2 vols. (unpublished manuscript, 1955), 83, as cited in Durth and Gutschow, *Träume in Trümmern*, 2:469.

67. Koshar, "Altar, Stage, and City," esp. 45–49.

68. Nietzsche, "On the Uses and Disadvantages of History for Life," 79, 83.

69. On preservation as the "art of the single case," see Rudolf Pfister's book review of Hans Hoermann, *Methodik der Denkmalpflege* (Munich, 1938), in *DKD* 40 (1938): 109; for Dagobert Frey's remark, see his "Der Denkmalpfleger: Robert Hiecke zum sechzigsten Geburtstage," *DKD* 38 (1936): 296–97, here 296.

70. Lakoff and Johnson, *Metaphors We Live By*, 9.

71. Shirer, *Berlin Diary*, 18.

72. Lurz, *Kriegerdenkmäler*, 5:136–38.

73. On *Triumph of the Will*, see Kracauer, *From Caligari to Hitler*, 301–2; on *Die Fahne*, see Werner Rittich, "Malerei im Haus der Deutschen Kunst," *KDR*, 6, Folge 11, Ausg. B (November 1942): 270 for the quote and 267 for the painting.

74. "Von Schlageter-Gedenken zur Hitler-Tat," *Volksparole* 29 (May 1933).

75. For one such primer, see Schumacher, *Deutschland-Fibel*, 95–8, here 95; on the *Heimat* museums, see Provinzialverwaltung to RP Düsseldorf, 10 November 1938, and RP to Oberpräsident of Rhine province, 5 July 1939, both in NWHSADü, Regierung Düsseldorf, 56235.

76. Stephenson, "Widerstand gegen soziale Modernisierung," 108–10.

77. An example of the traditional concerns of Nazi-inspired preservation can be found in Alexander Heilmeyer, "Neue Wege der Denkmalpflege," *KDR* 3, Folge 10, Ausgabe A (October 1939): iii–iv, which deals with a Bavarian press tour of castles and fortresses; for Nazi tourism, see Reichel, *Der schöne Schein*, 243–54; on the popularity of the Cologne inventory, see Clemen, *Der Dom zu Köln*, vii, ix; for aerial views of famous landmarks, see *Deutsches Land in 111 Flugaufnahmen*; and for the Drachenfels, see "Der Drachenfels wird umgestaltet," *Rheinische Landeszeitung*, 18 September 1936.

78. Projektgruppe "Heimatkunde des Nationalsozialismus," *Nationalsozialismus im Landkreis Tübingen*, 156; the ordinance on street names is quoted in Burkhard Meier, "Zur Umbenennung historischer Strassennamen," 231; "Das ist nationaler Kitsch," *Düsseldorfer Nachrichten*, 30 May 1933; "Gegen die Kitschplage: Eine Ausstellung in Köln," *Düsseldorfer Nachrichten*, 22 June 1933.

79. On Rhenish *Heimat* associations, see "Zusammenstellung der Heimatvereine," Oberpräsident, Verwaltung des Provinzialverbandes, Düsseldorf, 1938, ALVR, 11254.

80. On Düsseldorf, see Heimatverein "Alde Düsseldorfer," Rundbrief, 1 September 1941, SADü, XX 492.

81. For the following, see "Die Lage des Eifelvereins," *Kölnische Zeitung*, 13 June 1933; "Mitteilungsblatt des Eifelvereins" 1/44 (3 January 1944), typescript in ALVR, 11169.

82. Vorsitzender, Eifelverein, to Parteiamtliche Prüfungskommission der NSDAP, 23 March 1937, ALVR, 11169.

83. Cited in Projektgruppe "Heimatkunde des Nationalsozialismus," *Nationalsozialismus im Landkreis Tübingen*, 126; Hans Hörmann, "Das Hilfswerk 'Alt-Rothenburg,'" *DKD* 41 (1939): 18–20, here 20.

84. Ditt, *Raum und Volkstum*, 222–25.

85. Ibid., 225–30.

86. Metternich to RP Aachen, 11 December 1936, and Metternich to RP Aachen, 14 February 1936, both in NWHSADü, RP Aachen, 16819.

87. Scheffler, "Deutsches Land und Deutsche Menschen," 8.

88. Dagobert Frey, "Kunstdenkmäler im besetzten Polen," *DKD* 41 (1939): 98–103, here 98; H. Keuth, "Aufgaben der Denkmalpflege in Lothringen," *DKD* 43 (1942/43): 101–7, here 101.

89. Dagobert Frey, "Kunstdenkmäler im besetzten Polen," *DKD* 41 (1939): 98–103.

90. On Frey, see Nicholas, *Rape of Europa*, 75; on the Baltic, see Niels von Holst, "Denkmalpflege in den Baltischen Landen," *DKD* 43 (1942/43): 1–7.

91. For the following, see Franz Graf Wolff Metternich, "Der Kriegskunstschutz in den besetzten Gebieten Frankreichs und in Belgien: Organisation und Aufgaben," *DKD* 43 (1942/43): 26–35; Günther-Hornig, *Kunstschutz in den von Deutschland besetzten Gebieten*.

92. Kracauer, *From Caligari to Hitler*, 284–85, 287–88.

93. Nicholas, *Rape of Europa*, 119–45; Petropoulos, *Art as Politics*, 129–30.

94. Günther Grundmann, "Die Bedeutung Schinkels für die deutsche Denkmalpflege," *DKD* 42 (1940/41): 122–29, here 122, 123.

95. Durth and Gutschow, *Träume in Trümmern*, 1:244–45. Bahn's comments appeared in his "Um die alte Heimat," *Hamburger Anzeiger*, 7 February 1944.

96. Wentzel, "Die deutschen Glasmalereien von historischem Wert," 67–78.

97. Adenauer, "Heiteres und Besinnliches aus ernster Zeit," 45–49; Durth and Gutschow, *Träume in Trümmern*, 1:57, 243–47; P. J. Bauwers, "Werden und Wirken der Gesellschaft," *Mitteilungsblatt der Gesellschaft der Freunde des Wiederaufbaues der Stadt Köln*, December 1947, unpaginated.

98. Hans Bahn, "Die denkmalpflegerische Lage in Hamburg 1943, Ein Überblick und ein Ausblick," *DKD* 44 (1944): 28–35; for the quotes, 29, 35.

99. See, for instance, Kinder, "Die Generalbebauungspläne 1941 und 1944," 26–27. See also Dähn, "Die Zerstörung Hamburgs," 28. The postwar situation is covered by Ostermeyer, "Der Generalbebauungsplan, 1947," and Sill and Strohmeyer, "Der Aufbauplan von 1950." For the problem of continuity in German town planning, see Diefendorf, *In the Wake of War*, chaps. 6 and 7; Durth and Gutschow, *Träume in Trümmern*, 1:59, 162–63, 172–73, 193–96, 218, 237.

100. H. Schuster, "Die Herstellung der Glocke," *DKD* 44 (1944): 17.

101. Boberach, *Berichte des SD und der Gestapo*, 433–34, 614–15, 618, 627, 839; Lurz, *Kriegerdenkmäler*, 5:107.

102. Andreas-Friedrich, *Battleground Berlin*, 6; on the air-raid communities, see Kussmann, "Sieben Wochen in der Front," 17; on revelers and prostitutes among the ruins, see the memoir literature discussed in Schäfer, *Das gespaltene Bewußtsein*, 139–40.

103. On Lübeck, see Robert Hiecke, "Erich Blunck Post Festum zum 70. Geburtstag," *DKD* 43 (1942/43): 23, and "Zur Geschichte des Bombenangriffs auf Lübeck," 18–19; for the SA official Haake's comment, see typescript of his speech for the exhibit "Der Rhein und das Reich," Braunschweig, 18 October 1942, ALVR 12720.

104. Alvensleben, *Lauter Abschiede*, 8; Boberach, *Berichte des SD und der Gestapo*, 887–88, 892–93.

105. Boberach, *Berichte des SD und der Gestapo*, 813.

106. For two of many examples, see ibid., 777, 883.

107. Heimatverein "Alde Düsseldorfer," Rundbrief, 31 December 1943, for the call for solidarity, and Rundbrief, November 1942, for the description of the loss of the club meeting place, both in SADü, XX 492.

108. On Goebbels, see Schäfer, *Das gespaltene Bewußtsein*, 132. The statement on ruins as a deposit for the future was made by Haake in an 18 October 1942 speech for the opening of "Der Rhein und das Reich," a cultural exhibit held in Braunschweig; see the text of the address in ALVR 12720. For Hitler, see Speer, *Spandauer Tagebücher*, 309.

109. Speer, *Spandauer Tagebücher*, 309; Heimatverein "Alde Düsseldorfer," Rundbrief, November 1942, SADü, XX 492.

110. See Herbert, "Good Times, Bad Times," esp. 101–10.

Chapter 5

1. Hermand, *Kultur im Wiederaufbau*, 42.

2. Fulbrook, *Divided Nation*, 163, 176.

3. Just, *The Translator*, 131.

4. Günter Grass, *Kopfgeburten, oder Die Deutschen sterben aus* (Darmstadt, 1980), 23, as cited in Bullivant, "Continuity or Change?," 205.

5. Schwarz, "Modernisierung oder Restauration?," 280; see also Kleßmann, *Die doppelte Staatsgründung*, 63.

6. Beyme, *Der Wiederaufbau*, 37; Durth and Gutschow, *Träume in Trümmern*, 1:285; the letter from Langhoff was published in the *St. Galler Tageblatt* and the U.S.-controlled *Neue Zeitung* in 1946 and reprinted in Glaser, "So viel Anfang war nie," 9; Becher, "Für ein Deutschland," 33.

7. For these points, see Beyme, "Reconstruction in the German Democratic Republic," esp. 190–91.

8. Jansen, "Wohnungspolitik," esp. 18–21; Pike, *Politics of Culture in Soviet-Occupied Germany*.

9. See Diefendorf, *Rebuilding Europe's Bombed Cities*, for numerous examples.

10. Sill and Strohmeyer, "Der Aufbauplan von 1950," 51.

11. Zander, "Städtebaulicher Denkmalschutz," 80.

12. Beyme, "Reconstruction in the German Democratic Republic," 193.

13. Diefendorf, *In the Wake of War*, 69.

14. Huse, *Denkmalpflege*, 188; Bachmann, "Land Sachsen," 119–26.

15. Kleßmann, *Die doppelte Staatsgründung*, 59–63; Kershaw, *Popular Opinion and Political Dissent*, 159–79, 334–57.

16. Reichel, *Politik mit der Erinnerung*, 188; Haspel, "Zwischen Kronprinzenpalais und Stalinallee," 45; Zuchold, "Abriss der Ruinen." The Dresden story is told by Wolfgang Mischnick, a young member of the Dresden Liberal Democrats and later Free Democratic politician in Bonn in *Von Dresden nach Bonn*, 265–66.

17. Fischer, "Denkmalpflege zwischen Verdrängung und Trauerarbeit," 41–44; on churches, see Nerdinger, "Einführung in die Ausstellung," 196; on Munich, see Schleich, *Die zweite Zerstörung Münchens*, 21–22; on the general issue of architectural traces of Nazism, see Reichel, *Politik mit der Erinnerung*.

18. Noelle and Neumann, *Jahrbuch der öffentlichen Meinung, 1947–1955*, 125; Niethammer, *"Die Jahre weiß man nicht,"* 1:92.

19. De Gaulle quoted by Rousso, *Vichy Syndrome*, 27; for Adenauer, see Gesellschaft für christliche Kultur, "Kirchen in Trümmern," 115, where the future chancellor is paraphrased by participants; for Adenauer's ambivalence, see Schwarz, *Adenauer*, 554–55.

20. Durth and Gutschow, *Träume in Trümmern*, 2:479–85; Reichel, *Politik mit der Erinnerung*, 72; Meinecke, *Die deutsche Katastrophe*; Kulturbund, *Um Deutschlands neue Kultur*, esp. 29–30; for the postage stamps, see *Michel Deutschland-Spezial*, 603.

21. See Schulte-Wülwer, "Gedenkstätten," 227–29.

22. For the following, see Dietzfelbinger, "Reichsparteitagsgelände Nürnberg," 69, 73, n. 14; Reichel, *Politik mit der Erinnerung*, 52–59.

23. Diefendorf, *In the Wake of War*, 74, 75; Strauß, "Denkmalpflege in der Ostzone"; Stark, "Das Berliner Ensemble 'Unter den Linden,' " 82.

24. On the conservator as defense lawyer, see Oskar Karpa, "Wiederaufbau des Marktplatzes zu Hildesheim," *DKD* 11 (1953): 16; Hans Reuther, "Oskar Karpa," *DKD* 21 (1963): 98–99.

25. P. J. Bauwers, "Werden und Wirken der Gesellschaft," *Mitteilungsblatt der Gesellschaft der Freunde des Wiederaufbaues der Stadt Köln*, December 1947, unpaginated.

26. Beseler, "Baudenkmale," xiv, where Lill is cited; Huse, *Denkmalpflege*, 191; Durth and Gutschow, *Träume in Trümmern*, 1:258–59; Stark, "Das Berliner Ensemble 'Unter den Linden,' " esp. 82–85; Diefendorf, *In the Wake of War*, 77, 84–87; Seydewitz, *Die unbesiegbare Stadt*, 42–46.

27. Beseler, "Baudenkmale," xiv; for Hannover, see Diefendorf, *In the Wake of War*, 78; for the East, see Hans Berger, "Tendenzen der Denkmalpflege," 4.

28. Rave to Kultusminister, Düsseldorf, 6 January 1947, and Denkmal- und Museumsrat Nordwestdeutschland, "Grundsätze der Denkmalpflege beim Wiederaufbau alter Städte," n.d. [ca. 1947], unpaginated, both in NWHSADü, NW 60, 595; Durth and Gutschow, *Träume in Trümmern*, 1:257; Günter, "Schutz historischer Industrieanlagen," 137.

29. Hermand, *Kultur im Wiederaufbau*, 277–79.

30. Hans Berger, "Tendenzen der Denkmalpflege," 4.

31. For the West German statement, see the protest against the planned demolition of the Stuttgart "New Castle" in "Resolution der Landesdenkmalpfleger zum beabsichtigten Abbruch des Neuen Schlosses zu Stuttgart," *DKD* 12 (1954): 78; for the East, see Seydewitz, *Zerstörung und Wiederaufbau von Dresden*, 11.

32. Zimmermann, "Wiederaufbau des Frankfurter Goethehauses?," 51–54, with addendum by Lill, 54.

33. Huse, *Denkmalpflege*, 193.

34. Diefendorf, *In the Wake of War*, 69, 75, 79.

35. Beseler and Gutschow, *Kriegsschicksale Deutscher Architektur*, 1:v; on the DDR, see Eckardt, *Schicksale deutscher Baudenkmale*; on the Rhineland, see Bader, *Berichte über die Tätigkeit der Denkmalpflege*.

36. Wentzel, "Die deutschen Glasmalereien von historischem Wert," 68, 70; Rave, "Westfalen," 96; on the Wewelsburg under Nazism, see Hüser, *Wewelsburg*; Strauß, "Denkmalpflege in der Ostzone," 85.

37. On the Rhineland, see Beseler, "Kriegsschäden und Wiederaufbau," 59–61; for the national estimate, see Beseler and Gutschow, *Kriegsschicksale Deutscher Architektur,* 1:xii.

38. Schulte-Wülwer, "Gedenkstätten," 228.

39. Zuhorn, "50 Jahre Deutscher Heimatschutz," 55; DHB and Arbeitsgemeinschaft westdeutscher Heimatbünde, Report, Düsseldorf, 24 November 1952, NWHSADü, NW 60, 1661; for shop owners, see Oberstadtdirektor of Krefeld to Cultural Ministry, 21 December 1949, NWHSADü, NW 60, 596.

40. Doppelfeld, "Grabung in der Kirche St. Ursula zu Köln," 65–69; "Berichte der ehemaligen Arbeitsstellen des Instituts für Denkmalpflege der DDR," *DKD* 49 (1991): 20.

41. Wilhelm Neuß, "Einführung," 8; Frenken, "Die Hauptpfarrkirche St. Remigius," 35. On war damage to the two churches, see Beseler and Gutschow, *Kriegsschicksale Deutscher Architektur,* 1:675–76, 726–27.

42. Grundmann, "Zehnjahresbericht über die Tätigkeit," 52; Michael Siegel, *Denkmalpflege als öffentliche Aufgabe,* 66; Diefendorf, *In the Wake of War,* 74.

43. Grundmann, "Tätigkeitsbericht des Denkmalschutzamtes"; Grundmann, "Zehnjahresbericht über die Tätigkeit," esp. 46–47, 52; Herrbach, "Georg Lill"; Wolff Metternich, "Lebenslauf," 11–14; "Robert Hiecke," *DKD* 11 (1953): 70–72.

44. Josef Maria Ritz, "Vorwort," *DKD* 10 (1952): 1.

45. Kornfeld, "50 Jahre Rheinischer Verein," 15; Ruland, "Kleine Chronik des Rheinischen Vereins," 34–36.

46. Diefendorf, *In the Wake of War,* 70–71.

47. Strauß, "Denkmalpflege in der Ostzone," 79, 82–84; Hans Berger, "Tendenzen der Denkmalpflege," 4; Seydewitz, *Die unbesiegbare Stadt,* 243.

48. Gesellschaft für christliche Kultur, "Kirchen in Trümmern," 25, 43.

49. Bullivant, "Continuity or Change?," 202.

50. Gesellschaft für christliche Kultur, "Kirchen in Trümmern," 57.

51. The quote comes from a supporter of the restoration, who paraphrased the opponents' point of view: A. Ress, "Zur Frage der Alten Pinakothek," *DKD* 10 (1952): 138.

52. Beseler and Gutschow, *Kriegsschicksale Deutscher Architektur,* 2:1400; Brix, "Monumente der NS- und Trümmer-Zeit," 183.

53. Gesellschaft für christliche Kultur, "Kirchen in Trümmern," 115.

54. Ibid., 119.

55. Beseler, "Der Wiederaufbau der Kölner Kirchen," 229; Beseler and Gutschow, *Kriegsschicksale Deutscher Architektur,* 1:528.

56. Schwarz, in a letter to Mies van der Rohe, May 1947, as quoted in Diefendorf, "Städtebauliche Traditionen," 263.

57. Paul Ortwin Rave, "Sieben Jahre Denkmalpflege in Berlin," *DKD* 10 (1952): 120–24, here 123.

58. Strauß, "Denkmalpflege in der Ostzone," 79–80.

59. On East Germany, see Fulbrook, *Divided Nation,* esp. 299–303.

60. Denkschrift, RHB Aachen, n.d. [ca. 1948], NWHSADü, NW60, 1665.

61. Ritter, *German Resistance,* 173–76.

62. Jean Paul Richter is quoted in Pinson, *Modern Germany,* 20.

63. Milward, *European Rescue of the Nation-State;* Tipton and Aldrich, *Economic and Social History of Europe,* 91.

64. Lill, "Vorwort [1946]," 7.

65. Bürgermeister Arntz, "Gedenken zu dem Plan des Wiederaufbaues der Stadt Münstereifel," typescript, n.d. [ca. 1949], NWHSADü, NW60, 598.

66. Christian Wallenreiter, "Wohnungsbau statt Denkmalpflege?," *DKD* 10 (1952): 2–5, here 3.

67. Typescript of Busley's speech, n.d. [ca. Fall 1948], NWHSADü, NW60, 1669, 2:230.

68. Paul Ortwin Rave, "Sieben Jahre Denkmalpflege in Berlin," *DKD* 10 (1952): 120–24, here 120; on the rubble women, see Diefendorf, *In the Wake of War*, 22–23.

69. These and the following quotes are from the Busley typescript, NWHSADü, NW60, 1669, 2:230–32.

70. On plundering in the *Gestapo-Gelände*, see Young, *Texture of Memory*, 83, and Rürup, *Topographie des Terrors*, 188; plundering of historic buildings in private hands was especially widespread in the Westphalian countryside, as noted in Rave, "Westfalen," 96; for briquettes and bread, see Loest, *The Monument*, 148; for U.S. military plundering, see Alford, *Spoils of World War II*; on fashion, see Kohl, "Krieg der Röcke," 300–301.

71. *Michel Deutschland-Spezial*, 892, 894; Oberkreisdirektor, Kreisverwaltung Rees, to Kultusminister, Nordrhein-Westfalen, 9 February 1951, NWHSADü, NW60, 1670; "Das Amt für kölnisches Volkstum," *Unser Koeln* 5/6 (November/December 1948): 13. The cultural minister of Saxony after reunification, Hans Joachim Meyer, recalled in "Zwischen Palast und Platte," 9, that his parents had left him with lifelong images of wartime destruction by taking him around to church ruins and other destroyed buildings in Rostock when he was a child.

72. On "ruin films," see Ulfilas Meyer, "Trümmerkino," 258–67; one of the most famous photojournalistic accounts was Bourke-White, *Dear Fatherland, Rest Quietly.* On postwar photography, see Barnouw, *Germany 1945.*

73. Diefendorf, *In the Wake of War*, 73.

74. Walter Dirks, "Mut zum Abschied: Zur Wiederherstellung des Frankfurter Goethehauses," *Frankfurter Hefte* 1 (1947): 819–28, excerpted in Huse, *Denkmalpflege*, 198–201; on Dirks's Christian socialism, see Hermand, *Kultur im Wiederaufbau*, 59–60; see also Reichel, *Politik mit der Erinnerung*, 72–74.

75. Durth, "Utopia im Niemands-Land," 220–21; Albert Rapp, head of the Historical Museum, Frankfurt am Main, to Oberbürgermeister, 2 October 1948, as reprinted in Durth and Gutschow, *Träume in Trümmern*, 2:527–32, here 528.

76. For the following, see the excerpts of Hartmann's speech in Huse, *Denkmalpflege*, 202–4.

77. Franz Meunier, "Illusion als Schicksal," *Baukunst und Werkform* 2 (1948): unpaginated, as cited in Durth and Gutschow, *Träume und Trümmern*, 2:488.

78. See for example, Mischnick, *Von Dresden nach Bonn*, 263–66.

79. Diefendorf, *In the Wake of War*, 272–73; Diefendorf, "Städtebauliche Traditionen," 271.

80. Verkehrs- und Heimatverein Solingen to RP Düsseldorf, 15 June 1950, NWHSADü, Regierung Düsseldorf, 56245, pt. 2; Beseler and Gutschow, *Kriegsschicksale Deutscher Architektur*, 1:720; "Heimatvereine gegen 'Reißbrett-Mörder,' " *Rheinische Post*, 18 April 1953.

81. " 'Jonges' sorgen sich um die Altstadt," *Rheinische Post*, 15 January 1953.

82. Zimmermann, "Wiederaufbau des Frankfurter Goethehauses?," 54; on Münster, see Huse, *Denkmalpflege*, 188; Diefendorf, *In the Wake of War*, 88–89.

83. The words are those of Joseph Busley, as reported in a North Rhine Westphalian cultural ministry representative's Reisebericht über eine Besprechung der Vertreter des Heimatbundes in den Ländern Nordrhein-Westfalen und Niedersachsens, 27 July 1948, NWHSADü, NW 60, 1661. The meeting was held on 21 July.

84. Ludwig Eltz to Oberstadtdirektor, Köln, 13 March 1949, SKK, Bez. 1, Bd. 1, Altermarkt 20/22.

85. Höhn, "Frau im Haus und Girl im *Spiegel*," 63; Mischnick, *Von Dresden nach Bonn*, 202.

86. Seydewitz, *Zerstörung und Wiederaufbau von Dresden*, 39, 161, 254; on Mönchen-Gladbach, see "Heimatschau mal anders gesehen," *Freiheit*, 25 October 1950.

87. Karwelat, "Ein Berliner Stadtplan von 1946," 11, 13.

88. Museum für Geschichte der Stadt Dresden, *Biografische Notizen*; Seydewitz, *Zerstörung und Wiederaufbau von Dresden*, 263, 291; Azaryahu, "Street Names and Political Identity," 587–88.

89. "Hunderttausende feierten Geburtstag," *Der Mittag*, 10 July 1950; Seydewitz, *Zerstörung und Wiederaufbau von Dresden*, 309, where the author rejects such anti-Communist criticism as slanderous.

90. Arnold, "Volkstum, Heimat und Staat," 8; Bürgermeister Wittlich, Mehs, to Busley, 6 January 1948, NWHSADü, NW60, 1667; Kreisdirektor, Landkreis Ahaus, Vreden, to Kultusministerium Nordrhein-Westfalen, 11 May 1949, NWHSADü, NW60, 1670.

91. For expellees, see Arbeitsgemeinschaft der westdeutschen Heimatbünde, "Bericht Königswinter," typescript, December 1951, in NWHSADü, NW60, 1672.

92. Oberkreisdirektor, Kreisverwaltung Rees, to Kultusminister, Nordrhein-West-falen, 9 February 1951; for the Vreden proposal, see Kreisdirektor, Landkreis Ahaus, to Kultusministerium Nordrhein-Westfalen, 17 May 1949, both in NWHSADü, NW60, 1670. On war damage in Vreden, see Beseler and Gutschow, *Kriegsschicksale Deutscher Architektur*, 1:727–28.

93. See Wentzel, "Die deutschen Glasmalereien von historischem Wert," 78.

94. Buchsteiner, "Arbeiter und Tourismus," 172–74.

95. *Die schöne Heimat*.

96. This according to a book review of the series quoted on the back of the 1952 volume.

97. For the following, see *Die schöne Heimat*, 2, 87, 139; on St. Lorenz, see Beseler and Gutschow, *Kriegsschicksale Deutscher Architektur*, 2:1438–40.

98. *Die schöne Heimat*, 2.

99. Italics in the original.

100. For the following, see Weyers and Köck, *Die Eroberung der Welt*, 98–117.

101. Chair of the Verein der Freunde Kalkar to Busley, 14 November 1947, NWHSADü, NW60, 596; Beseler and Gutschow, *Kriegsschicksale Deutscher Architektur*, 1:510–11; "Das Amt für kölnisches Volkstum," *Unser Koeln* 5/6 (November/December 1948): 13; "Hunderttausende feierten Geburtstag," *Der Mittag*, 10 July 1950.

102. Morgenbrod, "Die Liebe zur Heimat war ungebrochen," 346–47; Wilhelm Wei-denhaupt to Kultusminister, Nordrhein-Westfalen, 1 March 1947, and memo from Joseph Busley, 14 March 1947, both in NWHSADü, NW60, 1668, Bd. I, 391–93; Hei-matverein Düsseldorfer Jonges, *50 Jahre Heimatverein*, 22, 27; " 'Jonges' sorgen sich um die Altstadt," *Rheinische Post*, 15 January 1953.

Chapter 6

1. On the symbolic importance of Robinson Crusoe in the early 1950s, see Enssle, "Five Theses on German Everyday Life," 14.

2. Bertolt Brecht, "Germany, 1952," in *Gesammelte Werke*, vol. 10 (Frankfurt am Main: Suhrkamp, 1967), as reprinted in McClelland and Scher, *Postwar German Culture*, 176.

3. Korte, "Erinnerungsspuren," 71.

4. Beyme, "Reconstruction in the German Democratic Republic," 191; Fulbrook, *Divided Nation*, 195, 204.

5. The speakers were Federal Foreign Minister von Brentano and the archbishop of Munich-Freysing, Cardinal Döpfner. They are quoted in "900 Jahre Dom zu Speyer," *Bulletin des Presse- und Informationsamtes der Bundesregierung* 171 (13 September 1961): 1634–35.

6. Bundesparteitag der CDU, 26.–29. April 1956, Stuttgart (Hamburg, n.d.): 23, as quoted in Heckel et al., *Kulturpolitik in der Bundesrepublik*, 65.

7. For statistics on the age of residential buildings, see Statistisches Bundesamt, *Statistisches Jahrbuch für die Bundesrepublik Deutschland* (1960), 268; (1965), 289; (1970), 240; and (1976), 561. The number for the DDR is for 1971.

8. Hans Magnus Enzensberger, "Bin ich ein Deutscher?," *Die Zeit*, 12 June 1964, reprinted in McClelland and Scher, *Postwar German Culture*, 190–95, here 191, 192, 195.

9. Korte, "Erinnerungsspuren," 71.

10. On "overcoming" the future, see the typescript "Theses on the Deutscher Gemeindetag conference 'Give the Town a Future,'" 28 April 1964, BAK, ZSg. 1, 30/1.

11. Nothnagle, "From Buchenwald to Bismarck," 93.

12. Kopp, *Die Wendung zur "nationalen" Geschichtsbetrachtung*, 5–6.

13. *Neues Deutschland*, 14 March 1951, as quoted in Falk Jaeger, "Die Bauhausbauten in Dessau als kulturhistorisches Erbe in der sozialistischen Wirklichkeit," *DKD* 39 (1981): 159–86, here 164; for Liebknecht, see Haspel, "Zwischen Kronprinzenpalais und Stalinallee," 39–40.

14. For the quote from the *Handbuch für Architektur*, published in East Berlin in 1954, see Helas, "Die Architektur der 50er Jahre in der DDR," 51. The Becher poem is cited by Goralczyk, "Architektur und Städtebau der 50er Jahre in der DDR," 69. For the characterization of DDR architecture, see Gerd Hatje, Hubert Hoffmann, and Karl Kaspar, *New German Architecture*, trans. H. J. Montague (New York: Praeger, 1956), as excerpted in McClelland and Scher, *Postwar German Culture*, 408–17, here 409. On urban planning and historic places in the Eastern bloc, see Rosenberg and Hruska, *Städtebau in West und Ost*, 79.

15. Mohr, "Vorwort," 1.

16. Ewald, "Kulturdenkmale," 59; E. Neuß, "Technische Denkmale," 80; Riesenberger, "Heimatgedanke und Heimatgeschichte in der DDR," 336–37.

17. Warneken and Warneken-Pallowski, "Kommunale Kulturpolitik," 402, 405.

18. Koonz, "Between Memory and Oblivion," esp. 265–69.

19. Grundmann, "Tätigkeitsbericht des Denkmalschutzamtes," 73.

20. Beseler, "Kriegsschäden und Wiederaufbau," 59; Schleich, *Die zweite Zerstörung Münchens*, 8; Kultusministerium, Niedersachsen, to Bundesministerium des Innern, 26 March 1959, BAK, B106, 33136.

21. Gebhard, "Schutz und Pflege des Bauernhauses"; Bendermacher, "Die 'Minderen Dinge,'" 291; Heinz Wolff, "Pflaster in alten Städten," *DKD* 19 (1961): 69–87; Löber, "Die Sicherung technischer Kulturdenkmale," 312; Schafft, "Schiffahrtsbezogene Denkmale," 18–21; Schlippe, "Erster Bericht des Amtes für Denkmalpflege der Hansestadt Lübeck," 109, 113; Klewitz, "Tagung der Vereinigung," 118–19. For the debate on the nineteenth century, see Heinrich Kreisel, "Die Beurteilung der Kunst der letzten hundert Jahre und die Denkmalpflege," *DKD* 15 (1957): 82–87, and Peter Hirschfeld, "Wie weit ist das späte 19. Jahrhundert 'denkmalschutzwürdig'?," *DKD* 17 (1959): 75–77.

22. Goralczyk, "Denkmale und Denkmalpflege in Berlin und in der Mark Brandenburg," 52.

23. Deiters, "Ein Beitrag zur Denkmalpflege in der DDR," 27.

24. Goralczyk, "Denkmale und Denkmalpflege in Berlin und in der Mark Brandenburg," 47; Falk Jaeger, "Die Bauhausbauten in Dessau als kulturhistorisches Erbe in der sozialistischen Wirklichkeit," *DKD* 39 (1981): 164; Helbig, "Denkmale der Volksarchitektur," 128–29.

25. Klewitz, "Tagung der Vereinigung," 121, 118.

26. J. M. Ritz, "Betrachtungen zur Denkmalpflegetagung 1955 in Westfalen," *DKD* 14 (1956): 62.

27. "Berichte der ehemaligen Arbeitsstellen des Instituts für Denkmalpflege der DDR: Berlin," *DKD* 49 (1991): 20. The view taken in this report contrasts sharply with Goralczyk, "Denkmale und Denkmalpflege in Berlin und in der Mark Brandenburg," esp. 44–42, which was written before the dissolution of the DDR. Goralczyk stressed that even in the first years of rebuilding, historic preservation had an important role in all regime initiatives.

28. Helas, "Berichte," 430; on the plaque, see Reinhard Meier, "Dresden," 161.

29. Deiters, "Ein Beitrag zur Denkmalpflege in der DDR," 28; on the Kulturbund, see Heider, *Politik—Kultur—Kulturbund*, 57, 219–20; Kleßmann, "Relikte des Bildungsbürgertums in der DDR"; on preservationist volunteers in another socialist state, see Winters, "Historic Preservation in Czechoslovakia."

30. Grundmann, "Zehnjahresbericht über die Tätigkeit," 49.

31. Bendermacher, "Die 'Minderen Dinge,'" 294–97.

32. Grundmann, "Zehnjahresbericht über die Tätigkeit," 50; Deiters, "Ein Beitrag zur Denkmalpflege in der DDR," 28; Kreisel, "Die Tagung und Besichtigungsfahrten der Denkmalpfleger," 234.

33. Grundmann, "Zehnjahresbericht über die Tätigkeit"; Heinrich Kreisel, "Inventarisation und Denkmalpflege," *DKD* 18 (1960): 69–71; Hervé, "Bericht aus Frankreich (Elsaß)," 79.

34. Ernst Borgwardt and Wolfgang Teuchert, "Tagung der deutschen Denkmalpfleger," *DKD* 21 (1963): 50–73, here 50; for Taut, see Heinrich Kreisel, "Die Farbgebung des Äußeren alter Bauwerke," *DKD* 21 (1963): 111–36; for more on color, see Ellger, *Konservator im Alltag*, 40–43.

35. Josef Maria Ritz, "Vorwort," *DKD* 10 (1952): 1.

36. Rörig, "Die Stadt in der deutschen Geschichte," 13, 32.

37. Christian Wallenreiter, "Wohnungsbau statt Denkmalpflege?," *DKD* 10 (1952): 3.

38. Ernst Sauermann, "Die Deutsche Glocke und Ihr Schicksal im Krieg," *DKD* 10 (1952): 14–32, here 10; Walther Zimmermann, "Glocken und Kunstlandschaft," *DKD* 10 (1952): 33–35, here 33.

39. Schleich, *Die zweite Zerstörung Münchens*, 20–23; the citation is from Brix, "Monumente der NS- und Trümmer-Zeit," 180.

40. Kier, "Zur Vermittelbarkeit von Bauten aus der NS-Zeit als Objekte der Denkmalpflege," 55.

41. Beseler and Gutschow, *Kriegsschicksale Deutscher Architektur*, 2:1373–74; Diefendorf, *In the Wake of War*, 94; Brix, "Munich: Victory Arch"; Brix, "Munich: Residenz and Nationaltheater."

42. See editor's introduction and Karl Fischer, "Wiederaufbau der Bayerischen Staatsoper, des Nationaltheaters zu München," *DKD* 21 (1963): 1–18, here 1 for both quotes.

43. Ibid., 5.

44. Brix, "Munich: Residenz and Nationaltheater," 43.

45. For the following, see Haspel, "Zwischen Kronprinzenpalais und Stalinallee," 42–43; Stark, "Das Berliner Ensemble 'Unter den Linden,'" 82, 85.

46. Heinrich Kreisel, "Die Beurteilung der Kunst der letzten hundert Jahre und die Denkmalpflege," *DKD* 15 (1957): 86.

47. On the Berlin synagogues, see Reichel, *Politik mit der Erinnerung*, 202–7; on Worms, see Ernst Borgwardt and Wolfgang Teuchert, "Tagung der deutschen Denkmalpfleger," *DKD* 21 (1963): 65–67, and Beseler and Gutschow, *Kriegsschicksale Deutscher Architektur*, 2:1018–29.

48. For the following, see H. K. Zimmermann, "Die neue Altstadt in Frankfurt am Main," *DKD* 14 (1956): 41–44.

49. Ibid., 42.

50. Ibid.

51. Ibid.

52. Bader, "Xanten," 152.

53. Gebhard, "Schutz und Pflege des Bauernhauses," 132, 138–39.

54. Ibid., 137.

55. Werner Bornheim gen. Schilling, "1945–1970—25 Jahre Denkmalpflege," *DKD* 28 (1970): 12.

56. Gebhard, "Schutz und Pflege des Bauernhauses," 140.

57. Clemen, *Die deutsche Kunst und die Denkmalpflege*, 9, 15, 49–50.

58. Klewitz, "Tagung der Vereinigung," 114; Kreisel, "Die Tagung und Besichtigungsfahrten der Denkmalpfleger," 242.

59. Niels von Holst, "Sowjetische Denkmalpflege in Riga und Reval," *DKD* 12 (1954): 67–70, here 70; Hans Reuther, "Dresden Zehn Jahre nach der Zerstörung," *DKD* 13 (1955): 58–69, here 58. For a subsequent account of DDR conservation efforts, see Hartwig Beseler, "Denkmalpflege in der DDR in der Selbstdarstellung (Sammelbericht)," *DKD* 32 (1974): 147–52. On von Holst in the war, see Petropoulos, *Art as Politics*, 111–13, 319.

60. Niels von Holst, "Sowjetische Denkmalpflege in Riga und Reval," *DKD* 12 (1954): 70.

61. Günther Grundmann, "Umsonst alle Proteste! Zum Abbruch des Potsdamer Stadtschlosses und des Braunschweiger Schlosses," *DKD* 18 (1960): 82, 83, 84.

62. Kornfeld, "50 Jahre Rheinischer Verein," 14.

63. Bader, "Xanten," 146–47, 149; "Von Trümmerbergen zum 'Kolner Stil,'" *Kölnische Rundschau*, 5 May 1955.

64. Bendermacher, "Neuß," 45.

65. Kühn, "Die kleine Stadt," 12.

66. Grundmann, "Tätigkeitsbericht des Denkmalschutzamtes," 74.

67. The terms are used in Bendermacher, "Neuß," 45.

68. See Moeller, *Protecting Motherhood*.

69. For the following, see Noelle and Neumann, *Jahrbuch der öffentlichen Meinung, 1947–1955*, 123, 125, 126, 132; *1957*, 150; *1958–64*, 230; Merritt and Merritt, *Public Opinion in Semisovereign Germany*, 54–55.

70. Noelle and Neumann, *Jahrbuch der öffentlichen Meinung, 1957*, 107. Whereas 51 percent of respondents from the "upper stratum and higher middle stratum" favored historical reconstruction, 43 percent favored it in the "broader middle stratum" and 46 percent in the "lower stratum." In the case of increasing age and higher education, however, the percentages favoring reconstruction always went up.

71. "Alle Kriegsschäden beseitigt," *Frankfurter Neue Presse*, 27 November 1954, as reprinted in Peter and Wolf, *Arbeit, Amis, Aufbau*, 28; "Aus Ruinen wuchs das zweite Dortmund," *Westdeutsche Allgemeine Zeitung*, 3 April 1958, Jubiläums-Ausgabe: "Zehn Jahre Aufbau an der Ruhr."

72. For the following, see Borger and Zehnder, *Köln*, 306.

73. Baedeker, *Deutschland in einem Bande*, 283.

74. "Von Trümmerbergen zum 'Kölner Stil,'" *Kölnische Rundschau*, 5 May 1955.

75. "Die Trümmerflora weicht dem Aufbau," *Frankfurter Rundschau*, 15 May 1954, as reprinted in Peter and Wolf, *Arbeit, Amis, Aufbau*, 22–23.

76. *Göttingen Tageblatt*, 8 July 1964, reprinted in Nissen, *Göttingen gestern und heute*, 114–15.

77. "Muß die Spitzhacke erbarmungslos wirken?," *Düsseldorfer Nachrichten*, 21 December 1955.

78. "Der Dolchstoß des Konservators," *Rheinische Post* (Ausgabe: Kempen), 29 October 1960.

79. Mitscherlich, *Die Unwirtlichkeit unserer Städte*, 32.

80. Ibid.

81. "Herbstliche Blumen dichten die schlichten Särge," *General-Anzeiger*, 17 October 1959.

82. Archenholz, *Die verlassenen Schlösser*, 258, 259, 260.

83. Seydewitz, *Zerstörung und Wiederaufbau von Dresden*, 358. The 1982 edition was titled *Die unbesiegbare Stadt* and included an introduction by Hans Modrow, then first secretary of the Dresden SED.

84. "Die Liefergasse ist geliefert," *Rheinische Post*, 20 December 1955.

85. "Keine falsche Pracht am Tußmann-Bau!," *Düsseldorfer Nachrichten*, 13 August 1957.

86. "Sünde wider den Geist der Denkmalpflege," *Mittag*, 24 August 1957.

87. "Neanderkirche wird freigelegt," *Rheinische Post*, 24 July 1957.

88. "Schutz der Baudenkmale in Dülken," *Rheinische Post*, 12 December 1957.

89. For the following, see Grundmann, "Umsonst alle Proteste! Zum Abbruch des Potsdamer Stadtschlosses und des Braunschweiger Schlosses," *DKD* 18 (1960): 82–87.

90. "Stiftung Dom zu Lübeck: Ein Aufruf und seine Folgen," *Frankfurter Allgemeine Zeitung*, 15 April 1961.

91. Hans-Jürgen Usko, "Jetzt ist Lübeck wieder Stadt der sieben Türme," *Die Welt*, 24 April 1961.

92. Staatliche Zentralverwaltung für Statistik, *Statistisches Jahrbuch der Deutschen Demokratischen Republik*, 317.

93. "Vereine, Veranstaltungen, Nachrichten, Personalia," *RHP* 1 (1964): 83–84; Interior Ministry, Rheinland-Pfalz, to Federal Interior Ministry, 8 June 1963, BAK, B106, 33158.

94. Gerteis, *Das unbekannte Frankfurt*.

95. Ibid., 175.

96. Ibid., 215. The photograph appears on p. 214.

97. Ibid., 220.

98. "Alte Bonner Straßen erzählen ihre Erlebnisse," *Bonner Rundschau*, 24 January 1965.

99. "Alte Bonner Straßen erzählen ihre Erlebnisse," *Bonner Rundschau*, 13 December 1964.

100. See "Alte Bonner Straßen erzählen ihre Erlebnisse," *Bonner Rundschau*, 3 January 1965.

Chapter 7

1. Bentmann, "Der Kampf um die Erinnerung," 213.

2. Fulbrook, *Divided Nation*, 168.

3. Grass, *Two States—One Nation?*, 63. Grass made the remark in a 1967 speech before the Bonn Press Club.

4. Mommsen, " 'Wir sind wieder wer,' " 203, 205.

5. Peter Ludz, "The German Democratic Republic from the Sixties to the Seventies," Harvard Center for International Affairs Occasional Papers, no. 26, November 1970, as cited in Fulbrook, *Divided Nation*, 204.

6. Hans Magnus Enzensberger, "middle class blues," in *poems for people who don't read poems*, trans. Michael Hamburger (New York: Atheneum, 1968), as reprinted in McClelland and Scher, *Postwar German Culture*, 184–85.

7. Beyme, *Der Wiederaufbau*, 213.

8. For the following periodization, see ibid., esp. 334–63.

9. Durth, *Inszenierung der Alltagswelt*, 9.

10. Trommler, Glaser, and Schwenger, "Kulturpolitik der Bundesrepublik Deutschland," 381.

11. Kreißig, Tressler, and von Uslar, *Kultur in den Städten*, 13–17, 79.

12. Statistisches Bundesamt, *Statistisches Jahrbuch für die Bundesrepublik Deutschland* (1970), 240.

13. Dölling, "Protection and Conservation of Historical Monuments," 11.

14. Nelles and Oppermann, *Stadtsanierung und Bürgerbeteiligung*, 20.

15. See Durth, *Inszenierung der Alltagswelt*, for a lively critique; the figures for displaced populations are cited in Günter, "Von der Denkmalpflege zum Städteschutz," 94; on neatness, se Relph, *Modern Urban Landscape*, 183–85.

16. "Editorial"; Boyer, *City of Collective Memory*, 47; Lange, "Altstadt und Warenhaus"; Relph, *Modern Urban Landscape*, 213–25.

17. Marcuse, "Die museale Darstellung des Holocaust," 88.

18. Herbert, "Der Holocaust in der Geschichtsschreibung der Bundesrepublik Deutschland," 38–39.

19. Domansky, "Die gespaltene Erinnerung," 188.

20. Behrens-Cobet and Reichling, " 'Bilder erhalten, die den Schlaf stören,' " 80–81, 82; Diner, "Zur Ideologie des Antifaschismus," 26.

21. Michael Siegel, *Denkmalpflege als öffentliche Aufgabe*, Anhang I, 293–94; Klaus Driessen, "Systematischer Vergleich der Denkmalschutzgesetze in der Bundesrepublik," *DKD* 32 (1974): 72–84; Wörner, "Législation des monuments historiques," 8–9; Hönes, "Kulturdenkmal und öffentliches Interesse," 22; Stich, "Maßnahmen der Stadterhaltung und des Denkmalschutzes."

22. Peter Goralczyk, "Rückblick auf Organisation und Recht der Denkmalpflege in der DDR," *DKD* 49 (1991): 11–15.

23. Dieterich, "Staatliche Hilfen zur Finanzierung der Erhaltung 'Alter Städte,' " 102; Föhl, *Bauten der Industrie und Technik*, 35–6.

24. Ruland, "Kleine Chronik des Rheinischen Vereins," 45–46.

25. For the quote, see "Rheinischer Verein für Denkmalpflege und Heimatschutz," *Rheinische Heimatpflege* 7 (1970): 175. For membership, see Rheinischer Verein für Denkmalpflege und Landschaftsschutz, *Satzung und Mitgliederverzeichnis*, 14–73, which lists 2,385 domestic individual members. If one includes foreign, corporative, and other special categories of members, the RVDL had "more than 3,000 members" at the end of 1971, 4,295 in March 1977, and 5,761 in October 1980, as noted in Ruland, "Kleine Chronik des Rheinischen Vereins," 47, 51, 54. Women made up 13 percent of the membership in 1971 compared with just 4 percent more than fifty years earlier.

26. Manfred Sack, "Brüderschaft mit der Historie," *Die Zeit*, 2 January 1976; Föhl, *Bauten der Industrie und Technik*, 35; Haindl, "Denkmalpflege in der sozialen Verantwortung."

27. Beseler, "Berufsbild und Berufsausbildung der Denkmalpfleger," 280, 281; Beseler, "Die Zukunft der Vergangenheit"; Michael Siegel, *Denkmalpflege als öffentliche Aufgabe*, 80.

28. Rommel, *Abschied vom Schlaraffenland*, 87.

29. Bornheim is quoted in "Bericht über die Jahresversammlung vom 2. bis 4. Juni 1973 in Hachenburg (Westerwald)," *RHP* 10 (1973): 228–249, here 236.

30. Beseler, "Die Zukunft der Vergangenheit."

31. Willibald Sauerländer, "Erweiterung des Denkmalbegriffs?," *DKD* 33 (1975): 117–30.

32. Ibid., 123.

33. For the above, see ibid., 125, 129.

34. Goslar *Stadtbaurat* E. D. Kohl is quoted in Manfred Sack, "Löwe mit Dauerwellen," *Die Zeit*, 18 June 1976.

35. Tomaszewski, "Denkmalpflege," 238, 239.

36. Manfred Sack, "Rudi Arndts Disneyland," *Die Zeit*, 2 May 1975.

37. Stahn, *Das Nikolaiviertel am Marx-Engels-Forum*.

38. Hans Joachim Meyer, "Zwischen Palast und Platte," 13–14; Manz, *Lebensniveau im Sozialismus*, 193.

39. Gotthard Voß, "Berichte der ehemaligen Arbeitsstellen des Instituts für Denkmalpflege der DDR: Halle," *DKD*, 49 (1991): 36–44, here 40.

40. Beseler, "Denkmal," 136; on Czechoslovakia, see Fitch, *Historic Preservation*, 366; the quote comes from Günter Kabus, Institut für Städtebau und Architektur der DDR, as cited by Joachim Nawrocki, "Der gewisse Kniff," *Die Zeit*, 16 January 1976, 17, which also contains data on DDR finances for restoration of old residential neighborhoods;

Kulturbund, *Technische Denkmale*; Günter, "Schutz historischer Industrieanlagen," 137, where the author is much too optimistic about the DDR's efforts in this area; Edgar Lehmann, "Die Anfänge der Neubearbeitung des Handbuchs der Deutschen Kunstdenkmäler von Georg Dehio in der DDR," *DKD* 49 (1991): 93–95.

41. Topfstedt, "Denkmale der Architektur und des Städtebaues der DDR," 14–16.

42. From an article by the assistant to Minister of Culture Werner Rackwitz, in the *Thuringische Landeszeitung*, 18 May 1978, as reprinted in "Zeugen der Kulturgeschichte," *DKD* 36 (1978): 130.

43. "Bericht über die Jahresversammlung vom 27. bis 30. Juni 1975 in Aachen," *RHP* 12 (1975): 202–17, here 216.

44. Werner Bornheim gen. Schilling, "Franz Graf Wolff Metternich," *DKD* 37 (1979): 204–8.

45. Franz Graf Wolff Metternich, "Denkmalpflege und Landschaftsschutz im Rheinland: Ein Rückblick und Ausblick," *RHP* 7 (1970): 193–96, here 193, 194.

46. Georg Mörsch, "Wer bestimmt das öffentliche Interesse an der Erhaltung von Baudenkmalen? Mechanismen und Problematik der Auswahl," *DKD* 38 (1980): 126–29, here 126, 127. Mörsch's article was the reprinted text of a talk given at a conference in Göttingen in 1975.

47. Debold and Debold-Kritter, "Das Konzept der Stadterhaltung von Bologna," 95–110; Günter, "Von der Denkmalpflege zum Städteschutz," 101; Negt and Kluge, *Öffentlichkeit und Erfahrung*, 447–55.

48. Benjamin, "Theses on the Philosophy of History," 256–57.

49. Boström and Günter, "Von Bürgerinitiativen zu Arbeiterinitiativen," 8–9; Günter and Günter, "Architekturelemente und Verhaltensweisen," 9, 10–12. For the inventory, see Günter, *Oberhausen*.

50. Führ and Stemmrich, *"Nach gethaner Arbeit verbleibt im Kreise der Eurigen,"* 77–80; Nelles and Oppermann, *Stadtsanierung und Bürgerbeteiligung*, 49; Rolf Düdder, "Wo die Hütte Heimat wird," *Die Zeit*, 31 January 1975; Günter, "Schutz von Denkmälern der Sozialgeschichte," 118.

51. For the following, see Günter and Günter, "Architekturelemente und Verhaltensweisen," 7, 18, 20–21, 56; on digging for one's past, see Benjamin, "Berlin Chronicle," 26; on "touch," see Günter, "Von der Denkmalpflege zum Städteschutz," 112; on workers' settlements as exploited colonies, see Günter, "Schutz von Denkmälern der Sozialgeschichte," 118, 124.

52. Boström and Günter, *Arbeiterinitiativen im Ruhrgebiet*, 9.

53. Günter and Günter, "Die Arbeiter machen ihre eigene Architektur," 70; the mineworker is cited in Günter, "Schutz historischer Industrieanlagen," 131.

54. Nelles and Oppermann, *Stadtsanierung und Bürgerbeteiligung*, 60, 63–4, 87, 93; on Borchers, see also Georg Mörsch, "Günther Borchers," *DKD* 38 (1980): 174–75, and Föhl, *Bauten der Industrie und Technik*, 35.

55. On historic preservation and social networks, see Appleyard introduction and, more broadly, Castells, *City and the Grassroots*.

56. Boström, Günter, and Vogt, "Entwicklung der Arbeitersiedlungen," 19.

57. Günter and Günter, "Architekturelemente und Verhaltensweisen," 8.

58. Brix, *Lübeck*.

59. See Brix's forward to ibid., 5.

60. *Reiseführer*, 97.

61. Both quotes in Brix's forward to *Lübeck*, 5.

62. "Denkmalschutz als Volksbewegung," *Frankfurter Allgemeine Zeitung*, 21 January 1975.

63. Michael Siegel, *Denkmalpflege als öffentliche Aufgabe*, 77–78; Beyme, *Die Wiederaufbau*, 232; Hönes, "Kulturdenkmal und öffentliche Interesse," 18.

64. Michael Siegel, *Denkmalpflege als öffentliche Aufgabe*, 78.

65. White, *Content of the Form*, 187.

66. Calvino, *Invisible Cities*, 15.

67. Ibid., 16.

68. Pfuel, "Eine Zukunft für unsere Vergangenheit," 11.

69. Hagelüken, "Auf den Barrikaden der Geschichte."

70. For profiles of the participants, see Haist, "Lebenswege."

71. Rieger, "Kunst- und Denkmalpflege und der moderne Tourismus," 99.

72. Statistisches Bundesamt, *Statistisches Jahrbuch für die Bundesrepublik Deutschland* (1970), 253; "Vereine, Veranstaltungen," *RHP* 10 (1973): 330; Helene Blum, "Ein Publikum erfährt Geschichte und Kunst: Erste Bilanz des neuen Kreismuseums Zons," *RHP* 10 (1973): 313–16; Hans Caspary, "Denkmalpflege im Hunsrück: Probleme einer im Umbruch befindlichen Landschaft," *RHP* 12 (1975): 87–100; *Reiseführer*, 5, 40.

73. Rieger, "Kunst- und Denkmalpflege und der moderne Tourismus," 100; Statistisches Bundesamt, *Statistisches Jahrbuch für die Bundesrepublik Deutschland* (1976), 296.

74. Rieger, "Kunst- und Denkmalpflege und der moderne Tourismus," 100.

75. Neil Smith, "Gentrification," 32.

76. Hiltrud Kier, "Stadt Köln," in "Bedrohte Denkmäler, Bedrohte Landschaft," *RHP* 10 (1973): 62.

77. For both quotes, see Waldemar Haberey, "Bonner Bürgerhäuser," *RHP* 8 (1971): 25–32, here 30.

78. Lynch, *Good City Form*, 261; Friedrichs, "Urban Renewal Policies and Back-to-the-City Migration."

79. Grassnick, "Kulturdenkmale als Mittel der Werbung"; Durth, *Inszenierung der Alltagswelt*, 11.

80. Otto Kaufmann, "Eine oberbergische Spar- und Darlehnskasse treibt Heimatpflege," *RHP* 8 (1971): 38–45.

81. Benjamin, "Berlin Chronicle," 40.

82. Engeli, "Städtische Geschichts- und Heimatvereine," 7, 2; Michael Siegel, *Denkmalpflege als öffentliche Aufgabe*, 73–74, 79–80; Pfuel, "Eine Zukunft für unsere Vergangenheit," 11; Müller, "Bürgerinitiativen in der politischen Willensbildung."

83. "Bonner Bürgerinitiativen: Was sind ihre Ziele—und wer steckt dahinter?," *General Anzeiger* (Bonn), 12 April 1980; Günter, "Von der Denkmalpflege zum Städteschutz," 97–98; "Sayner Hütte," in "Bedrohte Denkmäler, Bedrohte Landschaft," *RHP* 10 (1973): 323–26; Boström and Günter, "Von Bürgerinitiativen zu Arbeiterinitiativen," 8–9.

84. On alternative culture, see Trommler, Glaser, and Schwenger, "Kulturpolitik der Bundesrepublik Deutschland," 383–84. For examples, see Manfred Sack, "Kultur auf Schleichwegen," *Die Zeit*, 1 August 1975, and "Bildungsburg und Fischhalle," *Die Zeit*, 8 August 1975.

85. Castells, *City and the Grassroots*, 318.

86. For the following, see Schulz, "Zum Beispiel Eppsteinerstraße 47," which includes a narrative of the occupation as well as texts of some of the original documents of the *Hauskollektiv*. For comparative material on England, see Korfmacher, "Squatting."

87. Schulz, "Zum Beispiel Eppsteinerstraße 47," 86–87.

88. For the following, see ibid., 87–88.

89. For the following, see ibid., 89–93.

90. See Eley, "Nazism, Politics, and the Image of the Past," 200–202.

91. Frei, "Geschichte aus den 'Graswurzeln'?," 35–37, 39.

92. Paul and Schoßig, "Geschichte und Heimat," 23.

93. Benjamin, "Theses on the Philosophy of History," 255.

94. Paul and Schoßig, "Geschichte und Heimat," 23.

95. Till, "Place and the Politics of Memory," chaps. 2 and 3.

96. Pfuel, "Eine Zukunft für unsere Vergangenheit," 3, 4.

97. Ibid., 6.

98. Ibid., 3, 10, 11.

99. Gotthard Voß, "Berichte der ehemaligen Arbeitsstellen des Instituts für Denkmalpflege der DDR: Halle," *DKD*, 49 (1991): 42.

100. "Bericht über die Jahresversammlung vom 27. bis 30. June 1975 in Aachen," *RHP* 12 (1975): 202–17, here 202, 204, 216.

101. Hartwig Beseler, "Berichte der Landesdenkmalämter (BRD) zum Denkmalschutzjahr 1975: Schleswig-Holstein," *DKD* 34 (1976): 18–19; Beseler, "Die Zukunft der Vergangenheit"; Manfred Fischer, "Berichte der Landesdenkmalämter (BRD) zum Denkmalschutzjahr 1975: Hamburg," *DKD* 34 (1976): 8–10; Klotz, Günter, and Kiesow, *Keine Zukunft für unsere Vergangenheit?*; Günter, "Von der Denkmalpflege zum Städteschutz," 91.

102. Günther Kühne, "Stadtbildstürmer," *Die Zeit*, 10 October 1975.

103. Spagnoli, *Berlino*, 150.

104. Schleich, *Der zweite Zerstörung Münchens*, 7, 56, 187.

105. Beseler, "Die Zukunft der Vergangenheit"; Kiesow, "Europäische Denkmalschutzjahr," 251.

Conclusion

1. Kimmelmann, "It Was Big, It Was Fun, and That's Enough"; Christo and Jeanne-Claude, *Verhüllte/Wrapped Reichstag*.

2. Kundera, *Unbearable Lightness of Being*, 4, 5, 6.

3. Greenfield, *Nationalism*, 18.

4. See the podium discussion in Deutsches Nationalkomitee für Denkmalschutz, *Verfallen und vergessen*, 102–12.

5. Hobsbawm, *Nations and Nationalism*, 11.

6. Fulbrook, *Divided Nation*, 316.

7. Fitch, *Historic Preservation*, 328.

8. Clemen, *Die deutsche Kunst und die Denkmalpflege*, 9.

9. Lynch, *What Time Is This Place?*, 1.

10. Boyer, *City of Collective Memory*, 377.

11. Benjamin, "Theses on the Philosophy of History," 255.

12. Passerini, *Fascism in Popular Memory*.

13. Hobsbawm, *Nations and Nationalism*, 163.

Archival Sources

Archiv des Landschaftsverbandes Rheinland, Brauweiler
 Provinzial-Verwaltung der Rheinprovinz
Bundesarchiv Koblenz
 B106 Bundesministerium des Innern
 R36 Deutscher Gemeindetag 1921–1945
 Zsg. 1. Zeitgeschichtliche Sammlungen
Historisches Archiv der Stadt Köln
 Kulturangelegenheiten
Nordrhein-Westfälisches Hauptstaatsarchiv Düsseldorf (incl. Schloß Kalkum)
 NW60 Kultusministerium
 Regierung Aachen
 Regierung Düsseldorf
Stadtarchiv Düsseldorf
 Abteilung XX: Vereine
Stadt Köln, Konservator
 Bezirk 1, Alter Markt

Published Primary Sources

Institut für Zeitgeschichte. *Akten der Parteikanzlei der NSDAP.* Munich: K. G. Saur,
 1984. Microfiche.
Preußischer Landtag. *Stenographische Berichte über die Verhandlungen des Preußischen
 Landtages,* 1921–22. Microfilm.
Preußisches Herrenhaus. *Stenographische Berichte über die Verhandlungen des Preußi-
 schen Herrenhauses,* 1903–7. Microfilm.
Staatliche Zentralverwaltung für Statistik. *Statistisches Jahrbuch der Deutschen Demo-
 kratischen Republik.* Berlin: Staatsverlag der DDR, 1982.
Statistisches Bundesamt. *Statistisches Jahrbuch für die Bundesrepublik Deutschland.*
 Stuttgart and Mainz: Kohlhammer, 1960, 1965, 1970, 1976.

Stenographischer Bericht der Kriegstagung für Denkmalpflege Brüssel, 1915. Berlin: Ernst & Sohn, 1915.

Tag für Denkmalpflege. *Dreizehnter Tag für Denkmalpflege in Augsburg, 1917.* Berlin: Ernst & Sohn, 1917.

——. *Dritte gemeinsame Tagung für Denkmalpflege und Heimatschutz, Eisenach, 23. und 24. September 1920. Stenographischer Bericht.* Berlin: Ernst & Sohn, 1920.

——. *Gemeinsame Tagung für Denkmalpflege und Heimatschutz, Salzburg, 14. und 15. September 1911: Stenographischer Bericht.* Berlin: Ernst & Sohn, 1911.

——. *Tag für Denkmalpflege und Heimatschutz, Breslau, 1926: Tagungsbericht.* Berlin: Guido Hackebeil, 1927.

——. *Tag für Denkmalpflege und Heimatschutz, Dresden, 1936: Tagungsbericht.* Berlin: Deutscher Kunstverlag, 1938.

——. *Tag für Denkmalpflege und Heimatschutz, Köln, 1930: Tagungsbericht.* Berlin: Deutscher Kunstverlag, 1931.

——. *Tag für Denkmalpflege und Heimatschutz, Würzburg und Nürnberg, 1928: Tagungsbericht.* Berlin: Guido Hackebeil, 1929.

——. *Zweiter Tag für Denkmalpflege, Freiburg, 23–24 September 1901: Stenographischer Bericht.* Karlsruhe: Müller'sche Hofbuchdruckerei, 1901.

Contemporary Periodicals, Newspapers, and Newsletters

Der Baumeister, Beilage (1933, 1936)
Bonner Rundschau (1964–65)
Bulletin des Presse- und Informationsamtes der Bundesregierung (1961)
Die Denkmalpflege (1899–1923, 1930–33)
Denkmalpflege und Heimatschutz(1923–30)
Deutsche Kunst und Dekoration (1923–25)
Deutsche Kunst und Denkmalpflege (1934–present)
Düsseldorfer Nachrichten (1930, 1933, 1955, 1957)
Frankfurter Allgemeine Zeitung (1961, 1975)
Freiheit (1950)
General-Anzeiger Bonn (1959, 1980)
Hamburger Anzeiger (1944)
Heimatschutz (1909)
Heimatschutz-Chronik (1917)
HEUTE (1947–48)
Kölner Tageblatt (1917)
Kölnische Rundschau (1955)
Kölnisches Tageblatt (1917)
Kölnische Volkszeitung (1930–31)
Kölnische Zeitung (1894–1933)
Die Kunst im Deutschen Reich, Ausg. A. (1939–42)
Die Kunst im Deutschen Reich, Ausg. B: *Die Baukunst* (1938–44)
Kunst und Künstler (1914–15)
Localanzeiger, Cologne (1909)
Der Mittag (1950)
Mittag (1957)
Mitteilungen des Bundes Heimatschutz (1907)

Mitteilungen des Rheinischen Vereins für Denkmalpflege und Heimatschutz (1907–18)
Mitteilungsblatt der Gesellschaft der Freunde des Wiederaufbaues der Stadt Köln (1947)
Mitteilungsblatt des Eifelvereins (1944)
Mitteilungsblatt für den Reichsbund Volkstum und Heimat (1933)
National Zeitung (1937)
Rheinische Heimatpflege (1934, 1964–82)
Rheinische Landeszeitung (1936)
Rheinische Post (1952–60)
Rheinischer Heimatbund (1939–40)
Rheinische Zeitung (1913)
Unser Koeln (1948)
Volksparole (1933)
Wasmuths Monatshefte für Baukunst; Monatshefte für Baukunst und Städtebau (1913–33)
Westdeutsche Allgemeine Zeitung (1958)
Westdeutscher Beobachter (1940–41)
Die Welt (1961)
Die Zeit (1974–76)
Zeitschrift des Rheinischen Vereins für Denkmalpflege und Heimatschutz (1919–38)

Books, Articles, Dissertations, and Papers

Abelein, Manfred. *Die Kulturpolitik des Deutschen Reiches und der Bundesrepublik Deutschland: Ihre verfassungsgeschichtliche Entwicklung und ihre verfassungsrechtlichen Probleme.* Cologne: Westdeutscher, 1968.

Adenauer, Hanna. "Heiteres und Besinnliches aus ernster Zeit." In *Festschrift für Franz Graf Wolff Metternich*, edited by Josef Ruland, 45–49. Neuß: Gesellschaft für Buchdruckerei, 1973.

Alford, Kenneth D. *The Spoils of World War II: The American Military's Role in the Stealing of Europe's Treasures.* New York: Carol Publishing, 1995.

Les Allemands destructeurs de cathédrales et de trésors du passé. Paris: Librairie Hachette, 1915.

Alvensleben, Udo von. *Lauter Abschiede: Tagebuch im Kriege.* Edited by Harald von Koenigswald. Frankfurt am Main: Propyläen, 1971.

Anderson, Benedict. *Imagined Communities: Reflections on the Origins and Spread of Nationalism.* Rev. ed. London: Verso, 1991.

Andreas, Horst. "Wilhelm Heinrich von Riehl." *Rheinische Heimatpflege* 2 (1973): 129–30.

Andreas-Friedrich, Ruth. *Battleground Berlin: Diaries, 1945–1948.* Translated by Anna Boerresen. New York: Paragon House, 1990.

Applegate, Celia. *A Nation of Provincials: The German Idea of Heimat.* Berkeley: University of California Press, 1990.

Appleyard, Donald. Introduction to *The Conservation of European Cities*, edited by Donald Appleyard, 2–49. Cambridge, Mass.: MIT Press, 1979.

Archenholz, Bogislav von. *Die verlassenen Schlösser: Ein Buch von den großen Familien des deutschen Ostens.* Stuttgart: Deutscher Bücherbund, 1967.

Architekten- und Ingenieur-Verein Hamburg, ed. *Hamburg und seine Bauten, 1929–1953.* Hamburg: Hoffmann and Campe, 1953.

Arnold, Karl. "Volkstum, Heimat und Staat." In *Fünfzig Jahre Deutscher Heimatbund: Deutscher Bund Heimatschutz*, edited by Deutscher Heimatbund, 7–11. Neuß: Gesellschaft für Buchdruckerei, 1954.

Auffarth, Sid, and Adelheid von Saldern, eds. *Altes und neues Wohnen: Linden und Hannover im frühen 20. Jahrhundert.* Seelze-Velber: Kallmeyer, 1992.

Azaryahu, Maoz. "Street Names and Political Identity: The Case of East Berlin." *Journal of Contemporary History* 21 (1986): 581–604.

Bachmann, W. "Land Sachsen." In *Die Kunstpflege: Beiträge zur Geschichte und Pflege deutscher Architektur und Kunst*, edited by Georg Lill, 19–26. Berlin: Deutscher Kunstverlag, 1947.

Bader, Walter. "Zur Denkmalpflege in Nordrheinland." In *Berichte über die Tätigkeit der Denkmalpflege in den Jahren 1945–1955*, edited by Walter Bader, 13–36. Jahrbuch der rheinischen Denkmalpflege, vol. 20. Kevelaer: Butzon & Bercker, 1956.

——. "Xanten: Die Kleinstadt Xanten oder die Gefährdung eines Stadtbildes." In *Die Kleine Stadt: Gestaltung der rheinischen Klein- und Mittelstädte*, edited by Rheinischer Verein für Denkmalpflege und Heimatschutz, 136–56. Jahrbuch des Rheinischen Vereins für Denkmalpflege und Heimatschutz, 1959. Neuß: Gesellschaft für Buchdruckerei, 1960.

——, ed. *Berichte über die Tätigkeit der Denkmalpflege in den Jahren 1945–1955.* Jahrbuch der rheinischen Denkmalpflege, vol. 20. Kevelaer: Butzon & Bercker, 1956.

Baedeker, Karl. *Deutschland im einem Bande: Handbuch für Reisende.* Leipzig: Karl Baedeker, 1906.

Baird, Jay W. *To Die for Germany: Heroes in the Nazi Pantheon.* Bloomington: Indiana University Press, 1990.

Baldwin, Peter, ed. *Reworking the Past: Hitler, the Holocaust, and the Historians' Debate.* Boston: Beacon, 1990.

Barnouw, Dagmar. *Germany 1945: Views of War and Violence.* Bloomington: Indiana University Press, 1996.

Bataille, George. *L'erotisme.* Paris: Editions de Minuit, 1957.

Baudoui, Rémi. "Between Regionalism and Functionalism: French Reconstruction from 1940 to 1945." In *Rebuilding Europe's Bombed Cities*, edited by Jeffry M. Diefendorf, 31–47. Hampshire: Macmillan, 1990.

Bausinger, Hermann. "National Orientations in Tourism." Unpublished paper, European Forum, European University Institute, Florence, Italy, May 1994.

Becher, Johannes R. "Für ein Deutschland—schön wie nie [1945]." In *. . . einer neuen Zeit Beginn: Erinnerungen an die Anfänge unserer Kulturrevolution 1945–1949*, edited by Institut für Marxismus-Leninismus beim ZK der SED and Kulturbund der DDR, 33–37. Berlin: Aufbau, 1981.

Behrenbeck, Sabine. "Heldenkult oder Friedensmahnung? Kriegerdenkmale nach beiden Weltkriegen." In *Lernen aus dem Krieg? Deutsche Nachkriegszeiten 1918/1945*, edited by Gottfried Niedhart and Deiter Riesenberger, 344–64. Munich: Beck, 1992.

Behrens-Cobet, Heidi, and Norbert Reichling. " 'Bilder erhalten, die den Schlaf stören': KZ-Gedenkstätten in Ostdeutschland." *Werkstatt Geschichte* 6 (December 1993): 80–85.

Belting, Hans. *Die Deutschen und ihre Kunst: Ein schwieriges Erbe.* Munich: Beck, 1992.

Bendermacher, Justinus. "Die 'Minderen Dinge.' " In *Erhalten und gestalten: 75 Jahre Rheinischer Verein für Denkmalpflege und Landschaftsschutz*, edited by Rheinischer

Verein für Denkmalpflege und Landschaftsschutz, 277–302. Neuß: Gesellschaft für Buchdruckerei, 1981.

——. "Neuß: Wandel der Kleinstadt." In *Die Kleine Stadt: Gestaltung der rheinischen Klein- und Mittelstädte*, edited by Rheinischer Verein für Denkmalpflege und Heimatschutz, 44–70. Jahrbuch des Rheinischen Vereins für Denkmalpflege und Heimatschutz, 1959. Neuß: Gesellschaft für Buchdruckerei, 1960.

Benjamin, Walter. "A Berlin Chronicle." In *Reflections: Essays, Aphorisms, Autobiographical Writings*, edited by Peter Demetz, 3–60. New York: Schocken, 1986.

——. *Illuminations: Essays and Reflections*, edited by Hannah Arendt. New York: Schocken, 1969.

——. "Moscow." In *Reflections: Essays, Aphorisms, Autobiographical Writings*, edited by Peter Demetz, 97–130. New York: Schocken, 1986.

——. *Moscow Diary*. Translated by Richard Sieburth. Cambridge, Mass.: Harvard University Press, 1986.

——. *Reflections: Essays, Aphorisms, Autobiographical Writings*, edited by Peter Demetz. New York: Schocken, 1986.

——. "Theses on the Philosophy of History." In *Illuminations: Essays and Reflections*, edited by Hannah Arendt, 253–64. New York: Schocken, 1969.

——. "The Work of Art in the Age of Mechanical Reproduction." In *Illuminations: Essays and Reflections*, edited by Hannah Arendt, 217–52. New York: Schocken, 1969.

Bentmann, Reinhard. "Der Kampf um die Erinnerung: Ideologische und methodische Konzepte des modernen Denkmalkultus." In *Denkmalräume-Lebensräume*, edited by Ina-Maria Greverus, 213–46. Hessische Blätter für Volks- und Kulturforschung, vol. 2/3. Gießen: Schmitz, 1976.

Berger, Hans. "Tendenzen der Denkmalpflege in der DDR." *Deutsche Kunst und Denkmalpflege* 49 (1991): 2–8.

Berger, John. *About Looking*. New York: Pantheon, 1980.

Bergmann, Klaus. *Agrarromantik und Großstadtfeindschaft*. Meisenheim: Anton Hain, 1970.

Berliner Geschichtswerkstatt, ed. *Sackgassen: Keine Wendemöglichkeit für Berliner Straßennamen*. Berlin: Nishen, 1988.

Bermann, Marshall. *All That Is Solid Melts into Air: The Experience of Modernity*. New York: Viking Penguin, 1982.

Bernold, Monika. "Anfänge: Zur Selbstverortung in der populären Autobigraphik." *Historische Anthropologie* 1, no. 1 (1993): 5–24.

Beseler, Hartwig. "Baudenkmale: Zeugnisse architektonischer Überlieferung im Umbruch." In *Kriegsschicksale Deutscher Architektur: Verluste, Schäden, Wiederaufbau. Eine Dokumentation für das Gebiet der Bundesrepublik*, edited by Hartwig Beseler and Niels Gutschow, 1:ix–xl. Neumünster: Karl Wachholtz, 1988.

——. "Berufsbild und Berufsausbildung der Denkmalpfleger." In *Denkmalräume-Lebensräume*, edited by Ina-Maria Greverus, 279–86. Hessische Blätter für Volks- und Kulturforschung, vol. 2/3. Gießen: Schmitz, 1976.

——. "Denkmal." In *Kulturpolitisches Wörterbuch: Bundesrepublik Deutschland/Deutsche Demokratische Republik im Vergleich*, edited by Wolfgang Langenbucher, Ralf Rytlewski, and Bernd Weyergraf, 133–37. Stuttgart: Metzler, 1983.

——. "Kriegsschäden und Wiederaufbau in Zahlen." In *Berichte über die Tätigkeit der Denkmalpflege in den Jahren 1945–1955*, edited by Walter Bader, 59–61. Jahrbuch der rheinischen Denkmalpflege, vol. 20. Kevelaer: Butzon & Bercker, 1956.

——. "Der Wiederaufbau der Kölner Kirchen (Stand: 1. Juli 1953)." In *Berichte über die Tätigkeit der Denkmalpflege in den Jahren 1945–1955*, edited by Walter Bader, 225–63. Jahrbuch der rheinischen Denkmalpflege, vol. 20. Kevelaer: Butzon & Bercker, 1956.

——. "Die Zukunft der Vergangenheit." *Die Zeit*, 24 January 1975.

Beseler, Hartwig, and Niels Gutschow, eds. *Kriegsschicksale Deutscher Architektur: Verluste, Schäden, Wiederaufbau. Eine Dokumentation für das Gebiet der Bundesrepublik*. 2 vols. Neumünster: Karl Wachholtz, 1988.

Beyme, Klaus von. "Reconstruction in the German Democratic Republic." In *Rebuilding Europe's Bombed Cities*, edited by Jeffry M. Diefendorf, 190–208. Hampshire: Macmillan, 1990.

——. *Der Wiederaufbau: Architektur und Städtebaupolitik in beiden deutschen Staaten*. Munich: Piper, 1987.

Blessing, Werner. "The Cult of the Monarchy: Political Loyalty and the Workers' Movement in Imperial Germany." *Journal of Contemporary History* 13 (1978): 357–75.

Boberach, Heinz, ed. *Berichte des SD und der Gestapo über Kirchen und Kirchenvolk in Deutschland, 1934–1944*. Mainz: Matthias-Grünewald, 1971.

Bollerey, Franziska, Kristiana Hartmann, and Margret Tränkle. *Denkmalpflege und Umweltgestaltung: Orientierung und Planung im Stadtbereich. Stadtgestaltung zwischen Denkmalpflege und Schrebergarten*. Munich: Heinz Moos, 1975.

Boockmann, Hartmut. "Das ehemalige Deutschordens-Schloß Marienburg, 1772–1945: Die Geschichte eines politischen Denkmals." In *Geschichtswissenschaft und Vereinswesen im 19. Jahrhundert*, edited by Hartmut Boockmann, Arnold Esch, Hermann Heimpel, Thomas Nipperdey, and Heinrich Schmidt, 99–161. Veröffentlichungen des Max-Planck-Instituts für Geschichte, vol. 1. Göttingen: Vandenhoeck & Ruprecht, 1972.

Borger, Hugo, and Frank Günter Zehnder. *Köln: Die Stadt als Kunstwerk. Stadtansichten vom 15. bis 20. Jahrhundert*. Cologne: Greven, 1986.

Borrmann, Norbert. *Paul Schultze-Naumburg, 1869–1949, Maler-Publizist-Architekt: Vom Kulturreformer der Jahrhundertwende zum Kulturpolitiker im Dritten Reich*. Essen: Richard Bacht, 1989.

Boström, Jörg, and Roland Günter. "Von Bürgerinitiativen zu Arbeiterinitiativen." In *Arbeiterinitiativen im Ruhrgebiet*, edited by Jörg Boström and Roland Günter, 8–9. Westberlin: Verlag für das Studium der Arbeiterbewegung, 1976.

——, eds. *Arbeiterinitiativen im Ruhrgebiet*. Westberlin: Verlag für das Studium der Arbeiterbewegung, 1976.

Boström, Jörg, Roland Günter, and Hans Georg Vogt. "Überblick über die Entwicklung der Arbeitersiedlungen im Ruhrgebiet." In *Arbeiterinitiativen im Ruhrgebiet*, edited by Jörg Boström and Roland Günter, 10–21. Westberlin: Verlag für das Studium der Arbeiterbewegung, 1976.

Bourdieu, Pierre. "Cultural Reproduction and Social Reproduction." In *Knowledge, Education, and Cultural Change: Papers in the Sociology of Education*, edited by Richard Brown, 77–112. London: Tavistock, 1973.

——. *Distinction: A Social Critique of the Judgement of Taste*. Translated by Richard Nice. Cambridge, Mass.: Harvard University Press, 1984.

Bourke-White, Margaret. *"Dear Fatherland, Rest Quietly": A Report on the Collapse of Hitler's "Thousand Years."* New York: Simon and Schuster, 1946.

Boyer, M. Christine. *The City of Collective Memory: Its Historical Imagery and Architectural Entertainments*. Cambridge, Mass.: MIT Press, 1994.

Bracher, Karl Dietreich. *The German Dictatorship: The Origins, Structure, and Effects of National Socialism.* Translated by Jean Steinberg. New York: Praeger, 1970.

Breckmann, Warren G. "Disciplining Consumption: The Debate about Luxury in Wilhelmine Germany, 1890–1914." *Journal of Social History* 24 (1990): 485–505.

Bredt, F. W. *Friedhof und Grabmal.* Mitteilungen des Rheinischen Vereins für Denkmalpflege und Heimatschutz, vol. 10, no. 1. Düsseldorf: Schwann, 1916.

Brix, Michael. "Monumente der NS- und Trümmer-Zeit: Bewertungsprobleme der Denkmalpflege—Beispiel München." *Kunstchronik* 36 (April 1983): 178–84.

——. "Munich: Residenz and Nationaltheater." In *The Conservation of Historical Monuments in the Federal Republic of Germany,* edited by Regine Dölling, 40–43. Translated by Timothy Nevill. Munich: Heinz Moos, 1974.

——. "Munich: Victory Arch (Siegestor)." In *The Conservation of Historical Monuments in the Federal Republic of Germany,* edited by Regine Dölling, 39–40. Translated by Timothy Nevill. Munich: Heinz Moos, 1974.

——, ed. *Lübeck, die Altstadt als Denkmal: Zerstörung, Wiederaufbau, Gefahren, Sanierung.* Munich: Heinz Moos, 1975.

Brix, Michael, and Monika Steinhauser. "Geschichte im Dienst der Baukunst." In *Geschichte allein ist zeitgemäß: Historismus in Deutschland,* edited by Michael Brix and Monika Steinhauser, 199–327. Lahn-Gießen: Anabas, 1978.

Brown, G. Baldwin. *The Care of Ancient Monuments.* Cambridge: Cambridge University Press, 1905.

Buchsteiner, Thomas. "Arbeiter und Tourismus." Ph.D. diss., Eberhard-Karls-Universität, Tübingen, 1984.

Bullivant, Keith. "Continuity or Change? Aspects of West German Writing after 1945." In *The Culture of Reconstruction: European Literature, Thought, and Film, 1945–50,* edited by Nicholas Hewitt, 191–207. Hampshire: Macmillan, 1989.

Bültemann, Manfred. *Architektur für das Dritte Reich: Die Akademie für Deutsche Jugendführung in Braunschweig.* Berlin: Wilhelm Ernst & Sohn, 1986.

Burleigh, Michael. *Germany Turns Eastwards: A Study of "Ostforschung" in the Third Reich.* Cambridge: Cambridge University Press, 1988.

Buzard, James. *The Beaten Track: European Tourism, Literature, and the Ways to Culture, 1800–1918.* Oxford: Clarendon, 1993.

Calvino, Italo. *Invisible Cities.* Translated by William Weaver. San Diego: Harcourt Brace Jovanovich, 1974.

Campbell, Joan. *The German Werkbund: The Politics of Reform in the Applied Arts.* Princeton, N.J.: Princeton University Press, 1977.

Carr, David. *Time, Narrative, and History.* Bloomington: Indiana University Press, 1986.

Castells, Manuel. *The City and the Grassroots: A Cross-Cultural Theory of Urban Social Movements.* Berkeley: University of California Press, 1983.

Certeau, Michel de. *The Practice of Everyday Life.* Translated by Steven Rendall. Berkeley: University of California Press, 1984.

Chartier, Roger. "Texts, Printings, Readings." In *The New Cultural History,* edited by Lynn Hunt, 154–75. Berkeley: University of California Press, 1989.

Choay, Françoise. *The Modern City: Planning in the Nineteenth Century.* Translated by Marguerite Hugo and George R. Collins. New York: Braziller, 1969.

Christo, and Jeanne-Claude. *Verhüllter/Wrapped Reichstag, Berlin, 1971–1995.* Cologne: Benedikt Taschen, 1995.

Clemen, Paul. *Die deutsche Kunst und die Denkmalpflege: Ein Bekenntnis.* Berlin: Deutscher Kunstverlag, 1933.

——. "Entwicklung und Ziele in Deutschland und Österreich." In *Gemeinsame Tagung für Denkmalpflege und Heimatschutz, Salzburg, 14. und 15. September 1911: Stenographischer Bericht,* edited by Tag für Denkmalpflege, 51–64. Berlin: Wilhelm Ernst & Sohn, 1911.

——. "Der Krieg und die Kunstdenkmäler." In *Kunstschutz im Kriege: Berichte über den Zustand der Kunstdenkmäler auf den verschiedenen Kriegsschauplätzen und über die deutschen und österreichischen Maßnahmen zu ihrer Erhaltung,* vol. 1, *Die Westfront,* edited by Paul Clemen, 1–10. Leipzig: E. A. Seeman, 1919.

——, ed. *Der Dom zu Köln.* Vol. 6, pt. 3, of *Die Kunstdenkmäler der Rheinprovinz.* Düsseldorf: Schwann, 1938.

——. *Kunstdenkmäler der Stadt und des Kreises Düsseldorf.* Vol. 3, pt. 1, of *Die Kunstdenkmäler der Rheinprovinz.* Düsseldorf: Schwann, 1894.

——. *Die Kunstdenkmäler des Kreises Geldern.* Vol. 1, pt. 2, of *Die Kunstdenkmäler der Rheinprovinz.* Düsseldorf: Schwann, 1891. Reprint, Moers: August Steiger, 1979.

——. *Kunstschutz im Kriege: Berichte über den Zustand der Kunstdenkmäler auf den verschiedenen Kriegsschauplätzen und über die deutschen und österreichischen Maßnahmen zu ihrer Erhaltung.* Vol. 1, *Die Westfront.* Leipzig: E. A. Seeman, 1919.

Clifford, James. *The Predicament of Culture: Twentieth-Century Ethnography, Literature, and Art.* Cambridge, Mass.: Harvard University Press, 1988.

Confino, Alon. "The Nation as a Local Metaphor: Heimat, National Memory, and the German Empire, 1871–1918." *History & Memory* 5, no. 1 (Spring/Summer 1993): 42–86.

——. *The Nation as a Local Metaphor: Württemberg, Imperial Germany, and National Memory.* Chapel Hill: University of North Carolina Press, 1997.

Cosgrove, Denis, and Stephen Daniels, eds. *The Iconography of Landscape: Essays on the Symbolic Representation, Design, and Use of Past Environments.* Cambridge: Cambridge University Press, 1988.

Dähn, Arthur. "Die Zerstörung Hamburgs im Kriege, 1939–45." In *Hamburg und seine Bauten, 1929–1953,* edited by Architekten- und Ingenieur-Verein Hamburg, 28–38. Hamburg: Hoffmann and Campe, 1953.

Daniels, Stephen, and Denis Cosgrove. "Introduction: Iconography and Landscape." In *The Iconography of Landscape: Essays on the Symbolic Representation, Design, and Use of Past Environments,* edited by Denis Cosgrove and Stephen Daniels, 1–10. Cambridge: Cambridge University Press, 1988.

Debold, Peter, and Astrid Debold-Kritter. "Das Konzept der Stadterhaltung von Bologna: Thesen zur Übertragbarkeit." In *Lübeck, die Altstadt als Denkmal: Zerstörung, Wiederaufbau, Gefahren, Sanierung,* edited by Michael Brix, 95–110. Munich: Heinz Moos, 1975.

Dehio, Georg. "Denkmalschutz und Denkmalpflege im neunzehnten Jahrhundert." In *Konservieren nicht restaurieren: Streitschriften zur Denkmalpflege um 1900,* edited by Marion Wohlleben, 88–103. Bauwelt Fundamente, vol. 80. Braunschweig: Vieweg & Sohn, 1988.

Deiters, Ludwig. "Ein Beitrag zur Denkmalpflege in der DDR." In *Deutscher Preis für Denkmalschutz 1988,* edited by Deutsches Nationalkomitee für Denkmalschutz, 26–28. Schriftenreihe des Deutschen Nationalkomitees für Denkmalschutz, vol. 38. Bonn: Deutsches Nationalkomitee für Denkmalschutz, 1988.

Dellheim, Charles. *The Face of the Past: The Preservation of the Medieval Inheritance in Victorian England.* Cambridge: Cambridge University Press, 1983.

"Denkmalpflege." *Meyers Großes Konversations-Lexicon.* 6th ed. Vol. 4. Leipzig: Bibliographisches Institut, 1906.

"Denkmalpflege." *Meyers Lexicon.* 8th. ed. Vol. 2. Leipzig: Bibliographisches Institut, 1937.

Deutsche Burgen und feste Schlösser. Königstein im Taunus: Karl Robert Langewiesche, 1927, 1940.

Deutsche Dome des Mittelalters. Königstein im Taunus: Karl Robert Langewiesche, 1933.

Deutscher Heimatbund, ed. *Fünfzig Jahre Deutscher Heimatbund: Deutscher Bund Heimatschutz.* Neuß: Gesellschaft für Buchdruckerei, 1954.

Deutsches Land in 111 Flugaufnahmen. Königstein im Taunus: Karl Robert Langewiesche, 1941.

Deutsches Nationalkomitee für Denkmalschutz, ed. *Verfallen und vergessen oder aufgehoben und geschützt? Architektur und Städtebau der DDR: Geschichte, Bedeutung, Umgang, Erhaltung.* Schriftenreihe des deutschen Nationalkomitee für Denkmalschutz, vol. 51. Bonn: Deutsches Nationalkomitee für Denkmalschutz, 1995.

Diefendorf, Jeffry M. *In the Wake of War: The Reconstruction of German Cities after World War II.* New York: Oxford University Press, 1993.

——. "Konstanty Gutschow and the Reconstruction of Hamburg." *Central European History* 18, no. 2 (June 1985): 143–69.

——. "Städtebauliche Traditionen und der Wiederaufbau von Köln vornehmlich nach 1945." *Rheinische Vierteljahrs-Blätter* 35 (1991): 252–73.

——, ed. *Rebuilding Europe's Bombed Cities.* Hampshire: Macmillan, 1990.

Dieterich, Hartmut. "Staatliche Hilfen zur Finanzierung der Erhaltung 'Alter Städte.'" *Zeitschrift für Stadtgeschichte, Stadtsoziologie und Denkmalpflege* 4, no. 1 (1977): 99–114.

Dietzfelbinger, Eckart. "Reichsparteitagsgelände Nürnberg: Restaurieren, Nutzen, Vermitteln." In *Architektur und Städtebau der 30er/40er Jahre: Ergebnisse der Fachtagung in München, 1993,* edited by Werner Durth and Winfried Nerdinger, 64–73. Schriftenreihe des Deutschen Nationalkomitees für Denkmalschutz, vol. 48. Bonn: Deutsches Nationalkomitee für Denkmalschutz, 1994.

Diner, Dan. "Zur Ideologie des Antifaschismus." In *Erinnerung: Zur Gegenwart des Holocaust in Deutschland-West und Deutschland-Ost,* edited by Bernhard Moltmann, Doron Kiesel, Cilly Kugelmann, Hanno Loewy, and Dietrich Neuhaus, 21–29. Frankfurt am Main: Haag and Herchen, 1993.

——, ed. *Ist der Nationalsozialismus Geschichte? Zu Historisierung und Historikerstreit.* Frankfurt am Main: Fischer Taschenbuch, 1987.

Ditt, Karl. *Raum und Volkstum: Die Kulturpolitik des Provinzialverbandes Westfalen, 1923–1945.* Veröffentlichungen des Provinzialinstituts für Westfälische Landes- und Volksforschung des Landschaftsverbandes Westfalen-Lippe, vol. 26. Münster: Aschendorfsche Verlagsbuchhandlung, 1988.

Dodd, Philip. "Englishness and the National Culture." In *Englishness: Politics and Culture, 1880–1920,* edited by Robert Colls and Philip Dodd, 1–28. London: Croom Helm, 1986.

Dölling, Regine. "Protection and Conservation of Historical Monuments in the Federal Republic of Germany." In *The Conservation of Historical Monuments in the Federal*

Republic of Germany, edited by Regine Dölling, 9–23. Translated by Timothy Nevill. Munich: Heinz Moos, 1974.

———, ed. *The Conservation of Historical Monuments in the Federal Republic of Germany.* Translated by Timothy Nevill. Munich: Heinz Moos, 1974.

Domansky, Elisabeth. "Der Deutsche Werkbund." In *Bürgerliche Gesellschaft in Deutschland: Historische Einblicke, Fragen, Perspektiven,* edited by Lutz Niethammer, 268–74. Frankfurt am Main: Fischer, 1990.

———. "Die gespaltene Erinnerung." In *Kunst und Literatur nach Auschwitz,* edited by Manuel Köppen, 178–96. Berlin: Erich Schmidt, 1993.

———. " 'Kristallnacht,' the Holocaust, and German Unity: The Meaning of November 9 as an Anniversary in Germany." *History & Memory* 4, no. 1 (Spring/Summer 1992): 60–94.

Dominick, Raymond H. *The Environmental Movement in Germany: Prophets and Pioneers, 1871–1971.* Bloomington: Indiana University Press, 1992.

Doppelfeld, Otto. "Grabung in der Kirche St. Ursula zu Köln." In *Rheinische Kirchen im Wiederaufbau,* edited by Wilhelm Neuß, 65–69. Mönchen-Gladbach: Kühlen, 1951.

Dubrow, Gail Lee. "Restoring a Female Presence: New Goals in Historic Preservation." In *Architecture: A Place for Women,* edited by Ellen Perry Berkeley and Matilda Mc-Quaid, 159–70. Washington, D.C.: Smithsonian Institution Press, 1989.

Durth, Werner. *Inszenierung der Alltagswelt: Zur Kritik der Stadtgestaltung.* Braunschweig: Vieweg & Sohn, 1977.

———. "Utopia im Niemands-Land." In *So viel Anfang war nie: Deutsche Städte, 1945–1949,* edited by Hermann Glaser, Lutz von Pufendorf, and Michael Schöneich, 214–23. Berlin: Siedler, 1989.

Durth, Werner, and Niels Gutschow. *Träume in Trümmern: Planungen zum Wiederaufbau zerstörter Städte im Westen Deutschlands, 1940–1950.* Vol. 1, *Konzepte.* Vol. 2, *Städte.* Braunschweig: Vieweg, 1988.

———, eds. *Architektur und Städtebau der Fünfziger Jahre.* Schriftenreihe des Deutschen Nationalkomitees für Denkmalschutz, vol. 33. Bonn: Deutsches Nationalkomitee für Denkmalschutz, 1990.

———. *Architektur und Städtebau der Fünfziger Jahre: Ergebnisse der Fachtagung in Hannover.* Schriftenreihe des Deutschen Nationalkomitees für Denkmalschutz, vol. 41. Bonn: Deutsches Nationalkomitee für Denkmalschutz, 1990.

Durth, Werner, and Winfried Nerdinger, eds. *Architektur und Städtebau der 30/40er Jahre: Ergebnisse der Fachtagung in München, 1993.* Schriftenreihe des Deutschen Nationalkomitees für Denkmalschutz, vol. 48. Bonn: Deutsches Nationalkomitee für Denkmalschutz, 1994.

Eckardt, Götz, ed. *Schicksale deutscher Baudenkmale im zweiten Weltkrieg: Eine Dokumentation der Schäden und Totalverluste auf dem Gebiet der Deutschen Demokratischen Republik.* 2 vols. Munich: Beck; DDR-Berlin: Henschelverlag, 1978.

"Editorial: Denkmalpflege und Postmoderne." *Kunstchronik* 36 (April 1983): 161–62.

Eksteins, Modris. *Rites of Spring: The Great War and the Birth of the Modern Age.* New York: Doubleday, 1989.

Eley, Geoff. "Nazism, Politics, and the Image of the Past: Thoughts on the West German *Historikerstreit,* 1987–1988." *Past & Present* 121 (November 1988): 171–208.

Eley, Geoff, and Ronald Grigor Suny. "Introduction: From the Moment of Social History to the Work of Cultural Representation." In *Becoming National: A Reader,* edited by Geoff Eley and Ronald Grigor Suny, 3–37. New York: Oxford University Press, 1996.

Ellger, Dietrich. *Konservator im Alltag: Aufsätze und Vorträge*. Bonn: Habelt, 1987.

Engelbrechten, Julius Karl, and Hans Volz, eds. *Wir wandern durch das national-sozialistische Berlin: Ein Führer durch die Gedenkstätten des Kampfes um die Reichshauptstadt*. Munich: Zentralverlag der NSDAP, Franz Eher Nachf., 1937.

Engeli, Chr. "Städtische Geschichts- und Heimatvereine: Zum Ergebnis einer Umfrage." *Informationen zur modernen Stadtgeschichte 1974* 8 (1974): 1–9.

Englund, Steven. "The Ghost of Nation Past." *Journal of Modern History* 64, no. 2 (June 1992): 299–320.

Enssle, Manfred J. "Five Theses on German Everyday Life after World War II." *Central European History* 26, no. 1 (1993): 1–19.

Epstein, Klaus. *The Genesis of German Conservatism*. Princeton, N.J.: Princeton University Press, 1966.

Evans, Richard J. *Death in Hamburg: Society and Politics in the Cholera Years, 1830–1910*. London: Penguin, 1987.

———. *In Hitler's Shadow: West German Historians and the Attempt to Escape from the Nazi Past*. London: I. B. Taurus, 1989.

Ewald, V. G. "Kulturdenkmale." In *Einführung in die Heimatgeschichte*, edited by Hubert Mohr and Erik Hühns. East Berlin: VEB Deutscher Verlag der Wissenschaften, 1959.

Falke, Otto von. "Die Einrichtung des Kunstschutzes auf den deutschen Kriegsschauplätzen." In *Kunstschutz im Kriege: Berichte über den Zustand der Kunstdenkmäler auf den verschiedenen Kriegsschauplätzen und über die deutschen und österreichischen Maßnahmen zu ihrer Erhaltung*. Vol. 1: *Die Westfront*, edited by Paul Clemen, 11–15. Leipzig: E. A. Seeman, 1919.

Faulenbach, Bernd. *Ideologie des deutschen Weges: Die deutsche Geschichte in der Historiographie zwischen Kaiserreich und Nationalsozialismus*. Munich: Beck, 1980.

Feder, Gottfried. *Die neue Stadt: Versuch der Begründung einer neuen Stadtplanungskunst aus der sozialen Struktur der Bevölkerung*. 2nd ed. Berlin: Julius Springer, 1939.

Findeisen, Peter. *Geschichte der Denkmalpflege Sachsen-Anhalt: Von den Anfängen bis zum Neubeginn*. Berlin, DDR: Verlag von Bauwesen, 1990.

Fischer, Manfred F. "Denkmalpflege zwischen Verdrängung und Trauerarbeit." In *Architektur und Städtebau der 30er/40er Jahre: Ergebnisse der Fachtagung in München, 1993*, edited by Werner Durth and Winfried Nerdinger, 38–45. Schriftenreihe des Deutschen Nationalkomitees für Denkmalschutz, vol. 48. Bonn: Deutsches Nationalkomitee für Denkmalschutz, 1994.

Fiske, John. *Reading the Popular*. Boston: Unwin Hyman, 1989.

———. *Understanding Popular Culture*. Boston: Unwin Hyman, 1989.

Fitch, James Marston. *Historic Preservation: Curatorial Management of the Built World*. Charlottesville: University Press of Virginia, 1990.

Flores, Richard R. "Private Visions, Public Culture: The Making of the Alamo." *Cultural Anthropology* 10, no. 1 (1995): 100–116.

Föhl, Axel. *Bauten der Industrie und Technik*. Schriftenreihe des Deutschen Nationalkomitees für Denkmalschutz, vol. 47. Bonn: Deutsches Nationalkomitee für Denkmalschutz, n.d.

Forster, Kurt W. "Monument/Memory and the Mortality of Architecture." *Oppositions* 25 (Fall 1982): 2–19.

Foucault, Michel. *The Order of Things: An Archaeology of the Human Sciences*. New York: Vintage, 1973.

Frei, Alfred Georg. "Geschichte aus den 'Graswurzeln'? Geschichtswerkstätten in der historischen Kulturarbeit." *Aus Politik und Zeitgeschichte* B2/88 (8 January 1988): 35–46.

Frenken, Gerhard. "Die Hauptpfarrkirche St. Remigius zu Viersen." In *Rheinische Kirchen im Wiederaufbau*, edited by Wilhelm Neuß, 35. Mönchen-Gladbach: Kühlen, 1951.

Friedländer, Saul. *Reflections of Nazism: An Essay on Kitsch and Death.* Translated by Thomas Weyr. New York: Harper & Row, 1984.

——, ed. *Probing the Limits of Representation: Nazism and the "Final Solution."* Cambridge, Mass.: Harvard University Press, 1992.

Friedrichs, Jürgen. "Urban Renewal Policies and Back-to-the-City Migration." *Journal of the American Planning Association* 53, no. 1 (Winter 1987): 70–79.

Führ, Edward, and Daniel Stemmrich. *"Nach gethaner Arbeit verbleibt im Kreise der Eurigen": Arbeiterwohnen im 19. Jahrhundert.* Wupperthal: Peter Hammer, 1985.

Fulbrook, Mary. *The Divided Nation: A History of Germany, 1918–1990.* New York: Oxford University Press, 1992.

Gall, Ernst. "Georg Dehio." In *Neue Deutsche Biographie*, 3:563–64. Berlin: Duncker & Humblot, 1956.

Gebhard, Torsten. "Schutz und Pflege des Bauernhauses." *Deutsche Kunst und Denkmalpflege* 12 (1954): 132–40.

Geertz, Clifford. *The Interpretation of Cultures.* New York: Basic Books, 1973.

Geisberg, Max, ed. *Die Stadt Münster.* Vol. 41 of *Bau- und Kunstdenkmäler von Westfalen.* Münster: Aschendorfsche Verlagsbuchhandlung, 1935.

Gerteis, Walter. *Das unbekannte Frankfurt.* Neue Folge. Frankfurt am Main: Frankfurter Bücher, 1961.

"Zur Geschichte des Bombenangriffs auf Lübeck 28./29. März 1942: Auszüge aus amtlichen und parteiamtlichen Berichten." *Zeitschrift des Vereins für Lübeckische Geschichte und Altertumskunde* 37 (1957): 5–28.

Gesellschaft für christliche Kultur, ed. "Kirchen in Trümmern: Zwölf Vorträge zum Thema Was Wird aus den Kölner Kirchen [1948]." Reprinted in *Köln: Die Romanischen Kirchen in der Diskussion 1946/47 and 1985*, edited by Hiltrud Kier and Ulrich Krings, 19–126. Stadtspuren: Denkmäler in Köln, vol. 4. Cologne: J. P. Bachem, 1986.

Gillis, John, ed. *Commemorations: The Politics of National Identity.* Princeton, N.J.: Princeton University Press, 1994.

Glaser, Hermann. "So viel Anfang war nie." In *So viel Anfang war nie: Deutsche Städte, 1945–1949*, edited by Hermann Glaser, Lutz von Pufendorf, and Michael Schöneich, 8–23. Berlin: Siedler, 1989.

Goetz, Walter. "Georg Dehio." *Archiv für Kulturgeschichte* 23 (1933): 1–2.

Gollwitzer, Heinz. "Zum Fragenkreis Architekturhistorismus und politische Ideologie." *Zeitschrift für Kunstgeschichte* 42 (1979): 1–14.

Goralczyk, Peter. "Architektur und Städtebau der 50er Jahre in der DDR." In *Architektur und Städtebau der Fünfziger Jahre: Ergebnisse der Fachtagung in Hannover*, edited by Werner Durth and Niels Gutschow, 62–79. Schriftenreihe des Deutschen Nationalkomitees für Denkmalschutz, vol. 41. Bonn: Deutsches Nationalkomitee für Denkmalschutz, 1990.

——. "Denkmale und Denkmalpflege in Berlin und in der Mark Brandenburg." In *Denkmale in Berlin und in der Mark Brandenburg: Ihre Erhaltung und Pflege in der*

Hauptstadt der DDR und in den Bezirken Frankfurt/Oder und Potsdam, edited by Institut für Denkmalpflege, Arbeitsstelle Berlin, 10–58. Weimar: Hermann Böhlaus Nachfolger, 1988.

Grass, Günter. *Two States—One Nation?* Translated by Krishna Winston with A. S. Wensinger. San Diego: Harcourt Brace Jovanovich, 1990.

Grassnick, Martin. "Kulturdenkmale als Mittel der Werbung." *Die Alte Stadt* 10, no. 1 (1983): 39–47.

Grautoff, Otto. "Die Denkmalpflege im Urteil des Auslandes." In *Kunstschutz im Kriege: Berichte über den Zustand der Kunstdenkmäler auf den verschiedenen Kriegsschauplätzen und über die deutschen und österreichischen Maßnahmen zu ihrer Erhaltung.* Vol. 1, *Die Westfront*, edited by Paul Clemen, 111–40. Leipzig: E. A. Seeman, 1919.

Greenfield, Liah. *Nationalism: Five Roads to Modernity.* Cambridge, Mass.: Harvard University Press, 1992.

Greverus, Ina-Maria, ed. *Denkmalräume-Lebensräume.* Hessische Blätter für Volks- und Kulturforschung, vol. 2/3. Gießen: Schmitz, 1976.

Groh, Dieter, and Peter Brandt. *"Vaterlandslose Gesellen": Sozialdemokratie und Nation, 1860–1990.* Munich: Beck, 1992.

Große Bürgerbauten deutscher Vergangenheit. Königstein im Taunus: Karl Robert Langewiesche, n.d. [ca. 1915].

Grossert, Werner. "Nachdenken über meine Stadt." In *Demontage . . . revolutionärer oder restaurativer Bildersturm?*, edited by Bernd Kramer, 67–72. Berlin: Karin Kramer, 1992.

Grundmann, Günter. "Denkmale." In *Hamburg und seine Bauten, 1929–1953*, edited by Architekten- und Ingenieur-Verein Hamburg, 226–31. Hamburg: Hoffmann und Campe, 1953.

———. "Tätigkeitsbericht des Denkmalschutzamtes der Hansestadt Hamburg für die Jahre 1946 bis 1951." *Deutsche Kunst und Denkmalpflege* 10 (1952): 73–75.

———. "Zehnjahresbericht über die Tätigkeit der Vereinigung der Landesdenkmalpfleger in der Bundesrepublik Deutschland, 1950–1960." *Deutsche Kunst und Denkmalpflege* 19 (1961): 46–54.

Günter, Roland. *Oberhausen.* Vol. 22 of *Die Denkmäler des Rheinlandes*, edited by Landeskonservator Rheinland. Düsseldorf: Schwann, 1975.

———. "Schutz historischer Industrieanlagen." In *Keine Zukunft für unsere Vergangenheit? Denkmalschutz und Stadtzerstörung*, edited by Heinrich Klotz, Roland Günter, and Gottfried Kiesow, 125–37. Gießen: Schmitz, 1975.

———. "Schutz von Denkmälern der Sozialgeschichte. Beispiel: Die Arbeitersiedlung." In *Keine Zukunft für unsere Vergangenheit? Denkmalschutz und Stadtzerstörung*, edited by Heinrich Klotz, Roland Günter, and Gottfried Kiesow, 118–24. Gießen: Schmitz, 1975.

———. "Von der Denkmalpflege zum Städteschutz." In *Keine Zukunft für unsere Vergangenheit? Denkmalschutz und Stadtzerstörung*, edited by Heinrich Klotz, Roland Günter, and Gottfried Kiesow, 91–117. Gießen: Schmitz, 1975.

Günter, Roland, and Janne Günter. "Die Arbeiter machen ihre eigene Architektur. Was heißt: basteln . . . ?" In *Arbeiterinitiativen im Ruhrgebiet*, edited by Jörg Boström and Roland Günter, 70–73. Westberlin: Verlag für das Studium der Arbeiterbewegung, 1976.

———. "Architekturelemente und Verhaltensweisen der Bewohner." In *Denkmalräume-Lebensräume*, edited by Ina-Maria Greverus, 7–56. Hessische Blätter für Volks- und Kulturforschung, vol. 2/3. Gießen: Schmitz, 1976.

Günther-Hornig, Margot. *Kunstschutz in den von Deutschland besetzten Gebieten, 1939–1945*. Tübingen: Institut für Besatzungsfragen, 1958.

Gurlitt, Cornelius. "Der deutsche Städtebau." In *Die deutsche Städte: Geschildert nach den Ergebnissen der ersten deutschen Städteausstellung zu Dresden 1903*, edited by Robert Wuttke, 2:23–45. Leipzig: Brandstetter, 1904.

———. "Die Dorfkirche." In *Sächsische Volkskunde*, edited by Robert Wuttke, 363–81. Dresden: Schönfeld, 1900.

Gusevich, Miriam. "Purity and Transgression: Reflections on the Architectural Avant-garde's Rejection of Kitsch." *Discourse* 10, no. 1 (1987/88): 90–115.

Gutschow, Niels. "Stadtplanung im Warthegau, 1939–1944." In *Der "Generalplan Ost": Hauptlinien der nationalsozialistischen Planungs- und Vernichtungspolitik*, edited by Mechtild Rössler and Sabine Schleiermacher, 232–70. Berlin: Akademie Verlag, 1993.

Gutzler, Helmut. "Reisen und Tourismus." In *Kulturpolitisches Wörterbuch: Bundesrepublik Deutschland/Deutsche Demokratische Republik im Vergleich*, edited by Wolfgang Langenbucher, Ralf Rytlewski, and Bernd Weyergraf, 600–602. Stuttgart: Metzler, 1983.

Gynz-Rekowski, Georg von, and Rainer Schulze, eds. *Harzansichten: Historische Postkarten um 1900*. Wernigerode: Verlag Jüttners Buchhandlung, n.d.

Hagelüken, Alexander. "Auf den Barrikaden der Geschichte." *Spuren Suchen* 7 (1993): 40–43.

Hager, Luisa. "Georg Hager." In *Neue Deutsche Biographie*, 7:489–90. Berlin: Duncker & Humblot, 1965.

Haiko, Peter. "The Architecture of the Twentieth Century: Journal of Modern Architecture, Its Contribution to the Architectural History of Modernism." In *Architecture of the Early XX. Century*. Reprint. New York: Rizzoli, 1989.

Haindl, Erika. "Denkmalpflege in der sozialen Verantwortung: Ein Wandel beginnt sich abzuzeichnen." In *Denkmalräume-Lebensräume*, edited by Ina-Maria Greverus, 263–77. Hessische Blätter für Volks- und Kulturforschung, vol. 2/3. Gießen: Schmitz, 1976.

Haist, Karin. "Lebenswege." *Spuren Suchen* 7 (1993): 44–47.

Halbwachs, Maurice. *The Collective Memory*. Translated by Francis J. Ditter Jr. and Vida Yazdi Ditter. New York: Harper & Row, 1980.

Hamann, Richard, and Jost Hermand. *Stilkunst um 1900*. Berlin: Akademie Verlag, 1967.

Hardtwig, Wolfgang. *Geschichtskultur und Wissenschaft*. Munich: Deutscher Taschenbuch, 1990.

Hartmann, Kristiana. "Städtebau um 1900: Romantische Visionen oder pragmatische Aspekte." In *Die Alte Stadt: Die Sicht der mittelalterlichen Stadtarchitektur im 19. und 20. Jahrhundert*, edited by Cord Meckseper and Harald Siebenmorgen, 90–113. Göttingen: Vandenhoeck & Ruprecht, 1985.

Hartung, Werner. *Konservative Zivilisationskritik und regionale Identität: Am Beispiel der niedersächsischen Heimatbewegung 1895 bis 1919*. Hannover: Verlag Hahnsche Buchhandlung, 1991.

Haspel, Jörg. "Zwischen Kronprinzenpalais und Stalinallee: Rekonstruktion und Destruktion in der Hauptstadtplanung." In *Verfallen und vergessen oder aufgehoben und geschützt? Architektur und Städtebau der DDR: Geschichte, Bedeutung, Umgang, Erhaltung,* edited by Deutsches Nationalkomitee für Denkmalschutz, 35–46. Schriftenreihe des Deutschen Nationalkomitees für Denkmalschutz, vol. 51. Bonn: Deutsches Nationalkomitee für Denkmalschutz, 1995.

Hebdige, Dick. *Hiding in the Light: On Images and Things.* London: Routledge, 1988.

Heckel, Erna, Horst Keßler, Dieter Ulle, and Klaus Ziermann. *Kulturpolitik in der Bundesrepublik von 1949 bis zur Gegenwart.* Berlin (East): Dietz; Cologne: Pahl Rugenstein, 1987.

Heider, Magdalena. *Politik—Kultur—Kulturbund: Zur Gründungs- und Frühgeschichte des Kulturbundes zur demokratischen Erneuerung Deutschlands, 1945–1954, in der SBZ/DDR.* Cologne: Verlag Wissenschaft und Politik, 1993.

"Heimatmuseen." In *Wörterbuch der deutschen Volkskunde,* 299–300. Stuttgart: Kröner, 1936.

Heimatverein Düsseldorfer Jonges, ed. *50 Jahre Heimatverein Düsseldorfer Jonges.* Düsseldorf: n.p., 1982.

Heiss, Friedrich. *Bei Uns in Deutschland: Ein Bericht.* Berlin: Volk und Reich, 1941.

Helas, Volker. "Die Architektur der 50er Jahre in der DDR." In *Architektur und Städtebau der Fünfziger Jahre,* edited by Deutsches Nationalkomitee für Denkmalschutz, 49–55. Schriftenreihe des Deutschen Nationalkomitees für Denkmalschutz, vol. 36. Bonn: Deutsches Nationalkomitee für Denkmalschutz, 1988.

——. "Berichte: Zur Denkmalpflege." In *Denkmale in Sachsen: Ihre Erhaltung und Pflege in den Bezirken Dresden, Karl-Marx-Stadt, Leipzig, und Cottbus,* edited by Institut für Denkmalpflege, Arbeitsstelle Dresden, 415–89. Weimar: Hermann Böhlaus Nachfolger, 1978.

Helbig, Jochen. "Denkmale der Volksarchitektur." In *Denkmale in Sachsen: Ihre Erhaltung und Pflege in den Bezirken Dresden, Karl-Marx-Stadt, Leipzig, und Cottbus,* edited by Institut für Denkmalpflege, Arbeitsstelle Dresden, 128–47. Weimar: Hermann Böhlaus Nachfolger, 1978.

Herbert, Ulrich. "Good Times, Bad Times: Memories of the Third Reich." In *Life in the Third Reich,* edited by Richard Bessel, 97–110. Oxford: Oxford University Press, 1987.

——. "Der Holocaust in der Geschichtsschreibung der Bundesrepublik Deutschland." In *Erinnerung: Zur Gegenwart des Holocaust in Deutschland-West und Deutschland-Ost,* edited by Bernhard Moltmann, Doron Kiesel, Cilly Kugelmann, Hanno Loewy, and Dietrich Neuhaus, 31–47. Frankfurt am Main: Haag and Herchen, 1993.

Herf, Jeffrey. *Reactionary Modernism: Technology, Culture, and Politics in Weimar and the Third Reich.* Cambridge: Cambridge University Press, 1984.

Hermand, Jost. *Kultur im Wiederaufbau: Die Bundesrepublik Deutschland, 1945–1965.* Munich: Nymphenburger, 1986.

Herrbach, Brigitte. "Georg Lill." In *Neue Deutsche Biographie,* 14:503. Berlin: Duncker & Humblot, 1984.

Hervé, Martina. "Bericht aus Frankreich (Elsaß)." In *Das Dorf im Wandel: Denkmalpflege für den ländlichen Raum,* edited by Deutsches Nationalkomitee für Denkmalschutz, 78–80. Schriftenreihe des Deutschen Nationalkomitees für Denkmalschutz, vol. 35. Bonn: Deutsches Nationalkomitee für Denkmalschutz, 1988.

Hewison, Robert. *The Heritage Industry: Britain in a Climate of Decline.* London: Methuen, 1987.

Hilger, Hans Peter. "Paul Clemen und die Denkmäler-Inventarisation in den Rheinlanden." In *Kunstverwaltung, Bau- und Denkmal-Politik im Kaiserreich,* edited by

Ekkehard Mai and Stephan Waetzoldt, 383–98. Kunst, Kultur, und Politik im deutschen Kaiserreich, vol. 1. Berlin: Mann, 1981.

Hitler, Adolf. *Mein Kampf*. Translated by Ralph Mannheim. Boston: Houghton Mifflin, 1943.

Hobsbawm, Eric. "Mass-Producing Traditions: Europe, 1870–1914." In *The Invention of Tradition*, edited by Eric Hobsbawm and Terence Ranger, 263–307. Cambridge: Cambridge University Press, 1983.

———. *Nations and Nationalism since 1780: Program, Myth, Reality*. Cambridge: Cambridge University Press, 1990.

Hobsbawm, Eric, and Terence Ranger, eds. *The Invention of Tradition*. Cambridge: Cambridge University Press, 1983.

Hoffmann, Godehard. *Rheinische Romanik im 19. Jahrhundert: Denkmalpflege in der Preussischen Rheinprovinz*. Cologne: J. P. Bachem, 1995.

Höhn, Maria. "Frau im Haus und Girl im *Spiegel*: Discourse on Women in the Interregnum Period of 1945–1949 and the Question of German Identity." *Central European History* 26, no. 1 (1993): 57–90.

Holston, James. *The Modernist City: An Anthropological Critique of Brasília*. Chicago: University of Chicago Press, 1989.

Hönes, Ernst-Rainer. "Die ehrenamtliche Tätigkeit in Natur- und Denkmalschutz." *Die Alte Stadt* 13, no. 4 (1986): 295–304.

———. "Kulturdenkmal und öffentliches Interesse." *Die Alte Stadt* 10, no. 1 (1983): 18–38.

Horion, Johannes. "Paul Clemen und die Rheinlande." In *Festschrift zum Sechzigsten Geburtstag von Paul Clemen*, edited by Wilhelm Worringer, Heribert Reiners, and Leopold Seligmann, 11–16. Düsseldorf: Schwann, 1926.

———. *Die rheinische Provinzial-Verwaltung: Ihre Entwicklung und ihr heutiger Stand*. Düsseldorf: Schwann, 1925.

Horne, Donald. *The Great Museum: The Re-Presentation of History*. London: Pluto, 1984.

Hosmer, Charles B. "The Broadening View of the Historical Preservation Movement." In *Material Culture and the Study of American Life*, edited by Ian M. G. Quimby, 121–39. New York: Norton, 1978.

Hotz, Walter. *Handbuch der Kunstdenkmäler im Elsass und in Lothringen*. Munich: Deutscher Kunstverlag, 1970.

Huse, Norbert, ed. *Denkmalpflege: Deutsche Texte aus drei Jahrhunderten*. Munich: Beck, 1984.

Hüser, Karl. *Wewelsburg, 1933–1945: Kult- und Terrorstätte der SS. Eine Dokumentation*. Paderborn: Verlag Bonifatius-Druckerei, 1982.

Hutter, Peter. *"Die feinste Barbarei": Das Völkerschlachtdenkmal bei Leipzig*. Mainz: Philipp von Zabern, 1990.

Iggers, Georg G. *The German Conception of History: The National Tradition of Historical Thought from Herder to the Present*. Rev. ed. Middletown, Conn.: Wesleyan University Press, 1983.

Institut für Denkmalpflege. *Denkmale der Geschichte und Kultur: Ihre Erhaltung und Pflege in der DDR*. 3rd ed. Berlin: Henschelverlag, 1976.

Institut für Denkmalpflege, Arbeitsstelle Dresden, ed. *Denkmale in Sachsen: Ihre Erhaltung und Pflege in den Bezirken Dresden, Karl-Marx-Stadt, Leipzig, und Cottbus*. Weimar: Hermann Böhlaus Nachfolger, 1978.

Jackson, J. B. *The Necessity for Ruins*. Amherst: University of Massachusetts Press, 1980.

Jackson, Peter. *Maps of Meaning: An Introduction to Cultural Geography*. London: Unwin Hyman, 1989.

Jaeger, Julius. *Alt-Duderstadt: Bilder aus einer tausendjährigen Stadt*. Duderstadt: Aloys Mecke, n.d. [ca. 1927].

Jahrtausend-Feier Markt Rohr (Ndb.) 26. Juni–4. Juli 1926. Abensberg: Buchdruckerei des "Hallertauer General-Anzeigers," n.d. [1926].

Jankowski, Stanislaw. "Warsaw: Destruction, Secret Town Planning, 1939–44, and Postwar Reconstruction." In *Rebuilding Europe's Bombed Cities,* edited by Jeffry M. Diefendorf, 77–93. Hampshire: Macmillan, 1990.

Jansen, Bernd. "Wohnungspolitik, Leitfaden durch ein kalkuliertes Chaos." *Kursbuch* 27 (May 1972): 12–31.

Jefferies, Matthew. "Back to the Future? The *Heimatschutz* Movement in Wilhelmine Germany." *History* 77 (1992): 411–20.

——. *Politics and Culture in Wilhelmine Germany: The Case of Industrial Architecture*. Oxford: Berg, 1995.

Jeismann, Michael. *Das Vaterland der Feinde: Studien zum nationalen Feindbegriff und Selbstverständnis in Deutschland und Frankreich, 1792–1918*. Stuttgart: Klett-Cotta, 1992.

Jokilehto, Jukka Ilmari. "A History of Architectural Conservation: The Contribution of English, French, German, and Italian Thought towards an International Approach to the Conservation of Cultural Property." 3 vols. Ph.D. diss., Institute of Advanced Architectural Studies, University of York, 1986.

Judt, Tony. "The Past Is Another Country: Myth and Memory in Postwar Europe." *Daedalus* 121, no. 4 (Fall 1992): 83–118.

Jung, Martina, and Richard Birkefeld. " 'Großes Aufräumen': Die Sanierung des Ballhofviertels in der hannoverschen Altstadt." In *Altes und neues Wohnen: Linden und Hannover im frühen 20. Jahrhundert*, edited by Sid Auffarth and Adelheid von Saldern, 61–76. Seelze-Velber: Kallmeyer, 1992.

Junghanns, Kurt. *Bruno Taut, 1880–1938*. 2nd ed. DDR-Berlin: Henschelverlag; Berlin (West): Elefanten, 1983.

Just, Ward. *The Translator*. Boston: Houghton Mifflin, 1991.

Kaes, Anton. *From Hitler to Heimat: The Return of History as Film*. Cambridge, Mass.: Harvard University Press, 1989.

Kaes, Anton, Martin Jay, and Edward Dimendberg, eds. *The Weimar Republic Sourcebook*. Berkeley: University of California Press, 1994.

Kammen, Michael. *Mystic Chords of Memory: The Transformation of Tradition in American Culture*. New York: Vintage, 1991.

Kampffmeyer, Hans. *Friedenstadt: Ein Vorschlag für ein deutsches Kriegsdenkmal*. 2nd ed. Jena: Diederichs, 1918.

Karwelat, Jürgen. "Ein Berliner Stadtplan von 1946—seiner Zeit voraus." In *Sackgassen: Keine Wendemöglichkeit für Berliner Straßennamen*, edited by Berliner Geschichtswerkstatt, 9–23. Berlin: Nishen, 1988.

——. "Neutempelhof: Statt Pazifistenecke ein 'Fliegerviertel.' " In *Sackgassen: Keine Wendemöglichkeit für Berliner Straßennamen*, edited by Berliner Geschichtswerkstatt, 27–45. Berlin: Nishen, 1988.

Keitz, Christine. "Die Anfänge des modernen Massentourismus in der Weimarer Republik." *Archiv für Sozialgeschichte* 33 (1993): 179–209.

Kershaw, Ian. *Popular Opinion and Political Dissent in the Third Reich: Bavaria, 1933–1945*. Oxford: Clarendon, 1983.

Kier, Hiltrud. "Glanz und Elend der Denkmalpflege in Köln, 1906 bis 1981." In *Erhalten und gestalten: 75 Jahre Rheinischer Verein für Denkmalpflege und Landschaftsschutz*, edited by Rheinischer Verein für Denkmalpflege und Landschaftsschutz, 241–64. Neuß: Gesellschaft für Buchdruckerei, 1981.

———. "Zur Vermittelbarkeit von Bauten aus der NS-Zeit als Objekte der Denkmalpflege." In *Architektur und Städtebau der 30er/40er Jahre: Ergebnisse der Fachtagung in München, 1993*, edited by Werner Durth and Winfried Nerdinger, 46–63. Schriftenreihe des Deutschen Nationalkomitees für Denkmalschutz, vol. 48. Bonn: Deutsches Nationalkomitee für Denkmalschutz, 1994.

Kiesow, Gottfried. "Europäische Denkmalschutzjahr 1975: Versuch einer Bilanz für Hessen." In *Denkmalräume-Lebensräume*, edited by Ina-Maria Greverus, 247–77. Hessische Blätter für Volks- und Kulturforschung, vol. 2/3. Gießen: Schmitz, 1976.

Kimmelman, Michael. "It Was Big, It Was Fun, and That's Enough." *New York Times*, 16 July 1995.

Kinder, Hans. "Die Generalbebauungspläne 1941 und 1944." In *Hamburg und seine Bauten, 1929–1953*, edited by Architekten- und Ingenieur-Verein Hamburg, 26–27. Hamburg: Hoffmann and Campe, 1953.

Klapheck, Richard. *Neue Baukunst in den Rheinlanden: Eine Übersicht unserer baulichen Entwicklung seit der Jahrhundertwende*. Zeitschrift des Rheinischen Vereins für Denkmalpflege und Heimatschutz, vol. 21, no. 1. Düsseldorf: Schwann, 1928.

Klemperer, Klemens von. *Germany's New Conservatism: Its History and Dilemma in the Twentieth Century*. Princeton, N.J.: Princeton University Press, 1957.

Kleßmann, Christoph. *Die doppelte Staatsgründung: Deutsche Geschichte, 1945–1955*. Göttingen: Vandenhoeck & Ruprecht, 1982.

———. "Relikte des Bildungsbürgertums in der DDR." In *Sozialgeschichte der DDR*, edited by Hartmut Kaelble, Jürgen Kocka, and Hartmut Zwahr, 254–70. Stuttgart: Klett-Cotta, 1994.

———. *Zwei Staaten, eine Nation: Deutsche Geschichte, 1955–1970*. Göttingen: Vandenhoeck & Ruprecht, 1988.

Klewitz, Martin. "Tagung der Vereinigung der Landesdenkmalpfleger in der Bundesrepublik Deutschland vom 20.–23. September 1961 in Berlin." *Deutsche Kunst und Denkmalpflege* 19 (1961): 114–24.

Klotz, Heinrich, Roland Günter, and Gottfried Kiesow, eds. *Keine Zukunft für unsere Vergangenheit? Denkmalschutz und Stadtzerstörung*. Gießen: Schmitz, 1975.

Kocka, Jürgen. "Bürgertum und bürgerliche Gesellschaft im 19. Jahrhundert: Europäische Entwicklungen und deutsche Eigenarten." In *Bürgertum im 19. Jahrhundert: Deutschland im europäischen Vergleich*, edited by Jürgen Kocka, 1:11–76. Munich: Deutscher Taschenbuch, 1988.

Kohl, Isolde M. Th. "Krieg der Röcke." In *So viel Anfang war nie: Deutsche Städte, 1945–1949*, edited by Hermann Glaser, Lutz von Pufendorf, and Michael Schöneich, 292–301. Berlin: Siedler, 1989.

Koonz, Claudia. "Between Memory and Oblivion: Concentration Camps in German Memory." In *Commemorations: The Politics of National Identity*, edited by John Gillis, 258–80. Princeton, N.J.: Princeton University Press, 1994.

Kopp, Fritz. *Die Wendung zur "nationalen" Geschichtsbetrachtung in der Sowjetzone*. Munich: Günter Olzog, 1955.

Korfmacher, Jochen. "Squatting—Rechtliche Grundlagen, Geschichte und Organisation." *Archiv für Kommunalwissenschaften* 20, no. 2 (1981): 185–206.

Kornfeld, Hans. "50 Jahre Rheinischer Verein für Denkmalpflege und Heimatschutz." In *Die Heimat lebt: Vermächtnis und Verpflichtung*, edited by Rheinischer Verein für Denkmalpflege und Heimatschutz, 9–18. Jahrbuch des Rheinischen Vereins für Denkmalpflege und Heimatschutz, 1955/56. Neuß: Gesellschaft für Buchdruckerei, 1956.

Korte, Karl-Rudolf. "Erinnerungsspuren: Das neue Gesellschaftsbewußtsein." In *Geschichtsbewußtsein der Deutschen: Materialien zur Spurensuche einer Nation*, edited by Werner Weidenfeld, 65–79. Cologne: Verlag Wissenschaft und Politik, 1987.

Koselleck, Reinhart. "Allemagne, le mémorial de l'oubli." *Libération*, 17 January 1994.

———. " 'Space of Experience' and 'Horizon of Expectation': Two Historical Categories." In *Futures Past: On the Semantics of Historical Time*, by Reinhart Koselleck, 267–88. Translated by Keith Tribe. Cambridge, Mass.: MIT Press, 1985.

Koselleck, Reinhart, and Michael Jeismann, eds. *Der politische Totenkult: Kriegerdenkmäler in der Moderne*. Munich: Fink, 1993.

Koshar, Rudy. "Against the 'Frightful Leveler': Historic Preservation and German Cities, 1890–1914." *Journal of Urban History* 19, no. 3 (May 1992): 7–29.

———. "Altar, Stage, and City: Historic Preservation and Urban Meaning in Nazi Germany." *History & Memory* 3, no. 1 (Spring 1991): 30–59.

———. "Building Pasts: Historic Preservation and Identity in Twentieth-Century Germany." In *Commemorations: The Politics of National Identity*, edited by John Gillis, 215–38. Princeton, N.J.: Princeton University Press, 1994.

Kracauer, Siegfried. *From Caligari to Hitler: A Psychological History of the German Film*. 1947. Princeton, N.J.: Princeton University Press, 1974.

Kratzsch, Gerhard. *Kunstwart und Dürerbund: Ein Beitrag zur Geschichte der Gebildeten im Zeitalter des Imperialismus*. Göttingen: Vandenhoeck & Ruprecht, 1969.

Krauß, Jutta. *Die Wiederherstellung der Wartburg im 19. Jahrhundert*. Leipzig: Kranichborn, 1990.

Kreisel, Heinrich. "Die Tagung und Besichtigungsfahrten der Denkmalpfleger im Juni 1962 in Niedersachsen und Mitteldeutschland." *Kunstchronik* 15 (September 1962): 234–46.

Kreißig, Gerald, Heidemarie Tressler, and Jochen von Uslar. *Kultur in den Städten: Eine Bestandaufnahme*. Cologne: Kohlhammer, 1979.

Kühn, Erich. "Die kleine Stadt." In *Die Kleine Stadt: Gestaltung der rheinischen Klein- und Mittelstädte*, edited by Rheinischer Verein für Denkmalpflege und Heimatschutz, 7–18. Jahrbuch des Rheinischen Vereins für Denkmalpflege und Heimatschutz, 1959. Neuß: Gesellschaft für Buchdruckerei, 1960.

Kulturbund der demokratischen Erneuerung Deutschlands, ed. *Technische Denkmale in der Deutschen Demokratischen Republik*. Weimar: Kunstdruck Weimar, 1973.

———. *Um Deutschlands neue Kultur*. Halle: Akademischer Verlag, 1946.

Kundera, Milan. *The Unbearable Lightness of Being: A Lovers' Story*. Translated by Michael Henry Heim. New York: Harper & Row, 1984.

Kurtz, Michael Joseph. "American Cultural Restitution Policy in Germany during the Occupation, 1945–1949." Ph.D. diss., Georgetown University, 1982.

Kussmann, Andreas. "Sieben Wochen in der Front: Kriegsende in Düsseldorf." In *1946, Neuanfang: Leben in Düsseldorf*, edited by Stadtmuseum Düsseldorf, 17–33. Düsseldorf: Rheinisch-Bergische Druckerei und Verlagsgesellschaft, 1986.

Ladd, Brian. *The Ghosts of Berlin: Confronting German History in the Urban Landscape.* Chicago: University of Chicago Press, 1997.

———. *Urban Planning and Civic Order in Germany, 1860–1914.* Cambridge, Mass.: Harvard University Press, 1990.

Lademacher, Horst. "Die nördlichen Rheinlande von der Rheinprovinz bis zur Bildung des Landschaftsverbandes Rheinland, 1815–1953." In *Rheinische Geschichte,* edited by Franz Petri and Georg Droege, 2:475–844. Düsseldorf: Schwann, 1976.

Lakoff, George, and Mark Johnson. *Metaphors We Live By.* Chicago: University of Chicago Press, 1980.

Landschaftsverband Rheinland, ed. *"Der Rhein ist mein Schicksal geworden": Paul Clemen, 1866–1947. Erster Provinzialkonservator der Rheinprovinz.* Cologne: Rheinland-Verlag, 1991.

Lane, Barbara Miller. *Architecture and Politics in Germany, 1918–1945.* Cambridge, Mass.: Harvard University Press, 1968, 1985.

Lange, Dieter. "Altstadt und Warenhaus: Über Denkmalpflege und Postmoderne." In *Die Alte Stadt: Denkmal oder Lebensraum?,* edited by Cord Meckseper and Harald Siebenmorgen, 157–83. Göttingen: Vandenhoeck & Ruprecht, 1985.

Laqueur, Thomas W. "Memory and Naming in the Great War." In *Commemorations: The Politics of National Identity,* edited by John Gillis, 150–67. Princeton, N.J.: Princeton University Press, 1994.

Lasch, Christopher. *The True and Only Heaven: Progress and Its Critics.* New York: Norton, 1991.

Lehner, Hans. "Das Bonner Provinzialmuseum und die städtischen und Vereinssammlungen Rheinischer Altertümer." *Bonner Jahrbücher,* Sonderabdruck 116, no. 3 (1907): 1–11.

Lehnert, Detlef, and Klaus Megerle, eds. *Politische Identität und nationale Gedenktage: Zur politischen Kultur in der Weimarer Republik.* Opladen: Westdeutscher, 1989.

Lenz, H. "Die altsächsischen Bauernhäuser der Umgegend Lübecks." *Zeitschrift des Vereins für Lübeckische Geschichte und Altertumskunde* 7 (1895): 262–90.

Leo, Annette. "Spuren der DDR." In *Demontage . . . revolutionärer oder restaurativer Bildersturm?,* edited by Bernd Kramer, 59–66. Berlin: Karin Kramer, 1992.

Lewis, Helena. *The Politics of Surrealism.* New York: Paragon House, 1988.

Lidtke, Vernon. *The Alternative Culture: Socialist Labor in Imperial Germany.* New York: Oxford University Press, 1985.

Lill, Georg. "Vorwort." In *Stadt und Bezirksamt Speyer,* edited by Bernhard Hermann Röttger, v. Vol. 3 of *Die Kunstdenkmäler von Bayern: Regierungsbezirk Pfalz.* Munich: Oldenbourg, 1934.

———. "Vorwort [1946]." In *Die Kunstpflege: Beiträge zur Geschichte und Pflege deutscher Architektur und Kunst, im Auftrag der deutschen Denkmalpfleger,* edited by Georg Lill, 7. Berlin: Deutscher Kunstverlag, 1947.

———, ed. *Die Kunstpflege: Beiträge zur Geschichte und Pflege deutscher Architektur und Kunst, im Auftrag der deutschen Denkmalpfleger.* Berlin: Deutscher Kunstverlag, 1947.

Linse, Ulrich. "Die Entdeckung der technischen Denkmäler: Über die Anfänge der 'Industriearchäologie' in Deutschland." *Technikgeschichte* 53, no. 3 (1986): 201–22.

Lobell, Mimi. "The Buried Treasure: Women's Ancient Architectural Heritage." In *Architecture: A Place for Women,* edited by Ellen Perry Berkeley and Matilda McQuaid, 139–57. Washington, D.C.: Smithsonian Institution Press, 1989.

Löber, Ulrich. "Die Sicherung technischer Kulturdenkmale: Eine Aufgabe der Denk-malpflege." In *Erhalten und gestalten: 75 Jahre Rheinischer Verein für Denkmalpflege und Landschaftsschutz*, edited by Rheinischer Verein für Denkmalpflege und Landschaftsschutz, 303–12. Neuß: Gesellschaft für Buchdruckerei, 1981.

Loest, Erich. *The Monument*. Translated by Ian Mitchel. London: Secker & Warburg, 1984.

Lowenthal, David. *The Past Is a Foreign Country*. Cambridge: Cambridge University Press, 1985.

Lüdtke, Alf. " 'Coming to Terms with the Past': Illusions of Remembering, Ways of Forgetting Nazism in West Germany." *Journal of Modern History* 65, no. 3 (September 1993): 542–72.

Lurz, Meinhold. *Kriegerdenkmäler in Deutschland*. 5 vols. Heidelberg: Esprint-Verlag, 1987.

Lützeler, Heinrich. "Paul Clemen." In *Neue Deutsche Biographie*, 3:281. Berlin: Duncker & Humblot, 1956.

Lynch, Kevin. *Good City Form*. Cambridge, Mass.: MIT Press, 1981.

——. *The Image of the City*. 17th ed. Cambridge, Mass.: MIT Press, 1985.

——. *What Time Is This Place?* Cambridge, Mass.: MIT Press, 1972.

MacCannell, Dean. *The Tourist: A New Theory of the Leisure Class*. New York: Schocken, 1976.

McClelland, Charles E., and Steven P. Scher, eds. *Postwar German Culture: An Anthology*. New York: Dutton, 1974.

Magirius, Heinrich. *Geschichte der Denkmalpflege Sachsen: Von den Anfängen bis zum Neubeginn 1945*. Berlin, DDR: Verlag von Bauwesen, 1989.

Mai, Ekkehard, and Stephan Waetzoldt, eds. *Kunstverwaltung, Bau- und Denkmal-Politik im Kaiserreich*. Kunst, Kultur, und Politik im deutschen Kaiserreich, vol. 1. Berlin: Mann, 1981.

Maier, Charles. *The Unmasterable Past: History, Holocaust, and German National Identity*. Cambridge, Mass.: Harvard University Press, 1989.

Mainzer, Udo. "Denkmalpflege im Rheinland Heute: Chancen und Grenzen." In *Erhalten und gestalten: 75 Jahre Rheinischer Verein für Denkmalpflege und Landschaftsschutz*, edited by Rheinischer Verein für Denkmalpflege und Landschaftsschutz, 185–224. Neuß: Gesellschaft für Buchdruckerei, 1981.

Manz, Günter, ed. *Lebensniveau im Sozialismus*. Berlin: Verlag Die Wirtschaft, 1983.

Marcuse, Harald. "Die museale Darstellung des Holocaust an Orten ehemaliger Konzentrationslager in der Bundesrepublik." In *Erinnerung: Zur Gegenwart des Holocaust in Deutschland-West und Deutschland-Ost*, edited by Bernhard Moltmann, Doron Kiesel, Cilly Kugelmann, Hanno Loewy, and Dietrich Neuhaus, 79–97. Frankfurt am Main: Haag and Herchen, 1993.

Meckseper, Cord, and Harald Siebenmorgen, eds. *Die Alte Stadt: Denkmal oder Lebensraum?* Göttingen: Vandenhoeck & Ruprecht, 1985.

Meier, Burkhard. "Der Denkmalpflegetag in Kassel, 5. bis 8. Oktober 1933." *Die Denkmalpflege* 35, no. 6 (1933): 193–209.

——. "Zur Umbenennung historischer Strassennamen." *Die Denkmalpflege* 35, no. 6 (1933): 230–31.

Meier, Reinhard. "Dresden: 'Elbflorenz' zwischen Zerstörung und Wiederaufbau." In *Die Normalisierung Deutschlands: Bonner Protokolle und Reportagen aus der DDR*, edited by Reinhard Meier, 160–63. Zurich: Verlag Neue Zürcher Zeitung, 1986.

Meinecke, Friedrich. *Die deutsche Katastrophe: Betrachtungen und Erinnerungen.* Wiesbaden: E. Brockhaus, 1946.

Merritt, Anna J., and Richard L. Merritt, eds. *Public Opinion in Semisovereign Germany: The HICOG Surveys, 1949–1955.* Urbana: University of Illinois Press, 1980.

Meyer, Hans Joachim. "Zwischen Palast und Platte." In *Verfallen und vergessen oder aufgehoben und geschützt? Architektur und Städtebau der DDR: Geschichte, Bedeutung, Umgang, Erhaltung,* edited by Deutsches Nationalkomitee für Denkmalschutz, 9–13. Schriftenreihe des Deutschen Nationalkomitees für Denkmalschutz, vol. 51. Bonn: Deutsches Nationalkomitee für Denkmalschutz, 1995.

Meyer, Ulfilas. "Trümmerkino." In *So viel Anfang war nie: Deutsche Städte, 1945–1949,* edited by Hermann Glaser, Lutz von Pufendorf, and Michael Schöneich, 258–67. Berlin: Siedler, 1989.

Michel Deutschland-Spezial-Katalog, 1983/84. Munich: Schwaneberger, 1983.

Mielke, Friedrich. *Die Zukunft der Vergangenheit: Grundlagen, Probleme, und Möglichkeiten der Denkmalpflege.* Stuttgart: Deutsche Verlags-Anstalt, 1975.

Miljutenko, Wladimir. "Wir dürfen nicht geschichtslos werden." In *Demontage . . . revolutionärer oder restaurativer Bildersturm?,* edited by Bernd Kramer, 23–30. Berlin: Karin Kramer, 1992.

Milward, Alan. *The European Rescue of the Nation-State.* Berkeley: University of California Press, 1992.

Mischnick, Wolfgang. *Von Dresden nach Bonn: Erlebnisse—jetzt aufgeschrieben.* Stuttgart: Deutsche Verlags-Anstalt, 1991.

Mitscherlich, Alexander. *Die Unwirtlichkeit unserer Städte: Anstiftung zum Unfrieden.* Frankfurt am Main: Suhrkamp, 1965.

Mittig, Hans-Ernst, and Volker Plagemann, eds. *Denkmäler im 19. Jahrhundert: Deutung und Kritik.* Munich: Prestel-Verlag, 1972.

Moeller, Robert G. *Protecting Motherhood: Women and the Family in the Politics of Postwar West Germany.* Berkeley: University of California Press, 1993.

——. "War Stories: The Search for a Usable Past in the Federal Republic of Germany." *American Historical Review* 101, no. 4 (October 1996): 1008–48.

Mohr, Hubert. "Vorwort." In *Einführung in die Heimatgeschichte,* edited by Hubert Mohr and Erik Hühns. East Berlin: VEB Deutscher Verlag der Wissenschaften, 1959.

Mommsen, Wolfgang. " 'Wir sind wieder wer': Wandlungen im politischen Selbstverständnis der Deutschen." In *Stichworte zur "Geistigen Situation der Zeit."* Vol. 1, *Nation und Republik,* edited by Jürgen Habermas, 185–209. Frankfurt am Main: Suhrkamp, 1979.

Morgenbrod, Horst. "Die Liebe zur Heimat war ungebrochen: Das Wiederwachen der Brauchtums- und Heimatvereine." In *1946, Neuanfang: Leben in Düsseldorf,* edited by Stadtmuseum Düsseldorf, 343–51. Düsseldorf: Rheinisch-Bergische Druckerei und Verlagsgesellschaft, 1986.

Mosse, George. *The Crisis of German Ideology: Intellectual Origins of the Third Reich.* New York: Grosset & Dunlap, 1964.

——. *Fallen Soldiers: Reshaping the Memory of the World Wars.* New York: Oxford University Press, 1990.

——. *The Nationalization of the Masses: Political Symbolism and Mass Movements in Germany from the Napoleonic Wars through the Third Reich.* New York: New American Library, 1975.

Müller, Martin. "Bürgerinitiativen in der politischen Willensbildung." *Aus Politik und Zeitgeschichte* B11/83 (19 March 1983): 27–39.

Museum für Geschichte der Stadt Dresden, ed. *Biografische Notizen zu Dresdner Straßen und Plätzen, die an Persönlichkeiten aus der Arbeiterbewegung, dem antifaschistischen Widerstandskampf und dem sozialistischen Neuaufbau erinnern.* Dresden: Polydruck, 1976.

Muthesius, Stefan. *Das englische Vorbild: Eine Studie zu der deutschen Reformbewegungen im späteren 19. Jahrhundert.* Munich: Prestel, 1974.

———. "The Origins of the German Conservation Movement." In *Planning for Conservation*, edited by Roger Kain, 37–48. New York: St. Martin's, 1981.

Naumann, Friedrich. *Werke*, edited by Heinz Ladendorf. 6 vols. Cologne: Westdeutscher Verlag, 1964–69.

Negt, Oskar, and Alexander Kluge. *Öffentlichkeit und Erfahrung: Zur Organisationsanalyse von bürgerlicher und proletarischer Öffentlichkeit.* Frankfurt am Main: Suhrkamp, 1972.

Nelles, Wilfried, and Reinhard Oppermann. *Stadtsanierung und Bürgerbeteiligung.* Göttingen: Otto Schwartz, 1979.

Nelson, Cary, Paula Treichler, and Lawrence Grossberg. "Cultural Studies: An Introduction." In *Cultural Studies*, edited by Cary Nelson, Paula Treichler, and Lawrence Grossberg. New York and London: Routledge, 1992.

Nerdinger, Winfried. "Einführung in die Ausstellung 'Bauen im Nationalsozialismus—Bayern 1933–1945' in Münchener Stadtmuseum." In *Architektur und Städtebau der 30er/40er Jahre: Ergebnisse der Fachtagung in München, 1993*, edited by Werner Durth and Winfried Nerdinger, 177–213. Schriftenreihe des Deutschen Nationalkomitees für Denkmalschutz, vol. 48. Bonn: Deutsches Nationalkomitee für Denkmalschutz, 1994.

Neuß, E. "Technische Denkmale." In *Einführung in die Heimatgeschichte*, edited by Hubert Mohr and Erik Hühns. East Berlin: VEB Deutscher Verlag der Wissenschaften, 1959.

Neuß, Wilhelm. "Einführung." In *Rheinische Kirchen im Wiederaufbau*, edited by Wilhelm Neuß. Mönchen-Gladbach: Kühlen, 1951.

Nicholas, Lynn H. *The Rape of Europa: The Fate of Europe's Treasures in the Third Reich and the Second World War.* New York: Knopf, 1994.

Niedhart, Gottfried, and Deiter Riesenberger, eds. *Lernen aus dem Krieg? Deutsche Nachkriegszeiten, 1918/1945.* Munich: Beck, 1992.

Niethammer, Lutz, ed. *"Die Jahre weiß man nicht, wo man die heute hinsetzen soll": Faschismus-Erfahrungen im Ruhrgebiet. Lebensgeschichte und Sozialkultur im Ruhrgebiet, 1930 bis 1960.* 2 vols. Berlin: Dietz, 1983.

Nietzsche, Friedrich. "On the Uses and Disadvantages of History for Life [1874]." In *Untimely Meditations*, by Friedrich Nietzsche, 57–123. Translated by R. J. Hollingdale. Cambridge: Cambridge University Press, 1983.

Nipperdey, Thomas. *Deutsche Geschichte, 1800–1866: Bürgerwelt und starker Staat.* Munich: Beck, 1984.

———. *Deutsche Geschichte, 1866–1918.* Vol. 1, *Arbeitswelt und Bürgerwelt.* Munich: Beck, 1993.

———. "Der Kölner Dom als Nationaldenkmal." In *Nachdenken über die deutsche Geschichte*, by Thomas Nipperdey, 156–71. Munich: Beck, 1986.

———. "Nationalidee und Nationaldenkmal im 19. Jahrhundert." In *Gesellschaft, Kultur, Theorie: Gesammelte Aufsätze zur neueren Geschichte,* by Thomas Nipperdey, 133–73. Göttingen: Vandenhoeck & Ruprecht, 1976.

Nissen, Walter, ed. *Göttingen gestern und heute: Eine Sammlung von Zeugnissen zur Stadt- und Universitätsgeschichte.* Göttingen: Stadt Göttingen, 1972.

Noelle, Elisabeth, and Erich Peter Neumann, eds. *Jahrbuch der öffentlichen Meinung, 1947–1955.* 2nd ed. Allensbach am Bodensee: Verlag für Demoskopie, 1956.

———. *Jahrbuch der öffentlichen Meinung, 1957.* Allensbach am Bodensee: Verlag für Demoskopie, 1957.

———. *Jahrbuch der öffentlichen Meinung, 1958–1964.* Allensbach: Verlag für Demoskopie, 1965.

Nora, Pierre. "Between Memory and History: *Les Lieux de Mémoire.*" *Representations* 26 (Spring 1989): 7–25. Special issue, "Memory and Counter-Memory."

———, ed. *Le lieux de mémoire.* 3 vols. Paris: Gallimard, 1984–92.

Nörthen, Martina. "Innerlich unsolide, im Äußeren gemein: Die Geschichte eines typischen Lindener Mietshauses." In *Altes und neues Wohnen: Linden und Hannover im frühen 20. Jahrhundert,* edited by Sid Auffarth and Adelheid von Saldern, 53–60. Seelze-Velber: Kallmeyer, 1992.

Nothnagle, Alan. "From Buchenwald to Bismarck: Historical Myth-Building in the German Democratic Republic, 1945–1989." *Central European History* 26, no. 1 (1993): 91–113.

Olsen, Donald J. *The City as a Work of Art: London, Paris, Vienna.* New Haven, Conn.: Yale University Press, 1986.

Ostermeyer, Friedrich K. "Der Generalbebauungsplan, 1947." In *Hamburg und seine Bauten, 1929–1953,* edited by Architekten- und Ingenieur-Verein Hamburg. Hamburg: Hoffmann and Campe, 1953.

Paschke, Uwe K. *Die Idee des Stadtdenkmals: Ihre Entwicklung und Problematik im Zusammenhang des Denkmalpflegegedankens. Mit einer Darstellung am Einzelfall der Stadt Bamberg.* Nürnberg: Hans Carl, 1972.

Passerini, Luisa. *Fascism in Popular Memory: The Cultural Experience of the Turin Working Class.* Translated by Robert Lumley and Jude Bloomfield. Cambridge: Cambridge University Press, 1987.

———, ed. *International Yearbook of Oral History and Life Stories.* Vol. 1, *Memory and Totalitarianism.* Oxford: Oxford University Press, 1992.

Paul, Gerhard, and Bernhard Schoßig. "Geschichte und Heimat." In *Die andere Geschichte: Geschichte von unten. Spurensicherung. Ökologische Geschichte. Geschichtswerkstätten,* edited by Gerhard Paul and Bernhard Schoßig, 15–32. Cologne: Bund-Verlag, 1986.

Peter, Antonio, and Werner Wolf, eds. *Arbeit, Amis, Aufbau: Alltag in Hessen, 1949–1955.* Frankfurt am Main: Insel, 1989.

Petropoulos, Jonathan. *Art as Politics in the Third Reich.* Chapel Hill: University of North Carolina Press, 1996.

Petsch, Joachim. *Baukunst und Stadtplanung im Dritten Reich.* Munich: Carl Hanser, 1976.

Petz, Ursula von. *Stadtsanierung im Dritten Reich, dargestellt am ausgewählten Beispielen.* Dortmund: Informationskreis für Raumplanung, 1987.

Pfuel, Curt Christoph von. "Eine Zukunft für unsere Vergangenheit: Über das Europäische Denkmalschutzjahr 1975." *Aus Politik und Zeitgeschichte* B10/75 (8 March 1975): 3–14.

Pike, David. *The Politics of Culture in Soviet-Occupied Germany, 1945–1949*. Stanford: Stanford University Press, 1992.

Pinckney, David H. *Napoleon III and the Rebuilding of Paris*. Princeton, N.J.: Princeton University Press, 1958.

Pinson, Koppel S. *Modern Germany: Its History and Civilization*. New York: Macmillan, 1966.

Pommer, Richard, and Christian F. Otto. *Weissenhof 1927 and the Modern Movement in Architecture*. Chicago: University of Chicago Press, 1991.

Porciani, Ilaria. "Il medioevo nella costruzione dell'Italia unita: La proposta di un mito." In *Italia e Germania: Immagini, modelli, Miti fra due popoli nell'Ottocento. Il Medioevo/ Das Mittelalter. Ansichten, Stereotypen und Mythen zweier Völker im neunzehnten Jahrhundert: Deutschland und Italien*, edited by Reinhard Elze and Pierangelo Schiera, 163–91. Bologna: Società editrice il Mulino; Berlin: Duncker & Humblot, 1988.

Prinz, Michael, and Rainer Zitelmann, eds. *Nationalsozialismus und Modernisierung*. Darmstadt: Wissenschaftliche Buchgesellschaft, 1991.

Projektgruppe "Heimatkunde des Nationalsozialismus," Ludwig-Uhland-Institut für empirische Kulturwissenschaft der Universität Tübingen. *Nationalsozialismus im Landkreis Tübingen: Eine Heimatkunde*. Tübingen: Tübinger Vereinigung für Volkskunde, 1989.

Puvogel, Ulrike, ed. *Gedenkstätten für die Opfer des Nationalsozialismus: Eine Dokumentation*. Schriftenreihe der Bundeszentrale für politische Bildung, vol. 245. Ulm: Franz Spiegel, 1987.

Rademacher, Hellmut. *Das deutsche Plakat: Von den Anfängen bis zur Gegenwart*. Dresden: VEB Verlag der Kunst, 1965.

Rave, Wilhelm. "Westfalen." In *Die Kunstpflege: Beiträge zur Geschichte und Pflege deutscher Architektur und Kunst*, edited by Georg Lill, 96–98. Berlin: Deutscher Kunstverlag, 1947.

Reichel, Peter. *Politik Mit der Erinnerung: Gedächtnisorte im Streit um die nationalsozialistische Vergangenheit*. Munich: Carl Hanser, 1995.

———. *Politische Kultur der Bundesrepublik*. Opladen: Leske and Budrich, 1981.

———. *Der schöne Schein des Dritten Reiches: Faszination und Gewalt des Faschismus*. Munich: Carl Hanser, 1991.

Reiseführer: Deutsche Demokratische Republik. Berlin: VEB Tourist Verlag, 1978.

Relph, Edward. *The Modern Urban Landscape*. Baltimore: Johns Hopkins University Press, 1987.

Renard, Edmund. "Die Denkmalpflege in der Rheinprovinz." In *Die Rheinische Provinzial-Verwaltung: Ihre Entwicklung und ihre Heutiger Stand*, edited by Johannes Horion, 443–70. Düsseldorf: Schwann, 1925.

Reulecke, Jürgen. *Geschichte der Urbanisierung in Deutschland*. Frankfurt am Main: Suhrkamp, 1985.

Reuther, Hans. "Oskar Hoßfeld." In *Neue Deutsche Biographie*, 9:652–53. Berlin: Duncker & Humblot, 1971.

Rheinischer Verein für Denkmalpflege und Heimatschutz, ed. *Die Heimat lebt: Vermächtnis und Verpflichtung*. Jahrbuch des Rheinischen Vereins für Denkmalpflege und Heimatschutz, 1955/56. Neuß: Gesellschaft für Buchdruckerei, 1957.

——. *Die Kleine Stadt: Gestaltung der rheinischen Klein- und Mittelstädte.* Jahrbuch des Rheinischen Vereins für Denkmalpflege und Heimatschutz, 1959. Neuß: Gesellschaft für Buchdruckerei, 1960.

——. *Der Kölner Dom in Gefahr.* Zeitschrift des Rheinischen Vereins für Denkmalpflege und Heimatschutz, vol. 19, no. 3. Düsseldorf: Schwann, 1927.

Rheinischer Verein für Denkmalpflege und Landschaftsschutz, ed. *Erhalten und gestalten: 75 Jahre Rheinischer Verein für Denkmalpflege und Landschaftsschutz.* Neuß: Gesellschaft für Buchdruckerei, 1981.

——. *Satzung und Mitgliederverzeichnis.* Neuß: Gesellschaft für Buchdruckerei, 1971.

Rieger, Paul. "Kunst- und Denkmalpflege und der moderne Tourismus: Zum Thema Reisen und Bildung." *Deutsche Kunst und Denkmalpflege* 28 (1970): 99–103.

Riegl, Alois. "The Modern Cult of Monuments: Its Character and its Origin." Translated by Kurt W. Forster and Diane Ghirardo. *Oppositions* 25 (Fall 1982): 20–51.

——. "Der moderne Denkmalskultus: Sein Wesen und seine Entstehung." In *Gesammelte Aufsätze,* by Alois Riegl, 144–93. Augsburg: Filser, 1928.

Riesenberger, Dieter. "Heimatgedanke und Heimatgeschichte in der DDR." In *Antimodernismus und Reform: Zur Geschichte der deutschen Heimatbewegung,* edited by Edeltraud Klueting, 320–43. Darmstadt: Wissenschaftliche Buchgesellschaft, 1991.

Ritter, Gerhard. *The German Resistance: Carl Goerdeler's Struggle against Tyranny.* Translated by R. T. Clark. London: Allen & Unwin, 1958.

Rollins, William H. "Aesthetic Environmentalism: The *Heimatschutz* Movement in Germany, 1904–1918." Ph.D. diss., University of Wisconsin, Madison, 1994.

Rommel, Manfred. *Abschied vom Schlaraffenland: Gedanken über Politik und Kultur.* Stuttgart: Deutsche Verlags-Anstalt, 1981.

Rörig, Fritz. "Die Stadt in der deutschen Geschichte." *Zeitschrift des Vereins für Lübeckische Geschichte und Altertumskunde* 33 (1952): 13–32.

Rosenberg, Alfred. *Der Mythus des 20. Jahrhunderts: Eine Wertung des seelisch-geistigen Gestaltenkämpfe unserer Zeit,* 91st–94th ed. Munich: Hoheneichen, 1936.

Rosenberg, Franz, and Emanuel Hruska. *Städtebau in West und Ost.* Hannover: Niedersächsische Landeszentrale für Politische Bildung, 1969.

Rössler, Mechtild. "Applied Geography and Area Research in Nazi Society: Central Place Theory and Planning, 1933 to 1945." *Environment and Planning D: Society and Space* 7 (1989): 419–31.

Rössler, Mechtild, and Sabine Schleiermacher. "Der 'Generalplan Ost' und die 'Modernität' der Großraumordnung: Eine Einführung." In *Der "Generalplan Ost": Hauptlinien der nationalsozialistischen Planungs- und Vernichtungspolitik,* edited by Mechtild Rössler and Sabine Schleiermacher, 7–11. Berlin: Akademie Verlag, 1993.

Roth, Martin. *Heimatmuseum: Zur Geschichte einer deutschen Institution.* Berlin: Mann, 1990.

Rothes, Walter. *Kriegs-Gedächtniskirchen.* Munich: Glaube und Kunst, 1916.

Rousso, Henry. *The Vichy Syndrome: History and Memory in France since 1944.* Translated by Arthur Goldhammer. Cambridge, Mass.: Harvard University Press, 1991.

Ruland, Josef. "Kleine Chronik des Rheinischen Vereins für Denkmalpflege und Landschaftsschutz." In *Erhalten und gestalten: 75 Jahre Rheinischer Verein für Denkmalpflege und Landschaftsschutz,* edited by Rheinischer Verein für Denkmalpflege und Landschaftsschutz, 13–56. Neuß: Gesellschaft für Buchdruckerei, 1981.

Rürup, Reinhard, ed. *Topographie des Terrors: Gestapo, SS, und Reichssicherheitshaupt-*

amt auf dem "Prinz-Albrecht-Gelände." Eine Dokumentation. Berlin: Willmuth
Arenhövel, 1987.

Rüsen, Jörn. Lebendige Geschichte, Grundzüge einer Historik III: Formen und Funktionen
des historischen Wissens. Göttingen: Vandenhoeck & Ruprecht, 1989.

Ruskin, John. The Seven Lamps of Architecture. 1880. New York: Dover, 1989.

Said, Edward. Orientalism. New York: Pantheon, 1978.

Saldern, Adelheid von. "Bauen, nichts als Bauen . . . Einleitung." In Altes und neues
Wohnen: Linden und Hannover im frühen 20. Jahrhundert, edited by Sid Auffarth and
Adelheid von Saldern, 7–14. Seelze-Velber: Kallmeyer, 1992.

Schäfer, Hans-Dieter. Das gespaltene Bewußtsein: Deutsche Kultur und Lebenswirklich-
keit, 1933–1945. Munich: Carl Hanser, 1982.

Schafft, Peter. "Schiffahrtsbezogene Denkmale in Schleswig-Holstein." In Aspekten und
Perspektiven der Hafendenkmalpflege, edited by Deutsches Nationalkomitee für
Denkmalpflege, 18–21. Schriftenreihe des Deutschen Nationalkomitees für Denk-
malschutz, vol. 40. Bonn: Deutsches Nationalkomitee für Denkmalschutz, 1989.

Schama, Simon. Landscape and Memory. New York: Knopf, 1995.

Scharf, Helmut. Kleine Kunstgeschichte des deutschen Denkmals. Darmstadt:
Wissenschaftliche Buchgesellschaft, 1984.

Scheck, Thomas. " 'Im Winkel des großen Vaterlandes': Denkmalpflege in Schleswig-
Holstein, 1892–1924." Zeitschrift der Gesellschaft für Schleswig-Holsteinische
Geschichte 116 (1991): 213–81.

Scheffler, Karl. "Deutsches Land und Deutsche Menschen." In Deutsches Land in 111
Flugaufnahmen. Königstein im Taunus: Karl Robert Langewiesche, 1941.

Schivelbusch, Wolfgang. Railway Travel: The Industrialization of Time and Space in the
Nineteenth Century. Leamington Spa: Berg, 1986.

Schleich, Erwin. Die zweite Zerstörung Münchens: Historische Aufnahmen aus dem
Stadtarchiv München und von vielen anderen. Stuttgart: J. F. Steinkopf, 1978.

Schlippe, Bernhard. "Erster Bericht des Amtes für Denkmalpflege der Hansestadt
Lübeck." Zeitschrift des Vereins für Lübeckische Geschichte und Altertumskunde 44
(1964): 108–16.

Schlungbaum-Stehr, Regine. "Altstadtsanierung und Denkmalpflege in den 30er
Jahren: Fallbeispiel Köln." In Architektur und Städtebau der 30/40er Jahre: Ergebnisse
der Fachtagung in München, 1993, edited by Werner Durth and Winfried Nerdinger,
84–89. Schriftenreihe des Deutschen Nationalkomitees für Denkmalschutz, vol. 48.
Bonn: Deutsches Nationalkomitee für Denkmalschutz, 1994.

Die schöne Heimat: Bilder aus Deutschland. Königstein im Taunus: Karl Robert Langewiesche, 1952.

Schor, Naomi. "Cartes Postales: Representing Paris 1900." Critical Inquiry 18, no. 2
(Winter 1992): 188–244.

Schorske, Carl. Fin-de-Siècle Vienna: Culture and Politics. New York: Random House,
1980.

Schubert, Dirk. "Gottfried Feder und sein Beitrag zur Stadtplanungstheorie." Die Alte
Stadt 13, no. 3 (1986): 192–211.

Schubert, Otto. "Cornelius Gurlitt." In Neue Deutsche Biographie, 7:327–28. Berlin:
Duncker & Humblot, 1965.

Schulte-Wülwer, Ulrich. "Gedenkstätten." In Kulturpolitisches Wörterbuch: Bundesrepublik Deutschland/Deutsche Demokratische Republik im Vergleich, edited by Wolf-

gang Langenbucher, Ralf Rytlewski, and Bernd Weyergraf, 227–29. Stuttgart: Metzler, 1983.

Schulz, Til. "Zum Beispiel Eppsteinerstraße 47: Wohnungskampf, Hausbesetzung, Wohnkollektiv." *Kursbuch* 27 (May 1972): 85–97.

Schumacher, Rupert von. *Deutschland-Fibel: Volk, Raum, Reich.* Berlin: Verlag "Offene Worte," n.d. [1935].

Schwarz, Hans-Peter. *Adenauer: Der Aufstieg, 1876–1952.* Stuttgart: Deutsche Verlags-Anstalt, 1986.

——. *Die Ära Adenauer: Gründerjahre der Republik, 1949–1957.* Stuttgart: Deutsche Verlags-Anstalt, 1981.

——. "Modernisierung oder Restauration? Einige Vorfragen zur künftigen Sozialgeschichtsforschung über die Ära Adenauer." In *Vom Ende der Weimarer Republik bis zum Land Nordrhein-Westfalen.* Vol. 3 of *Rheinland-Westfalen im Industriezeitalter,* edited by Kurt Düwell and Wolfgang Köllmann, 278–93. Wuppertal: Peter Hammer, 1984.

Sears, John F. *Sacred Places: American Tourist Attractions in the Nineteenth Century.* New York: Oxford University Press, 1989.

Seydewitz, Max. *Die unbesiegbare Stadt: Zerstörung und Neuaufbau von Dresden.* Leipzig: VEB F. A. Brockhaus, 1982.

——. *Zerstörung und Wiederaufbau von Dresden.* Berlin: Kongress-Verlag, 1955.

Sherman, Daniel J. "Art, Commerce, and the Production of Memory in France after World War I." In *Commemorations: The Politics of National Identity,* edited by John Gillis, 186–211. Princeton, N.J.: Princeton University Press, 1994.

Shirer, William. *Berlin Diary: The Journal of a Foreign Correspondent, 1934–1941.* New York: Knopf, 1941.

Siegel, Jerrold. "The Human Subject as a Language-Effect." *History of European Ideas* 18, no. 4 (1994): 481–95.

Siegel, Michael. *Denkmalpflege als öffentliche Aufgabe: Eine ökonomische, institutionelle, und historische Untersuchung.* Göttingen: Vandenhoeck & Ruprecht, 1985.

Sill, Otto, and Heinrich Strohmeyer. "Der Aufbauplan von 1950." In *Hamburg und seine Bauten, 1929–1953,* edited by Architekten- und Ingenieur-Verein Hamburg. Hamburg: Hoffmann and Campe, 1953.

Silverman, Debora L. *Art Nouveau in Fin-de-Siècle France: Politics, Psychology, and Style.* Berkeley: University of California Press, 1989.

Sitte, Camillo. *City Planning According to Artistic Principles.* Translated by George R. Collins and Christianne Crasemann Collins. New York: Random House, 1965.

Smith, Anthony. *The Ethnic Origins of Nations.* Oxford: Blackwell, 1986.

——. "The Nation: Invented, Imagined, Reconstructed?" In *Reimagining the Nation,* edited by Marjorie Ringrose and Adam J. Lerner, 9–28. Buckingham: Open University Press, 1993.

Smith, Neil. "Gentrification, the Frontier, and the Restructuring of Urban Space." In *Gentrification of the City,* edited by Neil Smith and Peter Williams, 15–34. Boston: Allen & Unwin, 1986.

Spagnoli, Lorenzo. *Berlino: XIX e XX secolo.* Bologna: Zanichelli, 1993.

Speer, Albert. *Spandauer Tagebücher.* Frankfurt am Main: Ullstein, 1975.

Speitkamp, Winfried. " 'Ein dauerndes und ehrenvolles Denkmal deutscher Kulturtätigkeit': Denkmalpflege im Kaiserreich 1871–1918." *Die Alte Stadt* 18, no. 2 (1991): 173–97.

———. "Denkmalpflege und Heimatschutz in Deutschland zwischen Kulturkritik und Nationalsozialismus." *Archiv für Kulturgeschichte* 70 (1988): 149–93.

———. "Das Erbe der Monarchie und die Denkmalpflege in der Weimarer Republik." *Deutsche Kunst und Denkmalpflege* 50, no. 1 (1992): 10–21.

———. "Die Hohkönigsburg und die Denkmalpflege im Kaiserreich." *Neue Museumskunde* 34 (1991): 121–30.

———. "Kulturpolitik unter dem Einfluß der Französischen Revolution: Die Anfänge der modernen Denkmalpflege in Deutschland." *Tel Aviver Jahrbuch für deutsche Geschichte* 18 (1989): 129–59.

———. *Die Verwaltung der Geschichte: Denkmalpflege und Staat in Deutschland, 1871–1933*. Göttingen: Vandenhoeck & Ruprecht, 1996.

Spode, Hasso. " 'Der deutsche Arbeiter reist': Massentourismus im Dritten Reich." In *Sozialgeschichte der Freizeit: Untersuchungen zum Wandel der Alltagskultur in Deutschland*, edited by Gerhard Huck, 281–306. Wuppertal: Peter Hammer, 1980.

Stahn, Günter. *Das Nikolaiviertel am Marx-Engels-Forum, Ursprung, Gründungsort, und Stadtkern Berlins: Ein Beitrag zur Stadtentwicklung*, 2nd ed. Berlin: VEB Verlag für Bauwesen, 1985.

Stark, Kurt. "Das Berliner Ensemble 'Unter den Linden': Zur Denkmalpflege-Geschichte in der Hauptstadt der DDR." In *Denkmale in Berlin und in der Mark Brandenburg: Ihre Erhaltung und Pflege in der Hauptstadt der DDR und in den Bezirken Frankfurt/Oder und Potsdam*, edited by Institut für Denkmalpflege Berlin, 78–87. Weimar: Hermann Böhlaus Nachfolger, 1988.

Steinberg, Rolf, ed. *Nazi-Kitsch*. Darmstadt: Melzer Verlag, 1975.

Steinert, Johannes-Dieter. "Aspekte der Denkmalpflege in Nordrhein-Westfalen, 1946–52." Unpublished manuscript, 1980.

Stephenson, Jill. "Widerstand gegen soziale Modernisierung am Beispiel Württembergs, 1939–1945." In *Nationalsozialismus und Modernisierung*, edited by Michael Prinz and Rainer Zitelmann, 93–116. Darmstadt: Wissenschaftliche Buchgesellschaft, 1991.

Stern, Fritz. *The Politics of Cultural Despair: A Study in the Rise of the Germanic Ideology*. New York: Anchor, 1965.

Sternberger, Dolf. *Panorama of the Nineteenth Century*. Translated by Joachim Neugroschel. New York: Urizen, 1977.

Stich, Rudolf. "Maßnahmen der Stadterhaltung und des Denkmalschutzes im Spannungsfeld zwischen Bundes- und Landesrecht sowie zwischen kommunaler Selbstverwaltung und staatlicher Einwirkung." *Die Alte Stadt* 10, no. 2 (1983): 85–102.

Strauß, Gerhard. "Denkmalpflege in der Ostzone." In *Die Kunstpflege: Beiträge zur Geschichte und Pflege deutscher Architektur und Kunst*, edited by Georg Lill, 79–86. Berlin: Deutscher Kunstverlag, 1947.

Sutcliffe, Anthony. *The Autumn of Central Paris: The Defeat of Town Planning, 1850–1970*. Montreal: McGill-Queen's University Press, 1971.

Tacke, Charlotte. *Denkmal im sozialen Raum: Nationale Symbole in Deutschland und Frankreich im 19. Jahrhundert*. Göttingen: Vandenhoeck & Ruprecht, 1995.

Taut, Bruno. *1920–1922, Frühlicht: Eine Folge für die Verwirklichung des neuen Baugedankens*, edited by Ulrich Conrads. Bauwelt Fundamente, vol. 8. Berlin: Ullstein, 1963.

Terdiman, Richard. "Deconstructing Memory: On Representing the Past and Theorizing Culture in France since the Revolution." *Diacritics* 15, no. 4 (Winter 1985): 13–36.

Thiesse, Anne-Marie. "La petite patrie enclose dans la grande: Régionalisme et identité nationale en France sous la Troisième République, 1870–1940." Unpublished paper, European Forum, European University Institute, Florence, 24–26 March 1994.

Till, Karen. "Place and the Politics of Memory: A Geo-Ethnography of Museums and Memorials in Berlin." Ph.D. diss., University of Wisconsin, Madison, 1996.

Tipton, Frank, and Robert Aldrich. *The Economic and Social History of Europe: From 1939 to the Present.* Baltimore: Johns Hopkins University Press, 1987.

Tobia, Bruno. *Una patria per gli italiani: Spazi, itinerari, monumenti nell'Italia unita, 1870–1900.* Bari: Laterza & Figli, 1991.

Tomaszewski, Andrzej. "Denkmalpflege zwischen 'Ästhetik' und Authentizität." *Die Alte Stadt* 11, no. 3 (1984): 227–40.

Topfstedt, Thomas. "Denkmale der Architektur und des Städtebaues der DDR: Zur Vorgeschichte ihrer Erschließung und zu Aspekten ihrer Erhaltung." In *Verfallen und vergessen oder aufgehoben und geschützt? Architektur und Städtebau der DDR: Geschichte, Bedeutung, Umgang, Erhaltung,* edited by Deutsches Nationalkomitee für Denkmalschutz, 14–19. Schriftenreihe des Deutschen Nationalkomitees für Denkmalschutz, vol. 51. Bonn: Deutsches Nationalkomitee für Denkmalschutz, 1995.

Tower, Beeke Sell. *Envisioning America: Prints, Drawings, and Photographs by George Grosz and His Contemporaries.* Cambridge, Mass.: Busch-Reisinger Museum, Harvard University, 1990.

Trommler, Frank, Hermann Glaser, and Hannes Schwenger. "Kulturpolitik der Bundesrepublik Deutschland." In *Kulturpolitisches Wörterbuch: Bundesrepublik Deutschland/ Deutsche Demokratische Republik im Vergleich,* edited by Wolfgang Langenbucher, Ralf Rytlewski, and Bernd Weyergraf, 379–90. Stuttgart: Metzler, 1983.

Tuan, Yi-Fu. "Space and Place: Humanistic Perspective." *Progress in Geography* 6 (1974): 236–45.

———. *Space and Place: The Perspective of Experience.* Minneapolis: University of Minnesota Press, 1977.

Upmann, Augustin, and Uwe Rennspieß. "Organisationsgeschichte der deutschen Naturfreundebewegung bis 1933." In *Mit uns zieht die neue Zeit: Die Naturfreunde. Zur Geschichte eines alternativen Verbandes in der Arbeiterkulturbewegung,* edited by Jochen Zimmer, 66–111. Cologne: Pahl-Rugenstein, 1984.

Uyttenhove, Pieter. "Continuities in Belgian Wartime Reconstruction Planning." In *Rebuilding Europe's Bombed Cities,* edited by Jeffry M. Diefendorf, 48–63. Hampshire: Macmillan, 1990.

Verbeek, Albert. "Paul Clemen, 1866–1947." In *Rheinische Lebensbilder,* edited by Bernhard Pohl, 7:181–201. Cologne: Rheinland-Verlag, 1977.

Vierhaus, Rudolf. "Bildung." In *Geschichtliche Grundbegriffe: Historisches Lexicon zur Politisch-Sozialer Sprache in Deutschland,* edited by Otto Brunner, Werner Conze, and Reinhart Koselleck, 1:508–51. Stuttgart: Klett-Cotta, 1972.

Virilio, Paul. *The Vision Machine.* Translated by Julie Rose. Bloomington: Indiana University Press, 1994.

Vogts, Hans, ed. *Die Kunstdenkmäler der Stadt Köln.* 2 vols. Pt. 4, *Die Profanen Denkmäler.* Vol. 7, pt. 4, of *Die Kunstdenkmäler der Rheinprovinz.* Düsseldorf: Schwann, 1930.

Vondung, Klaus. "Deutsche Apokalypse, 1914." In *Das Wilhelminische Bildungsbürgertum: Zur Sozialgeschichte seiner Ideen,* edited by Klaus Vondung, 153–71. Göttingen: Vandenhoeck & Ruprecht, 1976.

Wächtler, Eberhard, and Otfried Wagenbreth, eds. *Technische Denkmale in der DDR*. Berlin: Kulturbund der DDR, 1973.

Warneken, Bernd-Jürgen, and K. Warneken-Pallowski. "Kommunale Kulturpolitik." In *Kulturpolitisches Wörterbuch: Bundesrepublik Deutschland/Deutsche Demokratische Republik im Vergleich*, edited by Wolfgang Langenbucher, Ralf Rytlewski, and Bernd Weyergraf, 401–7. Stuttgart: Metzler, 1983.

Warnock, Mary. *Memory*. London: Faber and Faber, 1987.

Weber, Max. "The Nation." In *From Max Weber: Essays in Sociology*, edited by H. H. Gerth and C. Wright Mills, 171–79. New York: Oxford University Press, 1958.

Weindling, Paul. *Health, Race, and German Politics between National Unification and Nazism, 1870–1945*. Cambridge: Cambridge University Press, 1989.

Wentzel, Hans. "Die deutschen Glasmalereien von historischem Wert." In *Die Kunstpflege: Beiträge zur Geschichte und Pflege deutscher Architektur und Kunst*, edited by Georg Lill, 67–78. Berlin: Deutscher Kunstverlag, 1947.

Weyers, Dorle, and Christoph Köck. *Die Eroberung der Welt: Sammelbilder vermitteln Zeitbilder*. Detmold: Westfälisches Freilichtmuseum Detmold, 1992.

White, Hayden. *Content of the Form: Narrative Discourse and Historical Representation*. Baltimore: Johns Hopkins University Press, 1987.

Whyte, Iain Boyd. *Bruno Taut and the Architecture of Activism*. Cambridge: Cambridge University Press, 1982.

Winnig, August. *Der Deutsche Ritterorden und seine Burgen*. Königstein im Taunus: Karl Robert Langewiesche, 1956.

Winters, Stanley B. "Historic Preservation in Czechoslovakia: The Château of Staré Hrady." *Canadian Slavonic Papers* 31, no. 3–4 (September–December 1989): 267–82.

Witt, Carl, ed. *Engere Heimat: Beitrag zur Geschichte der ehemaligen Ämter Liebenburg und Wöltingerode (des jetzigen Kreises Goslar)*. 3rd rev. ed. Salzgitter (Harz): Carl Witt, 1917.

Wohlleben, Marion. "Vorwort." In *Konservieren nicht restaurieren: Streitschriften zur Denkmalpflege um 1900*, edited by Marion Wohlleben, 7–33. Bauwelt Fundamente, vol. 80. Braunschweig: Vieweg & Sohn, 1988.

——, ed. *Konservieren nicht restaurieren: Streitschriften zur Denkmalpflege um 1900*. Bauwelt Fundamente, vol. 80. Braunschweig: Vieweg & Sohn, 1988.

Wolff Metternich, Franz Graf. "Lebenslauf." In *Festschrift für Franz Graf Wolff Metternich*, edited by Josef Ruland, 11–14. Neuß: Gesellschaft für Buchdruckerei, 1973.

Wörner, Hans Jakob. "Législation des monuments historiques." *Monuments historiques* 166 (1989): 4–10.

Wright, Patrick. *On Living in an Old Country: The National Past in Contemporary Britain*. London: Verso, 1985.

Wünderich, Volker. "Von der bürgerlichen zur proletarischen Kommunalpolitik: Zum Defizit der kommunalpolitischen Konzeption in der Arbeiterbewegung vor 1914." In *Provinzialisierung einer Region: Zur Entstehung der bürgerlichen Gesellschaft in der Provinz*, edited by Gert Zang, 434–63. Frankfurt am Main: Syndikat, 1978.

Young, James. *The Texture of Memory: Holocaust Memorials and Meaning*. London: Yale University Press, 1993.

Zander, Deiter. "Städtebaulicher Denkmalschutz in Mecklenburg-Vorpommern, 1945–1989." In *Verfallen und vergessen oder aufgehoben und geschützt? Architektur und Städtebau der DDR: Geschichte, Bedeutung, Umgang, Erhaltung*, edited by Deutsches Nationalkomitee für Denkmalschutz, 79–83. Schriftenreihe des Deutschen National-

komitees für Denkmalschutz, vol. 51. Bonn: Deutsches Nationalkomitee für Denkmalschutz, 1995.

Zenz, Emil. *Die Stadt Trier im 20. Jahrhundert.* Vol. 1, *1900–1950.* Trier: Spee, 1981.

Zerner, Henri. "Alois Riegl: Art, Value, and Historicism." *Daedalus* 105, no. 1 (Winter
1976): 177–88.

Zimmer, Jochen, ed. *Mit uns zieht die neue Zeit: Die Naturfreunde. Zur Geschichte eines
alternativen Verbandes in der Arbeiterkulturbewegung.* Cologne: Pahl-Rugenstein,
1984.

Zimmermann, H. K. "Wiederaufbau des Frankfurter Goethehauses?" In *Die
Kunstpflege: Beiträge zur Geschichte und Pflege deutscher Architektur und Kunst,* edited
by Georg Lill, 51–54. Berlin: Deutscher Kunstverlag, 1948.

Ziolkowski, Theodore. *German Romanticism and Its Institutions.* Princeton, N.J.: Princeton University Press, 1990.

Zöller-Stock, Bettina. *"Bruno Taut": Die Innenraumentwürfe des Berliner Architekten.*
Stuttgart: Deutsche Verlags-Anstalt, 1993.

Zuchold, Gerd. "Der Abriss der Ruinen des Stadtschlosses und der Bauakademie in Ost-
Berlin." *Deutschland Archiv* 2 (1985): 178–207.

Zuhorn, Karl. "50 Jahre Deutscher Heimatschutz und Deutsche Heimatpflege:
Rückblick und Ausblick." In *Fünfzig Jahre Deutscher Heimatbund: Deutscher Bund
Heimatschutz,* edited by Deutscher Heimatbund, 13–58. Neuß: Gesellschaft für
Buchdruckerei, 1954.

INDEX

Page numbers in *italics* refer to illustrations.

Ford, Henry, 176
Forster, Georg, 61
France: Third Republic in, 7; national patrimony in, 20; preservation in, 27, 36; war destruction in, 78, *82–84*, 200; reaction to German destructiveness in, 80; German preservationists' attitude toward, 94–95; German war cemeteries in, *96, 97, 97*, 98; German preservation in, 190
Franco-Prussian War, 86, 147
Frankfurt am Main, 67, 79, 104, 135–36, 155, 165, 211; and Main River bridge, 101–2; and Goethe House, 135–36, 208, 210, 213, 219, 229, 231–32, 233, 335; and *Altstadt*, 177, *178*; and Paulskirche, 208, 231, 284; and Römerberg, 265, *276*, 302, *303*; reconstruction of, 265–67, 274; rubble flora in, 275–76, *276*; and St. Leonhard Church, 284–86, *285*; cathedral of, *294*; trial of Auschwitz guards in, 296; and Westend, 320
Frankfurt an der Oder, 208
Frankfurter Allgemeine Zeitung, 283, 314
Frankfurter Hefte, 229
Frankfurter Neue Presse, 274
Frankfurter Rundschau, 275
Frey, Dagobert, 121, 126–27, 179, 188–89
Friends of Nature Tourists' Association, 133–34
Friends of the National Theater, 262
Frühlicht, 130–31, 133
Fuchs, Carl Johannes, 27, 123
Fulbrook, Mary, 199, 333

Garden City, 28, *105*, 155, *157*
Gaulle, Charles de, 207
Gebhard, Torsten, 267–68
Geertz, Clifford, 10
Gender: preservation and, 52, 54, 272–73. See also Women
General Anzeiger (Bonn), 319
General Plan East, 154, 155
Genovevaburg, 141, 145, *146*
Gerbeck, Willi, 2

German Democratic Republic, 202; and reconstruction, 202, 203, 204, 205–6, 208, *248*; and heritage, 208, 254, 303–6, 336; West German preservationists' attitude toward, 222, 257, 269–71; economic growth in, 247; residential housing in, 249; and national identity, 250–53, 291–92; architecture in, 251–52; creates Institut für Denkmalpflege, 254; meaning of ruins in, 255–57; *Heimat* museums in, 284; and New Economic System, 291, 292; antifascist memory in, 297; and European Cultural Heritage Year, 325. *See also* Preservation: and Communism
German National Committee for Historic Preservation, 12, 326, 332
German Urban League, 247, 293
Germany at Zero Hour, 228
Gerteis, Walter, 284–86
Geschichtswerkstätten. See History Workshops
Gießen, 273
Goch, 174
Goebbels, Joseph, 153–54, 177, 187; celebrates World War II bombing, 195, 235
Goerdeler, Carl, 223
Goering, Hermann, 190
Görlitz, 316
Goethe, Johann Wolfgang von, 29, 102, 103, 208, 229, 231
Göttingen, 277; Jacobikirche bells in, *138*
Goslar, 156, 316
Gothic style, 26, 100, 126, 313
Grass, Günter, 200, 226, 290
Great Britain: preservation in, 11, 28
Greece: preservation in, 36
Greenfield, Liah, 331
Greenfield Village, 176
Gropius, Walter, 26, 121
Grosz, Georg, 130
Grundgesetz, 202
Grundmann, Günther, 190–91, 216, 253, 257, 270–71
Gruppe 47, 219
Günter, Roland, 308, 309–12, 326, 334, 373 (n. 40)
Güstrow, 75

Holland, 200
Holocaust. *See* Memory: of Holocaust
Holst, Niels von, 189, 269–70
Honecker, Erich, 250, 291
Hopefulness: as conservative ideology,
    21–22, 148, 149, 196, 240–41, 267,
    269, 333, 336
Horion, Johannes, 116
Hoßfeld, Oskar, 17, 30–31, 51
Howland, Richard H., 283
Hunsrück, 316
Hutten-Czapski, Graf von, 43

Impressionism, 77
International Committee of Monuments,
    Artistic and Historical Sites, and
    Archaeological Excavations, 257, 324
Italy: unification of, 19; *borghese* in, 21;
    preservation in, 49, 307; number of
    monuments in, 300

Jackson, J. B., 77
James, Henry, 80
Jatho, Karl, 137
Jeanne-Claude, 329
Jean Paul (Richter, Johann Paul
    Friedrich), 224
Jena, 70–71
Jugendstil, 40, 45, 158, 317
Just, Ward, 199

Kalkar, 241
Kampfbund für deutsche Kultur, 167
Kampffmeyer, Hans, 105–6, 130
Karlsruhe, 111
Karpa, Oskar, 210
Kassel, 114, 155
Kempen, 277
Kier, Hiltrud, 317
Kiesow, Gottfried, 293, 295, 327
Klapheck, Richard, 122, 123
Klenze, Leo von, 261, 262
Knef, Hildegard, *230*
Knilling, Eugen von, 94
Knobelsdorff, Georg Wenzeslaus von,
    171, 263, 283
Koblenz, 48, 141
Kochenhof, 122

Kölnische Rundschau, 271
Kölnisches Tageblatt, 60
Kölnische Volkszeitung, 137
Kölnische Zeitung, 99
Körber, Kurt A., 315
Kohl, Helmut, 329, 333
Kokoschka, Oskar, 275
Kollwitz, Käthe, 220
Kommern, 316
Koselleck, Reinhart, 18, 21
Kraft durch Freude, 184
Kreisel, Heinrich, 258, 269
Krupp, Alfred, 69, 319
Krupp firm, 309, 310
Kühne, Günther, 326–27
Kulmbach, 69
Kultur, 333; defined, 21; and World
    War I, 77, 100; in Weimar Republic,
    121, 123, 148; after World War II, 212,
    238–40, 249
Kundera, Milan, 329–30, 339
Die Kunstpflege, 214, 217
Kyffhäuser monument, 23–24

Ladd, Brian, 342 (n. 8)
Lagarde, Paul de, 21, 51
Lampmann, Gustav, 122
Lamprecht, Karl, 22
Lane, Barbara Miller, 26
Langbehn, Julius, 21
Lange, Fritz, 250
Langhoff, Wolfgang, 202
Lasch, Christopher, 21–22
League of Industrialists, 70
Leistung: defined, 151–52; culture of,
    152–66; and racism, 153; and artistic
    activity, 153–54; and architecture,
    157–58, *158*; and urban renewal,
    163–64, 174; and preservation,
    166–70, 177, 179–80, 282; in postwar
    era, 208, 274, 291; socialist version of,
    291
Lemcke, Hugo, 113
Leonhardt, Rudolf, 251
Lezius, Heinrich, 36
Lichtwark, Alfred, 27
Liebknecht, Karl, 205
Liebknecht, Kurt, 251

Liebknecht Portal, 205, 306. *See also*
  Berlin: and castle
Lieux de mémoire. See Memory: sites of
Lill, Georg, 172, 210, 213, 216, 225
Lindner, Werner, 86–87, 93, 98–99, 104
Lippe-Detmold, 109
Loest, Erich, 227
Lorenz, Adolf Friedrich, 204
Louvain, 78
Lubitsch, Ernst, 117
Ludwig II (king of Bavaria), 263
Ludwigstein (castle), 117
Lübeck, 47, 123, 254, 312–13, 324; city
  hall in, *48*; historical society in, 67,
  259; bombing of, 191, 193–94; com-
  mercialization of monuments in, 283;
  monument restoration in, 283
Lüdtke, Alf, 321, 349 (n. 93)
Lüneburg, 36
Luftwaffe, 191
Luther, Martin, 303–4
Lutzeler, Heinrich, 218
Lynch, Kevin, 5, 336

MacCannell, Dean, 63
Maertens, Hermann, 24
Magdeburg, 130, 131, 133, 306; Taut's
  facade in, *132*
Mainz, 112
Malraux, André, 258
Mann, Thomas, 75
Marcuse, Herbert, 238
Marienburg, 29, *46*, 46–47, 57, 62, 140,
  159, 335, 347 (n. 62)
Marksburg (Braubach), 141, *143*
Markt Rohr, 145–47
Marshall Plan, 202
Mataré, Ewald, 220
Maximilianskirche. *See* Munich
May, Ernst, 114, 121, 122, 123
Mayen, 141, 145
Mechenich-Kommern, 253
Medick, Hans, 321
Mehring, Franz, 72
Mehs, 237
Meier, Burkhard, 167
Meier, Hans, 324
Meinecke, Friedrich, 80, 208

Memory: of Nazism, xii, 5, 6, 196,
  199–209 passim, 220–32 passim,
  235–36, 254, 270, 295–98, 326–28;
  compared to history, 6; of Holocaust,
  6, 208–9, 242, 252–53, 286–87,
  296–98, 322, 336, 337, 338; sites of,
  6–7; study of, 6–11, 338, 342–43
  (nn. 5, 10, 11); and national identity,
  7–8, 9, 10, 20–22, 44–59 passim, 99–
  106, 116–28 passim, 170–80, 218–27,
  258–73 passim, 306–13, 315, 327–28,
  337, 338; and future, 9; as discourse,
  10–11; and narratives, 18, 344 (n. 3);
  and *Bürgertum*, 20–21, 22, 70, 72; and
  photography, 23, 229; and national
  optics, 23–29; antiquarian, 25, 35, 66,
  260, 287, 336–37, 338; monumental,
  25, 35, 66, 260, 336–37, 338; and local
  museums, 67–68; Protestant, 69; of
  workers, 71–73, 196, 207, 305, 308–11;
  of 1848, 72–73; of war dead, 85–87, 95,
  96, 97–98, 159; critical, 135, 222–23,
  235–37, 243, 260, 268, 287, 295–98,
  307–13, 316, 336; Catholic, 137; and
  Leistung, 152; Nazi use of, 152–66
  passim, 180–85; of Weimar Republic,
  159–60; of Jews, 162, 264, 286–87; and
  family research, 186; and "silence,"
  199–200; of urban ills, 203; of Hitler,
  205, 273, 296; of post–World War II
  era, 207, 247; of Kaiserreich, 207, 273;
  and victimization, 208; of World War
  II, 215, 278–81; of Prussia, 237, 250,
  254, 279–80; and Robinson Crusoe,
  246, 367 (n. 1); popular, 260; crisis of,
  261; of resistance and persecution, 296;
  of Kristallnacht, 297; ungovernability
  of, 300; and scholastic competition,
  315–16; and new history movement,
  322–23. *See also* Monuments; Preservation
Mendelsohn, Erich, 129–30, 326–27
Mendelssohn, Moses, 159
Messel, Alfred, 26
Meyer, Hans Joachim, 365 (n. 71)
Milward, Alan, 224
Mischnick, Wolfgang, 205–6, 362 (n. 16)
Mitscherlich, Alexander, 277–78

international movement, 35; and legislation, 36–37, 44, 68–69, 77, 109–10, 111, 169, 216, 217–18, 253, 298, 325; organization of, 36–39, 40–44, 79–81, 85–87, 113, 166–70, 216–18, 253–58, 298–99; and conservators, 37–40, 115, 179, 191, 210, 211–12, 213, 254, 255, 257–58, 263–64, 277, 282–83, 297–301, 302, 307, 317; obstacles to, 43–44, 68–73, 110, 112, 117–18, 186–87, 209–11; and modernity, 44–47, 60, 122–24, 265–71, 277, 297; and national identity, 44–59, 87–99, 116–28, 170–80, 218–27, 258–73, 306–13, 326–28, 330–31, 333, 336; "colonialist" vision of, 47–48; and youth, 48–49; and urbanism, 51; and "uncultured," 51, 92–93, 225–27, 272; and gender, 52, 54, 95; and medical metaphors, 59, 91–92, 171–72, 173; public reception of, 59–73, 99–106, 126, 128–48, 180–88, 192–97, 227–43 passim, 273–87, 289–90, 309–12, 314–18, 325–28, 370 (n. 70); and the economy, 69–70, 121, 139, 215, 217; and war commemoration, 85–86, 93, 95, 97–98, 138–39; and language, 90, 92; and racism, 94, 120–21, 171–72, 224, 359 (n. 55); and Occident, 94–95, 121, 222, 223–25, 306, 325; and Weimar constitution, 108–9; "negative," 159–60, 162; and Nazism, 166–67, 169–70, 187–88; and theme parks, 176–77; privileged marginality of, 177, 179–80, 196; in World War II, 188–92; and Allied authorities, 205, 205–6, 207, 208, 210, 217, 218, 222, 223, 226, 232, 269–70; and Communism, 217, 222–23, 303–6, 313, 368 (n. 27); and international opinion, 231, 232, 283; and postmodernism, 295, 339; and memory of Nazism in, 297; socially mediated, 301–2; jubilee-, 303–4; and neo-Marxist Left, 307–13; and gentrification, 317–18; and citizens' initiatives, 319; alternative, 319–23; and European Cultural Heritage Year, 323–28. *See also* Memory; Monu-

ments; National identity; Reconstruction; Rhenish Association for the Preservation of Historic Sites; Tag für Denkmalpflege; Urban Planning; *individual cities and regions*

Project Group on Regional Social History, 321

Prussia: Law Code of 1794 in, 29; conservator of monuments in, 29, 37, 39–40, 115; early preservation in, 29–30; inventorying of monuments in, 36; 1907 law in, 37, 44; Rhine province of, 39, 113–14, 114–15; provincial government in, 39, 346 (n. 49); preservation debates in, 43; Ministry of War in, 78. *See also* East Prussia

Puttkamer, Robert von, 57

Quast, Ferdinand von, 29, 40
Quedlinburg, 169, 269, 316

Ratzel, Friedrich, 27
Rave, Paul Ortwin, 171, 214, 222, 226
Rave, Wilhelm, 211
Ravensbrück, 297, 305
Reber, Franz von, 88
Reconstruction, 202–9, 210, 215–16, 261–64, 292; discourse of, 119–20, 191, 195–96, 240–41, 267; criticism of, 229–33, 265–71, 277–78; Cultural Heritage Year as end of, 324
Regensburg, 324
Regions. See *Heimat*; *Heimatschutz*; Rhenish Association for the Preservation of Historic Sites; Rhineland; *individual cities and regions*
Rehort, Carl, 2
Reich Association for Heritage and Heimat (RVH), 166, 167, 171
Reich Federation for Heimat Art, 99–100, 352 (n. 61)
Reich Founding Day, 117
Reich Office for Area Planning, 154
Reichstag building, 23; 1933 fire in, 162; restoration of, 205
Reims cathedral, 77, 80–81, *82–84*; postcard of, 99
Renard, Edmund, 114, 123, 144

Schumacher, Fritz, 100, 164
Schwarz, Hans-Peter, 200
Schwarz, Rudolf, 218, 222, 232
Schwelm, Benedict von, 1, 2
Schwering, Ernst, 236
Seidl, Gabriel von, 88
Severing, Carl, 116
Seydewitz, Max, 280–81, 366 (n. 89),
    370 (n. 83)
Shirer, William, 180
Siebengebirge, 29
Siegel, Jerrold, 343 (n. 24)
Siegel, Michael, 12
Siegesallee, 23
Sippenforscher. See Memory: and family
    research
Sitte, Camillo, 24–25
Smith, Anthony D., 8, 334
Social Democratic Party (SPD), 21, 71,
    134, 291, 310, 311, 314; and preserva-
    tion, 72, 135–36, 270; and urban
    renewal, 163, 164. *See also* Workers
Society for Christian Culture, 218
Society for Research on Jewish Monu-
    ments, 67
Society for the Friends of Reconstruction
    of Cologne, 210
Solingen, 232
Sombart, Werner, 27
*Sozialistische Einheitspartei Deutsch-
    lands* (SED), 203, 252, 297, 303. *See
    also* German Democratic Republic
Speer, Albert, 165, 166, 175, 191, 195,
    252
Speitkamp, Winfried, 12
Spengler, Oswald, 116
Speyer, 112, 172, 173, 247
Squatters, 320–21
Stalinstadt, 251
Staudte, Wolfgang, 228
Stein, Karl Freiherr vom, 250
Stern, Ernst, 128–29, *129*
Sternberger, Dolf, 62
Stralsund, 313, 316
Strasbourg, 31; cathedral in, *32, 32*, 334
Strauß, Gerhard, 222
Street names, 98, 156, 184, 235–36
Study Group for Urban History, Urban

Sociology, and Monument Preserva-
    tion, 319
Stuttgart, 121–22; Old Castle in, 123–24,
    124
Syberberg, Hans-Jürgen, 296
Symbols: national, definition of, 10; pub-
    lic, 35–36, 335. *See also* Bürgertum;
    Monuments; National identity;
    Nazism; Preservation
Synagogues, 162, 264, 287

Tag für Denkmalpflege, 115; founding
    of, 40; at Freiburg, 40, 51, 57; social
    composition of, 40–41; at Salzburg, 41,
    43; at Dresden (1900), 57; at Augs-
    burg, 79; at Eisenach, 109, 117, 125; at
    Cologne, 113, 121, 125–28, 136–37,
    166–67; at Würzburg and Nuremberg,
    114, 122–23; at Kassel, 166–67,
    170–71, 355 (n. 48); at Dresden (1936),
    169–70
Taut, Bruno, 26, 107, 108, 121, 132, 148,
    155, 258; and Peace City, 106; and
    preservation, 130–33, 136, 312, 356
    (n. 58)
Tessenow, Heinrich, 139, 204
Thingstätte, 151
Thoma, Hans, 27
Tietze, Hans, 176
Toepfer, Alfred, 315
Totenburgen, 159
Tourism, 63, 145, 146, 182–84, 204, 209,
    238, 283, 316–17; and national iden-
    tity, 60–64; and preservation, 60–64,
    316; social, 133–35; and SA, 159, 161;
    and class struggle, 313
Touristenverein Naturfreunde. *See*
    Friends of Nature Tourists' Association
Treitschke, Heinrich von, 19
Trendelenburg, Friedrich, 79, 85
Trier, 48, 70, 71, *141*, 324
Triumph of the Will, 153, 180
Tröger, Annemarie, 321
Troeltsch, Ernst, 22
Trümmerfrauen, 226, 234
Tußmann, Heinrich, 281
Tzara, Tristan, 130